D1408685

Exam 70-217

MCSE

Windows® 2000
Directory Services
Infrastructure

TRAINING GUIDE

New
Riders

Damir Bersinic, MCT, MCSE+I, MCDBA
Rob Scrimger, MCT, MCSE+I, MCDBA, MCP+SB

MCSE Training Guide (70-217): I&A Windows 2000 Directory Services Infrastructure

International Standard Book Number: 0-7357-0976-9

Library of Congress Catalog Card Number: 00-100502

Printed in the United States of America

First Printing: August, 2000

04   03   02   01   7   6   5

Interpretation of the printing code: The rightmost double-digit number is the year of the book's printing; the rightmost single-digit number is the number of the book's printing. For example, the printing code 00-1 shows that the first printing of the book occurred in 2000.

Trademarks

Warning and Disclaimer

PUBLISHER
David Dwyer

ASSOCIATE PUBLISHER
Al Valvano

EXECUTIVE EDITOR
Stephanie Wall

ACQUISITIONS EDITORS
Stacey Beheler
Ann Quinn

MANAGING EDITOR
Gina Brown

PRODUCT MARKETING MANAGER
Stephanie Layton

MANAGER OF PUBLICITY
Susan Nixon

DEVELOPMENT EDITOR
Susan Brown Zahn

PROJECT EDITOR
Keith Cline

COPY EDITOR
Amy Lepore

TECHNICAL REVIEWERS
Emmett Dulaney
Kelly Held
Brian Komar

SOFTWARE DEVELOPMENT SPECIALIST
Michael Hunter

INDEXER
Cheryl Lenser

PROOFREADER
Marcia Deboy

COMPOSITOR
Wil Cruz

MANUFACTURING COORDINATOR
Jim Conway

COVER DESIGNER
Aren Howell

INTERIOR DESIGNER
Louisa Klucznik

Contents at a Glance

Table of Contents

Part II: Final Review

About the Authors

Damir Bersinic, an MCT, MCSE+Internet, MCDBA, and Oracle Certified DBA and Trainer, has over 17 years of industry experience working with SQL Server, Oracle, Microsoft Windows NT and BackOffice, and other advanced products. He began working with Windows 2000 when it was still called Windows NT 5.0 and has provided consulting and training on Active Directory and migrating to Windows 2000 to a number of companies. He is President and founder of Bradley Systems Incorporated, a Microsoft Certified Solution Provider focusing on database, Internet, and system integration consulting and training. His extensive work with Windows NT and BackOffice has allowed him to provide high-level consulting and other assistance to clients from Canada to Europe to Australia and New Zealand.

He is an avid fan of Formula 1 and CART racing and can be found in front of his large-screen TV on almost all race weekends. In his spare time (a concept that is somewhat foreign) he likes to listen to music and enjoy time with his wife. He can be reached via email at damir@bradsys.com.

Rob Scrimger is a trainer and consultant who lives and works in Canada. He started with computers in 1979 and through a lot of luck and on-the-job training has managed to do everything but design the boards (he is taking an electronics course though). When he's not working on computers, Rob enjoys good food and good friends, preferably on a boat. Currently Rob is certified in every product in the MCSE stream, holding every Microsoft certification except the MCSD. He plans on adding that by the time this book goes to press. He is also A+ and Network+ certified.

ABOUT THE TECHNICAL REVIEWERS

Brian Komar, MCSE+I, MCT, is an independent consultant currently doing lots of work with Microsoft Corporation. Tasks include acting as the technical lead for the Windows 2000 security course, reviewing published materials, delivering Windows 2000 MOC courses, consulting, and speaking at several conferences on Windows 2000 Active Directory and Security design topics.

In his spare time, Brian enjoys traveling with his wife Krista.

Emmett Dulaney, MCSE, MCP+I, i-Net+, A+, Network+, CNA, is the author of over a dozen books on certification. The former Certification Corner columnist for *Windows NT Systems Magazine*, he is the cofounder of DS Technical Solutions and an instructor for Indiana University/Purdue University of Fort Wayne, Indiana.

Dedication

Damir:

I would like to dedicate this book to my wife Visnja for her understanding and patience.

Rob:

To the light bulbs.

Acknowledgments

Damir:

Thanks to Stacey and the staff at New Riders for their patience, and Darko and the folks at the office for their understanding and support.

Rob:

I want to thank my family for putting up with me working full time and writing. I'd also like to thank Damir for lending a hand when it was needed and Brian for keeping things honest.

Tell Us What You Think!

As the reader of this book, *you* are our most important critic and commentator. We value your opinion and want to know what we're doing right, what we could do better, what areas you'd like to see us publish in, and any other words of wisdom you're willing to pass our way.

As the Executive Editor for the Certification team at New Riders Publishing, I welcome your comments. You can fax, email, or write me directly to let me know what you did or didn't like about this book— as well as what we can do to make our books stronger.

Please note that I cannot help you with technical problems related to the topic of this book, and that due to the high volume of mail I receive, I might not be able to reply to every message.

When you write, please be sure to include this book's title, author, and ISBN number (found on the back cover of the book above the bar code), as well as your name and phone or fax number. I will carefully review your comments and share them with the author and editors who worked on the book.

Fax: 317-581-4663

Email: stephanie.wall@newriders.com

Mail: Stephanie Wall
           Executive Editor
           Certification
           New Riders Publishing
           201 West 103rd Street
           Indianapolis, IN 46290 USA

How to Use This Book

New Riders Publishing has made an effort in the second editions of its Training Guide series to make the information as accessible as possible for the purposes of learning the certification material. Here, you have an opportunity to view the many instructional features that have been incorporated into the books to achieve that goal.

CHAPTER OPENER

Each chapter begins with a set of features designed to allow you to maximize study time for that material.

List of Objectives: Each chapter begins with a list of the objectives as stated by Microsoft.

Objective Explanations: Immediately following each objective is an explanation of it, providing context that defines it more meaningfully in relation to the exam. Because Microsoft can sometimes be vague in its objectives list, the objective explanations are designed to clarify any vagueness by relying on the authors' test-taking experience.

OBJECTIVES

This chapter looks at the DNS server that comes with Windows 2000 as it relates to the Active Directory. Although it concentrates on how to integrate with Active Directory, the chapter starts with a brief discussion of the basics of DNS. After that, a discussion of the installation is presented along with a look at the roles of a DNS server. After these basics are covered, the chapter turns to how it works with Active Directory.

The following objectives from the exam are covered in this chapter:

Install, configure, and troubleshoot DNS for Active Directory.

- **Integrate Active Directory DNS zones with non-Active Directory DNS zones.**
- **Configure zones for dynamic updates.**

▶ This objective is included to make sure you are able to work with DNS both for Active Directory and for other types of computers on your network. Also, one of the important changes in DNS for Windows 2000 is the capability to deal with dynamic updates. This is important for Active Directory so it can register various services with the DNS server to allow clients to find LDAP servers and domain controllers.

Manage, monitor, and troubleshoot DNS.

- **Manage replication of DNS data.**

▶ In managing replication of DNS, you need to understand the difference between zone transfers for standard zones and Active Directory replication that handles replication of Active Directory–integrated zones.

CHAPTER 2

Configuring DNS for Active Directory

Chapter Outline: Learning always gets a boost when you can see both the forest and the trees. To give you a visual image of how the topics in a chapter fit together, you will find a chapter outline at the beginning of each chapter. You will also be able to use this for easy reference when looking for a particular topic.

STUDY STRATEGIES

This chapter looks at the general administration of servers. The discussion begins with a look at the roles a server can take on for the network. Then there is a discussion of the backup and recovery of servers, notably the three ways you can recover a domain controller. The remainder of the chapter looks at monitoring and maintaining servers on the network. As you read through the chapter, pay particular attention to the following points:

▶ You need to know the five operation master roles.

▶ You should note which roles are domain level and which are enterprise level.

▶ You should know both how to transfer the roles and how to seize the roles.

▶ You should know which servers can be reinstated if the role is seized.

▶ You should know the standard backup and restore options when using the Microsoft Backup program.

▶ You need to know the three ways to restore a domain controller and when you should use each.

▶ You should be familiar with the options available on NTDSUTIL.

▶ You should know what tools are available to monitor a server or the network and when they can be used.

Study Strategies: Each topic presents its own learning challenge. To support you through this, New Riders has included strategies for how to best approach studying in order to retain the material in the chapter, particularly as it is addressed on the exam.

INSTRUCTIONAL FEATURES WITHIN THE CHAPTER

These books include a large amount and different kinds of information. The many different elements are designed to help you identify information by its purpose and importance to the exam and also to provide you with varied ways to learn the material. You will be able to determine how much attention to devote to certain elements, depending on what your goals are. By becoming familiar with the different presentations of information, you will know what information will be important to you as a test-taker and which information will be important to you as a practitioner.

EXAM TIP

What Product Is Right for Your Environment? Expect questions on the exam that require you to identify the right product for a specific environment. To answer these questions you must understand the platform on which each product runs and for what use Microsoft intended it.

Exam Tip: Exam Tips appear in the margins to provide specific exam-related advice. Such tips may address what material is covered (or not covered) on the exam, how it is covered, mnemonic devices, or particular quirks of that exam.

Note: Notes appear in the margins and contain various kinds of useful information, such as tips on the technology or administrative practices, historical background on terms and technologies, or side commentary on industry issues.

WARNING

Dual-Booting Is Not Recommended Although it is possible to set up a dual-boot system with Windows 95/98, Windows NT, and Windows 2000, it is not recommended. Remember that you will need to install all applications multiple times (once for each OS supported) and no application/system settings are migrated or shared between the OSs.

Warning: In using sophisticated information technology, there is always potential for mistakes or even catastrophes that can occur through improper application of the technology. Warnings appear in the margins to alert you to such potential problems.

INTRODUCTION

Chapter 1 covers the installation of Windows 2000. The chapter starts with an overview of the Windows 2000 product line. During the discussion of the installation a number of questions are presented so that you will be fully prepared to complete the installation of Windows 2000. Topics include system requirements, disk configurations, file systems, licensing, and workgroup versus domain model. The installation process is also covered in detail so you will be able to identify the steps involved in installing Windows 2000.

Automated installations of Windows 2000 are also covered in this chapter. We explore the use of unattended text files, Remote Installation Services, and the process of imaging a hard drive. At the end of the chapter you will be able to identify the Windows 2000 technologies that assist in the automated installation of Windows 2000.

The chapter ends with a discussion of the upgrade process for legacy Windows 9x and Windows NT operating systems.

WINDOWS 2000 PRODUCTS

Windows 2000 represents the latest version of Microsoft's Windows NT technology. The Windows 2000 product line includes four versions of the product. This section briefly summarizes each of these products and the major differences among them.

Windows 2000 Professional is the workstation operating system of choice in a Windows 2000 environment. Windows 9x and Windows NT 4.0 Workstations must be replaced if companies are to fully utilize the features of Windows 2000 (software deployment, Group Policies, and Active Directory, to name a few).

Windows 2000 Server includes all of the features of Windows 2000 Professional, but it is optimized to offer network services. Windows 2000 Server is ideal for file and print services and Web services.

Windows 2000 Server offers improved network management and supports Microsoft Active Directory (AD). AD represents one of the most significant changes to the Microsoft Windows product line.

NOTE

Windows 2000 and the Alpha Platform Windows NT and Beta releases of Windows 2000 provide support for the Alpha platform. You should note that Microsoft has discontinued support for the Alpha platform.

STEP BY STEP

2.2 Installing the DNS Service

1. From the Start menu, choose Settings and then Control Panel.

2. In the Control Panel window, double-click the Add/Remove Programs icon.

3. In the Add/Remove Programs applet, click the Add/Remove Windows Components button.

4. This opens the Windows Components Wizard (see Figure 2.3). Select Network Services and click the Details button.

5. Choose Domain Name System (DNS) and then click OK.

6. Click Next in the Windows Components Wizard. If you are prompted, enter the path to your distribution files.

7. Finally, the last screen of the Windows Components Wizard will appear and let you click Finish.

8. Close the Add/Remove Programs dialog box by clicking Close. Then you can close the Control Panel by clicking the Close button.

FIGURE 2.3
The Windows Components Wizard starts.

Step by Step: Step by Steps are hands-on tutorial instructions that walk you through a particular task or function relevant to the exam objectives.

Figure: To improve readability, the figures have been placed in the margins wherever possible so they do not interrupt the main flow of text.

INTRODUCTION

One of the most common jobs a network administrator faces is managing servers. As you move into Windows 2000, there no longer are primary domain controllers, backup domain controllers, and member servers. However, there are several special types of servers of which you need to be aware and be able to manage including the schema master, the domain naming master, the PDC emulator, the RID master, and the infrastructure master.

Essentially, in addition to the tasks you learned about in the preceding chapter (managing users, computers, and groups), you need to be able to monitor your servers. You must perform backups and restores. You will also transfer the key server roles from one server to another.

SERVER ROLES

Install, configure, and troubleshoot the components of Active Directory.

• **Transfer operations master roles.**

The operation masters are critical to the operation of the network, and you need to make sure they are available when necessary. Some of these roles can be offline for a time without effect, while others have a dramatic impact if they are offline for even a short time.

In the next few sections, you will learn about each of the operations master roles. From there, the discussion will look at the placement of the roles and how to transfer the roles. Then you will see how to seize a role from a server that has crashed. Finally, there will be a look at the global catalog server.

Objective Coverage Text: In the text before an exam objective is specifically addressed, you will notice the objective is listed to help call your attention to that particular material.

CASE STUDIES

Case Studies are presented throughout the book to provide you with another, more conceptual opportunity to apply the knowledge you are developing. They also reflect the "real-world" experiences of the authors in ways that prepare you not only for the exam but for actual network administration as well. In each Case Study, you will find similar elements: a description of a Scenario, the Essence of the Case, and an extended Analysis section.

CASE STUDY: IMPLEMENTING DNS FOR SUNSHINE BREWING

ESSENCE OF THE CASE

As you look at the problems involved, you will see a few key issues. The following are the main issues:

► There are some locations that have slow links.

► The locations of the laptop computers used by the Executive and Sales users move and change IP addresses.

► There are five domains for which you need to provide resolution.

► Resolution for external addresses needs to be provided.

► The server addresses tend to remain static.

► Some of the systems on the network are UNIX based and will not be Active Directory clients.

SCENARIO

In this chapter, you learned about DNS and how it will be used in the Windows 2000 Active Directory. Now that you have some knowledge on the subject, it is time to see how it can be applied to a real-world situation. In this case study, you will see how DNS will be configured in the Sunshine Brewing company.

Before you can install Active Directory, before you create your first user, you will need to make sure you have a working DNS structure. As you will recall from the case study in Chapter 1, the network designers have broken the organization down into what will become five different domains. You now need to consider the practical side of the design and look at how you will make sure name resolution can take place across all the domains and all the locations that make up Sunshine Brewing.

Essence of the Case: A bulleted list of the key problems or issues that need to be addressed in the Scenario.

Scenario: A few paragraphs describing a situation that professional practitioners in the field might face. A Scenario will deal with an issue relating to the objectives covered in the chapter, and it includes the kinds of details that make a difference.

Analysis: This is a lengthy description of the best way to handle the problems listed in the Essence of the Case. In this section, you might find a table summarizing the solutions, a worded example, or both.

CASE STUDY: INSTALLING AND CONFIGURING ACTIVE DIRECTORY

continued

ANALYSIS

In looking at this scenario, there are a couple of factors driving the analysis. First, you need to ensure replication. The replication, however, does not need to be any faster than the time it takes a user to physically move between two offices.

This being said, the shorter distances such as Victoria to Los Angeles or Ottawa to New York or Paris to London all take over an hour in the air. This means we should aim for replication every three hours between the main sites and longer between the other sites such as between Cape Town and Buenos Aries.

The other consideration with respect to replication is that not all the locations will have a back link to another location and could become isolated if the main link goes down. To ensure that replication can continue in these cases, secondary sites links need to be configured between locations using the Internet and a *virtual private network* (VPN) or SMTP as the intersite transport.

SMTP is a choice because the certificate server is able to create a certificate for us, but that only handles the replication. Because you would also want to be able to move other traffic if the main link goes, the VPN makes more sense.

This leaves intersite replication within a location. This can be handled simply by having all the sites within a location use the same site link. Therefore, there is a site link per location. The replication within the site takes place using the defaults. In each location, one site is created to link the locations, and these sites are also part of a site link to at least one other site using the network and two more sites either using the network or a VPN connection. If site links are configured that use VPNs, the cost is set to double the value of the highest network-connected site link.

To control the replication, three hours is used as the interval for sites connected via T1 during the day. Another site link is created for each that replicates once every hour overnight. The timing for other types of connections is based on these timing for T1 connections.

CHAPTER SUMMARY

KEY TERMS

- Active Directory integrated
- Caching server
- Dynamic Host Configuration Protocol (DHCP)
- Dynamic updates
- Forward lookup
- Fully Qualified Domain Name (FQDN)
- Iterative query
- LDAP

Although by no means a full discussion of the DNS service that is part of Windows 2000, this chapter has presented the key information that you need to know to make the DNS service work with Active Directory. The key points you will need as you move on to the installation of Active Directory include the following:

◆ For Active Directory to function, the DNS server must support SRV records and should support dynamic updates.

◆ When a zone is integrated with Active Directory, the zone information is stored in Active Directory, which will then handle security and replication.

◆ Several tools can be used to help troubleshoot DNS including the DNS snap-in, IPCONFIG, and NSLOOKUP.

Key Terms: A list of key terms appears at the end of each chapter. These are terms that you should be sure you know and are comfortable defining and understanding when you go in to take the exam.

Chapter Summary: Before the Apply Your Knowledge section, you will find a chapter summary that wraps up the chapter and reviews what you should have learned.

EXTENSIVE REVIEW AND SELF-TEST OPTIONS

At the end of each chapter, along with some summary elements, you will find a section called "Apply Your Knowledge" that gives you several different methods with which to test your understanding of the material and review what you have learned.

Chapter 2 CONFIGURING DNS FOR ACTIVE DIRECTORY   77

APPLY YOUR KNOWLEDGE

Exercises

The following series of exercises will give you a chance to get the hands-on experience that is critical to relating the information in the chapter to real life. It is strongly recommended that you complete these exercises and work with the system before attempting the exam.

2.1 Installing the DNS Service

In this exercise, you will be led through the steps to install the DNS service on a Windows 2000 server. It is assumed that you have a clean copy of either Windows 2000 Server or Advanced Server loaded on a nonproduction system.

WARNING **Testing and Exercises!** Never perform testing or exercises on production equipment.

5. Choose Domain Name System (DNS) and then click OK.

6. Click Next in the Windows Components Wizard. You will see the system Reconfiguring Components and might be prompted to insert your Windows 2000 compact disc.

7. Finally, the last screen of the Windows Components Wizard will appear and enable you click to Finish.

8. Close the Add/Remove Programs dialog box by clicking Close. Then you can close the Control Panel by clicking the Close button.

2.2 Creating the Zones

Now that you have the DNS service installed, you will create a reverse and a forward lookup zone. These will be used throughout the exercises in this text.

Estimated time: 15 minutes.

1. Start the DNS snap-in by selecting Programs, Administrative Tools, DNS from the Start menu.

Exercises: These activities provide an opportunity for you to master specific hands-on tasks. Our goal is to increase your proficiency with the product or technology. You must be able to conduct these tasks in order to pass the exam.

Review Questions

1. How are dynamic entries created on the DNS server?

2. What is the filename of the file containing the entries that the Netlogon service will register?

3. What are the two types of transfers that can take place between DNS servers configured with standard zones?

4. How are entries replicated in the Active Directory–integrated mode?

Review Questions: These open-ended, short-answer questions allow you to quickly assess your comprehension of what you just read in the chapter. Instead of asking you to choose from a list of options, these questions require you to state the correct answers in your own words. Although you will not experience these kinds of questions on the exam, these questions will indeed test your level of comprehension of key concepts.

Exam Questions

1. Francóis is attempting to troubleshoot a DNS server problem. He has configured a Windows 2000 server as a DNS server, which he intends to use during the change from a Windows NT 4.0 domain structure to a Windows 2000 Active Directory tree structure.

   As he attempts to upgrade the existing NT 4.0 primary domain controller, all goes well. However, at one point during the installation, the system offers to install the DNS server on the system he is upgrading. What could be causing this to happen? (Choose all that apply.)

   A. The PDC is configured to use a different DNS server.

   B. The DNS server is not configured for dynamic updates.

   C. The wrong version of DNS was installed.

   D. This is normal behavior.

2. Damir is installing DNS on a UNIX system using an older version of BIND — 4.9.6. He configures the new server to act as a secondary for the zone he configured for the Windows 2000 rollout he is performing. When the zone transfers, there are several records that look like gibberish. What might be causing this?

Exam Questions: These questions reflect the kinds of multiple-choice questions that appear on the Microsoft exams. Use them to become familiar with the exam question formats and to help you determine what you know and what you need to review or study more.

Answers to Review Questions

1. Dynamic updates can be made on the DNS server either by a client capable of performing the update or by the DHCP server that provided the client with the address. See the section "The Update Process."

2. The Netlogon service on each domain controller will create a series of entries in the DNS server that will enable the clients to locate the services it provides on the network. These entries are stored in a file called NETLOGON.DNS that is located in the systemroot\system32\dns directory. See the section "Integrating DNS and Active Directory."

3. In Windows 2000, the DNS server supports both normal or full transfers (AFXR) as well as incremental transfers (IFXR) based on the serial number of the zone file located on the servers. See the section "Transferring Zone Information."

4. If a zone is configured as Active Directory integrated, replication will be handled by Active Directory, which defaults to every 5 minutes within a site and is controlled by the site links between sites. The DNS server(s) will poll every 15 minutes by default for updates to the information. See the section "Transferring Zone Information."

5. For a DNS server to work with Active Directory, it must support SRV, service locator, records. In addition, it should, but does not need to, support dynamic updates. See the section "Integrating DNS and Active Directory."

Answers and Explanations: For each of the Review and Exam questions, you will find thorough explanations located at the end of the section.

Suggested Readings and Resources

1. Microsoft Windows 2000 Resource Kit. *Deployment Planning Guide.* Microsoft Press, 2000.

2. Hill, Tim. *Windows 2000 Windows Script Host.* Macmillan Technical Publishing, 1999.

3. *Using Group Policy Scenarios* from Microsoft's Web site at http://www.microsoft.com/windows2000/library/howitworks/management/grouppolicy.asp.

4. *Introduction to Windows 2000 Group Policy* from Microsoft's Web site at http://www.microsoft.com/windows2000/library/howitworks/management/grouppolicyintro.asp.

5. *Windows 2000 Simplifies Top 15 Administrative Tasks* from Microsoft's Web site at http://www.microsoft.com/windows2000/library/howitworks/management/adminsave.asp.

6. *Windows Script Host: A Universal Scripting Host for Scripting Languages* from Microsoft's Web site at http://www.microsoft.com/windows2000/library/howitworks/management/winscrwp.asp.

7. *Windows 2000 Desktop Management Overview* from Microsoft's Web site at http://www.microsoft.com/windows2000/library/howitworks/management/ccmintro.asp.

8. *Step-by-Step Guide to Understanding the Group Policy Feature Set* from Microsoft's Web site at http://www.microsoft.com/windows2000/library/planning/management/groupsteps.asp.

9. *Step-by-Step Guide to User Data and User Settings* from Microsoft's Web site at http://www.microsoft.com/windows2000/library/planning/management/userdata.asp.

10. *Manage Change with the Windows 2000 Platform* from Microsoft's Web site at http://www.microsoft.com/windows2000/guide/server/solutions/managechange.asp.

11. *Group Policy Simplifies Administration* from Microsoft's Web site at http://www.microsoft.com/windows2000/guide/server/solutions/gpsimplifies.asp.

Suggested Readings and Resources: The very last element in every chapter is a list of additional resources you can use if you want to go above and beyond certification-level material or if you need to spend more time on a particular subject that you are having trouble understanding.

Introduction

MCSE Training Guide: Windows 2000 Directory Services Infrastructure is designed for technicians or system administrators with the goal of certification as a *Microsoft Certified Systems Engineer* (MCSE). It covers the Implementing and Administering a Microsoft Windows 2000 Directory Services Infrastructure exam (70-217). According to Microsoft, this exam measures your ability to install, configure, and troubleshoot the Windows 2000 Active Directory components, DNS for Active Directory, and Active Directory security solutions. In addition, this test measures the skills required to manage, monitor, and optimize the desktop environment by using Group Policy.

This book is your one-stop shop. Everything you need to know to pass the exam is in here, and Microsoft has approved it as study material. You do not have to take a class in addition to buying this book to pass the exam. However, depending on your personal study habits or learning style, you may benefit from buying this book *and* taking a class.

You should be aware that Microsoft assumes that candidates for the exam have a minimum of one year's experience implementing and administering network operating systems in medium to very large computing environments. Microsoft also assumes you are familiar with TCP/IP.

HOW THIS BOOK HELPS YOU

This book takes you on a self-guided tour of all the areas covered by the Implementing and Administering a Microsoft Windows 2000 Directory Services Infrastructure exam and teaches you the specific skills you'll need to achieve your MCSE certification. You'll also find helpful hints, tips, real-world examples, and exercises as well as references to additional study materials. Specifically, this book is set up to help you in the following ways:

◆ **Organization.** The book is organized by individual exam objectives. Every objective you need to know for the Implementing and Administering a Microsoft Windows 2000 Directory Services Infrastructure exam is covered in this book. We have presented the objectives in an order that is as logical as possible to enhance the learning experience. We have also attempted to make the information accessible in the following ways:

  • The full list of exam topics and objectives is included in this introduction.

  • Each chapter begins with a list of the objectives to be covered.

  • Each chapter also begins with an outline that provides you with an overview of the material and the page numbers where particular topics can be found.

  • The objectives are repeated where the material most directly relevant to it is covered (unless the whole chapter addresses a single objective).

  • The CD-ROM included with this book contains, in PDF format, a complete listing of the test objectives and where they are covered within the book.

◆ **Instructional Features**. This book has been designed to provide you with multiple ways to learn and reinforce the exam material. The following are some of the helpful methods:

- *Objective Explanations*. As mentioned previously, each chapter begins with a list of the objectives covered in the chapter. In addition, immediately following each objective is an explanation in a context that defines it more meaningfully.

- *Study Strategies*. The beginning of the chapter also includes strategies for approaching the studying and retaining of the material in the chapter, particularly as it is addressed on the exam.

- *Exam Tips*. Exam tips appear in the margin to provide specific exam-related advice. Such tips may address what material is covered (or not covered) on the exam, how it is covered, mnemonic devices, or particular quirks of that exam.

- *Chapter Summaries*. Crucial information is summarized at the end of each chapter.

- *Key Terms*. A list of key terms appears at the end of each chapter.

- *Notes*. These appear in the margin and contain various kinds of useful information such as tips on technology or administrative practices, historical background on terms and technologies, or side commentary on industry issues.

- *Warnings*. When using sophisticated information technology, there is always the potential for mistakes or even catastrophes that occur because of improper application of the technology. Warnings appear in the margin to alert you to such potential problems.

- *Case Studies*. Each chapter concludes with a case study. The cases are meant to help you understand the practical applications of the information covered in the chapter.

- *Exercises*. Found at the end of the chapters in the "Apply Your Knowledge" section, exercises are performance-based opportunities for you to learn and assess your knowledge.

◆ **Extensive Practice Test Options.** The book provides numerous opportunities for you to assess your knowledge and practice for the exam. The practice options include the following:

- *Review Questions*. These open-ended questions appear in the "Apply Your Knowledge" section at the end of each chapter. They enable you to quickly assess your comprehension of what you just read in the chapter. Answers to the questions are provided later in a separate section titled "Answers to Review Questions."

- *Exam Questions*. These questions also appear in the "Apply Your Knowledge" section. Use them to help you determine what you know and what you need to review or study further. Answers and explanations for them are provided in a separate section entitled "Answers to Exam Questions."

- *Practice Exam*. A Practice Exam is included n the "Final Review" section. The "Final Review" section and the Practice Exam are discussed below.

- *ExamGear*. The special Training Guide version of the *ExamGear* software included on the CD-ROM provides further practice questions.

NOTE For a description of the New Riders *ExamGear, Training Guide* software, please see Appendix D, "Using the *ExamGear, Training Guide Edition* Software."

◆ **Final Review.** This part of the book provides you with three valuable tools for preparing for the exam.

- *Fast Facts.* This condensed version of the information contained in the book will prove extremely useful for last-minute review.

- *Study and Exam Tips.* Read this section early on to help you develop study strategies. It also provides you with valuable exam-day tips and information on exam/question formats such as adaptive tests and case study–based questions.

- *Practice Exam.* A practice test is included. Questions are written in styles similar to those used on the actual exam. Use it to assess your readiness for the real thing.

The book includes several other features such as a section titled "Suggested Readings and Resources" at the end of each chapter that directs you toward further information that could aid you in your exam preparation or your actual work. There are valuable appendixes as well including a glossary (Appendix A), an overview of the Microsoft certification program (Appendix B), and a description of what is on the CD-ROM (Appendix C).

For more information about the exam or the certification process, contact Microsoft:

Microsoft Education: 800-636-7544

Internet:

ftp://ftp.microsoft.com/Services/MSEdCert

World Wide Web:

http://www.microsoft.com/train_cert

CompuServe Forum: GO MSEDCERT

WHAT THE IMPLEMENTING AND ADMINISTERING A MICROSOFT WINDOWS 2000 DIRECTORY SERVICES INFRASTRUCTURE EXAM (70-217) COVERS

The Implementing and Administering a Microsoft Windows 2000 Directory Services Infrastructure exam (70-217) covers the Active Directory topics represented by the conceptual groupings or units of the test objectives. The objectives reflect job skills in the following areas:

◆ Installing, Configuring, and Troubleshooting Active Directory

◆ Installing, Configuring, Managing, Monitoring, and Troubleshooting DNS for Active Directory

◆ Installing, Configuring, Managing, Monitoring, Optimizing, and Troubleshooting Change and Configuration Management

◆ Managing, Monitoring, and Optimizing the Components of Active Directory

◆ Configuring, Managing, Monitoring, and Troubleshooting Active Directory Security Solutions

Before taking the exam, you should be proficient in the job skills represented by the following units, objectives, and subobjectives.

Installing, Configuring, and Troubleshooting Active Directory

Install, configure, and troubleshoot the components of Active Directory.

◆ Install Active Directory.

◆ Create sites.

◆ Create subnets.

◆ Create site links.

◆ Create site link bridges.

◆ Create connection objects.

◆ Create global catalog servers.

◆ Move server objects between sites.

◆ Transfer operations master roles.

◆ Verify Active Directory installation.

◆ Implement an organizational unit (OU) structure.

Back up and restore Active Directory.

◆ Perform an authoritative restore of Active Directory.

◆ Recover from a system failure.

Installing, Configuring, Managing, Monitoring, and Troubleshooting DNS for Active Directory

Install, configure, and troubleshoot DNS for Active Directory.

◆ Integrate Active Directory DNS zones with non-Active Directory DNS zones.

◆ Configure zones for dynamic updates.

Manage, monitor, and troubleshoot DNS.

◆ Manage replication of DNS data.

Installing, Configuring, Managing, Monitoring, Optimizing, and Troubleshooting Change and Configuration Management

Implement and troubleshoot Group Policy.

◆ Create a Group Policy object (GPO).

◆ Link an existing GPO.

◆ Delegate administrative control of Group Policy.

◆ Modify Group Policy inheritance.

◆ Filter Group Policy settings by associating security groups to GPOs.

◆ Modify Group Policy.

Manage and troubleshoot user environments by using Group Policy.

◆ Control user environments by using administrative templates.

◆ Assign script policies to users and computers.

Manage and troubleshoot software by using Group Policy.

◆ Deploy software by using Group Policy.

◆ Maintain software by using Group Policy.

◆ Configure deployment options.

◆ Troubleshoot common problems that occur during software deployment.

Manage network configuration by using Group Policy.

Deploy Windows 2000 by using Remote Installation Services (RIS).

- ◆ Install an image on a RIS client computer.
- ◆ Create a RIS boot disk.
- ◆ Configure remote installation options.
- ◆ Troubleshoot RIS problems.
- ◆ Manage images for performing remote installations.

Configure RIS security.

- ◆ Authorize a RIS server.
- ◆ Grant computer account creation rights.
- ◆ Prestage RIS client computers for added security and load balancing.

Managing, Monitoring, and Optimizing the Components of Active Directory

Manage Active Directory objects.

- ◆ Move Active Directory objects.
- ◆ Publish resources in Active Directory.
- ◆ Locate objects in Active Directory.
- ◆ Create and manage accounts manually or by scripting.
- ◆ Control access to Active Directory objects.
- ◆ Delegate administrative control of objects in Active Directory.

Manage Active Directory performance.

- ◆ Monitor, maintain, and troubleshoot domain controller performance.
- ◆ Monitor, maintain, and troubleshoot Active Directory components.

Manage and troubleshoot Active Directory replication.

- ◆ Manage intersite replication.
- ◆ Manage intrasite replication.

Configuring, Managing, Monitoring, and Troubleshooting Active Directory Security Solutions

Configure and troubleshoot security in a directory services infrastructure.

- ◆ Apply security policies by using Group Policy.
- ◆ Create, analyze, and modify security configurations by using Security Configuration and Analysis and Security Templates.
- ◆ Implement an audit policy.

Monitor and analyze security events.

HARDWARE AND SOFTWARE YOU'LL NEED

As a self-paced study guide, *MCSE Training Guide: Windows 2000 Directory Services Infrastructure* is meant to help you understand concepts that must be refined through hands-on experience. To make the most of your studying, you need to have as much background on and experience with Windows 2000 Server or Advanced Server as possible. The best way to do this is to combine studying with work on Windows 2000 Server or Advanced Server. This section gives you a description of the minimum computer requirements you need to enjoy a solid practice environment. For portions of this book, you will need two computers to properly complete the exercises.

◆ Windows 2000 Server, Advanced Server, and Professional.

◆ A server and a workstation computer on the Microsoft Hardware Compatibility List.

◆ Pentium 166 (or better) processor. Pentium II 300 or better is recommended.

◆ 1GB (or larger) hard disk. Parts of the book require at least two 1GB partitions on the computer.

◆ Super VGA video adapter and monitor.

◆ Mouse or equivalent pointing device.

◆ CD-ROM drive.

◆ Network interface card (NIC). The card on the computer on which you will run Windows 2000 Professional should at least contain a PXE boot ROM.

◆ A presence on an existing network or use of a two-port (or more) miniport hub to create a test network.

◆ Internet access with Internet Explorer 5 shipped with Windows 2000.

◆ 128MB of RAM (256MB recommended for Windows 2000 Server).

It is easier to obtain access to the necessary computer hardware and software in a corporate business environment. It can be difficult, however, to allocate enough time within the busy workday to complete a self-study program. Most of your study time will occur after normal working hours, away from the everyday interruptions and pressures of your regular job.

ADVICE ON TAKING THE EXAM

More extensive tips are found in the "Final Review" section titled "Study and Exam Prep Tips," but keep this advice in mind as you study:

◆ **Read all the material.** Microsoft has been known to include material not expressly specified in the objectives. This book has included additional information not reflected in the objectives in an effort to give you the best possible preparation for the examination—and for the real-world experiences to come.

◆ **Do the Step by Steps and complete the exercises in each chapter.** They will help you gain experience using the specified methodology or approach. All Microsoft exams are task- and experienced-based and require you to have experience actually performing the tasks upon which you will be tested.

◆ **Use the questions to assess your knowledge.** Don't just read the chapter content; use the questions to find out what you know and what you don't. If you are struggling at all, study some more, review, and then assess your knowledge again.

◆ **Review the exam objectives.** Develop your own questions and examples for each topic listed. If you can develop and answer several questions for each topic, you should not find it difficult to pass the exam.

NOTE **Exam-Taking Advice** Although this book is designed to prepare you to take and pass the Implementing and Administering a Microsoft Windows 2000 Directory Services Infrastructure certification exam, there are no guarantees. Read this book, work through the questions and exercises, and when you feel confident, take the Practice Exam and additional exams using the *ExamGear, Training Guide Edition* test software. This should tell you whether you are ready for the real thing.

When taking the actual certification exam, make sure you answer all the questions before your time limit expires. Do not spend too much time on any one question. If you are unsure, answer it as best as you can and then mark it for review when you have finished the rest of the questions. This advice will not apply, however, if you are taking an adaptive exam. In that case, take your time on each question. There is no opportunity to go back to a question.

Remember, the primary object is not to pass the exam—it is to understand the material. After you understand the material, passing the exam should be simple. Knowledge is a pyramid; to build upward, you need a solid foundation. This book and the Microsoft Certified Professional programs are designed to ensure that you have that solid foundation.

Good luck!

NEW RIDERS PUBLISHING

The staff of New Riders Publishing is committed to bringing you the very best in computer reference material. Each New Riders book is the result of months of work by authors and staff who research and refine the information contained within its covers.

As part of this commitment to you, the NRP reader, New Riders invites your input. Please let us know if you enjoy this book, if you have trouble with the information or examples presented, or if you have a suggestion for the next edition.

Please note, however, that New Riders staff cannot serve as a technical resource during your preparation for the Microsoft certification exams or for questions about software- or hardware-related problems. Please refer instead to the documentation that accompanies the Microsoft products or to the applications' Help systems.

If you have a question or comment about any New Riders book, there are several ways to contact New Riders Publishing. We will respond to as many readers as we can. Your name, address, or phone number will never become part of a mailing list or be used for any purpose other than to help us continue to bring you the best books possible. You can write to us at the following address:

New Riders Publishing
Attn: Executive Editor
201 W. 103rd Street
Indianapolis, IN 46290

If you prefer, you can fax New Riders Publishing at 317-817-7448.

You also can send email to New Riders at the following Internet address:

nrfeedback@newriders.com

NRP is an imprint of Pearson Education.
To obtain a catalog or information, contact us at nrmedia@newriders.com. To purchase a New Riders book, call 800-428-5331.

Thank you for selecting *MCSE Training Guide: Windows 2000 Directory Services Administration.*

EXAM PREPARATION

What is Active Directory? This is one of the first questions many people will have as they start to look at Windows 2000. The simple answer is, of course, that Active Directory is the directory service used in Windows 2000. This answer, though completely correct, is not overly useful.

This book begins by taking a look at what a directory service does and then at how Active Directory performs those functions. There are no formal Microsoft objectives discussed in this chapter. The point of this chapter is to give you an overview of Active Directory. Once you are armed with this information, the discussion will move on to cover how you implement the various pieces that make up directory services and how to deal with them on a day-to-day basis. This book does not cover the design of an Active Directory infrastructure. *MCSE Training Guide: Designing an Active Directory Infrastructure* provides coverage of that topic.

CHAPTER 1

Understanding Active Directory

STUDY STRATEGIES

▶ Pay close attention to how Microsoft has worked DNS into Active Directory.

▶ Make sure you understand classes and attributes and the comparison with tables and columns in a database.

▶ Make sure you know the three common elements in Active Directory.

INTRODUCTION

This chapter is included to cover the basics, the information you will need to know before you go on to learn about the details. The information you will cover here is the foundation for the information you will see in the rest of the text.

The chapter starts with a discussion of directory services in general and builds on the history of previous systems. Then it looks at directory services for what it is, a database. The basics of a database are discussed, and you will see how the directory service is built from the ground up. Then the chapter turns to the objects you will see in Active Directory and provides you with an introduction to the objects. Finally, the information is brought together to make sure you have a full and complete understanding of how the system works.

WHAT IS A DIRECTORY SERVICE?

This is a good starting point because you will need to understand why directory services are required before you will be able to understand what is significant about Active Directory.

As a starting point, consider networks such as NetWare 3.12 or Windows for Workgroups 3.11. These networks provided the basic requirements of a network; that is, they gave you a service (a program that runs in the background) that allowed users to connect to a station. They also provided a service that would automatically redirect requests to the network if the resource were on the network.

This is, of course, the basis of networking a server service and a redirector, or workstation, service. The server service accepts client requests and acts on them. The redirector service, called the Workstation service in Microsoft networking, decides whether the resources a user requests are on the local system or the network. Networks also need to provide authentication, the capability to identify the users connecting to a server, so that only people who are supposed to connect to a network resource are able to connect. A system that is going to share its resources (disk, printer, and so on) on the network needs a list of the people who are allowed to use the resource or, as was the case in Windows for Workgroups, a password users must know to connect to resources.

This is where directory services come into play. The directory is, in fact, the list of users allowed to connect to a system. This list further enables you to specify which users are allowed to use which resources; you can set security using a username. The directory service is the program that runs in conjunction with the server service to establish the username. This service, in essence, provides the authentication, and the server service provides the actual access to the resource.

In networks like NetWare 3.12, the directory was separate for each server on the network. This meant that a user needing access to multiple servers required a username and password for each server. This also meant the administrator would need to add the user to each of the servers and set the initial password to enable the user to connect. Further, the user would need to manage his password on multiple servers. NetWare 3.12 did provide a method to change passwords on multiple servers, but even this was not foolproof.

All this led to a lot of extra management on the part of the administrator and didn't provide a truly enterprise approach to networking. A couple of the networks of the day did have ways to get around this problem. LAN Manager, the precursor to Windows NT, had developed a way to centralize the directory on a group of servers. One server would have the original directory, the primary domain controller, where all changes would be made, and then one or more servers would make a copy of this directory. The other servers couldn't change the directory, but they could use it to authenticate users. In this model, a user would authenticate with a domain controller and then would be able to connect with any server for which that user had rights. In reality, this method separated the authentication and the server services even more.

The user would log on at his local computer to make sure he was allowed access to the network. This authentication would be sent across the network to a domain controller, which would actually perform the authentication. After this, all connections over the network to other servers were also authenticated against a domain controller. In fact, Windows NT 4.0 uses this same basic system for authentication to this day. The upshot was that, rather than every server having to keep a separate directory, the domain controllers took over this responsibility. Because only one controller had a write-enabled copy, there was now in fact only one directory for all the computers. The trick was that all the computers had to belong to the same domain (group of computers and users for administrative purposes), so the servers would recognize other servers with the same directory. If you connect to a server in a domain, it will find a domain controller for its domain to authenticate your logon request.

The other network operating system that had moved beyond the directory-per-server problem was Banyan VINES. Banyan's approach to the problem was somewhat different. Rather than creating large directories that were at times clumsy and hard to work with, they chose to continue to split the work across multiple servers. However, rather than having one directory per server with no real organization, they imposed a structure: a hierarchy on the directories. This let them easily create an enterprise-capable network. They could always add another branch to the network like a tree growing a new limb.

This was based on the X.500 specifications, which described a method of working with a directory in a hierarchy. In essence, this meant that a starting point was defined as the organization; the organization encompasses all the namespace of the enterprise network. That namespace was then broken down into organizational units that could be further subdivided. Users could belong to any organizational unit. When users needed to be authenticated, the correct organizational unit could be found, and the user authenticated against his home server. This meant that a user would have a simple username and a fully distinguished name such as ScrimR@Research@ScrimTech.

Perhaps this discussion has gone a little astray, so a summary is needed. A directory is a list of objects on a network that users need to find or that are required for the authentication of users. The "service" part of directory service is used to authenticate a user against the directory or to answer user queries about objects.

At this point, you should hopefully have an idea as to what a directory is used for, and perhaps you are beginning to see why an enterprise-level directory is required to perform these tasks in a very large network. Hopefully, you are also beginning to see that a directory is, in and of itself, a list.

LOOKING AT ACTIVE DIRECTORY

How does all this relate to Active Directory? Another good question. The answer is fairly simple. Active Directory (like Novell's Novell Directory Services) was built based on the technology that had preceded it. Microsoft already had a working system using the domain model. When they moved this up to Windows NT, they added the capability to tie domains together using trust relationships. This lets the domain controllers know about domains other than their own. Thus, if they need to validate a user, they can now pass that request to domain controllers in another domain. This enabled network designers to go beyond the basic domain, but it complicated authentication and increased administration because trust relationships also had to be managed.

The domain model itself was sound and worked well. Users were able to log on and function on the network without many problems. The difficulty with Windows NT's directory services only started when you had to move beyond the single domain. It caused extra traffic every time a user used a resource in another domain. It increased traffic as the domain controllers maintained the trust relationships. It meant a lot of traffic when permissions were being set because the entire directory would have to be read from remote domains each time a user from that domain was given permission. So trusts turned out to be workable but somewhat cumbersome.

Two things had to happen to make trusts a truly workable solution:

◆ A global list of each domain's directory would need to be available at each domain.

◆ A system to automatically manage trust relationships would be required.

The first problem you might associate with this scheme is that, by providing a list of all the objects in the directory from all the domains in an organization, you would create a great deal of background traffic. For example, listing the entire directory describing all objects in an organization with 80,000 users and even more computers would require a very powerful server and a lot of traffic to replicate the information. Further, if there were any differences in the structure of any of the domain databases you were trying to pull together, everything would quickly fall apart. These are obviously valid concerns, and Active Directory takes these concerns into account.

Before the discussion covers how these concerns are addressed, you need to understand what exactly is in the directory. It has already been stated that the directory is a list. A list on a computer is normally kept in a database. Keeping this in mind, the discussion will now look at the directory in terms of being a database.

Building a Database

The term "database" has been known to scare some people. However, everyone deals with databases in their simple form nearly every day. A database is basically a list such as a grocery list or a phonebook. The difference between a list and a database is twofold. First, a database is stored on a computer; second, a database has had structure imposed on it.

Consider for a moment a grocery list.

	Milk
Dozen	Eggs
	Bacon
	Bread

In this case, you have a list you might write when your spouse calls and asks you to pick these up on your way home. This is a database, and for each record (line or row), you have two pieces of information: the quantity and the description. When the quantity is not given, you can assume the default quantity (probably 1 in this case). This simple list can be rewritten as follows:

Quantity	*Description*
1	Milk
12	Eggs
1	Bacon
1	Bread

In a similar way, we could create a list of the users on the network:

User ID	Logon	First Name	Last Name	Domain
S-2882-234-23	SCRIM	Rob	Scrimger	ScrimTech
S-2322-321-99	JUUDY	Juudy	Jamieson	ScrimTech
S-2332-233-23	TAWNI	Tawni	Scrimger	ScrimTech

Looking at the table, we now have a key value: the user ID. This is an internal number used by the system to identify the user for security purposes. This is known as the *security identifier* (SID) in Windows NT and Windows 2000. Actual SIDs are much longer. In addition to the SID, the logon, first name, last name, and domain are all attributes used to describe the entity—all objects have a common name that has to be unique just like the SID. This list in a database would be a table; the attributes, which are the columns, define the table. As it relates to Active Directory, this also defines a class of object because a table stores all the entities of a single class.

To reduce the number of times you will have to create the same column, Microsoft splits attributes and classes. The attributes are created first, and then classes are built from the attributes available. Just like other databases, you can store information as words, as numbers, or as a logical yes/no. The classes store data as the attribute type. If you are familiar with databases, you could compare this to user-defined data types.

"Class" is a term used to describe a type of thing. In the preceding table, a user class is defined, and all users in this directory will have the attributes as shown. If you wanted to store information on computers, you could define another table that contained the attributes you wanted to store about computers. The same carries through for any type of thing (technical term for the stuff) you wanted to put into directory services.

You could also add another column if you want. You could add another attribute to the class definition. In making these modifications, you are extending the information stored in Active Directory. If you need to keep an employee number for each employee, for example, you could add an attribute and attach it to the users table. If you need to keep the asset tag number for equipment, you can add this information. What we have is an extensible architecture.

An extensible architecture provides an architecture in which the information you store is not limited by the manufacturer but can be added to as needed.

Perhaps you're wondering what this has to do with the two points that were brought up earlier: the need for a global list of each domain's directory and the requirement for a central method of managing trust relationships. This capability to add attributes and classes as required would, if anything, make it impossible to have a list of each domain's directory because each one could be different. However, this is not the case. In fact, every domain in your enterprise will have the exact same schema. This is accomplished through the use of a schema master. The schema master (like the PDC of old) is the only system with a write-enabled copy of the schema.

Because it would be impractical to track every attribute for all the objects in the enterprise, Active Directory enables you to mark certain attributes (columns) to be copied up to the global catalog. The global catalog is used to provide the list of objects in each domain's directory to all the users in your enterprise. Because you can tell Active Directory which attributes to include in the global catalog, you can control how much data is moved between global catalog servers.An extensible architecture provides an architecture in which the information you store is not limited by the manufacturer but can be added to as needed.

At this point, we have for each domain a directory (a database). Certain attributes from each domain will be copied to a global catalog that is then shared across all domains. This still doesn't help with the problem of trust relationships and doesn't explain the actual enterprise structure. Therefore, let's turn the discussion in that direction.

Building a Hierarchy

As previously stated, the domain model is a relatively good model for a small- to medium-size network. The problems that were encountered tended to have to do with larger organizations that needed to expand beyond a single domain. The problem had to do with locating resources across essentially an unstructured collection of domains and with maintaining the trust relationships.

The first answer that might occur to you is to expand the domain model so that a domain could contain enough objects to remove the need to go to multiple domains. This has been done to a degree. The new domains will be able to hold many more objects than the existing Windows NT domains (millions versus tens of thousands). However, the domain still has a place. Domains act as security and replication boundaries.

So if domains will continue to exist, the next best thing to do would be to impose some structure on them. This would make it easier to find objects as well as aid in the replication across domains for items such as the global catalog. Rather than reinvent the wheel, Microsoft decided to borrow existing technology to provide the backbone, the method of tying domains together.

Nearly everyone these days has had occasion to use an Internet browser. Few people probably ever consider what a remarkable achievement it is that you can enter any Web address for a site, anywhere in the world, and be connected (most of the time) with that site. This is fairly amazing considering the number of sites and the general complexity of the Internet. What makes this happen is the *domain name system* (DNS), probably the largest example of a hierarchical database on the planet.

DNS works by declaring the entire Internet to be one contiguous namespace. This provides a starting point that is known on the Internet as the root domain. You don't see it when you enter an address, rather it is implied. The root domain (all of the namespace) is then broken down into smaller sections. On the Internet, these are called top-level domains. Top-level domains, in turn, are broken down into second-level domains. From there, the process can continue ad infinitum.

When you look for an Internet site, the request (in theory) goes to the root domain. Because the root domain doesn't house the names of all the servers, it will redirect your query to a server responsible for the namespace you are seeking. If you were looking for `www.newriders.com`, for example, the root-level server would realize you are looking for a server in the .com domain and would send you (actually your DNS server) to the .com domain server. Your request would be directed to the server responsible for that namespace. From there, the .com server would determine that you are looking for a computer in the newriders.com namespace and would send you to the server that handles that part of the namespace. Now you could ask the server responsible for that newriders.com namespace for the address directly.

This might sound inefficient, but consider the number of records you would search if all the records were on the same server. Also, consider how big those servers would need to be to accommodate all the requests from users. By using the hierarchical model, DNS avoids having to search one large database and avoids overloading any single server.

Now, if you were to put the previously discussed directory database at each level rather than just having a database of host names at the lower levels, you would have effectively imposed a structure to Windows NT domains. Further, if one of the attributes you include in the global catalog is the distinguished name for any object (the full name including the domain and Organizational Unit (OU) to which the object belongs), you could then easily find and connect to any object anywhere in the enterprise. This is exactly what Microsoft has done in building Active Directory.

Because there is a structure to the domains, you can now create a system that will take care of the trust relationships because the structure can be deduced from the names. The domain naming master handles this in Active Directory. This system ensures that all domains have names that fit the namespace.

So now we have the three keys to making Active Directory work, and in fact, we have the three elements common to all domains in Active Directory:

◆ A common schema

◆ A common global catalog

◆ A common configuration

OBJECTS IN ACTIVE DIRECTORY

Now that you have an understanding of the structure and purpose of Active Directory, it seems appropriate to introduce the objects that are part of Active Directory. Some objects are very obvious: users, computers, and groups. Some objects are not so obvious:

organizational units and sites. The next few sections will look at each object and its use. First, however, we need to define an object as it relates to Windows 2000.

Basically everything is an object.

Obviously, this is a little on the vague side. However, it is perfectly accurate. Windows 2000 (as well as other versions of Windows) treat everything as an object primarily to simplify security. The easiest way to view an object is as a container; an object holds something. A file object holds data. A group object holds a list of members. Some objects, like printers or users, are holding a place rather than actually holding something tangible; such objects are known as leaf-level objects.

All objects will have the following attached to them:

◆ **Methods.** All objects will have some basic methods in common such as creating the object, opening the object, and deleting the object. In addition, most objects have methods that are specific to them. Think of methods as verbs, the actions that you can perform on the object or that the object can perform.

◆ **Properties.** All objects have properties or attributes that distinguish them from other objects. These attributes are the things that make objects different from one another. At the very least, objects have a name and type; beyond this, the properties are type specific with a good number of common attributes between similar types.

◆ **Collections.** When a property or attribute could have more than a single value (such as the ingredients in a can of soup), these values are stored as a collection, an array of values. The number of members in the collection is usually not known.

Relating this back to the previous discussion of databases, methods would be performing an action on a row. You might add a row, edit the information in a row, or remove a row from a table. These methods would generally be known as create, update, and delete. Notice that you can use the same verbs for everything in the operating system including files, printers, computers, and so on. This is what makes using objects terribly efficient. The number of verbs (actions) the computer needs to understand is greatly reduced, and general routines can be created to handle these functions. This makes programs easier to write, but it also makes the security easier to implement because all the objects are accessed the same way.

The properties would, of course, relate to the columns in the table. There are the obvious ones such as the name of the object and the type of object. Other properties are required such as the owner of the object. Collections would actually be a multiple-value field, that is, a field where you could enter many different values such as big and blue to describe the sky. This isn't technically how it will be implemented, but it is a good way to think of them.

A key collection that is placed on each object is the *discretionary access control list* (DACL). This is where the security model becomes both strong and simple. Because everything in the operating system is accessed the same way and everything has a DACL, it was easy for Microsoft to create a security reference model. For this model to work, though, we need to ensure that any process, user, service, or program that will attempt to access an object has a security context.

A security context simply means that we know which object (remember, users are objects) is attempting to access another object. A process is the general term we use to describe a program that is running. A process can be a background process, such as a service, or a foreground process, such as the program a user is running. When you log on to Windows 2000, you are authenticated against the directory services, and a program called Explorer.exe is running. This is the shell that you run in; it manages your desktop and puts the taskbar on the screen, and it handles the action you take on your desktop such as clicking the Start menu.

When you are authenticated and Explorer is started for you, information about you is attached to it. The information is your unique object ID (which is your SID) and the unique object IDs for the groups to which you belong to (their SIDs); together, they form the access token. When you run a program like Word, the IDs attached to Explorer (your user process) are compared to the ACL on the Word executable (and supporting files). If you have permission, the system will launch Word in another process and will attach your credentials (your object ID and those of the groups to which you belong) to the process.

Background processes also start under a given security context. They can be started using a username and password, just like you logging on, or they can start under the system account. The system account is actually the computer's local account, and it is stored in a local account's database.

By using the preceding process and by treating everything like an object, Windows 2000 maintains security regardless of how a user accesses an object. Now that object access has been explained, it is appropriate to look at some of the objects that will be in Active Directory.

Computers

The computer object is just that, a computer in the enterprise. This object is used in the background to enable the computers to be grouped together for management purposes. The account also lets the computer authenticate user logons because the computer will know which domain to use for authentication. When the text turns to a discussion of group policies, you will also find that you can apply security policies, select options, and even assign software to group objects (accounts) in a domain.

Users

Users are obviously a big part of the network, and without them, the network would be pointless (though faster). A user object holds the user's account, and this is what will enable the user to connect to the domain.

Groups

A group object (account) will contain a list of users that belong to the group. It will also, in Windows 2000, be able to contain other groups. These objects are also used when placing permission on other objects so that, rather than adding each user account, you can work with a larger group of users in one step. Groups, therefore, are also used to gather together a number of user accounts into a single object.

Printers

In Windows 2000, you have the option of creating a printer object in Active Directory if you share your printer. This is used primarily to enable users to search Active Directory. The printer is still an object on the local machine that acts as a print server, and that computer will handle the security.

Shared Folder

Like printers, shares can also be published in Active Directory. This, again, will be primarily to enable users to search for the share. The computer hosting the share will be responsible for checking the object permissions when the share is accessed.

CASE STUDY: AN INTRODUCTION TO SUNSHINE BREWING

ESSENCE OF THE CASE

As you read through the scenario, think about the parts of Active Directory that you have read about. In this case, there are two ways you can go with the design: use the locations as demarcation or use the functions as demarcation. Because administration is handled in the four main offices, you will be replicating information to all the offices. This replication will cause stress on some of the lower-speed lines, possibly saturating them.

INTRODUCTION

In this chapter, you have been introduced to the basic concepts of Active Directory. The chapter will hopefully provide you with the foundation in concepts that you will need to truly understand the information you will see in the remaining chapters.

In keeping with the introductory nature of this chapter, you will now read about Sunshine Brewing. This company and the associated network will serve as the foundation for the case studies that will appear at the end of each chapter. The case study is a chance to see some of the ways in which the technology you are reading about can be applied to the real world.

SCENARIO

Just like in project management, most of the work of networking is done during the planning or design phase. Because this book is about

continues

CASE STUDY: AN INTRODUCTION TO SUNSHINE BREWING

continued

implementation, it is actually predicated on the design principles discussed in the *MCSE Training Guide: Windows 2000 Directory Services Design*.

Sunshine Brewing is a multinational corporation with major centers in Ottawa, Sydney, Cape Town, and London. There are a series of smaller branch offices throughout the world. These are located in Victoria, Los Angeles, Mexico City, Houston, New York, Buenos Aires, St. John's, Paris, Moscow, Beijing, and Tokyo.

After extensive studies, the company has decided that they will use Windows 2000 with Active Directory as their primary network. In addition, they will also need to use UNIX for monitoring and controlling the production facilities.

Sunshine Brewing plans to provide both Internet and intranet access to all employees. Information will need to flow easily from location to location because teams are often drawn up from human resources across the entire organization. Provision will also have to be made for the sales and IT staff who travel frequently but still need to access resources in their home locations.

Before you can go much further, you will need to look at the physical network. You need to look at the number of users at each location and the role they play in the organization. The physical connections between the sites will also need to be addressed both as to the speed and the reliability. Table 1.1 breaks down the user community by location for you as a basis for the network.

TABLE 1.1

THE DISTRIBUTION OF USERS AT SUNSHINE BREWING

Branch	Exec.	R&D	IT	Adm.	Sales	Prod.
Ottawa	145	352	450	742	1,274	854
London	23	120	180	521	963	562
Cape Town	18	136	196	436	954	632
Sydney	32	224	251	357	965	843
Victoria	1	5	0	42	89	236
Los Angeles	2	6	0	61	109	310
Mexico City	3	12	0	72	174	400
Houston	2	15	0	66	98	350
New York	2	23	0	96	131	298
Buenos Aires	1	8	0	45	67	245
St. John's	1	4	0	35	64	198
Paris	1	16	0	41	134	201
Moscow	1	6	0	24	54	126
Beijing	1	2	0	88	140	320
Tokyo	2	4	0	48	98	264

CASE STUDY: AN INTRODUCTION TO SUNSHINE BREWING

As you probably guessed, the breakdown of the users into these six groups is not accidental. These represent the main roles in the company, and each of the roles has a different set of requirements from the network.

REQUIRMENTS

The following list is an overview of the different requirements for the users:

- **Exec. (235 users).** The executive users require 24-hour access from anywhere. Frequently, the executives travel between the offices and to other locations. They need to be able to use email, access an office suite, and be able to connect to server-based applications internally using a Web browser.

- **R&D (933 users).** The research and development users don't travel but do need to be able to collaborate with R&D users in other branches. In addition to email and an office suite, they need access to specialized applications. Research users also have the option of working at home or at the office, and at the office, they have shared desk areas where any research user can sit down and work. They want to ensure that all applications are available on each of the shared systems but would also like to have the users able to keep their own desktop settings.

- **IT (1,077 users).** The IT department in each location takes care of the local computers, both of the production systems that are running UNIX, and the Windows-based systems used by the other users.

The IT staff frequently travels to the branch offices to maintain and upgrade systems and will need access to their email from any branch. They will also need to be able to access troubleshooting tools located on various servers across the network.

- **Adm. (2,674 users).** The administration users are probably the easiest to deal with; they don't travel and only need to be able to work with email and an office suite. Each is assigned a fixed desk and computer.

- **Sales (5,314 users).** Sales users travel constantly and are rarely in the office. They use laptops exclusively to access their email, the order-processing application, and an office suite. They occasionally will stop by the office, and a space has been provided in each branch for about half of the sales staff to be in at any one time. The space provided includes only network connections, and the users will work on their laptops even in the office.

- **Prod. (5,839 users).** The production users are responsible for making sure that production and shipping is handled. They primarily use the UNIX systems, but also need access to email. They use Web browsers to access the production software.

As you can see, the requirement for each different type of user is varied, and this will need to be accommodated. In addition to the local software on their systems, they will need to access servers on a corporate level. This includes the UNIX servers that will control production and the accounting system that runs

continues

CASE STUDY: AN INTRODUCTION TO SUNSHINE BREWING

continued

on a SQL server in the Ottawa office. In addition, they need to access the sales tracking system that links the accounting system and the production system that has been specially built based on the Exchange servers used for email. Finally, the research staff makes frequent use of Exchange public folders for collaboration.

Another consideration is the remote access for the Executive and Sales users. This will be handled by finding an ISP local to each site and then getting the users an account with that ISP (most of which will bulk discount.) For some users, a global ISP will be used, and this could be considered for all users depending on price. The users will then use a virtual private network to access the local office through its Internet connection.

So far, you have learned about the user community and the locations; but before you can make decisions about the domain structure, the number of subnets, the sites, or the placement of servers, you need to know about the physical network.

Sunshine Brewing has been building the network for some time and therefore doesn't have a single technology that is across the board. The locations vary in the type and quality of network and in the type and quality of connection to the other offices and the Internet. The following list describes the technology in the different locations.

- **Ottawa (3,817 users).** The network in Ottawa has been upgraded a few times over the years and is now running 100Mbps Ethernet. The main protocol in use is

TCP/IP, and all of the desktop systems and servers are cycled out every two years. The facility is a collection of three buildings: one for production, one for warehousing, and one for offices. The three buildings are linked using a redundant fiber backbone providing high-speed connections between them. The buildings are using a combination of routing and switching so no more than 50 desktop systems and no more than 5 servers are local to any segment. In cases in which servers need to communicate with each other, a separate network card connects the servers; in the case of Microsoft products, this backbone runs the NetBEUI protocol.

The Ottawa location is currently connected to the Internet using a 100Mbps connection. In addition, there are T1 links between this office and London and 512Kbps Frame Relay links to Sydney and Cape Town. There is also a 512Kbps link to the St. John's office and an OC3 link to New York.

- **London (2,369 users).** The London office is similar to the Ottawa office but consists of two buildings: one for production and warehousing and the other for offices. The buildings are linked using a redundant fiber backbone providing high-speed connections between them. The buildings are using a combination of routing and switching such that no more that 120 desktop systems and no more than 10 servers are local to any segment. The office building uses 100Mbps Ethernet, and the production and warehousing site uses 10Mbps Ethernet.

CASE STUDY: AN INTRODUCTION TO SUNSHINE BREWING

The London office is connected to the Internet by a T1 link. There is also the connection to Ottawa using a T1 as well as a connection to Paris using a T1 and to Moscow using a 256Kbps leased line. An additional T1 connects the London office to the Tokyo office.

- **Cape Town (2,372 users).** The Cape Town office was acquired during a takeover of a rival brewing company. The existing Token Ring network is still in use, although the wiring has been upgraded to enable the network to run at 16Mbps. Again, there are two buildings as in London, and the buildings are linked using a redundant fiber backbone providing high-speed connections between them. The buildings are using routing such that no more that 150 desktop systems and no more than 15 servers are local to any segment.

The Cape Town office is connected to the Internet using a 512Kbps leased line. In addition, it is connected to the Buenos Aries office using a 512Kbps link and to the Ottawa office using 512Kbps.

- **Sydney (2,672 users).** Sydney is also broken down into two buildings, but the buildings are connected using a leased 768Kbps line because they are not physically close enough to use fiber. This office is currently using a 10Mbps Ethernet network. The buildings are using switching such that no more that 80 desktop systems and no more than 5 servers are local to any segment.

The Sydney office is connected to the Internet using a T1 link. It is connected to Ottawa using a 512Kbps line and to Tokyo using a T1 line.

- **Victoria (373 users).** The Victoria office, like all the branches, is a combined facility with the production, warehousing, and office space all in one location. The network is a routed 100Mbps Ethernet network with four network segments.

The Victoria office is connected to the Internet using business ADSL (768Kbps uplink speed). There is also a T1 link to the Los Angeles office.

- **Los Angeles (488 users).** The Los Angeles office uses 100Mbps Ethernet as well. It has five segments across routers locally. There is a T1 connection to the Internet in addition to the T1 connection to the Victoria office and a T3 connection to the New York office. There is also a T3 connection with Tokyo.

- **Mexico City (661 users).** In Mexico City, the network is running Token Ring at 4Mbps. The network is split into 10 separate rings, and routing is used between them. There is a 256Kbps link to the Internet and a 512Kbps link to the Houston office.

- **Houston (531 users).** The Houston office uses 100Mbps Ethernet and uses switching between the seven network segments. There is a T1 connection to the Internet in addition to the 512Kbps link to Mexico City and a T1 connection to the New York.

continues

CASE STUDY: AN INTRODUCTION TO SUNSHINE BREWING

continued

- **New York (550 users).** This network is using a switched fiber backbone and then uses 100Mbps to the desktop. There are six segments in the network. There is a T1 connection to the Internet in addition to the T1 connection to Houston, the T3 connection to Los Angeles, and the OC3 connection to Ottawa.

- **Buenos Aires (366 users).** In Buenos Aires, the network is running 10Mbps Ethernet with routers connecting the seven segments. There is a 256Kbps connection to the Internet in addition to the 512Kbps connection to Cape Town.

- **St. John's (302 users).** The St. John's office uses 100Mbps Ethernet with a switch between the six network segments. There is a business ADSL connection to the Internet along with the 512Kbps link with the Ottawa office.

- **Paris (393 users).** The Paris office also uses 100Mbps Ethernet and uses switching technology between the eight network segments. There is a 512Kbps link to the Internet and a T1 connection to the London office.

- **Moscow (211 users).** The Moscow office uses ARCnet at 2Mbps and is routing between the five network segments. There is a 128Kbps link to the Internet and the 256Kbps link to London.

- **Beijing (551 users).** The Beijing office uses 10Mbps Ethernet with bridges between the six network segments. There is a 128Kbps link to the Internet and a 256Kbps link to Tokyo.

- **Tokyo (416 users).** The Tokyo office is using fiber to the desktop and connects each system directly to one of their switches. They have a T1 link to the Internet and also have a 256Kbps link to Beijing, a T1 link with London, a T1 link with Sydney, and a T3 link with Los Angeles.

Within North America, the WAN links tend to be 95% reliable; elsewhere, it is closer to 75% reliability. Each location has demand-dial routes set up using RRAS to try to compensate for downtime, and this has brought your overall WAN link uptime to around 98%.

Corporate information is kept on each of the main sites; however, region-specific information will be kept in the appropriate branch office. This information will need to be available to all users.

ANALYSIS

The first big decision you need to make is how you will integrate the private and public DNS names. In this case, there are several countries involved, and probably the organization will register a domain in each country to have a local feel. This means you will have several different

CASE STUDY: AN INTRODUCTION TO SUNSHINE BREWING

names on the external network. That combined with concerns about accidentally exposing servers or addressing to the Internet leads to the conclusion that an internal address will be used. The obvious one would be SunshineBrewing.local, so this is what you'll see in the case studies.

The breakdown of the domains is more of a problem and would really require study as to how much change to expect. Little change would mean there would be little that needed to replicate. This company has 16,072 employees worldwide, which means that anything much over a 5% turnover rate per month could be an issue. There is also the password policy you will need to consider; if the passwords are changed frequently, you will have an increase in the replication within the domain.

There are basically three types of replication that need to be accounted for in the design: the global catalog, which is sent between domains frequently; the schema and configuration partitions, which are sent between domains but not frequently; and the domain partition, which contains all the domain information, which is sent frequently but only within the domain.

Conversations with the human resources department in this case can help you make the decision as can deciding on a password policy. In the case of Sunshine Brewing, the monthly turn over is about 2%. The password policy will require a password change every 60 days. Given this and given the very different needs of the

users, the Sunshine Brewing domain will be broken down by function rather than location. This should make administration easier although it will increase replication.

The design, then, is to have the SunshineBrewing.local domain, which will house the IT staff and Executive, and then create a child domain for each of the four remaining functions: Research.SunshineBrewing.local, Administration.SunshineBrewing.local, Sales.SunshineBrewing.local, and Production.SunshineBrewing.local.

Now that the structure is in place, you need to determine what organizational units and sites you will create. This is fairly simple. There were two demarcations you could have used for domain names: function and geography. Because function was used to create the domains, you will normally use geography to break this down further. Within each domain, there will therefore be an OU for each location.

From a network standpoint, you will need to control replication between locations, and therefore, you will create a site for each. In the large locations, you also need to consider the effect of replication on the network. This means you might need to break up the offices. Remember, though, that the Sales users are not always in the office, so you don't need to account for all of them. To keep this simple for purposes of example, the larger offices will be broken into two or three sites by building.

continues

CASE STUDY: AN INTRODUCTION TO SUNSHINE BREWING

continued

This is the basis for the network. In the case studies that follow, you will see how the DNS is configured, look at setting up the domains, and learn how to create the sites and OUs. Later, you will look at monitoring the network and learn the issues to look for as well as how to back up the network.

There will also be a discussion of how group policies are created, how to use them with roving users, and how to use them to manage the desktop environment. You will see an example of rolling out software and how to maintain it using group policies. Finally, you'll see how the RIS server can be used in this environment to help role out Windows 2000 Professional.

CHAPTER SUMMARY

At this point, it is probably worth taking all the information that has been presented and pulling it together.

Active Directory is a database that contains multiple tables, one for each class or type of object. The tables contain a unique ID and various attributes (properties) about the objects listed. From each of these tables, key fields are copied to the global catalog, which is replicated between all the domains in the enterprise. The structure of the database is common throughout the enterprise and is maintained on the schema master. Domains are used in Windows 2000 for administrative and replication boundaries. The domains are linked together in a hierarchy based on the DNS system.

This chapter has been an introduction to Active Directory and an overview of how it works. The following questions will help you review the material covered.

APPLY YOUR KNOWLEDGE

Review Questions

1. What is created in Active Directory for each type of object it lists?

2. What is the purpose of the global catalog?

3. What does the schema master do?

4. Every object has at least three attributes. What are the attributes?

5. What three things are common to all domains in Active Directory?

Answers to Review Questions

1. Each type or class of object creates a table that contains the unique identifier for the object and attributes related to the object type. See the section "Building a Database."

2. The global catalog maintains a partial set of attributes for all the objects stored in the Active Directory forest. The domains publish these attributes to the global catalog, creating a complete list of all the objects in the enterprise. See the section "Building a Database."

3. The schema must be the same for all domains within the enterprise. To ensure that this is the case, the only version of the schema that can be written to is the one on the schema master. See the section "Building a Database."

4. Every object, at the very least, needs to have ID, a common name, and a class. The full name needs to be unique across the enterprise and includes the full domain name. In addition, each object in Active Directory has a SID, or security identifier. See the section "Building a Database."

5. The three common elements to all domains are the schema, the global catalog, and the configuration. See the section "Building a Hierarchy."

This chapter looks at the DNS server that comes with Windows 2000 as it relates to the Active Directory. Although it concentrates on how to integrate with Active Directory, the chapter starts with a brief discussion of the basics of DNS. After that, a discussion of the installation is presented along with a look at the roles of a DNS server. After these basics are covered, the chapter turns to how it works with Active Directory.

The following objectives from the exam are covered in this chapter:

Install, configure, and troubleshoot DNS for Active Directory.

- **Integrate Active Directory DNS zones with non-Active Directory DNS zones.**

- **Configure zones for dynamic updates.**

▶ This objective is included to make sure you are able to work with DNS both for Active Directory and for other types of computers on your network. Also, one of the important changes in DNS for Windows 2000 is the capability to deal with dynamic updates. This is important for Active Directory so it can register various services with the DNS server to allow clients to find LDAP servers and domain controllers.

Manage, monitor, and troubleshoot DNS.

- **Manage replication of DNS data.**

▶ In managing replication of DNS, you need to understand the difference between zone transfers for standard zones and Active Directory replication that handles replication of Active Directory–integrated zones.

CHAPTER 2

Configuring DNS for Active Directory

▶ The DNS component of the Active Directory implementation exam is likely to be fairly small. You primarily need to concentrate on the following points:

- Creating DNS forward and reverse lookup zones

- Configuring DNS zones to accept dynamic updates

- Configuring secondary zone files

- Integrating Active Directory–integrated zones with other DNS servers

- Configuring a zone as Active Directory integrated

INTRODUCTION

Probably the most important aspect of Active Directory is that it is hierarchical. This is what enables Active Directory to use the concept of namespace, allowing an almost infinite number of objects to be stored and represented. This enables an organization to have a single root, or main, domain and then break this down into more and more precise sections.

Consider for a moment almost any company with whom you have dealt. Nearly all companies break down their organization into several different sections by function. For example, many companies have executive, accounting, human resources, sales, production, and marketing sections.

This structure builds a hierarchy with the executive at the top and the other sections reporting to that executive. Further, if you were to look at any one of the sections—accounting, for example—you could break this down to a VP, manager, or supervisor overseeing accounts payable and accounts receivable. This leads to another level of hierarchy (see Figure 2.1).

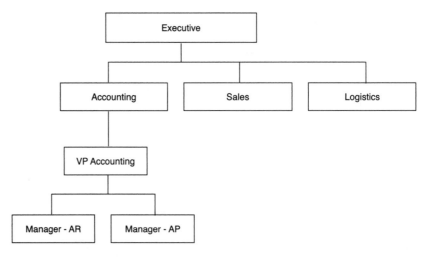

FIGURE 2.1
The organization chart for this example.

To take this further, you might break New Riders down by different divisions or by geographic location. Then you might have www.shipping.newriders.com and www.production.newriders.com.

Levels in an FQDN

These parts of the FQDN represent different levels in the namespace hierarchy. The example, www.newriders.com, tells us that from the root domain there is a com domain, in the com domain there is a newriders domain, and in that domain there is a server called www.

Part of Name	Represents	Level
Trailing period (.)	Root domain	Root
Com	Com domain	Top level
Newriders	Newriders domain	Second level
www	Server name or alias	–

Various bodies on the Internet manage the root and top-level domains. There is only one root domain, and this acts as the starting point for all names; it represents the starting point for the Internet namespace.

There are several top-level domains such as .com, .edu, and .gov that are intended to be used only within the United States. This is not always the case, and many foreign companies have registered as .com, .org, or .net. In other countries, the top-level domain is the country code such as .ca or .au.

The second level is where the hierarchy flattens out considerably. This is where companies, organizations, or individuals can start to register their names. In the previous example, newriders would have registered with the com domain. It is critical to register with the domain above you, the parent domain; otherwise, the resolution process discussed in the following "Resolving an FQDN" section will not work.

When you register your name, you are responsible for providing name resolutions for that part of the namespace. Therefore, you need to create one or more DNS name servers. If you are registering a domain on the Internet, you are generally required to provide two name servers. The theory behind this is that at least one will always be available. After the server is created, you can add entries for your domain in a zone file.

Understanding Zones

Any server you want to be available to the Internet needs to have an entry in a zone file. A name server is authoritative for a zone if it hosts the zone file used to resolve DNS queries for that zone. This can be somewhat confusing because many people will draw a parallel at this point between a zone and a domain. In most cases, this is not a problem because normally the two are the same. However, in some cases, an organization might decide to take the namespace it controls and further break it down.

For example, you work at newriders.com and want to separate the book publishing from the electronic publishing. You could, in fact, create a subdomain called electronic to separate that business out. This means you now would have the main domain called newriders.com and a subdomain called electronic.newriders.com. These could now be separate zone files, or they could be in the same zone file. If they are on the same server, they will be in the same zone file.

If they are on separate servers, then they are definitely two separate zones. In this case, you need to add *Name Server* (NS) records in the newriders.com zone that point at the name servers for electronic.newriders.com. This is the delegation process, the same process that happens on the Internet name servers when you register your domain; they add the NS records for your subdomain. These NS records are required to allow the process of name resolution to happen.

Resolving an FQDN

When you enter an address to browse, your operating system uses the resolver previously mentioned. The resolver queries your configured DNS server for the IP address of the name you entered. If the local DNS server has a zone file (is authoritative) for the zone you are querying, it will return the information to you from this file.

Unless you only browse for servers within your organization's namespace, the local DNS server will not be authoritative for the requested domain. This means that the server must now go out and find the address you are requesting. It does this by querying other DNS servers in the hierarchy for their best answer to the question, starting with the root and working down until it finds the server that is authoritative for the domain you are seeking.

For example, if you enter http://www.newriders.com into a browser, the browser will need to look this up using a resolver. It will first query the local DNS server. If this server cannot answer the query, the DNS server will then check the root-level server. The root-level server does not know the full path but does know where the com domain is located. Because this is all the root domain knows about your request, it will return the address of one or more *com domain* (COM-DOM) servers.

Your local DNS server will now query one of the COM DOM servers for the address you entered. Again, that server doesn't know where the host is but does know where the *newriders.com domain* is (NEWRIDERS-DOM). It will, therefore, return the NS records for the domain.

Your local DNS server will now query the name servers for NEWRIDERS-DOM, which will hopefully return the IP address for the server www. This means your server now knows the address and can return the address to the resolver on your system. The resolver on your system lets the browser know so it can open the page from the other company's Web server. This whole process is shown in Figure 2.2.

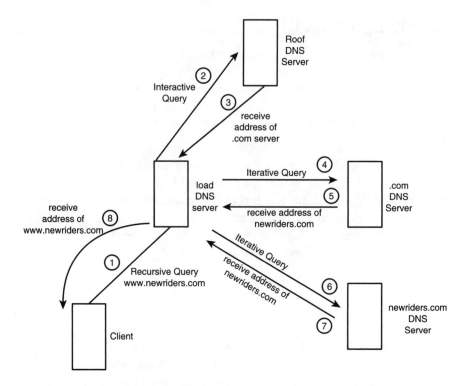

FIGURE 2.2
The steps in resolving a DNS query.

As you might have noticed, there are actually two types of queries in this discussion:

- ◆ **Recursive.** The query from your system to the local DNS server is the recursive query. Recursive queries require that the remote server return an authoritative answer or a "not found" message.

- ◆ **Iterative.** The other queries that came from your DNS server and queried the other DNS servers on the Internet are iterative. Several iterative queries (iterations) can be sent to locate an authoritative answer; each requests the best answer the other server can give.

The answers will be cached on the local server for a period of time specified by the remote server, known as the *time to live* (TTL). This means your next query to http://www.newriders.com will be answered from the cache on your local DNS server.

INSTALLING DNS

As is hopefully clear by now, DNS provides the hierarchy for Active Directory; therefore, you will first need to have a working DNS server before you can install Active Directory. You will normally install Windows 2000 as a server and then configure the DNS server service; after that is done, you will be able to install the Active Directory.

This part of the chapter assumes you can install Windows 2000 and concentrates on installation and configuration of the DNS server.

Prerequisites

Before you can install the DNS server, you need to have a working Windows 2000 Server or Windows 2000 Advanced Server. The system needs to be configured with TCP/IP and have disk space to hold the records that will be installed.

Although it is not required, you should confirm the computer name before you proceed. This will ensure that the correct information can be verified when DNS is installed. To confirm the name, follow these steps:

STEP BY STEP

2.1 Verifying Your Computer Name

1. Right-click the My Computer icon and choose Properties.

2. Click the Network Identification tab and make sure the full computer name is correct.

3. If required, click Properties and correct the name.

NOTE

Auto-Configuration With final release, you do not have to configure the DNS server beforehand. The Active Directory Installation Wizard will auto-configure the DNS service on the domain controller. It will configure only the forward lookup zone and will configure the zone as an Active Directory–integrated zone using secure updates.

NOTE

Network Service Installs In NT 4.0, Network Services were installed and removed using the Network Control Panel applet. In Windows 2000, Network Services are treated as regular components and are installed using the Add/Remove Programs applet.

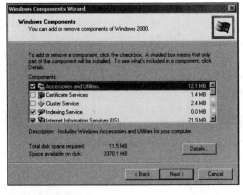

FIGURE 2.3
The Windows Components Wizard starts.

The Process

The process is as simple as the following Step by Step shows.

STEP BY STEP

2.2 Installing the DNS Service

1. From the Start menu, choose Settings and then Control Panel.

2. In the Control Panel window, double-click the Add/Remove Programs icon.

3. In the Add/Remove Programs applet, click the Add/Remove Windows Components button.

4. This opens the Windows Components Wizard (see Figure 2.3). Select Network Services and click the Details button.

5. Choose Domain Name System (DNS) and then click OK.

6. Click Next in the Windows Components Wizard. If you are prompted, enter the path to your distribution files.

7. Finally, the last screen of the Windows Components Wizard will appear and let you click Finish.

8. Close the Add/Remove Programs dialog box by clicking Close. Then you can close the Control Panel by clicking the Close button.

This process installs the DNS server. Next you need to create the reverse and forward lookup zones for your network, and then you can install Active Directory. Forward lookups resolve a name to an IP and reverse lookups do—well—the reverse.

ROLES FOR DNS SERVERS

Now that the DNS server is installed, you need to decide what role the DNS server will play in your organizational scheme. The role of the server depends on the zone files it has; because a server can have many different zone files, it can fill different roles. The main roles you will configure include

◆ Cache only

◆ Primary

◆ Secondary

Each of these roles will be explained in the following sections. Then the section titled "Integrating DNS and Active Directory," which covers a new role: Active Directory integrated.

Cache Only

This is the simplest type of server to configure because all you have to do is install the DNS server service. After this is done, other computers can point at this server to provide name resolution for names on the Internet or intranet. Because there are no zone files on this type of server, it will always have to find the resolution on other servers. Because it will then cache these, this type of server is known as a cache-only server. In addition, the server can be configured to use a forwarder; your local server can recursively ask another DNS server to resolve the name. This is useful in a large organization because a single large server can resolve the queries and cache them for multiple servers. This means that the chance of an address being in the cache on the central server is much greater.

Primary

A primary, actually in this version a standard primary, is the server that maintains the original zone file. Windows 2000 DNS server can host multiple primary zones.

The information for a primary zone is normally kept in the registry. It is also kept in a file located in c:\winnt\system32\dns for default installations. This is important because this enables zone transfers between Microsoft DNS servers and other types of DNS servers.

There are two types of primary zones you will need to deal with: forward and reverse. Forward lookup zones resolve an FQDN or host name to an IP address, as you saw earlier. The reverse zone does the reverse. It resolves IP addresses to FQDNs. Configuring each of these is covered in the following sections, starting with reverse. Reverse lets the DNS server create reverse lookup records for you automatically.

Reverse Lookup Zones

Shameless Plug If you are new to TCP/IP, you should spend some time learning it. TCP/IP and Windows NT 4.0 are discussed in *MCSE Training Guide: TCP/IP, 2nd Edition*.

One of the many confusing subjects is how a reverse lookup zone works. Like so many "confusing" topics, though, it is really very simple. You should know that forward lookups resolve names moving from right to left, from the root domain to the top level to the second level. Looking at an IP address, you might notice it is the other way around. That is, the last number is changed for each host instead of the first octet. Therefore, the same process will work, only it would need to go backward, or from left to right.

If you wanted the DNS server to work in reverse, you would in essence have to rewrite the resolvers and the name servers. Because there are many thousands of them already out there, this would be far too large a task. So if you cannot reverse the process, reverse the data. Take the numbers of the address and reverse them. Now, instead of looking up 152.124.25.14, your resolver will look up 14.25.124.152 reading from right to left, just like it does with an FQDN.

After you have created the reverse lookup zone, the DNS snap-in will update it as you change the forward lookup zones. Therefore, the first zone you should configure is the reverse lookup zone. The following Step by Step covers creating a reverse lookup zone.

STEP BY STEP

2.3 Creating a Reverse Lookup Zone

1. First you need to start the DNS management tool by selecting Programs, Administrative Tools, DNS from the Start menu.

2. The Microsoft Management Console starts and loads the DNS Manager snap-in (see Figure 2.4).

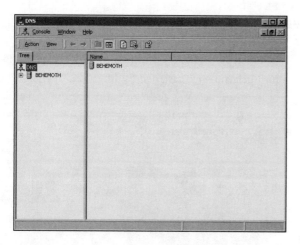

FIGURE 2.4
The DNS Manager snap-in loaded in the MMC.

3. Expand the server you are configuring, and on Reverse Lookup Zones right-click. From the context menu, choose New Zone. This will start the New Zone Wizard.

4. Click Next to bypass the Welcome to the New Zone Wizard screen.

5. On the next screen (see Figure 2.5), you can choose the type of zone, either Standard Primary or Standard Secondary. Active Directory-integrated is grayed out because Active Directory is not installed. Because this is the first zone, you should choose Standard Primary and click Next.

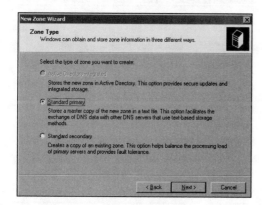

FIGURE 2.5
Choosing the type of zone to create.

continues

continued

6. Enter the first part of the IP address for which the zone will provide IP-to-FQDN resolution. This should be the number you were assigned by InterNIC or the portion of a private network address that is common to all hosts. Verify the filename the wizard created and, if it's okay, click Next (see Figure 2.6).

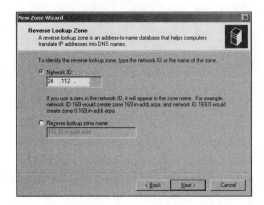

FIGURE 2.6
Entering the IP address of the network for the reverse lookup zone.

> **NOTE**
>
> **Using a File from a BIND Server**
> If you already have created this file on another server, regardless of type, you can copy the file to the systemroot\system32\dns directory and then enter the zone name in the Reverse Lookup Zone Name field and the filename on the next screen.

7. Next you need to enter a filename. If this is a new zone, a suggested name will appear and you can click Next. Otherwise, you should enter the zone filename in the Use this existing file: text box and click Next (see Figure 2.7).

FIGURE 2.7
Entering the filename information.

8. The next page of the wizard will confirm your choices. If everything is correct, click Finish. If there are errors, go back and correct them.

After this is configured, you can configure the forward lookup zone. There are additional properties you can configure for the zone; however, some of these depend on the information in the forward zone. This will be covered later in the chapter in the section "Configuring a Reverse Lookup Zone."

Forward Lookup Zones

The process for creating a standard forward lookup zone is similar to that of creating a reverse lookup zone. The following Step by Step walks you through the process.

STEP BY STEP

2.4 Creating a Forward Lookup Zone

1. First you need to start the DNS management tool by selecting Programs, Administrative Tools, DNS from the Start menu.

---

2. The Microsoft Management Console starts and loads the DNS snap-in.

---

3. Expand the server you are configuring and right-click Forward Lookup Zones. From the context menu, choose New Zone. This will start the New Zone Wizard.

---

4. Click Next to bypass the Welcome to the New Zone Wizard screen.

---

5. On the next screen, you can choose the type of zone, either Standard Primary or Standard Secondary. Active Directory-integrated is grayed out because Active Directory is not installed. Because this is the first zone, you should choose Standard Primary.

---

continues

continued

6. In the Name: text box, enter the name of the domain you are creating (see Figure 2.8) and then click Next.

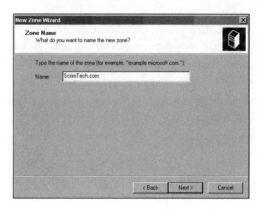

FIGURE 2.8
Entering the domain name for a forward lookup zone.

7. Next you can enter the filename to use for the zone, or if you copied a zone file from another server, you can enter the filename (see Figure 2.9). When this is done, click Next.

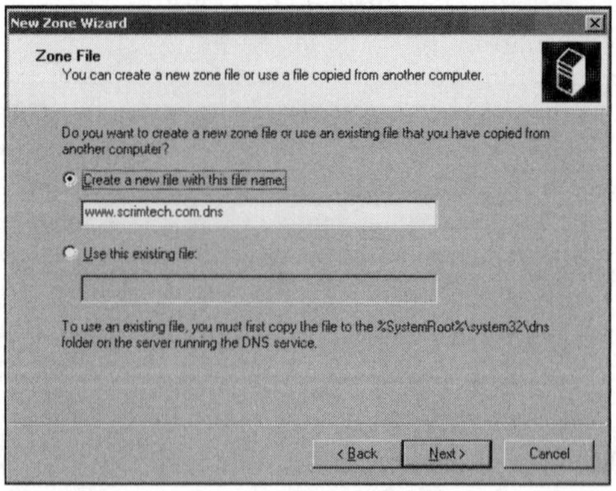

FIGURE 2.9
Enter the zone file filename.

8. On the next screen, you can confirm the choices you've made. If they are correct, click Finish. Otherwise, you should use the Back button to go back and correct the information.

As you can see, configuring a forward lookup zone is very simple. After this is done, you will normally configure additional properties of the zone. Then you will configure secondary servers.

Configuring Primary Zones

Now that you have created the zone you will use, you should configure the zones. This is simply a matter of configuring the options you want to use and possibly adding some host names.

In general, configuring the zone is a simple matter; the following steps will get you into the property sheets for the zones.

STEP BY STEP

2.5 Configuring a Forward Lookup Zone

1. Open DNS in Administrative Tools.

2. Expand the server that contains the zone, forward or reverse, to configure.

3. Expand the Reverse or Forward Lookup Zones folder.

4. Right-click the zone to configure and choose Properties.

When you are configuring a primary zone, the following series of options are available.

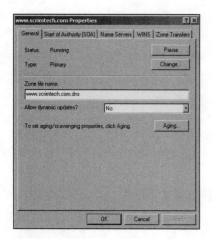

FIGURE 2.10
The General tab for a forward lookup zone.

General

The General tab (see Figure 2.10) enables you to configure some of the basic information about the zone. The options available include:

◆ **Status.** This tells you the current status of the zone and enables you to pause a zone (by clicking the Pause button) or to start a paused zone (by clicking the Start button).

◆ **Type.** This enables you to change the type of zone between primary, secondary, and Active Directory-integrated. This can be used to change the server role in a case a primary server crashes. It can also be used if you want to later change a server that was used during installation to an Active Directory–integrated server.

◆ **Zone file name.** This enables you to change the name that stores the zone file information without data loss. You should note that the zone information is actually in the registry, and the file is updated occasionally for compatibility with BIND secondary servers. You can force an update by choosing Update Server Data Files from the context menu.

◆ **Allow dynamic updates?** This is a new feature that works with DHCP to enable the client or the DHCP server to update the DNS zone dynamically. This is discussed further in the section "Integrating Active Directory and DNS."

◆ **Aging.** Because systems will be able to register themselves, you will occasionally end up with records that are no longer valid from a computer that is removed or perhaps a laptop for a user who visits the office. Aging enables you to configure whether the system will verify and occasionally delete records that are dynamically created. If you click the Aging button, there are three options you can set:

  • **Scavenge stale resource records.** This check box enables or disables scavenging. Aging and scavenging is a process that removes old dynamic resource records if the system has not reregistered its name. This can be configured at the server level or the zone level.

  • **No-refresh interval.** This is the period of time that a record is assumed to be okay. The client system will keep the record for at least this period of time.

- **Refresh interval.** This is the period of time that the client system has to refresh its record after the no-refresh interval has expired.

Start of Authority

The *Start of Authority* (SOA) record (see Figure 2.11) is used to find the server that has authority for a domain. The tab enables you to configure the normal DNS parameters that are part of the SOA record. These options include the following:

◆ **Serial number.** This is the serial number for the zone file. This will change incrementally each time the file is changed. Secondary servers will compare their version number to that of the primary and will copy (AXFR) the file if they are different. You can set this number to a higher value to force a change to be copied to a secondary server. A Windows 2000 server can also use an incremental zone transfer (IXFR), which only transfers the changes since the previous version number, reducing the amount of information being transferred.

◆ **Primary server.** This is the name of the primary server. This server has the read/write version of the zone file.

◆ **Responsible person.** This is the email address of the person in charge of the zone. The @ sign in the address is replaced by a period so the record can be correctly stored in the zone file. This is because the @ sign in a zone file means "this zone."

◆ **Refresh interval.** This value sets how often secondary servers will attempt to contact the primary to verify the version number and transfer the zone if required.

◆ **Retry interval.** If a secondary server cannot connect to the primary server at the refresh interval, it will retry the attempt at this interval.

◆ **Expires after.** This is the period after which a secondary server will stop resolving an address for a zone file it could not verify.

◆ **Minimum (default) TTL.** This setting is passed to other servers during name resolution and tells them how long they can cache the entry.

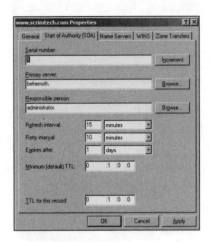

FIGURE 2.11
The SOA tab for a forward lookup zone.

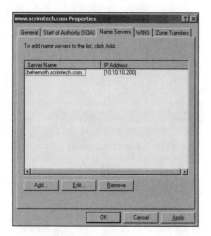

FIGURE 2.12
On this tab you can add, edit, or remove name servers for your domain.

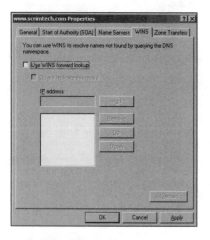

FIGURE 2.13
The WINS tab in a forward lookup zone.

◆ **TTL for this record.** You can change which server is the primary server at any time. This is because an expiry time was added to the SOA record. The servers will check to see if they are still the primary when this TTL expires.

Name Servers

The Name Servers tab (see Figure 2.12) lists the name servers in this zone. Listing a server here will create an NS record for the zone. These should match the servers registered with the domain one level up; the domain one level up will return these records when another server queries for your domain.

WINS

In a pure Windows 2000 network, you should not need this record because your systems will all register directly with the DNS server. However, if you need to support older Windows clients, you might configure the WINS tab (see Figure 2.13.) This will provide the server with the IP address of one or more WINS servers that it can query if it doesn't have the name you are looking up. The DNS server will query for the host name on the WINS server and can then append the zone file filename to create the FQDN.

The options on this tab include the following:

◆ **Use WINS forward lookup.** This will enable or disable this functionality.

◆ **Do not replicate this record.** If this is not checked, the WINS record will not be included in zone transfers to configured secondary DNS servers. All the DNS servers would then know about and use the WINS server. This should be selected if some of the secondary servers are non-Microsoft servers and do not support WINS resource records.

◆ **IP address.** This is where you can add, remove, or order the IP address(es) of the WINS server you want to use.

◆ **Advanced.** This will open another dialog box with the following options:

   • **Cache time-out.** When an address is resolved using the WINS server, this setting controls how long the DNS server will keep the entry in cache.

- **Lookup time-out.** This will determine how long the DNS server will wait for the WINS server to respond before giving up.

Zone Transfers

The last of the tabs in the forward lookup zone configuration is the Zone Transfers tab (see Figure 2.14). This tab configures how zone transfers, copying the zone from a primary server to a secondary, take place. You can configure this at the server with the primary zone file or at a server with a secondary file. At the secondary server, this will affect other secondary servers that get their copy of the zone file from it. In this role, it is a master server.

The options available include the following:

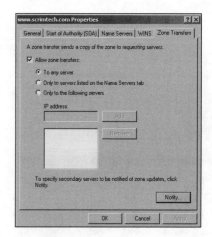

FIGURE 2.14
The Zone Transfers tab for a forward lookup zone.

◆ **Allow zone transfers.** This enables you to disable the capability to transfer the zone. You will almost always have this enabled. The only reason to disable it is to perform a massive update to the zone or if you only have a single primary server.

◆ **To any server.** This enables your zone to be transferred to any server that requests it. This should be avoided because it could give hackers information about your environment that could be used to help them break in.

◆ **Only to servers listed on the Name Servers tab.** This option is the most likely to be used because it will ensure that all secondary servers will be able to retrieve a copy of the zone information.

◆ **Only to the following servers.** In some cases, you will need to control where servers get their copy of the zone file. This is true if you are creating a multitiered DNS architecture, which you might do if your network includes slow links. If you choose this option, you should list the servers in the space provided.

◆ **Notify.** This button opens a dialog box that enables you to control which servers will be notified when the zone information changes. The options available are as follows:

- **Automatically notify.** Turn this feature on or off. Turning this feature on could increase the bandwidth usage; however, it will ensure that the secondary servers are kept up-to-date.

- **Servers listed on the Name Servers tab.** This setting automatically notifies all the servers listed in the Named Servers tab.

- **The following servers.** This enables you to control which servers are notified.

Configuring a Reverse Lookup Zone

Configuring a reverse lookup zone is almost identical to configuring a forward lookup zone. The only difference is the size of the tabs and the WINS-R tab.

WINS-R

Because this is the only tab (see Figure 2.15) that is different, it is the only one included here. This WINS-R record will point at the forward zone file; the name of that zone will be appended to records returned in reverse queries.

The options available are as follows:

◆ **Use WINS-R lookup.** This enables or disables the use of a WINS server for reverse lookups.

◆ **Do not replicate this record.** This prevents the WINS-R record from being replicated to other DNS servers. This should be used if there are local WINS servers where the other DNS servers are located.

◆ **Domain to append to returned name.** This option sets the domain portion of the FQDN that will be returned.

◆ **Advanced.** This opens the Advanced Options tab. There are three options available on that tab:

- **Cache time-out.** This is how long the name will be cached on the DNS server.

- **Lookup time-out.** This is how long the DNS server will wait, assuming the WINS server is not available.

- **Submit DNS name as NetBIOS scope.** This appends the DNS domain name entered in the Domain to Append to Returned Name field as the NetBIOS scope in the query to the WINS server.

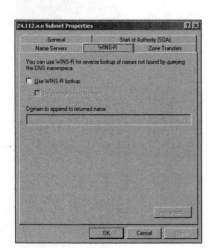

FIGURE 2.15
The WINS-R tab, which only requires that you enter the forward lookup zone.

Secondary

In addition to the primary server, you need to configure one or more servers to act as secondary servers. As you probably guessed from the discussion of configuring a forward lookup zone, a secondary server copies the zone file from another server. This could be the primary server or another secondary server. In this case, the secondary is also a master server. The following Step by Step describes the process of setting up a secondary server.

STEP BY STEP

2.6 Configuring a Secondary Server

1. Open DNS in Administrative Tools and expand the server that will be a secondary.

2. Right-click the Forward or Reverse Lookup Zones folder and choose New Zone.

3. Click Next to bypass the Welcome to the New Zone Wizard screen.

4. Choose Standard Secondary and then click Next.

5. Type the name of the domain for which you are configuring a secondary zone (see Figure 2.16) and then click Next.

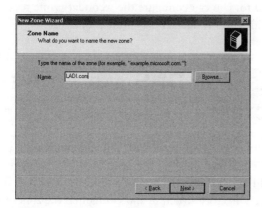

FIGURE 2.16
Entering the name of the zone to secondary.

continues

continued

6. Enter the IP address of the master server, the server from which you will copy the zone (see Figure 2.17), and click Next.

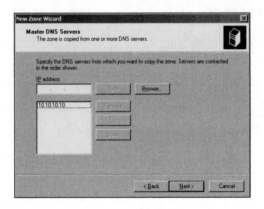

FIGURE 2.17
Enter the master server IP address.

7. On the last screen of the wizard, verify the information and then click Finish. The zone information might take a few moments to copy.

If you need to, you can configure the secondary zone properties. These are identical to the primary zone properties.

INTEGRATING DNS AND ACTIVE DIRECTORY

After you have the DNS server installed and configured, you can perform the last few steps to prepare to install Active Directory. You now should have created the reverse and forward lookup zones for your Active Directory structure and configured the zones to allow updates.

There are a couple different ways that the Active Directory zone can be integrated into your organization. This should be decided by the people who planned the Active Directory structure. The three common methods include the following:

◆ Use the same domain internally and externally. (For example, just use the DNS name you registered with the InterNIC, such as MCP.com.)

◆ Use a subdomain of the external domain. (For example, create a subdomain from your public domain for Active Directory, such as AD.MCP.com.)

◆ Use a separate domain internally. (For example, use a different name internally such as MCP.local. Because you are not registering with the InterNIC, any top-level domain can be used. Microsoft recommends .local.)

Whichever way you have decided to integrate the public and private networks, you should configure the reverse and forward lookup zones first.

Configuring Active Directory Integration

You will need to configure the zones you use for Active Directory as Active Directory–integrated zones. This is a simple process done on a domain controller running DNS and involves the following steps.

STEP BY STEP

2.7 Configuring a Zone as Active Directory Integrated

1. Open DNS in Administrative Tools and expand the server that manages the domain until you can see the domain, both forward and reverse. The server that manages the domain must be a domain controller as well as a DNS server.

2. Right-click on the domain. Note that you will need to click on it first so it has focus. Choose Properties.

continues

continued

3. Beside the Type, click the Change button.

4. Select Active Directory-integrated and then click OK.

5. Click OK to confirm the change. Click OK again to close the Zone Type dialog box.

6. Click OK to close the Properties dialog box and, if desired, close the DNS snap-in.

Remember that you do not have to use an Active Directory–integrated zone if you are using non-Microsoft servers or if you don't want zone information to be published in Active Directory. If you are going to create an Active Directory–integrated zone, you must use a domain controller as the DNS server.

Allowing Updates

Install, configure, and troubleshoot DNS for Active Directory.

▶ Configure zones for dynamic updates.

This is an important issue because the domain controllers will need to create several records so that users will be able to find them. These include service records, A or host records, and PTR or reverse lookup records. You will need to configure all the zones used in Active Directory to allow updates so that the servers and the clients can update their own records. This is done on the General tab of the zone properties, as you saw previously in the section "Configuring a Primary Zone."

For a standard zone, you will have the choices of Yes or No. Yes allows updates and No does not allow updating. If the type to zone is Active Directory integrated, you will also have the option to allow Only Secure Updates. When the zone is integrated with Active Directory, the zone information is moved into the Active Directory; therefore, you can apply permissions. If Only Secure Updates is selected, then computers with computer accounts in the forest where the DNS server is located will be able to register a computer.

The Update Process

The update process can be initialized either from the client or from the *Dynamic Host Configuration Protocol* (DHCP) server. If the client knows about dynamic DNS (for example, Windows 2000), it will perform the update. Otherwise, you will need to configure the DHCP server to process updates.

Windows 2000 clients will, by default, update the information on the DNS server. There are several instances in which the client will update the information on the DNS server:

◆ A change to one or more local IP addresses.

◆ The IP address leased from the DHCP server is refreshed or changed, either as a matter of course or by a user issuing the IPCONFIG /RENEW command.

◆ A user at the system forces the update using IPCONFIG /REGISTERDNS.

◆ The system or, in some cases, a service restarts.

◆ The computer name is changed.

◆ Updates are sent by Windows 2000 clients every 24 hours.

In any of these cases, the system will need to update the information. The update process follows these steps:

1. The DHCP client will send a SOA query for the domain name with which it is registered. This query will be used to find a server where the update can be processed.

2. An authoritative server responds to the query with the address for the primary server, the one with the primary zone file. In the case of an Active Directory-integrated zone, any DNS server will be able to perform the update because the information is stored as part of Active Directory.

3. The client will attempt to contact the server to perform the update. If the update fails, the client will query for the NS records for the domain. The client will then query the first name server for a SOA record and will try the server listed in this record.

> **NOTE**
>
> **DHCP Servers** A DHCP server is any server that runs a DHCP service, or daemon. This service will provide clients with an IP address and subnet mask. In addition, other configuration options can also be sent depending on the type of client requesting the address.

4. The client then sends the update. The server will now attempt to process the update. It first needs to make sure updates are allowed, and if the server is Active Directory integrated, it will also check whether the computer performing the update has the necessary permissions to perform the update.

Changes in Zones Used for Active Directory

There are several important things that will take place in DNS when you are working with Active Directory. Some of these changes only take place in Active Directory-integrated zones, whereas others are made as requirements of Windows 2000. This section will look at those changes, including the following:

◆ In Active Directory-integrated zones, any domain controller running DNS will be able to accept dynamic registrations.

◆ The Netlogon service will register with the DNS server(s) so that users can locate the services.

◆ You can apply security to DNS updates.

◆ Zone information becomes part of the Active Directory and is replicated using AD replication.

The Netlogon service registers additional names for a domain controller; these names enable the users to locate *Lightweight Directory Access Protocol* (LDAP) servers. This, in turn, enables users to search for logon servers or for other objects in the Active Directory.

The entries that the Netlogon service registers are stored in a file on the domain controller in c:\winnt\system32\config, by default, in a file named NETLOGON.DNS. The file contains entries to register the server services including LDAP, Kerberos, and the Global Catalog service. The contents look like the following:

```
mydom.local. 600 IN A 10.10.10.200
_ldap._tcp.mydom.local. 600 IN SRV 0 100 389
comp.mydom.local.
```

```
_ldap._tcp.pdc._msdcs.mydom.local. 600 IN SRV 0 100 389
comp.mydom.local.
_ldap._tcp.gc._msdcs.mydom.local. 600 IN SRV 0 100 3268
comp.mydom.local.
_ldap._tcp.a3c99adb-f3fe-4a88-8ea8-
7fc4945be8d6.domains._msdcs.mydom.local. 600 IN SRV 0 100
389 comp.mydom.local.
gc._msdcs.mydom.local. 600 IN A 10.10.10.200
2b8e8e62-6f26-4d89-ab0e-29ce9cec8458._msdcs.mydom.local.
600 IN CNAME comp.mydom.local.
_kerberos._tcp.dc._msdcs.mydom.local. 600 IN SRV 0 100 88
comp.mydom.local.
_ldap._tcp.dc._msdcs.mydom.local. 600 IN SRV 0 100 389
comp.mydom.local.
_kerberos._tcp.mydom.local. 600 IN SRV 0 100 88
comp.mydom.local.
_gc._tcp.mydom.local. 600 IN SRV 0 100 3268
comp.mydom.local.
_kerberos._udp.mydom.local. 600 IN SRV 0 100 88
comp.mydom.local.
_kpasswd._tcp.mydom.local. 600 IN SRV 0 100 464
comp.mydom.local.
_kpasswd._udp.mydom.local. 600 IN SRV 0 100 464
comp.mydom.local.
_ldap._tcp.Default-First-Site-Name._sites.mydom.local. 600
IN SRV 0 100 389 comp.mydom.local.
_ldap._tcp.Default-First-Site-
Name._sites.gc._msdcs.mydom.local. 600 IN SRV 0 100 3268
comp.mydom.local.
_kerberos._tcp.Default-First-Site-
Name._sites.dc._msdcs.mydom.local. 600 IN SRV 0 100 88
comp.mydom.local.
_ldap._tcp.Default-First-Site-
Name._sites.dc._msdcs.mydom.local. 600 IN SRV 0 100 389
comp.mydom.local.
_kerberos._tcp.Default-First-Site-Name._sites.mydom.local.
600 IN SRV 0 100 88 comp.mydom.local.
_gc._tcp.Default-First-Site-Name._sites.mydom.local. 600 IN
SRV 0 100 3268 comp.mydom.local.
```

Each line of the file registers a different service with the DNS server. The format for the lines is as follows:

```
service.protocol.name ttl class SRV preference weight port
target
```

The first part, `service.protocol.name`, lets the DNS server know what service is being registered and which transport protocol it will use. The choices of transport protocol are limited to either TCP or UDP. The `ttl` is the time to live. This is the length of time that the clients will be able to cache this entry. The class is always set to IN, which indicates that this is an Internet entry, followed by `SRV`, which tells the DNS server this is a service locator record.

When several servers provide the same service, the preference value indicates which record(s) should be returned first when a query is sent for that service with lower values first. If more than one server is at the same preference, then the weight is used to determine which server to try first. The port identifies which port the service is on. This information is passed to the client so that nonstandard ports can be used. Finally, the target is added as either an IP address or a host name.

For the moment, it is not important what specific entries are registered. At this point, you only need to know that the file exists and that it is used to register network services.

The other changes all affect Active Directory–integrated zones. These changes come about because the entries are now part of the Active Directory. The entries will be treated as objects in the Active Directory and therefore can have security applied to them. This allows for secure updates. This also means that the updates can be performed on any DNS server that handles this zone because Active Directory uses multimaster replication.

TRANSFERRING ZONE INFORMATION

Manage, monitor, and troubleshoot DNS.

▶ Manage replication of DNS data.

Whether your zone is integrated or not, you need to replicate the zone amongst the DNS servers. The next few sections cover how this is done.

In the Standard Environment

When you are configuring zone transfers in the standard DNS environment, you simply create a secondary server. You configure another DNS server to copy the zone file from the primary server or another secondary server. The zone transfer uses the parameters defined in the SOA record for the zone (discussed previously in the section "Configuring Primary Zones").

To configure a DNS server to act as a secondary server for an existing zone, you need to perform the following steps.

STEP BY STEP

2.8 Configuring a Secondary Server

1. Open DNS in Administrative Tools and expand the server that is to be the secondary.

---

2. Expand the server's information and the forward or reverse lookup zones.

---

3. Right-click on Forward Lookup Zones or Reverse Lookup Zones, whichever is appropriate, and choose New Zone.

---

4. Click Next to skip the welcome screen of the Welcome to the New Zone Wizard.

---

5. On the next screen, choose Standard Secondary and then click Next.

---

6. Enter the name of the zone and then click Next.

---

7. Enter the IP address of the master name server, either the primary server or a secondary that is already running. You can enter more than one server, and the DNS service will try them in order if it cannot connect to the first one. Click Next when this is done.

---

8. Click Finish to complete the setup.

After this is configured, the zone information will now be transferred according to the information you configured in the SOA record or if you specifically force a transfer. There are actually two types of transfers that can take place: full and incremental.

During the initial replication for the zone file, a full (AFXR) zone transfer will take place. If, however, both the primary server and the secondary server support incremental (IFXR) zone transfers, subsequent transfers will only need to transfer records that have changed.

> **NOTE**
> **Patience** It may take a few moments for the initial transfer to take place.

The incremental zone transfer uses the serial number of the zone file to track changes. When a secondary requests the IXFR, the serial numbers are compared. If they are the same, no zone transfer is performed. If they are different, the primary DNS server will send the changes that have occurred since the last zone transfer to the secondary server. It determines which records by comparing the serial number that the secondary has in the SOA resource record with the serial number that the secondary DNS server has in its version of the SOA resource record. All resource records that have been added or modified between the two serial numbers are transferred to the secondary zone. This reduces the network overhead but increases the overhead on the DNS server because it must track the changes.

In the Active Directory Environment

During the discussion of the Active Directory–integrated zone, you may have noticed that the servers were no longer primary or secondary but rather just integrated. This is because the information is loaded from Active Directory. It is actually Active Directory that will handle the replication. Instead of performing zone transfers, the DNS servers will poll Active Directory for updates every 15 minutes; this is set in the zone properties.

This is why all the domain controllers in an Active Directory–integrated zone that run DNS will be able to accept updates. They have a write-enabled copy of the zone.

You should be aware that the zone data is stored within the domain where the DNS servers are located. The problem with this is that data in Active Directory–integrated zones can only be replicated within a single domain using Active Directory replication. You can, therefore, only configure one domain to use Active Directory–integrated zones. All other domains need to use secondary DNS servers to the Active Directory–integrated zone.

In a Mixed Environment

Install, configure, and troubleshoot DNS for Active Directory.

▶ Integrate Active Directory DNS zones with non-Active Directory DNS zones.

Because this is not a perfect world—which would be boring—chances are you will need to be able to integrate DNS servers used to manage the Active Directory–integrated zones with other DNS servers that exist in your environment.

Microsoft has spent considerable effort ensuring that they are RFC compliant. This means that a Microsoft DNS server should be able to work with all other types of DNS servers on the market. Primarily, these will be *Berkeley Internet Name Domain* (BIND) systems.

These servers will be able to act as if they are secondary servers to the Active Directory–integrated servers. When transfers are made between two DNS servers running on Windows 2000 servers, the information that is transferred is compressed. This causes a transfer to a non-Windows 2000 server to fail. This option can be turned off in the DNS snap-in using Step by Step 2.9.

> **N O T E** **BIND Versions** Turning off compression is only required for BIND version 4.9.4 or earlier. This is not likely to be a requirement because you need BIND 4.9.6 as a minimum to support SRV resource records and 8.1.2 for full dynamic update compatibility with Windows 2000.

STEP BY STEP

2.9 Configuring Windows 2000 DNS for Old BIND Secondary Servers

1. Open DNS in Administrative Tools and right-click on the server.

2. Choose Properties from the context menu.

3. On the Advanced tab, make sure the BIND Secondaries option is checked.

4. Close the Properties dialog box.

Even if this option is set correctly, there may be problems if the server receiving the records is not able to understand some of the records. For example, if the server does not support SRV records, these records could show up incorrectly or could cause the transfer to fail.

TROUBLESHOOTING DNS

Because the DNS service is required for Active Directory to function, you will need to know how to troubleshoot. Several tools, in addition to the DNS snap-in, can be used to troubleshoot DNS problems. The following sections look at these tools.

Cannot Create Dynamic Entries

There are a couple fairly simple items you should check when you are troubleshooting a DNS server problem if you cannot create your dynamic entries on the server. These items are presented in the following sections.

Security

The first thing you should check is whether the computer is allowed to add entries dynamically to the DNS server. This is controlled under the zone properties on the Security tab.

The key settings to look for here are the Authenticated Users and Everyone. The Authenticated Users should be allowed to create child objects. This may sound strange because the user will log on long after the computer starts. Remember that computers also have accounts and are considered to be part of Authenticated Users; it is the computer account that will be used to update the information. The Everyone group should have permissions to Read so that users will be able to query the DNS server.

Wrong DNS server

You should check the DNS configuration to make sure the client is pointing at a DNS server that supports dynamic updates or is a secondary server to one that does. You should also make sure that the domain name entered is correct and that it matches a domain on the server with which you are attempting to register.

DNS Snap-in

The DNS snap-in provides a basic testing tool for the DNS service as well as the capability to enable logging. These options can be found by opening the server properties in the DNS Manager. Two tabs can be of use when trying to troubleshoot a DNS problem: Logging and Monitoring.

Logging

On the Logging tab, you can turn on logging options that will enable you to log the activity of the DNS server. There are several different items that you log:

◆ **Query.** This logs queries received by the server.

◆ **Notify.** This logs notifications that the server receives from other DNS servers.

◆ **Update.** This logs the dynamic update requests received from clients.

◆ **Questions.** This logs the information portion of the Std. Query packets sent to the server.

◆ **Answers.** This option logs the information portion of the Std. Response packets returned by the server.

◆ **Send.** This logs the number of iterative queries sent by the server.

◆ **Receive.** This logs the number of iterative queries received by the server.

◆ **UDP.** This logs the number of requests received using the *User Datagram Protocol* (UDP).

◆ **TCP.** This logs the number of requests received using the *Transmission Control Protocol* (TCP).

◆ **Full packets.** This logs the number of full packets sent or received by the server.

◆ **Write through.** This logs the number of records written by the DNS server to the zone file.

The log files can be found in the c:\winnt\system32\dns directory by default. This can let you see what the service is or is not doing with the requests it receives.

Monitoring

The Monitoring tab enables you to test the DNS server to make sure it is able to function correctly. You can select the test type, simple or recursive, and then can either choose the Test Now button or choose to have the test performed on an ongoing basis.

Using NSLOOKUP

The NSLOOKUP command is actually a fairly complex command that has both a command line and an interactive interface. For the purposes of quick testing, it is sufficient to understand the command line. There are two main types of queries you will send using the NSLOOKUP command: forward and reverse queries.

Most of the time, you will send a basic forward lookup query in which you will attempt to resolve a name from a client to ensure that the DNS server is able to find the client. There are a couple results to the basic query:

◆ The host is found, but you receive timeout errors. This is common if the reverse lookup zone doesn't have an entry for the DNS server or if there is no reverse lookup zone at all.

◆ The host is resolved with the full FQDN but not with the name alone. This is normally a result of an incorrect configuration on the client. Make sure the DNS setting includes the correct domain name information.

The basic query sent to the DNS server cyclops.scrimtech.com looks like this:

```
C:\>nslookup behemoth.scrimtech.local
Server:  cyclops.scrimtech.com
Address:  24.142.192.45

Name:    behemoth.scrimtech.local
Addresses:  10.10.10.200, 24.112.93.248
```

The other type of query is the reverse query. This can be helpful if you cannot find a host that you know exists. By querying the IP address of the known host, you will be able to tell what name is being associated with the host, as in the following example:

```
C:\>nslookup 207.236.145.38
Server:  cyclops.scrimtech.com
Address:  24.142.192.45

Name:    virgile.hq.newroma.com
Address:  207.236.145.38
```

Using IPCONFIG

The IPCONFIG command has been revamped from NT 4.0 to include three new switches that affect the interaction with DNS. These switches, as well as /ALL, can be useful when you are attempting to troubleshoot DNS problems.

◆ **/ALL.** This provides you with information about the configuration of each network connection on your computer, including the DNS server used by each of the cards.

◆ **/FLUSHDNS.** This clears all the cached information you have received from the DNS servers. You can try this to force the station to reread the information from the DNS server.

◆ **/REGISTERDNS.** This renews any DHCP leases you currently have and also reregisters all the dynamic entries you have created on the DNS server.

◆ **/DISPLAYDNS.** This shows the entries currently in cache from the DNS server. This enables you to ensure that the DNS server is providing the correct information.

Starting and Stopping Netlogon

As you might remember from the review of the NETLOGON.DNS file in the section "Changes in Zones Used for Active Directory," there are many entries added dynamically to the DNS server by the Netlogon service. You can quickly reregister this information by stopping and starting the Netlogon service.

CASE STUDY: IMPLEMENTING DNS FOR SUNSHINE BREWING

ESSENCE OF THE CASE

As you look at the problems involved, you will see a few key issues. The following are the main issues:

▶ There are some locations that have slow links.

▶ The locations of the laptop computers used by the Executive and Sales users move and change IP addresses.

▶ There are five domains for which you need to provide resolution.

▶ Resolution for external addresses needs to be provided.

▶ The server addresses tend to remain static.

▶ Some of the systems on the network are UNIX based and will not be Active Directory clients.

▶ Some of the internal applications are Web based, and you need to be able to advertise these in DNS.

▶ You want computers to be dynamically registered.

▶ You need to support SRV records.

▶ You need to control the replication.

SCENARIO

In this chapter, you learned about DNS and how it will be used in the Windows 2000 Active Directory. Now that you have some knowledge on the subject, it is time to see how it can be applied to a real-world situation. In this case study, you will see how DNS will be configured in the Sunshine Brewing company.

Before you can install Active Directory, before you create your first user, you will need to make sure you have a working DNS structure. As you will recall from the case study in Chapter 1, the network designers have broken the organization down into what will become five different domains. You now need to consider the practical side of the design and look at how you will make sure name resolution can take place across all the domains and all the locations that make up Sunshine Brewing.

ANALYSIS

The best choice in this case is an Active Directory–integrated zone for the root domain. The other domains will be child domains of this domain.

CASE STUDY: IMPLEMENTING DNS FOR SUNSHINE BREWING

It is obvious that you will need to create a domain that Active Directory will be able to use. In this case, Windows 2000 DNS servers that will also be domain controllers will handle the DNS. The first server will be installed, and DNS will be loaded on the server. That server will also be the server that you will install as the first server in your tree. After you install Active Directory, you will convert the zone to Active Directory integrated and will ensure that DNS is installed on all the domain controllers for the root domain.

This will require that you install a domain controller for the root domain in every location. On the upside, however, is the fact that an Active Directory–integrated domain will use multiple master replication. This means a user that dials in to the Victoria office will register with the domain name server in that office rather than trying to register with the one in Ottawa. Further, you will be able to control replication using the same site links that will be created to control all the other forms of replication.

Because the only addresses that will change will tend to be those of the laptop users, the fact that replication is not happening instantly shouldn't cause any problem. If you configure the zone with a longer refresh interval, you might find the laptop users are on and off again before their entries have to be replicated anyway.

Because you can add other records to an Active Directory–integrated zone, the requirements of the UNIX servers and the Web-based network applications are handled.

All that remains is to handle the resolution of the external addresses. This can be handled simply by configuring the DNS server to forward the requests through the firewall to a caching-only server on the outside of your network. This means the domain controller running the Active Directory–integrated zone is not exposed but is still able to resolve external addresses.

CHAPTER SUMMARY

KEY TERMS

- Active Directory integrated
- Caching server
- Dynamic Host Configuration Protocol (DHCP)
- Dynamic updates
- Forward lookup
- Fully Qualified Domain Name (FQDN)
- Iterative query
- LDAP
- Master server
- Name server
- Namespace
- Netlogon
- Notification
- NSLOOKUP
- Primary server
- Recursive query
- Resolver
- Reverse lookup
- Scavenging
- Secondary server
- Service records (SRV)
- Start of Authority (SOA)
- Time to live (TTL)
- Windows Internet Naming System (WINS)
- Zone
- Zone transfer

Although by no means a full discussion of the DNS service that is part of Windows 2000, this chapter has presented the key information that you need to know to make the DNS service work with Active Directory. The key points you will need as you move on to the installation of Active Directory include the following:

- ◆ For Active Directory to function, the DNS server must support SRV records and should support dynamic updates.

- ◆ When a zone is integrated with Active Directory, the zone information is stored in Active Directory, which will then handle security and replication.

- ◆ Several tools can be used to help troubleshoot DNS including the DNS snap-in, IPCONFIG, and NSLOOKUP.

APPLY YOUR KNOWLEDGE

Exercises

The following series of exercises will give you a chance to get the hands-on experience that is critical to relating the information in the chapter to real life. It is strongly recommended that you complete these exercises and work with the system before attempting the exam.

2.1 Installing the DNS Service

In this exercise, you will be led through the steps to install the DNS service on a Windows 2000 server. It is assumed that you have a clean copy of either Windows 2000 Server or Advanced Server loaded on a nonproduction system.

WARNING	**Testing and Exercises!** Never perform testing or exercises on production equipment.

Estimated time: 10 minutes.

1. From the Start menu, choose Settings and then Control Panel.

2. In the Control Panel window, double-click the Add/Remove Programs applet.

3. In the Add/Remove Programs dialog box, click the Add/Remove Windows Components button. This will take a moment.

4. This opens the Windows Components Wizard. Select Network Services and click the Details button.

5. Choose Domain Name System (DNS) and then click OK.

6. Click Next in the Windows Components Wizard. You will see the system Reconfiguring Components and might be prompted to insert your Windows 2000 compact disc.

7. Finally, the last screen of the Windows Components Wizard will appear and enable you click to Finish.

8. Close the Add/Remove Programs dialog box by clicking Close. Then you can close the Control Panel by clicking the Close button.

2.2 Creating the Zones

Now that you have the DNS service installed, you will create a reverse and a forward lookup zone. These will be used throughout the exercises in this text.

Estimated time: 15 minutes.

1. Start the DNS snap-in by selecting Programs, Administrative Tools, DNS from the Start menu.

2. Expand your server, click Reverse Lookup Zones, and then right-click Reverse Lookup Zones. From the context menu, choose New Zone. This will start the New Zone Wizard.

3. Click Next to bypass the introduction screen.

4. On the next screen, choose Standard Primary and click Next.

5. Enter the first part of the IP address of the server. You can use IPCONFIG at a command line to find this. Then click Next.

APPLY YOUR KNOWLEDGE

> **NOTE**
>
> **What to Enter for Your Reverse Zone**
> It can be confusing when you look at this dialog box to determine what to enter. This can vary depending on how you are connected to the Internet or if you are connected at all. As a rule of thumb, if your address starts with 1 through 126, enter only the first number. If the address starts with 128 through 191, enter the first two numbers; if your address is 192 or above, enter the first three numbers. For example, if your address is 173.23.92.2, you would enter 173.23.

6. Notice that the filename is automatically entered for you in the Create a New File with this File Name box. Click Next to continue.

7. Confirm your choices on the next page and click Finish.

8. Click on Forward Lookup Zones and then right-click on the Forward Lookup Zones. From the context menu, choose New Zone. This will start the New Zone Wizard again.

9. Click Next to bypass the introduction screen.

10. On the next screen, choose Standard Primary and click Next.

11. In the Name text box, enter a name for your domain, TestDom.local. Click Next.

12. On the next screen, notice the filename that is suggested: testdom.local.dns. Click Next to accept this filename.

13. On the next screen, confirm the choices you made and click Finish when they are correct.

2.3 Configuring for Dynamic Updates

Now that you have a forward and reverse lookup zone, you will configure these zones to allow dynamic updates. This relates to the exam objective "Configure zones for dynamic updates." This will also set up your system to install Active Directory.

Estimated time: 5 minutes.

1. On the reverse lookup zone that you created, right-click and choose Properties.

2. On the General tab, confirm that the Allow Dynamic Updates? field is set to Yes.

3. Click OK to close the properties.

4. Repeat steps 1 through 3 for the forward lookup zone.

2.4 Configuring a Zone Transfer

In this exercise, you will set up the DNS server on your Windows 2000 system to act as a secondary server. The exercise requires that you have another system acting as a DNS server from which you can transfer the information. If you have another computer, you can use the steps in exercise 1 and 2 to create another DNS server. Be sure to use a different domain name. If you have an existing domain, you can use that. Failing that, use the defaults in the exercise. You will receive an error, but you will get a chance to walk through the steps. This should help you with the exam objective "Manage replication of DNS data."

Estimated time: 10 minutes.

APPLY YOUR KNOWLEDGE

1. Right-click on Forward Lookup Zones and choose New Zone.

2. Click Next to bypass the introduction screen.

3. Choose Standard Secondary and click Next.

4. Enter the name of the domain to transfer, the name you created on the other computer, or use LADI.com as a test domain. Click Next to continue.

5. In the IP address box, enter the IP address of your other DNS server or use 10.10.10.10 if none is available. Click Add. Click Next to continue.

6. Review the information on the final screen and then click Finish.

7. If you are transferring a real zone, click on the new zone in the DNS console.

8. If the information has not transferred yet, right-click and choose Transfer from Master. After a minute, press F5 to refresh the display.

Review Questions

1. How are dynamic entries created on the DNS server?

2. What is the filename of the file containing the entries that the Netlogon service will register?

3. What are the two types of transfers that can take place between DNS servers configured with standard zones?

4. How are entries replicated in the Active Directory–integrated mode?

5. What type of record must a DNS server support if it will be used by Active Directory?

6. What is the difference between a master server and primary server?

Exam Questions

1. Francóis is attempting to troubleshoot a DNS server problem. He has configured a Windows 2000 server as a DNS server, which he intends to use during the change from a Windows NT 4.0 domain structure to a Windows 2000 Active Directory tree structure.

   As he attempts to upgrade the existing NT 4.0 primary domain controller, all goes well. However, at one point during the installation, the system offers to install the DNS server on the system he is upgrading. What could be causing this to happen? (Choose all that apply.)

   A. The PDC is configured to use a different DNS server.

   B. The DNS server is not configured for dynamic updates.

   C. The wrong version of DNS was installed.

   D. This is normal behavior.

2. Damir is installing DNS on a UNIX system using an older version of BIND — 4.9.6. He configures the new server to act as a secondary for the zone he configured for the Windows 2000 rollout he is performing. When the zone transfers, there are several records that look like gibberish. What might be causing this?

APPLY YOUR KNOWLEDGE

A. BIND cannot be used to back up a Windows 2000 DNS server.

B. The Windows 2000 DNS server is in Active Directory–integrated mode.

C. The UNIX server does not support Unicode characters.

D. The version of BIND in use does not support SRV records.

3. Brian is setting up a test environment for the Windows 2000 rollout project at his company. He configures several domain controllers. Each will have DNS running on it. The zone is configured as an Active Directory–integrated zone on one server already. What should he do to configure the zone transfers?

A. He needs to configure the existing DNS server as a primary server and the others as secondary.

B. He needs to configure the existing DNS server as a primary server, one DNS server as a master, and the rest as secondary.

C. He should configure the zone on the other servers as Active Directory integrated when he adds them.

D. Nothing. Active Directory will automatically handle replication.

4. Judy is using Windows 2000 servers for DNS in her environment. The servers are standalone servers that will be used for server-based applications. She wants to create a new zone called MS-TEST.INT on one of the servers. How should she configure the zone?

A. Standard primary

B. Standard secondary

C. Active Directory integrated

D. BIND compatible

5. Eric is attempting to find a problem with a Windows 2000 DNS server that does not seem to resolve Std. Query packets sent to it. Which of the following should he log to help him resolve the problem? (Choose all that apply.)

A. Query

B. Notify

C. Questions

D. TCP

6. Tawni is considering how to configure DNS in her company to integrate Windows 2000 Active Directory within the existing DNS configuration. What options does she have?

A. She can use the same domain internally and externally.

B. She can use a subdomain of the public domain.

C. She can use a separate domain with a nonstandard suffix.

D. All of the above.

7. Sam is installing the first domain controller in a new domain, which will be the root of her organization's tree. The DNS server in use supports the SRV records but does not support dynamic updates. What must she do after installing the new domain controller to make sure all the correct records are in the DNS server?

A. She should use the IPCONFIG/ REGISTERDNS command.

B. She should manually create the records required.

C. She should stop and start the Netlogon service.

D. She cannot use this DNS server.

8. Your company has seven locations around the world. You are currently documenting the DNS structure in place for the resolution of internal names. There is a primary DNS server located in the Ottawa head office. In addition, you have a secondary DNS server located in each of the other offices: Calgary, Washington, Mexico City, Dundee, Paris, and Bonn. The Paris and Bonn servers transfer the zone from the Dundee server, and the Mexico City server gets the zone from the Washington server. In your documentation, which servers should you list as master servers?

A. Only Ottawa.

B. Ottawa, Dundee, and Washington.

C. All the servers.

D. There is no such thing as a master server.

9. You are currently using a BIND server for your internal name resolution. You have around 300 internal servers in the BIND servers zone file, and you want to move these records to the new Windows 2000 DNS server you have installed. Which of the following methods is the best way to do this?

A. Copy the domain file to the Windows 2000 Server in the winnt/system32/dns directory before you create the zone.

B. Copy the domain file to the Windows 2000 Server in the winnt/system32/dns directory after you create the zone.

C. Copy the file to any location on the Windows 2000 server and then use the DNS snap-in to import the file.

D. You will need to manually enter the information again.

10. You are on location in a branch office that is being set up. You set up the DNS server that will perform local resolution and are configuring it as a secondary DNS server to your primary in the head office. Then you try to transfer the zone, but you are unable to do so. What is the most likely cause of the problem?

A. You need to configure the local server as an IP forwarder.

B. You need to configure the primary with the address of the secondary.

C. You need to install RIP v2, the protocol used to transfer zones.

D. You cannot create a secondary if the primary is AD integrated.

11. You are working on a server that is having intermittent problems. Occasionally, users are unable to locate the server, and until now, the local administrator has simply restarted the computer to fix the problem. The server is located in a branch office and uses a DNS server in your head office. Which of the following could solve the problem without restarting the computer?

APPLY YOUR KNOWLEDGE

A. Stop and start the Netlogon service.

B. Use the IPCONFIG /REGISTERDNS command.

C. Use the NETSTAT /UPDATEDNS command.

D. Use the REGWINS command.

12. Your manager has asked you to look into a problem for her. Every time she uses the NSLOOKUP command, she gets a timeout error. It isn't a critical error because she also gets the resolution she wants, but it doesn't look good. What should you check?

   A. The type of DNS zone she gets the error searching

   B. The DNS server's configuration

   C. The configuration of the forward lookup zones

   D. The configuration of the reverse lookup zones

13. You have configured a central DNS server that can access the Internet through your firewall. You want to be able to provide name resolution inside your network for Internet addresses using this one server to maximize caching and to minimize redundant traffic to the Internet.

   You will have DNS servers local to the subnets on the network, but you want them to resolve the name from a local zone file or by sending the request to the central server. What options should you set on the local DNS servers? (Choose all that apply.)

   A. Set the address of one or more secondary servers.

B. Set Enable Forwarders option on and enter an IP address for the central server.

C. Set the Use WINS Forward Lookup option on and enter an IP address of the central server.

D. Set the Do Not Use Recursion option on.

14. You are planning the implementation of Active Directory for your company. You are looking at the options for integrating the internal and external company names. The company already has MTP.com registered and is using this currently on the Internet. The company does not want the internal network to be visible at all to the external world. Which of the following methods for integrating the DNS names should you use?

   A. Use the same domain name internally and externally.

   B. Use a subdomain of your external name internally.

   C. Create a tree in your forest for the Internet name.

   D. Use a completely different name internally than you do externally.

15. You are troubleshooting a problem with the DNS server. The server does not seem to be able to resolve the addresses for some of the hosts in the network but is working fine for the rest. Everything looks fine in the DNS snap-in. What should you use to determine why the server is unable to resolve the addresses?

   A. Use the NETSTAT command.

   B. Use the Network Monitor utility.

C. Use the NSLOOKUP command.

D. Use the Monitoring tab in the DNS servers properties.

Answers to Review Questions

1. Dynamic updates can be made on the DNS server either by a client capable of performing the update or by the DHCP server that provided the client with the address. See the section "The Update Process."

2. The Netlogon service on each domain controller will create a series of entries in the DNS server that will enable the clients to locate the services it provides on the network. These entries are stored in a file called NETLOGON.DNS that is located in the systemroot\system32\dns directory. See the section "Integrating DNS and Active Directory."

3. In Windows 2000, the DNS server supports both normal or full transfers (AFXR) as well as incremental transfers (IFXR) based on the serial number of the zone file located on the servers. See the section "Transferring Zone Information."

4. If a zone is configured as Active Directory integrated, replication will be handled by Active Directory, which defaults to every 5 minutes within a site and is controlled by the site links between sites. The DNS server(s) will poll every 15 minutes by default for updates to the information. See the section "Transferring Zone Information."

5. For a DNS server to work with Active Directory, it must support SRV, service locator, records. In addition, it should, but does not need to, support dynamic updates. See the section "Integrating DNS and Active Directory."

6. The primary server contains the original, write-enabled zone file. This file is copied to secondary servers throughout an enterprise. In some cases, a secondary server will get its copy of the zone file from another secondary, which then becomes its master server. See the section "Transferring Zone Information."

Answers to Exam Questions

1. **A, B.** In this case, the most likely cause is that the server does not accept dynamic updates. When the installation routine runs, it will verify that the configured DNS server supports dynamic update. If it does not, then it offers to install DNS locally. The other possibility is that the Windows NT 4.0 server was not using the new Windows 2000 server as the DNS server in its TCP/IP configuration. Again, the system will find that the server does not support dynamic updates and will offer to install DNS.

   Answer C is obviously not right because there is only one version of DNS that comes with Windows 2000. Answer D is also incorrect because this is warning us that the DNS server is not able to perform updates. See the section "Troubleshooting DNS."

2. **C.** Because the transfer didn't fail, we can eliminate answers A, B, and D. This means that answer C is the only possible answer. This will actually happen depending on the version and operating system in use. See the section "Transferring Zone Information."

APPLY YOUR KNOWLEDGE

3. **D.** Because this is an Active Directory–integrated zone, there will be no primary or secondary servers. Remember that they are actually called standard primary and standard secondary. This means A and B cannot be correct. Answer D is true because the configuration will be replicated automatically to each new domain controller. Answer C could cause replication conflict and is also more work than required. See the section "Transferring Zone Information."

4. **A.** In this case, you will not necessarily be using Active Directory because the system running DNS is not necessarily a domain controller. Therefore, answer C is not correct. Because all of the types of zones you are able to create can be seconded by a BIND server, answer D is incorrect. This leaves either answer A or B. Because the zone does not exist yet, there is nowhere to transfer from; this makes A the correct answer. See the section "Transferring Zone Information."

5. **A, C.** In this case, Eric should log the query, questions, and answers to determine what is happening. There is no point in logging notifies because these are simply telling a secondary server to copy a zone file, and tracking what comes over TCP could miss or duplicate information. See the section "Troubleshooting DNS."

6. **D.** All of these are valid ways to integrate the zone you will use for Active Directory. See the section "Integrating DNS and Active Directory."

7. **B.** In a case in which you are using a DNS server that does not support dynamic updates, you will need to create the records for the global catalog server, the LDAP services, and the Kerberos services. The specific records that will be required are listed in the NETLOGON.DNS file. The IPCONFIG / REGISTERDNS is used to register the name of the computer with the DNS server if it is dynamic. She could have stopped and started NetLogon to reregister the services, but again, this only works for DNS servers that perform dynamic updates. See the section "Integrating DNS and Active Directory."

8. **B.** A master server is the server from which a secondary will retrieve its copy of the zone file. The Ottawa server is the master for the Calgary, Washington, and Dundee servers. The Washington server is the master server for Mexico City, and the Dundee server is the master server for Paris and Bonn. Answer A is the definition of a primary server, and answer C is the definition of an authoritative server (a server that can answer a query about a domain). See the section "Copying Zone Information."

9. **A.** The easiest way to do this is to copy the files to the directory noted and then create the zone file in the DNS snap-in. During the creation process, you will have the opportunity to name the file; select the existing file and the entries should appear. You could also configure the server as a secondary and transfer the zone; once done, you could then change the zone to primary. If you copy the file after the zone is created, it will be overwritten the next time the system updates the zone files. Answer C is wrong because there is no import command. See the section "Primary."

10. **B.** The most likely cause of the problem is that the primary or AD-integrated zone is configured to only transfer the zone to known servers. This means you need to connect to the primary or an AD-integrated server and add the new server as a

secondary. Configuring the server as an IP forwarded would allow the resolution to take place, but all resolution would need to cross the WAN link, and the local server would not have a copy of the zone files. RIP v2 is a routing protocol and has nothing to do with zone transfers. See the section "Secondary."

11. **B.** The problem here is that the server is dynamically registering with the server in head office. This can cause a server not to register correctly. In this case, you might be tempted to choose both A and B; however, there is no mention in the question that this is a domain controller. The NETSTAT command does not have an UPDATEDNS switch, and there is no REGWINS command. See the section "Using IPCONFIG."

12. **D.** This is an all-too-common error caused by the DNS server attempting to perform a reverse lookup on itself. The problem lies in the reverse lookup zone file, which is either missing or does not contain an entry for the DNS server. Because your manager always seems to get the error, the type of query is not important. There is no configuration option that will stop the reverse lookup, so you cannot fix it in the configuration. Finally, because she does get the resolution, the problem does not lie in the forward lookup zone. See the section "Troubleshooting DNS."

13. **B, D.** In this case, you want the server to forward requests to the central DNS server. Therefore, you need to enable forwarders. Because you don't want this server to perform queries of its own to the Internet, you need to turn off recursion. There is no need to set the

secondary server to perform this task, and WINS has nothing to do with resolving Internet names that are FQDNs. See the section "Roles for DNS Servers."

14. **D.** In this case, you want to keep the two zones completely separate. The best way to do this is to have two completely different domains such as MTP.com and MTP.local. The .local is a Microsoft suggestion. Using the same name internally and externally could lead to some of the namespace accidentally getting out. Using a subdomain can cause the same problem. And, of course, creating a subnet domain for the Internet wouldn't work. See the section "Integrating DNS and Active Directory."

15. **B.** The NETSTAT command does not enable you to troubleshoot DNS; it is used to check network status. It could let you look quickly at the connections to other DNS servers, but that is all. The NSLOOKUP utility would let you query the server to see if the record is there. Because other queries are not finding the record, this solution is not likely to either. You would, of course, check the DNS snap-in for the record and for the server configuration before going this far. The Monitoring tab enables you to determine whether the system can or cannot make a query. The Network Monitor is the only tool that will actually let you see the request; this is sent to and from the DNS server. See the section "Troubleshooting DNS."

Suggested Readings and Resources

1. *Windows 2000 Server Resource Kit TCP/IP Core Networking Guide.* Microsoft, 2000.

2. *Windows 2000 Domain Name System Overview.* White paper. Microsoft, 2000.

3. Scrimger, Rob and Kelli Adams. *MCSE Training Guide: TCP/IP 2nd Edition.* New Riders Publishing, 1999.

Now that you have had an introduction to the concepts of Active Directory and have reviewed DNS, it is time to start looking at how to work with Active Directory. Some of the objectives and subobjectives from the units "Installing, Configuring, and Troubleshooting Active Directory" and "Managing, Monitoring, and Optimizing the Components of Active Directory" are covered in this chapter. The other objectives and subobjectives are covered in other chapters.

The first part of this chapter will look at the logical structure of Active Directory. The last part of the chapter will show you how to create a root domain.

Install, configure, and troubleshoot the components of Active Directory.

- **Install Active Directory.**
- **Verify Active Directory installation.**
- **Create sites.**
- **Create subnets.**
- **Create connection objects.**
- **Create site links.**
- **Create site link bridges.**
- **Move server objects between sites.**
- **Create global catalog servers.**

▶ This objective is included primarily to make sure you can install Active Directory and verify that it is installed. This objective also is included to ensure that you can configure a domain to match the physical network. You should know the requirements for installation, primarily the DNS server requirements. You should also understand the changes made to the system due to the installation.

CHAPTER 3

Building Your Active Directory Structure

The domain configuration aspect of this objective requires that you know how to set up Active Directory based on the network. This includes creating sites, which are collections of subnets, and then making sure replication is possible using site links and site link bridges. You also need to know how to create a connection object. Using connection objects, you can override the system-generated connections. Finally, you need to know how to create a global catalog server.

Manage and troubleshoot Active Directory replication.

- **Manage intrasite replication.**

- **Manage intersite replication.**

▶ This objective is included to ensure that you are familiar with the replication process and are able to recognize and resolve replication issues. An important aspect of managing and troubleshooting Active Directory replication includes understanding the Knowledge Consistency Checker and how it works with site links to build the replication topology. You also need to know how to control the replication topology with the NTDS settings.

STUDY STRATEGIES

This chapter covers three main topics: logical structure, physical structure, and replication. You should understand how these work together to move information around an Active Directory network. Most notably, you should pay attention to the following:

▶ The installation of domain controllers and their differences depending on where they are logically located

▶ The creation and use of sites and site links

▶ The role and function of the Knowledge Consistency Checker

▶ The ways in which replication takes place and how replication works

▶ How to use global catalog servers and where they should be placed

INTRODUCTION

The domain controllers serve as the backbone to the network, and being able to implement them in a logical manner is key to the success of any Windows 2000 deployment. In this chapter, you will look at how to roll out the domain controllers and how to configure replication between these controllers. Keeping your organization running smoothly requires the replication of information about both the structure of and the objects in Active Directory.

The chapter begins with a discussion of the logical structures that make up the Active Directory and then moves on to installing domain controllers. After that, the physical world is introduced, and the discussion will turn to subnets and sites. This leads to the discussion of the replication of Active Directory both within a site and between sites.

UNDERSTANDING AD's LOGICAL STRUCTURE

Although some of the following information has already been introduced, it is worth taking a closer look at the logical structures that make up Active Directory.

The discussion will begin with a look at domains and the purpose of domains, which are the building blocks of the logical structure. Then the discussion will turn to the ways in which you can tie domains together into trees and, eventually, how trees can expand to make up a forest.

Domains

The basic unit you deal with is the domain, just like Windows NT 4.0. By breaking your enterprise into different domains, you achieve several benefits:

- ◆ Domains enable you to organize objects within a single department or a single location. Within the domain, all information about the objects is available.

◆ Domains act as a security boundary; domain administrators have complete control over all the resources within the domain. Group policies can be applied at the domain level. Group policies determine how resources can be accessed, configured, and used.

◆ Domain objects can be made available to other domains and can be published in the Active Directory.

◆ Domain names follow the DNS naming structure. This permits an infinite number of child domains.

◆ Domains enable you to control replication; objects stored in the domain are only fully replicated to other domain controllers in the domain.

There are two ways to create Active Directory domains: by upgrading a Windows NT 4.0 domain or by installing a Windows 2000 Server and then promoting it to be a domain controller.

After you have created a root domain, you can then move on to create trees. A tree always starts with the root domain but then can branch out to include other domains. This provides you with the first level of hierarchies within Active Directory.

Trees and Forests

When you are controlling the domain, you are dealing with the working level of the network. Users are located in domains. Computers are located in domains. To tie the domains together, you need to organize them into a logical structure. This structure will either be a domain tree or a forest.

Obviously, this is why we had the discussion on DNS in Chapter 2, "Configuring DNS for Active Directory." The DNS hierarchy is used in Windows 2000 to tie the various domains together and to create the domain tree. If you start with a domain such as Widgets.com, for example, you could create a single domain that contains all the objects in your enterprise. However, this might not be practical if your organization has offices in two major geographical areas and if each area works independently from the other. In this case, you might opt to create separate domains that could be independently managed. In Figure 3.1, you will notice that there is a Widgets.com as well as an East.Widgets.com and a West.Widgets.com. In this case, the top domain is simply a pointer to one or the other of the lower-level domains.

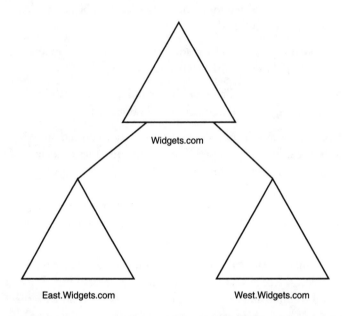

FIGURE 3.1
A sample domain tree for Widgets.com broken down using geography.

If you were to break the organization down along the lines of an organizational chart, the tree might look more like Figure 3.2. In this figure, there is a domain for sales and marketing, a domain for logistics (production and shipping), and a domain for research and development. The administration and other support roles, in this case, would be in the top-level domain.

Remember from Chapter 1, "Understanding Active Directory," that throughout this enterprise, there would be a single schema, a common global catalog, and transitive two-way trust relationships.

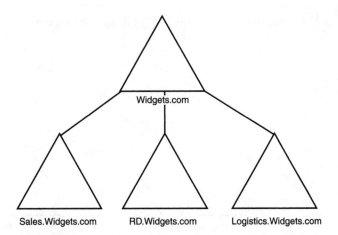

FIGURE 3.2
A sample domain tree for Widgets.com broken down by function.

There are some cases, however, in which a domain tree will not
work. In cases in which different parts of the organization need to
have separate public identities, you cannot use the same structure
if the internal naming is to mirror the external nature. In a case
such as this, you might have more than one tree. However, it is still
important to keep the three common elements: shared schema,
shared configuration, and the global catalog. To do this, one of the
domains will become the root of the enterprise. The other domains
will be children even though their names look different. In Figure
3.3, Stuff.com has been added. Convention dictates that the line
joining the new tree to the forest is drawn to the top of the root to
show that it is not just a child domain.

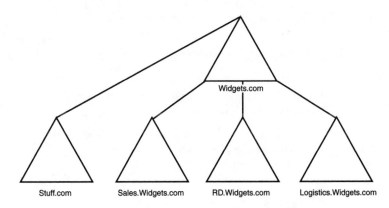

FIGURE 3.3
A sample domain forest.

From here, you could add children to Stuff.com (see Figure 3.4).

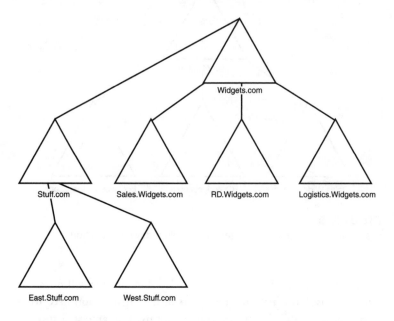

FIGURE 3.4
An expanded domain forest.

After you have installed the first domain controller for the first domain, you can begin to build the hierarchy by using DCPROMO to create other domain controllers. During the promotion, you will have the option of creating new domain controllers in the existing domain, a new controller for a new child domain, or a new root controller for a new tree in the forest.

The combination of trees and forests provides you absolute flexibility in the design of your domain structure and, therefore, in the design of your Active Directory.

Now that you have knowledge of domains, which provide your first level of hierarchy, it makes sense to move on and talk about *organizational units* (OUs). OUs provide the secondary level of hierarchy. They let you break down a domain into logical units that you can control, to a degree, independently.

Organizational Units

The capability to delegate control of part of a domain to a user or a group of users is new to Windows 2000. This is achieved through the use of organizational units. An organizational unit is a container within the Active Directory you create. After you create the container, you can move computers, users, and other objects into the container.

After this is accomplished, you could delegate control of those objects in the container to a set of users or groups. As a domain administrator, you would still have control, but the people you delegate can also control these objects. This enables you to create workgroup administrators who can handle a limited section of your domain. You can also apply group policies to the organizational unit that are different from those policies you applied to the domain.

Figure 3.5 shows an example of how the Widgets.com network could be fit into a single domain while still providing local administrators to deal with a group of users and computers.

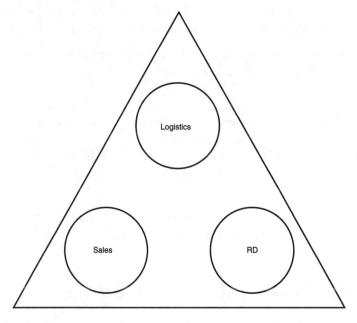

FIGURE 3.5
The Widgets.com network designed using organizational units.

You can even create organizational units within another organizational unit. This enables you to create a hierarchy of organizational units within a domain.

You need to decide for your organization whether you should use domains or organizational units to manage users, computers, and the other objects in Active Directory. The following guidelines should be used to decide whether to use domains or organizational units:

◆ Use domains if the organization is one in which different users and resources are managed by completely different sets of administrators.

◆ Use domains for a network in which parts of the network are separated by a slow link. This can also be accomplished using sites, which we will see later in the section "Working in the Physical Network."

◆ Use organizational units to mimic the structure of your organization.

◆ Use organizational units to delegate administrative control over smaller groups of users, groups, and other objects.

◆ Use organizational units if this particular part of your company is likely to change later.

As you can see, the logical structure of Active Directory is used to build a hierarchy that enables you to organize users within any size of organization. Using domains, you can create security and replication boundaries; and then using organizational units, you can further divide domains into manageable sections.

The planning of the Active Directory structure is the domain of the network planners. As the implementer, you now need to create the root domain and the rest of the tree and then the organization units.

INSTALLING THE FIRST DOMAIN

Install, configure, and troubleshoot the components of Active Directory.

• **Install Active Directory.**

Obviously, this is an important objective because all the other work you will do depends on the capability to install Active Directory. This section starts with an examination of the root installation and then looks at verifying installations. From there, the discussion will turn to the other types of installations.

Now that you are familiar with the logical structure of Active Directory, it is time to look at the installation of Active Directory. The installation is a simple process. Before beginning installation, however, you will want to have planned the structure of your enterprise.

Prerequisites

As you have probably guessed, a number of necessary items and tasks need to be completed before you install Active Directory. The following is a list of the key items that need to be in place:

◆ You need to have a Windows 2000 Server, Advanced Server, or Data Center Server installed and running.

◆ You should have a DNS server installed with a forward lookup zone configured. The DNS server needs to support *Service* (SRV) records and should allow for dynamic updates and standard zones incremental transfers.

◆ You need to be sure that the correct DNS server is selected for the computer you are making a domain controller and that the name of the computer is correct. The computer also needs to have TCP/IP installed and correctly functioning.

◆ You need to be sure that you have an NTFS partition on the computer you are making into a domain controller. You also need to have enough space for the directory (1GB is recommended).

◆ You need to be sure that the system time zone is correct. You also need to be sure that the correct time is set on the system.

In addition to the physical systems in place to install the domain controller, you need to know the name of the domain controller to install. You also need to know the domain name for the domain you are creating.

Naming Your Domain

There are several different ways you can decide to name the domain. The three main choices are:

◆ **Use your organization's real Internet domain name.** This would mean that your internal and external identities would be the same, and the risk is that your Active Directory structure could easily become exposed to the public Internet.

◆ **Use a subdomain under your existing Internet domain.** In other words, create something like AD.widgets.com as the starting point for the Active Directory. This makes it easier to separate the public and private structure. However, this approach adds complexity to the naming system.

◆ **Use a totally separate name internally.** This means you can keep the public and private parts of the network completely separate. Microsoft suggests that you can use .local if you plan to separate the internal and external naming of the organization. You might use Widgets.com for the Internet and Widgets.local for the Active Directory.

The domain name, of course, should be decided before you begin to perform the installations. Naming domains will require probably a lot of discussion. Assuming you have all the required information and the prerequisites are met, it is time to install Active Directory.

The Installation Process

The installation of the root domain is very straightforward, and the complete process is outlined in the following Step by Step.

STEP BY STEP

3.1 Installing Active Directory

1. From the Start menu, choose Run. Enter **dcpromo** and then click OK.

2. Click Next to pass the introductory screen of the Active Directory Installation Wizard.

3. Choose Domain Controller for a New Domain and then click Next (see Figure 3.6).

4. Choose Create a New Domain Tree and then click Next (see Figure 3.7).

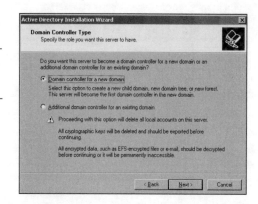

FIGURE 3.6
Creating a new domain.

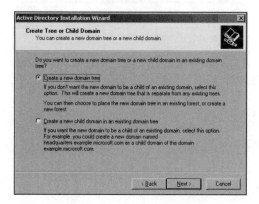

FIGURE 3.7
Creating a new domain tree.

5. Choose Create a New Forest of Domain Trees and click Next (See Figure 3.8).

6. Enter the Full DNS name for the new domain and click Next (See Figure 3.9).

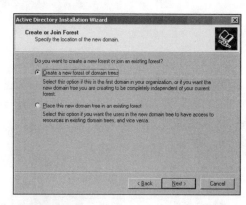

FIGURE 3.8
Creating a new domain tree in a new forest.

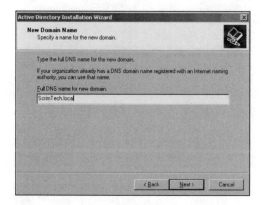

FIGURE 3.9
Entering the name for your new domain.

NOTE If the first part of the name is the name for your existing NT domain, you will receive a warning, and the down-level (NetBIOS) domain name will include a number to differentiate it from the existing domain. This will not happen when you upgrade an existing PDC (see Figure 3.10).

continues

FIGURE 3.10
The error indicates that the domain name
exists as an NT 4.0 domain.

continued

7. Confirm the down-level (NetBIOS) domain name
(see Figure 3.11).

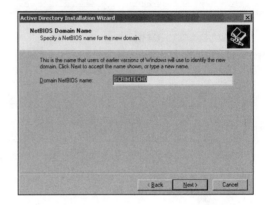

FIGURE 3.11
The down-level domain name (used by non-Active Directory clients).

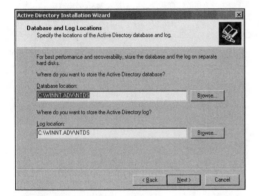

FIGURE 3.12
Specifying where the directory services
database and log should be located.

8. Confirm the location of the Active Directory database and
log files. It is best to place these on different drives for
recoverability. Both must be located on a drive formatted
with NTFS (see Figure 3.12).

9. Confirm the location of the SYSVOL directory (which
replaces the Netlogon share). This must be located on
a drive formatted with NTFS 5 (see Figure 3.13).

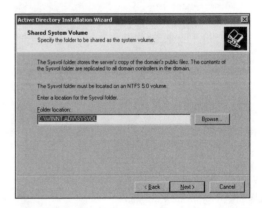

FIGURE 3.13
Choosing the location for the SYSVOL.

10. The wizard now confirms your DNS server. You will receive a warning if it does not find the server (see Figure 3.14).

FIGURE 3.14
You will receive this error if the system cannot find your DNS server.

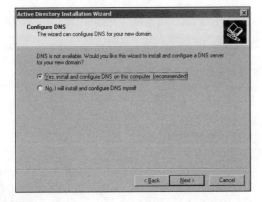

FIGURE 3.15
The installation will offer you the choice of installing DNS if it was not found.

11. Next you will receive a security warning about pre-Windows 2000 RAS security. In NT 4.0 and prior, the RAS server had to allow clients to read domain information before authentication. If you run down-level RAS servers, you need to allow the weaker permissions. Choose the appropriate option and click Next (see Figure 3.16).

12. Next you are prompted to enter the directory services Restore-mode password. You should make this a secure password and should safely store the password so it can't be forgotten (see Figure 3.17).

NOTE If the DNS server could not be located, the wizard will offer to install and configure it for you (see Figure 3.15). If you want the wizard to do this, click Yes. If you choose No, the installation will continue. You will receive numerous startup errors, however, and Active Directory will not work until you correct the problem. It is recommended that you allow the wizard to install and configure DNS if it cannot find an appropriate DNS server.

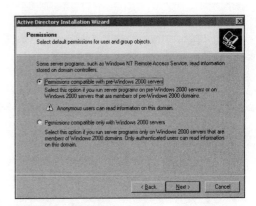

FIGURE 3.16
This dialog box warns you about NT 4.0 RAS security.

continues

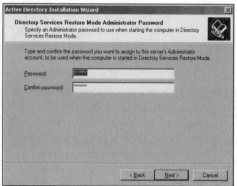

FIGURE 3.17
Entering the directory services Restore-mode password.

FIGURE 3.19
The final dialog box summarizes your installation.

continued

13. The next screen will summarise all the choices you have made to this point. You should review the entries and, if necessary, use the Back button to go back and change any of the options that are not correct (see Figure 3.18).

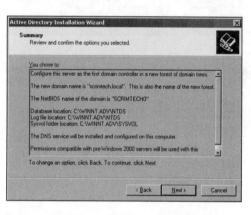

FIGURE 3.18
Confirming all the choices you made.

14. Assuming that all has gone well, you should now get a final screen confirming the installation of Active Directory. Click Finish and then restart the computer (see Figure 3.19).

At this point, Active Directory will be installed. After the system has restarted, you might want to verify the installation.

Verifying the Installation

Install, configure, and troubleshoot the components of Active Directory.

• **Verify Active Directory installation.**

After the installation of Active Directory, you should verify that the installation worked and that the system is running correctly. This will ensure that the other servers you add to the domain and the other domains you add to the tree will install correctly.

It is a fairly simple matter to verify that Active Directory is installed on the computer. All you need to do is verify that the following options are now in the Administrative Tools folder on the Start menu.

- ◆ **Active Directory Users and Computer.** This is used to manage users and computers as well as organizational units within your domain.

- ◆ **Active Directory Domains and Trusts.** This is used to manage domains and trust relationships with NT 4.0 domains.

- ◆ **Active Directory Sites and Services.** This is used to configure the directory services site and the replication between sites.

You can also use the following steps to make sure Active Directory is installed.

STEP BY STEP

3.2 Verifying That Active Directory Is Installed

1. Open Active Directory Users and Computers.

2. Click on the Domain Controllers folder.

3. Verify that your computer is listed.

Getting the first domain controller installed and running correctly is critical because all the other installations will need to communicate with this system as they proceed.

After you have your first domain controller, you will need to add others. The next few sections cover the differences for the various types of setups you will need to perform.

OTHER INSTALLATIONS

Now that you have a working domain controller, you will want to add at least one other domain controller for redundancy. In most cases, you will add several more domain controllers to a domain. In addition, you need to be able to add other domains to your domain tree or more trees to the forest. This section looks at these types of installations.

Adding a Domain Controller

To provide redundancy and load balancing, you need to add more domain controllers to the domains you create. The process for adding a domain controller is straightforward. You begin with a computer with Windows 2000 Server, Advanced Server, or Data Center Server installed. Then you do the following.

STEP BY STEP

3.3 Adding a Domain Controller to an Existing Domain

1. From the Start menu, choose Run. Enter **dcpromo** and then click OK.

2. Click Next to pass the introductory screen of the Active Directory Installation Wizard.

3. Choose Additional Domain Controller for an existing domain and then click Next.

4. You will be asked for your network credentials. The credentials you provide should be those of a member of the Domain Admins group. When you have entered the credentials, click Next to continue.

5. Next you will be asked for the name of the domain you want to join. This is the full DNS name of the domain. You should make sure the system is using a DNS server that can resolve the name. After this is entered, click Next to continue.

6. You will now be asked where you want to put the database and the log for Active Directory. This needs to be on an NTFS partition. Enter the location for these files and then click Next to continue.

7. Next you need to enter the location of the SYSVOL directory. This also needs to be on an NTFS partition; after you have entered the location, click Next to continue.

8. You will be asked for the Active Directory Restore-mode password. Enter the password and click Next.

9. Next you will get the summary screen. Click the Finish button and the Active Directory information will be copied.

10. When the copy is finished, you are prompted to restart the computer.

You should now be able to add a domain controller to an existing domain. Using multiple domain controllers is important for redundancy and for load balancing. The next section looks at adding a child domain to an existing domain.

Adding a Child Domain

As you build the Active Directory structure for your organization, you will probably need to add child domains. The process is more like creating a new domain than adding a domain controller. The basic steps follow.

STEP BY STEP

3.4 Adding a Child Domain to a Domain Tree

1. From the Start menu, choose Run. Enter **dcpromo** and then click OK.

2. Click Next to pass the introductory screen of the Active Directory Installation Wizard.

3. Choose Domain Controller for a New Domain and then click Next.

4. Choose Create a New Child Domain in an Existing Tree and then click Next.

continues

continued

> **5.** Enter the network credentials for a user in the Enterprise Admins group from the parent domain and then click Next.
>
> **6.** Enter the DNS name for the new domain and the parent domain and click Next.
>
> **7.** Confirm the down-level (NetBIOS) domain name and click Next.
>
> **8.** Confirm the location of the Active Directory database and log files. It is best to place these on different drives for recoverability. Both must be located on a drive formatted with NTFS.
>
> **9.** Confirm the location of the SYSVOL directory (which replaces the Netlogon share). This must be located on a drive formatted with NTFS 5.
>
> **10.** Next you get a security warning about pre-Windows 2000 RAS security. In NT 4.0 and prior, the RAS server had to allow clients to read domain information before authentication. If you run down-level RAS servers, you need to allow the weaker permissions. Choose the appropriate option and click Next.
>
> **11.** You will be asked for the Active Directory Restore-mode password. Enter the password and click Next.
>
> **12.** Assuming all has gone well, you should now get a summary screen confirming the installation of Active Directory. Click Next and then restart the computer.

After this installation, you would proceed to add more domain controllers to the new domain using the steps in Step by Step 3.3.

Remember that child domains act as boundaries for replication and security. Child domains become part of the same namespace. In some cases, this isn't what you require, and you need to create a new tree, making a forest.

Creating a Forest

Creating a forest is the final setup we'll discuss. Your internal organization will probably use one naming scheme, so creating a forest is not a common event. In any case, the process is almost identical to that of adding a child domain. The following steps help you to create a forest.

STEP BY STEP

3.5 Adding a Root Server in a Forest

1. From the Start menu, choose Run. Enter **dcpromo** and then click OK.

2. Click Next to pass the introductory screen of the Active Directory Installation Wizard.

3. Choose Domain Controller for a New Domain and then click Next.

4. Choose Create a New Domain Tree and then click Next.

5. Choose Place this New Domain Tree in an Existing Forest and then click Next.

6. Enter the network credentials for a user in the Enterprise Admins group from the root domain and then click Next.

7. Enter the DNS name for the new domain and click Next.

8. Confirm the down-level (NetBIOS) domain name and click Next.

9. Confirm the location of the Active Directory database and log files. It is best to place these on different drives for recoverability. Both must be located on a drive formatted with NTFS.

10. Confirm the location of the SYSVOL directory (which replaces the Netlogon share). This must be located on a drive formatted with NTFS 5.

> **NOTE**
>
> **DNS Support** Because this domain will be the start of a new tree, it will also be the start of a separate namespace. If the DNS server is not set up correctly, you will have the same options as you did during the installation of the initial domain controller as seen in Step by Step 3.1.

continues

continued

11. You next get a security warning about pre-Windows 2000
RAS security. In NT 4.0 and prior, the RAS server had to
allow clients to read domain information before authentication. If you run down-level RAS servers, you need to
allow the weaker permissions. Choose the appropriate
option and click Next.

12. You will be asked for the Active Directory Restore-mode
password. Enter the password and click Next.

13. Assuming all has gone well, you should now get a final
screen confirming the installation of Active Directory.
Click Finish and then restart the computer.

As you can see, building the logical structure of Active Directory is
fairly simple, and with good planning, it should go fairly smoothly.
Remember that domains act as security and replication boundaries,
and this is the key reason for using them.

If you were to put hundreds of domain controllers in a single
domain, perhaps in different locations, you would still have a
replication problem. This problem is addressed by using sites that
enable you to further control replication. This requires addressing
the physical network.

WORKING IN THE PHYSICAL NETWORK

Now that you have seen how to configure the logical portion of
Active Directory, it is time to look at configuring the physical side.
The physical parts of Active Directory, sites and subnets, are used to
control replication. By creating sites and later site links, you will be
able to determine at what times replication can occur and how often
during that period it will happen.

One of the key parts of using Active Directory is the TCP/IP
requirement. TCP/IP is not required simply to enable Windows
2000 to use the DNS system, although that is very important.

TCP/IP enables you to break your enterprise into sites and to control replication between sites. You will also be able to apply group policies to sites, enforcing certain settings for all the computers in a single location.

A site is very simply one or more IP subnets connected by high-speed links. This is perhaps a little vague. High-speed is relative to your environment. Many factors need to be examined when determining what exactly is meant by high-speed. If your domain contains three million objects, your password policy requires passwords to be changed every seven days, and you experience a high turnover of employees, then a 10Mbps LAN might not be able to keep up with the replication required. On the other hand, if you have a few hundred objects in the Active Directory and there are few changes in your environment and only two domain controllers, you might find that a 128Kbps ISDN link is fine.

As a rule of thumb, consider anything that runs T1 (1.54Mbps) and below to be a slow link. In these cases, you want to consider the effect of replication on the link. You probably need to create two sites so you can control the replication between them.

The good news is that sites follow what most organizations already do with their networks. Also, sites are very easy to create and manage in Active Directory. Normally, you already have sites defined in your network, breaking the segments into manageable sections. These sections are normally implemented to control the traffic because this is also the point of sites; the translation from the physical segments into sites is very straightforward.

Working with Sites

Install, configure, and troubleshoot the components of Active Directory.

• Create sites.

If you were to allow uncontrolled replication on your network, you would have many problems with available bandwidth. This is notably the case when you have a link to a remote office. In these cases, you need to remember that sites are used to control replication traffic and to create the sites you need to control the traffic.

You need to be able to create and manage sites within the Active Directory. The following sections outline how to create and remove sites. Then you will see how to add subnets to a site and how to move domain controllers to a site.

Adding a Site

Adding a site is a very simple procedure. The following steps are involved.

STEP BY STEP

3.6 Creating a Site

1. Start Active Directory Sites and Services.

2. Right-click on the Sites folder and choose New Site (see Figure 3.20).

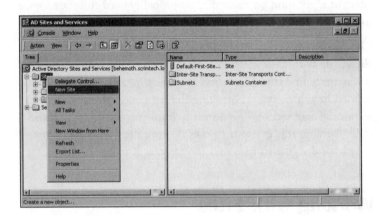

FIGURE 3.20
Choose New Site from the context menu.

3. In the New Object – Site dialog box, enter the name of the new site (see Figure 3.21). Letters and numbers are allowed, but spaces and special characters are not.

4. Click one of the site links and then click OK. Site links are covered later in this chapter.

5. You will get a message telling what the next steps are (see Figure 3.22). Click OK to continue.

As you can see, creating a site is a simple process. You can also rename and delete sites.

Renaming a Site

Renaming a site is as simple as renaming a file. The following steps are all you need to do to rename a site.

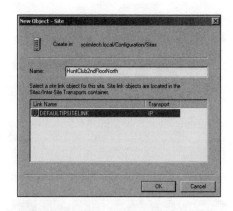

FIGURE 3.21
Enter the name of the new site.

STEP BY STEP

3.7 Renaming a Site

1. Open Active Directory Sites and Services.

2. Open the Sites folder and click on the site you want to rename.

3. Click once again or right-click and choose Rename.

4. Enter the new name and press Enter.

FIGURE 3.22
A message tells you what the next steps are to complete the site.

Renaming is useful when you are reorganizing your network or if a remote office changes purpose. Renaming is also useful when a site no longer is needed.

Deleting a Site

Deleting a site is just as simple as renaming a site. You should make sure the site is empty before you delete the site; otherwise, some objects could be lost. The following Step by Step walks you through deleting a site.

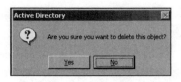

FIGURE 3.23
The confirmation dialog box.

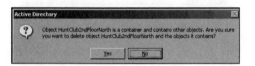

FIGURE 3.24
This dialog box is warning you that other objects could be deleted along with the site.

STEP BY STEP

3.8 Deleting a Site

1. Open Active Directory Sites and Services.

2. Open the Sites folder and click on the site you want to delete.

3. Press the Delete key or right-click and choose Delete. You will get a confirmation dialog box (see Figure 3.23).

4. If you're sure you want to delete the site, click Yes. You will get a warning about a site being a container object and that deleting the site will delete the other objects (see Figure 3.24).

5. Choose Yes to complete the deletion.

Again, you normally only delete sites if you are reorganizing your physical network.

In addition to creating, renaming, and deleting sites, you should be aware of and be able to set the properties of the sites in your network.

Site Properties

There are some properties you can set for the sites you create in the Active Directory. The following sections describe the properties that can be set for a site. To set the properties, right-click on the site name and choose Properties. This will bring up the Properties dialog box (see Figure 3.25).

The following are the properties you can set on each tab:

◆ **Site.** Enter a description for the site on this tab.

◆ **Location.** This enables you to enter a location for the site.

◆ **Object.** This enables you to see the full name of the object and other details such as when it was created. There is nothing you can edit on this tab.

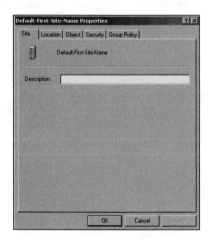

FIGURE 3.25
The site Properties dialog box.

◆ **Security.** This enables you to set the security for the object in Active Directory. The default security enables administrators to manage the site and enables others to read the information.

◆ **Group Policy.** This enables you to assign group policies to the site and create and modify the policies.

Remember that a site is defined as a group of IP subnets connected using high-speed networking. This means you need to be able to work with subnets as well.

Working with Subnets

Install, configure, and troubleshoot the components of Active Directory.

- **Create subnets.**

Now that you can create and delete sites, you need to be able to populate the sites. This is a matter of deciding which subnets should be in a site and creating them in Active Directory. Decisions about which subnets to include will depend on the network design and how you will actually control the location of objects in Active Directory.

Subnets need to be added, deleted, and moved between sites. In addition, like the other objects in Active Directory, you can set various properties for subnets. The next few sections show you how to perform these functions.

Adding a Subnet

Adding a subnet is very simple, as you will see in the following Step by Step.

STEP BY STEP

3.9 Creating a Subnet in Active Directory

1. Open Active Directory Sites and Services.

2. Right-click on the Subnets folder and choose New Subnet.

continues

FIGURE 3.26
The dialog box used to add subnets.

continued

3. In the dialog box, enter the IP address and subnet mask for a system on that subnet.

4. The system automatically converts the information to network ID/number of bits notation (see Figure 3.26).

5. Select the site to which you want to add the subnet and then click OK.

Again, adding a subnet is very simple, but before you click OK, you should make sure you have entered the correct information. Sometimes you will need to delete a subnet.

Deleting a Subnet

Deleting a subnet is as simple as adding a subnet. Follow the following steps to learn how to delete a subnet.

STEP BY STEP

3.10 Deleting a Subnet

1. Open Active Directory Sites and Services.

2. Open the Subnets folder and click on the subnet to delete.

3. Press the Delete key or right-click and choose Delete. You will get a confirmation dialog box.

4. Click Yes to confirm the deletion.

Although you can delete subnets, it is far more common to move a subnet to a different site. This happens as the network changes and the distribution of users and servers changes.

Moving a Subnet

There will be times when you need to move a subnet. This can happen when the network grows or shrinks or as the bandwidth between sites is increased.

The steps for moving a subnet are, again, very simple, as shown in the following Step by Step.

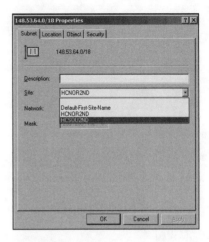

FIGURE 3.27
Moving a subnet is easy in the Properties dialog box.

STEP BY STEP

3.11 Moving a Subnet to Another Site

1. Open Active Directory Sites and Services.

2. Open the Subnets folder and click on the subnet you want to move.

3. Right-click and choose Properties.

4. In the Properties dialog box (see Figure 3.27) on the Subnet tab, use the Site drop-down list to choose the site to which you want to move the subnet.

5. Click OK to complete the move.

In most cases, even moving subnets is a rare occurrence. Moving subnets only happens when the physical network is reorganized.

As you can see, there are other tabs in this dialog box. The following list describes the other options you can set on each tab.

- ◆ **Subnet.** This tab enables you to enter a description for the subnet and move it to another site.

- ◆ **Location.** This enables you to enter a location for the subnet.

- ◆ **Object.** This enables you to see the full name of the object and other details such as when it was created. There is nothing you can edit on this tab.

- ◆ **Security.** This enables you to set the security for the object in Active Directory. The default security enables administrators to manage the site and enables others to read the information.

Now that you have created the sites, you need to move the domain controllers into the sites and configure the replication between the sites.

REPLICATING ACTIVE DIRECTORY INFORMATION

Replication is the process of taking information from one system and copying it to another system. In Windows 2000, replication is a very important element. Changes can occur at any domain controller, not just at a primary domain controller, which was the case in Windows NT 4.0.

In addition to the multiple-master replication model for the domain objects, there is additional information that needs to be replicated throughout the organization. The following is a list of the key information that needs to be replicated.

This section looks at Active Directory replication, starting with an overview of how it works. From there, the specifics of the intrasite replication will be discussed including a look at connections. After that, the discussion turn to how you can control replication between sites. Finally, there will be a quick look at how you configure a global catalog server.

- ◆ **Schema information.** You saw in Chapter 1, "Understanding Active Directory," that this is the actual structure of the database that holds information about the objects in your enterprise. You might recall that all the domains and, therefore, all the domain controllers need to use the same schema for Active Directory to work correctly. The schema must be replicated to all domain controllers.

- ◆ **Configuration information.** This is the overall design of the entire enterprise. It includes the domains, their names, and where they fit into the hierarchy. It also includes other information such as the replication topology. This information is used by all the domain controllers and therefore is replicated to all domain controllers.

- ◆ **Domain data.** This is the information you store about the objects making up your domain. All the information is replicated within a domain by the domain controllers. The global catalog servers throughout the enterprise replicate a subset of the information.

As you can see, there are two levels of replication. There is the replication within a domain and the replication handled by the global catalog servers. The replication within a domain is primarily handled by the domain controllers. This replication is principally interested in the replication of all the objects in the domain with all the attributes for each of the objects.

The global catalog servers handle the other replication. At least one global catalog server is required in the enterprise. There should also be one global catalog server for each domain and for each site in the enterprise.

The global catalog servers are responsible for replication of the following information:

◆ The schema information for the forest

◆ The configuration information for all domains in the forest

◆ A subset of the properties for all directory objects in the forest (replicated between global catalogs only)

◆ All directory objects and all their properties for the domain in which the global catalog is located

Now that you know what is replicated, we will look at how replication works.

How Replication Works

Replication is based on the *Update Sequence Number* (USN) in Active Directory. The USN tracks, for each domain controller, the number of changes it has made to its version of the directory. As a change is made, the current USN is assigned to the object, and the USN for the domain controller is incremented.

Each domain controller keeps track of its own USN and the USNs for its replication partners. Periodically (every five minutes by default), the server checks for changes on its replication partners. Requesting any changes since the last-known USN for the partner accomplishes this check. The partner can then send all the changes since the USN number.

A domain controller could be offline for a period of time, and after it comes back, it will quickly be able to get back up-to-date.

There is a danger here. Assume a domain controller receives an update. It makes the change and then updates its USN. The domain controller that made the change originally now requests the USN for the server that got the change. Its USN is updated, and therefore, the change is requested. The system that originated the change now has its own change back. If the system made the change and updated its USN, this whole cycle would repeat ad infinitum.

To avoid this scenario, Active Directory tracks the number of originating writes that have occurred for each attribute. The number of times a user changed the value, rather than the number of times it was changed using replication, is tracked. In the preceding case, the first system in which the change was made will find that it has the correct originating write value and will not make the change.

There is also the possibility that two different users could be changing the same attribute of the same object at the same time on two different controllers. When these changes both start to replicate, a conflict will be detected. Windows 2000 will choose the change with the newer time stamp (the more recent change) to resolve the conflict. If the two changes were made at the same millisecond, then the change with the higher globally unique ID will win.

Now that you have seen the theory of replication, it is time to see how the replication is configured within a site and between sites.

Replication Within a Site

Manage and troubleshoot Active Directory replication.

- **Manage intrasite replication.**

Although there is little you need to do with intrasite replication, it is important for you to understand how it works and the components involved. This serves as a basis for intersite replication.

Replication within a site is handled by Active Directory. There is no need for you to take any action. The *Knowledge Consistency Checker* (KCC) evaluates the domain controllers in the site and automatically creates a replication topology. In general, the KCC configures connections so that each domain controller replicates with at least two other domain controllers.

The KCC automatically adjusts the replication topology as the network conditions change. As domain controllers are added or removed (or just moved), the KCC continues to make sure that each domain controller replicates with at least two others. Within a site, replication does not use compression, and in some cases (such as a password change), the replication is completed on an immediate basis.

Replication within a site is quite easy to work with; there is nothing to do. The KCC does most of the work for you by creating the correct connection objects to link all your servers together.

Connection Objects

Install, configure, and troubleshoot the components of Active Directory.

- **Create connection objects.**

Connection objects serve as the backbone for replication; they define network paths through which replication can occur. You need to know what these are and how they are defined; you should also be able to define them yourself.

The KCC essentially manages the replication within a site by creating connection objects between the various domain controllers in the site. The KCC also creates connection objects between sites where required.

A connection represents a permanent or temporary network path that can be used for replication. Normally, you will not create the connection objects within a site yourself. It is assumed that all the paths between servers are of equal speed, and therefore, the KCC should be able to handle creating the connection objects.

You can create connections within a site. You can also edit the connections created by the KCC; however, you should be careful when doing this. In the case of a connection that you create, the connection is never evaluated by the KCC and is never deleted until you do so. This could cause problems if your network changes and you neglect to remove the connection you created. In cases in which you edit the connection that the KCC makes, the changes you make will be lost when the KCC next updates the connections.

The main reason you might want to create a connection object is to specify the bridgehead servers that will be used to link to sites. The bridgehead servers will be the main method of replication across a site link. To create a connection object, follow these steps.

STEP BY STEP

3.12 Creating a Connection Object Manually

1. Open Active Directory Sites and Services.

2. Expand the Sites folder and then expand the site for which you want to create a link.

3. Expand the Servers folder for the site and then expand the server that will be part of the connection.

4. On the NTDS Settings, right-click and choose New Active Directory Connection.

5. In the dialog box that appears, choose (or find) the server to which you want to create the link and then choose OK.

Connection objects, as you have seen, provide the network paths for replication. This is true whether the connection is within a site or is used to link two sites together.

Replication Between Sites

Manage and troubleshoot Active Directory replication.

- **Manage intersite replication.**

The capability to manage intersite replication is critical for administrators on Windows 2000 networks. Without this capability, the replication would easily saturate WAN connections and make Windows 2000 Active Directory unmanageable.

When the replication within a site is not compressed, replication between sites will be. Within a site, Active Directory assumes a high-speed connection and, to save processing time, does not compress the data. Between-site bandwidth is assumed to be lower. Therefore, Active Directory compresses the data being transferred between sites.

Active Directory also enables the replication between the sites to be scheduled so that it only happens during scheduled hours. During those hours, you still have the option of changing the interval of the replication. Before you can set this up, you need to move a domain controller to another site. Then you need to create a connection between that domain controller and one in another site.

Because replication is done between domain controllers, you need to add domain controllers to the site to which they physically belong. Clients within a site also look for a domain controller in the site to log on to, and by moving a domain controller to the site, you decrease the logon times, increasing satisfaction with the network.

Moving Domain Controllers

Install, configure, and troubleshoot the components of Active Directory.

- **Move server objects between sites.**

The capability to control replication and to ensure that users are able to log on within a reasonable amount of time requires that you be able to locate domain controllers near the users. This requires that you occasionally move a domain controller between sites.

The purposes of a site are to help manage the replication between domain controllers and to manage replication across slow network links. In addition to creating the site and adding subnets to that site, you need to move domain controllers into the site.

To move a domain controller, follow these simple steps.

STEP BY STEP

3.13 Moving a Domain Controller

1. Open Active Directory Sites and Services.

2. Expand the Sites folder and then expand the site where the server is currently located.

3. In the site, expand the Servers folder.

4. Right-click on the server and choose Move.

5. From the dialog box (see Figure 3.28), choose the destination subnet and click OK.

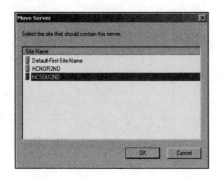

FIGURE 3.28
Select the destination subnet for the server and click OK.

Moving a domain controller to a site is part of creating and managing sites within Active Directory.

Now that you have moved the domain controllers to different sites, you need to create a site link between the sites. This provides the path through which replication to this site takes place.

Connecting Sites

Install, configure, and troubleshoot the components of Active Directory.

- **Create site links.**

The key to controlling replication is to create sites. Sites enable you to create site links that enable you to control when a link exists and how often replication can take place while the link is available. Multiple site links can be used to create different replication schedules at different times or to provide redundant links with higher costs.

Now that you have moved the domain controllers to different sites, you need to create a site link between the sites. This provides the path through which replication to this site takes place.

By creating and configuring site links, you provide the KCC with information about what connection objects to create to replicate directory data. Site links indicate where connection objects should be created. Connection objects use the network to exchange directory information.

Follow these general steps to create a site link.

STEP BY STEP

3.14 Creating a Site Link

1. Open Active Directory Sites and Services.

2. Expand the Sites folder and then the Inter-Site Transports.

3. Right click on the IP or SMTP folder, depending on the protocol you want to use (see the following discussion of the protocols), and then choose New Site Link.

4. Enter a name for the site link in the Name text box. From the Sites Not in This Site Link list, choose the site this will connect and click the Add button. Click OK when you're finished.

When creating site links, you have the option of using either IP or SMTP as the transport protocol for the site link.

◆ **SMTP replication.** SMTP can only be used for replication over site links. SMTP is asynchronous, meaning it typically ignores all schedules. Beware if you choose to use SMTP over site links; you must install and configure an enterprise certification authority. The *certification authority* (CA) signs SMTP messages that are exchanged between domain controllers, ensuring the authenticity of directory updates.

◆ **IP replication.** IP replication uses *Remote Procedure Calls* (RPC) for replication. This is the same for both intersite and intrasite replication.

After the site link is created, you can go back and set the other properties of the site link. You do this by locating the site link in the IP or SMTP folder and then bringing up the properties of the link.

The General tab on the Properties sheet sets the properties for the site link. There are also Object and Security tabs, which are the same as the tabs previously discussed. The items you can configure follow:

◆ **Description.** This is a description of the link for your information.

◆ **Site in This Site Link.** This area can be used to add domain controllers to and remove them from a site link.

◆ **Cost.** This is a relative value, and it is used by Active Directory to decide what route to use when replicating information. The cheapest available route is used based on the overall cost. This is easy to determine between two sites. When the sites are not directly connected, however, all the combinations of sites that link the two will be evaluated, and the total costs through all the sites are compared.

N O T E

Creating Your Own Certificate
If you don't need to authenticate with external sources, you can use the certificate server that comes with Windows 2000 to create the certificate.

◆ **Replicate Every.** This is the interval at which replication takes place over this link.

◆ **Change Schedule.** This button enables you to change when the site link is available for replication. Replication during the period that the link is available occurs at a frequency determined by the interval.

Site connectors provide the flexibility required to work with the physical network within a domain. In some cases, you might want to control which servers are used for replication. To do this, you need to configure a bridgehead server.

Bridgehead Servers

A bridgehead server is the main server used for intersite replication. You can configure a bridgehead server for each site you create for each of the intersite replication protocols. This enables you to control which server in a site is used to replicate information to other servers. Step by Step 3.15 walks you through the configuration of a bridgehead server.

STEP BY STEP

3.15 Configuring a Server as a Bridgehead Server

1. Open Active Directory Sites and Services and expand the Sites folder.

2. Expand the site in which you want to create a bridgehead server and then expand the Servers folder.

3. Right-click on the server and choose Properties.

4. In the Transports available for intersite transfer area, select the protocol or protocols for which this server should be a bridgehead and click Add.

5. Click OK to set the properties and then close Active Directory Sites and Services.

The capability to configure a server as a bridgehead server gives you greater control over the resources that used for replication between two sites or in cases such as a site link bridge between multiple sites.

Site Link Bridges

Install, configure, and troubleshoot the components of Active Directory.

- **Create site link bridges.**

In many cases, you do not need to deal with site link bridges. By default, all site links are automatically bridged, a property known as transitive site links. In some cases, you will want to control through which sites data can flow. In these cases, you need to create site link bridges.

By default, all the site links you create are bridged together. This bridging enables all the sites to communicate with each other. If this is not physically possible because of the structure of your network, you need to disable the automatic bridging and create the appropriate site link bridges.

For example, consider the diagram in Figure 3.29. You see three sites (1, 2, and 3) directly connected to each other. In this case, automatic bridging would work fine. However, Site 4 is connected using a low-speed connection, and therefore, you would not want it to replicate with all the other sites. In this case, you would want Site 4 to replicate only with Site 1.

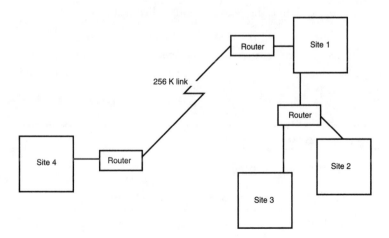

FIGURE 3.29
A network example in which automatic bridging would be problematic.

To resolve this replication problem, you would turn off automatic bridging. Then create a site link containing the three sites that are directly connected. Create a second site link between Site 1 and Site 4. Then create a site link bridge that gives Active Directory a way to get information from Sites 2 and 3 to Site 4 through Site 1 and vice versa.

To disable the automatic bridging, follow these steps.

STEP BY STEP

3.16 Disabling Transitive Site Links (Automatic Bridging)

1. Open Active Directory Sites and Services.

2. Expand the Sites folder and then the Inter-Site Transports.

3. Right-click on the transport for which you want to turn off the automatic bridging and choose Properties (see Figure 3.30).

4. On the General tab, clear the Bridge all site links check box and click OK.

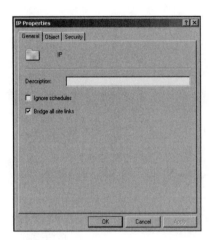

FIGURE 3.30
The IP inter-site transport properties dialog box.

On the General tab, notice that there is also an option to ignore all schedules. This option is only used to force changes to flow through whether or not replication was currently scheduled.

After you have ensured that transitive site links exist—in other words, that automatic bridging is off—you will need to create the site link bridge (or bridges). This process is outlined in the following Step by Step.

STEP BY STEP

3.17 Creating a Site Link Bridge

1. Open Active Directory Sites and Services.

2. Expand the Sites folder and then the Inter-Site Transports.

3. Right-click on the transport you want to use and choose New Site Link Bridge.

4. In the Name box, enter a name for the site link bridge.

5. From the list of Site links not in this bridge, select the site links you want to add. Remove any extra site links in the Site links in this bridge box. Click OK when the correct site links are part of the bridge.

Until now, we have dealt with the replication of the domain information. You need to consider the replication of the schema and configuration partitions and of the global catalog. This is handled by global catalog servers.

Global Catalog Servers

Install, configure, and troubleshoot the components of Active Directory.

- **Create global catalog servers.**

Global catalog servers provide essential information that is used to glue together all the parts of the Active Directory. The global catalog server ensures that the schema and configuration information is distributed to all the domains and it also handles universal group membership. It also provides a method of locating objects in Active Directory.

At the beginning of the preceding discussion on replication, you were told that the global catalog servers would replicate with each other. This replication is accomplished as though the global catalog servers were all in one domain and the KCC handles the replication. Your only choice is whether a domain controller will be a global catalog server. The following Step by Step outlines how to make a domain controller a global catalog server.

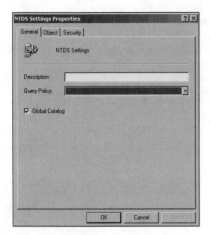

FIGURE 3.31
In the NTDS properties, you can configure a server as a global catalog server.

STEP BY STEP

3.18 Configuring a Server as a Global Catalog Server

1. Open Active Directory Sites and Services.

2. Expand the Sites folder and expand the site where the server is located. Expand the Servers folder and then expand the server.

3. Right-click the NTDS Setting and choose Properties (see Figure 3.31).

4. If the server should be a global catalog server, make sure the Global Catalog check box is checked. Otherwise, clear the check box. Click OK and you're finished.

One of the key jobs of an administrator is to keep the directory information up-to-date and to ensure that all the domain controllers have the correct information. Replication makes this possible. You need to understand this for both the exam and real life.

CASE STUDY: INSTALLING AND CONFIGURING ACTIVE DIRECTORY

ESSENCE OF THE CASE

There are a few points that you need to consider as you look at this case:

▶ Some of the physical locations only have a link to one other location. Some form of backup link is needed.

▶ Some of the locations are large and probably need multiple controllers. These locations might require multiple sites.

▶ To ensure that locating objects around the world is possible and that users can log on from anywhere, global catalog servers are required at each site.

▶ Because the domains are divided by function instead of geography, each location requires at least one domain controller for each domain.

▶ The overall size of any domain is comparatively small. Combined with low turnover and infrequent password changes, there should be minimal replication.

▶ Because there are domain controllers from each domain local to the location, users are able to make changes that are reflected at their locality, meaning replication does not have to happen immediately.

SCENARIO

In this chapter, you have looked at the physical and logical configuration of Active Directory. In addition, you have seen how to install the domain controller and child domains as well as how to install another tree in the forest.

The other major topic discussed was replication. You should now understand the three partitions of Active Directory: schema, configuration, and domain. You should also understand how these partitions would be replicated.

Recall from the previous case studies that Sunshine Brewing is located in 15 different cities around the world with some of those locations having multiple sites. You might also recall that the domain structure was to follow reporting lines instead of geography because of the very different needs of the users around the world.

Now it is time to implement this in the real world and to look at the concerns and issues that will be faced.

The scenario is very simple. You need to install an Active Directory tree that spans the globe. In addition, you need to ensure that replication is able to keep all the domains in all the locations up-to-date without saturating the bandwidth between any of the locations.

With these facts in mind and considering the general purpose of the network, the following analysis presents a solution for this scenario.

continues

CASE STUDY: INSTALLING AND CONFIGURING ACTIVE DIRECTORY

continued

ANALYSIS

In looking at this scenario, there are a couple of factors driving the analysis. First, you need to ensure replication. The replication, however, does not need to be any faster than the time it takes a user to physically move between two offices.

This being said, the shorter distances such as Victoria to Los Angeles or Ottawa to New York or Paris to London all take over an hour in the air. This means we should aim for replication every three hours between the main sites and longer between the other sites such as between Cape Town and Buenos Aries.

The other consideration with respect to replication is that not all the locations will have a back link to another location and could become isolated if the main link goes down. To ensure that replication can continue in these cases, secondary sites links need to be configured between locations using the Internet and a *virtual private network* (VPN) or SMTP as the intersite transport.

SMTP is a choice because the certificate server is able to create a certificate for us, but that only handles the replication. Because you would also want to be able to move other traffic if the main link goes, the VPN makes more sense.

This leaves intersite replication within a location. This can be handled simply by having all the sites within a location use the same site link. Therefore, there is a site link per location. The replication within the site takes place using the defaults. In each location, one site is created to link the locations, and these sites are also part of a site link to at least one other site using the network and two more sites either using the network or a VPN connection. If site links are configured that use VPNs, the cost is set to double the value of the highest network-connected site link.

To control the replication, three hours is used as the interval for sites connected via T1 during the day. Another site link is created for each that replicates once every hour overnight. The timing for other types of connections is based on these timing for T1 connections.

CHAPTER SUMMARY

This chapter provided opportunities for hands-on work with Active Directory. As you can see, the structure of Active Directory is basically organized into two parts: the logical and the physical designs. The logical design consists of organizational units that break down the administration of domains, domains that make up the root and branches of a tree, and trees that make up forests.

There is also the physical design that takes the enterprise and breaks this down into high-speed networks. On the physical side, there are multiple sites that make up the network and a Knowledge Consistency Checker that tracks all the site links building the connections forming the replication topology. You have the option of creating your own connections and of modifying the replication topology using your own site link bridges. All these things are put into place to ensure your ability to replicate all the objects in your domain.

In addition, you need to create global catalog servers, typically one per site and one per domain. These global catalog servers replicate the enterprise-wide information such as the global catalog (a list of the objects from all domains with a subset of the attributes), the schema, and the configuration information.

Moving on, you will see how to create and manage objects in Active Directory in Chapter 4, "Administering Active Directory Services," and how to manage the servers and the special roles some of them take on in Chapter 5, "Managing Servers."

KEY TERMS

- Child domain
- Configuration partition
- Connection objects
- DCPROMO
- Domain partition
- Forest
- Knowledge Consistency Checker
- NTFS
- Originating write
- RAS
- Remote procedure call
- Schema partition
- Simple Mail Transfer Protocol
- Site
- Site link bridges
- site links
- Subnet
- SYSVOL
- Tree
- Update Sequence Number

APPLY YOUR KNOWLEDGE

Exercises

During these exercises, you will need to have at least two computers with which you can work. The computers will be promoted and demoted a few times, so if the computer contains any important information, you should back this information up before you proceed.

3.1   Preparing the DNS Server

In this exercise, you will create a DNS standard primary zone that will be used for the remaining exercises. This exercise assumes you have a system with Windows 2000 Server or Advanced Server and the DNS server installed. If this is not the case, refer to Chapter 2, "Configuring DNS for Active Directory," for how to install DNS.

Estimated time: 10 minutes.

1. From the Start menu, choose Programs, Administrative Tools, DNS.

2. Expand your local server and click on the Forward Lookup Zones to set the focus.

3. Right-click on Forward Lookup Zones and choose New Zone.

4. Click Next to skip the introductory screen. Then choose Standard Primary and click Next.

5. Enter **W2KBrewing.com** as the domain name and click Next.

6. On the next screen of the wizard, verify that the filename is W2KBrewing.com.dns and then click Next.

7. Click Finish to complete the creation of the zone.

8. Expand Forward Lookup Zones (if it isn't already expanded) and click on W2KBrewing.com.

9. Right-click W2KBrewing.com and choose Properties.

10. In the Allow dynamic updates? drop-down text box, choose Yes. Click OK and then close the DNS Manager.

11. Right-click on My Network Places and choose Properties.

12. On the connection for your network card, right-click and choose Properties.

13. Double-click the Internet Protocol and make sure your primary DNS server entry contains your IP address. (Hint: Make sure your IP address is the same as the IP address listed above.)

14. Click OK to close the TCP/IP properties and then click OK again to close the connection properties. Close the My Network Places Properties.

3.2   Install a Root Domain Controller

Now that the DNS server is configured to work with Active Directory (that is, it supports SRV records and allows dynamic updates), you can install Active Directory. This exercise assumes that the drive on which Windows 2000 is installed is NTFS. If it is not, use the **CONVERT** command to change it to NTFS.

Estimated time: 20 minutes.

1. From the start menu, choose Run and enter **dcpromo**.

2. Click Next to pass the introductory screen of the Active Directory Installation Wizard.

3. Choose Domain Controller for a New Domain and then click Next.

APPLY YOUR KNOWLEDGE

4. Choose Create a New Domain Tree and then click Next.

5. Choose Create a New Forest of Domain Trees and click Next.

6. Enter **W2KBrewing.com** as the full DNS name for the new domain and click Next.

7. Confirm that the down-level domain name is W2KBrewing.

8. Observe the default locations for the Active Directory database and log file. Click Next to accept the default.

9. Observe the location of the SYSVOL directory. Click Next to accept the default.

10. Next you'll receive the security warning about pre-Windows 2000 RAS security. Click Next to continue.

11. Enter **password** as the Directory Services Restore-mode password and click Next to continue.

12. Review the summary screen to make sure all the selections are correct and click Next to continue. If they are not, use the Back button to return and correct them.

13. Click Finish and restart your computer when prompted.

3.3   Verifying the Installation of Active Directory

In this exercise, you will verify that Active Directory was correctly installed and that the correct resource records have been added to the DNS server.

Estimated time: 5 minutes.

1. Log on to the domain controller you just created as the administrator. The password is the same as the administrator password was before you promoted the system.

2. From the Start Menu, choose Start, Programs, Administrative Tools.

3. Verify that you now have these Active Directory tools: Users and Computers, Sites and Services, and Domains and Trusts.

4. Click on DNS to open the DNS Manager.

5. Expand the server and then the Forward Lookup Zones and click on W2Kbrewing.

6. There should be four subfolders: _msdcs, _sites, _tcp, and _udp.

7. Close the DNS Manager.

3.4   Adding a Second Domain Controller

In this exercise, you will add a second domain controller to your domain. This enables you to create sites and configure site links and bridges. This exercise should be performed on a server running Windows 2000 Server or Advanced Server, but not the server installed in Exercise 3.2. The drive that Windows 2000 is installed on also needs to be NTFS.

Estimated time: 15 minutes.

1. Log on to the server as an administrator.

2. Right-click on My Network Places and choose Properties.

3. Right-click on the connection for your network card and choose Properties. Double-click Internet Protocol.

APPLY YOUR KNOWLEDGE

4. For the primary DNS server, enter the address of your existing server. This address was created in the preceding exercises.

5. Close the TCP/IP properties by clicking OK and then close the connection properties by clicking OK. Close the Connections dialog box.

6. From the Start button, choose Run, enter **dcpromo**, and then press Enter.

7. Click Next to skip the introductory screen.

8. Choose Additional domain controller for an existing domain and click Next.

9. For the network credentials, enter **Administrator** for the username, your administrator password, and the domain **W2Kbrewing.com** as the domain and click Next.

10. In the Domain to Join text box, enter **W2Kbrewing.com** and click Next.

11. Accept the default for the database and log locations by clicking Next.

12. Accept the default for the SYSVOL location by clicking Next.

13. When the completion screen is displayed, click Finish and then restart the computer when prompted.

3.5 Managing Sites and Replication

In this exercise, you will create sites and subnets. You will also move one of the domain controllers to a different site. You will configure site links and site link bridges. Finally, you will be configuring a domain controller as a global catalog server. This exercise can be completed from either computer.

This exercise is configuring the network shown in Figure 3.32.

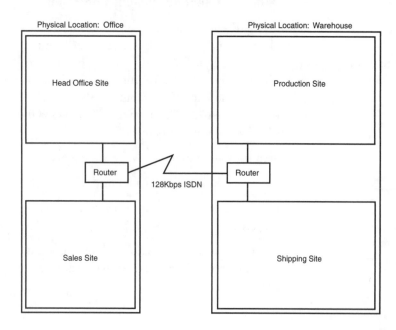

FIGURE 3.32
A sample network for Exercise 3.5.

APPLY YOUR KNOWLEDGE

Estimated time: 20 minutes.

1. Log on as the Administrator.

2. Open Active Directory Sites and Services (Start, Programs, Administrative Tools).

3. Expand the Sites folder and observe the default contents.

4. Right-click on the Sites folder and choose New Site.

5. Enter **HeadOffice** and click DEFAULTIP-SITELINK in the list of site links. Click OK to add the site.

6. Read the message and then click OK to clear it.

7. Using steps 4 through 6 as a reference, add the following sites:

   • Production

   • Shipping

   • Sales

8. Expand the Inter-Site Transports folder and right-click on IP. Choose New Site Link.

9. Enter **Warehouse** as the site link name.

10. Click Production in the list of Sites that are not in this link and click Add. Do the same for Shipping. Click OK to create the site link.

11. Create another site link called Office that contains the HeadOffice and Sales sites.

12. Expand the Default-First-Site-Name and then expand the Servers folder. Your two servers should be listed.

13. Right-click on one of the servers and choose move. Select HeadOffice from the list and click OK.

14. In the same way, move the other server to Production.

15. Right-click the Subnets folder and choose New Subnet.

16. Enter the IP address **10.1.1.0** with a subnet mask of **255.255.255.0**. Select HeadOffice as the site for this subnet and click OK.

17. Using steps 15 and 16, add these additional subnets:

IP Address	Mask	Site
10.1.2.0	255.255.255.0	HeadOffice
10.1.3.0	255.255.255.0	HeadOffice
10.2.1.0	255.255.255.0	Production
10.2.2.0	255.255.255.0	Production
10.3.1.0	255.255.255.0	Sales
10.3.2.0	255.255.255.0	Sales
10.4.1.0	255.255.255.0	Shipping

18. Under Inter-Site Transports, right-click on IP and choose Properties.

19. Clear the check box for Bridge All Site Links and click OK.

20 Right-click IP again and choose New Site Link Bridge.

21. Enter **Crosstown** as the name and add the Office and Warehouse site links. Click OK to create the bridge.

22. Expand the HeadOffice site and the Servers folder under it. Expand your server and right-click the NTDS Settings.

APPLY YOUR KNOWLEDGE

23. Choose New Active Directory Connection. Click the other domain controller in the list and click OK.

24. Using steps 22 and 23, create a connection from the server in Production to the server in HeadOffice.

25. Right-click either server and choose Properties. In each case, choose IP from the available list of transports for intersite data transfer. Click Add to make this the preferred bridgehead server. Click OK.

26. Repeat step 25 for the other server.

27. Right-click the NTDS Settings for either server and choose Properties. Make sure the Global Catalog is selected and click OK. Repeat for the other server.

28. Close the Sites and Services manager.

Review Questions

1. What are two main reasons for creating a domain?

2. What is the purpose of an organizational unit?

3. What is the difference between a site link and a site link bridge?

4. When would you create an Active Directory connection?

5. What is the definition of a site?

6. What is difference between a forest and a tree?

7. What type of server is used to replicate the schema for an enterprise?

8. What options can you set on a site link to control replication?

9. If you create site link bridges manually, what must you do to make sure your site link bridges are used?

10. What can you do to force replication across all site links to take place?

Exam Questions

1. Colin installs a Windows 2000 Server that will be used during the installation of the Active Directory structure for his organization. He installs the DNS server, creates the domain, and configures it for dynamic updates.

    When he tries to install the first domain controller, he gets a message that the domain controller for the domain is not available. He decides to continue the installation and fix the problem later. What problem will he need to fix later?

    A. The DNS server needs to be stopped and started.

    B. The server he is installing needs to point to the DNS server.

    C. Only Active Directory–integrated DNS can be used when installing Active Directory. Colin should have chosen to have the wizard install it.

    D. The DNS server needs to be configured for dynamic updates, not the zone.

APPLY YOUR KNOWLEDGE

2. Sally is a network administrator and is currently installing Windows 2000 with Active Directory. She has noticed that the replication between the 15 domain controllers is taking a lot of the bandwidth on her 10Mbps Ethernet network.

   The location she is working in has three floors. Sally wants to create a separate site for each floor. She has created the three sites and the site links between them, but it doesn't seem to have made a difference. What should she do next?

   A. She needs to reboot all the domain controllers.

   B. She needs to wait for the Knowledge Consistency Checker to calculate the new connections.

   C. She needs to move the domain controllers to the subnets in the Sites and Services manager.

   D. There is nothing she can do except upgrade to 100Mbps Ethernet.

3. Marc is the administrator for a network that is part of an Active Directory tree. His network is divided into four different sites spread across two large floors in a downtown office tower.

   To work on the hardware on a domain controller, he has shut it down. Everything is going well until a user calls and tells Marc that he can't find the resources in another domain in the tree. What could be the problem?

   A. The site link between that domain the local domain is on the domain controller on which Marc is working.

   B. The other domain has lost its primary domain controller.

   C. The replication is not scheduled until later in the day.

   D. The system Marc is working on is the global catalog server for the site.

4. Harvey has created a Windows 2000 Active Directory structure for his organization. He has set up a single domain containing the 700 users and their computers. The company is divided into two offices with a 56Kbps link between them.

   Harvey configures two sites, one for each office, and he configures a site link between them using SMTP. The replication between the sites doesn't seem to be working. What should Harvey do?

   A. He needs to create an enterprise certification authority.

   B. He needs to install Microsoft Exchange.

   C. He needs to install an SMTP-based mail system.

   D. He needs a connection faster than 56Kbps.

5. You are writing out the procedures for creating a site for a new administrator who is starting up a new office for your organization. Which of the following is the best method for creating a site?

   A. Create the site, select the site link, add the subnets, and then move in the domain controllers.

   B. Move the domain controllers, create the site, add the subnets, and then select the site links.

   C. Create a temporary site link bridge, add the domain controllers, rename the site that's created, and then add subnets.

APPLY YOUR KNOWLEDGE

D. Create the subnets and then create a site by grouping them. Next create the links and then move in the domain controllers.

6. You are explaining Active Directory replication to your manager to try to convince him that you will need to upgrade your network from the current 2Mbps ARCnet. You are explaining the differences between intersite and intrasite replication. Which of the following is true only of intersite replication?

   A. Managed by the Knowledge Consistency Checker.

   B. Uses remote procedure calls over the Internet Protocol.

   C. Sends the data in a compressed format.

   D. Defined by connection objects.

7. You have a single remote site on your network, and you want to make sure you use the link as little as possible for replication. You create a site link for your office, and then you create a site link between the main site and the remote site. You create a site link bridge so that data going to the remote site will all flow through the main site.

   You monitor the link, and you notice that replication is still taking place from sites other than the main site. What should you do to correct this?

   A. Check for and correct manually created link objects.

   B. Make sure the Ignore Schedule option is not selected.

   C. Make sure the Enable option is set on the site link bridge.

   D. Make sure the Bridge all site links option is not selected.

8. You are helping colleagues study for the 70-217 exam. You are currently studying Active Directory replication and the various partitions. You give them the following four choices listed and ask them to pick out the one that is not a partition of Active Directory. Which item should they choose?

   A. Schema

   B. Configuration

   C. Global catalog

   D. Domain

9. Users in the two remote sites you manage are complaining that the links to the head office where you work are slow. They report that the links have been slow for the last couple days. You check the links and find that they are, in fact, running at 100% capacity. When you investigate further, you determine the cause of the problem is Active Directory replication. When you check the site links you have created, the information is correct that the links should only be checking for changes every four hours during the day and every two hours at night. What else should you check?

   A. You should check the schedule on the site link bridges.

   B. You should check the Ignore Schedule option.

   C. You should make sure other operators are not forcing the replication for some reason.

   D. You should check how many users have been added in the previous 24 hours.

10. Your company has two separate locations, one of which is in Tokyo and the other in Cape Town. Each location has its own IT department, and each controls all its own users, computers, and groups. Currently, you have a 512Kbps Frame Relay link between them, and the link is close to 100% capacity. The company is currently running as a single domain. You are asked, as the Windows 2000 expert, to suggest the best way to reduce the load on the link. Which of the following do you suggest?

    A. The network is optimal now. Do nothing.

    B. You suggest two sites, one for each location.

    C. You suggest two organization units, one for each location.

    D. You suggest two domains, one for each location.

11. You are writing up a document that will be used as a reference by administrators on your network. You currently have 74,234 users on the network, and your network spans the globe. You are summarizing the steps involved in the creation of a site before you go into details. Which of the following is the correct series of steps that you will summarize?

    A. Create the subnets, name the site, and then move the subnets.

    B. Create the site and connect it to a site link, create the subnets, and then move a controller to the site.

    C. Create the site link and then the site, move a domain controller to the site, and then create the subnets.

D. Create the site and make sure the site links are correct, create the subnets, and then move the servers to it.

12. You are adding a remote site to your network that will be connected using a 128Kbps ISDN line. The ISDN line is expected to be busy during the day, approximately 80% utilized, and to only have 30% utilization at night. You want to ensure that replication does not use too much bandwidth during the day but that at night it will have sufficient bandwidth to complete any synchronization. The network designers have told you that you must have the capability to replicate at least once during the day. Which of the following will best deal with these requirements?

    A. Create a site link that will only replicate at night and manually force the replication once a day.

    B. Create a site link used during the night that has an interval of 30 minutes and one during the day with an interval of 6 hours.

    C. Create a site link used during the night with a cost of 10 and a day schedule with a cost of 99.

    D. Create a site link used during the night with the default cost and interval and another site link available only from noon until 1 p.m.

13. You have two sites that are linked using a fractional T1 connection. You are working to optimize the replication traffic between the sites. Each site contains one high-end domain controller that is dedicated to global catalog. You want to ensure that replication over the site link uses these two controllers. What should you do to ensure this?

APPLY YOUR KNOWLEDGE

A. Create connections objects that link these servers.

B. Create a site link bridge that links these servers.

C. Make sure the site link specifies these servers as the bridgehead servers.

D. Create a separate site for each server and link these sites. Then configure a site link between each of the servers and the other servers on their network.

14. You have configured the site links and site link bridges for your network. Replication is working, and all the sites are receiving the updates to Active Directory. You are describing the network you're working on to a colleague, and she tells you that you didn't need to configure site link bridges. Why didn't you have to create the site link bridges?

A. The KCC will create the site link bridges for you.

B. The sites will be automatically bridged.

C. The domain naming master will handle this for you.

D. The global catalog will handle this for you.

15. Your network is very stable. The users don't change much and neither do the computers. The structure in place is working, and you rarely change anything in Active Directory. You have been working on a bandwidth problem between the main site and a remote site and have determined that there is some replication traffic going across the link during the day. What can you do to remove this traffic?

A. Create a site link that only replicates at night.

B. Create a site link bridge that only replicates at night.

C. Create two site links, one that replicates on a slow schedule during the day and another that replicates more frequently at night.

D. Create two site link bridges, one that replicates on a slow schedule during the day and another that replicates more frequently at night.

Answers to Review Questions

1. Domains create a replication and a security boundary within your organization. Users who are members of the Enterprise Administrators security group have the capability to control all domains. However, users who are members of the Domain Admins security group only have control over their own domain. See the section "Understanding AD Logical Structure."

2. An organizational unit can be used to delegate control of a selected group of computers, users, and other objects within a domain to a user or group. This effectively creates an administrator-type account with a limited scope. Organizational units can also be used to apply group policies. See the section "Organizational Units."

3. A site link is used to describe a network path that exists directly between two sites, whereas a site link bridge describes a path between two sites that uses a third site to which both of the sites have a site link. See the section "Replication Between Sites."

APPLY YOUR KNOWLEDGE

4. Normally, you don't need to create Active Directory connections. The exception is a case in which the Knowledge Consistency Checker will not be able to correctly find the connection between two servers. Connections represent a direct network path between two servers. See the section "Connection Objects."

5. A site is best defined as one or more IP subnets interconnected using a high-speed (above T1) network. See the section "Working with Sites."

6. A tree is a structure that starts at a root domain containing only direct descendants. All the domains share a common namespace. A forest enables you to create the same type of structure; however, there is more than one namespace. See the section "Trees and Forests."

7. Whereas the domain controllers for a domain are responsible for the replication of objects that belong to the domain, the global catalog servers replicate the information about the enterprise including a list of all objects, the schema, and configuration information. See the section "Global Catalog Servers."

8. The options you can set on a site link include the scheduled periods during which the site link is available and the interval (frequency) at which the controllers check for updates. See the section "Replication Between Sites."

9. By default, all site links are bridged. This means that all the sites can be reached through any combination of site links. If you are going to manage this manually, you need to disable the automatic site link bridging in the IP or SMTP properties. See the section "Replication Between Sites."

10. Site links are only available during scheduled times. If you need to force them all to be available, you need to select the Ignore All Schedules option in the IP or SMTP properties. See the section "Replication Between Sites."

Answers to Exam Questions

1. **B.** In this case, the most likely cause is that the new domain controller is not pointing at the right DNS server. The DNS service in Windows 2000 can host both dynamic and nondynamic zones. In this question, it is set on the zone level, so answer D is incorrect. The switch between modes does not require stopping and starting, so answer A is incorrect. Answer C is interesting because it leads to a chicken-and-egg problem, but it is definitely wrong. See the section "Installing the First Domain."

2. **C.** Although an upgrade to 100Mbps would probably make all of Sally's users happy, this is not required and it makes answer D wrong. If you needed to reboot all the servers in your organization every time you added a site, no one would use the operating system. This means answer A is wrong. There might be a delay of a few minutes, but there wouldn't be that long of a delay in recalculating the connections. Answer B is wrong. C is the correct answer. This makes sense because the domain controllers are all still in the site and would continue to replicate at the same rate. See the section "Moving Domain Controllers."

3. **D.** In this case, answer A is wrong because site links are between sites in the same domain. Answer B is also wrong because there are no

APPLY YOUR KNOWLEDGE

longer PDCs, only domain controllers. Replication scheduling is set on a site link, and the resources the user wants are in another domain, so answer C is also wrong. This leaves answer D, which is correct. Because the global catalog replicates the entire set of objects from the enterprise (with a few attributes) so that resources can be found, it makes sense that the users can't find the resource without the global catalog server. See the section "Global Catalog Server."

4. **A.** If you are using SMTP for your site links, you need to have an enterprise certification authority. The authority will be used to sign the SMTP packets being sent. The SMTP packets are sent between servers in the sites involved in the site link and do not actually use mail servers, meaning answers B and C are incorrect. SMTP (email) can run over a modem that is as slow as 110 baud (that's what was available way back when); therefore, answer D is incorrect. See the section "Replication Between Sites."

5. **A.** In this case, the best answer is to create the site first, so answers B, C, and D are wrong. You are asked for the site link that the site will be part of during the creation of that site. This means you are selecting the site link as you create it. You can then add subnets and domain controllers (in any order). See the section "Replicating AD Information."

6. **C.** In this case, the only difference listed is that it will use compression on the data. The other differences are that you can schedule the replication between sites and set the interval to check for updates. You can also have different links with different costs between two sites, and between

sites you could use SMTP. After you define a site link, the KCC handles the connections for you, so answer A is not correct. The intersite replication can use SMTP, but it also uses RPC over IP, so answer B isn't right. Answer D is incorrect because the KCC automatically establishes all required links for you. See the section "Replicating Active Directory Information."

7. **D.** In this case, you might have a problem with a manually created connection, but even a manually created connection has to follow the site link information, so answer A is incorrect. Answer B would be a problem because replication would happen continuously; however, this would not ignore the site link bridge. Answer C is not a valid option. This means that answer D must be and is correct. This option is on by default, and you need to make sure it is off if you need to create site link bridges. See the section "Replication Between Sites."

8. **C.** There are three partitions that make up Active Directory: the schema partition that contains all the attributes and classes defining the database, the configuration partition used to hold the domain configuration and trust information, and the domain partition, which is the information about every object in each domain. The global catalog is a subset of the attributes and is not actually a separate partition. See the section "Replicating Active Directory Information."

9. **B.** Site link bridges do not have schedules, so answer A is not correct. Although other operators might be forcing replication across the link, you should probably assume they would not be continually doing this for an entire week, meaning answer C is wrong. Answer D falls for a

APPLY YOUR KNOWLEDGE

similar reason. It should not take a week for Active Directory replication to complete unless you're using a 110-baud modem. This leaves answer B, which makes sense. This option can be used to force replication if required but should be turned off immediately so that the site link schedules are again respected. See the section "Replication Between Sites."

10. **D.** In a case like this, in which you have administration on both sides of the link and the locations are essentially running separately either because of geography such as this case or because of business line, you will normally consider a domain. Remember that a domain is a replication and a security boundary. The network is obviously not optimal if you are looking into it. The idea of two sites could work if there was only administration in one site or if the units had to work closely together. This is not the case here. Using an organizational unit, although useful for applying policy and delegating control, does not let you schedule replication and would not fix the problem in this case. See the section "Understanding AD Logical Structure."

11. **B.** When you are creating a site, first create the site name and choose the site link to which it belongs. If the site link is not appropriate, you should create a new one. Next you create the subnets that will be part of the site, and then you move or create domain controllers in the site. You should also configure the Licensing Site Settings. See the section "Working with Sites."

12. **D.** In this case, you would use two site links so that everything is automatic. The night schedule is fine with the default or could even be made more frequent. All you need to do additionally is replicate once a day, and doing that replication

during lunchtime probably will cause the least interruption. See the section "Replication Between Sites."

13. **A.** By creating a connection, a network path, between these servers, you will have specified the path replication should take. You could also configure the server objects as the bridgehead servers for that replication protocol; however, that would cause them to be used as the main servers for all site links using that protocol. The site link does not have an option to specify the bridgehead servers, and a site link bridge is used to link sites, not servers. The last option, D, might work if you turned off the automatic site bridging. See the section "Connection Objects."

14. **B.** Although the KCC won't actually create site link bridges, it will create the required connections so that all the sites will receive the Active Directory updates. The domain naming master deals with domains, so answer C is wrong; the global catalog has nothing to do with this, meaning answer D is wrong. See the section "Site Link Bridges."

15. **A.** In this case, you can force replication if there is a problem, but after the network reaches a stable point, there is not so much need for replication. Answers B and D are wrong because they talk about site link bridges, and answer C is not the best answer because there would still be replication during the day. See the section "Replication Between Sites."

Suggested Readings and Resources

- *Windows 2000 Server Resource Kit. Deployment Planning Guide.* Microsoft, 2000.

- Archer, Scott. *MCSE Training Guide: Windows 2000 Directory Services Design.* Indianapolis: New Riders Publishing, 2000.

This chapter helps prepare you for the Microsoft exam by covering the "Manage Active Directory Objects" objective and parts of the "Install, Configure, and Troubleshoot the Components of Active Directory," objective.

Manage Active Directory objects.

- **Move Active Directory objects.**

- **Publish resources in Active Directory.**

- **Locate objects in Active Directory.**

- **Create and manage accounts manually or by scripting.**

- **Control access to Active Directory objects.**

- **Delegate administrative control of objects in Active Directory.**

▶ This is obviously a key objective, and it is included to make sure you can add user and computer accounts to the directory.

One of the key changes in the directory services from NT 4.0 is the capability to set permissions on objects in Active Directory. You must be able to set the permissions and understand the implications of setting objectives.

Active Directory also has the capability to list printers and shares on the network. As with adding users and computers, you need to be able to add these objects, by publishing them, to the Active Directory.

In addition to adding users, computers, shares, and printers, you also need to know how to find these objects both from the administrative point of view and the user's perspective.

CHAPTER 4

Administering Active Directory Services

Active Directory includes the capability to delegate the administration of parts of the directory to other users or groups. Your ability to perform the steps required to delegate will be tested.

You must be able to move users within a domain, between OUs, and between domains. This is also new to Active Directory; in NT 4.0, you had to delete and re-create the object to move it.

Install, configure, and troubleshoot the components of Active Directory.

- **Implement an organizational unit (OU) structure.**

▶ Organizational units in Active Directory are intended to take the place of resource domains. This objective is included, along with the delegation objective, to ensure that you can work effectively with OUs.

STUDY STRATEGIES

This chapter deals with a lot of different topics, all related to the basic functions of an administrator. You may have already performed these functions. Keep this in mind as you read through the chapter. In particular, you should pay attention to the following:

▶ Note the management of objects, including their creation, modification, moving, and deletion.

▶ Although it's not an exam topic, you should understand how groups work and the AGgdLP (**A**ccounts are grouped in **G**lobal **g**roups that belong to **d**omain **L**ocal groups that have the **P**ermissions).

▶ Understand what a universal group does.

▶ Pay attention to the descriptions of the tabs used for searches.

▶ Make note of how to use organizational units.

▶ Review the options for sharing directories and how the share gets into Active Directory. This should include printers.

INTRODUCTION

The management of objects on a network is a large portion of the job of a network administrator. This chapter takes a look at some of the key components of network administration and how to perform the required functions.

This chapter starts with the addition of user and computer accounts and then looks at how to manage groups of users and computers at one time. After you have seen how to add the users and computers to your network, you will see how to locate objects in the Active Directory, both as an administrator and as a user.

This will show you how easy it is to find and work with Active Directory. The discussion will then turn to the security of the objects in the Active Directory. There will also be a discussion of organizational units and the delegation of authority. This involves setting up a user or group to manage a portion of the Active Directory.

After that, you will see how to move objects in the directory, both within a domain as well as between domains. The addition of shares and printers will then be discussed, followed by a look at how to monitor and troubleshoot Active Directory.

PERFORMING BASIC ADMINISTRATION

Manage Active Directory objects.

- **Create and manage accounts manually or by scripting.**

Every system and user that participates on a Windows 2000 network needs to have some sort of security context, some form of identification. This means that the capability to create and manage user and computer accounts is key to making the network function correctly. A user or computer account is used to perform the following functions:

◆ Authenticate the identity of the user or computer

◆ Authorize or deny access to domain resources

◆ Administer other security principals

◆ Audit actions performed using the user or computer account

Because users need to have a computer to log on to, it makes sense to start this discussion by looking at computer accounts.

Computer Accounts

In Windows 2000, the management of computer accounts has been expanded so that computer accounts can be managed almost like a user account. Any computer running Windows 2000 or Windows NT 4.0 can join the domain and therefore will be authenticated when the computer starts up.

By having the computer authenticate, the network can audit the activity from the computer and can manage the computer from a central location. This is only possible for Windows 2000 and Windows NT 4.0 computers. Windows 95 and Windows 98 do not have the advanced security features of the other operating systems, and although a user can use them as a workstation, the computer cannot be managed.

Managing Computers

The main tool you use to manage the computers on a network is Active Directory Users and Computers snap-in. This tool enables you to add, delete, move, and manage the computer accounts. By default, only the group Domain Admins has permission to add and manage computers for a domain.

You can perform several different actions on a computer; however, you will start by seeing how to add a computer. This can be done either from the computer itself (see Step by Step 4.1) or from Active Directory Users and Computers.

STEP BY STEP

4.1 Adding a Computer to a Domain from the Computer

1. Right-click My Computer on the desktop and choose Properties from the context menu.

2. Click the Network Identification tab and choose the Properties button.

continues

continued

3. Enter the domain you want the computer to join.

4. If required, check the Create a computer account in the domain box and enter a username and password combination that has permissions to add computers to the domain. This is required if you are adding the computer without having first created the account.

5. Click OK. You should get a message welcoming you to the domain.

Using these steps, you can easily add a computer to the domain as you are installing the system.

You can also create the computer account before you install the computer. In this case, the person performing the installation does not need to be a member of the Domain Admins group because he or she doesn't need to create the computer account in the domain. Follow Step by Step 4.2 to add a computer account to the domain before the computer is added.

STEP BY STEP

4.2 Adding a Computer Account

1. Open Active Directory Users and Computers.

2. In the console tree, click Computers or click the container in which you want to add the computer.

3. Right-click the container in which you want to add the computer, point to New, and then click Computer.

4. Type the computer name in the New Object - Computer dialog box and click Next (see Figure 4.1). If you want, you can change the group or user that is allowed to add the computer to the domain. You can also create an account for a Windows NT computer by checking Allow pre-Windows 2000 computer to use this account.

5. If the computer you are adding is a managed computer, you can add the globally unique identifier to Active Directory by selecting This is a managed computer and entering the ID. Click Next when you have completed this screen.

6. On the next screen of the wizard, click the Finish button to add the computer account.

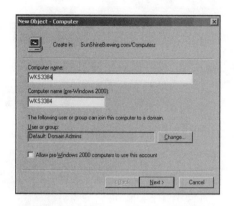

FIGURE 4.1
On this screen, you enter the name of the computer to add.

After you have added the computer account to Active Directory, you might want to set the computer account properties. Several items can be set, and some are for information only. To change the properties, follow Step by Step 4.3.

STEP BY STEP

4.3 Modifying Computer Account Properties

1. Open Active Directory Users and Computers.

2. In the console tree, click the container that contains the computer whose properties you want to modify.

3. In the details pane, right-click the computer and then click Properties.

4. Set the properties as desired and then click OK.

The first two Step by Steps showed you how to create the computer account, and this one showed you how to set the properties for the computer accounts. Many different properties can be set for a computer.

The following list explains the options you can set on each of the tabs in the Properties dialog box.

◆ **General.** On this tab, you will see the computer name, the DNS name, and the role of the computer. You can add a description. You also can set the computer as Trust computer for delegation. This enables the local system account on the computer to request services from another system on the network.

◆ **Operating System.** This tab provides you with information about the operating system running on the computer including the name, version, and service pack.

◆ **Member Of.** This enables you to control the group membership of the computer. Windows 2000 enables computers to be put into groups for administrative purposes and Group Policy filtering. To add a computer to a group, choose Add and select the group from the list that appears. If you want to remove the computer from a group, click the group name and click Remove. The Set Primary Group option is discussed later in this chapter.

◆ **Location.** This enables you to enter a location for the computer.

◆ **Managed By.** This screen enables you to set the user account or group account that will manage the computer. If you have entered the contact information for the user, it will appear here.

◆ **Object.** This is the object's full name, creation data, and update information.

◆ **Security.** This is where you can set the security on the object. This does not set the security on the computer but on the object in Active Directory. This is covered in detail later in this chapter.

Occasionally, you will have to remove a computer from the Active Directory. You might remove a computer when it joins a different domain or if the computer is being scrapped. Follow Step by Step 4.4 to delete a computer account.

STEP BY STEP

4.4 Deleting a Computer Account

1. Open Active Directory Users and Computers.

2. In the console tree, click the folder in which the computer is located.

3. In the details pane, right-click the computer and then
   click Delete.

4. Confirm the deletion by clicking Yes in the dialog box
   that appears.

Deleting a computer account, like deleting any other object,
removes the object and the *security identifier* (SID) for the object.
This means that deleting the object, which Windows 2000 identifies
by its SID, is final. Creating a new object of the same name creates a
different SID and therefore a different object.

The main reason for creating computer accounts in Active Directory
is to manage the computers on your network. This includes putting
them in groups and controlling their properties using group policies,
but it can also include working with the Computer Management
snap-in as shown in Step by Step 4.5.

STEP BY STEP

4.5 Managing a Computer

1. Open Active Directory Users and Computers.

2. In the console tree, click the container that contains the
   computer you want to manage.

3. In the details pane, right-click the computer and then
   click Manage.

This enables you to manage all aspects of the computer, and it gives
you critical information you will need for troubleshooting from a
central location on the network.

Occasionally, computers will crash. When this happens, you might
have to reload or even rebuild the computer. In Windows NT, this
meant you had to remove the computer from the domain and then
add the computer back into the domain. The computer would then
have a new SID, and according to the domain, it would be a
completely different computer.

In Windows 2000, computers can be members of groups, can be assigned managers, and can have group policies that apply to them. If the SID changed, then all of these would need to be reset. To save you from doing that, you can reset the computer account. This breaks the computer connection with the domain and enables you to add the computer back in without loosing these settings. Step by Step 4.6 walks you through resetting a computer account.

STEP BY STEP

4.6 Resetting a Computer Account

1. Open Active Directory Users and Computers.

2. In the console tree, click the container that contains the computer you want to reset.

3. In the details pane, right-click the computer and then click Reset Account.

4. Click Yes to confirm the resetting of the account.

5. Click OK to close the confirmation message.

By resetting a computer account, you can rejoin a computer to the domain. This means it will still have the same name and the same SID, and it enables you to replace a computer without having to reset security information.

Along the same vein, you might also need to suspend a computer's account for a period of time. For example, you should disable the computer account if you send a computer out for service so that the computer cannot be used to break into your network. Follow Step by Step 4.7 to learn how to disable a computer account.

STEP BY STEP

4.7 Disabling a Computer Account

1. Open Active Directory Users and Computers.

2. In the console tree, click the folder that contains the computer you want to disable.

3. In the details pane, right-click the desired computer and then click Disable Account.

4. Click Yes to confirm the resetting of the account.

5. Click OK to close the confirmation message.

The computer, once disabled, will not be able to reconnect to the network until the account is enabled again.

Of course, if you disable a computer account, you need to be able to enable the account when the computer is back. Follow Step by Step 4.8 to learn how to enable a computer account.

STEP BY STEP

4.8 Enabling a Computer Account

1. Open Active Directory Users and Computers.

2. In the console tree, click the folder that contains the computer you want to enable.

3. In the details pane, right-click the desired computer and then click Enable Account.

4. Click OK to close the confirmation message.

Now that you have seen how to manage computer accounts, you need to learn about managing users. This enables you to create the user accounts, enabling your users to work with the computers on the network.

User Accounts

A user account enables a user to log on to computers and domains with an identity that can be authenticated and authorized for access to domain resources. Every user needs his or her own user account and password. User accounts also are used as service accounts for some applications such as Microsoft SQL Server 2000 and Microsoft Exchange 2000.

Just like Windows NT before it, Windows 2000 provides two predefined user accounts that you can use to log on to a computer running Windows 2000. These predefined accounts are the Guest and Administrator accounts.

Generally, the Guest account is disabled within a domain except in cases in which security is not a concern. The Administrator account is the account you will use to create and manage all aspects of Active Directory.

Much of the management of user accounts parallels what you saw with computer accounts. A few more options are available, though, for user properties.

Managing Users

Probably the most obvious place to start looking at the management of user accounts is with the creation of user accounts. Follow Step by Step 4.9 to add a user account.

STEP BY STEP

4.9 Adding a User Account

1. Open Active Directory Users and Computers.

2. In the console tree, click the folder to which you want to add the user.

3. Right-click the folder to which you want to add the user, point to New, and then click User.

4. In First name, type the user's first name.

5. In Initials, type the user's initials.

6. In Last name, type the user's last name.

7. Modify Full name as desired.

8. In User logon name, type the name with which the user will log on and, from the drop-down list, choose the suffix that must be appended to the user logon name. These two together make up the *user principal name* (UPN). This is normally the same as the user's email address.

9. If the user will use a different name to log on from down-level computers, change the user logon name as it appears in User logon name (pre-Windows 2000) to the different name.

10. Review the entries (see Figure 4.2) and then click the Next button.

11. In Password and Confirm password, type the user's password.

12. Select the appropriate password options. The following choices are available:

- **User must change password at next logon.** This forces the user to change his or her password when he or she first logs on. Consider this option before using it. If the user has never worked with Microsoft networking before, changing the password during the first logon could be confusing.

- **User cannot change password.** This prevents the user from being able to change his or her password and forces the administrator to manage passwords for all the users on the network. This can be used on shared accounts or for other accounts you want to control.

- **Password never expires.** You will probably be setting account policies on your network including how often a user can and must change his or her password. This option indicates that this account is not bound by those settings. This is used mainly for service accounts.

- **Account is disabled.** You can create accounts that are disabled. This is useful if the user will not actually be on the network for some time, but you are creating accounts. This is also useful for creating a template account that can be copied to create user accounts. When the account is copied, this option will be cleared.

13. Review the settings (see Figure 4.3) and then click Next to continue.

14. Click Finish to create the user account.

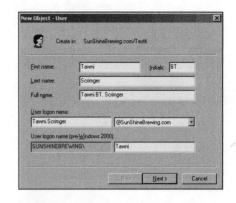

FIGURE 4.2
The first screen of the Add User Wizard is used to enter the user's identity.

FIGURE 4.3
The second screen of the Add User Wizard is used to set the password and options.

Creating user accounts is an important part of any administrator's job. A user account is required for every user accessing the network.

As you probably guessed, the options you see here are not all of the options you can set for the user. Normally, after you have created a user account, you then edit the account to set the remaining properties for the user. Step by Step 4.10 shows you how to edit the properties.

STEP BY STEP

4.10 Modifying User Account Properties

1. Open Active Directory Users and Computers.

2. In the console tree, click the folder that contains the desired user account.

3. Right-click the user account and then click Properties.

4. Change the properties as required and then click OK to complete the modifications.

You will want to set a number of user properties as shown in the following sections. The steps you have just seen can be used to access all of them.

Given the complexity of some of the tabs you can set for the user options, the next part of the discussion will look at each tab and the available options.

The General Tab

The General tab (see Figure 4.4) enables you to set general user properties. A description of each of the properties is included in the following list:

◆ **First name.** This is the first name of the user.

◆ **Initials.** This is the middle initial(s) of the user.

◆ **Last name.** This is the last name of the user.

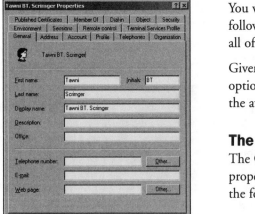

FIGURE 4.4
The General tab of the user Properties dialog box.

◆ **Display name.** This is the name that shows up in groups and distribution lists and when a user works with the **Find** command.

◆ **Description.** This is a description of the user. Generally, this is the user's title.

◆ **Office.** This is the location for the user's office.

◆ **Telephone number.** This is the phone number for the user. You can list other numbers using the Other button.

◆ **E-mail.** This is the user's email address. This is normally the same as the user's principal name but not always.

◆ **Web page.** This is one or more Web pages that pertain to the user.

The Address Tab

The information on the Address tab (see Figure 4.5) provides the user's mailing address. A description of the properties is included in the following list:

◆ **Street.** This is the street address for the user.

◆ **P.O. Box.** This is for organizations using mail drops.

◆ **City.** This is the city in which the user is located.

◆ **State/province.** This is the state or province in which the user is located.

◆ **Zip/Postal Code.** This is the user's zip or postal code.

◆ **Country/region.** This drop-down box enables you to specify the user's country or region.

The Account Tab

This tab enables you to control the account settings for the user including changing the username used to log on (see Figure 4.6). A description of the properties is included in the following list:

◆ **User logon name.** This is the name the user will use to log on to the network. You can change the logon name and the extension. Changing the extension does not move the user to a different domain.

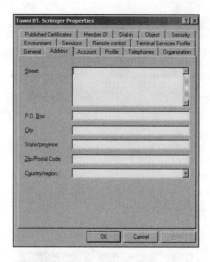

FIGURE 4.5
The Address tab of the user properties dialog box.

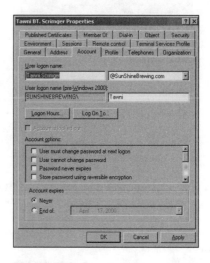

FIGURE 4.6
The Account tab of the user Properties dialog box.

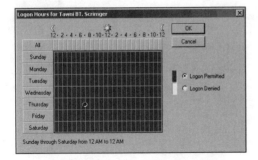

FIGURE 4.7
You can set the logon hours using this dialog box.

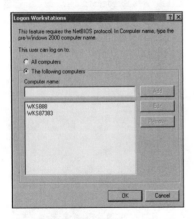

FIGURE 4.8
You can configure the computers onto which a user is allowed to log on.

◆ **User logon name (pre-Windows 2000).** This is the down-level logon name for systems not running Windows 2000.

◆ **Logon Hours.** This enables you to set the hours that the user is allowed to log on to the network. These should be set to the user's work hours in high-security environments (see Figure 4.7).

◆ **Log On To.** This enables you to set the computers onto which the user is allowed to log on (see Figure 4.8).

◆ **Account is locked out.** This option is only available if the account has been locked out. This happens if the user tries to guess a password more times than the effective security policy allows.

◆ **Account options.** This is a series of options that can be set for the account.

  • **User must change password at next logon.** This forces the user to change his password when he next logs on to the domain.

  • **User cannot change password.** This prevents the user from changing his password.

  • **Password never expires.** This sets the account so that it is exempt from the account policies such as account lockout.

  • **Store password using reversible encryption.** This option is required to support Macintosh computers. It stores the password with encryption that can be unencrypted so that users are able to log on. Enable this for users logging on from Apple computers.

  • **Account is disabled.** This account cannot be used. This option can be used for a person who is going to be away from the office for an extended period or if you are creating template accounts.

  • **Smart card is required for interactive logon.** If you are using a smart card system, you can set this option so that extra encryption can be used on the account information.

- **Account is trusted for delegation.** You can set this option to allow the user to delegate control of a portion of the namespace to other users. This enables a user who is in charge of an OU to delegate part of the responsibility to another user or group.

- **Account is sensitive and cannot be delegated.** This prevents a user from being able to delegate control of this account.

- **Use DES encryption types for this account.** By default, Active Directory uses Kerberos for security. This configures this account to use DES encryption instead.

- **Do not require Kerberos preauthentication.** This option should be set if you are not using the Windows 2000 implementation of Kerberos for authentication.

◆ **Account expires.** This sets the expiration date for the account.

The Profile Tab

The Profile tab (see Figure 4.9) sets the user's home directory, logon script, and the location for the user profile. A description of the properties is included in the following list:

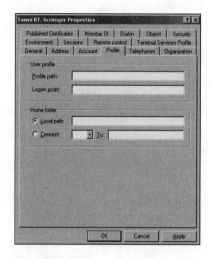

FIGURE 4.9
The Profile tab of the user Properties dialog box.

◆ **Profile path.** This is the network location for the user's profile. By entering a location using a universal naming convention name, you are able to configure the user to work with a roaming or mandatory user profile.

◆ **Logon script.** This is the name of the batch file that should be run when the user logs on. This is generally for down-level clients. Only the name is required because the file will be in the SYSVOL share on the domain controllers. The file can be either a BAT or CMD file. If you use BAT, Windows NT or Windows 2000 starts a DOS emulation session to run the file. A CMD file will be run in 32-bit mode. The extension is not included in this box.

◆ **Home folder.** This sets the user's home folder to a directory on the local computer or to a shared directory on the network.

NOTE

The USERNAME Variable The %USERNAME% variable can be used to create a directory with the same name as the user's pre-Windows 2000 logon name. This can be used for the profile path (for example, \\server\share\%USERNAME%) or for the home folder.

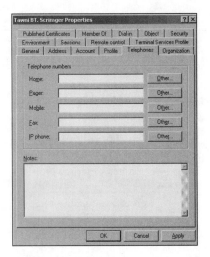

FIGURE 4.10
The Telephone tab of the user Properties dialog box.

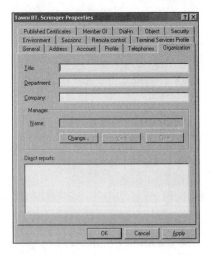

FIGURE 4.11
The Organization tab of the user Properties dialog box.

The Telephones Tab

As one would expect, this tab is used to track the various phone numbers that a user could have (see Figure 4.10). There are really only two sections on this tab, as shown in the following list:

◆ **Telephone numbers.** This is where you can list the phone numbers you have for a person. This includes the capability to list more than one number for any of the categories.

◆ **Notes.** This area is set aside for your comments about the user.

The Organization Tab

The Organization tab (see Figure 4.11) is used to enter information about a user's role within the organization. A description of the properties is included in the following list:

◆ **Title.** This is the user's title.

◆ **Department.** This is the department for which the user works.

◆ **Company.** This is the name of the company for which the user works.

◆ **Manager.** This is the name of the user's manager. The name is selected from the users already in Active Directory.

◆ **Direct reports.** This is a list of the people that report to this user. This is built automatically by Active Directory.

The Terminal Server Tabs

The next four tabs all deal with configuration settings for Terminal Server. These tabs only apply if you have Terminal Server installed.

On the Environment tab (see Figure 4.12), you can set options that control the user's environment when he or she uses Terminal Server. A description of the properties is included in the following list:

◆ **Starting program.** This section enables you to set a program to start automatically when the user logs on.

◆ **Client devices.** This enables you to control whether client drives and printers are remapped when the user starts a new session.

The Sessions tab (see Figure 4.13) can be used to configure session timeout and reconnection settings. A description of the properties is included in the following list:

◆ **End a disconnected session.** This tells the computer how long to wait before closing a session if the user is disconnected. The user can reconnect to the same session during this time.

◆ **Active session limit.** This is the maximum duration for a session on the Terminal Server for this user.

◆ **Idle session limit.** This is how long a session will be kept open without any user action.

◆ **When session limit is reached or connection is broken.** This tells the system what to do when one of the preceding settings is exceeded.

◆ **Allow reconnection.** This enables you to set which station the user can reconnect from if the session has been disconnected.

The Remote Control tab (see Figure 4.14) enables you to set the options for taking control of the user session. A description of the properties is included in the following list:

◆ **Enable remote control.** This turns on the capability to take control of a user's session.

◆ **Require user's permission.** If this is set, the user will be advised when someone is taking over his or her session and will be asked whether to permit it.

◆ **Level of control.** This sets whether you are able to simply view the session or perform actions in the session.

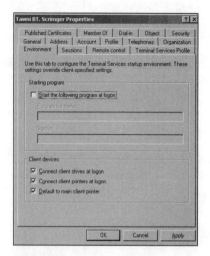

FIGURE 4.12
The Environment tab of the user Properties dialog box.

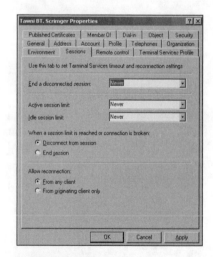

FIGURE 4.13
The Sessions tab of the user Properties dialog box.

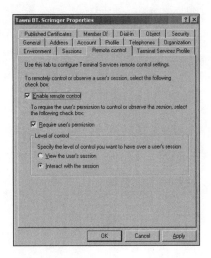

FIGURE 4.14
The Remote Control tab of the user properties dialog box.

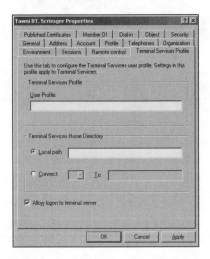

FIGURE 4.15
The Terminal Service Profile tab of the user properties dialog box.

The last of the Terminal Server tabs is Terminal Services Profile (see Figure 4.15). This enables you to change the user's profile location and home directory when he or she uses a Terminal Server. A description of the properties is included in the following list:

◆ **User Profile.** This tells the server where the user's profile should be taken from and stored.

◆ **Terminal Services Home Directory.** This is the directory to use as a home directory when the user uses Terminal Server.

◆ **Allow logon to terminal server.** This determines whether the user is allowed to log on to Terminal Server.

The Published Certificates Tab

The Published Certificates tab (see Figure 4.16) enables you to control the certificates available for the user.

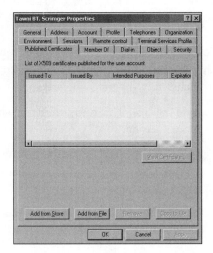

FIGURE 4.16
The Published Certificates tab of the user properties dialog box.

You can add certificates from a local certificate store or from a file. These are X.509 certificates that can be used for Internet authentication and that are also in the encrypted file system.

The Member Of Tab

The Member Of tab (see Figure 4.17) manages which groups a user belongs to and which group is the user's primary group.

Use the Add and Remove buttons to add or remove the user from groups. The user's primary group applies only to users who log on to the network from a Macintosh or to users who run POSIX applications. Unless you are using these services, there is no need to change the primary group from Domain Users, which is the default value.

The Dial-in Tab

On the Dial-in tab (see Figure 4.18), you can set the user dial-in options. A description of the properties is included in the following list:

◆ **Remote Access Permission.** Here you can choose to allow or deny the user dial-in permissions or to have permissions left up to Remote Access Policy.

◆ **Verify Caller-ID.** This information is used to set the caller ID that will be given by a RADIUS system.

◆ **Callback Options.** This enables you to set whether the user should be given the option of a callback, which can save long-distance charges. You can also set a number to call back to, which adds security because the user must be at a preassigned number.

◆ **Assign a Static IP Address.** This enables you to assign the use a static IP address.

◆ **Apply Static Routes.** This enables you to configure routing for the remote system.

The Other Tabs

The Object and Security tabs provide additional control. The Object tab is for information purposes only. It lets you know what the full name of the object is, when it was created, when it was updated, and the Update Sequence Number.

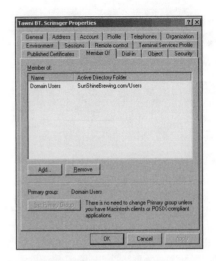

FIGURE 4.17
The Member Of tab of the user Properties dialog box.

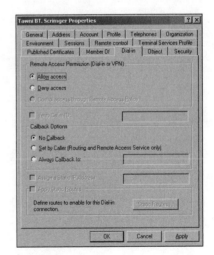

FIGURE 4.18
The Dial-in tab of the user Properties dialog box.

The Security tab enables you to set security on the Active Directory object. This is covered later in this chapter in the section "Permissions in Active Directory Services."

Other User Management Functions

In addition to adding an account, there are several other functions you might have to perform on user accounts. This section looks at how to perform some of these functions.

At times, you will need to delete a user account. Remember that, after a user account has been deleted, all permissions and memberships associated with that user account are deleted. The SID for each account is unique; therefore, a new user account with the same name as a previously deleted user account does not automatically assume the permissions and memberships of the previously deleted account. To delete a user account, follow the steps in Step by Step 4.11.

STEP BY STEP

4.11 Deleting a User Account

1. Open Active Directory Users and Computers.

2. In the console tree, click Users or click the folder that contains the user account.

3. Right-click the user account and then click Delete.

4. Confirm the deletion in the dialog box that appears.

Occasionally, you will need to rename a user. This might happen when a new employee is replaces an employee that has left the organization or if one of your users changes his or her name for legal reasons. To rename a user account, follow Step by Step 4.12.

STEP BY STEP

4.12 Renaming a User Account

1. Open Active Directory Users and Computers.

2. In the console tree, click the container that contains the desired user account.

3. In the details pane, right-click the user account and then click Rename.

4. Type the new name or press Delete, and then press Enter to display the Rename User dialog box.

5. In Rename User, Name, type the username.

6. In First name, type the user's first name.

7. In Last name, type the user's last name.

8. In Display name, type the name used to identify the user.

9. In User logon name, type the name with which the user will log on and, from the drop-down list, click the suffix that should be appended to this name.

10. If required, change the down-level logon name.

11. Click OK.

There are obviously many reasons you might need to rename a user account including marriage, a legal name change, or replacing a user.

There will also be times when you need to disable a user account. Disabling user accounts is a good practice when a user leaves the organization or is going to be gone for an extended period of time. In the case of a user who leaves, you can later rename the account if a replacement is hired.

You can also create disabled user accounts with common group memberships. Disabled user accounts can be used as account templates to simplify user account creation. Follow the steps in Step by Step 4.13 to learn how to disable a user account.

STEP BY STEP

4.13 Disabling a User Account

1. Open Active Directory Users and Computers.

2. In the console tree, click Users or click the folder that contains the desired user account.

3. In the details pane, right-click the user.

4. Click Disable Account.

5. Click OK to close the confirmation message.

If you disable an account when a user will be away for an extended period of time, you save yourself the task of re-creating the account when the user returns. This is also useful because you can create a disabled account with the settings you need and then just copy to add a bunch of users.

Obviously, you will at some point delete the account or re-enable the account. Disabled accounts have an X in a red circle on their icon in Active Directory Users and Computers. Follow Step by Step 4.14 to learn how to enable a disabled user account.

STEP BY STEP

4.14 Enabling a Disabled User Account

1. Open Active Directory Users and Computers.

2. In the console tree, click Users or click the folder that contains the desired user account.

3. In the details pane, right-click the user and then click Enable Account.

4. Click OK to close the confirmation dialog box.

Another function you will need to perform, probably more often than other functions, is resetting a user's password because he or she forgot it. Always make sure you are talking to the user who is requesting a changed password (and not an imposter). Resetting a user password is presented in Step by Step 4.15.

STEP BY STEP

4.15 Resetting a User Password

1. Open Active Directory Users and Computers.

2. In the console tree, click the folder that contains the desired user account.

3. In the details pane, right-click the user whose password you want to reset and then click Reset Password.

4. Type and confirm the password. Passwords can be up to 128 characters in length and can contain letters, numbers, and most special characters.

5. If you want to require the user to change this password at the next logon process, select the User must change password at next logon check box.

6. Click OK to reset the password and then OK to close the confirmation dialog box.

As you can now see, managing users is not overly complicated. However, you will likely spend a good deal of time performing these operations. Working with users and user accounts is a large part of a network administrator's job.

Using Templates

You can use template accounts to create a shell that can be copied to create new user accounts. This is done by creating a fake user account and setting the groups and other options for the account. Then, when you need another account for a section, you have a template. You can copy the template and then edit the details to personalize the account. Copying a user account is demonstrated in Step by Step 4.16.

> **WARNING**
>
> **Service Account Password** Any services authenticated with a user account must be reset if the password for the service's user account is changed.

STEP BY STEP

4.16 Copying a User Account

1. Open Active Directory Users and Computers.

2. In the console tree, click the folder that contains the desired user account.

3. In the details pane, right-click the user account you want to copy and then click Copy.

4. In First name, type the user's first name.

5. In Last name, type the user's last name.

6. Modify Full name to add initials or reverse the order of first and last names.

7. In User logon name, type the name with which the user will log on and, from the list, click the desired suffix.

8. Set the User logon name (pre-Windows 2000) as required.

9. In Password and Confirm password, type the user's password.

10. Select the appropriate password options.

11. If the user account from which the new user account was copied was disabled, click Account is disabled to clear the check box and enable the new account.

12. Click OK when you done.

Using templates and copying them to create new user accounts saves you a great deal of time over creating each user account manually. The process is, as you saw, twofold: Create a user account with the basic information, which is disabled, and then copy it as required.

The management of users and computers is one of the most basic functions of a network administrator. In each case, you have to add, edit, and remove accounts many times over the life of a network. As you have seen, this is thankfully a simple task and is essentially the same for users and computers. There are other ways you can create and manage objects in Active Directory, though, and you should be aware of them.

OTHER TOOLS FOR MANAGING OBJECTS

In addition to what you have already seen, there are a couple tools of which you need to be aware for both the exam and real life. This includes the directory exchange utilities LDIFDE and CSVDE and the ADSI interface. These tools and how they can be used is the focus of this section.

Directory Exchange Utilities

The two directory exchange utilities enable you to import users and other directory objects including attributes and classes. They have been included to give you a way of dealing with large numbers of updates at the same time and either having to spend a week implementing the changes or spending the time to create a program for a "one-off" job.

Using LDIFDE

The *LDAP Data Interchange Format* (LDIF) *Directory Exchange* (LDIFDE) utility can be used to import data to or export data from Active Directory. Because the LDIF standard is an industry standard for importing or modifying LDAP directories, the LDIFDE utility can be used to perform these functions in Windows 2000. This command is run from the command line, and the operation is controlled partially by the options selected and partially by the information in the file.

The command line looks like the following.

```
LDIFDE -i -f -s -c -v -t -d -r -p -l -o -m -n -j -g -k -a
-b -? -u
```

There are a number of parameters resulting from the flexibility of the command. These can be broken down into three main parts: common options, export options, and import options. The following list describes the options available.

◆ **-f filename** This option provides the utility with the name of the file to import from or export to.

◆ **-u** This option tells the command that the file you are using should be Unicode.

◆ **-s servername** This tells the command on which domain controller to perform the operation. If this is not given, a domain controller from the domain the user is currently logged on to will be used.

◆ **-c distinguishedname distinguishedname** This tells the command to replace every occurrence of the first distinguished name with the second name listed.

◆ **-t portnumber** If the LDAP server you are using is not on the standard port 389, you can enter the port number. The port number for the global catalog, for example, is 3268.

◆ **-v** This tells the command to use Verbose mode, which returns more information.

◆ **-?** This provides you with online help.

◆ **-a distinguishedname password** This tells the command what username and password to send to the LDAP server for authentication. For password, you can enter an "*" and receive a prompt for the password, which will be hidden.

◆ **-b username domain password** This enables you to use the standard logon information rather than a distinguished name. For password, you can enter an asterisk (*) and receive a prompt for the password, which will be hidden.

◆ **-i** This sets the command to Import mode. The default is Export mode, which requires no switch.

◆ **-k action** This option enables you to set the action that should be taken if there is an error.

◆ **-d distinguishedname** This specifies the starting point for an export. The root of the current domain is used if this is not included.

◆ **-r LDAPfilter** This option enables you to filter which records are to be exported using an LDAP property as criteria.

◆ **-p LDAPsearchscope** This option enables you to specify the scope of the LDAP search. The options are base, one-level, or the entire subtree.

◆ **-l LDAPattributelist** This option sets the list of LDAP attributes you want to export. The default is all attributes.

◆ **-o attributelist** This option enables you to omit specific attributes from a export. This way, you can create a LDAP file that is importable to another LDAP-compliant system that does not support so many attributes.

◆ **-m** This option tells the command to exclude Active Directory–specific information in the export file. This is used if you are planning to import the same list back in after making changes.

◆ **-n** This option tells the command not to export binary values. By default, these values are exported.

◆ **-j filepath** This option sets the path for the log file generated during an export.

◆ **-g** This option turns off paged searches during an export.

As you can see, there are a number of options. Most of them, however, are used in the export function. For the exam, you should be familiar with basic import and export functionality.

The file you will be working with is a text file, and you will be able to edit it as such. The following is a sample of the file:

```
dn: CN=Scrim,CN=Users,DC=ScrimTech, DC=com
changetype: add
cn: Scrim
description: Rob Scrimger
objectClass: user
sAMAccountName: Scrim
```

This file can be created by you, or it can be created if you export the directory by the LDIFDE command. In either case, you can edit the file until the information is correct, and then you would import it using the following syntax:

```
ldifde -i -f import.ldf
```

As you can see, the LDIFDE utility is a quick way to get a list of users from Active Directory, to import a list from another source into Active Directory, or even to export a list of attributes to modify and then reimport them afterward. The utility works exclusively with LDIF files, though, and you may have to use CSVDE if your file is a comma-separated file.

Using CSVDE

The other tool available is the CSVDE, which works with comma-separated value files. This type of file is useful if you are working with programs such as Excel when you are cleaning up files that should be imported or exported.

This command is very similar to the LDIFDE command; the most notable difference is that it can only be used to add records to Active Directory. It cannot modify them. The file is also simpler in that it consists of a header row of attribute names and then a number of records with those attributes, one per line similar to the following list:

```
dn,cn,firstName,surname,description,objectClass,
➥sAMAccountname
"cn=Heidi Hagan,cn=Users,dc=ScrimTech,dc=com",Heidi
Hagan,Heidi,Hagan,VP - Research,user,HHagan
"cn=Wayne Cassidy,cn=Users,dc=ScrimTech,dc=com",Wayne
Cassidy,Wayne,Cassidy,Manager,user,WCassidy
```

If you look closely, you will notice there is no changetype included in the file. This is why you cannot perform modifications. The command line is almost identical to LDIFDE, and the options present have the same meaning as they did for LDIFDE.

```
CSVDE -i -f -s -c -v -t -d -r -p -l -o -m -n -e -j -g -k -a
-b -? -u
```

Although they are slightly different, both LDIFDE and CSVDE are able to move information into or out of Active Directory. You also will want to be able to address Active Directory programmatically. To do this, you need to use the ADSI.

Scripting Using the ADSI

As you can see, it is easy enough to create and import a list of users into Active Directory. Because the classes and attributes and their definitions are also part of Active Directory, it is also possible to add these with the utilities you have just seen. However, there are going to be times when you will want to work interactively with Active Directory. The best way to do this is to work with the *Active Directory Service Interface* (ADSI).

This interface can be used from various languages, including the Windows Scripting Host, to interact with Active Directory. ADSI conforms to the *Component Object Model* (COM) and supports standard COM features.

A full discussion of creating ADSI scripts is best left for discussions on programming, which is well beyond the scope of this text. For our purposes, you should be aware that ADSI exists and works with any language including the Windows Scripting Host. To give you an idea of how simple the interface is, the following example is included:

```
Dim objDomain
Dim objUser

Set
objDomain=GetObject("LDAP://OU=Users,DC=ScrimTech,DC=com")
Set objUser = objDomain.Create("user","cn=Dave Shapton")
objUser.Put "samAccountName","DShapton"
objUser.Put "givenName","Dave"
objUser.Put "sn","Shapton"
objUser.Put "userPrincipalName","DShapton@ScrimTech.com"
objUser.SetInfo
MsgBox "User created " & objUser.Name
Set objDomain = Nothing
MsgBox "Finished"
WScript.Quit
```

In this case, the first two lines are creating placeholders for the objects that will be created. Next, the connection is made to the LDAP server using the LDAP:// component. A user object is then created with the new name. Next, various attributes are set. Then the info is saved. A dialog box tells you that the user was created, and the program ends.

Again, it is a simple program, but it begins to show you what is possible. For the exam, all you need to know is that ADSI exists. You need to understand groups more fully.

GROUPS IN WINDOWS 2000

Obviously, you don't want to have to manage 70,000 users one at a time. You need to be able to group together users and computers so that you can work with many users or computers at the same time.

As you start to learn about groups in Windows 2000, it is worth looking back over all the information you are able to store about users. One of the intents of Windows 2000 is to bring together directory services from the network side and from the email side. A large part of the information you can store for users is information that you normally, until now, would have stored in the email system.

This becomes even more evident as you start to look at groups because there are two main types of groups you are going to be able to create in the Windows 2000 directory services:

◆ **Distribution groups.** These groups are used exclusively for email and cannot be used to set security.

◆ **Security groups.** These groups can be used to group together users or to assign permissions to objects on the network or in Active Directory. These groups can also be used for email.

Although the distribution groups are a valid object in the Windows 2000 Active Directory, the rest of the discussion concentrates on security groups. You will examine the main functions of groups, domain modes, strategies for using groups, built-in and predefined groups, predefined global groups, special identities, and the management of groups.

There are two main functions that a group in the Windows 2000 Active Directory takes on: Groups are used to gather users accounts into a single entity to simplify the administration of users, and groups assign permissions to objects and resources. The difference is in the scope of the group.

◆ **Global.** Global groups typically are used to gather user accounts together and should normally not be given permissions. The users gain permissions from adding the global group to a local group that has permissions. Global groups can contain users from the local domain only. They are available in the domain in which they are created and in other domains in the tree or forest.

◆ **Local.** Local groups are used to gather permission to perform functions within a domain. The local group in a Windows NT domain is available only on the computer on which it is created. In Windows 2000, the local group is available on all systems in the domain that run Windows 2000 and are referred to as domain local groups.

◆ **Universal.** Universal groups combine the capabilities of the global and local groups. They can contain users and groups from any domain in the tree or forest and can be assigned rights to resources or objects in any domain. This group removes the boundaries of domains from management. It increases the amount of replication required between global catalog servers because global catalog servers manage these groups. These groups are only available in native mode.

Domain Modes

The actual use and scope of the groups depend on the mode in which you are running the domain. There are two domain modes in which you can run a Windows 2000 domain:

◆ **Mixed mode.** In this mode, you can use both Windows NT and Windows 2000 domain controllers in the same domain. This is the default domain mode, and it provides you with the functionality needed during the upgrade process.

◆ **Native mode.** In this mode, you can take advantage of several group enhancements including the capability to work with universal groups.

Windows 2000 native mode is only available for domains that have no Windows NT 4.0 domain controllers. If you have upgraded all the domain controllers that you plan to and have removed all Windows NT domain controllers, you can upgrade to native mode. Changing domain modes is addressed in Step by Step 4.17.

STEP BY STEP

4.17 Changing Domain Modes

1. Open Active Directory Domains and Trusts.

2. Right-click the domain to convert and choose Properties.

3. On the General tab (see Figure 4.19), click the Change Mode button.

continues

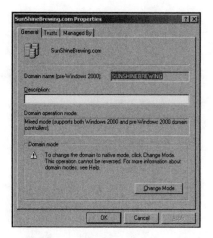

FIGURE 4.19
From the General tab, click the Change Mode button.

continued

4. You will receive a warning that you will not be able to return to mixed mode. Click Yes to continue.

5. Click OK to finish the operation.

6. You will receive a warning that the information could take 15 or more minutes to replicate. Click OK to close the message.

The following table summarizes the effect of domain modes on groups.

TABLE 4.1

EFFECT OF DOMAIN MODES ON GROUPS

Type of Group	Function	Mixed Mode	Native Mode
Universal	What can be included as members	Not available	Accounts, global groups, and universal groups from any domain
	What it can be a member of	Not available	Can be put into other groups in any domain
	What it is used for	Not available	Can be assigned permissions in any domain
	Can be converted to other types	Not available	Not available
Global	What can be included as members	Accounts from the same domain	Accounts and other global groups from the same domain
	What it can be a member of	Local groups in any domain	Can be put into other groups in any domain
	What it is used for	Can be assigned permissions in any domain	Can be assigned permissions in any domain

Type of Group	Function	Mixed Mode	Native Mode
	Can be converted to other types	Not available	Can be converted to universal scope as long as it is not a member of any other group having global scope
Domain local	What can be included as members	Accounts and global groups from any domain	Accounts, global groups, and universal groups from any domain as well as domain local groups from the same domain
	What it can be a member of	Not available	Can be put into other domain local groups in the same domain
	What it is used for	Can be assigned permissions in the local domain	Can be assigned permissions only in the same domain
	Can be converted to other types	Not available	Can be converted to universal scope as long as it does not have as its member another group having domain local scope

You need to plan for the use of groups. The following section covers strategies for using groups.

Strategies for Using Groups

Planning how you are going to use groups before deploying Windows 2000 will save you a lot of work trying to retrofit groups into your network. The first step in planning your groups, as you might have guessed, is to determine the domain mode you will be using. Local, global, and universal groups offer the administrator varying levels of control.

Using Domain Local Groups

Normally, you use domain local groups to assign permissions. By using a domain local group to hold the permissions, you are able to use global groups and universal groups from any domain to add users to the permissions.

For example, you have a printer and allow accountants in your domain to use it. You could take a global group that has the accountants in it and add it to a local group with permissions on the printer. If you later need to add an accounting group from another domain, you can simply add the global group. Or, if you needed to switch the permissions to another printer, you can just give the local group permissions on that printer.

Using local groups enables you to work with multiple global groups that need access to multiple local resources through a single entity.

Using Global Groups

Global groups should normally be used to gather users from a domain into a collective entity that can be used in the local domain or any other domain in the tree or forest. Because groups with global scope are not replicated outside their own domain, accounts in a group having global scope can be changed frequently without generating replication traffic to the global catalog.

Using Universal Groups

Use groups with universal scope to consolidate groups that span domains. To do this, add the accounts to groups with global scope and nest these groups within groups with universal scope. Using this strategy, any membership changes in the groups with global scope do not affect the groups with universal scope.

This is important because any changes to universal group membership cause the entire membership of the group to be replicated to every global catalog in the forest.

When working with groups, it is important to remember that global groups are used to gather users, and local groups are used to assign permissions. The addition of a global group to a local group is what gives the users rights. Universal groups enable you to gather global groups and add them to multiple local groups across domains.

In addition to the groups you will create, there are several built-in groups you can use to manage your network.

Built-In and Predefined Groups

During the installation of the domain, several groups are created by default. These groups represent various roles users will take on your network, and they are included to help you set up the management of you network. The groups appear either in the Builtin folder for local groups or in the Users folder for global groups.

Built-In Local Groups

The groups placed in the Builtin folder for Active Directory Users and Computers include the following:

◆ Account Operators

◆ Administrators

◆ Backup Operators

◆ Guests

◆ Print Operators

◆ Replicator

◆ Server Operators

◆ Users

◆ Power Users (found on Professional and standalone servers only)

These groups have domain local scope and are primarily used to assign permissions to users who have some administrative role in that domain. The following table shows the default rights for each of these groups as well as the general rights for all users, which is a special group called Everyone.

TABLE 4.2

RIGHTS ASSIGNED TO THE BUILT-IN ADMINISTRATION GROUPS

User Right	Allows	Groups Assigned This Right by Default
Access this computer from the network	Connect to the computer over the network.	Administrators, Everyone, Power Users
Back up files and file folders	Back up files and folders regardless of file and folder permissions.	Administrators, Backup Operators
Bypass traverse checking	Move through a folder in which a user has no permissions to enable him or her to get a subfolder.	Everyone
Change the system time	Set the time for the computer.	Administrators, Power Users
Create a pagefile	This right has no effect.	Administrators
Debug programs	Debug various low-level objects such as threads.	Administrators
Force shutdown from a remote system	Shut down a remote computer.	Administrators
Increase scheduling priority	Increase the processing priority of a process.	Administrators, Power Users
Load and unload device drivers	Install and remove device drivers.	Administrators
Log on locally	Log on at the physical computer.	Administrators, Backup Operators, Everyone, Guests, Power Users, and Users
Manage auditing and the security log	Configure auditing and view and clear the security log. Members of the Administrators group can always view and clear the security log.	Administrators

User Right	*Allows*	*Groups Assigned This Right by Default*
Modify firmware environment variables	Modify system environment variables stored in nonvolatile RAM on computers that support this type of configuration.	Administrators
Profile a single process	Perform performance sampling on a process.	Administrators, Power Users
Profile system performance	Perform profiling performance sampling on the computer.	Administrators
Restore files and file folders	Restore backed-up files and folders regardless of file and folder permissions.	Administrators, Backup Operators
Shut down the system	Shut down the computer.	Administrators, Backup Operators, Everyone, Power Users, and Users
Take ownership of files or other objects	Take ownership of files, folders, printers, and other objects on (or attached to) the computer.	Administrators

In addition to the local groups that are added, several other predefined groups are global in scope.

Predefined Global Groups

The predefined groups placed in the Users folder for Active Directory Users and Computers are as follows:

◆ Cert Publishers

◆ Domain Admins

◆ Domain Computers

◆ Domain Controllers

- Domain Guests
- Domain Users
- Enterprise Admins
- Group Policy Admins
- Schema Admins

These groups enable you to collect different types of users and link them to the built-in local groups. By default, all users are member of the Domain Users groups, and all computers are added to Domain Computers. These groups can be used to manage the bulk of the users and computers on your network. By default, the Domain Users group in a domain is a member of the Users group in the same domain.

The Domain Admins group is used for the administrators of the domain. The Domain Admins group is a member of the local Administrators group. You should only add users to this group if they need to have full administrator privileges within the domain.

The buil-in and predefined groups can be used to manage most of your network. These groups in conjunction with the groups you will create make management simple and easy.

Special Identities

There are three special groups to which users can belong. Users become members of these groups not by you adding them to the group but by the actions they take themselves. These groups are as follows:

- **Everyone.** This represents all current users of a system whether they connect across the network or log on locally.

- **Network.** This group includes any user using a resource across the network.

- **Interactive.** This group is for users physically at the computer.

Although the special identities can be assigned rights and permissions to resources, you cannot modify or view the memberships of these special identities. You do not see them when you administer groups and cannot place the special identities into groups. Group scopes do not apply to special identities. Users are automatically assigned to these special identities whenever they log on or access a particular resource.

Managing Groups

Now that you have seen some of the theory behind groups, it is time to see how administrators work with groups. This section shows you how to add, edit, and delete groups and how to add and remove members. Use the following Step by Step to learn how to add a group.

STEP BY STEP

4.18 Adding a Group

1. Open Active Directory Users and Computers.

2. Right-click the folder in which you want to add the group, point to New, and then click Group.

3. Type the name of the new group. By default, the name you type is also entered as the pre-Windows 2000 name of the new group. However, you can change this if required.

4. Click the Group scope you want.

5. Click the Group type you want.

6. Verify the information (see Figure 4.20) and click OK.

FIGURE 4.20
Verify the information and click OK.

Remember that you add global groups to gather users you want to manage as a single entity. Local groups are created to gather rights. You should always check to see if an existing group meets your needs because this reduces the overall number of groups and in general reduces the permissions checking.

As with the user options, there are more options you can set. To edit these options, you need to edit the group properties. Use Step by Step 4.19 to learn how to modify group properties.

STEP BY STEP

4.19 Modifying Group Properties

1. Open Active Directory Users and Computers.

2. Click the folder that contains the group.

3. In the details pane, right-click the group and then click Properties.

4. Change the properties as required and click OK.

Although you can change all the properties of groups, you normally change the membership of groups. This enables you to add or remove users from the group. You might also change the manager of a group if the management is being delegated.

There are six tabs you use to configure groups. The following is a list of the tabs and what you can configure on each of the tabs:

◆ **General.** This enables you to change the down-level name of the group. You can also add a description and an email address, change the scope and type of group, and add notes.

◆ **Members.** This tab enables you to add or remove members. "Surprisingly," it does this by having you click Add or Remove.

◆ **Member Of.** Like users, groups can be members of other groups. This tab enables you to add the group to or remove the group from other groups.

◆ **Managed By.** This enables you to set the user who is the manager for the group. The information about that user is then displayed.

◆ **Object.** This tells you the name, creation, update dates, and Update Sequence Number for the object.

◆ **Security.** This enables you to set security on the object in Active Directory. This is discussed in more detail later in this chapter.

There will be times when you want to delete a group. Remember, though, that just like a user, a unique SID represents a group. When you delete the group, you are deleting the SID. Creating a new group with exactly the same name does not provide the rights and permissions that were assigned to the group without you assigning them again. Use Step by Step 4.20 to learn how to delete a group.

STEP BY STEP

4.20 Deleting a Group

1. Open Active Directory Users and Computers.

2. In the console tree, double-click the domain node.

3. Click the folder that contains the group.

4. In the details pane, right-click the group and then click Delete.

5. Click Yes in the confirmation dialog box.

When you finish using a group and are sure no one else is using it, you should delete it to make sure there are no stray permissions on the group. This also removes the object from Active Directory.

Remember that you can either open the group properties to add the user or open the user properties to add the user to a group. You can also use these to see what groups a user belongs to or which users are members of a group.

As with all network operating systems, groups are a key management tool. They enable you to manage a large number of users quickly and easily. Although groups are not officially part of the exam, questions about them have appeared in some cases. Make sure you understand both the types of groups (security and distribution) and the scope of groups (global, universal, and local).

As you move into the next section, you will learn how to locate objects. This is useful when you want to create groups.

LOCATING OBJECTS IN DIRECTORY SERVICES

Manage Active Directory objects.

- **Locate objects in Active Directory.**

As the number of objects you store in Active Directory increases, you obviously need some method of finding the objects so you can work with them. In addition, there would be little point in configuring Active Directory to create a list of all the objects across your enterprise if the users were not able to locate the objects. In this section, you will see how to locate objects in Active Directory from both the administrative interface and the user interface.

Finding Objects in the Management Interface

When you are working with the users and computers that make up your network, you need to be able to find the object you want to manage. This can be done using either the **Find** command located in the context menu for the domain or the **Find** icon on the toolbar. Step by Step 4.21 walks you through using the Find command to locate an object.

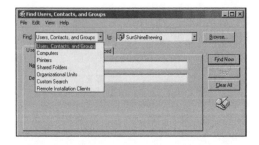

FIGURE 4.21
The Find dialog box, showing what you can find.

STEP BY STEP

4.21 Locating an Object Using the Find Command

1. Open Active Directory Users and Computers from the Administrative Tools menu.

2. On any domain, right-click and choose Find from the context menu.

3. In the Find text box, select what you want to find (see Figure 4.21).

4. In the In text box, select which domain to search or select that you want to search all of Active Directory (see Figure 4.22).

5. Depending on your selection, you can now fill in the option for which you are searching. The following is a list of the search possibilities:

- **Users, Contacts, and Groups.** In this case, you can enter a name or description.

- **Computers.** When searching for computers, you can enter the name of the computer, the name of the owner, or the role in the domain (domain controller or workstation/server).

- **Printers.** For printers, you can search by printer name, location, or model.

- **Shared Folders.** For shared folders, you have the option of searching by name or by keywords associated with the shared folder.

- **Organizational Unit.** If you need to search for an OU, your only choice is to enter the name.

- **Custom Search.** This option enables you to specify exactly what you want to search and to search on several criteria. The custom search main screen is the same as the Advanced option for all the other searchable items. The Advanced option is described in more detail later in this chapter.

- **Remote Installation Clients.** This enables you to search by the globally unique identifier or by the remote installation server to which it is assigned.

You do not have to enter the full value for a text field. Search normally finds what you are looking for using a word or two. For example, you can find all the people with the last name Smith by entering **Smith** in the search box.

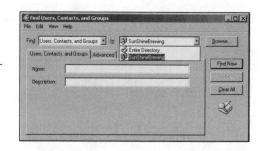

FIGURE 4.22
The Find dialog box, showing search options.

continues

FIGURE 4.23
You can search for printers based on features.

continued

6. If you are searching for a printer, you could click the Features tab and search for a printer based on its available features (see Figure 4.23).

7. Click Find Now and the system performs the search, placing the results in a results window (see Figure 4.24).

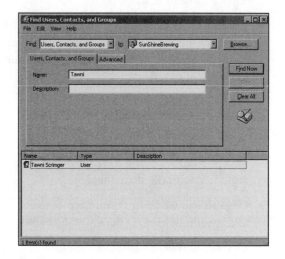

FIGURE 4.24
The results of a search.

After you have found the object or objects for which you were looking, you can select them and use the right-click to bring up the context menu. This gives you the same options as locating the object manually and then right-clicking.

Advanced Search

By performing an advanced search, or using Custom Search, you can be more specific about the objects you are trying to find. The objects you can search for appear along with a list of their attributes. Use Step by Step 4.22 to explore the Advanced search options.

STEP BY STEP

4.22 Advanced Searches

1. In the Find dialog box, choose the object to find and then click the Advanced tab (see Figure 4.25).

2. Click the Field button to drop down the list of fields on which you can search. Click on the desired field (see Figure 4.26).

3. Choose the type of condition from the Condition drop-down list (see Figure 4.27).

4. If required, enter a value in the Value box.

5. Click Add to add the condition to the list. You can remove a condition by clicking the condition and then clicking Remove.

6. Repeat steps 2 through 5 for each additional condition for which you are searching. The conditions are treated like a logical AND.

7. Click the Find Now button to execute the search.

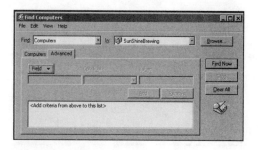

FIGURE 4.25
The Advanced search tab.

FIGURE 4.26
The options you can search for depend on the object you choose. In some cases, you have a list of objects with fields listed in a fly-out menu.

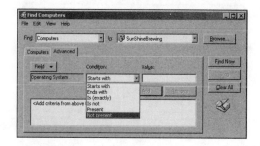

FIGURE 4.27
You can use several conditions, all of which expect a value other than Present or Not present (which tests for the existence of the attribute).

Being able to use the advanced search functions enables you to find the objects you need quicker and without having so many objects appear. The advanced search also enables you to access characteristics to find groups of objects with a common setting.

Finding objects in the administrative tools is useful for you as an administrator, but users also need to be able to find Active Directory objects.

Finding Objects as a User

Users also need to be able to search for objects in Active Directory. The users can easily find either printers or people using the Search tools on the Start menu. Step by Step 4.23 walks you through a search for a printer.

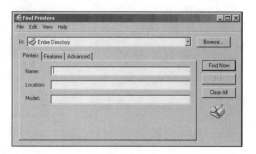

FIGURE 4.28
The interface is displayed for users to find printers.

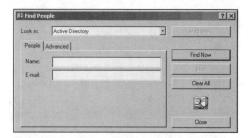

FIGURE 4.29
The Find People dialog box can search Active Directory or any other LDAP provider.

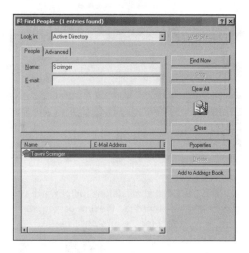

FIGURE 4.30
The results are displayed in a results pane.

STEP BY STEP

4.23 Searching for a Printer as a User

1. Choose Start, Search, For Printers to bring up the dialog box shown in Figure 4.28.

2. Enter the search criteria as seen in Figure 4.28 or leave the Find Printers dialog box empty to find all printers.

3. Click Find Now.

When the user finds a printer, he or she can right-click on the printer and choose Connect to use the printer. Finding people is similar to finding printers. Step by Step 4.23 walks you through finding people with Active Directory.

STEP BY STEP

4.23 Finding People Using Active Directory

1. Choose Start, Search, For People to bring up the Find People dialog box.

2. In the Look in drop-down list box, choose Active Directory (see Figure 4.29).

3. Enter the name or other information you are looking for and then click Find Now (see Figure 4.30).

Using this tool, users can find other users on the network and can access information about them. They also can use this to send email to other users.

Now you should understand that you need to be able to locate objects both as an administrator and as a user.

You might be wondering about the security if just anybody can find objects on your network. This is not a concern because the objects are all protected by an access control list.

At this point, you have seen how to work with user and computer accounts and how to manage them using groups. You should also know how to find the objects in Active Directory. The next section takes you into organizational units you can use to delegate control of some of the objects to other users or groups.

CREATING AN ORGANIZATIONAL UNIT

Install, configure, and troubleshoot the components of Active Directory.

- **Implement an organizational unit (OU) structure.**

As your network begins to grow, you will find that you have a large number of users to organize. You will also find that you will need to separate the users so you can manage groups of users together. Ideally, you want to be able to delegate the control of groups of users to others on the network.

Organizational groups enable you to logically organize the users, computers, and other resources in your network. Using organizational units enables you to maintain centralized control of the network. It also enables you to group users and computers for the delegation of control and for the application of group policies.

Consider, for example, a network of some 8,000 users. You have a couple of choices as to how you split this network apart. You can create a root domain and then create child domains. You can also create a single domain and then split the network up using organizational units. Even in a network in which you have split the enterprise into child domains with a single root domain, you can use OUs to organize the users within a domain.

Where to Create OUs

The choice between domains or organizational units is part of the network design. Typically, domains act as replication and security boundaries. If these are not created, your logical division in the network will be done using OUs.

STEP BY STEP

4.24 Creating an Organizational Unit

1. Open Active Directory Users and Computers.

2. Right-click the folder under which you want to create the new OU. Within Active Directory, an OU acts like a folder.

3. From the context menu, choose New, Organizational Unit.

4. Enter the name of the organizational unit and click OK.

After you have created the OU, you can move users and computers into the OU or just create them in the OU. In addition, you can create other objects in the OU such as groups, printers, shared folders, and other organizational units.

Remember, the main reason for creating an OU is to enable you to delegate authority for the OU to another user or group. This is done by setting permissions on the OU so that a user or group can have control.

PERMISSIONS IN ACTIVE DIRECTORY SERVICES

Manage Active Directory objects.

- **Control access to Active Directory objects.**

Every object in Active Directory has a *security ID* (SID), a unique number identifying the object. When a user logs on to Windows 2000, the system generates an access token, which is attached to the user's initial process (Explorer) by default. The access token is made up of the SID of the user and the SID of any group to which the user belongs, along with other information.

The access token is then attached to each process the user launches. It is used to compare object permissions to determine whether the user has access to the object. In Windows 2000, this includes access to the object in Active Directory.

Each object has a security descriptor, which includes the SID of the owner, the SID of the principal group of the owner, and a *discretionary access control list* (DACL) along with a *system access control list* (SACL). The SID of the owner is used to give the owner access to change permissions. The SID of the group is used for group access from POSIX applications and from Services for Macintosh. The SACL controls the local systems access to the object.

The DACL is filled with access control entries. An *access control entry* (ACE) contains a SID, the type of access the entry represents, and whether the access is granted or denied. When object access is attempted (you try to read an object's attributes, for example), the access token for your session is read, and each SID is compared with the first ACE. If this gives one of the SIDs in your access token permission, that's it. You have access. On the other hand, if this denies you the access you need, that is also it—you are denied access. Denies are always listed first. If your access is not resolved on the first ACE, then the next is checked and so on until you either have the rights you require or you are denied access.

By setting the permission on object, you can set the actions people can perform on the objects. This is how you can allow other users or groups in the network to manage parts of your organization.

Object-Level Permissions

Before you can set or even see the object-level permissions, you need to be able to see the advanced settings for the objects in the Active Directory. This can be turned on under the View option in the menu. If you click View, you will see the Advanced Features option. If there is a check mark, it is turned on. Otherwise, it is off. The option acts as a toggle; if you choose it when it is off, it will turn on and vice versa.

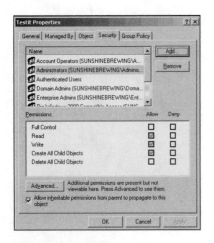

FIGURE 4.31
The Security tab for an organization unit.

N O T E

Inherited Permission   If the permissions are grayed out, they are inherited from a higher level of the Active Directory. The next section, "Permissions Inheritance," talks more about this.

With the advanced features turned on, you can view and set object-level permissions. You do not normally do this; rather, you create an OU and then delegate control of the OU to a user or group. However, Step by Step 4.25 covers the procedure.

STEP BY STEP

4.25 Setting Permissions on an Object

1. Open Active Directory Users and Computers.

2. Find the object for which you want to set permissions and right-click. From the context menu, choose Properties.

3. Click the Security tab. If this tab does not appear, close the dialog box and verify that you have Advanced Features turned on from the View menu.

4. In the Name list, locate the user or group for which you want to review or change permissions (see Figure 4.31). If the desired user or group is not listed, click Add and choose the user or group.

5. In the Permissions box, choose the permissions you want to grant or deny and check those boxes. Clearing a checked box removes the permission. The permissions are defined in the following list.

6. Click OK to apply the permissions.

As you saw, there are five different permissions you can set. The permissions are fairly straightforward. The following list reviews the permissions:

◆ **Full Control.** This enables the user or group to perform any action on the object within Active Directory. Full Control encompasses all the permissions that follow:

   • **Read.** This enables a user to read the object and the properties associated with the object. This is the default permission for everyone so that he or she can find the object when searching Active Directory.

- **Write.** This enables the user to change the properties of the object.

- **Create All Child Objects.** This enables a user or group with permissions to create objects. For example, you can create users and computers within container objects such as organizational units.

- **Delete All Child Objects.** This enables a user to delete the child objects from a container object, such as an OU, even if he or she did not create the object.

If you look back at Figure 4.31, you will notice that there is also an Advanced button. This enables you to get into greater specificity with the permissions as well as configuring the auditing and letting you take ownership of the object. Step by Step 4.26 walks you through setting advanced permissions.

STEP BY STEP

4.26 Setting Advanced Permissions

1. From the Object tab of the object properties dialog box, click the Advanced button.

2. From the Permission Entries list on the Permissions tab (see Figure 4.32), choose the entry to change and click View/Edit or click Add and choose a user from the list.

3. In the Permission Entry dialog box (see Figure 4.33) for the object, click on the tab you want to set permissions. Choose either Object, which controls the entire object, or Properties, which controls access to individual properties of the object.

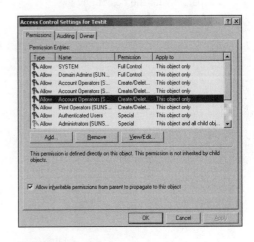

FIGURE 4.32
The Access Control Settings for objects are fine-tuned using this dialog box.

continues

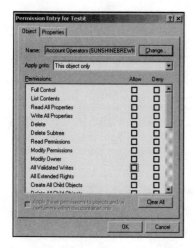

FIGURE 4.33
Advanced permissions can be set
separately for the object and the
properties of the object.

continued

> **4.** As you complete each tab, choose the appropriate Apply
> setting. These affect the scope of the setting. You can click
> the Clear All button to clear all the properties at once.
>
> **5.** Click OK to continue.

Normally, you do not set the advanced permissions yourself.
Advanced permissions are set through the Delegation of Control
Wizard. You can also use these steps to check the permissions, and
this is more common.

A large number of permissions can be set, and these are presented in
the following list. These are more for your information than for the
exam itself.

Permissions you can set on the object include the following:

◆ **Full Control.** This gives the user or group full control of
the object. It is included here so you can control the scope to
which it is applied.

◆ **List Contents.** This enables a user or group to list the
contents of a container object only.

◆ **Read All Properties.** This enables a user or group read all the
properties of an object.

◆ **Write All Properties.** This enables a user or group to write to
all the properties of an object.

◆ **Delete.** This gives the user or group permission to delete the
object.

◆ **Delete Subtree.** This enables the user or group to delete the
object and all objects it contains.

◆ **Read Permissions.** The user or group is allowed to read the
permissions on the object.

◆ **Modify Permissions.** The user or group is allowed to modify
the permissions on the object.

◆ **Modify Owner.** If this permission is given, the user or group
is allowed to change the owner (take ownership) of the object.

◆ **All Validated Writes.** This enables the user or group to perform any write operation on the object.

◆ **All Extended Rights.** This gives the user or group access to the extended rights on the object.

◆ **Create/Delete All Child Objects.** The user or group is able to create child objects and, with the Delete permission, delete all child objects including those belonging to others.

◆ **Create/Delete *named* Objects.** This series of entries is similar to Create/Delete All Child Objects, except the rights cover only the object type named. For example, this is how you can delegate control of computers within an OU.

On the Properties tab, you can selectively give or deny a user the capability to read and write the properties of the object. Consider carefully using these settings. These settings force Active Directory to check permissions on a column-by-column basis.

The options for the scope break down in a manner similar to the properties. The permissions can be set to affect the current object only, the current object and its children, only the children, or a specific type of object.

Permissions you set on an object can actually affect other objects, too.

Permissions Inheritance

The objects created in a container inherit permissions set on container objects in Active Directory.

This means that, if you set permissions on an OU and then create another OU within it, the permissions that are set on the top-level OU flow down to the lower-level OU and onto the objects created within it.

Although this is the default behavior, this is not always the desired behavior. For this reason, you have the option of blocking the inheritance of permissions. This is done on the Security tab. Step by Step 4.27 explores blocking inherited permissions.

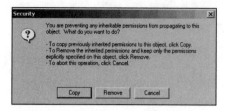

FIGURE 4.34
You have two options regarding the inheritable permissions when you clear the check box.

STEP BY STEP

4.27 Blocking Permissions Inheritance

1. Open Active Directory Users and Computers.

2. Find the object for which you want to set permissions and right-click. From the context menu, choose Properties.

3. Click the Security tab. If this tab does not appear, close the dialog box and verify that you have Advanced Features turned on from the View menu.

4. Clear the Allow inheritable permissions from the parent to propagate to this object check box.

5. A dialog box appears asking what you want to do with the inherited permissions already on the object (see Figure 4.34).

6. To keep the permissions, click Copy; to remove them, click Remove.

After you have cleared this check box, permissions are not inherited again unless you recheck the box. This is true even if you move the object to another container.

In most cases, you won't set these permissions directly; you will delegate control of an organizational unit that contains the objects.

Delegating Administrative Control

Manage Active Directory objects.

- **Delegate administrative control of objects in Active Directory.**

Combining the use of organizational units and permissions provides you with the capability to delegate the management of portions of Active Directory to other users. This means you can create an organizational unit and give a user or group the rights they need to manage that OU, effectively creating a workgroup or local administrator within a single domain.

Applying the required Full Control permissions using the Security tab can delegate control; however, you should use the Delegation of Control Wizard. This wizard enables you to completely delegate control or to delegate only partial control of an OU, as you will learn in Step by Step 4.28.

STEP BY STEP

4.28 Delegating Control with the Wizard

1. In Active Directory Users and Computers, right-click the OU for which you want to delegate control.

2. Choose Delegate Control from the context menu.

3. Click Next to bypass the introductory screen.

4. On the next screen, use the Add button to add the users and/or groups to which you will delegate control and then click Next.

5. On the next page of the wizard, you are asked what you want to allow the user or group to do. You can choose one or more common tasks from the list. You have the option of customizing what you are delegating. The common tasks include the following:

   • Create, delete, and manage user accounts.

   • Reset passwords on user accounts.

   • Read all user information.

   • Create, delete, and manage groups.

   • Modify the membership of a group.

   • Manage Group Policy links.

6. If you selected Create a custom task to delegate, you are asked to specify the object or objects over which the user or group will have control.

continues

continued

7. You then see a list of the general permissions, as described in the preceding bulleted list. You can also see the permissions from the advanced permissions by checking the Property-specific and/or Create/deletion of specific child objects check boxes.

8. Choose the rights the user or group should have and click Next.

9. Review the information and click Finish.

The main reason for creating organization units is so you can delegate control. The delegation adds the required permissions. This can be run more than once and adds more permissions as required.

Understanding the permissions you can set on objects is important because they control the actions of the users and, in some cases, the administrators. It is permissions that make delegation of control and secure dynamic updates possible. You also need to be able to set permissions on printers and shared folders.

Managing Shares

A share is a part of your disk that you allow people to access across the network. The point at which you create the share and all the directories below it are accessible through the share. This is the primary method for allowing your users to access data on servers.

Obviously, sharing directories is not part of managing Active Directory. This section is included to make sure you have the basics and can understand the publishing of shares in Active Directory and the permissions you can set.

When you share a directory, you create a name representing the directory on the network, which users can access using a *universal naming convention* (UNC) name. Creating a share is a simple process you can accomplish in several different ways. Step by Step 4.29 walks you through creating a share from the command line.

STEP BY STEP

4.29 Creating a Share from the Command Line

1. Open a command prompt (Start, Programs, Accessories, Command Prompt).

2. Enter the command **NET SHARE ShareName=Path**.

- ShareName is the name to which users to connect.

- Path is the path on the disk you want to share.

3. Press Enter.

Although you won't normally use the command line to create a share, you need to know how to do this so you can create scripts to automate some of your administrative functions. This is also very useful if you take advantage of the Telnet service included in Windows 2000. It can also be used to get a list of the directories you have shared and their names. Step by Step 4.30 helps you learn how to retrieve a list of shares.

STEP BY STEP

4.30 Retrieving a List of Shares at the Command Line

1. Open a command prompt (Start, Programs, Accessories, Command Prompt).

2. Enter the command **NET SHARE** and press Enter.

This is a very quick and useful way to find out what is shared on your computer.

In most cases, you create shares from your computer using Explorer, the Computer Management snap-in, or the Active Directory Users and Computers snap-in. This uses the graphical user interface to create the share. Step by Step 4.31 shows you how to create shares using the Explorer.

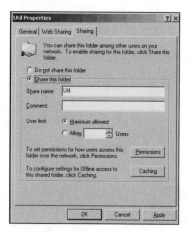

FIGURE 4.35
A folder's Properties dialog box showing the Sharing tab.

STEP BY STEP

4.31 Sharing a Directory using the Explorer

1. Open Explorer (right-click My Computer and choose Explore).

2. Locate the directory you want to share.

3. Right-click the Directory and choose Sharing.

4. In the Properties (see Figure 4.35) dialog box, click Share this folder.

5. A default share name should appear. If desired, change the share name.

6. Enter a comment to describe the share and its contents.

7. Set the number of simultaneous users with the User limit option. The choices are Maximum allowed or Allow a specific number. If you choose Allow, enter the number allowed.

8. Set the Permissions and Caching options as required.

9. Click OK to share the folder and close the Properties dialog box.

This is a common way to create shares. You need to know it because you will occasionally need to create a share this way. You may have to step a user through creating a share this way.

You can also create share from Computer Management. To get to the Computer Management snap-in, you can either open Computer Management from the Administrative Tools menu, or you can open Directory Users and Computers. Then you can right-click the computer where you want to create the share and choose Manage from the context menu. Step by Step 4.32 walks you through using Computer Management to create a share.

STEP BY STEP

4.32 Creating a Share in Computer Management

1. Expand the System Tools folder, expand Shared Folders, and then expand Shares.

2. Right-click the Shares folders and choose New File Share.

3. In the Select a Folder to Share dialog box, locate the folder you want to share by expanding the drive and the subfolders and then clicking the folder. The folder name appears in the Folder Name dialog box. You can also simply enter the name.

4. Click Next and you will see the Set Permission dialog box. If you choose to change permissions, you have the choice of applying the permissions to the share only or to the share and the files and folders within.

5. Click Next and enter the name to which you want users to connect in the Name text box. Optionally, you can enter a description of the share.

6. Select the operating system with which you want to share the folder.

7. Click Next and the final dialog box of the wizard will confirm your choices. Click Finish to create the share.

8. If you want to create another share, click Yes in the Create Shared Folder Wizard dialog box. Otherwise, click No.

Sharing a folder is a very basic operation on the network, and it is one you will do many times. Another type of sharing in Windows 2000 is called *Distributed File System* (DFS). A full discussion of DFS is beyond the scope of this text; however, you should be aware of its existence for the exam.

DFS enables you create a single share point such as \\server\DFS to which users can connect. Under this share, you will create DFS child nodes, which are in fact pointers to other shares on the network. This means a user only needs to connect to the main share and then could change to other shares by changing "directories." There are two types of DFS: standalone and domain. A standalone DFS is like a regular share, and you might publish it in Active Directory. A domain DFS provides you with the capability to have a child node that points at more than one server. This, in combination with the file replication system, makes the file system fault tolerant and allows for load balancing. Domain DFS becomes part of Active Directory and is automatically published.

However you decide to share files, you need to set permissions.

Share Permissions

When you create a share, the information in the share is exposed to the network. You need to set the permissions for the users that will access the share to ensure that only the users who are supposed to use the share are doing so. The effective permissions for a share are a combination of the share permissions and the NTFS permissions if, as it should be, the share is on an NTFS drive.

Normally, you set the share permissions to be more liberal than the NTFS permissions because the same share permissions are used for the shared directory and all subdirectories. The permissions through the share are compared to the NTFS permissions, and the more restrictive permissions are applied.

If a user is given control of a file through NTFS but only Read permissions to the share, the Read permissions win, and the user cannot exercise the rights he or she has been given. On the other hand, if the user has control through the share and control only on the one file but nothing on the other files, he or she will be able to work with that one file. The permissions of the share and file combine and are equal, so the user can access the file. The control permission with no permission combines to give the users no permissions on the other files in the directory.

The following are the six main NTFS rights that a user can have for a file:

◆ **Read (R).** This gives the user the capability to read the information.

◆ **Write (W).** This gives the user the capability to change the information and save the changed version.

◆ **Execute (X).** This enables a user to load an executable and run the code.

◆ **Delete (D).** This enables the user to delete a file or folder.

◆ **Permissions (P).** This permission enables the user to change the permissions on a file.

◆ **Take Ownership (O).** This enables the user to take ownership of the file, giving him or her the capability to change permissions.

The standard permissions are a combination of these rights and let the user perform different functions. There are three permissions you can either give or deny users: Read (RX), Change (RWXD), and Full Control (RWXDPO). Step by Step 4.33 walks you through setting shared folder permissions.

NOTE | **Denying Permissions** Microsoft suggests that you use the Deny permission sparingly. Deny overrides all other permissions even if a user has Full Control. Depending on where the Deny permission is set, it could be hard to track down. Remember that if you do not give a user permissions, the user does not have them. If you are careful about the permissions you give, you should not have to use Deny.

STEP BY STEP

4.33 Setting Shared Folder Permissions

1. Open the share properties (see Step by Step 4.32).

2. Click the Permissions button.

3. Click Add and add the groups or users that should have access by clicking on the user and then clicking Add. If the user is in a different domain, use the Look in drop-down list to choose the domain.

4. When all the users are added, choose the type of access to grant and then click OK.

5. Repeat steps 2 through 4 as required. If you need to remove a user, click the user and then click Remove.

6. Click OK when you are finished and close the share Properties dialog box.

In addition to setting the share permission, you should also set the NTFS permissions. This is done in a similar manner by right-clicking in Explorer the file or folder on which you want to set permissions and then choosing Properties. From there, you can choose the Security tab and set NTFS permissions.

Publishing a Share

Manage Active Directory objects.

- **Publish resources in Active Directory.**

By publishing a share, users can find the share in Active Directory. Publishing a share is a simple process done in Directory Users and Computers. This is demonstrated in Step by Step 4.34.

STEP BY STEP

4.34 Publishing a Share in Active Directory

1. Open Active Directory Users and Computers.

2. Expand the domain in which you want to publish the share and locate the folder under which you want to publish it.

3. Right-click the folder and choose New, Shared Folder.

4. Enter the name you want to appear in Active Directory and the name of the share it represents.

5. Click OK.

The inclusion of a share within Active Directory makes it easier for the user to locate shares. Many users do not understand the meaning of UNC names, and this is a means to make it easier to find the share that is needed.

Just as you can publish folders, you can also publish printers to make them easier to find.

PUBLISHING PRINTERS

Manage Active Directory objects.

- **Publish resources in Active Directory.**

Publishing printers makes them available to Active Directory, which means that users can search for them and then attach them as required. In Windows 2000, you can do this on the Sharing tab of the printer's Properties sheet by clicking List in Active Directory.

If the printer is not connected to a Windows 2000 computer, you need to add it in Directory Users and Computers. This is demonstrated in Step by Step 4.35.

STEP BY STEP

4.35 Publishing a non-Windows 2000 Printer in Active Directory

1. Open Active Directory Users and Computers.

2. Expand the domain in which you want to publish the share and locate the folder under which you want to publish it.

3. Right-click the folder and choose New, Printer.

4. Enter the network path for the printer.

5. Click OK.

This makes the printer an object in Active Directory that users can then search for. Although this section is brief, printers are one of the objects added to Active Directory by default, and you need to know how to add them. In addition, you need to know how to move them.

Moving Objects Within the Directory

Manage Active Directory objects.

- **Move Active Directory objects.**

As time goes by, you will be adding organizational units and rearranging users. This happens as companies reorganize or as employees change jobs within an organization. The process for moving objects in Active Directory is a very simple one if you are moving users between organizational units. If you need to move a user to a different domain, you need to use the MOVETREE utility. Step by Step 4.36 walks you through the process of moving an object between OUs.

FIGURE 4.36
The popup enables you to choose the organizational unit to which you want to move the object.

STEP BY STEP

4.36 Moving an Object Between Organizational Units

1. In Active Directory Users and Computers, locate the object to move.

2. Right-click the object and choose Move from the context menu.

3. In the list that pops up, choose the organizational unit to which to move the object and click OK (see Figure 4.36).

Being able to move objects enables you to deal with the shifts in your organizational structure that occur over time. This capability used to require third-party utilities. Having the capability to move objects built in to Active Directory Users and Computers should make the life of administrators easier.

Moving an object between domains is a little more difficult than moving between OUs. This is because the SID is made up of the SID for the domain along with the relative identifier. To move an object between domains, you need to use the MOVETREE utility.

The **MoveTree** command requires that you provide the source and destination server and the source and destination distinguished names. The servers can be any servers in the source or destination domain. The syntax is as follows:

```
MoveTree [/operation] [/s source_server] [/d
destination_server] [/sdn source_name]
[/ddn destination_name] [/u Domain\Username] [/p Password]
[/verbose]
```

The operation can be Start to start the operation, Check to check the directory tree, or Continue to continue a failed move operation. If you need to move an organizational unit called Marketing from the Office domain to a new domain called Marketing, for example, the command might look like this:

```
Movetree /start /s ADSRV1.office.local /d
➥ADSRV1.marketing.office.local
        /sdn cn=marketing,dc=office,dc=local /ddn
➥cn=Users,dc=marketing,dc=office,dc=local
        /p office\administrator /p password
```

Moving objects within a domain is simple and straightforward. This capability makes it much easier for you to manage a network, because users often move from job to job within an organization. The moving of objects from one domain to another is more difficult. However, the capability to do this saves you money on the third-party utilities that used to be required to accomplish this task.

CASE STUDY: ADMINISTERING ACTIVE DIRECTORY

ESSENCE OF THE CASE

We want to look at the creation of the organizational units and the placement of servers. There is little that you really need to consider as long as you keep a few basic points in mind.

- ▶ Each site requires at least one global catalog server and should have at least one domain controller from each domain.

- ▶ There are five domains based on the user's function in the organization rather than his or her location.

- ▶ The sites were created for the different locations, and the sites have been configured to replicate so that information should not be more than three hours out-of-date at any major location.

- ▶ There are 15 sites, 4 of which are major offices and the other 11 of which are minor offices.

SCENARIO

This chapter has presented a great deal of information. Most of it does not affect the design of the network directly but rather affects the policies that need to be followed on the network. There need to be policies about the creation and use of the types of groups and about the addition of objects to Active Directory.

Policies also need to be developed to deal with the delegation of control of organizational units and what that control will entail. Further, Sunshine Brewing should set standards for different levels of security on documents and should determine the permissions and auditing requirements for these documents.

This case study looks at the creation of organizational units and at the placement of global catalog servers. By ensuring that the sites are in place as discussed in the preceding chapter and by ensuring the correct placement of servers and the creation of appropriate organizational units, we can facilitate whatever policy is created.

Again, this is a fairly straightforward example in which you need to both make sure there is a global catalog server in each site and create organization units.

ANALYSIS

The organizational units will be perhaps a little numerous; however, because they exist only as objects within Active Directory, this is not a problem. For each of the domains, you will end up having a separate organizational unit for each location.

CASE STUDY: ADMINISTERING ACTIVE DIRECTORY

This will enable you to manage all the users of one type at the domain level or to manage all the users of one type at the same location at the OU level. This will make the application of site-level Group Policy more difficult because you will need to define it in one domain and link to it from the other domains. This means that site-level policies should be defined in the root domain that will need to have at least one domain controller in each location.

As for the global catalog servers, in this case, we will look at configuring the bridgehead servers for the site links to act as the global catalog servers.

CHAPTER SUMMARY

This chapter looked at the basic administration of Active Directory. Here you have seen how to create objects of different types, move the objects, and set permissions on the objects. You have also seen how to create organizational units and how to delegate control of those organizational units to other users and groups.

KEY TERMS

- Distribution group
- Domain local group
- Global group
- Inheritance
- Local group
- Mixed mode
- MOVETREE
- Native mode
- Object-level permissions
- Rights
- Security group
- Security principal
- Universal group

APPLY YOUR KNOWLEDGE

Exercises

4.1   Creating Accounts in Active Directory

In this exercise, you will use Active Directory Users and Computers to create user and computer accounts that will be used in the remaining exercises.

Estimated time: 15 minutes.

1. Open Active Directory Users and Computers.

2. Expand your domain.

3. Right-click the Users folder and then select New, User from the context menu.

4. For the First name, enter **Sales**; for the Last name, enter **Admin**.

5. For the User name, enter **SalesAdmin** and then click Next.

6. On the password page of the wizard, clear the User must change password at next logon option, enter **Trojan** as the password, and confirm the password information.

7. Click Next and then click Finish on the confirmation screen.

8. Using steps 3 through 7 as a guide, add the following users.

First Name	Last Name	User Name	Password
Marylou	Scott	Mscott	eastern
Anne	Sheard	Asheard	eastern
Judy	Jamieson	Jjamieson	eastern
Ralph	Smith	Rsmith	eastern
Krista	Bailey	Kbailey	eastern
Dan	Harris	Dharris	western

First Name	Last Name	User Name	Password
Peter	Loke	Ploke	western
Helen	Burke	Hburke	western
Mark	Spence	Mspence	western
Jim	Xu	Jxu	western

9. Right-click the Computer folder and then select New, Computer from the context menu.

10. For the Computer name, enter **WKS5542**.

11. Click Next and then click Finish on the confirmation screen.

12. Using steps 9 through 11 as a guide, add the following computers:

> WKS8726
> WKS8652
> WKS0823
> WKS0564
> WKS8762
> WKS7645
> WKS2735
> WKS0012
> WKS3218

4.2   Creating Organization Units

In this exercise, you will create the Sales OU, and within the Sales OU, you will create two more OUs called Eastern and Western.

Estimated time: 5 minutes.

APPLY YOUR KNOWLEDGE

1. If Active Directory Users and Computers is not open, open it.

2. Right-click your domain and choose New, Organizational Unit.

3. Enter **Sales** as the name of the OU and click OK.

4. If you need to, expand your domain and locate the OU you just created.

5. Right-click the Sales OU and choose New, Organizational Unit from the context menu.

6. Enter the name **Eastern** as the new OU name and click OK.

7. Repeat steps 5 and 6 to create the Western OU.

4.3 Delegating Control of an Organizational Unit

In this exercise, you delegate control of the Sales OU to the SalesAdmin account.

Estimated time: 10 minutes.

1. If Active Directory Users and Computers is not open, open it.

2. Open the Users folder and locate the SalesAdmin account.

3. Right-click the SalesAdmin account and choose Move.

4. In the list of folders, choose the Sales organizational unit and click OK.

5. Click the Sales OU and verify that the SalesAdmin account is there.

6. Right-click the Sales OU and choose Delegate Control from the context menu.

7. Click the Next button to bypass the introductory screen.

8. On the next screen, click the Add button. Select the SalesAdmin user and click Add and then OK. Click Next to go to the next screen.

9. On the next screen of the wizard, check the following options and then click Next.

   • Create, delete, and manage user accounts.

   • Reset passwords on user accounts.

   • Read all user information.

   • Create, delete, and manage groups.

   • Modify the membership of a group.

10. Review the information and click Finish.

4.4 Moving Objects in Active Directory

In this exercise, you will move the users that should be in the Eastern organizational unit within the Sales OU to that OU.

Estimated time: 5 minutes.

1. If Active Directory Users and Computers is not open, open it.

2. Click the KBailey user object. With the Ctrl key pressed, click the remaining four accounts for the eastern region (MScott, ASheard, JJamison, and RSmith).

3. Right-click any of the highlighted accounts and choose Move.

4. In the list of folders, expand the Sales organizational unit and then click on the Eastern OU. Click OK.

APPLY YOUR KNOWLEDGE

5. Expand the Sales OU and click the Eastern OU. Verify that the accounts are there.

6. Move the remaining five accounts to the Western OU under Sales (DHarris, PLoke, HBurke, Mspence, and JXu).

4.5   Finding a User

In this exercise, you use the Search tool to find a user account.

Estimated time: 5 minutes.

1. Choose Start, Search, For People to bring up the Find People dialog box.

2. In the Look in drop-down list box, choose Active Directory.

3. Enter the name **Dan** and then click Find Now.

4. Verify that the information for Dan Harris appears.

4.6   Publishing a Share

In this exercise, you will publish a share in Active Directory.

Estimated time: 5 minutes.

1. Open Explorer by right-clicking My Computer and choosing Explore.

2. Click on the C: drive and, in the right pane, right-click in a blank area.

3. From the context menu, choose New, Folder from the menu. Enter the name **PubTest** for the folder and press Enter.

4. Right-click the PubTest directory and choose Sharing.

5. In the Properties dialog box, click Share this folder and then click OK to accept the defaults.

6. Open Active Directory Users and Computers.

7. Expand your domain and then the Sales OU.

8. Right-click the Sales OU and choose New, Shared Folder.

9. Enter **SalesFiles** as the name you want to appear in Active Directory and **\\\servername\PubTest** as the share name (where *servername* is the name of your server).

10. Click OK.

11. Verify that the folder appears in the Sales OU. If it does not, try right-clicking Sales and choosing Refresh from the context menu.

Review Questions

1. What is the main purpose of organizational units?

2. What protocol is used to search Active Directory?

3. What is the purpose of groups?

4. What is the greatest number of levels you should nest in OUs?

5. What is the effect of delegating control of an organizational unit?

6. If you set permissions on an organizational unit, what happens to the permissions of the object in the OU?

7. What do you need to do to publish a printer in Active Directory?

APPLY YOUR KNOWLEDGE

8. If you move an object within a domain, what tool should you use?

9. If you move an object to another domain, what happens to the permissions on the object if you have cleared the Inherit Permissions check box?

10. What does the Advanced tab on the Search screen let you do?

Exam Questions

1. Jon is in charge of a network that has a single Windows 2000 domain. The network has 700 users at present and services the entire company.

    Jon has been dealing with the human resources department for the past few days and, after several discussions, has agreed to let them deal with their own computer accounts. What must he do to allow them to manage their own computers? (Choose two.)

    A. He needs to create a new domain.

    B. He needs to create a new OU.

    C. He needs to create a new site.

    D. He needs to set individual permissions on the computer accounts.

    E. He needs to use the Delegation of Control Wizard.

2. Wanda is troubleshooting a problem that a user named Ralph is having in Active Directory. Ralph has permissions to manage an OU; he is trying to change the account information for a user that has just changed jobs. Ralph is unable to change the information. What should Wanda check?

    A. She should check whether the user really has permissions to manage the OU.

    B. She should check whether the account has been moved to the correct OU.

    C. She should check whether the Inherit Permissions option is checked.

    D. She should check the database integrity.

3. You are planning to move several computers to better organize them. To what can computers be added? (Choose all that apply.)

    A. Domains

    B. Sites

    C. Organizational units

    D. Groups

    E. Trusts

4. Sally is trying to publish a printer in Active Directory. The printing device is attached to a Windows 95 computer and is managed from a Windows 2000 computer. What must she do to create the printer in Active Directory?

    A. She needs to share the printer from the Windows 95 computer.

    B. She needs to share the printer from the Windows 2000 computer.

    C. She needs to add a file share on the Windows 95 computer.

    D. She needs to manually add the printer to Active Directory because it is attached to a Windows 95 computer.

APPLY YOUR KNOWLEDGE

5. David is trying to move an object from cn=user, dc=sunshine, dc=com to cn=accounting, dc=sunshine, dc=com. What must he do to move the user?

   A. He needs to delete the user from the first location and re-create the user in another location.

   B. He needs to right-click the user and select the correct OU.

   C. He needs to use the **MoveTree** command as the command line.

   D. He needs to use NTDSUTIL to move the user.

6. David is trying to move an object from cn=user, dc=sunshine, dc=com to cn=accounting, dc=hq, dc=sunshine, dc=com. What must he do to move the user?

   A. He needs to delete the user from the first location and re-create the user in another location.

   B. He needs to right-click the user and select the correct OU.

   C. He needs to use the **MoveTree** command as the command line.

   D. He cannot move the user.

7. Sam is creating groups in a new domain in an Active Directory tree. She has a group of users in the domain that need to have access to resources in three other domains. What type of groups should she use?

   A. Global

   B. Universal

C. Domain local

D. Local

8. Tom is troubleshooting a permissions problem for Danielle. Danielle has a file she needs to upload to a server once a week. The file is then read by all the executive-level users in the organization.

   Danielle currently has to go to the server, log on to the server, and then copy the file to the server from a floppy. She wants to be able to connect to the share that the executives use to read the file to upload the file to the server weekly. What should Tom check?

   A. The NTFS permissions

   B. The permissions on the Everyone group

   C. The share permissions

   D. The permissions on the file object in Active Directory

9. A computer running in your network recently crashed. The system was an older P233MMX with 64MB of RAM, and you'll be replacing the system with a new multiprocessor computer.

   Because you are changing the hardware abstraction layer from a single processor to a multiprocessor, you realize you have to reload the computer. What should you do in Active Directory to make sure you can easily add the computer to the domain?

   A. Rename the existing computer account.

   B. Move the existing computer account to the Lost and Found folder.

   C. Delete the computers account.

   D. Reset the computers account.

APPLY YOUR KNOWLEDGE

10. Dave has a group of users in a domain, and he wants to apply a different Group Policy to them. What should he do to apply the Group Policy?

    A. Create a global group.

    B. Create a universal group.

    C. Create a new domain.

    D. Create an organizational unit.

11. Glen is on the help desk and gets a panic call from a user named Tim. Tim's boss Leslie is at a meeting in Rome and needs a document on her hard drive; she is currently not able to get at her email and needs a copy right away. What should Glen have Tim do?

    A. Copy the document to a floppy and send it by courier.

    B. Print the document and fax it.

    C. Locate a printer in Active Directory in the Rome office and print it there.

    D. Tell Tim to have Leslie call and help her get at her email.

12. The human resources department has come to you with a problem. It has a shared directory with the HR updates, but it seems no one can find them because no one seems to have read them. The department wants to make sure users can locate the documents. What can you do to make sure they can locate the documents?

    A. Create a new group and put the documents there.

    B. Create a mailing list and have HR mail the document to all users.

    C. Publish the HR share in Active Directory.

    D. Locate the directory in a new DFS root.

13. Sam is creating groups in a new domain in an Active Directory tree. She has a resource on a Windows 2000 domain controller in the domain that will be accessed by groups from the local domain and from four other domains. What type of groups should she use?

    A. Global

    B. Universal

    C. Domain local

    D. Local

14. In an effort to reduce the number of calls handled by the help desk in your organization, you have decided to create a group of "user mentors" that will receive extra training and some extra permissions on the network. These users will be able to manage the user computers, which are grouped in a single OU in each of your six domains. They also will be able to reset the password of the users that are also grouped in an OU in each domain. The users that will be part of the program are scattered throughout the six domains. What type of group should you use to delegate the permissions they will need?

    A. Global.

    B. Universal.

    C. Domain local.

    D. Don't use a group; use an OU.

APPLY YOUR KNOWLEDGE

15. Sally is attempting to share a directory. Which tool should she use?

    A. Explorer

    B. Active Directory Sites and Services

    C. Active Directory Users and Computers

    D. Server Manager

Answers to Review Questions

1. The main purpose of an organizational unit is to enable you to delegate the control of a set of users, computers, and other objects in Active Directory. This is done either by manually setting permissions on the organizational unit or by using the Delegation of Control Wizard. See the section "Creating an Organizational Unit."

2. Although you don't see it called LDAP, the protocol used to search Active Directory is Lightweight Directory Access Protocol, which was originally defined in the X.500 specifications. See the section "Locating Objects in Active Directory."

3. The purpose of groups is to collect users or rights. Global groups are used to gather users into a manageable unit and to make this group available in the local domain and all the other domains. The local group typically is used to gather the rights you want to assign. Users gain the rights when you add the global group to the local group. Universal groups act as a bridge between global and local groups that can span many domains. See the section "Groups in Windows 2000."

4. Microsoft recommends that you do not nest organizational units beyond three layers. This is primarily because each OU level, in addition to the domain and site to which a user belongs, can have group policies assigned to it. The loading of more than five Group Policy documents would cause the logon process to become unreasonably slow. See the section "Creating an Organizational Unit."

5. When you delegate control of an organizational unit, you are really setting the permissions on the OU and the objects in the OU so that the delegate can control whatever the permissions allow. See the section "Delegating Administrative Control."

6. When you set permissions on an OU, the objects in the OU inherit the changes you make. This is the normal behavior and can be overridden by blocking inheritance. See the section "Permissions Inheritance."

7. If the printer is on a Windows 2000 computer, all you need do is share the printer and check the List in Directory box. This is checked by default. See the section "Publishing Printers."

8. Moving an object within a domain can be done using the **Move** command on the context menu for the object. If you need to move the object between domains, you need to use Movetree. See the section "Moving Objects Within the Directory."

9. The permissions will stay the same. The permissions on an object on which you have cleared the inheritance will stay the same whether or not the object is moved. See the section "Moving Objects Within the Directory."

APPLY YOUR KNOWLEDGE

10. The Advanced tab enables you to specify, in detail, what you are looking for by giving you a list of the objects for which you can search and the attributes that are available to search. See the section "Advanced Search."

Answers to Exam Questions

1. **B, E.** The best choice here is to create an OU and then use the Delegation of Control Wizard to give control to the HR users. You could create a domain (A), but this would add a layer of complication to the network that is not required. Although he could set the permissions on each individual computer (D), this is more work than necessary to accomplish the same functionality as creating an OU and delegating. Creating a site (C) does not allow for any delegation of control. See the section "Delegating Administrative Control."

2. **C.** In this case, you can tell that the user account has been moved, and the likely problem is that the inherit permissions check box has been cleared. Answer A is possible, but the user is supposed to have the permission, and according to the question, it is just the one account he cannot access. Again, answer B is possible. However, because the user has probably done this before, you can assume he is looking in the right place and seeing the account. As for checking the integrity, this is possible, but you would probably have other symptoms appearing. See the section "Moving Objects Within the Directory."

3. **A, C, D.** A computer account can be part of a domain, organizational unit, or group. This provides extra control that was not available in

NT 4. The site is not a container for computers (except domain controllers), and trusts are the links between. See the sections "Computer Accounts," "Groups in Windows 2000," and "Creating an Organizational Unit."

4. **B.** In Windows 2000, printers that are shared are automatically published in Active Directory, and because this printer is controlled from a Windows 2000 system, that is all that is required. Because the printer is attached to the Windows 95 system, answers A and D are incorrect. File shares are separate from the printer in Active Directory, so answer C is incorrect. See the section "Publishing Printers."

5. **B.** In this case, the object is moving from one OU to another in the same domain. The **Move** command from the context menu handles this. Answer A is wrong and would cause all user permissions to be lost. Answer C is wrong because the move is within a domain. Answer D is wrong because the NTDSUTIL is used for maintenance, not to move users. See the section "Moving Objects Within the Directory."

6. **C.** In this case, the user is being moved from one domain to another domain. The **Move** command on the context menu only works within a single domain, so answer B is incorrect. Answer A would work, but all the user information and permissions would be lost, and the user would have a new SID, so this is not the best answer. Answer C is correct here because this is the purpose of the **MoveTree** command. Answer D is incorrect because answer C is correct. See the section "Moving Objects Within the Directory."

7. **A.** Global groups are available in the domain in which they are created and in other domains within a forest. Local and domain local groups

APPLY YOUR KNOWLEDGE

are only available in the domain in which they are created and therefore will not work in this case, so answers C and D are wrong. A universal group is used if you have users from multiple domains that all need access to resources in multiple domains, so answer B is not right. See the section "Strategies for Using Groups."

8. **C.** In this case, you can rule out NTFS permissions because the user is able to perform the operation locally. Therefore, answer A is incorrect. The Everyone group doesn't have permissions, which is good because this is executive information, so answer B is wrong. File objects are not part of Active Directory; therefore, answer D is wrong. This leaves share permissions, which is correct. Remember that share and NTFS permissions are combined, and the lower permission is used. Because Danielle has the NTFS permissions, she can do it locally. We can therefore assume the share permissions are wrong. See the section "Managing Shares."

9. **D.** Renaming the computer account would leave a dead computer account in the Active Directory that would never be used. Therefore, answer A is wrong. The Lost and Found directory is where the system puts orphaned objects it finds, and it is not used by users, so answer B is wrong. Deleting the account and re-creating it will lose all the group memberships and Group Policy information, so this is also wrong. Resetting the account keeps the account and enables you to add the computer to the domain again; therefore, it is the best answer in this case. See the section "Computer Accounts."

10. **D.** Because you can apply Group Policy at the OU level, this is the best answer. Answers A and B could be possible if you were to use Group Policy filtering; however, this is not the best way to perform the action because all the other users would also need to load the policy file. There is no need to create a new domain for most of Group Policy, so answer C is incorrect. See the section "Creating an Organizational Unit."

11. **C.** This is a simple question to make sure you know that you can search Active Directory. Answer A would work; however, the cost and time involved makes it impractical. Answer B is probably what most users would do; however, there is also a cost involved, and the faxed copy would not be as clear. Answer D is also possible; however, answer C is easier because Tim's boss is probably busy. See the section "Locating Objects in Active Directory."

12. **C.** Although a news group could be used, this would not make the HR documents easy to find because the user would need to check the news server and look at the new groups. The mailing list could also work but would greatly increase the load on the mail server and the network. Locating the directory in a new DFS root would make it easier to get to but not easier to find. This leaves C as the answer, which makes sense because the capability to publish a share is included to make it easier to find. See the section "Managing Shares."

13. **C.** A local group is used on standalone servers and Windows 2000 Professional, so answer D is incorrect. Global groups are used to make the users in a domain available to other domains, so answer A is incorrect because this is a resource. Universal groups, answer B, are used to take users from many domains and give them rights in many domains. This leaves a domain local group, answer C, which is correct. The global

APPLY YOUR KNOWLEDGE

group from the local domain and the other four domains would be added to this domain local group to give the users rights. See the section "Strategies for Using Groups."

14. **B.**   In this case, you are taking users that are part of multiple domains and providing them rights in multiple domains. The correct tool to do this is a universal group. Global groups enable you to bunch users, which will be used in other domains, and local groups are used to hold the rights and normally have global groups as members. In this case, you could perform the action using a combination of global and local groups; however, the universal group does it with greater easy and is the right answer. See the section "Strategies for Using Groups."

15. **A.**   There are three utilities Sally can use. The **NET** command, Explorer, and the Computer Management snap-in. The only one listed is Explorer. Sites and Services is used to control sites in Active Directory and some services; Users and Computers is used to manage Active Directory objects and can be used to open the Computer Management snap-in for a computer. The Server Manager could do this in NT 4; however, this is Windows 2000. See the section "Managing Shares."

Suggested Readings and Resources

1. *Microsoft Windows 2000 Server Manual.* Microsoft Press, 2000.

2. Microsoft Windows 2000 Resource Kit. *Deployment Planning Guide.* Microsoft Press, 2000.

This chapter covers some of the objectives and subobjectives from the units on "Installing, Configuring, and Troubleshooting Active Directory" and "Managing, Monitoring, and Optimizing the Components of Active Directory." Other objectives and subobjectives from these units are covered in other chapters.

Install, configure, and troubleshoot the components of Active Directory.

- **Transfer operations master roles.**

▶ This objective is included because of the importance of the operations masters. You need to understand what the various operations masters do and the effects of them being online. In addition, you should be able to transfer the operations master roles whether or not the previous master is available.

Back up and restore Active Directory.

- **Perform an authoritative restore of Active Directory.**

- **Recover from a system failure.**

▶ Backup and recovery are important aspects of managing a network. This includes backing up and recovering the directory services. This objective is included to make sure you are able to perform a normal recovery either by installing a replacement controller or by restoring from backup. In addition, you need to fully understand what an authoritative restore is and when you need to use it.

Manage Active Directory performance.

- **Monitor, maintain, and troubleshoot domain controller performance.**

- **Monitor, maintain, and troubleshoot Active Directory components.**

▶ This objective is included primarily to make sure you know how to monitor and maintain the Active Directory database. You need to know what tools are available and what tools you should use.

CHAPTER 5

Managing Servers

This chapter looks at the general administration of servers. The discussion begins with a look at the roles a server can take on for the network. Then there is a discussion of the backup and recovery of servers, notably the three ways you can recover a domain controller. The remainder of the chapter looks at monitoring and maintaining servers on the network. As you read through the chapter, pay particular attention to the following points:

▶ You need to know the five operation master roles.

▶ You should note which roles are domain level and which are enterprise level.

▶ You should know both how to transfer the roles and how to seize the roles.

▶ You should know which servers can be reinstated if the role is seized.

▶ You should know the standard backup and restore options when using the Microsoft Backup program.

▶ You need to know the three ways to restore a domain controller and when you should use each.

▶ You should be familiar with the options available on NTDSUTIL.

▶ You should know what tools are available to monitor a server or the network and when they can be used.

INTRODUCTION

One of the most common jobs a network administrator faces is managing servers. As you move into Windows 2000, there no longer are primary domain controllers, backup domain controllers, and member servers. However, there are several special types of servers of which you need to be aware and be able to manage including the schema master, the domain naming master, the PDC emulator, the RID master, and the infrastructure master.

Essentially, in addition to the tasks you learned about in the preceding chapter (managing users, computers, and groups), you need to be able to monitor your servers. You must perform backups and restores. You will also transfer the key server roles from one server to another.

SERVER ROLES

Install, configure, and troubleshoot the components of Active Directory.

- **Transfer operations master roles.**

The operation masters are critical to the operation of the network, and you need to make sure they are available when necessary. Some of these roles can be offline for a time without effect, while others have a dramatic impact if they are offline for even a short time.

In the next few sections, you will learn about each of the operations master roles. From there, the discussion will look at the placement of the roles and how to transfer the roles. Then you will see how to seize a role from a server that has crashed. Finally, there will be a look at the global catalog server.

Operation Masters

In Active Directory, changes to user accounts, computer accounts, shares, and the like can be made on any domain controller. This provides a great deal of flexibility. Some changes, however, should be made only in one place (changing the schema, for example).

Active Directory gets around this limitation by using a group of servers called operations masters. These servers are responsible for a role within the enterprise or within each domain. You need to know about and be able to transfer five operations masters if a server is being brought down for service or crashes.

◆ **Schema master.** There is only one schema master for the entire enterprise. The schema master has the original version of the schema and is the only place where the schema can be changed.

◆ **Domain naming master.** The server performing this role is responsible for the addition and removal of domains within the entire enterprise; therefore, there is only one in the enterprise. This server ensures the uniqueness of the domain name and makes sure it fits within the enterprise namespace. The information about the logical structure of the Active Directory namespace is used in managing the trust relationship between the domains.

◆ **Relative ID (RID) master.** Every object created on a domain controller has a *security ID* (SID). In Active Directory, this is a combination of the domain's security ID plus a unique ID within the domain. The RID master is responsible for creating the second part of the security ID; it generates a series of them for each domain controller and gives these identifiers to the controllers. Because the entire SID is only unique in the domain, it is considered a relatively unique ID. Obviously, there must be a RID master for each domain.

◆ **PDC emulator.** To support down-level clients, one of the domain controllers in a domain takes on the role of *primary domain controller* (PDC) emulator. This domain controller is responsible for replicating the Active Directory domain with the NT 4.0 *backup domain controllers* (BDCs). If your domain is in native mode, the PDC emulator receives preferential replication of password changes. If a down-level client then attempts to log on and is serviced by another controller that has not received the update, that controller forwards the logon request to the PDC emulator.

◆ **Infrastructure master.** This server maintains the user-to-group mappings for its domain. As users are renamed or moved to a different container, the infrastructure master updates the references and replicates them to the other domain controllers. Each infrastructure master handles the accounts within its own domain, even for groups from other domains.

Each of these roles needs to be managed to make sure it is available to the other systems on the network and to make sure there is recoverability in case of a system crash. This involves planning the correct locations for these servers.

Planning Operations Master Locations

When you first start to install your domain structure by installing your first domain controller, you are setting the location for all the roles previously mentioned. As the enterprise grows and you add child domains, the first domain controller you install in each of the domains is the domain operations masters (RID, PDC emulator, and infrastructure) for that domain.

Generally, this works fine for a small domain located within a single building or for a forest that has few domains with few controllers. As you start to move beyond these basics, you might consider moving some of the domain operations masters. Planning the operations masters in a domain is discussed first in the next section, followed by a discussion of planning the operations masters in a forest.

Planning the Operations Masters in a Domain

In a domain with only one domain controller, that controller handles all the operations master roles. Because you are normally going to have multiple domain controllers, you have some choice as to which controllers to use for the various operations master roles. Generally, this should be one of the more powerful systems on the network. In addition, you can specify a standby operations master; this system should have a good connection to the operations master.

Usually, you keep the operations master roles together on the same server. This means you don't have to keep track of the different roles.

However, if you have a large number of changes to groups or if you have a large number of down-level clients or are constantly adding users and computers, you might consider separating the roles. Normally, you separate the roles by moving the PDC emulator to another system. If you do this, make sure the system to which you move the role has good network connectivity with the standby operations master.

Planning the Operations Masters in a Forest

There is no advantage to separating the schema master and the domain naming master. These are both operations that are performed only on occasion. The server that houses these roles should be near the stations used for administration. Other than this logistical concern, there is little need to change their location.

Now that you have seen how to plan for the location of the operations masters, you also need to know how to transfer these roles.

Setting Operations Master Roles

Transferring a master role moves the role from one server to another when both of the servers are available. The steps are similar for each of the roles you might have to move, as you will see in the next few sections.

Transferring the Schema Master Role

To transfer the schema master role, follow Step by Step 5.1.

STEP BY STEP

5.1 Transferring the Schema Master Role

1. Open the Active Directory Schema snap-in. You need to add this snap-in to the Microsoft Management Console if you haven't previously done so.

continues

NOTE

If you haven't added the snap-in already, you can do so by going Start, Run and entering MMC. When you click OK, an empty console appears. Choose Console, Add/Remove Snap-in, and then click the Add button. From the list, choose Active Directory Schema and click Add. Then Close the Add Standalone Snap-in dialog box and click OK to return to the console.

This snap-in might not be on your system. To add the snap-in, right-click Adminpak.msi in the source file directory and follow the instructions.

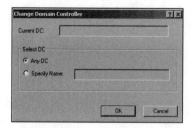

FIGURE 5.1
You can select a specific controller or let the system choose a controller.

continued

2. Right-click Active Directory Schema and click Change Domain Controller.

3. You can either click Any DC to let the system choose one or select Specify Name and enter the name of the controller you want to have in the role of schema master (see Figure 5.1). This sets the focus to that controller; make sure you have set the focus to a system other than the current schema master.

4. Right-click Active Directory Schema again and choose Operations Master.

5. Click Change.

The schema master is one of the enterprise-level roles, and it only causes you problems when an administrator or a software installation attempts to modify the schema. After you have the schema master in place, you do not move it unless you are going to replace the system on which it resides. This is also true of the domain naming master.

Transferring the Domain Naming Master Role

You want to make sure the domain naming master, like the schema master, is on a subnet that contains another domain controller so that all changes are quickly replicated to the second controller. Typically, you have the schema master and the domain naming master on the same controller with another controller located on the same subnet for backup purposes.

Use the procedure in Step by Step 5.2 to change the location of the domain naming master role.

STEP BY STEP

5.2 Changing the Location of the Domain Naming Master Role

1. Open Active Directory Domains and Trusts (Start, Programs, Administrative Tools).

2. Right-click Active Directory Domains and Trusts and choose Connect to Domain Controller.

3. Choose the domain either by entering its name or by using the Browse button. Normally, you should keep the domain naming master in the root domain. Then choose a controller to which to move the role from the list of available domain controllers. Click OK to connect to the controller. This sets the focus on the controller that will perform the role (see Figure 5.2).

4. Right-click Active Directory Domain and Trusts again and choose Operations Master.

5. Click Change to move the role.

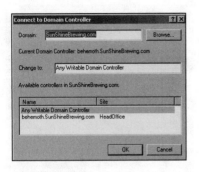

FIGURE 5.2
Choose the domain controller to which you want to move the role.

Transferring the Domain-Level Master Roles

The operation masters at the domain level also typically are on a single controller with another controller on the same subnet for backup purposes. You might occasionally have to move these roles to perform maintenance on the controller or if the server is about to crash. Step by Step 5.3 describes how to move one or all of the domain-level master roles.

STEP BY STEP

5.3 Transferring Domain-Level Operation Masters

1. Open Active Directory Users and Computer from the Administrative Tools menu.

2. Right-click Active Directory Users and Computers and choose Connect to Domain Controller.

3. Choose the domain controller to which you want to move the role and choose OK. This sets the focus to the domain controller.

continues

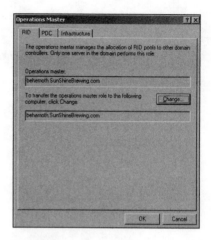

FIGURE 5.3
Choose the tab for the role you need to change and then click Change to move the role.

continued

4. Right-click Active Directory Users and Computers again and choose Operations Masters (See Figure 5.3).

5. Choose the operations master by selecting the tab that corresponds to the role you want to change. On that tab, click Change to move the role. Click Change on all the tabs to move all the roles.

As you can see, it is easy to move the operation master roles if the systems are both online. If this is not the case, you need to consider which master has failed and how long the system will be down. In some cases, you might have to seize the role.

Recovering from a Master Failure

As in Windows NT 4.0, if a system crashes, you need to take some action to correct the problem. In this case, you seize the role from the system that previously had it and give it to the standby system. This is a drastic step in some cases because the entire network could become corrupted if you were to later return the original master to service. The PDC emulator and the infrastructure master, however, can be brought back online. To seize a server role, follow the steps shown in Step by Step 5.4.

STEP BY STEP

5.4 Seizing a Operation Master

1. Start a command prompt and type **ntdsutil**.

2. At the NTDSUTIL prompt, enter **roles**.

3. You should now get the fsmo maintenance prompt; enter **connections**.

4. At the server connections prompt, enter **connect to server** followed by the FQDN name of the standby server.

5. Enter **quit** to return to the fsmo maintenance prompt.

6. Enter **seize** followed by the role to seize.

7. You are prompted to confirm your seize with a dialog box (see Figure 5.4).

8. Type **quit** to exit fsmo maintenance, and then type **quit** again to exit the NTDSUTIL.

> **N O T E**
>
> **Transferring Roles** You can also use NTDSUTIL to transfer the operations master roles by using the **transfer** command rather than the **seize** command.

FIGURE 5.4
Confirm the **seize** command.

The complete session could look like the following screen dump.

```
C:\>ntdsutil
ntdsutil: roles
fsmo maintenance: connections
server connections: connect to server behemoth
Binding to behemoth ...
Connected to behemoth using credentials of locally logged
➥on user
server connections: quit
fsmo maintenance: seize PDC
Attempting safe transfer of PDC FSMO before seizure.
FSMO transferred successfully - seizure not required.
Server "behemoth" knows about 5 roles
Schema - CN=NTDS
Settings,CN=BEHEMOTH,CN=Servers,CN=HeadOffice,CN=Sites,CN=
➥Configuration,DC=SunShineBrewing,DC=com
Domain - CN=NTDS
Settings,CN=BEHEMOTH,CN=Servers,CN=HeadOffice,CN=Sites,CN=
➥Configuration,DC=SunShineBrewing,DC=com
PDC - CN=NTDS
Settings,CN=BEHEMOTH,CN=Servers,CN=HeadOffice,CN=Sites,CN=
➥Configuration,DC=SunShineBrewing,DC=com
RID - CN=NTDS
Settings,CN=BEHEMOTH,CN=Servers,CN=HeadOffice,CN=Sites,CN=
➥Configuration,DC=SunShineBrewing,DC=com
Infrastructure - CN=NTDS Settings,CN=BEHEMOTH,CN=Servers,
➥CN=HeadOffice,CN=Sites,CN=Configuration,DC=SunShineBrewing,
➥DC=com
fsmo maintenance: quit
ntdsutil: quit
Disconnecting from behemoth ...
```

The roles you can seize are as follows:

Schema master

Domain naming master

RID master

PDC

Infrastructure master

Seizing a role should be the method of last resort because this can cause problems on the network. The only "special" server that you can have multiples of is the global catalog server.

Global Catalog Servers

In addition to the roles you already have seen, there is another role that a server can play within your enterprise: the role of global catalog server. The global catalog server keeps a listing of all information about objects in its domain plus all the objects located in the other domains throughout the enterprise but only a subset of the other domain object's properties.

The global catalog is used to contain some enterprise-wide information such as the membership of certain groups, specifically universal groups. The other main function of the global catalog is to enable users and other processes to search the entire enterprise for objects that are required.

The first domain controller in the domain is the global catalog server by default. You can add more global catalog servers if you want or drop existing ones. However, there must always be at least one global catalog server per forest. To configure a domain controller as a global catalog server, follow the steps shown in Step by Step 5.5.

STEP BY STEP

5.5 Configuring a Domain Controller to Host the Global Catalog

1. Open Active Directory Sites and Services.

---

2. Expand the Sites folder and then expand the folder for the site that contains the domain controller you want to manage.

---

3. In the site, open the Servers folder and then expand the server you want to configure.

---

4. On the NTDS Settings object, right-click and choose Properties.

5. On the General tab, check the Global Catalog check box to make the domain controller a global catalog server. Clear the check box if you don't want the system to act in this role. Click OK when you're finished.

In this section, you learned about the operations master roles and their purpose. You also looked at the placement of the servers and how to transfer or seize the operations master roles. The purpose of the discussion is to make sure you are able to control and recover from problems with a server. Another important aspect of recovering from a system error is using the backup and recovery utility.

BACKING UP AND RESTORING SERVERS

System backup is critical in every production environment. There are always going to be problems requiring you to recover information that was accidentally either lost or destroyed due to a system failure of some kind.

The version of Backup that ships with Windows 2000 is a drastic improvement over the previous versions. The most notable improvement is that you can now use media other than tape when performing backups. The Backup program enables you to perform all of the following:

◆ Back up selected files and folders.

◆ Restore backed-up files to the same or a different disk.

◆ Create an Emergency Repair Disk.

◆ Make a copy of remote storage data and data in mounted drives.

◆ Make a copy of the system state data including the registry, the Active Directory database, and the certificate service database.

◆ Schedule backups to automate the process.

In the next few sections, you will learn about the Backup utility and how to use it to back up and restore a Windows 2000 server.

Backup Types

As a rule, the first decision you need to make concerns the type and frequency of the backups you will perform as well as what you will back up. The backup utility in Windows 2000 enables you to back up FAT or NTFS partitions local to the system you are using to run the backup software. The backup utility also enables you to back up FAT or NTFS partitions to which you are connected across the network.

There are five different types of backup you can perform to prevent data loss. These can be used singly or in combination. The following list describes the five types of backups you can perform.

◆ **Copy.** This type of backup simply takes the files you select and copies them to the backup media. The archive attribute is not changed during this type of backup. This is useful when you need to perform a quick backup before installing new software because it does not interfere with full or incremental backups.

◆ **Daily.** This backup method uses the date attribute of a file to copy any files that have changed during the day the backup is performed. This type of backup doesn't change the archive attribute either and, therefore, does not affect other types of backups. This is a quick method of grabbing the changes that take place during the day, and it can be used in conjunction with other types of backups to recover to the minute.

◆ **Differential.** During a differential backup, all the files where the archive attribute is set are backed up. The attribute, however, is not reset. This means you can fully back up a system and then perform differential after differential. When restoring, you only need to restore the full backup and the last differential. The downside is that the size of the backup increases greatly over time.

◆ **Incremental.** This backs up all the files that have changed since the last full or incremental. It backs up the files and then resets the archive attribute to indicate the file has been backed up. With this type of backup, you would need to restore a full backup and then each incremental in sequence from that point forward.

◆ **Normal.** This is the full backup, and it simply copies all the selected files and clears the archive attribute as it is backed up. To effectively work with any other type of backup, you need to have first done a normal backup that can serve as a baseline.

Normally, you choose to work either with normal and incremental backups or with normal and differential. In either method, you normally perform a full backup weekly and then the differential or incremental daily. Using incremental backups reduces the amount of space required to hold the backups and the amount of time required to perform the daily backups. However, the recovery process takes longer. Using differential takes more backup space and more time, but the recovery time is reduced because only the normal and the last differential need to be restored.

Permissions Required for Backups

Obviously, if just anyone could go through and perform a backup, then users could easily grab data off a system. By restoring that data somewhere else, users could access information they should not have. Therefore, you need to have the correct permissions to perform a backup.

To perform a backup, you generally need to be a member of either the Backup Operators or Administrators group. You need to be in one of these groups for the local system and for any system you are backing up remotely. This enables you to back up data that is not your own.

WARNING

Using Read Permissions
Remember that any user with read or higher permissions is able to copy and therefore read information.

There are a couple precautions you might want to take when performing backups to make sure they don't become a security risk. One of the options you have during backup is to Allow Only the Owner and the Administrator Access to the Backup Data. This option prevents a person who gets hold of the tape, or another backup device, from restoring the files. Further, you can change the

Group Policy (covered in Chapter 6, "Using Group Policy to Manage Users") so that Backup Operators can only back up data and not restore it.

Backing Up System State Data

The system state data is special data you need to plan to back up. This data cannot be backed up from across the network. It must be backed up from the local system. The system state data can include:

◆ The registry

◆ The COM+ class registration database

◆ The boot files, including the system files

◆ The certificate services database

◆ The Active Directory service database

◆ The system volume (SYSVOL)

◆ The cluster service information

Not all of these components are applicable to all configurations of Windows 2000. However, if you configure the backup system to back up system state data, the preceding items that are present will be backed up. You do not have the choice to backup up individual pieces of the system state data; due to the interaction between the components, backup is an all-or-nothing deal.

When restoring system state data, you need to start the system in a special mode known as Directory Services Restore mode. This is one of the choices from the F8 menu. You do have the choice to restore the system state data to an alternate location. This, however, only restores the registry files, system volume information, cluster service database, and the system boot files. The other information is not restored. This is because the COM+ registration database is built as components are installed, and they typically need to be reinstalled if the source files are in different locations. The certificate information also needs to be rebuilt because the certificate server needs to be reinstalled and will, therefore, have a new signing key.

The Active Directory database does not need to be restored. It is assumed that you will have more domain controllers and that, therefore, they will be able to restore the information through the process of replication. If the Active Directory database were restored (as it is if you don't choose an alternate location), it would be replaced anyway.

This can lead to a problem if part of your Active Directory is lost by accident. For example, if an *organizational unit* (OU) were accidentally deleted, restoring it from a backup would not restore the OU. To restore a deleted object from Active Directory, you need to perform an authoritative restore.

Authoritative Restores

In cases such as a deleted OU, you could force a full restore to the normal location. This will, in fact, restore the Active Directory database. The problem is that the original *Update Sequence Numbers* (USNs)—every change to an object updates the sequence number, and the highest number is considered the most recent state—will be restored with the object. This means the USN of the deleted object that is still in Active Directory will be higher than the one of the restored object, forcing the object to be deleted again.

If the OU were restored, during the next replication, the USNs would tell the local system that the OU had been deleted. Therefore, the OU would be deleted again and would not be replicated to the other domain controllers. To get around this problem, you use NTDSUTIL to perform an authoritative restore.

The process is straightforward in that you still perform the restore process. However, before you restart the server, you run NTDSUTIL to mark the part of the Active Directory you are trying to recover. The process simply sets the USNs to a higher number. When you start the server and replication begins, the number on the copy you have is higher and is replicated to the other domain controllers.

Remember that, if you are simply trying to recover a broken computer, you need to perform a regular restore. This type of restore replaces the information, and then the replication process brings the system back up-to-date. If you restore to an alternate location, only part of the system state data is recovered, and the replication again brings the system up-to-date.

You need to perform an authoritative restore only if part of the Active Directory database is lost.

Performing Backups

Now that the theory is covered, it is time to look at how to perform backup and restore operations in detail. As you might guess, this section concentrates on using the backup utility that comes with Windows 2000.

The Backup program that comes with Windows 2000 enables you to back up to tape or to a file. When you use a file, you need to give the location and a name for the file. The default extension of .BKF (backup file) is optional. However, it is best to use defaults so that other users are aware of the file type. The file can be located on any fixed or removable media on the system or a share on a remote computer. If you use a tape, it must be local to your system.

The basic steps involved in a backup are as follows:

1. Using the tree view in the Backup program, select the files and folders you want to back up.

2. Choose the backup media you are using: either a file or a tape. Identify the file or tape you will use.

3. Choose the options you want such as the type of backup you want to perform and whether you want to log the backup. You can also select whether to back up data from mounted drives, specify files types not to backup, and whether to verify the backup.

4. Set any advanced options and select the schedule for the backup.

You can also use the wizard incorporated to configure the backup.

Using the Backup Wizard

Step by Step 5.6 walks you through the process of using the Backup Wizard to configure a backup.

STEP BY STEP

5.6 Performing a Backup Using the Backup Wizard

1. Open the Backup program (Start, Programs, Accessories, System Tools, Backup).

2. Click the Backup Wizard button (see Figure 5.5).

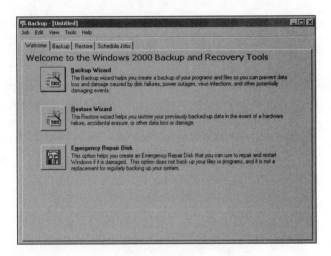

FIGURE 5.5
In the Backup program, click the Backup Wizard option.

3. Click Next to pass the introduction screen.

4. Choose what to back up and then click Next.

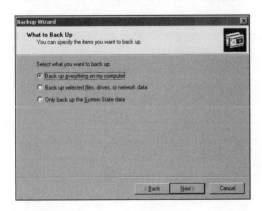

FIGURE 5.6
Choose what you want to back up.

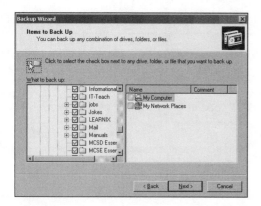

FIGURE 5.7
Select the files you want to back up.

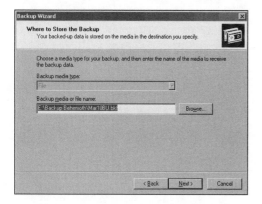

FIGURE 5.8
Choose the location and name for the backup.

FIGURE 5.9
The summary screen gives you the chance to select Advanced options.

5. If you choose to back up selected files, you will see a tree representing the drives and files on your computer. Select the files or folders to back up by expanding the tree and then placing a check in the boxes in front of the files or folders you want to back up (see Figure 5.7).

6. Select the backup media, either tape or a file, and choose the tape drive or files to use (see Figure 5.8).

7. On the next screen, you can click Finish and the backup begins. If you click the Advanced button, you will have further choices (see Figure 5.9).

8. The first advanced option asks what type of backup to perform (see Figure 5.10). Choose the type you want. You also have the option of backing up files that have been moved to remote storage (archived). Check the box if you want to do this and then click Next.

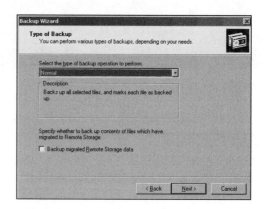

FIGURE 5.10
Choose the type of backup and whether you want to include archived data.

9. The next screen provides you with the option to verify the backup after it is finished (see Figure 5.11). This is a good idea. You can also choose to use hardware compression if it is offered by the tape drive. Set the options and click Next.

10. Next you can choose to overwrite the existing data or
append it. If you choose to overwrite, you also have the
option of allowing only the owner of the backup and the
administrator to have access. Click Next to continue (see
Figure 5.12).

11. Next you have the option to set the backup label and
the media label (see Figure 5.13). Set these and then
click Next.

12. The next screen gives you the option of performing the
backup now or scheduling it (see Figure 5.14). Select the
option you want and click Next.

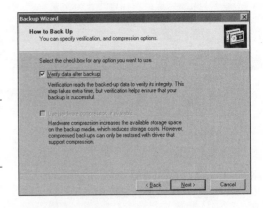

FIGURE 5.11
You should normally let the Backup program
verify the backup after it is finished.

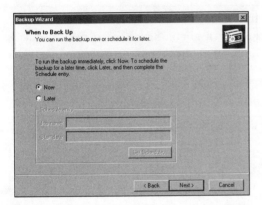

FIGURE 5.14
Choose when you want this backup to be performed.

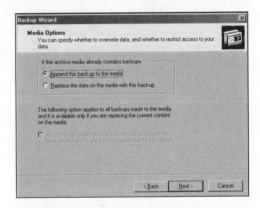

FIGURE 5.12
Choose whether to append to the existing data.

13. If you choose Later, you are prompted for the username
and password to run the job. Enter these and then you
can enter the job name. Click the Set Schedule button to
set the schedule. (The scheduling options are covered in
Step by Step 5.7.) Click Next to continue.

14. Now you can click Finish and the job will run or will be
scheduled to run (see Figure 5.15).

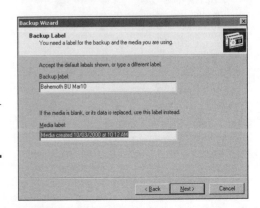

FIGURE 5.13
Enter a backup and media label.

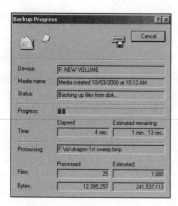

FIGURE 5.15
The backup then runs.

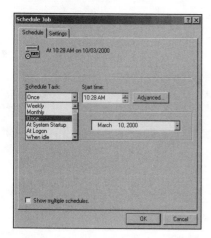

FIGURE 5.16
Choose the frequency for the job.

If you choose to set a schedule, multitudes of options are available including the capability to have multiple schedules. Step by Step 5.7 walks you through the scheduling of a backup.

STEP BY STEP

5.7 Scheduling a Backup

1. On the When to Back Up page of the wizard, click Later. If you are prompted, enter a username and password to perform the backup.

2. Enter a job name in the Job Name dialog box and click Set Schedule.

3. In the Schedule Job dialog box, you first need to select how often to run the job. From the Schedule Task drop-down list, choose the frequency (see Figure 5.16).

4. Depending on the choice you make, you will now be given eight different choices.

   • **Daily.** For daily jobs, you can select what time to run the job and whether backup runs every day or less frequently.

   • **Weekly.** For weekly tasks, you can again choose whether backup occurs every week or less frequently. You also get to choose the time at which the task runs. In addition, you can choose on which days of the week the backup runs.

   • **Monthly.** Again, you can choose what time the job runs; however, you also can choose which day of the month either by the numeric day or by the occurrence of a weekday (for example, the first Tuesday). In addition, you can choose in which months the schedule will run from the Select Months button.

   • **Advanced.** The Advanced button is available for daily, weekly, and monthly schedules; it enables you to add a start date for the task and an end date. In addition, you can have the job run multiple times during the days it runs. For example, you can have it rerun every so many minutes or hours, or you can have it run until a given time with the option of killing the job at that time.

- **Once.** This runs the job at one given date and time.

- **At System Startup.** This runs the job whenever the system is started.

- **At Logon.** This has the job run whenever a user logs on at the system.

- **When Idle.** This runs the job whenever the system is idle for a given number of minutes.

5. If you need to select more than one schedule for the backup job to run, you can select Show Multiple Schedules and create more schedules for the job.

6. Click on the Settings tab (see Figure 5.17) to select the options for the schedule.

7. Select the options you require. The following are the available options.

- **Delete the task if not scheduled to run again.** This removes the task from the task list if it is not scheduled to run again.

- **Stop the task if it runs for.** This enables you to set a limit on how long the job can run. If the time you enter is exceeded, the job is terminated.

- **Idle Time.** You can select to start the task only if the computer has been idle for at least a specified span of time. This prevents any scheduled task from running unless the computer has been idle for a specified period. You can set the number of minutes the computer needs to be idle, and you can set how long the system should wait before the giving up on the job. You can also select to stop the task if the computer becomes busy again.

continues

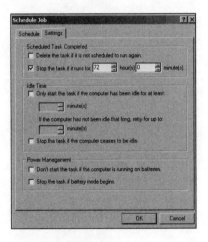

FIGURE 5.17
The Settings tab covers other options for the task.

continued

> **NOTE**
>
> **Editing Scheduled Tasks** To edit a scheduled task, open Start, Programs, Accessories, System Tools, Scheduled Tasks and double-click on the task.

- **Power Management.** The options here enable you to stop a task from running if the computer is on battery power and to stop the task if that system goes to battery during the task.

8. Click Next when the schedule is set.

This section has covered the basics of backing up a server on your network. Of course, if you have backups, you also need to know how to perform a restore.

Performing a Non-Authoritative Restore

Being able to restore the information on a domain controller, or any other server, is important. This section looks at the basic restore. The next section looks at an authoritative restore.

The basics of restoring information to the server are fairly simple, as shown in Step by Step 5.8.

STEP BY STEP

5.8 Performing a Basic Restore

1. Choose the files you want to restore. In a lot of cases, you will be restoring files lost due to accidental deletion, and this makes the process easy. The Backup program, which is also used to restore, provides you with a tree view of the information in the backup and enables you to select what to restore.

2. You need to select a location to which to restore the files. The program gives you three choices: You can restore the data to the original directory structure. You can restore the data to a different directory with the directory structure intact. You can restore the data to a different directory without the directory structure (all the files in one folder).

3. Choose what to do if the file you are restoring currently exists on the disk. The options are Do Not Replace, Replace If Newer, or Always Replace.

4. You are now ready to perform the restore or set the advanced options and perform the restore. The advanced options include restoring the security settings, the removable storage database, and the junction point data.

Restoring a Domain Controller— Non-Authoritative

Back up and restore Active Directory.

•**Recover from a system failure.**

There are a couple ways you can restore a domain controller. You can allow replication to restore the Active Directory data to its current state on the network. This means you will be completely up-to-date. You can also restore the system state information from a backup.

Before you can perform either of the restores, you need to correct the problem with the system or reinstall the computer. If you need to rebuild the computer, you should make sure the number and size of the disk volumes and their format are the same.

Restoring Using Replication

The easiest way to restore a domain controller is to use replication. This is normally done when you have to rebuild the computer due to a hardware problem or complete corruption of the operating system. This procedure works only if the system is not currently a domain controller (that is, the computer is freshly installed, and you have not run DCPROMO). Any extra services that were running on the system need to be reinstalled and configured; otherwise, the entire configuration will be lost.

The process is very simple and relatively quick. Step by Step 5.9 walks you through the process of restoring a domain controller using replication.

WARNING

Restoring to FAT   If the information was backed up from an NTFS partition under Windows 2000, the data should be restored to the same partition. Several features of the NTFS file system are backed up including the permissions, encryption settings, and remote storage information, and they cannot be restored if the target drive is FAT. Some, not all, of these features can be restored to an NTFS partition under NT 4.0.

STEP BY STEP

5.9 Restoring a Domain Controller Using Replication

1. Using a working system, open Active Directory Sites and Services and delete the reference to the domain controller.

2. Use the Active Directory Installation Wizard to promote the system to a domain controller.

This process creates a working domain controller with all the current Active Directory information. Even if you plan to fully restore a system that is dead, you normally reinstall the computer and should follow this procedure to start the process.

Restoring from a Backup

If the domain controller had other services configured on it, you need to restore the entire domain controller. You need to back up the files and system state data before you begin this process.

Before you can restore system state data, you need to restart the computer and enter the Directory Services Restore mode. To do this, follow Step by Step 5.10.

STEP BY STEP

5.10 Starting Your Computer in Directory Services Restore Mode

1. Turn the computer on if it is not already on. From the Start menu, choose Shutdown and then choose Restart from the Shutdown menu.

2. As the computer starts, a message prompts you to select the operating system to start. Do so, and then press F8.

3. Use the arrow keys to choose Directory Services Restore Mode and press Enter.

4. When prompted, log on to the system. During the logon, you should get a warning that you are running in safe mode (see Figure 5.18).

Now that your system is in the correct mode, you can use the Restore program to restore the system state data and any other data you require such as the files required for services. To restore system state data, follow Step by Step 5.11.

STEP BY STEP

5.11 Restoring System State Data

1. Open the Backup program (Start, Programs, Accessories, System Tools, Backup).

2. Click the Restore Wizard button.

3. Click Next to bypass the introduction screen.

4. On the next screen, you are given the choice of which backup to restore (see Figure 5.19).

   If the backup does not appear, click the Import button and locate the file that contains the backup. After you have entered the filename, click OK and the backup appears in the list (see Figure 5.20).

5. Click Next to go to the Completing the Restore Wizard page. Click Finish to restore.

6. If the system asks you to confirm the filename to restore, verify that it is correct and click OK. The restore then begins (see Figure 5.21).

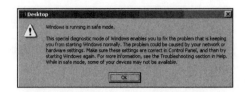

FIGURE 5.18
This warning appears to remind you that you are in safe mode.

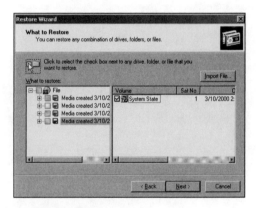

FIGURE 5.19
Select the backup you want to restore.

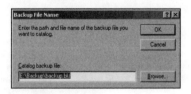

FIGURE 5.20
You can import the backup device if it is not listed.

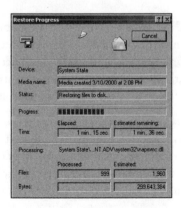

FIGURE 5.21
The system is restoring the system state data.

continues

continued

>   **7.** When the restore is complete, click Close to close the
>   dialog box and then close the Backup program.
>
>   **8.** Restart the computer in normal mode.

After you restart, the system should be back to normal except that it
might be out-of-date. This should clear up in short order, though, as
replication brings in changes from all the other domain controllers
in the domain.

This, of course, brings up a question: What if you are restoring the
Active Directory to restore one or more objects that had been
deleted? Unfortunately, this type of restore won't work because it
replicates with the other domain controllers and makes the local
copy of Active Directory like every other copy. To restore a deleted
object, you must perform an authoritative restore.

Performing an Authoritative Restore

Back up and restore Active Directory.

- **Perform an authoritative restore of Active Directory.**

Normally, when you restore a domain controller from backup, the
information restored is exactly what was on the system. In most
cases, this is exactly what you want to happen. However, if you are
trying to undo the deletion of an Active Directory object, this won't
work.

The attribute Update Sequence Number for the object being
restored is lower than the last USN on the version of the object in
the Active Directory of the other domain controllers. This means
that, when replication starts the other domain controllers, having
a higher USN on the object forces the local controller to delete
this object.

To prevent this, you need to perform an authoritative restore. An
authoritative restore follows exactly the same steps outlined in Step
by Step 5.11 with the addition of one other step before you restart
the computer. This additional step comes between the previous steps

7 and 8. The purpose of this step is to increase the attribute USN to force the other servers to accept this as the newest update to the object.

Step by Step 5.12 walks you through an authoritative restore.

STEP BY STEP

5.12 Updating the USN to Undelete an Object

1. Start a command prompt and enter **ntdsutil**.

2. At the NTDSUTIL prompt, enter **authoritative restore** and press Enter.

3. Enter **restore subtree** and the full name of the object you are restoring. This is made up of the cn= and dc= components of the object's name and should not contain any spaces.

4. A dialog box should appear asking if you're sure you want to restore the object. Check the object and click Yes if it is correct (see Figure 5.22).

5. After the restore finishes, you can restore another object, or you can type **quit** to exit Restore mode and then type **quit** again to exit NTDSUTIL.

6. Restart the computer.

FIGURE 5.22
Confirm that the object name is correct and click Yes.

The whole process looks like the following listing:

```
C:\>ntdsutil
ntdsutil: authoritative restore
authoritative restore: restore subtree
➥cn=testit,dc=sunshinebrewing,dc=com
Opening DIT database... Done.
The current time is 03-10-00 15:00.52.
Most recent database update occured at 03-10-00 13:51.56.
Increasing attribute version numbers by 10000.
Counting records that need updating...
Records found: 0000000018
Done.
```

continues

continued

```
Found 18 records to update.
Updating records...
Records remaining: 0000000000
Done.

Successfully updated 18 records.
Authoritative Restore completed successfully.
authoritative restore: quit
ntdsutil: quit

C:\>
```

Hopefully, you won't have to perform authoritative restores too often. However, as you can see, they are not overly difficult.

This section has covered the basics of backup and restore. This is a very important aspect of the administrator's job, and you should be sure you are familiar with this. Another major function is monitoring servers to make sure they are functioning correctly or to troubleshoot a problem.

OTHER ADMINISTRATIVE FUNCTIONS

Manage Active Directory performance.

- **Monitor, maintain, and troubleshoot domain controller performance.**

- **Monitor, maintain, and troubleshoot Active Directory components.**

In addition to being able to handle problems that can arise from time to time, you should also know how to monitor your servers, including your domain controllers. Monitoring your domain controllers enables you to keep them performing at their optimum level.

This section looks at monitoring in general and at the tools available to help with monitoring. Different problems you can have with domain controllers and how to fix them also are addressed.

The NTDSUTIL Command

One of the key utilities for managing Active Directory is NTDSUTIL. This is a command-line utility that performs several different functions. These functions include the following:

◆ **Authoritative Restore.** As you already have seen, the authoritative restore can be used to force an object to be recovered. Restoring the object from a backup and then updating the USN on the object does this.

◆ **Domain Management.** This option enables you to pre-create objects in Active Directory, such as child domains, so that the user physically installing the system does not need to have Enterprise Administrator privileges.

◆ **File.** This option enables you to manage NTDS.dit and related directory service database files. To manage these files, you need to start the computer in Directory Services Restore mode so the files are not open.

◆ **IPDeny List.** This enables you to create a list of IP addresses from which the server will reject LDAP queries. This setting affects the default LDAP policy and, as such, affects all domain controllers that do not have a specific LDAP policy.

◆ **LDAP Policies.** To ensure that domain controllers continue to work properly, you might need to specify limits for a number of LDAP operations. This option enables you to set those limits.

◆ **Metadata Cleanup.** In a case in which a domain controller has failed or a domain has been removed without using DCPROMO, there will still be information about the domain or server in the configuration data. This utility enables you to clean up these orphaned records.

◆ **Roles.** As you have seen, there are five operations master roles. These roles need to be available for certain functions on the network to take place. This command enables you to transfer or seize the operations master role.

◆ **Security Account Management.** This option enables you to find and clean up duplicate SIDs when there has been a problem with the RID master and there is a possibility of duplicate SIDs on the network.

◆ **Semantic Database Analysis.** The **files** command deals with the files that make up Active Directory. The semantic database analysis can be used to find problems with the linkages between logical structures. For example, it might find an orphaned user that is part of an OU that no longer exists. These inconsistencies should show up in the lost-and-found container as well.

The utility is very easy to use but does not provide a GUI interface. It is assumed that all these functions will eventually be available through a management interface. However, several of these functions might need to be performed at the recovery console, which is command line, so this utility will remain in place.

In addition to the NTDSUTIL used to examine and manage the Active Directory, there are also several utilities that can be used to monitor domain controllers and the network.

Monitoring a Domain Controller

Several tools can be used to monitor the systems on your network. The following sections examine the Task Manager, Event Viewer, Network Monitor, and Performance tools. Each of the tools has a particular use. Generally, you need to use more than one tool to find and resolve a problem.

Some of the tools are used more than others; most notably, the Task Manager can quickly determine whether more complete monitoring is required. This tool will be examined first.

Task Manager

One of fastest and easiest ways to check your system performance is to use the Task Manager. This tool was primarily meant for you to be able to start, stop, and view the tasks running on your system. In fact, however, Task Manager is also very useful as a troubleshooting tool.

To access the Task Manager, you can do any of the following:

◆ Press Ctrl+Shift+Esc.

◆ Right-click the taskbar and choose Task Manager.

◆ Press Ctrl+Alt+Del and click the Task Manager button.

After the Task Manager has started, you will notice that it has three different tabs: Applications, Processes, and Performance (see Figure 5.23).

Each of the tabs in the Task Manager shows you different information. The Applications tab tells you which applications are loaded and which of them are running. This is where you can end a task that is hung or frozen by selecting the application and clicking the End Task button. The New Task button can be used to start a new application.

The Processes tab enables you to see all the processes running on the system, including the applications and the services that make up Windows 2000. By default, you get the following columns in the Task Manager Processes tab.

◆ **Image Name.** This is the name of the process currently running. This enables multiple instances of the same program to run at the same time under different image names.

◆ **PID.** This is the process ID, which is used by the system to track the processes running within the Windows 2000 kernel.

◆ **CPU.** This is the current percentage of the CPU time being used by the process. This is a quick way to tell which process is hogging the CPU. If you click on a column label, such as CPU, it sorts the list by that column.

◆ **CPU Time.** This is the amount of time a process has spent actually executing.

◆ **Mem Usage.** This is the amount of memory the application is using on the system. This is another good counter if you need to quickly find out why you don't have enough memory or why you are experiencing excessive swapping to disk.

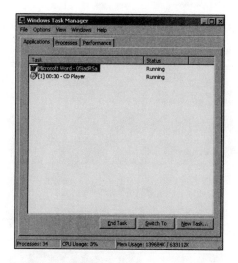

FIGURE 5.23
The Task Manager with Applications tab in front.

NOTE **Busy Applications** There are times when an application is overly busy and shows up as Not Responding. This does not always mean the application has crashed. The Task Manager queries the application to see if it is still responding to the system. There will be times when an application is so busy that it cannot respond to the system. Try waiting a few minutes before killing the application.

In addition to these counters, a number of other counters can be added. To add a counter, use the steps in Step by Step 5.13.

STEP BY STEP

5.13 Adding Columns in the Task Manager

1. In the Task Manager, choose View, Select Columns from the menu.

2. Place a check mark in the box beside the columns you would like to see.

3. Click OK.

There are numerous columns you can add. If you are not sure about the meaning of a column, you can use the Help item on the menu to get details.

The last tab is a quick overview of the performance. This is not meant to be the sole source of performance information; rather, it is a quick look at the status of the system at the current moment. There are six main sections to this tab. These are broken down in the following list:

◆ **CPU Usage.** This shows the current CPU usage and then graphs the usage for the last minute or so, depending on the update frequency you chose. Two options under the View item on the menu affect this area. CPU History refers to the graph where you can choose to have one graph per CPU or one total graph. The other option, Show Kernel Times, adds a second line, in red, to the graph showing Kernel-mode time. This is a quick check on the CPU for the system. If the processor(s) is (are) constantly over 80%, you should look at the Processes tab to see what service is having a problem. If no single process is overloaded, you should consider a system upgrade.

◆ **Mem Usage.** This shows the amount of memory currently in use. This can be a quick guide as to whether a system is over-loaded. If the amount of memory in use is greater than that physically in the system, you need more memory.

◆ **Totals.** This section tells you the total number of handles, threads, and processes.

◆ **Physical Memory (K).** This is the amount of physical memory in the system with a breakdown of the amount available and the amount used for system cache. Ideally, available memory should never drop below 4096K. Generally, the more memory available the better. However, if you find you have more than 65,536K free, you probably have too much memory in the system, or some services didn't start.

◆ **Commit Charge (K).** This is the total amount of memory committed to all the applications running on the system including both the physical RAM and the paging files. The Total is the amount currently committed. If this value is more than the total physical RAM, you might consider more memory for the system. The Limit is the amount of RAM and paging file space available. The Peak is the highest amount of memory committed since the system was last restarted.

◆ **Kernel Memory (K).** This is the memory allocated to kernel functions such as the server service and the RPC subsystem. The Total amount changes as the demands on the system increase. The Paged amount is the amount of memory that could, if required, be paged to disk. The Nonpaged memory is the core of the operating system and varies depending on the drivers installed. If you notice that this amount increases slowly but steadily on a system, you probably have a memory leak. A memory leak occurs when a driver or other program allocates and uses memory but then does not free the memory correctly. Eventually, this causes your system to need to be restarted. You should remove the drivers, one at a time, until you see the leak stop. At that point, you should find a newer version of the driver.

As you can see, the Task Manager is a helpful utility. You can use the Task Manager when you have an application that is acting up. You can also use it to check the status of your system. The limitation of the Task Manager is that it only enables you to see what is happening now. Occasionally, you need to know what has happened previously on the system; for this, you can use the Event Viewer.

Event Viewer

Windows 2000 can start even if there are problems with some services or devices. Although it is frustrating to sit there waiting for the service or device to fail so that the boot can continue, Windows 2000 does enable you to get into the system and fix the problem. After the system has started, you should look in the Event Viewer to determine the cause of the problem.

Parts of the Event Log

Like all the administrative tools in Windows 2000, the Event Viewer is a snap-in to the MMC. This has enabled Microsoft, and will enable other manufacturers, to add its logs to the Event Viewer. The six most common logs you will see are listed here for your reference (see Figure 5.24).

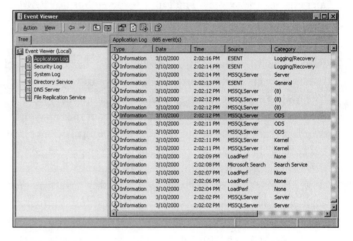

FIGURE 5.24
The Event Viewer is accessed using Programs, Administrative Tools, Event Viewer.

◆ **Applications Log.** Any application written to Microsoft standards has the capability to record information in the applications log. This log often tells you why Exchange Server is not working or the SQL server couldn't start.

◆ **Security Log.** Events that deal with the security of the system are tracked in this log. The information that is logged depends on the settings you select in the group policies. Remember, however, that excessive auditing is likely to affect system performance.

◆ **System Log.** All the device drivers and services as well as other system-related components record their errors in the system log. This is the log to look at when you get the `At least one driver or service has failed to start` message when you start Windows 2000.

◆ **Directory Service.** This is the log that tracks events related to the Active Directory database and its replication.

◆ **DNS Server.** This log tracks events that affect the DNS server. If you are having problems resolving network names or logging on, you should check this log.

◆ **File Replication Service.** This is the service that manages the replication of the files in the SYSVOL. If you find that group policies, or other information contained in the SYSVOL directory, fail to get to all the domain controllers, you should check this log.

It is a good habit to get into checking the event logs on a regular basis. Event logs can often tell you what problems occurred that you weren't aware of and can indicate which errors might occur in the future.

Configuring the Event Logs

The event logs store a good deal of information. The more services and applications on a system and the more auditing you require, the larger the amount of information you receive. To prevent the event logs from filling up, which can cause other problems, you should configure the logs to the size you think will be required. This ensures that the log information will be there when you need it. Step by Step 5.14 shows you how to configure the event log settings.

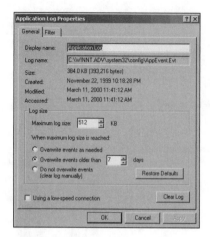

FIGURE 5.25
The General tab of the Application Log
Properties dialog box.

STEP BY STEP

5.14 Configuring Event Log Settings

1. Open the Event Viewer.

2. Right-click the log to configure and choose Properties (see Figure 5.25). Each property is individually configured.

3. On the General tab, configure the desired log options. The following is a list of the options you can set:

- **Display Name.** This is the name that will appear in the list.

- **Maximum Log Size.** This is the largest size to which the log can grow, set in kilobytes.

- **When Maximum Log Size Is Reached.** This tells the system what to do when the maximum size is reached. The choices are to overwrite events starting with the oldest, to overwrite only events older than a given number of days, or to not overwrite. Be aware that, with either the second or the third choice, actions could be performed on the server without being logged. For most of the logs, overwriting as needed is probably the best choice. The security log, though, should not have this setting. You can configure the server to crash on audit fail. This configuration prevents unlogged activity on the server.

- **Restore Defaults.** This restores the default log settings.

- **Clear Log.** This clears the log. You are asked whether you want to save the information first.

- **Using a Low-Speed Connection.** This is so you can let the system know you are connecting to the remote system using a slow connection.

4. Click OK to set the values.

Because the event logs are recorded separately at each of the computers in your network, you need to set these options for each computer in your network. This can be done either by going to each system or by connecting to them over the network.

Connecting to a Remote System

You can view and configure the logs on a remote system by using your Event Viewer to connect to the event logs on the remote system. This is done using the steps shown in Step by Step 5.15.

STEP BY STEP

5.15 Viewing the Event Log on a Remote Server

1. Open the Event Viewer and right-click the Event Viewer folder.

2. On the context menu, choose Connect to Another Computer.

3. In the Select Computer dialog box, either select Local Computer or select Another Computer and enter the name of the computer.

4. Click OK.

This enables you to check the status for remote systems without having to physically visit the system. This can be very useful if your clients are running Windows 2000 Professional because you can troubleshoot problems remotely using the event log.

Using the Event Log

The event log records all the activity on a system. Errors, along with the normal activity of a system, are recorded. Each type of event recorded in the event log is marked by an icon that makes it easier to quickly find problems. There are five icons you will see.

Information. This is not a critical event but rather just an occurrence that took place. An informational message can be useful when you are making sure processes are running correctly.

 Warning. This is a warning that something didn't work correctly. The error didn't stop the process; however, you should check the process. There is some kind of problem.

 Error. This is a critical error and indicates that the process was not able to continue because of the error. Some processes continue to retry forever, filling the log with these critical errors.

 Failure. This indicates that someone was trying to perform an action for which he or she was not given permissions. This only occurs in the security log and should be checked.

 Success. This indicates that an action was attempted and the user had the correct permissions to perform the action. This is generally a good sign. However, you can use this information to track down people who have managed to break in to your system.

In most cases, you can ignore the informational messages. The key issues are the Failure audits in the security log. These should be checked immediately because they indicate that someone is attempting to do something for which he has not been specifically granted permission.

In the other logs, you need to look at both the Warnings and the Errors. Normally, people start at the top of the log and move down when they first start to work with the event logs. The trick, however, is to find out where the errors start and then work up the log. Look at events from oldest to newest. This enables you to see the progression of the problem.

When you find the first or earliest event in the sequence that led to the failure, you should view the details of the event.

Viewing Event Details

Viewing the event details gives you more information about the event and sometimes even some usable data. All you need to do to view an event is double-click it (see Figure 5.26).

The Event Properties dialog box is divided into four main sections. The information at the top identifies the error and its source. There are three buttons that enable you to move about in the event log. The dialog box also contains the event Description and Data sections.

The section contains the following pieces of information:

◆ **Date.** The date of the event.

◆ **Time.** The time the event occurred.

◆ **Type.** The type of error (for example, Information, Warning, Error).

◆ **User.** The name of the user causing the error or running the process that caused the error.

◆ **Computer.** The name of the computer where the event occurred.

◆ **Source.** The process, a program or service, that reported the event.

◆ **Category.** Some services have several components to them, and this helps identify which part of the service had the problem.

◆ **Event ID.** The number you look up in TechNet. This is the internal number from the service that describes this event.

The buttons that enable you to move about in the event log include an up arrow. This enables you to move up the event log, or forward in time, by default. This option is good for following the sequence of events. The down arrow does the opposite. The other button enables you to copy the event to the clipboard so you can paste it into another application such as email.

The description is supposed to help you understand what the error is, and Microsoft has come a long way in making these useful in Windows 2000. Occasionally, you still need to refer to other sources, such as TechNet for the Microsoft Web site, for the more cryptic messages.

The data is occasionally useful and can be displayed either as bytes or as words. Displaying it as bytes is best because this gives you

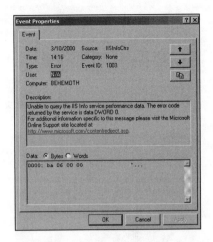

FIGURE 5.26
The details of an event.

readable characters on the right side. Displaying the message as words (16 bits of data makes a word) rarely ever gives you any useful information.

The process of going through the entire event log can take some time. To cut down the time required, you can filter the information listed in the log.

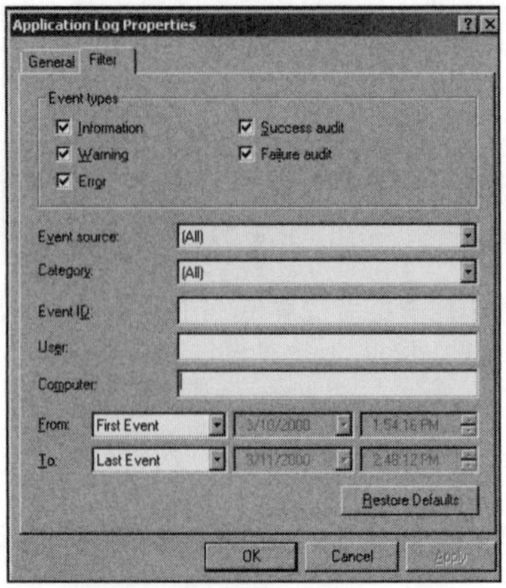

Filtering

There can be thousands of events listed in the event logs. To simplify the job of finding the problem, you can filter the log. Follow the steps shown in Step by Step 5.16 to filter a log.

FIGURE 5.27
The Filter tab of the Applications Log Properties dialog box.

STEP BY STEP

5.16 Filtering an Event Log

1. Open the Event Viewer.

2. Right-click the log you want to filter and choose Properties.

3. Click the Filter tab and choose the types of events you want to see (see Figure 5.27).

4. Click OK to apply the filter.

Filtering is one way to change the view of the events in the log. Other view options also are available, as discussed in the following section.

View Options

In addition to filtering the events, you can also use the View item from the context menu (see Figure 5.28) to affect how the information is listed.

NOTE
Status Bar You can tell whether a filter is applied by looking at the status bar above the list of events. To turn the filter off, go back to the Filter tab and click the Restore Defaults button.

The following options are available:

◆ **Choose Columns.** This enables you to choose which columns you see in the detail pane. By default, all the columns are shown.

◆ **All Records.** This turns off a filter if one is applied.

◆ **Filter.** This is another way to get to the data-filtering settings.

◆ **Newest First.** This lists the records from newest to oldest.

◆ **Oldest First.** This is the opposite of Newest First. Records are listed from oldest to newest.

◆ **Find.** This brings up a dialog box similar to the Filter dialog box. The difference is Find takes you to the next record, up or down, matching your entry.

◆ **Customize.** This enables you to customize your view of the Microsoft Management Console.

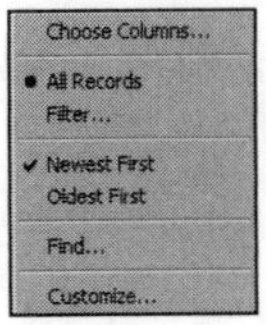

Now that you have seen most of the options that enable you to customize the view of the event logs, this section concludes with a quick look at saving and loading the log files.

Archiving Logs

In some cases, you might want to archive the event logs to review them at a later time. You might want to pass them through a custom application to look for problems. Saving and loading an event log is done from the context menu, as shown in Step by Step 5.17.

FIGURE 5.28
The View menu within the context menu. You need to click the log first to set the focus and then right-click.

STEP BY STEP

5.17 Saving and Retrieving Event Log Information

1. Open the Event Viewer.

2. Right-click the log with which you want to work.

3. Choose one of the following options:

   • **Open Log File.** This enables you to open a saved log file and view the contents.

continues

continued

- **Save Log File As.** This enables you to save the log file. You have the choice of Event log file, Text file, or Comma separated file.

- **New Log File.** This stops recording to the current log file and starts a new log file.

- **Clear All Events.** This clears the log file. You will be asked if you want to save the events, but the log is cleared.

Using these steps, you can keep track of the events from a system over a period of time and review them at a later date.

The Event Viewer is an important tool because it enables you to see what happened on the computer. It does not, however, enable you to track what is happening on the network. For this, you need to use the Network Monitor, one of the key diagnostic tools shipped with Windows 2000.

Network Monitor

Although a full discussion of the Network Monitor would be interesting, it is beyond the scope of this book. You are strongly encouraged to delve into the Network Monitor, however, so you can understand how to troubleshoot not only the local system but also the network to which it is attached.

As you prepare for the 70-217 exam, you need to know the function of the Network Monitor.

When a packet is sent on a broadcast-based network, such as Ethernet or Token Ring, the packet is received at every card on the subnet. Normally, the packet is evaluated, and the destination address is checked to see if it is a full broadcast or is intended for the local machine. If the packet is not destined to one of these addresses, it is discarded.

Network Monitor tells the card to enter promiscuous mode. The card begins grabbing all the packets on the network and storing them for analysis (see Figure 5.29).

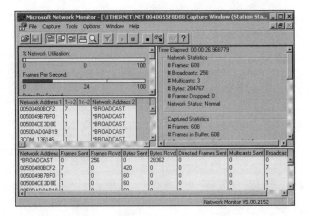

FIGURE 5.29
The Network Monitor capturing data.

The Network Monitor summarizes the data and reports the various
protocols on the network, the sessions between computers. It can
also enable you to actually see the traffic in a useful format (see
Figure 5.30) in which it has interpreted all the codes from the
network into understandable terms.

FIGURE 5.30
The view of the data that crossed the network while the capture ran.

You can even zoom in on the information and look at the different layers (see Figure 5.31).

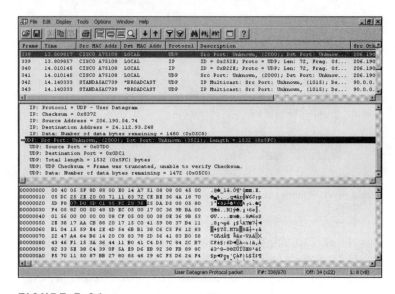

FIGURE 5.31
Looking at a packet of data in detail.

The Network Monitor enables you to see the information floating around on your network. This can be useful if you are having problems finding computers. You can see what the DNS query is and where it is going. If you can't authenticate, you can look at the session and authentication handshake. These are only two examples of what you can look for when using Network Monitor.

The Network Monitor enables you to see what is happening on the network. This might not help if the problem is the computer you are trying the fix. Therefore, Microsoft included the Performance tool, the other key diagnostic tool included in Windows 2000.

Performance

A full discussion of the Performance tool falls well beyond the scope of this book. As you prepare for the 70-217 exam, however, you need to know the purpose and use of the Performance tool.

There are, in fact, two parts to the Performance tool. There is the System Monitor, which enables you to graphically view the current activity or logged activity on a server. This enables you to see trends over a period of time and can give you up-to-the-minute information about your system.

The other portion of the Performance tool is Performance Logs and Alerts, which enables you to create log files of the activity on a server or to configure alerts that will fire when certain thresholds are reached. You can use these tools to help you in several different tasks.

◆ Profile the services running on a computer to let you know how many users it can support and what resources are left for other services. This can be used to optimize the services used on domain controllers.

◆ You can use Performance to create a baseline of the performance of a system. That way, when you make changes in an attempt to increase the performance, you can compare current performance with baseline performance to judge the net effect.

◆ Maintain the level of service by monitoring the performance and tuning the system by adding, or removing, resources as the usage on the system changes.

You can draw a parallel here between the Network Monitor and Performance. What Network Monitor does for you on the network, Performance does for you on the computer.

Objects

Performance works by reading various performance counters. All the Microsoft services have built-in counters that Performance reads. The values that are read can be graphed, logged, or checked against an alert.

The source of the counter, the service that the counter is built in to, is known from the Performance point-of-view as a Performance object. For example, the processor is a Performance object exposed by the kernel, and server is a Performance object exposed by the server service.

Each object has different counters you can read. There are some counters that most objects have such as the % Processor Time.

There are also counters specific to the object. For example, the Processor object has an Interrupts/Sec counter, and the Server object has a Logon/Sec counter.

In addition to choosing the object and the counter for the object, you also can choose which instance of the object you want to examine. This is required because you can have more than one instance of an object available. For example, you could run two copies of the same program, or more likely, you could have two or more physical disks in a computer.

The Performance tool is broken down into two main pieces: the System Monitor and the Performance Logs and Alerts. The System Monitor is where you do the analysis and look at the data that the computer is generating or that you captured previously.

System Monitor

System Monitor is used to analyze the data you collect. The information for the System Monitor can come from the live system or can be read from a log file. From the live system, you can select any available object to monitor and can add whatever counters you want for the instance you want to examine.

In addition, you can specify the update frequency when looking at live data or the time window you want to view for recorded logs.

The other part of the Performance tool is the capability to log the counters on the system so you can later look at them in the System Monitor. It can also be used to set up alerts that fire when certain counters for a specific instance of a performance object fall below or rise above a given value.

Performance Logs and Alerts

Performance logs record the same information that you graph in the System Monitor. In fact, the data is viewed using that tool. Counter logs can be created to record any of the objects and counters available and can be scheduled to start and stop recording at given times. You also need to specify an update frequency for the log files.

There is also a trace log you can create. This log tracks information about the starting and stopping of processes, or threads, or tracks disk I/O.

> **WARNING**
>
> **Update Frequency** Using a small update frequency—that is, many updates—affects system performance and causes the log to grow quickly, possibly filling the disk.

Alerts are the other part of Performance. Alerts enable you to configure a threshold value for a counter and have the system take an action when the value is exceeded (above or below). The specified action can be to send a network alert, start a counter log, or run a program.

Performance is the tool you use to determine the number of users a server can handle or to determine the source of a performance bottleneck.

You have now had a chance to see the main tools used for monitoring a domain controller or aspects of a domain controller. Several other tools are used to look at specific parts of Windows 2000 and Active Directory.

Other Troubleshooting Tools

In addition to the tools previously discussed, several others tools are part of the Resource Kit. The setup for these tools is found in the \SUPPORT\TOOLS folder on the Windows 2000 CD. Not all the tools are related to Active Directory, but you should be aware of the following ones:

- ◆ **ACLDiag.** This utility enables you to determine whether a user has been given access to a directory object. It can also be used to reset access control lists to their default state.

- ◆ **ADSIEdit.** This MMC snap-in enables you to view all objects in the directory and to modify the objects or set access control lists on them.

- ◆ **DNSCMD.** This utility checks the dynamic registration of DNS resource records.

- ◆ **DOMMAP.** This utility checks the replication topology and domain relationships.

- ◆ **DSACLS.** This enables you to check and edit the access control list on directory objects.

- ◆ **DSAStat.** This compares the information on domain controllers, looking for differences.

◆ **ESEUtil.** This utility works on the extensible storage engine and can repair, check, compact, move, and dump database files. The NTDSUtil calls these functions to perform various tasks.

◆ **NETDOM5.** This utility handles the batch management of trusts, joining computers to domains and verifying trusts and secure channels.

◆ **NETTest.** This utility can check end-to-end network connectivity as well as distributed services functions.

◆ **NLTest.** This program makes sure the locator service and secure channel are functioning.

◆ **NTDSUtil.** In addition to managing operations masters and allowing authoritative restores, this utility manages the database files using ESEUtil and lists site, domain, and server information.

◆ **REPAdmin.** This checks replication consistency between replication partners, monitors replication status, displays replication metadata, and forces replication events and Knowledge Consistency Checker recalculation.

◆ **REPLMon.** This program displays replication topology, monitors replication status, and can force replication events and Knowledge Consistency Checker recalculation.

◆ **SDCheck.** This tool enables an administrator to determine whether access control lists are being correctly inherited and whether access control list changes are being replicated from one domain controller to another.

◆ **SIDWalker.** This utility enables you to set the ACL on objects owned by accounts that have been moved, deleted, or orphaned.

These tools can be used after you determine where the problem lies to pinpoint the problem and to help you fix it. You should be familiar with the name and purpose of each of these tools for the exam. If you have time, you should also try each of the tools to have a feel for them.

The monitoring of servers is important for being able to fix problems before they occur. The tools you have just seen all have a place and time when they should be employed, and you should make sure you understand the use for each.

CASE STUDY: MONITORING AND MANAGING ACTIVE DIRECTORY

ESSENCE OF THE CASE

Looking back at the Sunshine Brewing company, you will remember that there are a number of locations you need to deal with and five different domains that span all the locations. This makes the recovery more difficult because you need to be able to recover any domain from any location. Some of the other factors to consider are listed here.

▶ There are few changes to the Active Directory, and although users might move from location to location, they will typically stay in the same line of work and therefore the same domain.

▶ You will need to have a global catalog server per site. There will be a large number of sites.

▶ For recoverability, you will control the operation masters in Ottawa.

▶ You will schedule all backups to happen automatically.

With all this in mind, there isn't a lot that requires analysis in this case.

SCENARIO

This case study deals with preparing for recovery. This is something that should be planned well in advance and should include where to get parts or other servers. You should also plan for locating servers in case the computer room is not available. Your plan should also deal with emergency power.

This case, however, deals specifically with the placement of servers and how the backup strategy will be planned.

ANALYSIS

To facilitate the operations master, a pair of domain controllers will be located in Ottawa, and a connection object will be created between them to make sure they are replication partners. One of these servers will be configured as the schema and domain naming master, and the other will be just a domain controller. For the domain-level operations masters, a similar pairing will be created in the Ottawa office for each of the domains.

In the Ottawa office, backups will be taken weekly with a differential taken each night for the servers configured as the operations master and backup. These backups will be kept for four weeks and then rotated back through the backups. There will also be monthly, quarterly, and yearly backups. The monthly backups will be kept on site until the next monthly backup, at which time they will be stored off site for 15 years.

CHAPTER SUMMARY

KEY TERMS

- Authoritative restore
- Backup
- Event Viewer
- Global catalog server
- Infrastructure master
- Network Monitor
- NTDSUTIL
- Operation masters
- PDC emulator
- Performance
- Restore
- RID master
- System state data
- Task Manager

This chapter looked at server roles including the two enterprise roles: schema master and domain naming master. It also looked at the three master roles found in each domain: the PDC emulator, the RID master, and the infrastructure master. You saw what purpose each role served and how to move the role to another server or seize the role when the server crash is unrecoverable.

Next you looked at the backup and restore options available in Windows 2000. The basics of backups—the different types and their uses—were discussed, and the Backup program was introduced. The restore process for servers that had other services was examined. You also learned how to reinstall basic servers. The discussion then covered the authoritative restore process and the requirements associated with this process.

Finally, you were introduced to some of the monitoring/troubleshooting tools available. These tools take a lot of practice, and you should work with them for a period of time before attempting the exam.

APPLY YOUR KNOWLEDGE

Exercises

5.1 Working with Server Roles

In this exercise, you will move the enterprise-level operations masters from one server to another. This exercise assumes you have two Windows 2000 servers or advanced servers installed and promoted to domain controllers in the same domain.

Estimated time: 10 minutes.

1. Log on to the second domain controller as the Administrator.

2. Locate your source files directory. This will be the CD you used to install, if you didn't copy the i386 directory to the hard disk for the installation.

3. Open Windows Explorer and locate the file ADMINPAK.MSI. Right-click the file and choose Install.

4. When the wizard appears, click Next to bypass the introductory screen.

5. On the next screen, choose Install All of the Administrative Tools and click Next.

6. When the installation finishes, click Finish.

7. Close Windows Explorer and then, from the Start menu, choose Run and enter MMC. Press Enter.

8. Choose Console, Add/Remove Snap-in from the menu.

9. In the Add/Remove Snap-in dialog box, click Add, locate Active Directory Schema, and then click Add.

10. Click Close to close the list of snap-ins and then click OK to close the Add/Remove Snap-in dialog box.

11. Right-click Active Directory Schema and, from the context menu, choose Change Domain Controller.

12. Click on Specific Name and enter the name of the second domain controller. Click OK.

13. Right-click Active Directory Schema again and choose Operation Master from the context menu.

14. Verify that the Current Focus and The Server Is Currently entries refer to two different servers. If they do not, go back to step 11 and enter the name of the other server.

15. Click Change.

16. Close the MMC. When prompted to save changes, click No.

17. Open Active Directory Domains and Trusts from the Administrative Tools menu.

18. Right-click Active Directory Domains and Trusts and choose Connect to Domain Controller.

19. Click the Browse button and choose your domain. From the list of servers, choose the one to which you have transferred the schema master role.

20. Right-click Active Directory Domains and Trusts again and choose Operations Master.

21. Verify that the server names are different in the Change dialog box. If they are not, go back to step 18 and choose another server.

22. Click Change.

23. Close Active Directory Domains and Trusts.

APPLY YOUR KNOWLEDGE

5.2   Backing Up System State Data

This exercise requires two computers. One of the computers will be used as the location to back up to, and the other will be backed up.

Estimated time: 15 minutes.

1. Log on to the system that will be used to hold the backup.

2. On that system, create a directory called Backup and share the directory.

3. Log on to the system you will back up as Administrator.

4. Right-click My Network Places and choose Map Network Drive from the context menu.

5. Choose drive O: and enter **\\your_other_servers _name\Backup** as the destination.

6. Open Active Directory Users and Computers.

7. Right-click your domain and choose New, Organizational Unit. Enter **Testit** and the name and click OK.

8. Expand your domain and right-click the Testit organizational unit. Choose New, User. Use the name David Smith with a username of Dsmith. Click Next.

9. On the password screen, click Next to accept the defaults and then click Finish.

10. Close Active Directory Users and Computers.

11. Choose Start, Programs, Accessories, System Tools, Backup to start the Backup program.

12. Click the Backup Wizard button; click Next to bypass the introduction screen.

13. On the What to Backup page, choose Only Back Up System State Data.

14. On the Where to Store the Backup page, enter **O:\State.bkf** and click Next.

15. On the Completing Backup Wizard screen, choose Finish.

16. When the backup completes, click Close and then close the Backup program.

5.3   Restoring a Domain Controller

In this exercise, you will restore the domain controller you backed up in Exercise 5.2. Before you restore the domain controller, you will add a user to the domain.

Estimated time: 15 minutes.

1. Open Active Directory Users and Computers.

2. On the Users folder, right-click and choose New, User from the context menu.

3. Enter **John White** as the name and **JWhite** as the username and then click Next.

4. Accept the defaults for the password information by clicking Next and then click Finish.

5. Wait for six minutes. This will ensure the replication has taken place.

6. Restart the computer you backed up.

7. When the boot menu appears, choose the operating system. As the Starting Windows message appears, press F8 to enter advanced startup options.

8. Choose Directory Services Restore Mode.

9. When prompted, press Ctrl+Alt+Del and log on as Administrator.

APPLY YOUR KNOWLEDGE

10. Click OK to close the message that warns you that the server is in safe mode.

11. Start the Backup program.

12. Click the Restore Wizard button.

13. Click Next to bypass the first screen.

14. Expand the File item in the left pane and choose the last backup. (This should be the backup you created in Exercise 5.2.) After the backup is selected (has a check mark), click Next to continue.

15. On the Completing the Restore Wizard page, click Finish to restore. If the system asks you to confirm the filename to restore, verify that it is correct and click OK.

16. When the restore is complete, click Close to close the dialog box and then close the Backup program.

17. When prompted, restart the computer.

18. When the system has restarted, log on as Administrator.

19. Open Active Directory Users and Computers.

20. Click the Users folder and look for John White. If he does not appear, wait a few minutes and then right-click the Users folders and choose Refresh.

5.4 Performing an Authoritative Restore

In this exercise, you will perform an authoritative restore for the domain controller you backed up in Exercise 5.3. In this case, you will recover the Testit organizational unit from an accidental deletion.

Estimated time: 25 minutes.

1. Open Active Directory Users and Computers.

2. On the Testit folder, right-click and choose Delete.

3. You will receive a warning dialog box that Testit is a container. The warning will ask if you're sure you want to delete it and all the objects it contains. Click Yes.

4. Wait for six minutes. This will ensure the replication has taken place.

6. Restart the computer you backed up.

7. When the boot menu appears, choose the operating system. As the Starting Windows message appears, press F8 to enter advanced startup options.

8. Choose Directory Services Restore Mode.

9. When prompted, press Ctrl+Alt+Del and log on as Administrator.

10. Click OK to close the message that warns you that the server is in safe mode.

11. Start the Backup program.

12. Click the Restore Wizard button.

13. Click Next to bypass the first screen.

14. Expand the File item in the left pane and choose the last backup. After the backup is selected (has a check mark), click Next to continue.

15. On the Completing the Restore Wizard page, click Finish to restore. If the system asks you to confirm the filename to restore, verify that it is correct and click OK.

16. When the restore is complete, click Close to close the dialog box and then close the Backup program.

APPLY YOUR KNOWLEDGE

17. When prompted, do not restart the computer.

18. Start a command prompt and enter **ntdsutil**.

19. At the NTDSUTIL prompt, enter **authoritative restore** and press Enter.

20. Enter **restore subtree** and the full name of the organizational unit you deleted earlier. For example, if your domain was ODIN.COM, you would enter dc=com,dc=odin,cn=Testit.

21. A dialog box asks whether you're sure you want to restore the object. Click Yes.

22. After the restore finishes, type **quit** to exit Restore mode, and then type **quit** again to exit NTDSUTIL.

23. Restart the computer.

24. When the system has restarted, log on as Administrator.

25. Open Active Directory Users and Computers.

26. Verify that the Testit organizational unit is back.

Review Questions

1. What is the role of domain naming master?

2. What must you restore before restoring an incremental backup?

3. You need to determine the number of users that a new type of server can handle. Which tool should you use?

4. What are the two components that make up the SID of an object in Active Directory?

5. What utility do you use to grab the schema master role if it has failed?

6. You have a server that cannot find other servers on the network. What tool can you use to determine what queries it is sending?

7. You have had to seize the schema master role. What precaution should you take with the server it has replaced?

8. When you start your computer, you get a message indicating that a service or device failed to start. What should you do to determine the cause of the problem?

9. You need to restore an organizational unit that was accidentally deleted. What must you do?

10. If you need to seize a role, what should you consider when choosing the server on which to place the role?

Exam Questions

1. Jon is attempting to promote a computer to be the first domain controller in a new child domain. Everything is going fine. When he enters the domain name, however, the system hangs.

   He retries the operation two more times after verifying that all the settings are correct, and he has the correct permissions. What should Jon do?

   A. Check to see if the infrastructure master is offline.

   B. Check to see if the DNS server is down.

   C. Check to see if the domain naming master is offline.

   D. None of the above.

APPLY YOUR KNOWLEDGE

2. Francóis is adding users to a domain. After adding the first 117 new users to the domain, he can add no more users. Why?

   A. The PDC emulator is not available.

   B. The domain he is adding to has the maximum 10,000 users.

   C. The DNS server is not able to register the new users.

   D. The RID master is offline.

3. Diane is on the help desk when a user calls. The user cannot change his network password. The user is on an old Windows 95 computer. Diane verifies the user's name and resets his password for him. He is still unable to change his password. What should Diane check next?

   A. She should make sure the user has a DNS entry in his TCP/IP configuration.

   B. She should make sure he has a valid TCP/IP address.

   C. She should make sure the PDC emulator is online.

   D. She should verify that file replication is running.

4. Bubba is working on a server that has been responding slowly lately. He attempts to tune the TCP window size and the SRTT values. He sets a working set size for one of the applications and tweaks a few other values. He thinks the server is running faster, but the users are still complaining; some are even saying it is worse.

   What should Bubba have done before he started tuning the TCP window size and the SRTT values to able to determine whether the performance is better or worse?

   A. He should have used a stopwatch to time several different applications running on the computer he was tuning. The times can be used to calculate the time each application took before and after the changes.

   B. He should have used the Network Monitor to determine the throughput of the server.

   C. He should have used a stopwatch to time several different applications running on a computer connected to the computer he was tuning. The times can be used to calculate the time each application took before and after the changes.

   D. He should have created a baseline using Performance and then compared it to the running values after the changes.

5. Which of the following are possible ways to recover a domain controller that has failed?

   A. Reinstall Windows 2000 and promote the domain controller.

   B. Reinstall Windows 2000 and restore the last backup.

   C. Reinstall Windows 2000 and perform an authoritative restore

   D. All of the above.

6. Which of the following are valid options for the Backup program when performing a backup? (Choose all that apply.)

   A. Verify After Backup.

   B. Use Software Compression.

   C. Allow User Access to Backup.

   D. Allow Only Owner and Administrators Access to the Backup.

APPLY YOUR KNOWLEDGE

7. Amanda is setting up the first domain controllers for her organization. She has set up four domain controllers so far. Suddenly, Amanda remembers that she needs to make changes to the schema for the customer. She adds the Active Directory Schema snap-in and attempts to change the schema. She is unable to change the schema. What is the likely cause?

   A. She does not have permissions.

   B. She cannot find the schema master.

   C. The schema can only be modified before other servers are added.

   D. This must be done interactively at the system that is the schema master.

8. Bobby has set up a backup schedule for the servers and is configuring the servers to perform backups. He configures the servers to do a full backup Sunday at 1 a.m. Further, he configures the servers to perform a differential backup Monday, Tuesday, Wednesday, Thursday, and Friday nights at 1 a.m.

   On Thursday at 2 p.m., a server that Bobby has configured this way goes down. What must he do to restore the server?

   A. He needs to restore the full backup and then the differential from Wednesday night.

   B. He needs to restore the full backup and then the differentials from Monday, Tuesday, and Wednesday.

   C. He needs to restore the differential from Wednesday night.

   D. He needs to restore the differentials from Monday, Tuesday, and Wednesday.

9. Bill is attempting to perform a restore on a domain controller he has just finished repairing. The repair involved replacing the drive that contained the SYSVOL directory. The drive is tested and is now formatted NTFS. Bill runs the Backup program and attempts to restore the domain controller. He receives an error. What is wrong?

   A. The drive is not using the same letter.

   B. The drive is not formatted using NTFS.

   C. The system needs to be restarted because the drive was formatted.

   D. The system needs to be restarted and started in the right mode.

10. What functions can you perform using NTDSUTIL? (Choose all that apply.)

    A. Change server roles.

    B. Change the backup options.

    C. Change update number of an object in Active Directory.

    D. Change permissions on an object in Active Directory.

11. Joanne works for a company with a multidomain network. Currently, she is creating new groups that will be used for a project that runs on SQL Server. She creates the groups and then adds the users. When she returns from lunch, Joanne notices that the users are no longer in the groups. What could the problem be?

    A. She does not have permissions to manage the users.

    B. The infrastructure master is not online.

APPLY YOUR KNOWLEDGE

C. She added the users to the wrong domain.

D. The groups have not replicated at the point she added the users.

12. Bobby has set up a backup schedule for the servers and is configuring the servers to perform backups. He configures the servers to do a full backup Sunday at 1 a.m. Further, he configures the servers to perform a differential backup Monday, Tuesday, Wednesday, Thursday, and Friday nights at 1 a.m.

    On Friday at 10 a.m., a server that Bobby has configured this way goes down. How much data is lost?

    A. Everything since the full backup

    B. Everything since the Tuesday differential

    C. Everything since the Wednesday differential

    D. None of the above

13. Which of the following utilities can you use to change the permissions on objects in Active Directory? (Choose all the apply.)

    A. NTDSUTIL

    B. ACLDiag

    C. DSACLS

    D. DSAStat

14. Frank is working on a connectivity problem and needs to be able to view the packets on the network. What should he do?

    A. Use Event Viewer.

    B. Use Performance.

    C. Use Network Monitor.

    D. Use NETSTAT.

15. Erin is attempting to connect to a resource in the HR domain. She is in the Sales domain and needs to access the HR resource to complete her overtime claim. When she calls the help desk, Mia verifies that she is a valid user and that she is properly logged on. Mia also verifies that Erin has permissions. Mia attempts to connect to the resource from her domain (Administration). She is also unable to connect. What should she check next?

    A. She should make sure the domain naming master is online.

    B. She should make sure the schema master is online.

    C. She should make sure the PDC emulator is online in the HR domain.

    D. She should make sure the infrastructure master is online in the Sales domain.

Answers to Review Questions

1. The domain naming master is responsible for the addition and removal of domains within the entire enterprise. Therefore, there is only one in the enterprise. This server ensures the uniqueness of the domain name and that it fits within the enterprise namespace. See the section "Server Roles."

2. To restore an incremental backup, you first need to restore the last full backup before the incremental. You also need to restore all the incremental backups that were performed in order. See the section "Backup Types."

APPLY YOUR KNOWLEDGE

3. In this case, you should use the Performance tool. This will enable you to profile the services that the server will run so you can determine how much load each service will place on the server. This information will enable you to estimate the number of users that the server can handle. See the section "Monitoring a Domain Controller."

4. The SID of an object is made up of the domain SID followed by a relative identifier supplied to the domain controller in batches from the RID master. See the section "Server Roles."

5. If you need to seize a role, you should use NTDSUTIL. This tool forcibly takes the role, even if the original server is not available. In most cases, you should make sure the previous server is never returned to service because this would place two of the same operations masters on the network. See the section "Recovering from a Master Failure."

6. In this case, you would use the Network Monitor to enable you to see the actual queries being sent and the responses, if any, from the other servers. See the section "Monitoring a Domain Controller."

7. After seizing the schema master role, you must make sure the previous server is never returned to the network because this would place two schema masters on the same network. See the section "Recovering from a Master Failure."

8. Whenever you get this message, the first place you should look is the Event Viewer. The event log should contain details about the error that occurred during startup. Remember to find a time before the error occurred and work your way forward in time. See the section "Monitoring a Domain Controller."

9. If you need to restore an Active Directory object that has been deleted, you need to perform an authoritative restore. This increases the change number on the object to one sufficiently high enough to force the object to replicate back to the other servers. See the section "Performing an Authoritative Restore."

10. The best server is a server that is on the same subnet as the previous server. This way, you can be assured that the server had the most up-to-date information possible. Failing this, you should check the Sites and Services to determine the replication partners for the server and then choose one of these. See the section "Recovering from a Master Failure."

Answers to Exam Questions

1. **C.** If you add a new domain to an existing domain tree, you need to be able to validate your name with the domain naming master. Answer A is incorrect because the new server will be the infrastructure master for its domain because this is a domain-level server. Answer B is incorrect because the DNS is required; however, the server would have given that as the error. Because answer C is correct, answer D is incorrect. See the section "Server Roles."

2. **D.** The PDC emulator receives priority replication. If it is not available, however, you can still add users, making answer A incorrect. There is no practical limit to the number of objects in a domain, so answer B is incorrect. Answer C is incorrect because users do not register with the DNS server. This means answer D must be

APPLY YOUR KNOWLEDGE

correct. If there are no relative identifiers, a server cannot add more objects. There is no way to create a SID. See the section "Server Roles."

3. **C.** In this case, the user was able to log on. Answers A and B, although possible, are not likely. Because this is an Active Directory exam, you can assume that if it worked yesterday, the problem is not a network problem. Because file replication is not required for logons, answer D can be ruled out here. Answer D could be valid if mandatory profiles had been mentioned. This leaves answer C, and because this is Windows 95, which is not an Active Directory client by default, it makes sense. The client computer requires a PDC to change passwords. See the section "Server Roles."

4. **D.** Bubba is playing with a lot of things that we haven't and won't discuss. This information is obviously useless except to tell you that Bubba needs more work and should stop playing in the registry. You will find that Microsoft does put a lot of irrelevant information in its questions, and you should be prepared to wade through it. Answers A and C involve a stopwatch and are, therefore, only measuring one aspect of the performance. This could be an indication but is neither accurate nor conclusive. Answer B is great if you are concerned about what exactly is going in and out of the network. However, quantitative measurement of network traffic is better handled along with memory, disk access, and CPU usage by the Performance tool. See the section "Monitoring a Domain Controller."

5. **A, B.** Both A and B recover a domain controller. Answer C describes how you can recover an object in Active Directory that was deleted. Answer D is incorrect because answer C

is incorrect. You will see questions like this in which you need to understand what the writer (me) was going for. Make sure you always read the question very carefully. See the section "Backing Up and Restoring Servers."

6. **A, D.** Answer B is incorrect, although you could confuse it with the capability to use hardware compression, and this is obviously what the question's writer (me) was going for. Answer C is incorrect because users are not allowed to do backup or restore operations. Answers A and D are both valid options. See the section "Backing Up and Restoring Servers."

7. **B.** In this case, you can assume that the person who installed all four domain controllers has the administrator password. The schema can be modified at any time, so answer C is incorrect. Answer D might seem like it makes sense because of the importance of the schema; however, this would not allow for remote administration, and nearly everything from Microsoft can be remotely managed. This leaves B, which, again, makes sense. See the section "Server Roles."

8. **A.** When you restore data, you always start with a full backup and then proceed to restore a series of incremental backups in order to a single differential. Answers C and D don't include the full backup. Answer B restores backups that do not need to be restored. See the section "Backing Up and Restoring Servers."

9. **D.** Whenever you attempt to restore a domain controller, you need to be in directory services Restore mode so that the SYSVOL directory is accessible. The drive letter should be the same but could actually be different, meaning answer A is incorrect. The question states that the drive

APPLY YOUR KNOWLEDGE

is NTFS. Answer B is incorrect. This does happen in exams (notably betas). You may encounter a case in which you don't have enough information. If you run across this, you basically have to guess. Normally, if there is an obvious answer, go for it and ignore the inconsistency. Answer C hasn't been true for a long time; you can partition and format a driver without having to restart the computer. See the section "Backing Up and Restoring Servers."

10. **A, C.** In this case, you have a simple question. Sometimes you get them. NTDSUTIL can change the Update Sequence Number of an object. This is how an authoritative restore works. It can also change, as well as seize, operations master roles. The Backup program works with backups, meaning answer B is incorrect. The utility to change permissions is DSACLS (or Directory Service Access Control Lists Setting), meaning answer D is incorrect. See the section "The NTDSUTIL Command."

11. **B.** If she didn't have permissions, she could not have moved them in the first place. Therefore, answer A is incorrect. Even if she had added the users, they would still be in the group if she had added them across a trust. Therefore, answer C is incorrect. Creating objects causes an immediate replication. Also, if she saw the group to add the users to it, it was obviously available. Therefore, answer D is incorrect. This leaves the infrastructure master, which is responsible for the mapping of users to groups. See the section "Server Roles."

12. **C.** In this case, there is no incremental backup, so answer B is out. The differentials are available, so answer C is the last backup and, therefore, where the data loss starts. If you lost everything back to the full backup, then differentials would be pointless. Therefore, answer A is out. Because C is correct, answer D cannot be correct. See the section "Backing Up and Restoring Servers."

13. **B, C.** NTDSUTIL is used to manage servers, not permissions. Therefore, answer A is eliminated. ACLDiag is used to view and reset the permissions. Resetting changes the permissions, so answer B is correct. DSCALS is specifically for this purpose, and answer C is correct. DSAStat is used to compare and find differences between the directory databases on two servers. It doesn't change things, so answer D is eliminated. See the section "The NTDSUTIL Command."

14. **C.** The only tool that captures and displays packages from the network is the Network Monitor. The Event Viewer (answer A) records events on the system, not packets in and out, and is therefore incorrect. The Performance tool can tell you many things about the server, but it can't let you see the contents of a packet. Answer B is incorrect. The NETSTAT command can be used to see the network sessions you have but will not capture and display the data; therefore, answer D is incorrect. See the section "Monitoring a Domain Controller."

APPLY YOUR KNOWLEDGE

15. **C.** This one is tricky. At first, you might think there is a problem with the server because no one can connect. However, this is not an option. So you have to start eliminating answers. The first to go is the schema master, which has little to do with day-to-day functions. Next you can eliminate the infrastructure master. Users were able to connect, so this is not a matter of groups. This leaves the domain naming master and the PDC emulator. This might hint at the trust relationship issue that is the problem here. This would lead you the domain naming master, but it manages the relationships. Relationships are actually handled on the PDC emulators. This means C is correct. See the section "Server Roles."

Suggested Readings and Resources

1. Microsoft Windows 2000 Server Resource Kit. *Microsoft Windows 2000 Server Operations Guide.* Microsoft Press, 2000.

2. Microsoft Windows 2000 Server Resource Kit. *Microsoft Windows 2000 Server Deployment Planning Guide.* Microsoft Press, 2000.

In this chapter, you learn to create and control Group Policy to manage users and groups at the site, domain, and *organizational unit* (OU) level. You are first presented with information on what Group Policy is and how it works including its scope, where it can be created, and how it is enforced. This is followed by a discussion on how to create Group Policy objects at different branches within Active Directory. The enforcement of Group Policy and setting security for the policies created are then outlined. Because it is unlikely that your organization is static and because business policies change on a regular basis, focus then is directed to the management of group policies, which includes delegation of administrative control as well as modification of Group Policy after it has been created. Finally, this chapter discusses the types of things that can be controlled using Group Policy including computer and user settings as well as their precedence. The chapter concludes with a case study and a section in which you can apply your knowledge and practice working with Group Policy.

This chapter covers some of the objectives and subobjectives from the unit "Installing, Configuring, Managing, Monitoring, Optimizing, and Troubleshooting Change and Configuration Management." The other objectives and subobjectives are covered in other chapters.

Implement and troubleshoot Group Policy.

- **Modify Group Policy inheritance.**
- **Create a Group Policy object (GPO).**
- **Link an existing GPO.**
- **Filter Group Policy settings by associating security groups to GPOs.**
- **Delegate administrative control of Group Policy.**
- **Modify Group Policy.**

CHAPTER 6

Using Group Policy to Manage Users

▶ Group Policy is one of the key features of Windows 2000. This feature enables you to control user and computer environments. The purpose of this objective is to help you become comfortable with the process of adding Group Policy to an Active Directory container, linking existing Group Policies to an Active Directory container, and deleting *Group Policy objects* (GPOs). You will also be tested on the inheritance of Group Policy between different Active Directory containers: sites, domains, and organizational units. Configuring security of Group Policy objects, including delegating administration of a Group Policy to other users, will also be tested.

Manage and troubleshoot user environments by using Group Policy.

- **Control user environments by using administrative templates.**

- **Assign script policies to users and computers.**

▶ The purpose of this objective is to help you become familiar with the process of creating and modifying Group Policy to manage user environments. This can be done in one of two ways: using administrative templates or using scripts.

Administrative templates modify registry settings for either or both the user and computer onto which the user is logging. You will be tested on the options available to manage what the user is able to do and when to use computer settings or user settings within the administrative templates.

In some cases, scripts might be necessary to provide more control over a user environment beyond that which is available through administrative templates. You will be tested on how to create scripts and how scripts are processed as well as what types of scripts are possible.

Manage network configuration by using Group Policy.

▶ The purpose of this objective is to make sure you are familiar with network elements that can be controlled using Group Policy. This includes redirection of certain folders, settings for how RAS and network connections work, and whether users are able to make changes to network settings.

OUTLINE

▶ When preparing the Group Policy elements for the Implementing and Administering a Microsoft Windows 2000 Directory Services Infrastructure exam, the best way to become proficient in the topic is to make use of it. In other words, it is imperative that you follow the Step by Steps and exercises in this chapter to understand how Group Policy functions and what kind of things it can be used to control. A thorough understanding of Group Policy inheritance, filtering, and the options surrounding these two areas is also required. You will be tested on your knowledge of not only how to configure Group Policy but also of how it works. The exam and review questions at the end of this chapter will also help you understand more about how it works.

▶ Because Group Policy is such a large topic in the Windows 2000 world, it has been broken down into three chapters in this book. A good understanding of what can be accomplished with Group Policy in all its areas (administrative templates, security settings, software deployment, and desktop configuration) is also recommended. For this reason, you should be comfortable with the information presented in this chapter as well as the next two chapters.

INTRODUCTION

One of the most powerful tools within the Windows 2000 Active Directory construct is the capability to use Group Policy to provide centralized control over users, groups, and computers within a large enterprise. Group Policy enables the administrator of a very large network to control what occurs on a user's desktop even if the user is many miles away. Group Policy also enables that same administrator to delegate some or all of this administrative capability to a local administrative resource. It is perhaps the single most powerful feature of Windows 2000 while at the same time being potentially the one that might cause the most grief if not properly implemented.

INTRODUCTION TO GROUP POLICY

A challenge facing any administrator of a Windows 2000 network is how to make sure users' desktops and other settings conform to corporate standards. This is especially true of large organizations with many users and even several sites in different and disparate locations. Active Directory provides a mechanism to ensure that administration of these settings can be controlled centrally. Active Directory also provides a mechanism to ensure that the settings apply to all users who require them, regardless of the user's location. This mechanism is Group Policy.

With Group Policy, an administrator can define the state of a user's work environment once. Windows 2000 Active Directory continually enforces these settings no matter which machine the individual uses or where he or she might happen to be. With Group Policy, an administrator is able to do the following:

◆ Enforce centralized control of user and computer settings at the site and domain level or, optionally, provide the capability for local administrators to incorporate local settings at the OU level. This is useful in large organizations with many geographical locations. It enables the administrator to enforce corporate requirements while allowing for local control of other settings. For example, all users must have the corporate intranet shortcut on their desktops, but they need to still be able to control other local applications such as Office 2000. (The version to be used in France would be French, while in the United Kingdom it would be English.)

◆ Provide a desktop environment that enables users to perform their duties while at the same time ensuring that critical applications cannot be modified or removed. This should result in lower technical support requirements because users cannot make damaging changes that result in machines becoming inoperable due to user error.

◆ Control what a desktop looks like and how a computer behaves, including which software is or can be installed. Group Policy allows control of user and computer registry settings, the invocation of scripts to modify the computer and user environments, security settings for computers and domains, and automatic installation (or even removal) of software. Group Policy allows control of the location of certain critical data folders such as the user's home directory and desktop working directory.

◆ Ensure that corporate policies, including business rules, and security requirements are enforced. In this way, it is possible to ensure that user passwords are a minimum length, that users change their passwords every 90 days, and that all users have a shortcut to the corporate intranet site on their desktop at all times.

Group Policy is a technology that can be applied at the site, domain, and organizational unit level within Active Directory. Because Group Policy is an Active Directory object, it can be used to enforce the previously mentioned settings on any Windows 2000 client computer. These clients include Windows 2000 Professional, Windows 2000 Server, Windows 2000 Advanced Server, and Windows 2000 Data Center Server.

Group Policy Components

Group Policy is an object within Active Directory. It is commonly referred to as a *Group Policy object* (GPO). The GPO includes settings that enable you to control many different aspects of the

NOTE

Group Policy on Windows NT 3.51 or Windows NT 4.0 Group Policy cannot be used to enforce settings on Windows NT 3.51 or Windows NT 4.0 clients. These operating systems do not support Active Directory. For Windows NT 3.51 and later clients, you still need to make use of system policies available in NT and used to enforce user and computer settings within the NT domain structure. The same also holds true for Windows 95 and Windows 98 clients. Basically, unless the client is a Windows 2000 computer, you cannot use Group Policy—use system policies instead.

computing environment. It is an object within Active Directory and can be associated with different Active Directory containers (sites, domains, and OUs). Because GPOs can be associated with different Active Directory containers, they can be used to enforce organization-wide (site and domain) or department-level (OU) rules.

Group Policy objects are actually composed of two parts: the *Group Policy container* (GPC) and the *Group Policy template* (GPT).

The GPC (see Figure 6.1) is an Active Directory object that includes GPO attributes and version information. Each GPO is represented by a *globally unique identifier* (GUID). The GUID is a 128-bit number that uniquely identifies the GPO within the forest, domain tree, and domain. The GUID cannot be changed or removed by the user and is automatically maintained by Active Directory. Version information is also attached to the GPO and is tracked within Active Directory. This information is attached to the GPC and is shared by domain controllers. Each domain controller uses the information contained within Active Directory and the GPC to make sure it is running the most recent version of a GPO. If it does not have the most recent version, replication occurs, transferring the most recent version from another domain controller. The following Step by Step shows you how.

NOTE

Preconfigured GPOs   When you install Active Directory and create the first domain controller in the first domain in the first forest, Windows 2000 Active Directory creates two Group Policy objects automatically: the Default Domain Policy and the Default Domain Controller Policy. These default policies will be copied to all domain controllers in all other domains created in the forest. If you wanted to have a default set of values in GPOs for all users and computers in the domain, you would modify the Default Domain Policy. Similarly, if you wanted all domain controllers in all domains to start out with the same settings, you would modify the Default Domain Controller Policy on that first domain controller. As you will find out later, domain administrators within the subdomains can modify these after the fact.

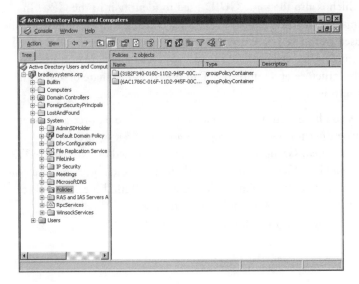

FIGURE 6.1
The Group Policy container within Active Directory Users and Computers.

STEP BY STEP

6.1 Viewing Group Policy GUIDs

1. To view the Group Policy container within Active Directory Users and Computers, click the View menu and select Advanced Features.

2. Expand the domain, the System container, and the Policies container to see the GUIDs representing all known GPOs within the domain.

The GPT is a set of folders and subfolders in the SYSVOL share on Windows 2000 domain controllers. Each GPO created always results in the creation of a folder hierarchy, which contains the physical files and settings required by the GPO. These include administrative templates, security settings, scripts, software installation info, and folder redirection settings. Windows 2000 clients connect to the SYSVOL shared folder to obtain these settings and apply what is contained within them.

Each GPT folder is named the same as the GUID of the GPO, which is also the same GUID used to identify it in the GPC. In this way, if you rename a GPO after creating it, the unique identifier used by Active Directory (the GUID) and the corresponding GPT structure, as well as the GPC, do not change. Figure 6.2 shows the structure of a sample GPT in the SYSVOL share of a domain controller.

As you have seen, Group Policy can be used to enforce a number of settings for both the computer and the user. As previously mentioned, Group Policy objects are composed of two parts: a GPC and a GPT. Group Policy can only be used to enforce computer and user configuration items on Windows 2000 machines. To enforce settings on other Microsoft operating systems (Windows NT, Windows 9x), you still need to use System Policy.

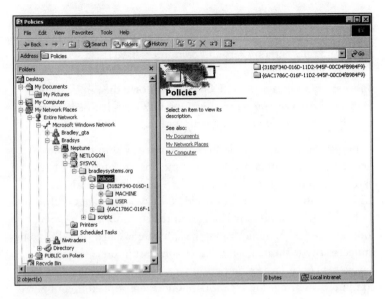

FIGURE 6.2
The Group Policy Template folder hierarchy within the SYSVOL share of a
Windows 2000 domain controller.

GROUP POLICY SCOPE

Group Policy has particular sets of rules it follows when applied
to users and computers. One set of these rules deals with what
happens at each Active Directory container where Group Policy
exists (inheritance), while another deals with how settings from
multiple GPOs are combined to provide an effective policy application. Finally, a third set of rules deals with how GPOs are processed
within the same Active Directory container. All of these areas are
addressed here.

Each GPO can be linked to one or more containers within Active
Directory because GPOs are composed of a separate Group Policy
container. In other words, you can create a single Group Policy
object with a predefined collection of settings to be applied (for
example, specify the desktop wallpaper to be the company logo).
This GPO can then be selectively linked to only the Sales and
Marketing organizational units within the Corporate domain,

while other organizational units such as R&D and Tech Support might not have these GPOs linked to them. In this way, GPOs make sure only certain users and computers have these settings enforced while others do not. The benefit derived is that it is unnecessary to create separate GPOs to enforce the same settings for several parts of your company. One GPO can be used for more than one organizational component within Active Directory.

Administrators can also link more than one GPO to the same Active Directory container. For example, instead of putting both user desktop settings and software installation information into one GPO, an administrator might decide to have a separate GPO for each item. In this way, any changes to the desktop, which are made through the GPO, do not cause the software installation GPO to be unnecessarily replicated. This makes administration easier and can have a beneficial impact on performance. When a user logs on or a computer is started, the appropriate GPOs are applied if configured for that container.

Group Policy Inheritance

When processing group policies, a clear inheritance hierarchy is followed (see Figure 6.3): x, then y, and then z. This means that if similar settings exist at different levels, the order in which the GPOs are applied determines which setting is the final one applied to the computer or user. In this way, it is possible for an administrator at an OU level to overwrite a setting defined at the domain or site level. As you will see later in this chapter, it is also possible for a higher-level (domain or enterprise) administrator to override this capability.

The first GPOs to be processed are those for the Active Directory site where the user's computer is physically located. The computer and user settings for the site are processed and applied to the registry. Because the site represents a physical location and because a single site can actually have more than one domain, it is important to start with the Group Policy that usually takes into account language and other regional differences. This is the Group Policy for the site where the computer and user are located.

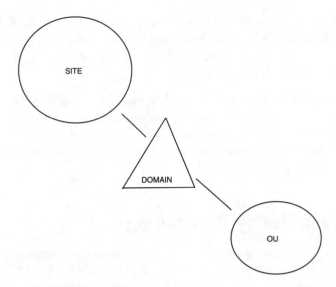

FIGURE 6.3
Group Policy inheritance during processing.

The next GPOs to be processed are those for a domain. Each
user, group, and computer is always associated with a domain.
Domain-wide policies affect all users and are primarily used to
enforce domain-wide security restrictions or general business rules
and settings that need to be in place. For enterprises that use a
domain structure to differentiate between different business units,
this ensures that each unit enforces its set of rules without affecting
the other parts of the company. As with the application of GPOs
to sites, computer and user settings defined within the policy are
applied to the registry.

The last GPOs to be processed are those for the OU in which
the user or computer is located within Active Directory. Active
Directory enables a domain or enterprise administrator to further
subdivide the users and computers within a domain into administrative units called OUs, so this policy should apply to the smallest
number of objects and should make sure a very specific set of rules
is also enforced. For example, you might have a Sales domain within
your corporate structure, and within that Sales domain, you might
decide to create a Telemarketing OU. The users placed in the
Telemarketing OU need to have a more restrictive series of desktop
settings than other salespeople in the organization. You accomplish

> **NOTE**
>
> **Local Group Policy Object** Each
> computer running Windows 2000
> also has a local GPO. In this way, it
> is possible to configure settings that
> apply only to this one computer and
> are not replicated to other Windows
> 2000 machines. When Active
> Directory is used, these settings can
> be overwritten by policies defined at
> the site, domain, or OU level. These
> settings are the least influential (that
> is, their settings have the lowest
> priority). In a non-Active Directory
> environment, as in a workgroup set-
> ting with no Windows 2000 domain
> controllers, these GPOs are the only
> ones that can be applied and thereby
> increase in importance.

N O T E

System Policy Processing In environments in which both Windows 2000 clients and Windows 9x or Windows NT 4.0 clients exist, you might still need to keep system policies around to enforce desktop and other settings. When a Windows 9x or Windows NT 4.0 client is used to log on to the network, it still processes System Policy and not Group Policy.

If Windows NT 4.0 domain controllers exist on the domain, they also supply System Policy to users when they log on to the domain. This can change the configuration of a client computers, even Windows 2000 clients, based on the policy settings. It is recommended that domain controllers be upgraded to Windows 2000 as quickly as possible.

Any computer upgraded to Windows 2000 still retains the registry changes made by Windows NT–style System Policy after the upgrade. This is because changes in the registry as a result of System Policy are not backed out during the upgrade.

this by associating a GPO with the Telemarketing OU and configuring the Group Policy with these settings. As with the application of GPOs to sites and domains, computer and user settings defined within the policy are applied to the registry.

Group Policy follows a specific path of inheritance, enabling the administrator to fine-tune the application of settings to users and computers. The inheritance hierarchy is always site, domain, and then OU, ending with the OU closest to the user or computer object to whom the GPO is being applied.

Group Policy Processing

As previously mentioned, GPOs can be linked to a site, domain, or OU within Active Directory. More than one GPO can be linked to the same container, and they will all be processed together, depending on the security and other settings configured.

The actual steps taken by Windows 2000 in the processing of Group Policy are quite simple. First, when a Windows 2000 computer starts up, it needs to communicate with domain controllers in the domain to update DNS and other settings and to make sure the domain controllers are aware it is running. During this procedure, the GPOs that contain computer settings that need to be applied to the Windows 2000 computer are processed and applied to the registry. At this time, any startup scripts that were created and assigned to the computer will run, thereby ensuring that computer settings are as expected.

When a user logs on to a Windows 2000 computer, any GPOs that have been associated with the site, domain, or OU to which the user belongs and that have been configured to run for that user, or the group of which that user is a member, will be applied. This means that two different users logging on to the same computer at different times might have completely different environments as a result of the policy settings applied to each. Further, after a user logs on to a computer, Windows 2000 also processes any logon scripts that have been configured to run for him or her or for a group of which he or she is a member.

Administrators can change what is contained in GPOs over time, and some of these settings might need to be applied within a very short time. This is why Windows 2000 provides for an automatic refresh of Group Policy while systems are running and users are still logged on. This ensures that Group Policy is consistently applied to all users and computers, even if the user never logs off or if the computer is never turned off. In this way, it is possible to have a consistent set of rules that are applied and followed throughout the enterprise or any portion thereof.

Domain controllers within Windows 2000 Active Directory refresh or reapply GPOs every 5 minutes. Windows 2000 member servers, considered clients in the processing of Group Policy, refresh Group Policy every 90 minutes, plus or minus a 30-minute stagger factor. This ensures that all the domain controllers and the servers to which users will be connecting have an up-to-date copy of any Group Policy. This does not mean GPOs are copied between domain controllers every 5 minutes; this only occurs when the GPOs have been modified. Part of the checking that takes place is whether a GPO needs to be refreshed. Refreshing occurs if the GPO changes, which can be determined by the version number of the GPO.

Windows 2000 clients also refresh GPOs but only every 90 minutes, plus or minus 30 minutes. The refresh internal itself is staggered among Windows 2000 client computers to ensure that network bandwidth does not get saturated because of GPO refresh. For example, let's say you have 200 or more clients connecting to a small number of servers and domain controllers. Each client communicates with domain controllers at different times for a GPO refresh but always within 90 minutes of the previous refresh. The initial check is to determine whether any GPOs have changed and need to be downloaded, followed by a download of any GPOs that have been modified. During this process, any changes that have been made to the GPO are applied immediately at the client, even if the user is still logged on.

The default refresh rate for a GPO can be changed within the GPO template. This means that, if the preceding default settings are too frequent, you can reduce the frequency of GPO refresh or vice versa. Caution should be used when changing the refresh rate. Changing the refresh rate can result in a long lag time between a change to a GPO and its application on a client computer (if the refresh interval was made longer such as 180 minutes instead of 90 for a client). Changing the refresh rate can cause network problems if the refresh internal is shortened because all clients need to communicate more frequently with domain controllers to see if a refresh is required.

N O T E **Refresh Rules** Software installation, offline files, and folder redirection settings, which can be configured in Group Policy, do not follow the refresh rules. These GPO settings are only applied when a computer starts up or a user logs on. For changes to the settings within a GPO to take effect, the machine needs to be restarted or the user needs to log off and then log on again. This is done to ensure that files needed by a user during a session are not directed to more than one location, thereby causing confusion.

N O T E **Connecting to the GPO** Because site, domain, and OU policies may all be processed, the client computer might actually connect to more than one domain controller. It does this if a site GPO is to be applied and the site GPO was defined in a domain other than the one of which the computer is a member. As a rule, the client must connect to a domain controller in the domain where the GPO was created. For domain GPOs and OU GPOs, this always is the domain in which the user logging on is defined; for sites, it is the site in which the GPO was defined.

One of the major changes in Windows 2000 is the capability to have Group Policy settings inherited at different levels of Active Directory (site, domain, or OU). Having GPO settings automatically reapplied to all domain controllers, member servers, and Windows 2000 clients to ensure an up-to-date list of settings is a key benefit. The combination of Group Policy inheritance (the order in which GPOs are evaluated) and processing (how GPOs are processed within the same container and on the network) is a very important point of discussion and is covered next.

Combining Group Policies

Implement and troubleshoot Group Policy.

- **Modify Group Policy inheritance.**

As you have seen so far, GPOs can be created at three levels: site, domain, and OU. It is also possible to create more than one policy at each level with differing or similar settings. Therefore, it is important to understand exactly what will happen if GPOs are combined and what the net effect of all the GPOs will be as a result. The process is a lot simpler than you might initially have thought because the rules are very straightforward.

When a computer starts up and a user logs on, the domain controller figures out which GPOs need to be applied for both the computer and the user. In doing so, the domain controller processes the GPOs for the computer first and then for the user and forwards to the client a list of GPOs to be applied. The client then connects to the SYSVOL folder of the domain controller, locates the GPT of the first GPO provided by the domain controller, and applies the Group Policy settings. This process is repeated for all GPOs that the domain controller specified to the client.

The process proceeds according to the Group Policy inheritance rules previously discussed (site, then domain, and finally OU). If, at any level of this processing, multiple GPOs apply to the computer and/or user at the same level (site, domain, or OU), they are processed, bottom to top, in the order in which they appear in the Group Policy tab of the container to which they are linked. In the example shown in Figure 6.4, if both GPOs applied to the same user or computer, the Password Policy would be applied first and then the Default Domain Policy. If any settings in the Password Policy (see Figure 6.5 for an example of password settings) also existed in the Default Domain Policy, the setting in the Default Domain Policy would take precedence.

FIGURE 6.4
Multiple GPOs can be linked to the same Active Directory container. Processing is bottom to top.

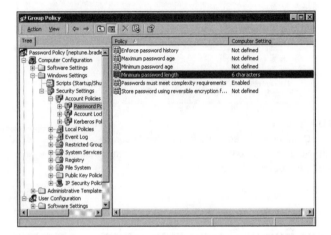

FIGURE 6.5
Password Policy settings for complexity and password length.

For example, consider the following scenario. You define a setting in the Password Policy. This policy states that passwords must be at least six characters in length and must also meet complexity requirements (that is, passwords must be a combination of uppercase letters, lowercase letters, numbers, or symbols). The Default Domain Policy also has a policy setting defined that states the password must be eight characters long, but there are no complexity requirements. In this situation, the result would be an effective policy that enforces a password of eight characters, as defined in the Default Domain Policy applied last. The policy also requires that password complexity be enforced, as specified in the Password Policy and not overridden by the Default Domain Policy because this setting was not specified (disabled) at the Default Domain Policy (see Figure 6.6).

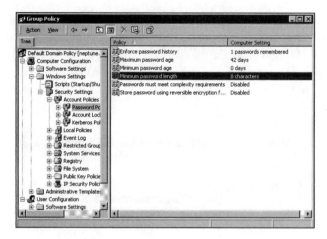

FIGURE 6.6
Default Domain Policy settings for password complexity and password length. Note that the password complexity setting is disabled, which means it is not changed at this level.

Group Policy Processing Rules

As previously mentioned, a series of rules are followed by Windows 2000 when applying Group Policy. Some of these already have been discussed, but it is beneficial to have the rules presented together.

◆ All Group Policy settings apply unless a conflict is encountered. This means the effective policy settings applied to a user or computer are the sum total of all site, domain, and OU GPOs that have been specified for the user and computer.

◆ A conflict may occur and is defined as the same setting being defined at more than one level or in more than one GPO at the same level (as shown in the preceding example). When a conflict is encountered, the rules of policy inheritance are followed until it is resolved.

◆ Policy inheritance follows the path of site, then domain, and finally OU.

◆ If more than one GPO is linked to the same Active Directory container, GPOs are processed from the bottom to the top as they are listed in the Group Policy tab for the container.

◆ The last setting processed always applies. This means that, when settings from different GPOs in the inheritance hierarchy conflict, the one that applies is the setting specified in the last container.

◆ When settings from GPOs linked to the same Active Directory container conflict, the GPO at the top of the list is the one that applies.

◆ If a setting is specified for a user as well as a computer at the same GPO level, the computer setting always applies when it conflicts with a user setting. In other words, at the same GPO level, computer settings take precedence over user settings.

Group Policy has a clearly defined scope, inheritance, and processing order. Group Policy can be applied to either the computer or the user, and the computer policy always has a higher priority when it conflicts with a user setting. Now you will find out how to actually create GPOs at different levels of Active Directory.

CREATING AND MANAGING GROUP POLICY

Implement and troubleshoot Group Policy.

- **Create a Group Policy object (GPO).**
- **Link an existing GPO.**

Creating GPOs is a relatively simple and straightforward process. As long as you have administrative rights either on the domain or within the OU in which you want to create the policy, it is quite simple. The following Step by Step shows you how to create a group policy for the domain.

STEP BY STEP

6.2 Creating a Group Policy for the Domain

1. Click the Start button and go to Programs, Administrative Tools, as shown in Figure 6.7.

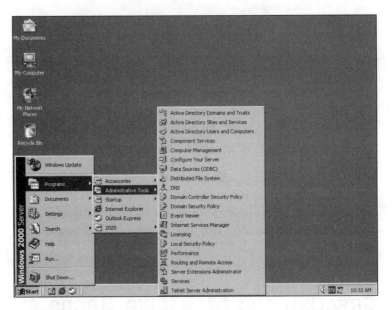

FIGURE 6.7
The Administrative Tools program group in Windows 2000.

2. Because you are creating a Group Policy for the domain, you would choose Active Directory Users and Computers as the program to start. This choice opens a *Microsoft Management Console* (MMC) similar to the one in Figure 6.8.

3. To create Group Policy, you need to right-click the Active Directory container within which you want to create the policy. In Windows 2000 Active Directory Users and Computers, you are permitted to create a GPO in the domain controller's container or at the domain itself. To create a domain-wide policy, right-click the domain name and select Properties. A screen similar to Figure 6.9 displays.

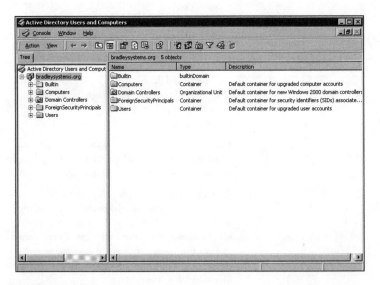

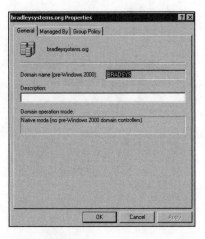

FIGURE 6.9
The Properties dialog box for the domain in
Active Directory Users and Computers.

FIGURE 6.8
The Active Directory Users and Computers Microsoft Management Console
snap-in main screen.

4. All containers in Active Directory that are capable of
having GPOs associated with them will present a dialog
box similar to the one in Figure 6.9. Selecting the Group
Policy tab in the dialog box presents a screen, similar
to Figure 6.10, listing the currently linked GPOs for
the container. If more than one GPO is linked to the
container, the order in which they are applied starts from
the bottom. This tab also gives you several options (by
way of buttons) for creating and managing Group Policy.
These options are as follows:

Button	What It Does
New	Enables you to create a new GPO at this container level and insert it at the bottom of the list of GPOs for this container. This GPO is linked automatically to this container and applies to normal users after it has been created.
Add	Enables you to link a GPO created in another Active Directory container to this container and insert it at the bottom of the list of GPOs for this container. The GPO linked also automatically applies to normal users after it has been linked.

continues

NOTE

Group Policy and Default Containers
It is not possible to associate a Group
Policy with the default Active Directory
containers Users, Computers, Built-In,
or Foreign Security Principals. This is
because the default domain GPO,
which is created when Windows 2000
Active Directory is installed, already
applies to the contents of these
containers. In other words, creating a
GPO in these containers would be
redundant because they are the
subject of any GPO created in the
domain or associated with domain
controllers.

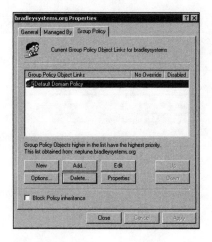

FIGURE 6.10
The Group Policy tab of an Active Directory
container that supports having a GPO
linked to it.

continued

Button	What It Does
Edit	Enables you to modify the attributes of the GPO and enable and disable policy settings. After editing of the GPO is completed, changes are applied to all users and computers affected by the policy using the normal refresh schedule as previously outlined.
Options	Enables you to set options for the GPO including whether it is enabled and whether its settings can be blocked at lower levels of the inheritance hierarchy.
Delete	Enables you to remove the link to the GPO for this container and optionally delete the GPT associated with the GPO. Deleting the GPT removes the GPO completely and does not allow it to be linked to any other containers. Simply deleting the link for the GPO leaves the GPT intact and allows it to be linked to other containers.
Properties	Brings up a dialog box that enables you to configure security for the GPO, disable portions of the GPO that are not being used, and search for all containers to which the GPO is linked. This last option provides a mechanism to ensure that completely removing a GPO will not cause problems within other parts of the enterprise.

Another option that can be set by the administrator is whether to block policy inheritance. This will be discussed in more detail in the "Group Policy Security" section later in this chapter.

A final set of buttons enables you to set the proper order for policy application within this container if it is linked to more than one GPO. As previously discussed, GPOs are applied within the same container from bottom to top as they appear on this screen. The Up and Down buttons enable you to specify which GPO will be the first to be applied (the one closest to the bottom) and which will be the last applied, potentially overriding other GPOs settings.

5. To create a new GPO that will automatically be linked to this container, click the New button. This adds a GPO to the bottom of the list and enables you to specify the name, as shown in Figure 6.11.

6. To add, or link, an existing GPO to this Active Directory container, click the Add button. You are then presented with a dialog box containing three tabs, similar to the dialog box in Figure 6.12. Because we can link GPOs to sites, domains, and OUs, the list of GPOs that have been created at the domain or OU level is presented under the Domains/OUs tab. The list of GPOs that apply to sites is presented under the Sites tab. For an alphabetical list of all the GPOs that this domain controller recognizes, and that most likely exist within the enterprise, you can click the All tab. You are presented with a list similar to the one shown in Figure 6.13.

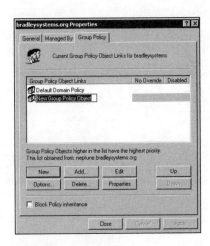

FIGURE 6.11
Creating a new GPO.

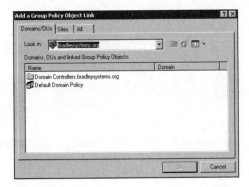

FIGURE 6.12
Adding a GPO link presents this dialog box.

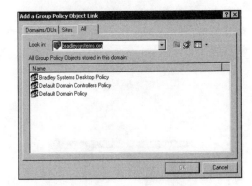

FIGURE 6.13
A list of all GPOs (in alphabetic order) in the enterprise can be found in the All tab of the Add a Group Policy Object Link dialog box.

7. Clicking the Edit button after highlighting a GPO on the list enables you to modify the settings of the GPO. If the GPO was created by another administrator at a higher level within Active Directory, you might not have the necessary permissions to perform this task, and you will be presented with an error message. If you do have the requisite permissions to change the GPO settings, you will be presented with a dialog box similar to the one in

continues

continued

Figure 6.14. As is evident in the figure, a great many options for both the user and the computer can be specified within Group Policy. The meaning of these settings is discussed later in this chapter.

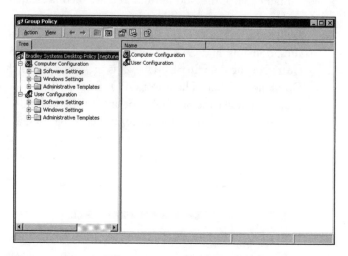

FIGURE 6.14
Group Policy settings can be modified using the MMC console. Clicking the Edit button opens it automatically.

FIGURE 6.15
The Options dialog box for a GPO enables you to disable a GPO or prevent changes downstream.

8. Clicking the Options button presents you with a dialog box containing check boxes, as shown in Figure 6.15.

The No Override check box enables an administrator to enforce particular GPOs settings, even if other GPOs further on in the inheritance hierarchy override the setting. The No Override option is typically used in situations in which a higher-level administrator at the domain level wants to make sure GPO settings encompassing corporate rules are not changed by lower-level administrators at the OU level. This is a way to ensure that higher-level settings are not tampered with by other GPOs.

The Disabled check box does exactly what it says: It does not enforce the GPO at this level. GPOs can be enabled or disabled. If you do not want a particular GPO to apply within the container, you can disable it using this option. This is also useful when you are configuring settings for a policy, and you do not want it to be enforced until all changes have been completed and for troubleshooting.

9. The Delete button presents you with the dialog box shown in Figure 6.16. This option enables you to delete a link from the current Active Directory container for the GPO or to permanently remove the GPO from Active Directory. To remove the link, you must have administrative permissions for the container. To permanently remove the GPO, you must have administrative permissions in the container where the GPO was initially created.

FIGURE 6.16
The Delete button presents a dialog box that enables you to remove a link for the GPO or to remove the GPO completely.

10. The dialog box presented when you click the Properties button is shown in Figure 6.17. The General tab initially shows the GUID within Active Directory for the GPO. You also are presented with the creation date and time for the GPO as well as the last change date/time and the number of revisions made to the computer and user section of the GPO. You also have the option to disable the user and/or computer portions of the GPO if they are not currently set, meaning they are not being used. Disabling one part or the other of the GPO makes download times quicker because not all parts of the GPT need to be downloaded and applied to the client.

Clicking the Links tab of the Properties dialog box presents a screen similar to the one in Figure 6.18. Clicking the Find Now button initiates a search for links to this GPO within the scope selected. This is a very useful way to ensure that any GPO you intend to permanently delete will not cause problems for other administrators relying upon this GPO.

FIGURE 6.17
The main Properties dialog box for a GPO showing the GUID, creation date/time, revisions, and domain for a GPO. Computer and user settings can also be disabled for the GPO.

Disable Computer Configuration and Disable User Configuration Settings
Selecting both the Disable Computer Configuration settings and Disable User Configuration settings check boxes on the General tab of the GPO Properties dialog box effectively results in no GPO settings being applied to either the user or computer. This action still forces the GPO to be processed when a user logs on. This is not the same as disabling the GPO in the Options dialog box because the GPO is still processed but no GPTs or scripts are downloaded. To completely disable GPO processing, use the Options dialog box.

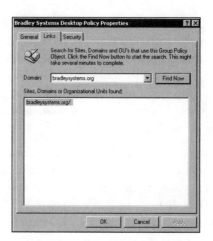

FIGURE 6.18
The Links tab enables an administrator to find out where a GPO is linked (being used).

The Security tab of the Properties dialog box enables you to grant and revoke permissions to administer this GPO. It also enables you to set permissions for those users who will have the GPO applied when they log on. This is discussed in more detail in the next section.

As shown by the preceding Step by Step, creating a GPO is a very straightforward process. Managing it after the fact is quite easy as well. The hard part is determining which settings to apply within the GPO and which users and computers should have the policy enforced. These are discussed later when you are introduced to Administrative Templates as well as in Chapter 7, "Software Distribution Using Group Policy" and Chapter 8, "Managing Security Using Group Policy."

GROUP POLICY SECURITY

Implement and troubleshoot Group Policy.

- **Filter Group Policy settings by associating security groups to GPOs.**
- **Delegate administrative control of Group Policy.**

One of the best features of Group Policy in Windows 2000 is the capability to determine which users and computers a GPO applies to as well as which users are allowed to administer the policy. Through the selective use of permissions and security, the administrator has the capability to provide very precise access to and application of any GPO created. This one feature is a vast improvement over the Windows NT 4.0 System Policy, which was used before Windows 2000.

When setting permissions for Group Policy, the administrator is able to configure two things:

◆ To whom the policy will apply

◆ Which users will be permitted to make changes to the policy as well as its inheritance

Both of these topics are discussed in detail in the next section. Configuration of permissions for both of these elements, as well as how inheritance takes place, is performed from the Properties dialog box of the container to which the GPO has been linked (refer to Figure 6.10).

Configuring Group Policy Security

In configuring Group Policy security, you should be concerned with a number of areas. First, you need to set permissions on Group Policy to determine to which users and computers the GPO will apply. You also need to specify permissions to enable other users to modify the policy. If you want to be very precise, you can configure advanced permissions for the GPO; this gives you extremely fine control of which privileges will be given to whom.

Setting Permissions to Use the Policy

Setting permissions is the initial stage in configuring Group Policy security. By default, Group Policy is applied to members of the Authenticated Users system group. If you do not want this to be the case and want to restrict the application of Group Policy to a specific set of users, computers, or groups, you would assign permissions explicitly. The following Step by Step walks you through setting permissions.

N O T E **Modifying GPO Security** Do not double-click the GPO name. This puts you into edit mode for the GPO. To modify GPO security, you need to select the GPO by clicking its name and then indicate that you want to modify the properties of the GPO by clicking the Properties button.

STEP BY STEP

6.3 Setting Permissions to Use a GPO

1. Click the Start button, go to Programs, Administrative Tools, and select Active Directory Users and Computers.

2. Right-click your domain name and select Properties. If the GPO whose permissions you want to modify is at the OU level, right-click the OU and select Properties.

3. In the dialog box that opens, select the Group Policy tab.

4. Click Default Domain Policy, or another policy for which you want to modify permissions, and then click the Properties button.

5. To place yourself in a position to modify the permissions for this GPO, click the Security tab. A screen similar to the one shown in Figure 6.19 displays. From this screen, it is possible to modify permissions for both administering and using the policy.

As Figure 6.19 shows, you are presented with a screen displaying a list of users and groups for whom the permissions for the GPO are currently set. As you click each user or group account, notice that the display at the bottom of the dialog box changes, indicating the different permissions for that particular group. In this way, it is possible to have different permissions for different users and computers for the same policy.

The Permissions section of the dialog box lists the standard permissions that can be applied to the GPO. The Permissions section also reveals whether these policies have been allowed (granted) or denied for the user, group, or computer specified earlier.

The standard permissions are as follows:

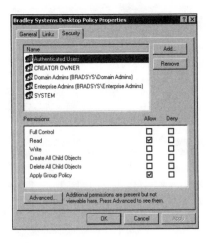

FIGURE 6.19
The Security tab of the Default Domain Policy Properties dialog box.

Permission	*Meaning*
Full Control	Enables the user or group to perform all tasks with this GPO. This includes modifying the GPO settings, adding or changing permissions for the GPO, creating and deleting all child objects, and deleting the GPO itself.

Permission	Meaning
Read	Enables the user, group, or computer to read the GPO. By being able to read the GPO, if the Apply permission is also specified, the user or computer is able to read the settings to be applied. Although Read permissions are required to apply a GPO, this permission can also be granted by itself to enable a user to read the contents of a GPO. For example, to change GPO settings, the administrator has to read the GPO even though it does not apply to him.
Write	Enables the user or group to modify the settings of a GPO. The administrator must have Write permissions to the GPO to change the effect of a GPO. This enables you to edit the policy settings. To make use of the Group Policy MMC snap-in to modify the GPO, you also need to have Read permissions so you can see the current settings.
Create All Child Objects	This permission enables you to add objects to GPO settings. For example, in the Software Installation setting, you need to associate packages with the GPO. This permission enables you to do so.
Delete All Child Objects	Enables you to remove a child object that might have been created for a GPO.
Apply Group Policy	This permission tells Active Directory to apply the settings specified within the Group Policy template to the user, group, or computer granted this permission. For a GPO to be fully applied, the user, group, or computer must also be given the Read permission.

NOTE

Denying Permission The capability to explicitly deny a particular permission is a new feature of Windows 2000. This feature should be used sparingly if at all. By explicitly denying a permission (placing a check mark in the Deny column), you are effectively stating that, regardless of any other permission allowed through the user's or group's membership in other groups, the permission will be denied. This is a dangerous practice to implement. It might make it difficult to determine where the root of a problem of GPO application actually exists. Instead of explicitly denying permission, it is recommended that you simply not check the Allow box for the permission you don't want to grant to the user or group. This does not grant the permission to the user or group and enables other group memberships to determine the effective permissions.

Each GPO you create will have a default set of permissions applying to several groups within Active Directory. The groups are as follows:

Group	Default Permissions Set
Authenticated Users	Read and Apply. Any user whose user account is affected by the container (site, domain, or OU) will have the GPO applied. Read permission is used to facilitate this. You have to be able to read the GPO to apply it.

continues

N O T E

Administrators and Group Policy
Members of the Domain Admins and
Enterprise Admins groups may still
have GPO settings applied to them
even though the Apply Group Policy
permissions might not have been
explicitly allowed to them. This is
because all users logging on to
a domain are members of the
Authenticated Users system group,
and this group has the Apply Group
Policy permissions checked Allow. If
you want to ensure that settings in a
particular GPO do not apply to Domain
Admins or Enterprise Admins, you
need to check the Deny check box for
Apply Group Policy for these groups.

continued

Group	Default Permissions Set
CREATOR OWNER	All check boxes cleared. This means no permissions are explicitly granted or denied. Permissions are inherited from other permissions specified.
Domain Admins	Read, Write, Create All Child Objects, and Delete All Child Objects. Members of Domain Admins are permitted to make any necessary changes to the GPO as well as read its current contents, but will not have the GPO applied to them when they log on.
Enterprise Admins	Same as Domain Admins. Enterprise Admins is a global group in mixed-mode domains and a universal group in native-mode domains.
SYSTEM	Same as Domain Admins. SYSTEM is the operating system account.
	SYSTEM is a built-in operating system account and does not belong to the Authenticated Users group; therefore, the default domain GPO does not apply to it.

6. To add a permission for a user or a security group, click the Add button. A dialog box similar to Figure 6.20 displays, showing all users, groups, and computers at the container level where you currently are located: the domain.

   Clicking on the arrow by the Look in list box presents the Active Directory domain structure. You can select the focus of the users, groups, and computers to which you want to apply the policy, and you can examine the entire contents of the directory (see Figure 6.21). In this way, you are able to narrow the scope of objects, which might number in the hundreds or thousands, to which you want to apply GPO permissions.

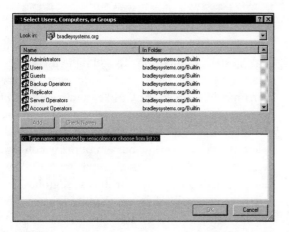

FIGURE 6.20
The Select Users, Computers, or Groups dialog box for Group Policy permissions.

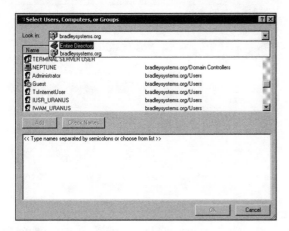

FIGURE 6.21
Selecting the scope of permission assignment.

Scrolling down the container reveals a list of groups, computers, and users to which permissions can be applied.

continues

continued

NOTE

Groups Are Better   When deciding whether to apply permissions to GPOs to either users or groups, remember that it is recommended that you apply permissions to groups rather than users. This is because it is very easy to add users and computers to and remove users and computers from groups. In Windows 2000, computers can be members of groups. You can have the permissions granted to the group automatically apply to every member of the group. Specifying permissions individually for users or computers on the GPO requires more maintenance and can also be more difficult to troubleshoot.

7. To select a user, simply locate his or her name in the list and click the Add button. To add more users, select another name and click Add. To add several users at one time, hold down the Ctrl key and click each of the users, groups, or computers to which you want to assign permissions and click Add when you have finished your selection. The area at the bottom of the window will fill with your selections, as shown in Figure 6.22. You also have the option to verify that the users, groups, and computers are still valid within Active Directory by clicking the Check Names button. To save your selection, click OK.

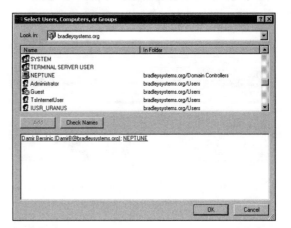

FIGURE 6.22
Selecting users, groups, and computers to which to apply permissions.

8. After you have saved the list of Active Directory objects to which you want to apply permissions, you are returned to the main Security window of the GPO Properties dialog box. The default permission applied to each object selected is Read, as shown in Figure 6.23. This means that these users, groups, or computers can read the GPO. It might also apply to them due to their permissions inherited from their membership in the Authenticated Users group, which has Read and Apply Group Policy permissions.

Setting Permissions to Manage the Policy

In larger enterprise environments, administration of a Windows 2000 Active Directory structure could be quite decentralized. At the same level in the Active Directory hierarchy, there might be many different administrators all with a specific set of tasks to perform. Group Policy encompasses many areas related to computer configuration and user environment settings. For this reason, it might be beneficial to have other individuals responsible for modifying GPO settings.

As an administrator, you can grant the capability to change and update settings of GPOs that have been created to other users who do not actually have administrative privileges on the container to which the GPO has been linked. This enables you to have the user make changes to the GPO but not modify the contents of the container in any other way. The user cannot create or remove any child objects within the container. In this way, an organization could have individuals responsible for configuring GPOs while not necessarily having influence over the structure of the Active Directory tree.

When a user has been granted administrative control of a GPO, he or she is able to make changes to the GPO settings but cannot create new GPOs within the same container. If a user has administrative privileges on a container to which the GPO is linked, that user also has administrative privileges for the GPO. Granting administrative privileges to a GPO is specifically useful when a user is responsible for testing GPO settings prior to large-scale implementation, when he or she is responsible for publishing and maintaining software applications propagated through the GPO, or when help desk personnel need to be able to make changes to the GPO settings to solve problems.

For users to make changes to GPO settings, they need two permissions: Read to be able to see the current settings, and Write to change them. However, the delegation of administrative control for a GPO is limited to Domain Admins or Enterprise Admins. This means that only users who are members of the Domain Admins or Enterprise Admins security group are able to grant the Write permission to other users, regardless of who owns the GPO.

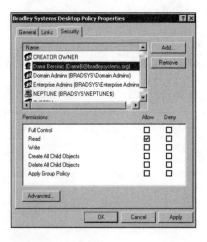

FIGURE 6.23
The default permission applied to new selections is Read.

NOTE

Permissions for a Group Policy
Permissions for a Group Policy are evaluated to the lowest level possible. This means that permissions set at a group level (for example, Sales) can be overridden by specifying a permission explicitly for a member of the group (for example, HeesH). Suppose you assign the permissions Read and Apply Group Policy to the group Sales and specify a permission setting for the user HeesH of Read only. All users of Sales will have the GPO applied except HeesH because a user-level setting takes precedence over a setting for any of the groups of which the user is a member. You have filtered the application of the GPO to all members of Sales except HeesH (which also means you removed the Authenticated Users group from the list of groups with permissions on the GPO).

To set permissions for a user to manage a Group Policy, perform the following steps.

STEP BY STEP

6.4 Setting Permissions to Manage a GPO

1. Click the Start button, go to Programs, Administrative Tools, and select Active Directory Users and Computers.

2. Right-click your domain name (or the organizational unit where the GPO is created) and select Properties.

3. In the dialog box that presents itself, select the Group Policy tab.

4. Click Default Domain Policy and then click the Properties button.

5. Click the Security tab to display existing permissions.

6. Click the Add button to be presented with a list of users, groups, and computers from which to choose.

7. Click the user or group you want to manage the GPO and then click Add.

8. Click OK when you are finished selecting all the users and groups to manage the policy. This returns you to the Security tab of the main Group Policy Properties dialog box.

9. Click the name of the user or group you added to the permission list for this GPO and check the Read and Write check boxes in the Allow column. Repeat this for each user or group you want to be able to manage the GPO.

10. When you are finished, select Apply and then OK to save your changes and exit the Group Policy Properties dialog box.

In most cases, when setting permissions for the application and modification of Group Policy, you make use of the default, combined permissions previously outlined. With these, you can

set to which users, computers, and groups the policy will be applied
as well as who has control over making changes to the policy. If you
need more specific control over permissions, you can make use of
the advanced permissions available.

Advanced Group Policy Permissions

Windows 2000 Active Directory provides for a vast number of
permissions that can be applied or denied to a user, group, or
computer. These are normally hidden from view to simplify the
assignment of permissions, but they are available should you desire
to change them.

Clicking the Advanced button in the Security tab of the Group
Policy Properties dialog box opens the dialog box shown in Figure
6.24. From here, you are able to view and modify the current
permissions, view and modify auditing, and view and change the
owner of the GPO on which you are focused.

In the Permissions tab of the Access Control Settings dialog box,
you can now see the type of permission (Allow or Deny). You
can see the names of users, groups, or computers to which the
permission applies (Name). The name of the permission is
displayed. Permissions might be Special, which means you need to
select View/Edit to see more, or Apply Group Policy. You can also
see to what these settings apply: the object and all child objects, just
this object, or only child objects. In the Permissions tab, you also
can Add, Remove, and View/Edit the specific permissions that have
been applied.

Selecting an existing user or group to whom permission has been
applied and then clicking View/Edit presents you with a dialog box
similar to the one shown in Figure 6.25. The specific permissions
included within the simplified selection shown in the Security tab
of the GPO Properties dialog box are shown. As you can see, the
permissions of Write, Read, Create All Child Objects, and Remove
Child Objects allowed to Domain Admins on the Security tab
actually break out into a much larger group of more specific
permissions. These include Read All Properties, List Contents, Read
Permissions, and Write Permissions, to name a few. These, and
many others, are the permissions presented in the Object tab of

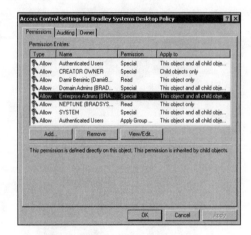

FIGURE 6.24

The Access Control Settings dialog box for
Group Policy can be opened by clicking
Advanced in the Group Policy Properties
Security tab.

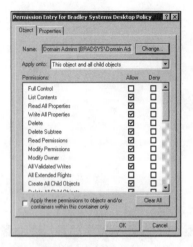

FIGURE 6.25

This detailed permission view in the Permission Entry dialog box is presented by clicking View/Edit in the Access Control Settings dialog box.

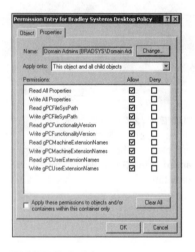

FIGURE 6.26

Permissions that can be applied to the properties of a GPO are shown in the Properties tab of the Permission Entry dialog box.

the Permission Entry dialog box. Permissions that apply only to the properties of the GPO are available on the Properties tab, as shown in Figure 6.26.

On either tab, you also will notice a few other items. First, the Name field provides you with the user, group, or computer to which these permissions apply, making sure you are aware for what or whom you are currently setting permissions. The Change button beside the Name field enables you to change to whom these permissions apply. In other words, the Change button enables you to assign this same set of permissions to another user, group, or computer from this dialog box.

The Apply onto list box enables you to specify at which level these permissions should apply: this object only, this object and all its children, its children only, computers only, groups only, sites, or users. A partial listing is shown in Figure 6.27, indicating the flexibility of permission assignment within Windows 2000. By selectively applying GPO permissions to only certain Active Directory objects, you can further narrow the scope of the policy and provide excellent control over the application of GPOs within your enterprise.

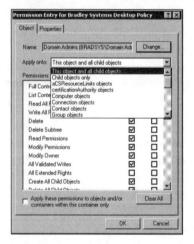

FIGURE 6.27

Permissions can be applied to many levels and types of objects.

The main part of the dialog box shows all the permissions that can be applied and those that have been allowed or denied to the named object indicated. You are able to check and uncheck permissions until you achieve the combination desired.

At the bottom of the dialog box, a couple other options also are available. To clear all the permissions that appear onscreen, instead of removing them one by one, you can select the Clear All button. This enables you to start fresh and apply only the permissions you require. It is usually a good idea to take note of what permissions existed before clearing them in case you want to get back to a known state.

The Apply these permissions to objects and/or containers within this container only check box is at the bottom of the screen. This limits the propagation of permissions to this level only and does not apply them to all lower levels. This is not that much of a concern for GPOs. In the NTFS file system permission assignment, for example, it can ensure that permissions are not overwritten two or more levels below where they were set. Permissions will be overwritten only at the level they were set.

By using permissions, the administrator can control to whom the policy will apply as well as who has the privilege to create or modify the policy settings. In this way, you are able to ensure that certain policies apply to a particular group of users or computers and that other policies do not.

Higher-level policies at the site or domain level can be configured to override settings for lower-level policies at the OU level. A lower-level administrator (at an OU, for example) also has the capability to block policy inheritance and not have settings from GPOs created at the site or domain level apply to his or her users (unless those GPOs have been configured with the No Override setting). These options are discussed in the next section.

> **NOTE**
>
> **Applying Advanced Permissions Settings** It is generally not a good idea to apply permissions at this level because it can be difficult to debug the application of a GPO after doing so. The simplified permissions available on the Security tab of the GPO Properties dialog box should provide most of the functionality required to properly apply and enforce Group Policy. Applying advanced permission settings can cause unexpected behavior in Group Policy unless it is carefully planned.

Group Policy Inheritance

In some cases, simply setting permissions to a GPO might not be enough. You might want to block GPOs from being applied to a part of Active Directory or force corporate standards to make sure they are adhered to by all parts of an organization. Finally, you might want to have a GPO apply only to certain users or computers and not to others. These three elements are called blocking, forcing, and filtering Group Policy and are discussed next.

Although not specifically an aspect of security, one very important element in determining how Group Policy is implemented is Group Policy inheritance. By using one or more of the methods of blocking, forcing, and filtering, you are able to fine-tune the application of Group Policy within your organization.

Using these same methods, you can force certain settings on all users (forcing), prevent higher-level policies from applying to a lower level such as an OU (blocking), or set permissions to make sure a policy applies only to the users it should (filtering). These methods are examined in the following sections.

Blocking Group Policy Inheritance

Group Policy can be set at the site, domain, and OU level. An administrator at the OU or domain level, however, might not want to have higher-level GPOs apply to his or her specific OU. Furthermore, because Active Directory allows for a tree-type structure for domains, a lower-level domain administrator in Paris might not want the English-language-specific settings configured in a GPO at the New York headquarters to overwrite the territory-specific settings he has configured for France. Essentially, blocking is beneficial when you need a specific set of GPO settings to be applied, and the inheritance of higher-level settings might be problematic because of regional differences or OU-specific characteristics. Blocking is most useful when an administrator for a container, such as an OU, needs to have total control over all characteristics of that container including GPOs.

When deciding whether to use blocking, it is important to be aware of two rules. First, when you decide to block policy inheritance, you are doing it for all GPOs higher up in the inheritance hierarchy. You cannot selectively decide which GPOs are blocked. It is an all-or-nothing proposition. Either all the GPO settings that have been configured at a higher level are blocked and any of their settings that you want applied have to be configured in your GPOs, or none of the GPO settings configured higher up are blocked. There is no middle ground; all GPOs are blocked or none are blocked.

The second rule to consider when deciding whether to use blocking is that higher-level administrators might not want certain GPOs blocked. In this case, they might force the application of a GPO whether or not you decide to block inheritance. Any forced

GPOs from a parent container, such as a site or domain, cannot be blocked at the child. This is to ensure that vital corporate settings exist everywhere. An example in which this might be useful is a GPO that ensures the automatic installation and updating of antivirus software at the site level. You might decide to block inheritance at the OU or domain level. If the GPO containing the settings for the antivirus software is configured to be forced, the software will be installed and maintained as specified in the site GPO.

To block Group Policy inheritance, perform the following steps.

STEP BY STEP

6.5 Blocking Group Policy Inheritance

1. Open the MMC used to administer the container at which you want to block GPO inheritance, either Active Directory Users and Computers or Active Directory Sites and Services.

2. Right-click the container at which you want to block Group Policy inheritance and select Properties.

3. In the dialog box presented, click the Group Policy tab.

4. Click the Block Policy inheritance check box, as shown in Figure 6.28, to block GPO settings from higher levels from being applied at this Active Directory container.

5. Click Apply and then OK to save your settings.

Setting a GPO to block policy inheritance is quite easy, but you must be aware of the consequences. After GPO settings are blocked at a particular Active Directory container, typically an OU, no higher-level settings will be applied to the container. This means that, if you want the behavior provided by the policies you just blocked, you need to create a GPO with the same settings. However, a higher-level administrator (for example, those at the domain level) might decide that certain GPOs cannot be blocked. They have the option to force GPOs to apply to all lower-level Active Directory containers. You will look at this next.

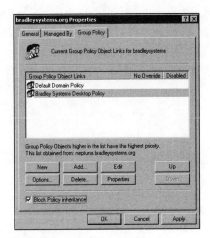

FIGURE 6.28
Block Group Policy inheritance by selecting the Block Policy inheritance check box.

Forcing Group Policy Settings

As a domain- or site-level administrator, you are responsible for a large number of users and computers within the organization. Lower-level administrators might be delegated administrative rights for their subdomain or OU. You want to be certain that several important settings, dictated by business policies, are not modified by lower-level administrators. These business policies might specify that a corporate logo must be used as desktop wallpaper by all users or that antivirus software must be installed on all machines. You create one or more GPOs with these corporate requirements configured and now need to ensure that they are applied across the entire enterprise. Group Policy enables you to do this by forcing these GPOs and their settings to all lower levels, whether or not GPO inheritance has been blocked.

When deciding whether to force a GPO to lower levels, always make sure this is the best way of accomplishing your goals. For example, you are considering forcing settings on lower-level containers within Active Directory that should only apply to the Sales department. Forcing this GPO from the domain level also changes settings for users in other departments and does not produce the desired result. When a GPO is forced, its settings override all lower-level settings whether or not they have been changed at the lower-level container.

When deciding whether to force GPO settings on lower levels of the hierarchy, ask yourself two questions: "Do all containers below this level HAVE TO have these settings?" and "Should lower-level administrators be able to change these settings?" If the answer to the first question is "Yes," then you might want to consider forcing the GPO. If the answer to the second question is "yes," then you might want to reconsider forcing the GPO. When the answer to the first is "yes" and the answer to the second is "no," this indicates that forcing the GPO is the best route so far.

To force GPO settings to be applied at all lower levels, perform the following steps.

STEP BY STEP

6.6 Forcing Group Policy Inheritance

1. Open the MMC used to administer the container from which you want to force GPO settings, either Active Directory Users and Computers or Active Directory Sites and Services.

2. Right-click the container containing the GPO whose settings you want to force and select Properties.

3. In the dialog box presented, click the Group Policy tab.

4. Click the Options button to bring up the GPO Options dialog box, as presented in Figure 6.29.

5. To force GPO settings to be applied to all lower levels, check the No Override check box.

6. Click OK to save your option settings.

7. Click Apply and then OK in the main Properties dialog box to save your settings.

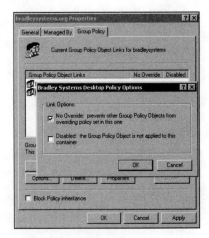

FIGURE 6.29
Force Group Policy settings to all lower-level containers by selecting the No Override option in the GPO Options dialog box.

Once again, it is important to reiterate that choosing to force GPO settings by selecting No Override in the Options dialog box forces the settings at that level to all lower-level Active Directory containers whether or not these same settings have been changed at the lower level. In other words, administrators who have configured the same settings at the subdomain or OU level will not have their settings applied.

Although blocking GPO settings and forcing GPO settings might provide you with much more functionality than what was available in Windows NT 4.0 System Policy, they still do not enable you to control which specific users will have the policy applied. This is done by filtering, or selectively applying permissions to, a GPO.

Filtering Group Policy

So far, you have seen how to block all GPOs from applying to a lower-level container and how to force GPO settings to all lower-level containers. However, you might want to have certain GPOs apply to some users, groups, or computers but not to others. The process used to selectively apply GPO settings is called filtering.

Filtering Group Policy means applying permissions on the GPO so it excludes certain users, security groups, or computers. In other words, filtering is really the careful management of permissions to ensure that the GPO applies only to the objects it should.

GPOs linked to Active Directory containers were discussed previously. When a GPO is linked to an Active Directory container, by default the Authenticated Users security group, which includes all users and computers, is granted the Read and Apply Group Policy permission. This means that, by default, GPO settings apply to everyone and everything unless other permissions are specified including Administrators. To filter Group Policy settings perform the following steps.

STEP BY STEP

6.7 Filtering Group Policy

1. Open the MMC used to administer the container from which you want to filter GPO settings, either Active Directory Users and Computers or Active Directory Sites and Services.

2. Right-click the container where the GPO settings you want to filter are located and select Properties.

3. In the dialog box presented, click the Group Policy tab.

4. Click the Properties button to open the GPO Properties dialog box.

5. Click the Security tab to see a list of users, groups, and computers that have been assigned permissions on the GPO.

6. If the user, group, or computer for whom you would like to filter the policy is not listed, click the Add button. You are then presented with a list of users, groups, and computers. Select the objects for which you want to filter the Group Policy settings and click Add and then OK.

7. As shown in Figure 6.30, to filter the application of GPO settings, clear the Read and Apply Group Policy check boxes under the Allow column in the Security tab. This ensures that the GPO settings do not apply to the user, computer, or security group for which you have cleared these permissions. Also clear the Allow column for Apply Group Policy for the Authenticated Users group or remove the Authenticated Users group.

An alternative way of filtering the policy is to check Deny for Apply Group Policy for the user, group, or computer to which you do not want the policy to apply. Deny always wins over Allow and is useful when you want to apply the GPO settings to most users with a few exceptions such as Administrators.

8. Click Apply and then OK to save your security settings.

9. Click Apply and OK on the main Properties dialog box to save your settings.

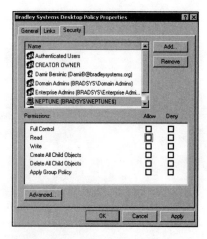

FIGURE 6.30
Clearing the Read and Apply Group Policy permissions for a user, security group, or computer filters the GPO and ensures that it does not apply to that object.

As you have learned, Group Policy inheritance can be blocked, forced, and filtered. Blocking policy inheritance means that GPO settings from higher-level Active Directory containers (sites and domains, typically) are not be applied to lower-level Active Directory containers (OUs). Forcing GPO settings is the opposite of blocking—ensuring that settings in a GPO created at a higher-level Active Directory container apply to all lower-level Active Directory container, regardless of whether GPO inheritance has been blocked. Filtering is the careful application of permissions to ensure that GPO settings only apply to the users and/or computers to which the Apply Group Policy permission has been granted.

All this is well and good, but what can you control using Group Policy? The next section discusses some of the reasons you would use Group Policy and how user and computer environments can be controlled using GPOs through administrative templates. Chapter 7, "Software Distribution Using Group Policy," and Chapter 8, "Managing Security Using Group Policy" provide more detail about other aspects of Group Policy.

MANAGING USER ENVIRONMENTS USING GROUP POLICY

Manage and troubleshoot user environments by using Group Policy.

- **Control user environments by using administrative templates.**
- **Assign script policies to users and computers.**

One of the challenges faced by administrators of Windows 2000, or any other network, is to make sure users have access to the resources required to do their jobs. Furthermore, as the resources required for users to do their jobs change, administrators must have a mechanism to propagate these changes to the affected users as quickly and as efficiently as possible. The ideal end result should be a lessening of the workload for administrators and properly configured environments for users.

Windows 2000 Group Policy enables the administrator, through the use of administrative templates and scripts, to configure user and computer environments once and then have these settings automatically applied to all users and computers requiring these settings. Administrative templates are changes made to the registry, while scripts are batch files, executable programs, or Windows Scripting Host files (such as VBScript or JavaScript). Changes made to GPOs within a container (for example, an OU) are automatically applied to all users and computers within that container, assuming permissions have been so configured. This means that any new user or computer added at the same container (for example, OU) level take on the settings specified without any additional configuration required on behalf of the administrator.

In managing user environments through the use of administrative templates and scripts, GPOs can be configured that enable you to do the following:

◆ Guarantee that all users have a standard corporate desktop.
Group Policy enables you to make sure corporate standards are
followed. These standards can include background wallpaper
for the desktop, a specific screen saver to be used, the characteristics of user passwords, frequency of password changes, and
logon messages. The idea is to guarantee that most of what
users need to have configured on their desktops, and what
they need to do their job, is configured for them. They do
not need to make changes to their settings to perform their
designated function but only if they want to step outside the
norm. This, however, can also be prevented if you so desire.

◆ Restrict users from accessing certain programs or parts of the
operating system. Although it might not be nice to say, some
users should not have access to parts of Windows 2000
because they might do more to harm themselves than to help
themselves. For example, you might want to restrict a user's
capability to open Control Panel to change system settings.
In situations in which a desktop configuration must be maintained as a corporate standard, users can be prevented from
making changes that deviate from that standard. Similarly,
you might want to ensure that users are not able to start the
command prompt or use the Run option on the Start menu
because this might load programs containing viruses.

The consequences of both of these examples can also result in
more help desk support calls, and this can increase the *total
cost of ownership* (TCO) for the organization. Generally, the
goal of restricting user access is twofold. Preventing users from
damaging their systems and minimizing any potential impact
their actions might have on support costs to the organization
is part of the goal. Providing users with all the requisite tools
to do their jobs is the other part of the goal.

◆ Guarantee that users always have the desktop settings, network
and printer connections, and programs they need to do their
job, no matter what machine they use to connect to the network. Windows 2000 Group Policy enables you to redirect
the location of user profiles and key folders to network drives.
This option enables the user to roam within the corporation
while still maintaining his or her desktop preferences as well
as network shares. You also are able to govern how large user

profiles can become and whether users can make changes to them. Shared printer and network drives that have been established for or by the user can also be reestablished whenever a user logs on to the network, no matter which computer is used to do so and even if the user is connecting remotely.

◆ Configure and restrict the use of certain Windows 2000 components such as Internet Explorer, Windows Explorer, and Microsoft Management Console. As an administrator, you can prevent users from executing certain Windows components through GPOs.

◆ Maintain a clean computer and desktop. One of the nice features of using GPOs to manage user environments is the capability to remove one user's settings from the desktop before another logs on. When a user logs off or restarts the machine, administrative templates can remove any desktop settings configured for that user from the computer and present a clean desktop and configuration for the next user logging on. In this way, one user's set of changes and configuration will not automatically impact or be inherited by the next. This reduces confusion for the next user and helps lower the TCO.

In the following sections, you will explore administrative template settings that affect users and those that affect computers. You also will learn to modify administrative templates. There will be times when you need to configure other aspects of the user environment such as ensuring that certain drive letters on the client machine are mapped to specific shares on the LAN. The following sections also discuss how to configure and use scripts in Group Policy and how to examine other configurable settings in Group Policy.

Administrative Template Settings

Manage and troubleshoot user environments by using Group Policy.

• **Control user environments by using Administrative Templates.**

When editing a GPO to configure or modify settings, you are presented with a Microsoft Management Console with the Group

Policy snap-in similar to Figure 6.31. As is evident in the figure, administrative templates can apply to both the computer configuration and the user configuration of the Group Policy. Although many settings apply to both, a few are specific to either the computer or the user.

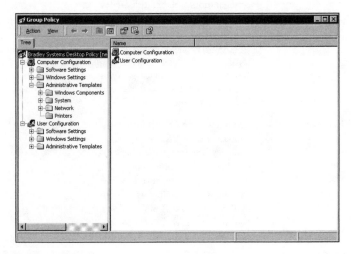

FIGURE 6.31
Some administrative templates apply to either the computer configuration or the user configuration of Group Policy.

The types of Administrative Template settings, what they control, and to what they apply are indicated in the following table.

Setting Type	Used to Control	Applies To
Windows Components	Parts of Windows 2000 and its tools. Here you are able to configure the behavior of parts of Windows 2000 including Internet Explorer, Microsoft NetMeeting, Windows Explorer, Windows Installer, Task Scheduler, and the Microsoft Management Console. The types of things that can be configured include whether the program can be launched, which portions of the program can be used, and how the program behaves once launched.	Computer User

continues

continued

Setting Type	Used to Control	Applies To
System	How parts of Windows 2000 operate including what happens at logon or logoff, DNS client suffix configuration, whether disk quotas are enforced, Group Policy characteristics such as refresh internal, and Windows File Protection—the capability for Windows 2000 to automatically replace critical system files that might have been overwritten by other programs.	Computer User
Network	Attributes of network connections such as whether RAS support is available for either dial-out or dial-in, whether modifications to network properties can be made, offline file configuration including whether the user can make use of offline files, and how and when synchronization takes place.	Computer User
Printer	Configuration of printers such as whether they can be published in Active Directory, whether to publish printers automatically, whether Web-based printing is permitted, and other settings such as computer location, the polling frequency for printers, and others.	Computer
Start Menu & Taskbar	The portions of the Start menu and taskbar that are available. This includes such things as whether the user has the **Search** command, **Run** command, Help, and Favorites visible on the Start menu. It also enables you to configure whether common program groups are visible to the user, whether Windows Update is an option, and many more. The idea here is to configure Start menu and taskbar settings that enable a user to perform his or her job but not provide the user with tools that could corrupt the his or her environment.	User

Setting Type	Used to Control	Applies To
Desktop	Active Desktop settings including whether to enable Active Desktop (it is enabled by default), permit or prohibit a user from making changes to desktop settings, specify a desktop wallpaper for the user, hide My Network Places icon from the user, save settings upon exit, and many others. Here you also can configure whether a user can perform Active Directory searches for computers and printers and how broad the scope of those searches can be.	User
Control Panel	The behavior of several aspects of Control Panel including whether it is enabled; which Control Panel applets are available to the user; whether the user is able to run Add/ Delete Programs to install and/or remove software; where the software can be installed from (CD, Web, network); control over display properties including the capability to add a screen saver, modify settings, enable or disable changing the wallpaper, and more; the addition, deletion, and modification of printers; and whether a specific language will be used by all users to whom the GPO applies.	User

The next sections will examine the administrative template settings that affect the user.

Administrative Template Settings That Affect the User

As previously indicated, administrative template settings that affect users can be broken down into six categories: Windows Components, Start Menu & Taskbar, Desktop, Control Panel, Network, and System. Each of these enables an administrator to lock down certain aspects of a user's experience. In the following sections, each of these categories is examined.

Administrative Template Windows Components Settings for Users

Windows Components administrative template settings enable you to configure the behavior and capabilities of six components of the Windows 2000 operating system (see Figure 6.32): Microsoft NetMeeting, Internet Explorer, Windows Explorer, Microsoft Management Console, Task Scheduler, and Windows Installer.

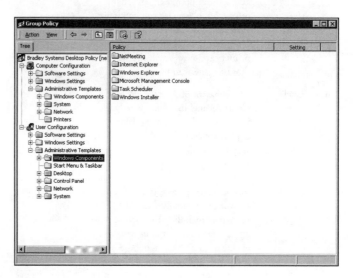

FIGURE 6.32
Administrative Templates Windows Components settings that can be changed for the user.

Microsoft NetMeeting

Using the template for Microsoft NetMeeting, you can specify some general settings (see Figure 6.33) such as whether the whiteboard feature is enabled and whether the user is allowed to enter Chat mode. You also have three additional folders with more settings that deal with configuration: Application Sharing, Audio & Video, and the NetMeeting Options Page.

In Application Sharing, you can set whether the user can share an application during a NetMeeting session, enable others to take control of the application, or enable sharing of the desktop.

When configuring Audio & Video, you can determine the amount of bandwidth a NetMeeting session is allowed to consume as well as whether video and audio can be used and their characteristics.

The Options Page settings enable you to specify what will be visible and modifiable by the users when they select options for NetMeeting.

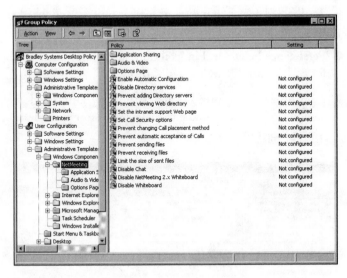

FIGURE 6.33
Administrative Templates settings for Microsoft NetMeeting that can be configured for the user.

Internet Explorer

Windows 2000 Group Policy enables you to be very precise about how *Internet Explorer* (IE) will behave for a user and how the user is able to configure IE. The settings that can be specified have to do with Internet Control Panel. You can configure a number of general Internet Explorer settings (see Figure 6.34) such as whether the user has the option to manage digital certificates, language settings, color settings, whether the user can customize the search page, and others. In addition, a number of other elements of IE can be set using Group Policy, including the following:

◆ **Internet Control Panel.** Which pages are available when users select Tools, Preferences in IE.

◆ **Offline pages.** The configuration of channels and subscriptions and the frequency of updates.

◆ **Browser menus.** The characteristics of the menus available and which options should be included. For example, disabling the source menu option to view the HTML source for a page.

◆ **Toolbars.** The configuration of toolbar buttons and whether they can be modified by the user.

◆ **Persistence behavior.** Limits the amount of disk space used for caching for different types of IE zones.

◆ **Administrator-approved controls.** Which controls and components the user is able to make use of (for example, Media Player or Shockwave).

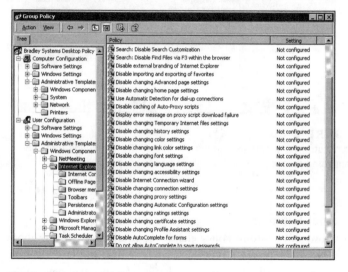

FIGURE 6.34
Administrative Templates Internet Explorer settings that can be configured for the user.

Windows Explorer

As an administrator, you also are able to configure the characteristics of Windows Explorer for the user through Group Policy Administrative Templates (see Figure 6.35). This enables you to specify whether the user is able to see other computers on the network by enabling or disabling Entire Network and Computers Near Me in Windows Explorer. You can also specify whether a user is allowed to have the option to map network drives from within Windows

Explorer. Other characteristics that can be set include the appearance of Windows Explorer, whether recent files are tracked and available to the user, and the behavior of shortcuts when a user is roaming.

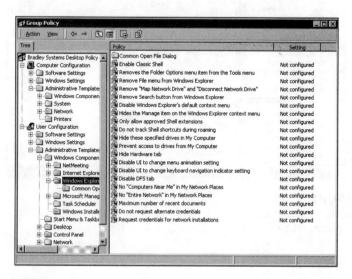

FIGURE 6.35
Administrative Templates Windows Explorer settings that can be configured for the user.

Microsoft Management Console

One of the nice features of administrative templates for configuring user settings, as it applies to administering Windows 2000, is the capability of a domain administrator to delegate authority but also lock down which Microsoft Management Console features are available to the junior administrators. With MMC settings in Group Policy (see Figure 6.36), a senior administrator can specify whether a junior administrator, or any other user, is able to modify the MMC consoles. You can also specify whether a junior administrator can make use of all or a subset of the MMC snap-ins available or can make changes to aspects of Group Policy that might have been configured. This control is possible because MMC, with its various snap-ins, is the main console for administering Windows 2000. Only the people who should have access to it have access; others are excluded.

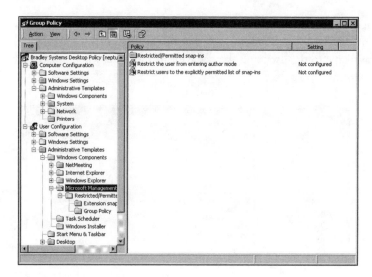

FIGURE 6.36
Administrative Templates Microsoft Management Console settings that can be configured for the user.

Task Scheduler

Windows 2000 provides for a Task Scheduler. This feature is much improved as compared to the AT scheduler in Windows NT. As shown in Figure 6.37, with Group Policy, you can set the behavior of the Task Scheduler for a user including whether he or she is able to delete tasks, create new tasks, or even run tasks. In this way, you can prevent unwanted jobs from running when they shouldn't or from running at all.

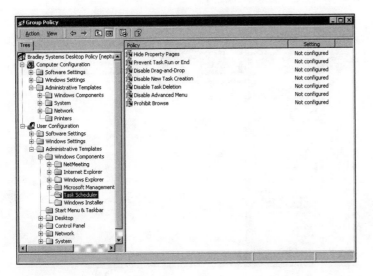

FIGURE 6.37
Administrative Templates Task Scheduler settings that can be configured
for the user.

Windows Installer

Windows Installer template settings are extremely useful in preventing users from installing software they should not have on their
machines. Using Windows Installer settings for the user (see Figure
6.38), you can configure the media search order for files to be
installed (that is, floppy, CD, or network). You can disable the
capability to install software from removable media (that is, floppy
or CD). You can also specify whether, during installation, the Install
program should run with administrative privileges.

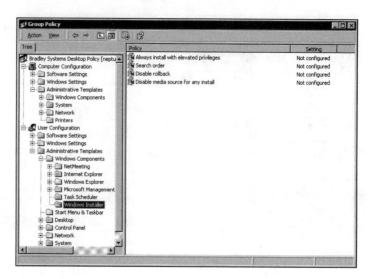

FIGURE 6.38
Administrative Templates Windows Installer settings that can be configured for the user.

As you have seen, with Windows Components administrative template settings for the user, you are able to configure the behavior of several key pieces of Windows 2000 for the user: Microsoft NetMeeting, Internet Explorer, Windows Explorer, Microsoft Management Console, Task Scheduler, and Windows Installer. Other parts of Windows 2000 can also be configured using Group Policy, such as the Start menu and the taskbar, which are discussed next.

Administrative Template Start Menu & Taskbar Settings for the User

Start Menu & Taskbar settings that can be configured for the user with Administrative Templates determine how the Windows Start menu appears as well as its functionality. You are able to specify (see Figure 6.39) whether the user has a **Run** command on his or her Start menu, allowing him or her to launch any program. Disabling the **Run** command prevents the user from running any program except those for which shortcuts already exist, although other methods (such as the command prompt or double-clicking a file in Windows Explorer) can still allow a user to launch a program. It also enables you to specify whether the Search, Help, Favorites,

and Documents menus are available from the Start menu. You
can also include or remove the common program groups, the user
program groups, or both/neither from the list of programs, thereby
further limiting what programs the user is able to run.

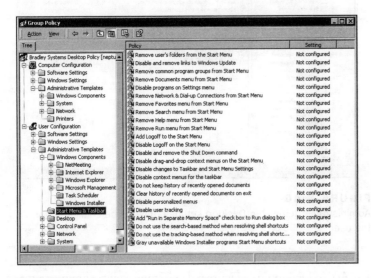

FIGURE 6.39
Administrative Templates Start Menu & Taskbar settings that can be
configured for the user.

As shown, Start Menu & Taskbar settings that can be configured
for the user with administrative templates determine how the
Windows Start menu appears as well as its functionality.

Administrative Template Desktop Settings for the User

Desktop settings that can be specified for the user with administrative templates include Active Directory and Active Desktop settings
as well as some general desktop configurations (see Figure 6.40).
Some of the general settings that can be configured include whether
My Documents appears on the desktop and/or the Start menu. You
also can determine whether changes to the desktop are saved when
the user logs off. This template enables you to choose whether
Internet Explorer, My Network Places, or even any icons appear on
the desktop. This template also enables you to determine whether
the user can make changes to the location of the taskbar.

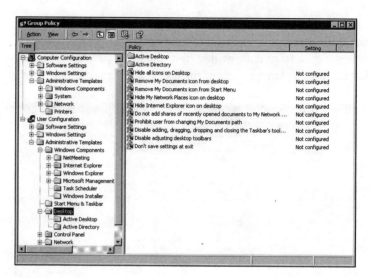

FIGURE 6.40
Administrative Templates Desktop settings that can be configured for
the user.

For Active Desktop (see Figure 6.41), Group Policy administrative
templates enable you to set whether Active Desktop is used, the
wallpaper that will be used, and whether that wallpaper is a bitmap
(BMP) file or another type such as a JPEG or GIF. You also can
configure whether the user is allowed to make changes to the desktop including adding, deleting, modifying, and even closing items.
A comprehensive Prohibit Changes setting can also be specified to
prohibit changes of any kind.

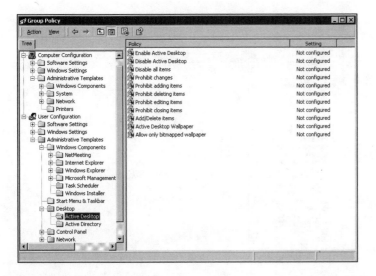

FIGURE 6.41
Administrative Templates Active Desktop settings that can be configured
for the user.

Only a few settings can be specified for the user for Active Directory
(see Figure 6.42). The settings available deal with the depth of
Active Directory searches (the number of objects returned in a single
search) and enabling you to configure whether the user can filter
those searches. These settings are intended for use in large organizations with tens of thousands of users and many more computers.
These setting primarily ensure that a search through Active
Directory does not take up a lot of time or consume a great deal
of network bandwidth or domain controller resources.

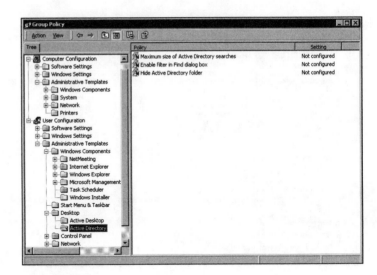

FIGURE 6.42
Administrative Templates Active Directory settings that can be configured for the user.

Desktop settings that can be specified for the user with administrative templates enable the administrator to predetermine elements of the desktop such as the wallpaper to be displayed, the redirection of key folders to a network drive for backup, and others. They are used to ensure that all desktops conform to corporate policies.

Administrative Template Control Panel Settings for the User

One of the areas of greatest potential concern to an administrator is the user changing his or her configuration without being fully aware of the consequences of the changes. You might have heard stories, or have firsthand experience, of a user making a change to his or her network configuration that disconnected him or her from the network and then calling for support to try and fix it. In some cases, a little bit of benevolent paternalism is useful to prevent users from shooting themselves in the foot (and some users do insist on shotguns!).

In administrative templates user settings that relate to Control Panel (see Figure 6.43), you can configure four main items: Add/Remove Programs, Display, Printers, and Regional Options (as well as some general setting). The most useful of these general settings is the capability to disable Control Panel. This is useful for a large chunk of the user base that does not need to make any changes to their systems or that only are allowed to run a corporate-standard desktop. If you would like to permit the user to make use of some of the applets in Control Panel, you are able to specify which ones to show or hide. This regulates the amount of potential damage a user can inflict upon his or her system.

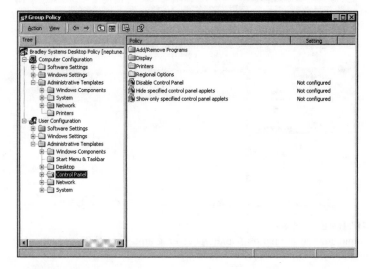

FIGURE 6.43
Administrative Templates Control Panel settings that can be configured for the user.

As previously mentioned, four of the items you can configure In administrative templates user settings relate to Control Panel: Add/Remove Programs, Display, Printers, and Regional Options. These items are discussed in the following sections.

Add/Remove Programs

In the Add/Remove Programs folder of the Control Panel administrative template for the user (see Figure 6.44), you can configure whether a user can make use of this applet. Further, if you decide to allow the user to run the Add/Remove Programs applet, you can specify whether the user is able to add, change, or remove programs. You can specify whether the user can add programs from a CD, floppy, the network, or from Microsoft (Windows Update capability). You also can allow or prevent a user from installing Windows Components, such as games or other parts of the operating system, that can be specified during the installation process of Windows 2000.

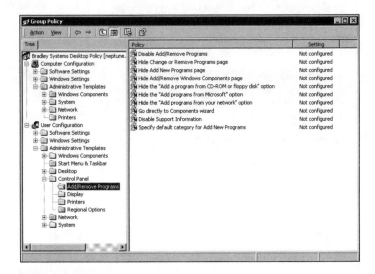

FIGURE 6.44
Administrative Templates Add/Remove Programs Control Panel settings that can be configured for the user.

Display

A key requirement of locking down a user's desktop is the capability to specify the way his desktop is displayed. This is controlled through the Display applet in the Control Panel, which also can be configured with Group Policy administrative templates (see Figure 6.45). As an administrator, you can specify whether a user can make any changes to his display settings and, if so, what these can include. Changes you might specify include such items as the display background or screen saver. You can specify password protection of the screen saver once enabled. This is useful to provide a minimal level of security when a user walks away from his desk. You can also control the capability of the user to change his resolution and number of colors.

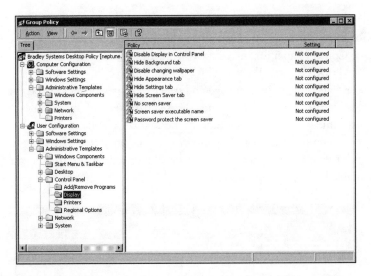

FIGURE 6.45
Administrative Templates Display Control Panel settings that can be configured for the user.

Printers

To control printers, administrative templates (see Figure 6.46) enable you to set whether a user can add or remove printers through the Printer applet in the Control Panel or by going to Settings, Printers from the Start menu. You can also specify where the user can search for printers that he or she might be allowed to add (a Web site, Active Directory, or the network).

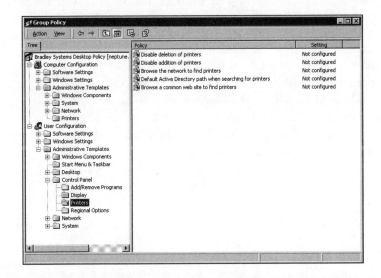

FIGURE 6.46
Administrative Templates Printers Control Panel settings that can be configured for the user.

Regional Options

Regional Options only has one setting in the administrative template for Control Panel for the user (see Figure 6.47). Regional Options are allowed or not allowed. This enables you to configure whether users can change the language and other territory- or region-specific characteristics of their machines. These characteristics include the date/time format, currency, and numeric format, such as decimal and thousand separators. If you want to guarantee that all users run with the same settings and are not be able to change them, you can disable this policy option.

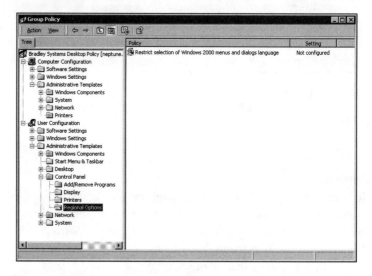

FIGURE 6.47
Administrative Templates Regional Options Control Panel settings that can be configured for the user.

In specifying Control Panel settings, the administrator is able to preconfigure with Group Policy which options in Control Panel are available to users to make changes to their computers and which are locked down. This ensures that users do not, through their own actions, cause their computers to stop functioning, thereby requiring support personnel to be dispatched.

Administrative Template Network Settings for the User

With Network settings for the user through Group Policy administrative templates, you are able to specify the behavior of Offline Files and Network and Dial-up Connections (see Figure 6.48).

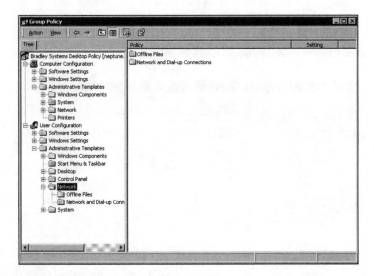

FIGURE 6.48
Administrative Templates Network settings that can be configured for the user.

Offline Files Network Settings

One of the nice features of Windows 2000, especially for individuals who travel a fair bit and make use of a notebook computer to connect to the office network, is the capability to configure certain network folders to be available offline. This can also be a problem for the administrator, however, who might not want certain files to be available offline (for example, source code for a new piece of software being developed for commercial resale). Administrative templates enable you to configure how offline files behave for the user (see Figure 6.49). You are able to specify whether this feature is turned off completely. You can control which folders users can make available offline and whether they can configure this themselves. You can specify the frequency of reminders about synchronization and offline file availability. Administrative templates enable you to determine what happens when a server becomes available (that is, whether cache copies of files should be used or the files should become unavailable). You also determine whether the Make Available Offline menu option is even shown for network file resources.

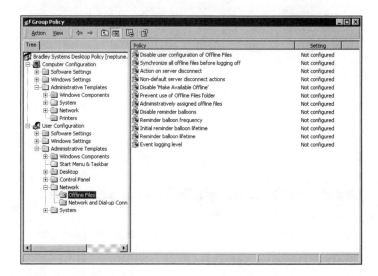

FIGURE 6.49
Administrative Templates Offline Files Network settings that can be configured for the user.

Dial-Up Connections

The other part of Network settings that can be configured for the user has to do with the behavior of dial-up connections and network configuration. Through these policy settings (see Figure 6.50), you can specify whether a user can add or remove RAS (that is, dial-up) connections for himself or all users. You can specify whether users can connect and disconnect using RAS or the network, can rename RAS connections, or can modify TCP/IP settings. This control enables you to lock down network settings that the user might want to change, but doing so could cause him grief. These same settings can be enabled for users who are more technically savvy and who understand the implications of making a change to TCP/IP settings or a RAS connection configuration.

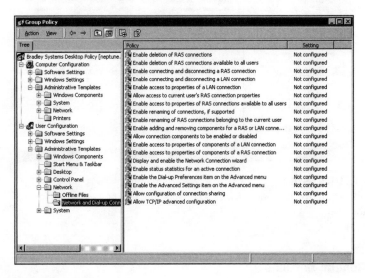

FIGURE 6.50
Administrative Templates Network and Dial-Up Connections settings that can be configured for the user.

In configuring network settings through Group Policy, you can control whether offline files will be enabled or disabled by default as well as their characteristics. The behavior of networking and dial-up connections also can be controlled.

Administrative Template System Settings for the User

The last set of configuration items that can be specified through administrative templates for the user deals with system behavior. This includes some general settings (see Figure 6.51) as well as two particular categories of system settings: Logon/Logoff and Group Policy.

N O T E

Disable the Use of Registry Editing Tools It is strongly recommended that you disable the use of registry editing tools for the majority of your users. The registry stores critical system settings and application information that is needed by Windows 2000 and to run most Windows 2000 applications. A modification of the registry by a user is an immediate action that cannot be rolled back unless the user remembers the changes he or she made during the modification. As such, it is quite possible that a user might cause a serious problem on his or her system by modifying the registry and not being aware of the consequences.

Disabling the user's capability to modify the registry still allows you to do so yourself. You can modify the registry either locally on the machine where the changes need to be made or remotely. Administrators, by default, have the capability to perform remote registry edits.

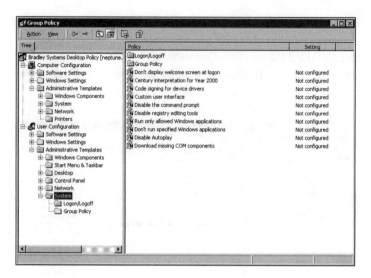

FIGURE 6.51
Administrative Templates System settings that can be configured for the user.

General Settings

In the general portion of System settings, you can specify whether a welcome screen is displayed to the user at logon. You also can control whether the user is able to use registry editing tools. You can lock down the applications that the user is able to run. For example, you can determine that only those applications whose EXE file is listed in the setting can be run and that all others cannot. You can disable Autoplay for CDs inserted into the CD-ROM drive. You also can disable the command prompt. These are probably the most restrictive settings that can be applied to a user and have the greatest immediate impact of what is permitted or denied for the user.

Logon/Logoff Settings

When dealing with Logon/Logoff settings for a user (see Figure 6.52), you can set the behavior of logon and logoff script execution. For example, you can determine whether these scripts are visible or run asynchronously. You govern the capability for a user to change his or her password or even to log off. You can limit the size of the user's profile, remove certain folders from the profile, and outline what programs run or are not run at logon.

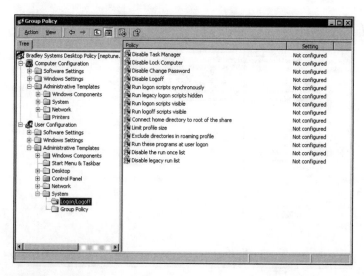

FIGURE 6.52
Administrative Templates Logon/Logoff System settings that can be configured for the user.

Group Policy

The Group Policy portion (see Figure 6.53) of the System settings of the administrative template for a user enables you to set which domain controllers are used to download the GPTs from a domain controller. You can determine how frequently the computer refreshes any policy from a domain controller. You also can determine whether administrative template (ADM) files should be automatically updated.

The System settings portion of administrative template settings for the user is quite powerful. It enables the administrator to preconfigure how Group Policy is applied to each user as well as whether the user is required to log on and, if so, whether a company-specific message is displayed. It allows even more precise control over a user's desktop by domain administrators.

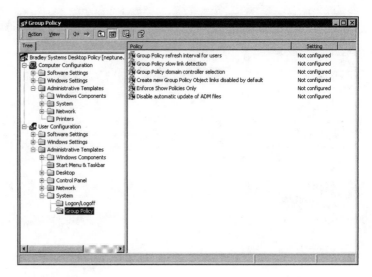

FIGURE 6.53
Administrative Templates Group Policy System settings that can be configured for the user.

The Usefulness of Administrative Template Settings for the User

Now that you have seen some of the things that can be set for the user when using administrative templates, it might be worthwhile to review what types of control this provides the administrator.

Using administrative templates to control user settings, the administrator is able to do the following:

◆ **Lock down user desktops.** Through proper configuration of Windows Components, Desktop, and Start Menu & Taskbar settings, you can control the appearance and capabilities of the desktop that a user can use.

◆ **Lock down user access to resources.** By making use of settings for Windows Components, Desktop, and Start Menu & Taskbar, you also can limit the user to a specific set of network folders, printers, and local resources. These are in addition to, and not a replacement for, proper NTFS and share permissions for these resources.

◆ **Lock down user access to administrative tools and applications.** Through specification of Windows Components, Desktop, Start Menu & Taskbar, and System settings, you can prevent users from making use of administrative tools such as Control Panel, MMC, registry editing tools, and other applications that might cause their configuration to become unusable.

A great many elements of a user's experience with a Windows 2000 computer can be controlled by an administrator through Group Policy. These include what programs can be run, how the desktop appears, what network functionality is available, and whether the user is required to log on, to name a few. User desktop settings are not the entire scope that can be affected by administrative templates. Computer settings also can be configured in Group Policy to make sure that a computer, no matter which user is logged on to it, has a predefined set of characteristics.

Administrative Template Settings That Affect the Computer

As previously mentioned, administrative templates apply to both the user and the computer. The number of areas in which you can configure administrative template settings for the computer is fewer than for the user (see Figure 6.54). You can configure four areas instead of six, and the number of settings available is also fewer. This is primarily because any setting configured for the computer applies to all users on that particular machine. Any user logging on to a machine for which computer settings have been configured through administrative templates has those settings apply. The settings that can be configured for the computer include Windows Components, System, Network, and Printer settings.

NOTE **Administrative Templates in Computer and User Portions of Group Policy** Any administrative template setting existing in both the computer portion and the user portion of Group Policy always has the computer setting apply. In other words, if you specify in the computer portion of the administrative template for a GPO that Autoplay of CD-ROMs should be disabled, but the user portion configures Autoplay to be enabled, the computer setting wins: Autoplay is disabled. This is because a user can log on to several machines and have the same GPO settings applied no matter where he or she logs on, while a computer can only exist once, and its configuration must be protected at the expense of user preferences.

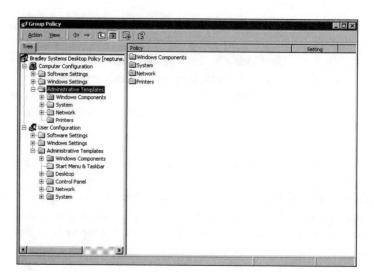

FIGURE 6.54
Administrative Templates settings that can be configured for the computer.

Generally, the number of items that can be configured for the computer using administrative templates is far fewer than the number of items to be configured for the user with the same portion of the administrative template. For example, even though the Windows Components folder appears in both the computer and user portions, the number of settings that can be configured for the user is much greater and more precise. This is because many of the settings are changes that need to be made to the user portion of the registry (HKEY_CURRENT_USER) instead of the computer portion (HKEY_LOCAL_MACHINE). It only makes sense that more changes need to be made to the user portion for application and other configuration settings than to the computer portion. The computer portion deals with the characteristics of the machine for all users (that is, a minimal required configuration), while the user portion deals with individual preferences, of which there might be many.

Administrative Template Windows Components Settings for the Computer

In the Windows Components portion of the administrative template for the computer (see Figure 6.55), you are presented with four areas of Windows 2000 for which you can configure settings: NetMeeting,

Internet Explorer, Task Scheduler, and Windows Installer. These all were also found in the user portion of the GPO, though the user portion also included MMC and Windows Explorer.

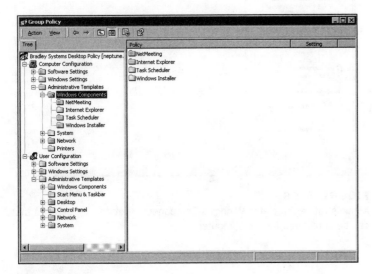

FIGURE 6.55
Administrative Templates Windows Components settings that can be configured for the computer.

NetMeeting

In the NetMeeting folder, only one setting (see Figure 6.56) can be configured for the computer: whether to allow remote desktop sharing. This is unlike the many settings available for the user. Remote desktop sharing is the capability of the desktop to be controlled remotely through NetMeeting. You configure this for the computer so that no one can access and take control of the computer remotely, a potential security risk.

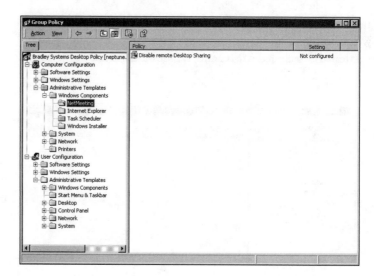

FIGURE 6.56
Administrative Templates Windows Components/NetMeeting settings that can be configured for the computer.

Internet Explorer

Using the computer settings related to Internet Explorer (see Figure 6.57), you can lock down proxy settings as well as security policies for all users on the computer. You also have the option to remove the Internet Explorer splash screen on the invocation of Internet Explorer. You can control whether IE checks for updates to itself or automatically installs any missing components because of a single user's interaction with a site requiring a component not currently installed. In other words, you can govern the look, feel, and behavior of IE for all users on the machine.

Task Scheduler

The Task Scheduler settings that can be configured for the computer (see Figure 6.58) are almost identical to those for the user. As previously mentioned, the computer setting always wins in the event of a conflict, so this is the preferred location for any setting that should apply to all users. These settings include whether any user on the computer can create or delete a task and whether the task's property pages are visible.

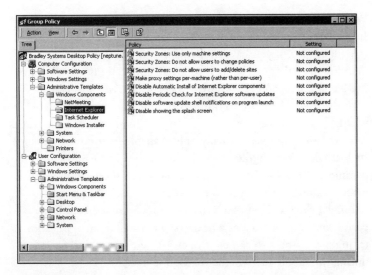

FIGURE 6.57
Administrative Templates Windows Components/Internet Explorer settings that can be configured for the computer.

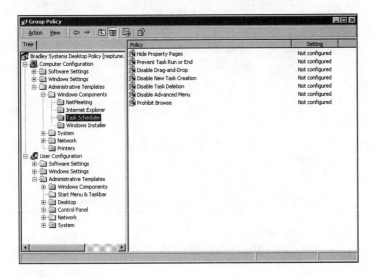

FIGURE 6.58
Administrative Templates Windows Components/Task Scheduler settings that can be configured for the computer.

Windows Installer

In configuring settings for Windows Installer at the computer level (see Figure 6.59), you have the capability to control whether Windows Installer can be used to install applications on Windows 2000 computers and how those installs behave when interacting with the user. These interaction settings include such options as whether the user has control over installs (that is, can make changes to installation options normally only available to administrators such as where certain files go and which type of program group—common or user—an application creates). Another option is whether a user is able to perform certain additional tasks such as browse the media or patch the application while his or her permissions are elevated as a result of the install of an application taking place. You also can control elevating the user's privileges during the install and whether to log the install.

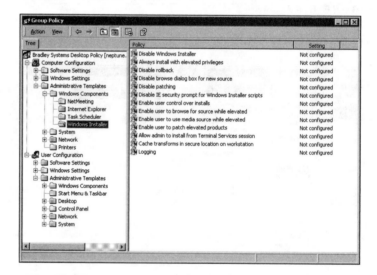

FIGURE 6.59
Administrative Templates Windows Components/Windows Installer settings that can be configured for the computer.

In configuring the behavior of Windows Components such as Windows Installer, Internet Explorer, NetMeeting, and Task Scheduler, you are ensuring that these apply to all users on the computers affected by the policy. You also can configure other system behavior such as quotas using System settings.

Administrative Template System Settings for the Computer

On the system side, administrative template settings that can be configured at the computer level (see Figure 6.60) deal with five areas: Logon, Disk Quotas, DNS Client, Group Policy, and Windows File Protection. Some general settings also can be configured that pertain to the computer as a whole. These include whether certain options appear on the Start menu if the user is logging on to Windows 2000 through a Terminal Services connection. The appearance of status messages to the user during boot, logon, logoff, or shutdown can be configured with this template. Finally, you can control which programs to run at startup.

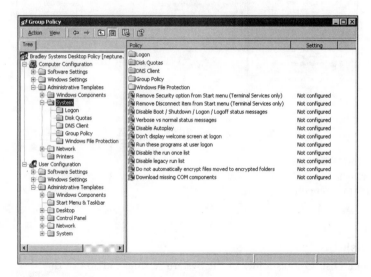

FIGURE 6.60
Administrative Templates System settings that can be configured for the computer.

Logon

During logon, Windows 2000 goes through a number of phases, and some of these require user interaction. The Logon portion of the System administrative template of the GPO (see Figure 6.61) enables you to specify what happens when some of these conditions are encountered. Here, you can set how startup scripts are run for the computer. This is different from logon scripts for the user, which are set in the user portion of this GPO. You can specify whether roaming profiles are deleted after a user logs off. You can force the download of a user profile even if logon is taking place over a slow network connection such as a modem dial-in. You can specify time-out settings for dialog boxes and profile downloads.

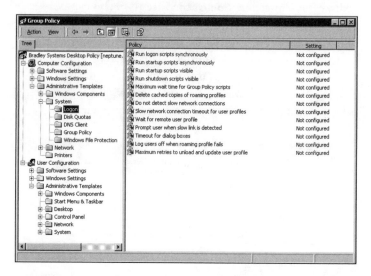

FIGURE 6.61
Administrative Templates System/Logon settings that can be configured for the computer.

Disk Quotas

The Disk Quotas folder of the System settings portion of the computer administrative template (see Figure 6.62) lets you enable or disable disk quotas for a machine. Disk quotas are used to limit the amount of disk space that any one user can occupy on a machine. Enabling disk quotas in the template provides the possibility of setting them at the file system level; disabling them in the policy turns off quota enforcement whether or not they are configured at the file system level. You also can specify what happens when a user exceeds his or her quota. You can establish the default quota limit. Finally, this portion of the template enables you to determine whether to log, in the Windows NT event log, when a user reaches a warning or maximum quota level.

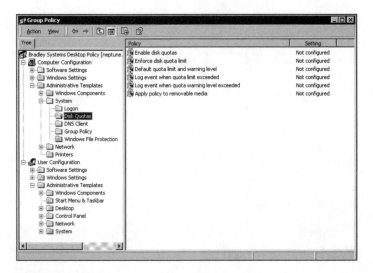

FIGURE 6.62
Administrative Templates System/Disk Quotas settings that can be
configured for the computer.

DNS Client

There is only one setting for the computer in the DNS Client
portion of the administrative template (see Figure 6.63); this setting
is the Primary DNS Suffix. This setting enables you to specify what
should be appended to the name of the machine to create a *fully
qualified domain name* (FQDN) for the host. This is required for
Active Directory functionality and host name resolution. Setting
the suffix here prevents all users, including administrators, from
changing it in the TCP/IP Properties dialog box for the computer's
network configuration.

Group Policy

Similar to the Group Policy portion of the user administrative
template (see Figure 6.64), the computer settings for Group Policy
within the System folder of the administrative template are used to
govern what happens during GPO processing for the computer. This
also controls the frequency of refreshes for both domain controllers
and other types of Windows 2000 computers. You also are able to
specify which portions of the GPO are processed for the computer,
including scripts, software installation policy, Encrypting File System
policy, and disk quota policy.

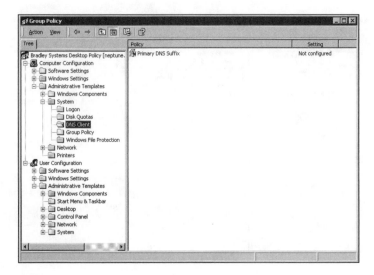

FIGURE 6.63
Administrative Templates System/DNS Client settings that can be configured for the computer.

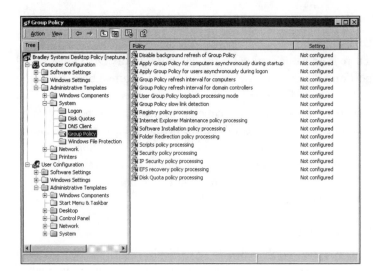

FIGURE 6.64
Administrative Templates System/Group Policy settings that can be configured for the computer.

Windows File Protection

Windows File Protection (WFP) is the capability of Windows 2000 computers to automatically replace critical system files when they have been overwritten by other applications such as an installer program for a piece of software. The Windows File Protection portion of the computer administrative template (see Figure 6.65) enables you to specify the frequency of scans by WFP. These scans determine whether any files need to be restored to their original state. You can determine the location of the WFP cache in case you want to move it from the default. You can determine whether a limit should be placed on the cache. The cache is used to store copies of Windows 2000 files that may be replaced by other programs, so they can be more easily restored without requiring you to insert a CD containing the original files. You also can determine whether the file scan progress window is hidden as the scans take place.

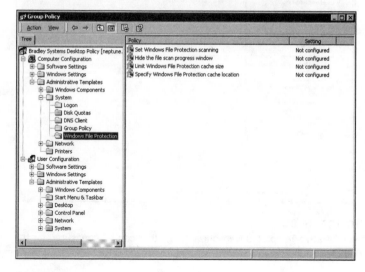

FIGURE 6.65
Administrative Templates System/Windows File Protection settings that can be configured for the computer.

Using the System settings portion of the administrative templates for the computer, you can configure logon, disk quota, DNS client domain name suffixes, Group Policy, and Windows File Protection behavior for all users on the computer. This ensures that these elements adhere to corporate policies that might have been established. Using Network settings, you also are able to configure how the computer behaves on the network.

Administrative Template Network Settings for the Computer
Manage network configuration by using Group Policy.

Like the user portion of the Network settings for the administrative template, the computer portion (see Figure 6.66) enables you to configure Offline File settings as well as Network and Dial-up Connections configuration.

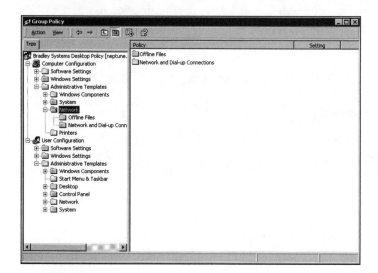

FIGURE 6.66
Administrative Templates Network settings that can be configured for the computer.

Offline Files

The Offline Files settings that can be configured from the computer portion of the administrative template (see Figure 6.67) are almost identical to the user settings. Here, you also find such options as whether to show the Make Files Available Offline option for a folder and balloon reminder settings. There also are other computer-level settings. These settings include the capability for you to configure whether offline files are supported on this machine. You can determine whether local copies of offline files should be erased from the hard drive after a user logs off. You also can determine the logging level for offline file events and the default cache size. In other words, settings that can impact many users and reduce disk space are available only on the computer portion of the administrative template.

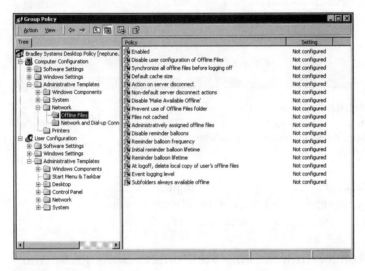

FIGURE 6.67
Administrative Templates Network/Offline Files settings that can be configured for the computer.

Network and Dial-Up Connections

The only setting that can be specified in the Network and Dial-up Connections folder of the Network portion of the computer administrative template is whether to allow configuration of connection sharing on the computer (see Figure 6.68). Connection sharing is a feature of Windows 2000 that enables users to configure their system as a gateway to the Internet for a small network of 2 to 10 users.

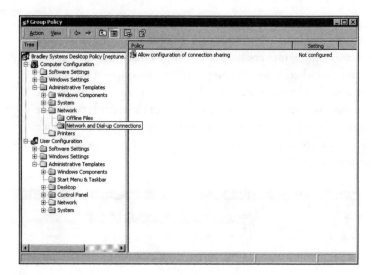

FIGURE 6.68
Administrative Templates Network and Dial-up Connections settings that can be configured for the computer.

With network settings for the computer, the administrator can configure the behavior of offline files and whether sharing of an Internet connection can be enabled on the computer.

Administrative Template Printers Settings for the Computer

The Printers portion of the computer administrative template (see Figure 6.69) enables you to specify whether printers defined on the computer can be published in Active Directory. You also can determine whether Web-based printing, a new Windows 2000 feature, should be allowed. This portion of the template enables you to specify whether printers on the computer are announced for browsing on the network. You can determine whether printers should be pruned and the pruning characteristics. Pruning is a feature of Windows 2000 domain controllers that automatically removes printers from Active Directory if they become unavailable and republishes them if they come back to life.

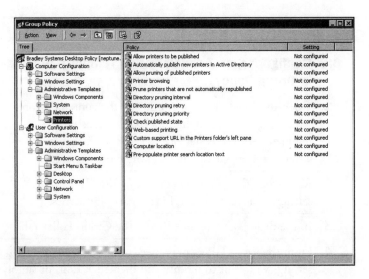

FIGURE 6.69
Administrative Templates Printer settings that can be configured for
the computer.

In specifying computer settings using administrative templates, you
can configure several aspects of behavior for the computer. These
aspects include Windows 2000 components such as IE or Windows
Installer, system behavior for things such as disk quotas and
Windows File Protection, and network and printer settings. These
elements are similar to those that can be configured for the user. In
cases in which user and computer settings conflict, the computer
setting always applies.

Having found out what the available options are for configuring
users and computers using administrative templates in Group Policy,
the next logical step is to implement them within a GPO.

Modifying Administrative Template Settings

Although a lot of time has been spent outlining just what kind of
settings can be applied to the user, the computer, or both, how to
actually implement an administrative template setting has not yet
been mentioned. Step by Step 6.8 provides you with the necessary
information to modify an administrative template.

STEP BY STEP

6.8 Configuring an Administrative Template Setting in Group Policy

1. Open the MMC used to administer the container from which you want to configure GPO administrative template settings, either Active Directory Users and Computers or Active Directory Sites and Services.

2. Right-click the container containing the GPO whose settings you want to modify and select Properties.

3. In the dialog box presented, click the Group Policy tab.

4. From the list of GPOs presented, click the one whose settings you want to modify and then click Edit, or simply double-click the GPO you want to edit. This starts an MMC console to edit the Group Policy.

5. Expand (press the + symbol next to) the Administrative Templates portion of either the Computer Configuration section of the GPO (if you want to modify a computer setting) or the User Configuration section of the GPO (if you want to modify a user setting). For example, if you want to enable disk quotas for all users on a set of computers, you would expand the Administrative Templates section of the Computer Configuration.

6. Continue to expand the folders at lower levels of the administrative template until you reach the folder containing the setting you want to modify. For example, to enable disk quotas, expand System and then Disk Quotas until the MMC console looks similar to Figure 6.70.

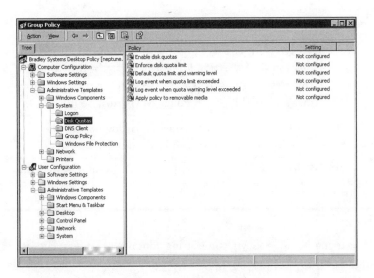

FIGURE 6.70
To enable disk quotas, expand the Administrative Templates, System, Disk Quotas folders of the Computer Configuration portion of the GPO.

7. To enable or disable a setting, double-click the setting you want to modify and then select the appropriate radio button: Enabled, Disabled, or Not Configured (as shown in Figure 6.71). Enabled means the policy setting will be enforced at this level, although it can be overridden at a lower level such as an OU. Disabled means the setting will not be enforced at this level. Not Configured means the setting will not be set at this time but will be inherited from a parent container such as a domain or site. Not Configured is the default for all settings when you create a new GPO.

8. As shown in Figure 6.72, it also is possible to get additional information about the setting you are going to change in the Windows 2000 Group Policy Editor. Clicking the Explain tab presents a short explanation of what the setting does and what will happen if you enable or disable the setting.

continues

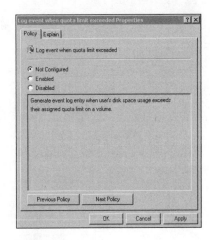

FIGURE 6.71
To enable disk quotas, click the Enable radio button in the setting Properties dialog box.

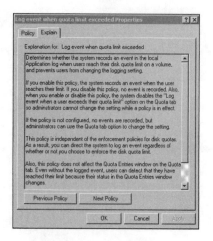

FIGURE 6.72
The Explain tab displays information on the effect of enabling a setting.

continued

9. To save your changes to the setting, click Apply and then OK to exit the setting Properties dialog box. If you have completed all the changes to the GPO that you want to make, close the Group Policy MMC to save the GPO.

10. Click OK to close the Properties dialog box for the container whose GPO you just modified.

11. Exit the Active Directory Users and Computers or Active Directory Sites and Services MMC.

Specifying Group Policy settings using administrative templates is quite simple. Pick the setting you want to enable or disable, click the appropriate button, and Group Policy is specified. The hardest part is determining which setting should be enabled or disabled, and it might require many hours of discussion to arrive at a cohesive policy. However, in some cases, administrative templates do not provide the functionality needed to properly configure a user's or computer's environment. For these eventualities, Microsoft Windows 2000 enables you to create scripts and have them enforced using Group Policy.

Configuring and Using Scripts in Group Policy

In this section, you will learn about scripts and how they are processed on Windows 2000 computers. You will then be shown how to attach a script to a GPO for the computer portion of the GPO (startup and shutdown scripts) or the user portion of the GPO (logon and logoff scripts).

The options available with administrative templates might not be sufficient to provide the complete environment needed by a user to perform his or her job. Examples of this include the automatic creation of certain shortcuts on the desktop or the establishment of printer and network shared folder connections at the time a user logs on. To have these changes take place automatically when a computer starts up or a user logs on, you can make use of Group Policy scripts.

Group Policy enables you to configure scripts that run when a machine starts up or shuts down. You can configure scripts that run when a user logs on or logs off to implement changes to the environment for all or a single user. You can also configure scripts to clean up any modifications made by others before the next user logs on or the system restarts. Scripts can be batch files (BAT or CMD), executable programs (EXE), or Windows Script Host scripts (VBScript or JScript). Generally, you make use of scripts when you want to implement a Group Policy and when the requirement cannot be met by any administrative template setting. You can set up a script to perform that task to achieve the desired result. With support for VBScript and *Windows Script Host* (WSH) in Windows 2000, scripts can be created to accomplish virtually any task.

Group Policy Script Processing Order

The order of execution of Group Policy scripts is quite specific, as is the application of any Group Policy setting. Similarly, if there is a conflict between different scripts, the setting found in the last script processed always prevails. This is significant because it is a slight departure from the application of administrative template settings.

When you specify an administrative template setting for both the user and the computer, the computer setting always takes precedence. Let's say in the System folder of the administrative template for the computer you configure Autoplay to be disabled, but you enable the same setting for the user. In this case, Autoplay remains disabled because the computer setting indicated it should be disabled. The reason for this result is that, when applying GPO settings, the configuration specified for the computer and the user are merged, and any conflicts resolved before the template settings are applied. In this way, the administrator can always be sure of the end result of any changes in the template setting.

When scripts are configured, scripts can be run at computer startup, user logon, user logoff, and computer shutdown. Each of these is a very distinct event (in fact, the user logon and logoff can occur many times before the computer shutdown), and scripts are processed when the event occurs. Because scripts are simply batch files, executable files, or WSH scripts, they do not have any way to really check for the previous state and then determine that settings specified within the script should not be applied. The assumption

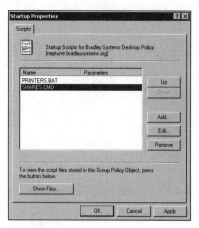

FIGURE 6.73
Startup script order of execution can be set in the Startup Properties dialog box under Windows Setting, Scripts, Startup in the Group Policy Editor.

Default Timeout Value The default timeout value for script processing is 10 minutes. This means that if a script has not completed processing in 10 minutes, it is assumed to have timed out, and the next script starts. If your scripts are complex and require more than 10 minutes to run, you can change the default timeout value by modifying the setting found at Computer Configuration, Administrative Templates, System, Logon, Maximum wait time for Group Policy Scripts. The setting applies to all scripts: startup, shutdown, logon, and logoff. This could make the process of logging on or off or starting or shutting down the machine lengthy. Setting the value too low could cause scripts to fail prematurely, not allowing the full configuration to be completed. It is generally recommended that default settings be maintained unless there is a good reason to change them.

is that all the settings should be applied no matter what. This blanket desire to apply all the settings specified in the script makes it possible for a setting configured in the user logon script to override one configured in the computer startup script. This is the way it is intended to work, and you, as the administrator, need to be aware of this. The actual processing order of scripts is as follows:

1. When a user starts a computer and logs on, two scripts run: startup scripts and logon scripts. Startup scripts run in sequential order (synchronously). Each script must complete or time out before the next one starts. Scripts run in the background and are hidden (not visible) to the user. In other words, the user cannot snoop and see what types of changes have been applied to the system as a result of the startup script. The order of execution of startup scripts is specified in the Startup Properties dialog box shown in Figure 6.73. It is found under Computer Configuration, Windows Settings, Scripts, Startup in the Group Policy Editor.

   Logon scripts run after the startup scripts and are run asynchronously by default with the possibility of more than one script executing at the same time. If conflicting settings appear in two or more logon scripts, the last setting to execute is the one that applies. This means that if using the default settings, it might not always be possible to predict what the end result of logon script execution will be if the same setting is applied in more than one script. As a general rule of thumb, do not apply the same setting in several scripts.

2. When a user logs off, logoff scripts run.

3. When a user shuts down or restarts the computer as part of the logoff process, shutdown scripts run.

Once again, it is important to note that startup scripts run at the time the computer starts, while logon scripts run when a user logs on. Similarly, logoff scripts run when a user logs off the computer, and shutdown scripts run when the computer is shut down. As previously mentioned, by default startup scripts run in the order specified in Group Policy, while logon scripts run in no particular order. If you have the same setting applied in more than one logon script, there is no way to predict the exact end result of the scripts unless you modify Group Policy Administrative Template settings for the user to run Logon and Logoff scripts synchronously.

Implementing Scripts Using Group Policy

Perhaps the hardest part of implementing scripts in Windows 2000 is their creation. This can be done using Notepad or any other editor, and it needs to take place prior to associating the script with the computer or user configuration of Group Policy. As previously mentioned, scripts can be BAT or CMD files, executable programs, or Windows Script Host files.

After you have created a script to be used to configure either a computer at startup or shutdown or a user environment at logon or logoff, you need to do two things. You must copy the file to a shared location where it can be downloaded and run. This is typically in a folder within the GPO structure located on the SYSVOL shared folder on a domain controller. You must also associate the script with a GPO. Step by Step 6.9 guides you through copying the file and associating it with a GPO.

STEP BY STEP

6.9 Implementing Scripts to Be Used in Group Policy

1. Open the MMC used to administer the container at which you want to add a script to Group Policy, either Active Directory Users and Computers or Active Directory Sites and Server.

2. Right-click the container containing the GPO where you want to add the script and select Properties.

3. In the dialog box presented, click the Group Policy tab.

4. From the list of GPOs presented, click the one to which you want to add a script and then click Edit, or simply double-click the GPO you want to edit. This starts an MMC console to edit the Group Policy.

5. To modify a startup or shutdown script, you would expand Computer Configuration, Windows Settings, and then Scripts to be presented with a choice similar to that in Figure 6.74. For the rest of the Step by Step, you will configure a logon script. To start the process, expand User Configuration in the Group Policy Editor.

continues

NOTE

BAT Files and CMD Files Although you can create and execute both batch (BAT) files and command (CMD) files in Windows 2000, they execute quite differently. Batch files execute within an *NT Virtual Machine* (NTVDM) and are designed to be compatible with DOS and MS Windows 3.x/95/98. They are inherently 16 bit, and if the BAT file hangs, it might cause the entire NTVDM to hang (if it is being shared with other applications). CMD files are 32 bit and execute in their own memory space using the CMD.EXE command interpreter. Any problem with a CMD file does not affect the execution of other programs because it is an isolated process. This distinction might be somewhat confusing because the commands you can put in a BAT file are by and large the same as those allowed in a CMD file.

continued

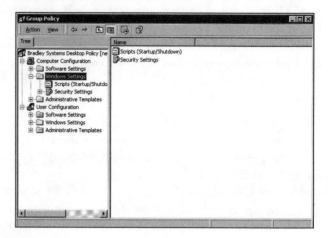

FIGURE 6.74
To create a startup or shutdown script, double-click the startup or
shutdown choices presented within the Computer Configuration portion
of the Group Policy Editor.

6. Expand Windows Settings. You will see a screen similar to
Figure 6.75.

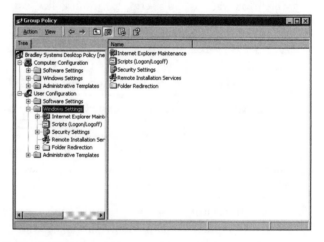

FIGURE 6.75
The Windows Settings folder of the User Configuration portion of the GPO
is where logon and logoff scripts are located.

7. Click Scripts and then double-click Logon or Logoff, depending on which type of script you want to create. Because you will be creating a logon script in this Step by Step, the Logon Scripts Properties dialog box, similar to the one shown in Figure 6.76, will be presented.

8. At this point, you have the option to Add a script. If scripts are already listed, you have the option to Edit their properties or Remove them. You also have the option to Show Files. This option shows the actual physical files on the hard drive that correspond to the scripts listed. To copy a script to the proper location for logon scripts, click Show Files to open a Windows Explorer window similar to Figure 6.77. To copy a file to the proper directory, open Windows Explorer and point to the folder where you created a logon script, click the script, and drag it to the Windows Explorer window opened by the Show Files button earlier.

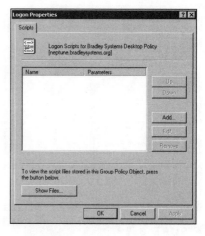

FIGURE 6.76
The Logon Properties dialog box where you can add and view the list of scripts.

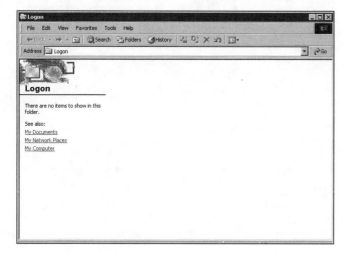

FIGURE 6.77
The Windows Explorer window shows the physical list of files in the Logon script GPT folder.

continues

NOTE

The Group Policy Template For a script file to be replicated to domain controllers and for it to be run as a Group Policy script, it must be physically located in the Group Policy template path on a domain controller. The default location of a logon script is on the domain controller's SYSVOL share under the folder structure of *<domain name>*\Policies\<GPO GUID>\User\Scripts\Logon. For a logoff script, it is in the same path except the final folder name is Logoff instead of Logon. Startup and shutdown scripts can be found in the folder structure of *<domain name>*\Policies\<GPO GUID>\Machine\Scripts\Startup or Shutdown folders within the SYSVOL share.

For scripts to run successfully, they must be copied to the preceding locations.

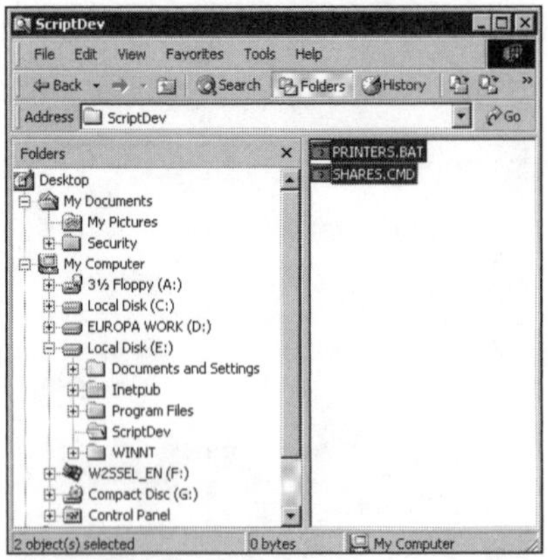

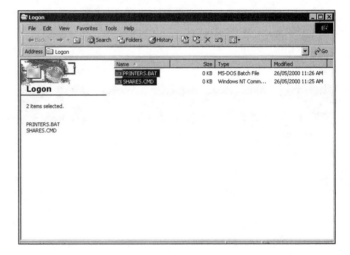

FIGURE 6.78
To copy a script from a folder on the hard drive to the appropriate folder within the GPT, just drag it from the source to the Windows Explorer opened when you clicked Show Files.

> **NOTE**
>
> **Adding Files to the Folders for Scripts**   Because of the permissions automatically configured by Windows 2000 when a domain controller is set up, only members of the Administrators, Domain Admins, or Enterprise Admins groups are able to add files to the folders used for scripts. This is because the GPT folder structure is one that needs to be preserved because it affects all users. If you attempt to copy a file to a script folder in the GPT and are told you do not have the proper permissions, contact your administrator.

continued

In Figure 6.78, for example, you have a folder called scripts on the E: drive of the machine. This folder is used to store a copy of the scripts that can be used in a GPO. (These scripts were created by the author and do not exist in your system. To simulate this behavior on your own system, create two scripts with the same names.) To copy the two files created (PRINTERS.BAT and SHARES.CMD) to the proper directory for them to be used as logon scripts, simply select and drag the files to the Logon Explorer window. The result is as shown in Figure 6.79. When you have finished copying all the files to the GPT folder, close the Windows Explorer window.

FIGURE 6.79
The Logon scripts folder in a Windows Explorer window after files have been copied to it.

9. To add a logon script after it has been copied to the proper folder, click Add in the Logon Properties dialog box. A dialog box similar to the one in Figure 6.80 enables you to type in the name of the script to add, specify additional parameters, or browse for the script file using the familiar Windows Explorer mechanism.

Click Browse to locate the files you created earlier and copied to the proper folder. Notice that you are automatically placed in the GPT folder for the type of script you are adding and can the files you copied earlier. Click one of them to assign them to this GPO. Click OK when you are done. To assign more scripts, repeat the preceding process.

10. After you have added your scripts, you are returned to the Logon Properties dialog box, which might look similar to Figure 6.81 after your scripts have been added. If you click one of the scripts, notice that the Edit and Remove buttons become available. To change the parameters for script execution or the location of the script, choose Edit. (Edit does not mean actually modify the script file but rather make changes to the execution parameters.) To make a script unavailable for execution, choose Remove. Remove does not delete the actual script file on disk; it only removes the link between the GPO and the script. You will need to manually remove the actual script file.

11. When you are satisfied that you have configured all the scripts properly, click Apply and then OK. This returns you to the Group Policy Editor.

12. To exit the Group Policy Editor MMC, close the application.

13. To exit the Properties dialog box for the Active Directory container containing the GPO, click OK.

14. You can optionally close the MMC console for Active Directory Users and Computers or Active Directory Sites and Services if you are done.

FIGURE 6.80
The Add a Script dialog box enables you to browse for the file and specify any parameters to be passed to the script when it runs.

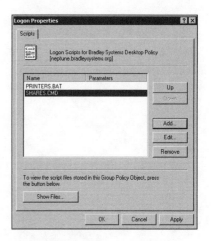

FIGURE 6.81
The Logon Properties dialog box after scripts have been added.

In terms of configuring and using scripts, the most important elements to keep in mind are that you need to determine what types of scripts are available (logon, logoff, startup, or shutdown) and why these scripts are necessary. Scripts are not shipped with Windows 2000 by default, so any you need must be created manually.

Scripts can be attached to GPOs and assigned to users and computers. Obviously, startup and shutdown scripts are assigned to computers. These scripts execute sequentially, and if settings within scripts conflict, the last setting processed is the one applied. Logon and logoff scripts only apply to users and are processed in no particular order (asynchronously), so conflicting settings might give unpredictable behavior.

Scripts should always be stored in the SYSVOL folder on a domain controller under the GUID of the GPO where they are used (as part of the Group Policy template). They need to be copied there manually by the administrator.

In addition to scripts and administrative templates, other settings can also be configured using Group Policy. These are summarized in the next section. Software settings and security settings are discussed in other chapters.

Other Settings Configurable Using Group Policy

In addition to administrative templates and scripts, a number of other settings are configurable through Group Policy. Several of these, including Software Installation, Security Settings, and Remote Installation Services, are covered in other chapters. Figure 6.82 shows the other Windows settings that can be configured. You will notice that the other settings for the computer (Software Settings and Security Settings) are covered in the chapters that follow. The next sections take a look at the settings that won't be covered later including Internet Explorer Maintenance and Folder Redirection.

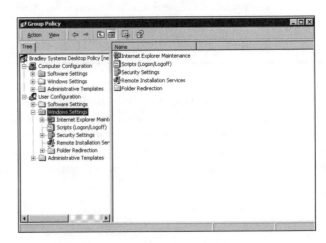

FIGURE 6.82
Other Windows settings for the Computer Configuration and the User Configuration that can be specified using Group Policy.

Internet Explorer Maintenance Settings for the User

Windows 2000 Group Policy enables the administrator to preconfigure several Internet Explorer settings outside of GPO administrative templates (see Figure 6.83). These include the Browser User Interface, Connection settings, several preconfigured URLs, IE Security settings, and Programs invoked automatically by IE.

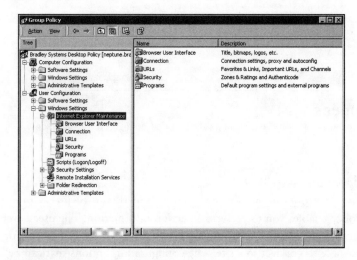

FIGURE 6.83
Internet Explorer settings configurable for the user through Group Policy.

Browser User Interface

The Browser User Interface settings (see Figure 6.84) available for you to specify for the user include the Browser Title configuration, which includes the title appearing on the toolbar as well as a background bitmap for the toolbar. Animated Bitmaps settings enable you to customize the animated bitmap that appears in the top-right corner of the browser as it is waiting for all data to be transferred from a Web site. You also can specify a Custom Logo that will appear in the top-right corner of the browser window after a Web page has been fully transferred. Finally, you can configure additional Browser Toolbar Buttons for the user or can remove the current toolbar buttons and replace them with a new set you have created. All these settings enable you control the appearance and behavior of the browser user interface.

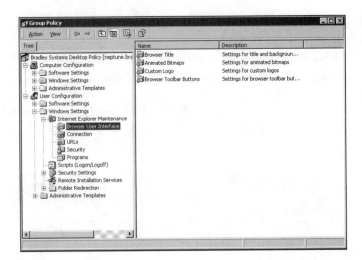

FIGURE 6.84
Browser User Interface settings that can be configured for the user.

Connection Settings

To make sure Internet Explorer works properly for the user, Group Policy enables you to preset connection information. The user never receives the dreaded error message telling him or her that it was not possible to connect to a site. The configuration options that can be specified (see Figure 6.85) include the capability to replace a user's Connection settings with a customized set of options. You can determine whether proxy server settings are automatically detected. You can manually set up a proxy server configuration and impose it upon the user. Finally, you also are allowed to specify the User Agent String, the identification information transmitted by the browser when it connects to a Web site.

Preconfigured URL Settings

The URL settings portion of Internet Explorer Maintenance (see Figure 6.86) enables you to make sure certain sites appear in the list of Favorites and Links for the user. You also have the option to remove existing Favorites that the user might have added or just replace those created by the administrator. This option enables you to update an older set of Favorites and Links with a more up-to-date version. Important URLs can also be specified; they include the home page for the user, the default search page, and an URL for online support. Finally, you also can preset Channels to which the user will subscribe.

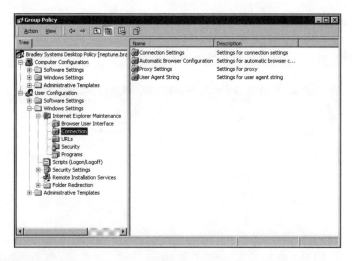

FIGURE 6.85
Internet Explorer Connection settings also can be specified using
Group Policy.

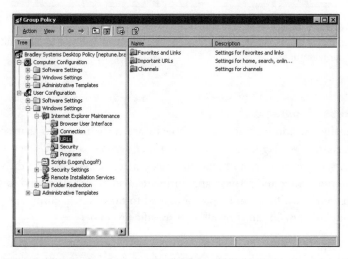

FIGURE 6.86
Internet Explorer URL settings enable the administrator to make sure sites
appear in Favorites (or Channels) and to import URLs to be included within
the list available to a user.

IE Security Zones

As an administrator, you might want to impose control over how
Internet Explorer security zones are configured as well as whether

Authenticode support should be enabled within Internet Explorer. Both of these can be specified through the Security option of Internet Explorer Maintenance (see Figure 6.87).

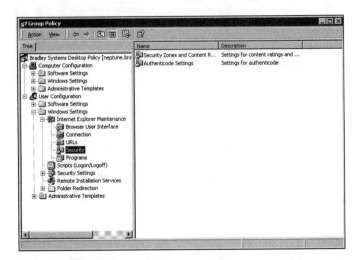

FIGURE 6.87
Internet Explorer Maintenance also enables the administrator to customize Security settings.

Preset Programs

Finally, the administrator also is able to preset the programs that will be started (see Figure 6.88) when the user decides to read Usenet newsgroups, retrieve and send Internet email, receive a call via the Internet, enter and retrieve appointments, edit a Web page, and look up contacts. These can be preconfigured to make sure a corporate standard is maintained by all, or a specific group of, users.

Configuring Internet Explorer settings enables the administrator to make sure all users have the same configuration for IE, which should reduce help desk calls and reduce TCO. Should a new set of short-cuts be required in IE, they can be centrally administered as can other configuration components of IE.

The last settings that can be configured for a user (other than those covered in future chapters) deal with folder redirection.

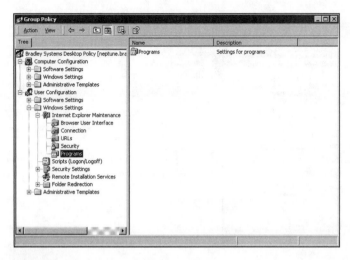

FIGURE 6.88
Program settings in Internet Explorer Maintenance enable the
administrator to specify which programs will be used for email.

Specifying Folder Redirection Settings for the User

Folder redirection, configurable through Group Policy (see Figure
6.89), is the selective placement of folders that all users make use
of on different volumes of local computers or on shared network
volumes where they can be backed up. Unlike Windows NT 4.0,
which provided this capability through roaming profiles, Windows
2000 Group Policy enables an administrator to selectively place a
folder on one location while another folder, which is also part of the
standard user profile, is kept local. Furthermore, the folders that are
redirected are not copied to the local machine, thereby saving disk
space.

An example of this could be the My Documents folder that is often
used to store an individual's current word processor, spreadsheet program, and other files. To make sure these files are backed up, the
administrator might decide to redirect them to a network share on a
hard drive that is backed up nightly. Other folders, such as desktop
shortcuts, the Start menu configuration, or the application data
folder may remain on the local drive.

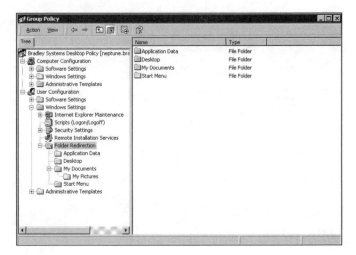

FIGURE 6.89
Folder Redirection settings that can be configured for the user through Group Policy.

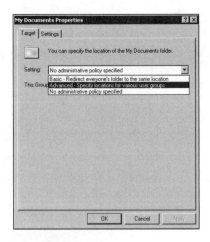

FIGURE 6.90
Folder redirection properties enable you to redirect folders for all users or selectively by group membership.

To redirect a folder to a location other than the default, select which folder you want to redirect, right-click the name, and select Properties. A dialog box like that shown in Figure 6.90 displays, enabling you to decide how to redirect the folder. You can redirect the folder to a common location for all users, Basic; redirect the folder to a different location for a user based on his or her group membership, Advanced; or leave the current settings intact.

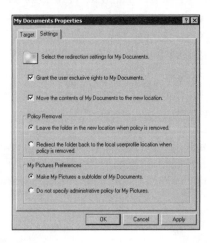

FIGURE 6.91
Basic configuration setting options that can be configured when all users' folders are redirected to the same location.

If you decide to redirect all users' folders to the same location, you can further configure the behavior of the folder. This configuration includes whether to move the current contents of the folder to the new location. You also have the option to grant only the user permissions to the redirected folder; this prevents others from seeing the contents of the folder when they should not have access. You can specify what will happen when the folder redirection policy is removed as well other settings based on which folder you are redirecting.

Microsoft stated that one of the design goals of Windows 2000 was to reduce the TCO of Windows 2000–based computers. With the combination of Active Directory and Group Policy, this goal has been largely achieved. Group Policy enables the administrator to configure user and computer settings at the site, domain, or OU level and to selectively apply these settings to users and computers. In configuring user and computer environments, the administrator can use administrative templates to specify settings. Administrative templates modify the registry entries on the target computer for either the user or the computer. In situations in which Administrative templates might not provide sufficient functionality, you are able to use scripts to configure other elements of the user and computer environment.

Naturally, proper planning is required to make sure the behavior received is the one expected and desired. Sometimes, despite the best planning, implementation might not always work as expected. This is when troubleshooting is required.

TROUBLESHOOTING GROUP POLICY

In some cases, it might be necessary to determine exactly what is happening with Group Policy because the configuration settings you've specified do not appear to be taking effect on users' computers. Windows 2000 provides for the capability to audit Group Policy processing. The audit enables you to determine exactly what is occurring and thereby help resolve the problem.

Group Policy Implementation Considerations

One of the best ways to ensure that Group Policy functions properly is to adhere to some of the recommendations from Microsoft regarding its proper implementation. These recommendations, summarized in the following list, should serve as a guideline to be used in your own environments when implementing Group Policy:

◆ **Minimize the number of GPOs you create.** Even though it is possible to create and enforce Group Policy at the site, domain, and OU level, this could be too much of a good thing. The ideal number of GPOs is the smallest number possible to accomplish any business requirement. If you do not need site-level GPOs, don't create them. You will probably want to implement one domain-level GPO, but you need to determine whether a second or a third would be beneficial. Create OU-level GPOs only if the OU has a very specific set of characteristics that are not shared by the rest of the users and computers on the domain. Minimalism creates fewer GPOs; fewer GPOs have a decreased potential to cause problems. Furthermore, the more GPOs that need to be processed when a user logs on, the longer the logon process will take.

◆ **Configure user-level settings rather than computer-level settings to control desktops.** Computer-level GPO settings only apply to a machine and affect the users logged on to that particular computer. User-level settings apply to the user, no matter which computer he or she uses to log on and connect to the network. Because the scope of user-level settings is potentially greater, they provide a better mechanism to control the user environment.

◆ **Use security group membership to filter the application of Group Policy.** By default, GPOs are enforced for members of the Authenticated Users group, which includes Administrators, Domain Admins, and Enterprise Admins. If certain GPOs should not be enforced for other users, place those users in a security group (preferably at the same level as the GPO from which you intend to filter them) and check the Deny permission box for Apply Group Policy to make sure GPO is not applied. Users who do not have an ACE indicating that a particular GPO should be applied to them have faster logons because GPO processing is bypassed for them.

◆ **Disable parts of a Group Policy that are not being enforced.** If you decide to only configure the user portion of a GPO and leave the computer portion intact, configure the options for the Group Policy so that the Computer Configuration settings are not downloaded and processed. This also improves the speed of GPO processing and results in considerable time saving during user logon.

◆ **After making a change to a GPO, log on as an affected user and test to make sure what should happen is, indeed, taking place.** The worst thing that an administrator can do with Group Policy is assume it will work. Just remember what you were taught about the word "assume." All settings and scripts should be fully tested before the policy is implemented. Through filtering, you can make sure only the test users are affected by the policy until it is ready to be released throughout the rest of the organization.

◆ **Perhaps this really should be the first point: Planning the implementation of Group Policy is paramount.** You should always ask yourself what it is you are trying to accomplish and why and what is the best way to get there? Group Policy could be the right answer. If so, plan its introduction and configuration very carefully and, as previously mentioned, test it as well. There is nothing worse for job security than an unplanned and premature implementation of a feature with widespread impact.

◆ **Limit the use of blocking and forcing, and, to a lesser extent, filtering of GPOs.** Blocking, forcing, and filtering could make it more difficult to determine where a problem actually originates and might also result in unpredictable behavior (unless carefully planned).

◆ **Do not delegate administrative control over GPOs to others unless you need to do so.** Too many cooks in the kitchen usually spoil the broth (or result in a very strange set of toppings for pizza). As an administrator, you should enjoy holding control, not giving it away. However, if you are the administrator of a large multinational conglomerate, you have to give some control away so be flexible.

As previously indicated, the cardinal principle to be followed when planning and implementing Group Policy is the KIS principle—Keep It Simple. Do not try to do too much with a single policy. At the same time, don't have so many policies that processing takes a long time. Keep common settings at the domain level and specific ones at the OU level. Don't have a GPO at each OU level (have one only where needed) and let policies flow through inheritance.

If this still does not work, you might have a simple common problem that can be easily solved.

Common Group Policy Problems

Despite the best planning, and even though you have followed all the recommendations laid out in the preceding list, it might still be possible for things to go awry. Some common problems and their solutions are presented in the following table.

Problem	Cause	Solution
Group Policy is not being applied to users and computers in a site, domain, or OU.	The most likely cause is that GPO inheritance has been blocked. A second possible reason for this behavior is that the GPO has been filtered to exclude the users and computers.	Configure No Override for the GPO to prevent lower-level administrators from blocking GPO settings.
	When multiple GPOs are applied (site, domain, and OU level), it is possible thatsettings at a higher-level (such as domain) GPO have been overwritten by a lower-level (such as OU) GPO.	Verify GPO security settings to make sure filtering has not been applied to broadly.
Group Policy is not being enforced for a security group in an OU to which it is linked.	Group Policy can be linked to sites, domains, or OUs. Because a GPO can be linked to an OU does not mean it will be applied to security groups in the OU. The determination of which security groups have the GPO applied is made by the permissions configured for the GPO.	Grant the security group Read and Apply Group Policy permissions.

Problem	Cause	Solution
An administrator cannot open a GPO to edit it.	Any user who needs to modify a GPO needs to have Full Control privileges for the GPO. If an administrator is unable to view the GPO settings and/or modify them, he or she most likely does not have sufficient permissions.	Grant the user or security group the Full Control permission for the GPO.
Attempting to edit a GPO returns a Failed to open the Group Policy object error.	This problem usually occurs when network problems exist. These could include physical problems with the network, the server being down, or most likely, *domain name system* (DNS) configuration.	Verify that a domain controller is available. Verify that the network is not experiencing problems. Verify DNS configuration and availability.

Most problems that occur as a result of Group Policy processing can easily be solved if you apply a logical approach to the problem-solving process. First, verify that domain controllers are around and that they contain the Group Policy templates in question. Second, walk through what should happen and the permissions assigned to the policy. Most problems either are permission-related or the GPO is not at the right level.

If more extensive checking of how GPOs are processed is required, you can always configure auditing.

Auditing Group Policy

In situations in which the problems you are experiencing are not easily classified and you have faithfully followed the recommended procedures for implementing Group Policy, Microsoft Windows 2000 provides the capability to configure auditing of Group Policy execution and modification.

To configure auditing for a GPO, follow the steps outlined in Step by Step 6.10.

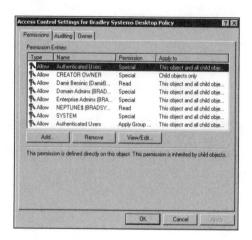

FIGURE 6.92
The advanced Access Control Settings dialog box for a Group Policy enables you to configure auditing.

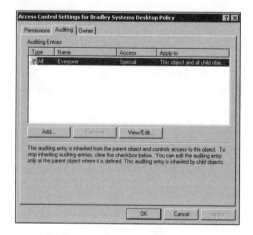

FIGURE 6.93
The Auditing tab of the advanced Access Control Settings dialog box for Group Policy.

STEP BY STEP

6.10 Configuring Auditing for Group Policy

1. Open the MMC used to administer the container at which you want to configure auditing for a Group Policy, either Active Directory Users and Computers or Active Directory Sites and Services.

2. Right-click the container containing the GPO for which you want to enable auditing and select Properties

3. In the dialog box presented, click the Group Policy tab.

4. Select the GPO for which you intend to configure auditing and click the Properties button.

5. From the Group Policy Properties dialog box, select the Security tab by clicking it.

6. Click the Advanced button to bring up the advanced security settings, as shown in Figure 6.92.

7. Click the Auditing tab to display the current auditing configuration for the Group Policy. A dialog box similar to Figure 6.93 opens. You might find a message at the bottom of the dialog box telling you that the auditing configuration presented is inherited from a parent container. If this is so, you might need to go to the parent container to remove the displayed auditing configuration.

8. To add an auditing configuration for the selected Group Policy, click the Add button. At this point, you are presented with a list of users, computers, and groups available on the domain. Select the user, group, or computer for which you want to enable auditing and click OK.

9. After selecting the user, group, or computer for which you are configuring auditing, you are shown a dialog box that enables you to configure auditing for a number of events for the GPO, as shown in Figure 6.94. As you can see, you can audit the successful or unsuccessful use of a GPO privilege or both. The list of available options is exactly the same as the list of available permissions for the GPO.

You also can set auditing of the manipulation of properties for the GPO by clicking the Properties tab. As you will also note, you can specify whether the auditing settings apply to the selected GPO container and all child containers, the selected container only, the child objects only, the computer objects only, and so on.

If you decide to apply auditing settings to children of the current container, you can limit the scope of propagation to the current level only by checking the Apply these auditing entries to objects and/or containers within this container only check box.

Finally, the Clear All button erases all the settings specified. In case you made an error and want to start from scratch or if problems exist with auditing and you want to reinitialize the settings, the Clear All button is an option.

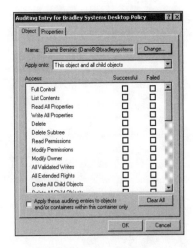

FIGURE 6.94
Auditing Entry dialog box for Group Policy.

10. When you have finished selecting which permissions and properties will be audited for the GPO, click OK to save you settings. You should select a minimum of Read and Apply Group Policy auditing for at least failures (or both failures and success) to see if a GPO is being applied.

11. Click Apply and then OK to exit the Access Control Settings dialog box.

12. Click OK to close the GPO Properties dialog box and save your settings.

13. Click OK to close the Active Directory container dialog box.

14. Exit your MMC console.

After you have configured auditing, you can view the results of auditing by opening Event Viewer and selecting the Security Log, as shown in Figure 6.95. This should provide you with information about GPO processing. This also tells you with which users and computers GPO processing is encountering problems.

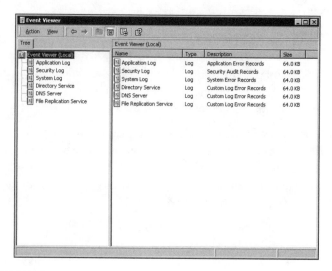

FIGURE 6.95
Auditing records for Group Policy are viewed in the Security Log of Event Viewer.

When troubleshooting Group Policy, first determine what is going wrong and for whom. Check GPO processing in terms of permissions for the GPO as well as inheritance and blocking. In situations in which the problem encountered is hard to track down, you can configure auditing to log success and/or failure events of GPO processing, which can be used to step through what is happening and, hopefully, determine the cause of the problem.

CASE STUDY: USING GROUP POLICIES TO CONFIGURE USER AND COMPUTER SETTINGS AT SUNSHINE BREWING

ESSENCE OF THE CASE

Specifically, you have received the following requests:

▶ The CEO has decided that all users should have a common desktop background wallpaper, the company logo, so that visitors to any Sunshine Brewing location will always be able to see the corporate identity displayed. Currently, users throughout the company can choose their own background.

▶ Sales managers in each office want to constantly remind the sales team of the current promotion by having it displayed on their desktop at all times.

▶ Users at corporate headquarters have been complaining that, when they want to take home documents on shared folders on servers to work on them, they have to keep remembering to copy them to the local disk on the notebook. Sometimes they forget, and they have to drive back to the office to get the files. They would like files they are working on to be automatically copied to the hard disk of their notebook computer and then copied back to the network when they log on.

▶ The help desk staff at headquarters has developed a Web site that provides answers to many common user questions. They would like this site to be

automatically added as a Favorite in all instances of Internet Explorer used within the company. Because IE5 is the corporate standard, this would ensure that any user in the company could go to the help desk site to have his or her questions answered instead of calling the help desk first. This would save time and resources for the help desk.

▶ Users are complaining that, when they want to find a printer close to them, they have to scroll down a long list when they use the Windows 2000 search feature to locate a printer. They want a list of printers near them displayed by default instead of all printers.

▶ The Admin heads in each office are finding that their staff spends a lot of time running games and other applications during office hours. They want the capability to restrict these users to only the accounting program, email, office suites, and Internet Explorer.

▶ All users, with the exception of IT and R&D, should only be able to run Add/Remove Programs and Display applets in Control Panel.

▶ Administrators for each department should be able to configure department-level settings, which might not have been identified yet.

continues

CASE STUDY: USING GROUP POLICIES TO CONFIGURE USER AND COMPUTER SETTINGS AT SUNSHINE BREWING

continued

You have been asked to come up with a plan that satisfies these requirements in the shortest possible time as well as ensuring that any changes to these settings can be made easily and applied to the user or computer without manual intervention.

The CIO and CEO want these requests implemented unless the operating system does not support them.

SCENARIO

In this chapter, you were introduced to Group Policy and how it can be used to manage user and computer environments. Sunshine Brewing has a large international implementation that can be helped by using Group Policy to configure user and computer settings throughout the enterprise.

The implementation of Active Directory sites, OUs, and domains at Sunshine Brewing has successfully taken place, as has the migration of user desktop and notebook computers to Windows 2000 Professional. The key user computers now all operate on the Windows 2000 platform. You, as the key administrator at Sunshine Brewing, now find yourself receiving requests from junior administrators at the different sites, as well as management, to have specific settings applied to these environments.

ANALYSIS

As you can see, the requests range from company-wide requirements to specific elements that deal only with a part of the organization. Your solution needs to incorporate all these elements while also being easy to administer. The best solution for these requirements is to make use of Windows 2000 Group Policy using Administrative Templates and Windows Settings configuration settings in the GPO.

The first requirement (common background wallpaper featuring the corporate logo) can be satisfied by creating a Group Policy at the domain level that includes the wallpaper to be used. You would specify the location of the wallpaper on a

CASE STUDY: USING GROUP POLICIES TO CONFIGURE USER AND COMPUTER SETTINGS AT SUNSHINE BREWING

network share that is replicated to other servers through a fault-tolerant DFS link. This could be part of the Default Domain Policy GPO installed by Windows 2000 Active Directory.

The requirement for sales users to have a background wallpaper that reflects the current promotion can be handled by creating a GPO at the site level that specifies the wallpaper containing the current promotion. Because you do not want this wallpaper to be modified by the domain-level policy, you would configure No Override for the site policy to make sure the setting is not changed. Further, to ensure that the GPO only applies to sales users in the site, you would filter the GPO so that its settings were applied only to members of the Sales security group.

To provide users not connected to the network with access to their files, or if the server hosting the files goes down, you would configure support for Offline Files using a GPO at the corporate HQ site in Ottawa and, using the GPO, specify which shared folders will have Offline Files turned on automatically. This way, users can work with their files while away from the office and, as long as they open a file before leaving, have it copied to their machine.

To assist the help desk staff in making sure all users have a Favorites link in IE to the help desk Web site, create a GPO at the domain level with No Override that adds the URL for the Web site to the users' list of Favorites. This way, the shortcut is always available to the user.

Searches in Active Directory default to the Entire Directory. To change the default search location for printers, create a GPO at the domain level that enables filtering of Active Directory searches by enabling the setting in Administrative Templates, Desktop, Active Directory. In this way, searches for printer objects default to only those printers physically close to the user's location.

To ensure that Admin users are able to run only specified applications, create a GPO at the Admin OU and specify which applications can be run by users. Any applications other than those appearing on the list will not be available to users.

To ensure that all users can only run Add/ Remove Programs and Display in Control Panel, restrict the list of applets that can be run to these two. To ensure that this policy does not apply to R&D and IT staff, filter the Group Policy by making sure the Apply Group Policy check box for these security groups is not checked.

Finally, to enable administrators at the OU level or site level to create new policies, delegate administrative control to these containers and grant necessary privileges such as Create Group Policy Container Object.

As you can see, using Group Policy can solve many complex requirements including those that might appear to be conflicting.

CHAPTER SUMMARY

KEY TERMS

- Administrative templates
- Blocking policy inheritance
- Folder redirection
- Forcing Group Policy
- GPO inheritance
- GPO scope
- Group Policy container
- Group Policy filtering
- Group Policy object
- Group Policy precedence
- Group Policy template
- GUID
- Logon/logoff scripts
- No Override
- Registry
- Startup/shutdown scripts

In this chapter, you were introduced to Group Policy and how it can be used to enforce a consistent configuration at the site, domain, and/or OU level. Group Policy is a very powerful feature of Windows 2000 and is a tremendous improvement over System Policy, which was available in Windows 9x and Windows NT.

By configuring Group Policy, you are able to specify how a computer is configured and whether users can make changes to certain computer configurations. You are can lock down the desktop and other characteristics of a user's environment no matter where he or she logs on to the domain from: his or her usual workstation, a remote machine through dial-up, another node in the same location, or a computer halfway around the world.

Group Policy is composed of two parts: a Group Policy container and a Group Policy Template. GPCs are Active Directory objects linked to a site, domain, or OU. GPTs are physical files, including administrative templates and scripts, that are stored within the Policies container for the SYSVOL share on domain controllers. Each GPT is stored in a folder with the same name as the GUID of the GPO for which it is a template.

Group Policy settings specified at a higher level, such as a domain or a site, are automatically inherited by all lower-level Active Directory objects such as OUs. A local administrator responsible for a subdomain or OU can block policy inheritance from higher levels such as a site, thereby ensuring that only his or her GPOs are processed. However, higher-level administrators have the option to override the blocking of GPO application at lower levels, thereby forcing GPO settings even if they are blocked at a lower level.

The order of Group Policy processing is always site, domain, and then OU. As it is possible to have OUs within OUs, it is possible for many GPOs to be processed when a user logs on or a computer starts up. It is recommended that fewer rather than more GPOs be created to provide for acceptable logon performance.

CHAPTER SUMMARY

Group Policy can be filtered to ensure that it is processed only by the users for whom it is intended. In this way, it is possible to selectively implement Group Policy for a security group, computer, or user. To ensure that proper application of Group Policy is taking place, the administrator is able to configure auditing for GPO processing and view the results in the Event Viewer. This is also a good troubleshooting tool when needed.

GPO settings can be applied through administrative templates or scripts. Administrative templates and scripts can be configured for both the computer and the user. If a conflict exists in the application of an administrative template setting between a user and a computer, computer settings always override user settings. For scripts, the last script to execute is the one whose settings are applied, regardless of whether the script is a user logon script or a system startup script.

In situations in which a GPO has been linked to an Active Directory container and the GPO only contains computer configuration settings, the administrator is able to speed up processing by setting a GPO option to only process the computer settings and not bother downloading the user settings on GPO application. The converse is also true and helps provide better performance in situations in which many scripts might need to be processed.

APPLY YOUR KNOWLEDGE

Exercises

All the exercises for this chapter assume you have installed Windows 2000 Server (or Advanced Server) on a computer. Your Windows 2000 Server must be configured as the domain controller of a domain for the exercises to work properly. You need to be able to log on to the domain as an administrator. Your user account must be a member of either the Enterprise Admins group or the Domain Admins group. If you know the password for the user Administrator, this is sufficient.

6.1 Creating Organizational Units, Users, Groups, and Moving Your Domain Controller

In this exercise, you will create two organizational units that will be used in future exercises. You also will create a security group and some users. Finally, you will move your domain controller into one of the OUs you just created to make sure the GPO settings you create in later exercises will be applied to your computer.

Estimated time: 20 minutes.

To create OUs, groups, and users, follow these steps:

1. Log on to the Windows 2000 Server domain controller as Administrator for your domain.

2. Click Start, Programs, Administrative Tools, Active Directory Users and Computers to open the MMC console for managing users and computers in your domain.

3. Right-click your domain and select New, Organizational Unit. In the dialog box that opens, type **Research**.

4. Repeat step 3 to add a Sales OU as well.

5. Right-click the Research OU and select New, Group. Enter **Developers** for the group name, **Domain Local** as the group scope, and **Security** as the group type.

6. Repeat step 5 to create a Domain Local Security group called Telemarketing in the Sales OU.

7. In the Sales OU, add three new users with logons of HowardH (Howard Ham), PhilC (Phillip Chambers), and NatashaW (Natasha Wilson). Make PhilC and NatashaW members of the Telemarketing group (but not HowardH). When prompted for a password, enter the word **password** for each user. Leave the rest of the settings at the default.

8. In the Research OU, add two new users with logins of RalphD (Ralph Downing) and TimC (Tim Clark) and make TimC a member of the Developers group. When prompted for a password, enter **password** for each user. Leave the rest of the settings at the default.

To move your domain controller to the Research OU, follow these steps:

1. If you have not already done so, start Active Directory Users and Computers and expand your domain.

2. Click Domain Controllers.

3. In the details pane, right-click your computer (which is also the domain controller) and select Move.

4. In the Move dialog box, expand your domain and click the Research OU and then OK.

5. Exit Active Directory Users and Computers.

APPLY YOUR KNOWLEDGE

6.2 Creating a Group Policy Object for Computers

In this exercise, you create a Group Policy to enable disk quotas on the Research OU computers as well as to enforce them, and you configure a default quota.

Estimated time: 20 minutes.

To create the Research Computer Policy, follow these steps:

1. While logged on as a Domain Administrator, start Active Directory Users and Computers.

2. Expand your domain, right-click the Research OU, and select Properties.

3. On the Group Policy tab, click New, type **Research Computer Policy** as the name, and press Enter.

To edit the Research Computer Policy administrative template settings, follow these steps:

1. Select the Research Computer Policy you created earlier and click Edit. This starts the Group Policy Editor MMC.

2. In the Group Policy console tree, expand Computer Configuration and then expand Administrative Templates.

3. In the console tree, expand System, click Disk Quotas, and in the details pane, double-click Enable disk quotas.

4. In the Properties dialog box, select Enabled and click OK.

5. In the details pane, double-click Default quota limit and warning level to bring up the Properties dialog box. Click Enabled and leave the default 100MB limit as is. Click OK to exit the dialog box and save you changes.

6. Double-click Enforce disk quota limit in the details pane, click Enabled to select the setting, and click OK to save your changes.

7. Close the Group Policy Editor MMC console.

8. Close Research OU Properties dialog box and exit Active Directory Users and Computers.

9. Restart your computer for the changes to take effect.

   To avoid restarting your computer, you can go to Start, Programs, Accessories and click Command Prompt to start a command prompt. In the Command Prompt window, type **secedit/ refreshpolicy user policy** and **secedit/ refreshpolicy machine policy** to refresh the user and machine policies on the domain controller. This might take a few minutes.

6.3 Creating a Group Policy Object for Users

In this exercise, you will create a Group Policy to remove the **Run** command from the Start menu of all telemarketing users as well as to disable the use of Control Panel for these same users.

Estimated time: 20 minutes.

To create the Telemarketing Users Policy, follow these steps:

1. While logged on as a Domain Administrator, start Active Directory Users and Computers.

2. Expand your domain, right-click the Sales OU, and select Properties.

3. In the Group Policy tab, click New, type **Telemarketing Users Policy** as the name, and press Enter.

APPLY YOUR KNOWLEDGE

To edit the Telemarketing Users Policy Administrative Template settings, follow these steps:

1. Select the Telemarketing Users Policy you created earlier, click Properties, and then click the Security tab.

2. Select the Authenticated Users group and click Remove.

3. Click Add and, in the list of users and groups in your domain, select the Telemarketing group and click Add and then OK.

4. With the Telemarketing group selected, make sure Allow Read and Allow Apply Group Policy are selected. Click OK to close the Properties dialog box.

5. Select the Telemarketing Users Policy and click Edit. This starts the Group Policy Editor MMC.

6. In the Group Policy console tree, expand User Configuration and then expand Administrative Templates.

7. In the console, click Start Menu & Taskbar and then, in the details pane, double-click Remove Run menu from the Start menu.

8. In the Properties dialog box, select Enabled and click OK.

9. In the Group Policy Editor MMC console, click Control Panel (two folders below Start Menu & Taskbar, with which you just worked).

10. Double-click Disable Control Panel in the details pane to bring up the Properties dialog box.

11. Click Enabled and then OK to close the Disable Control Panel Properties dialog box.

12. Close the Group Policy Editor MMC console.

13. Close the Sales OU Properties dialog box and exit Active Directory Users and Computers.

14. Restart your computer for the changes to take effect.

To avoid restarting your computer, you can go to Start, Programs, Accessories and click Command Prompt to start a command prompt. In the Command Prompt window, type **secedit /refreshpolicy user policy** and **secedit/ refreshpolicy machine policy** to refresh the user and machine policies on the domain controller. This might take a few minutes.

6.4   Verifying Group Policy Administrative Template Settings

In this exercise, you will log on as HowardH to verify that both the computer and user policy settings you have configured are being enforced.

Estimated time: 20 minutes.

1. If you are currently logged on to your computer, log off and log on again as HowardH with a password of password.

2. Click Start, Programs, Accessories, Windows Explorer to launch Windows Explorer.

3. Expand My Computer and click drive C. How much free disk space is shown as available in the details pane?

_____

_____

_____

APPLY YOUR KNOWLEDGE

4. Click another NTFS partition if available and verify the amount of free disk space available to HowardH. How much is available?

_____

_____

_____

5. Why is this much disk space available to the user on each NTFS partition?

_____

_____

_____

6. Click Start, Settings. Is Control Panel listed as one of the available settings options? Why or why not?

_____

_____

_____

7. Click Start. Is the Run menu available from the Start menu? Why or why not?

_____

_____

_____

8. Are the computer policy settings for the Research OU being enforced on your computer?

_____

_____

_____

9. Are the user policy settings for the Sales OU being enforced on your computer?

_____

_____

_____

10. Log off Windows 2000.

6.5   Implementing Logon and Logoff Script Policies

In this exercise, you will create a simple logon script that will connect users to a network share when they log on. You will create a GPO that will ensure that this logon script is applied to all users in the Research OU.

Estimated time: 20 minutes.

To create a share and logon script, follow these steps:

1. Log on to your computer as the administrator for your domain.

2. Start Windows Explorer and create a new folder at the root of the C: drive called CORPDATA.

3. Share this folder with the share name of CORPDATA. Leave the permissions and all other settings at their default values.

4. Create a new folder at the root of the C: drive. Call it **Scripts**.

5. Change to the Scripts folder and right-click and create a new text document. Leave the filename at the default and then double-click the filename to open Notepad.

6. From the File menu in Notepad, select Save As and name the file **"CORPDATA.CMD"** (with the double quotation marks). Save it as a file type of All Files. This is required because Notepad automatically appends the .TXT extension to the filename, which will not allow the file to be processed as a script.

7. While still in Notepad, enter the following text in the file:

   net use k: \\\\<*server*>\\corpdata

   where <*server*> is the name of your computer. Save the file and exit Notepad.

8. Close Windows Explorer.

To create a Group Policy for a logon script, follow these steps:

1. If you have not already done so, log on to your computer as the Administrator for your domain.

2. Start Active Directory Users and Computers and expand your domain to reveal the Research OU.

3. Right-click the Research OU and select Properties.

4. In the Properties dialog box, select the Group Policy tab and click New to add a new policy called Research Logon Script Policy.

5. Select the Research Logon Script Policy and click Edit to bring up the Group Policy Editor MMC console.

6. Expand User Configuration and then Windows Settings and click Scripts. Double-click Logon to bring up the Logon Properties dialog box.

7. Select Show Files to see a list of files in the GPT directory. You should see no files in the Logon folder window that appears.

8. Click the Start menu and select Run. In the Run box, enter **C:\\scripts** and press Return. A window with the contents of the C:\Scripts folder with the CORPDATA.CMD file you created earlier will appear.

9. Click the CORPDATA.CMD file and drag it to the Logon folder window. This copies the file to the proper GPT folder where it can be used by the Group Policy. Close both the Logon folder and Scripts folder windows.

10. In the Logon Properties dialog box, click Add and then Browse. Select CORPDATA.CMD from the list of files presented. To be sure the file is processed as a script, select Script Files as the file type to display in the Browse window. Click OK to exit the Add a Script dialog box.

11. Click OK to exit the Logon Scripts Properties dialog box.

12. Close the Group Policy Editor MMC Window.

13. Click Close to exit the Research Properties dialog box and then exit Active Directory Users and Computers.

14. Log off Windows 2000.

6.6 Verifying Group Policy Logon Script Settings

In this exercise, you will log on as RalphD and HowardH to verify that the logon script policy is being enforced.

Estimated time: 20 minutes.

1. If you are currently logged on to your computer, log off and log on again as RalphD with a password of password.

APPLY YOUR KNOWLEDGE

2. Click Start, Programs, Accessories, Windows Explorer to launch Windows Explorer.

3. Expand My Computer. Does a mapping to the CORPDATA share on your computer appear as mapped drive letter K? Why or why not?

_____

_____

_____

4. Log off and log on again as HowardH with a password of password.

5. Click Start, Programs, Accessories, Windows Explorer to launch Windows Explorer.

6. Expand My Computer. Does a mapping to the CORPDATA share on your computer appear as mapped drive letter K? Why or why not?

_____

_____

_____

7. Log off Windows 2000.

6.7   Linking an Existing GPO to an OU

In this exercise, you will link the Research Logon Script Policy to the Sales OU because Sales needs to have access to and communicate to clients the published released schedules placed in the CORPDATA share by the Research users.

Estimated time: 20 minutes.

1. Log on to the Windows 2000 Server domain controller as Administrator for your domain.

2. Click Start, Programs, Administrative Tools, Active Directory Users and Computers to open the MMC console for managing user and computers in your domain.

3. Expand your domain and then right-click the Sales OU and select Properties.

4. In the Group Policy tab, select Add to open the Add a Group Policy Object Link dialog box.

5. Click the All tab and select Research Logon Script Policy and then click OK.

6. In the Sales Properties dialog box, you should now see the Research Logon Script Policy added to the list.

7. Click OK to exit the Sales OU Properties dialog box and then close Active Directory Users and Computers.

8. Log off Windows 2000.

6.8   Verifying Group Policy Link and Logon Script Settings

In this exercise, you log on as RalphD and HowardH to verify that the logon script policy is being enforced.

Estimated time: 20 minutes.

1. If you are currently logged on to your computer, log off and log on again as RalphD with a password of password.

2. Click Start, Programs, Accessories, Windows Explorer to launch Windows Explorer.

APPLY YOUR KNOWLEDGE

3. Expand My Computer. Does a mapping to the CORPDATA share on your computer appear as mapped drive letter K? Why or why not?

_____

_____

_____

4. Log off and log on again as HowardH with a password of password.

5. Click Start, Programs, Accessories, Windows Explorer to launch Windows Explorer.

6. Expand My Computer. Does a mapping to the CORPDATA share on your computer appear as mapped drive letter K? Why or why not?

_____

_____

_____

7. Log off Windows 2000.

6.9 Delegating Administrative Control of Group Policy

In this exercise, you delegate administration of the Telemarketing Users Policy to HowardH, who is the manager of the sales department. Because your company is quite small, its resources are scarce. Howard has taken a few Windows 2000 courses and believes he is familiar with Active Directory and Group Policy. After giving him a quick test, you feel he is able to administer this policy for his part of the company.

Estimated time: 20 minutes.

1. Log on to Windows 2000 as the Administrator for your domain.

2. Start Active Directory Users and Computers and expand your domain. Right-click the Sales OU and select Properties.

3. Click the Group Policy tab, select the Telemarketing Users Policy, and select Properties.

4. Click the Security tab. What permissions does HowardH currently have for this Group Policy?

_____

_____

_____

5. Click Add to be presented with a list of users and groups in your domain.

6. Scroll down the list until you find HowardH, highlight his name by clicking it, and then select Add. Click OK.

7. What permissions does HowardH now have on the Group Policy?

_____

_____

_____

8. What permissions would HowardH need to be able to administer the GPO?

_____

_____

_____

9. Grant HowardH the required additional permissions to administer Group Policy while still making sure the policy applies to him. Click OK to exit the Telemarketing Users Policy Properties dialog box.

APPLY YOUR KNOWLEDGE

10. Close Active Directory Users and Computers.

11. Log off Windows 2000.

6.10 Testing the Delegation of Administrative Control of Group Policy

In this exercise, you test to see whether HowardH can successfully modify the Telemarketing Users Policy.

Estimated time: 20 minutes.

1. Log on to Windows 2000 as HowardH with a password of password.

2. Start Active Directory Users and Computers and expand your domain. Right-click the Sales OU and select Properties.

3. Click the Group Policy tab and select the Telemarketing Users Policy. Which of the six options at the bottom of the dialog box are available to HowardH?

_____

_____

_____

4. Click the Research Logon Script Policy. Is there a difference in the options available to HowardH for the Research Logon Script Policy and the Telemarketing Users Policy?

_____

_____

_____

5. Click the Telemarketing Users Policy and click Properties. Is HowardH able to change permissions to this GPO? Why or why not?

_____

_____

_____

6. Close the Telemarketing Users Policy Properties dialog box and click Edit. Does the Group Policy Editor MMC appear?

_____

_____

7. To modify the GPO as HowardH and to add Logoff to the Start menu, expand User Configuration, Administrative Templates, Start Menu & Programs. In the details pane, double-click Add Logoff to the Start Menu and select Enabled. Was HowardH able to modify the GPO setting? Why or why not?

_____

_____

_____

8. Click OK to exit the Add Logoff to the Start Menu Properties dialog box and then close the Group Policy Editor MMC.

9. Click OK to close the Sales OU properties dialog box and close Active Directory Users and Computers.

APPLY YOUR KNOWLEDGE

6.11 Filtering and Blocking Group Policy Inheritance

After much deliberation, it was decided that sales is a part of the company that should set its own policies for different users. Further, the Telemarketing Users Policy should only apply to users in the Telemarketing security group.

In this exercise, you will block policy inheritance for the Sales OU and filter policy inheritance to make sure the Telemarketing Users Policy is only enforced on users in the Telemarketing security group.

Estimated time: 20 minutes.

1. Log on to your computer as a domain-level Administrator.

2. Start Active Directory Users and Computers, expand your domain, and then right-click the Sales OU and select Properties.

3. Click the Group Policy tab. What do you need to do to make sure any higher-level policies are not enforced in this OU? Configure the setting that does not enforce higher-level GPOs on this OU.

   _____

   _____

   _____

4. Click the Telemarketing Users Policy and click the Security tab. What changes do you need to make to ensure that only the Telemarketing security group has this policy enforced? Perform the necessary changes.

   _____

   _____

   _____

5. Click OK to close the Telemarketing Users Policy Properties dialog box.

6. Click OK to close the Sales OU Properties dialog box and then close Active Directory Users and Computers.

7. Log off Windows 2000.

6.12 Testing Filtering Group Policy

In this exercise, you will log on to your computer as a member of the Telemarketing security group to test GPO filtering. You will also log on as HowardH and note any differences.

Estimated time: 20 minutes.

1. Log on to your computer as NatashaW, one of the users in the Telemarketing security group, with a password of password.

2. Click Start, Programs, Accessories, Windows Explorer to launch Windows Explorer.

3. Expand My Computer and click drive C. How much free disk space is shown as available in the details pane?

   _____

   _____

   _____

4. Click another NTFS partitio, if available and verify the amount of free disk space available to NatashaW. How much is available?

   _____

   _____

   _____

APPLY YOUR KNOWLEDGE

5. Why is this much disk space available to the user on each NTFS partition?

   _____

   _____

   _____

6. Click Start, Settings. Is Control Panel listed as one of the available settings options? Why or why not?

   _____

   _____

   _____

7. Click Start. Is the Run menu available from the Start menu?? Why or why not?

   _____

   _____

   _____

8. Are the computer policy settings for the Research OU being enforced on your computer?

   _____

   _____

   _____

9. Are the user policy settings for the Sales OU being enforced on your computer?

10. Log off Windows 2000.

11. Log on to your computer as HowardH with a password of password.

12. Click Start, Programs, Accessories, Windows Explorer to launch Windows Explorer.

13. Expand My Computer and click drive C. How much free disk space is shown as available in the details pane?

    _____

    _____

    _____

14. Click another NTFS partition if available and verify the amount of free disk space available to HowardH. How much is available?

    _____

    _____

    _____

15. Why is this much disk space available to the user on each NTFS partition?

    _____

    _____

    _____

16. Click Start, Settings. Is Control Panel listed as one of the available settings options? Why or why not?

    _____

    _____

    _____

17. Click Start. Is the Run menu available from the Start menu? Why or why not?

    _____

    _____

    _____

APPLY YOUR KNOWLEDGE

18. Are the computer policy settings for the Research OU being enforced on your computer?

   _____

   _____

   _____

19. Are the user policy settings for the Sales OU being enforced on your computer?

   _____

   _____

   _____

20. Log off Windows 2000.

Review Questions

1. What is the difference between a Group Policy container and a Group Policy template?

2. If you wanted to make sure a GPO for a site was applied to all users and computers in the site, what would you need to do?

3. To which users and computers do GPO settings apply to by default?

4. What is the difference between administrative templates and scripts?

5. What types of scripts are supported by Windows 2000 Group Policy?

6. What are the benefits that Group Policy provides to administrators?

7. You want to make sure all users in the domain have the same background wallpaper on their desktops: a corporate logo. The director of sales also wants to have a quarterly promo as the background for the sales staff members who are part of the Sales security group. How would you accomplish both goals?

8. If a computer setting in a GPO disables AutoPlay and a user setting in the same GPO enables AutoPlay, will AutoPlay be disabled or enabled?

9. What does the term forcing Group Policy mean?

10. What permissions are required if you want to grant a user administrative control of a GPO? Where would the permissions need to be set to enable the users to create additional GPOs in the same container?

11. If all Group Policies you have configured only deal with the user portion of the GPO, how could you improve performance of GPO processing?

Exam Questions

1. You are the administrator of LearnWin2K.com, an online training organization providing Windows 2000 training. You need to configure all the customer service machines so that Internet access is disabled. However, customer service supervisors need to be able to use the Internet. All customer service users are part of the CustomerService security group; customer service supervisors are also part of the CSSupervisors security group.

   Which of the following do you need to perform to satisfy these goals? (Choose the best answer.)

APPLY YOUR KNOWLEDGE

A. Create two GPOs, one to disable Internet access and the other to enable it. Grant the CustomerService security group Read and Apply Group Policy permissions on the first GPO; grant the CSSupervisors security group Read and Apply Group Policy permissions on the second.

B. Create two GPOs, one to disable Internet access and the other to enable it. Grant the CustomerService security group Read and Apply Group Policy permissions on the first GPO; grant the CSSupervisors security group Read and Apply Group Policy permissions on the second. Grant the CSSupervisors security group Read permissions on the first.

C. Create one GPO to disable Internet access. Grant the CustomerService security group Read and Apply Group Policy permissions.

D. Create one GPO to disable Internet access. Grant the CustomerService security group Read and Apply Group Policy permissions; grant the CSSupervisors security group only Read permissions on the GPO.

2. You have linked a GPO to the domain that removes the Run command from the Start menu for all domain users. While installing a new server in the accounting department, you notice that some of the Windows 2000 Professional computers still have the **Run** command available. Why would this occur? (Choose two correct answers.)

A. Accountants are not domain users.

B. You did not force the GPO settings.

C. Group Policy is not enforced on Windows 2000 Professional computers.

D. Policy inheritance was blocked at the Accounting OU level.

E. The users are not running Windows 98 on their client computers. To disable the **Run** command, users must run Windows 98.

3. You are finding that administering Group Policy is becoming more time consuming as your company grows. Departments also have been requesting more control at their own OU level. Each department has been assigned a junior administrator to handle its requirements. What do you need to do to delegate administration of each department's GPOs to these junior administrators? (Choose the best answer.)

A. Use the Delegation of Control Wizard to delegate control of the GPOs for their OU to them.

B. Grant them Full Control permissions on the GPOs linked to their OU.

C. Make them members of the OU Admins security group.

D. Grant them Read and Write permissions on the GPOs linked to their OU.

E. Make them members of the Domain Admins security group.

F. Grant them Read and Write permissions on their OU.

4. You are finding that administering Group Policy is becoming more time consuming as your company grows. Departments also have been requesting more control at their own OU level. Each department has been assigned a junior administrator to handle its requirements.

APPLY YOUR KNOWLEDGE

What do you need to do to allow these junior administrators to administer existing GPOs in their OUs and to create and remove GPOs if needed? (Choose all the best correct answers.)

A. Use the Delegation of Control Wizard to delegate control of the GPOs for their OU to them.

B. Grant them Full Control permissions on the GPOs linked to their OU.

C. Make them members of the OU Admins security group.

D. Grant them Read and Write permissions on the GPOs linked to their OU.

E. Make them members of the Domain Admins security group.

F. Grant them Read and Write permissions on their OU.

5. What is the order of application of Group Policy? (Choose the best answer.)

A. Computer, user, script

B. Site, domain, OU

C. Domain, site, OU

D. OU, site, domain

E. User, script, computer

6. You have configured Group Policy as follows:

At the domain level, you have GPO1 that removes Control Panel from the Settings menu.

At the site level, you have GPO2 that forces user passwords to be six characters long. GPO has been configured with No Override.

At the OU level, you have GPO3 that removes the Run command from the Start menu.

You have blocked policy inheritance at the OU level.

What is the result when a user logs on to a Windows 2000 Professional computer that is in the OU container? (Choose all correct answers.)

A. Control Panel is not available.

B. Control Panel is available.

C. User passwords must be six characters long.

D. User passwords can be any length.

E. Run is available on the Start menu.

F. Run is not available on the Start menu.

7. Group Policy is enforced on computers running which of the following operating systems? (Choose all correct answers.)

A. Microsoft Windows for Workgroups 3.11

B. Microsoft Windows 2000 Advanced Server

C. Microsoft Windows 95

D. Microsoft Windows NT 4.0 with Service Pack 6 or later

E. Microsoft Windows 2000 Professional

F. Red Hat Linux 6.1 with Samba installed.

8. What should you do if you want Group Policy options at the OU level to ensure that only computer configuration settings are applied for a GPO and that these settings are not affected by domain GPO configuration? (Choose the best answer.)

APPLY YOUR KNOWLEDGE

A. Enable Computer Configuration settings and No Override.

B. Enable Computer Configuration settings and Block Policy Inheritance.

C. Disable User Configuration settings and Block Policy Inheritance.

D. Disable User Configuration Settings and No Override.

E. Disable Computer Configuration settings and No Override

F. Enable User Configuration settings and Block Policy Inheritance.

9. You design a Group Policy structure with two GPOs, one at the domain level and the other at the Marketing OU level.

   • At the domain level, you specify a background wallpaper and assign the policy to Authenticated Users.

   • At the Marketing OU level, you enable Control Panel and assign the policy to the SalesPeople security group.

   • At the Marketing OU level, you specify a background wallpaper and assign it to the Salespeople security group.

   • At the domain level, you specify that users can only make use of the Add/Remove Programs and Display portions of Control Panel.

   • You configure the Marketing OU GPO with No Override.

   • You configure the domain-level GPO with No Override.

A user in the Marketing OU logs on to the network after you have saved your changes and after a refresh of the GPO has taken place on all domain controllers affected. What is the result of your GPO settings on the user desktop? (Choose all correct answers.)

A. Control Panel is enabled for the user.

B. Only Add/Remove Programs and Display properties are available in Control Panel.

C. The user has the domain-level background wallpaper.

D. The user has the background wallpaper specified in the Marketing OU GPO.

10. What are the default Group Policy refresh intervals for computers in the domain? (Choose two correct answers.)

A. Group Policy is refreshed on domain controllers every 15 minutes.

B. Group Policy is refreshed on member servers and workstations every 15 minutes.

C. Group Policy is refreshed on member servers and workstations every 90 minutes.

D. Group Policy is refreshed on domain controllers every 90 minutes.

E. Group Policy is refreshed on member servers and workstations every 5 minutes.

F. Group Policy is refreshed on domain controllers every 5 minutes.

APPLY YOUR KNOWLEDGE

11. You are the administrator of the factron.com domain. You have created the following Active Directory containers:

    • A Sales OU

    • A Development OU

    • A Finance OU

    In which Active Directory containers are you able to create a Group Policy? (Choose all correct answers.)

    A. Users

    B. Sales OU

    C. Finance OU

    D. Computers

    E. Development OU

    F. factron.com domain

    G. Domain Controllers

12. You modify the Offline Folder settings for users on an existing GPO that has been assigned to the SalesPeople security group. NatashaR, a member of the SalesPeople security group, is already logged on to the domain on a Windows 98 computer. When will the updated settings for Offline Folders take effect on her computer? (Choose the best answer.)

    A. The next time she logs on to the domain.

    B. Within 5 minutes.

    C. Within 90 minutes.

    D. Within 15 minutes.

    E. The next time the computer restarts.

    F. The new settings will not take effect.

13. Where are Group Policy template settings stored? (Choose the best answer.)

    A. In each Windows 2000 computer's %SystemRoot%\GPO folder

    B. In each domain controller's %SystemRoot\GPO folder

    C. On each domain controller's SYSVOL share in a folder with the same name as the GPO

    D. On each domain controller's SYSVOL share in a folder with the same name as the GUID of the GPO

    E. On each Windows 2000 computer's SYSVOL share in a folder with the same name as the GPO

    F. On each Windows 2000 computer's SYSVOL share in a folder with the same name as the GUID of the GPO

14. You create a logon script that maps LPT1 to a printer called HP5 on the DEVWORK file server. You create a startup script that maps LPT1 to a printer called LEXMARK on the DEVWORK server. You create another logon script that deletes any mapping to LPT1.

    You create a GPO at the Sales OU. You add the startup script to the Computer Configuration of the GPO. You also add both logon scripts to the User Configuration of the GPO. You assign the Sales security group the Apply Group Policy permission to the GPO and remove the Authenticated Users group from the list of groups with permissions on the GPO.

    HeesH, a member of the Sales security group whose computer account is defined in the Sales OU, logs on to the network. What will LPT1 be mapped to on his computer? (Choose the best answer.)

APPLY YOUR KNOWLEDGE

A. \\DEVWORK\HP5

B. \\DEVWORK\LEXMARK

C. The mapping will be deleted.

D. \\DEVWORK\HP5 and
\\DEVWORK\LEXMARK

E. The mapping cannot be predicted.

15. You are attempting to edit a GPO but receive the `Failed to Open Group Policy Object` error message. You connect to a share on the single domain controller on your site and verify that the domain controller is available and that the network is functioning properly. What is the most likely cause of the problem? (Choose the best answer.)

A. You do not have sufficient permissions to edit the GPO.

B. A DHCP server is not available.

C. The GPO is not authorized in Active Directory.

D. The DNS server is not available.

E. The WINS server is not available.

F. The GPO does not exist.

Answers to Exercises

6.4 Verifying Group Policy Administrative Template Settings

3. The amount of free disk space should be just under 100MB. The disk quota established by the policy is the default of 100MB for all users. Because drive C is where Windows 2000 is installed and is the default location for user profiles, you will have just under 100MB of free space.

4. The user should have 100MB of disk space available to him. This is the amount permitted for all users as established by the disk quota default in the computer policy.

5. You configured a computer policy that enforced and established a disk quota. The default disk quota assigned to each user is 100MB on each NTFS partition according to the policy. Because you did not change the default for HowardH's user account, he is allowed 100MB of disk space per the GPO settings.

6. No, Control Panel is not available under Settings. The Group Policy configured for the Sales OU disables Control Panel, and it should not appear if the policy is being enforced.

7. No, the Run menu is not available from the Start menu. The Run menu was removed for users in the Sales OU in the user settings of the Group Policy.

8. Yes, the computer policy settings are being enforced. Disk quotas have been established and enforced for all users on computers in the Research OU. A default quota of 100MB on each partition has been assigned to users.

9. Yes, user policy settings for the Sales OU are being enforced on the computer. The Run menu is not available from the Start menu, and Control Panel is also not available, as specified in the Group Policy.

APPLY YOUR KNOWLEDGE

6.6 Verifying Group Policy Logon Script Settings

3. A mapping to the CORPDATA share does appear as drive K on the machine. This is because RalphD is a user in the Research OU where the GPO has been defined and is subject to the scripts specified in the policy.

6. A mapping to drive K for the CORPDATA share does not appear in the list in Windows Explorer. HowardH is a user in the Sales OU and is not subject to the conditions and settings of the policy defined for the Research OU where the logon script is located.

6.8 Verifying Group Policy Link and Logon Script Settings

3. A mapping to the CORPDATA share does appear as drive K on the machine. This is because RalphD is a user in the Research OU where the GPO was originally defined, and he is subject to the scripts specified in the policy. Linking the policy to the Sales OU did not change the original relationship between the policy and the Research OU.

6. A mapping to drive K: for the CORPDATA share does appear in the list in Windows Explorer. HowardH is a user in the Sales OU and is now subject to the conditions and settings of the Research Logon Script Policy, which has been linked to the Sales OU.

6.9 Delegating Administrative Control of Group Policy

4. No permissions are assigned directly to HowardH at this time. Because HowardH is a member of the Domain Users built-in group, he has Read and Apply Group Policy permissions.

7. HowardH now has the Read permission on the GPO. The Apply Group Policy permissions check box is cleared, so he no longer has this permission on the GPO.

8. He would need Read and Write permissions to administer the GPO. If you wanted the policy to also apply to him, you would need to grant him the Apply Group Policy permission as well.

6.10 Testing the Delegation of Administrative Control of Group Policy

3. HowardH has the Properties and Edit options available. New, Add, Delete, and Options are grayed-out. This enables HowardH to edit the GPO contents and view the GPO properties. He cannot add, delete, change the order of application, block policy inheritance, override lower-level policies, or disable the Group Policy.

4. HowardH only has the Properties button available for the Research Logon Script Policy, which enables him to view the Properties of the GPO but not modify them. He cannot edit the Group Policy. He is able to edit the Telemarketing Users Group Policy.

5. HowardH is presented with a dialog box that states he is not able to change the permissions of the GPO. He needs to be given the Full Control or Change permissions to change the security settings of the GPO.

APPLY YOUR KNOWLEDGE

6. Yes, the MMC is displayed because HowardH has the Read and Write permissions on the GPO.

7. Yes, HowardH is able to make changes to the GPO settings because he has been given the Write permission on the GPO.

6.11 Filtering and Blocking Group Policy Inheritance

3. You need to block policy inheritance at the Sales OU level. To do this, check the Block Policy Inheritance check box in the bottom-left corner of the dialog box.

4. Remove Authenticated Users from the list of groups assigned permissions. Also clear the Apply Group Policy permission from user HowardH because he is not a member of the Telemarketing security group. Finally, add the Telemarketing security group to the list of groups with permissions and assign them the Read and Apply Group Policy permissions.

6.12 Testing Filtering Group Policy

3. The amount of free disk space should be just under 100MB. The disk quota established by the computer policy is the default of 100MB for all users. Because drive C is where Windows 2000 is installed and is the default location for user profiles, you have just under 100MB of free space. This is not due to the Telemarketing Users Policy but rather the computer policy applied to the machine, which is located in the Research OU.

4. 100MB of disk space should be available to the user. This is the amount permitted for all users as established by the disk quota default in the computer policy.

5. You configured a computer policy that enforced and established a disk quota. The default disk quota assigned to each user is 100MB on each NTFS partition according to the policy. Because you did not change the default for HowardH's user account, he is allowed 100MB of disk space per the GPO settings.

6. No, Control Panel is not available under Settings. The Group Policy configured for the Telemarketing security group of the Sales OU disables Control Panel, and it should not appear if the policy is being enforced.

7. No, the Run menu is not available from the Start menu. The Run menu was removed from the Telemarketing security group of the Sales OU in the user settings of the Group Policy. NatashaW is a member of the Telemarketing security group.

8. Yes, the computer policy settings are being enforced. Disk quotas have been established and enforced for all users on computers in the Research OU. A default quota of 100MB on each partition has been assigned to users.

9. Yes, user policy settings for the Sales OU are being enforced on the computer. The user is a member of the Telemarketing security group, which has the policy applied to it. The Run menu is not available from the Start menu, and Control Panel is also not available, as specified in the Group Policy.

13. The amount of free disk space should be just under 100MB. The disk quota established by the computer policy is the default of 100MB for all users. Because drive C is where Windows 2000 is installed and is the default location for user profiles, you have just under 100MB of free space. This is not due to the Telemarketing Users

APPLY YOUR KNOWLEDGE

Policy but rather the computer policy applied to the machine, which is located in the Research OU. HowardH is bound by this policy.

14. The user should have 100MB of disk space available to him. This is the amount permitted for all users as established by the disk quota default in the computer policy.

15. You configured a computer policy that enforced and established a disk quota. The default disk quota assigned to each user is 100MB on each NTFS partition according to the policy. Because you did not change the default for HowardH's user account, he is allowed 100MB of disk space per the GPO settings.

16. Yes, Control Panel is available under Settings. The Group Policy configured for the Telemarketing security group of the Sales OU does not apply to HowardH because he has had this policy filtered to not be applied to him.

17. Yes, the Run menu is available from the Start menu. The Run menu was removed from the Telemarketing security group of the Sales OU in the user settings of the Group Policy. HowardH, however, is not a member of the Telemarketing security group, so the policy setting does not apply to him.

18. Yes, the computer policy settings are being enforced. Disk quotas have been established and enforced for all users on computers in the Research OU. A default quota of 100MB on each partition has been assigned to users.

19. No, user policy settings for the Sales OU are not being enforced for this user on the computer. HowardH is not a member of the Telemarketing security group that has the policy applied to it. The Run menu is not available from the Start menu, and Control Panel is available.

Answers to Review Questions

1. A GPO consists of two parts: a Group Policy container and a Group Policy Template. The GPC is an Active Directory object that contains GPO attributes and version information. Domain controllers use the GPC to determine whether they have the most recent version of the GPO. The GPT is a folder hierarchy in the shared SYSVOL folder on domain controllers. The GPT contains all the GPO settings including administrative templates, scripts, software installation, folder redirection, and security settings for the GPO. See "Introduction to Group Policy" and "Group Policy Components."

2. To make sure a GPO for a site was applied to all users and computers in the site, you would select the No Override option for the GPO. This forces the GPO settings to be applied to all subsequent levels of the hierarchy, including domains and OUs, because GPOs for a site are processed first. See "Group Policy Security," "Group Policy Inheritance," and "Forcing Group Policy Settings."

3. GPO settings apply to members of the Authenticated Users group by default. At this level, all users that log on to the domain, as well as all computers that log on to the domain when started, have GPO settings applied to them. See "Group Policy Security" and "Configuring Group Policy Security."

4. Administrative template settings within GPOs make modifications to the registry in either the HKEY_LOCAL_MACHINE registry hive (if you modify the Computer Configuration of the administrative template) or the

HKEY_CURRENT_USER registry hive (if you modify the User Configuration of the administrative template). Scripts can be used to perform any task and to modify any setting, including registry settings, because they are either a BAT or CMD file, a VBScript or JScript script processed by Windows Script Host, or an executable (EXE) file. See "Managing User Environments Using Group Policy."

5. Windows 2000 Group Policy supports four types of scripts. For the computer, startup and shutdown scripts are available. For the user, logon and logoff scripts can be configured. See "Managing User Environments Using Group Policy" and "Configuring and Using Scripts in Group Policy."

6. Group Policy enables the administrator to set centralized and/or decentralized policies that provide control over computer and user environments. GPOs enable the administrator to make sure users have the application and requisite environmental settings to perform their jobs. They enable the administrator to have control over user and computer environments whether they are located in the next room or halfway around the world. Because GPO administration can be delegated to others, it enables a corporate administrator to make sure the local requirements are incorporated into any centralized administration of desktops that is desired. Finally, GPOs enable the administrator to make sure corporate policies and business rules can be enforced throughout the enterprise. See "Introduction to Group Policy" and "Group Policy Scope."

7. To make sure all users in the domain have the corporate logo as the background wallpaper on their desktop, you would create a GPO at the domain level and configure the wallpaper settings in the User Configuration portion of the administrative template settings of the GPO. You would also make sure the Domain Users security group has been assigned the Read and Apply Group Policy permissions on the GPO.

To ensure that members of the sales department have a quarterly promo as the background wallpaper on the desktop, you would create a GPO at the domain level and configure the wallpaper settings in the User Configuration portion of the administrative template settings of the GPO. You would also make sure the Sales security group has been assigned the Read and Apply Group Policy permission on the GPO. To not have this GPO applied to any other users in the domain, you would also remove the Domain Users security group from the list of users and groups assigned permissions on the GPO.

Next, to ensure that the sales users would not receive the background wallpaper that all other users are getting, you would filter the domain users Group Policy, add the Sales security group to the list of groups assigned permissions on the domain users GPO, and uncheck the Apply Group Policy permission so that the policy is not enforced for the Sales security group.

Finally, to ensure that these settings are not tampered with by lower-level administrators, you would set the No Override option for both GPOs. See "Managing User Environments Using Group Policy" and "Group Policy Scope."

8. AutoPlay will be disabled. Computer settings take precedence over user settings; hence, the computer setting of disable AutoPlay will win out. See "Group Policy Scope" and "Group Policy Processing."

APPLY YOUR KNOWLEDGE

9. Forcing Group Policy means you have configured the No Override option for the GPO. The end result is that the settings in the GPO with the No Override option set cannot be modified by lower-level GPOs even if the administrator at that lower level (domain or OU) has blocked policy inheritance. See "Group Policy Security."

10. For the user to be able to modify an existing GPO, he or she needs to be assigned both Read and Write permissions on the GPO. If you wanted them to create additional GPO objects within the same container, they would need to be granted permissions on the container in which the GPO is defined. Specifically, they would require the Create Group Policy Container Objects and Delete Group Policy Container Objects permissions on the Active Directory container. Granting them Read and Write permissions also works but might provide them with more privileges than you want. See "Group Policy Security," "Configuring Group Policy Security," and "Setting Permissions to Manage the Policy."

11. To improve performance of policy processing if only the user portion of the GPO is specified for your policy, you can check the Disable Computer Configuration settings on the General tab of the GPO Properties dialog box. This tells all computers applying the policy to only download the user configuration settings and not waste time downloading the computer portion because it is not used. See "Troubleshooting Group Policy."

Answers to Exam Questions

1. **D.** Internet access is enabled by default when you install Windows 2000. If you want to turn it off, you need to create a GPO that disables Internet access. Customer service supervisors are members of both the CustomerService security group and the CSSupervisors security group. If you only grant the CustomerService group Read and Apply Group Policy permissions, supervisors do not have Internet access. To correct this, grant the CSSupervisors only Read permissions on the GPO, thereby filtering the policy from them.

   Answer B also provides a solution that works, although creating two policies requires more administration than is actually needed with a single GPO. Because the question asked for the best answer, D is the only logical choice. See "Group Policy Scope" and "Group Policy Security."

2. **B, D.** The fact that some users have the Run command still available indicates that GPO inheritance was blocked at the Accounting OU level. Other GPOs were put in place, which allowed some users to have Run on the Start menu and others to have it removed. Had you forced the GPO settings to be applied by selecting the No Override option for the GPO, this behavior would not have occurred, and the Run command would be removed from all users. Both the lack of forcing the GPO and the capability of OU administrators to block policy inheritance are the cause of the problem. See "Group Policy Security" and "Group Policy Inheritance."

APPLY YOUR KNOWLEDGE

3. **D.** To allow the junior administrators to modify the GPOs in their OUs, you need to assign them Read and Write permissions to the GPOs in their OUs. Assigning them Full Control permissions also works, but it might give them more permissions than needed (for example, the capability to change a GPOs permissions or to specify options such as No Override). Granting them Read and Write permissions to the OU enables them to change other objects within the OU, again giving them higher permissions than necessary. You cannot use the Delegation of Control Wizard to delegate control of GPOs; the Delegation of Control Wizard can only be used to delegate administrative authority to the GPO's parent container such as OUs. Making users members of the Domain Admins group is never a good idea. See "Group Policy Security," "Configuring Group Policy Security," and "Setting Permissions to Manage the Policy."

4. **D, F.** The answer to this question is similar to the preceding, except you now need to have the users be able to change the contents of the parent OU container. To do this, they also have to have Read and Write permissions on the OU they will be controlling. In actuality, the junior administrators only require the Create Group Policy Container Objects permission and the Delete Group Policy Container Object permissions, but these were not available in the question. See "Group Policy Security" and "Configuring Group Policy Security."

5. **B.** Policies are always applied starting at the site level, then the domain level, and finally the OU level. This is because site-level GPOs can be used to configure computer and user settings that might take into consideration geographic local differences; domain-level GPOs specify settings applied to all users and computers in the domain. All these settings can be overwritten and/or modified at the OU level, which has the smallest number of Active Directory objects to be affected, both computers and users. In each stage, you are reducing the number of Active Directory objects to be affected by a GPO. See "Group Policy Scope."

6. **B, C, F.** Policy inheritance was blocked at the OU level, which means any higher-level GPOs will not be applied at the OU, where the **Run** command (GPO3) was removed from the Start menu (answer F). The site-level GPO (GPO2) was configured with No Override, so the fact the policy inheritance was blocked at the OU level has no effect. The policy still applies and states that passwords must be six characters long (answer C). Control Panel was disabled at the domain level (GPO1), but this GPO was not configured with the No Override option, so it was blocked at the OU level and was not processed. Hence, Control Panel is still available to users at the OU level (answer B). See "Group Policy Security" and "Group Policy Inheritance."

7. **B, E.** Group Policy is enforced only on computers running any variant of Windows 2000, which includes Windows 2000 Professional and Windows 2000 Advanced Server. It also includes Windows 2000 Server and Windows 2000 Data Center Server. See "Introduction to Group Policy."

8. **C.** Disable User Configuration Settings tells all computers downloading the policy to not bother with the user portion of the GPO and to only download the computer portion. Block Policy Inheritance prevents higher-level GPO settings

APPLY YOUR KNOWLEDGE

from being applied at the OU level unless they were configured with the No Override option. See "Group Policy Scope," "Combining Group Policies," "Group Policy Security," and "Group Policy Inheritance."

9. **B, C.** Because you configured the domain-level GPO with No Override, any conflicting settings between it and the Marketing GPO will ensure that the domain-level settings apply. In this case, the user gets the domain level wallpaper and Control Panel settings. See "Group Policy Security" and "Group Policy Inheritance."

10. **C, F.** The default Group Policy refresh internal is 5 minutes on domain controllers and 90 minutes, plus or minus a 30-minute stagger interval, on member servers and workstations. See "Introduction to Group Policy," "Group Policy Scope," and "Group Policy Processing."

11. **B, C, E, F, G.** You are able to create GPOs in the Sales, Finance, and Development OUs as well as the Domain Controllers container and at the domain level. You cannot create a GPO at the Users or Computers containers. See "Creating and Managing Group Policy" and "Introduction to Group Policy."

12. **F** Because NatashaR is using Windows 98, Group Policy is not enforced. GPO settings only apply to Windows 2000 Professional, Server, Advanced Server, and Data Center Server computers. System Policy applies to Windows 9x and Windows NT 4.0 computers. See "Introduction to Group Policy."

13. **D.** Group Policy templates are stored on each domain controller in the SYSVOL share in a folder with the same name as the globally unique identifier as the Group Policy object. See "Introduction to Group Policy" and "Group Policy Components."

14. **E.** The mapping cannot be predicted in this case because logon scripts run asynchronously. This means that both logon scripts will run at the same time, and whichever one is the last to apply the mapping for LPT1 is the one that wins. This could be either \\DEVWORK\LEXMARK or a deletion of the LPT1 mapping. See "Configuring and Using Scripts in Group Policy" and "Group Policy Script Processing Order."

15. **D.** The most likely cause of this problem is DNS configuration. If a DNS server with the SRV records needed to locate the GPO is not available, even though you might be able to communicate with the domain controller for file and printer sharing, you might not be able to open the GPO for modification because the domain controller host name could be resolved by another DNS server or a WINS server. Whether a DHCP server or WINS server is available won't have any bearing on this problem. You do not need to be authorized in Active Directory to modify a GPO; you only need to have the necessary permissions. Authorizing is done for DHCP and RIS servers. If the GPO did not exist, you would not be able to modify it. The only possible answer is D. See "Troubleshooting Group Policy."

Suggested Readings and Resources

1. Microsoft Windows 2000 Resource Kit. *Deployment Planning Guide.* Microsoft Press, 2000.

2. Hill, Tim. *Windows 2000 Windows Script Host.* Macmillan Technical Publishing, 1999.

3. *Using Group Policy Scenarios* from Microsoft's Web site at `http://www.microsoft.com/windows2000/library/howitworks/management/grouppolicy.asp`.

4. *Introduction to Windows 2000 Group Policy* from Microsoft's Web site at `http://www.microsoft.com/windows2000/library/howitworks/management/grouppolicyintro.asp`.

5. *Windows 2000 Simplifies Top 15 Administrative Tasks* from Microsoft's Web site at `http://www.microsoft.com/windows2000/library/howitworks/management/adminsave.asp`.

6. *Windows Script Host: A Universal Scripting Host for Scripting Languages* from Microsoft's Web site at `http://www.microsoft.com/windows2000/library/howitworks/management/winscrwp.asp`.

7. *Windows 2000 Desktop Management Overview* from Microsoft's Web site at `http://www.microsoft.com/windows2000/library/howitworks/management/ccmintro.asp`.

8. *Step-by-Step Guide to Understanding the Group Policy Feature Set* from Microsoft's Web site at `http://www.microsoft.com/windows2000/library/planning/management/groupsteps.asp`.

9. *Step-by-Step Guide to User Data and User Settings* from Microsoft's Web site at `http://www.microsoft.com/windows2000/library/planning/management/userdata.asp`.

10. *Manage Change with the Windows 2000 Platform* from Microsoft's Web site at `http://www.microsoft.com/windows2000/guide/server/solutions/managechange.asp`.

11. *Group Policy Simplifies Administration* from Microsoft's Web site at `http://www.microsoft.com/windows2000/guide/server/solutions/gpsimplifies.asp`.

This chapter covers an objective from the unit "Installing, Configuring, Managing, Monitoring, Optimizing, and Troubleshooting Change and Configuration Management." Other objectives and subobjectives from this unit are covered in other chapters. The exam objective addressed by this chapter follows:

Maintain and troubleshoot software by using Group Policy.

- **Deploy software by using Group Policy.**

- **Maintain software by using Group Policy.**

- **Configure deployment options.**

- **Troubleshoot common problems that occur during software deployment.**

▶ The deployment of software in any organization can be a daunting task. Windows 2000 Active Directory provides a method that can make the job easier: Group Policy. You will be tested on your understanding of software deployment within the Group Policy context. Different methods can be used to deploy software. These methods include assigning and publishing. Software can be deployed to users and computers. Software can be assigned to computers or users and published to users only. You need to fully understand both deployment concepts for the exam. The upgrade and removal of software also is a test item including the different ways these two tasks can be performed. The exam tests your knowledge of deployment options and how to modify software deployment to reflect specific requirements within the organization.

CHAPTER 7

Software Distribution Using Group Policy

▶ In preparing for the Microsoft exam, it is strongly recommended that you perform all the Step by Steps as well as the exercises for this chapter.

▶ An understanding of the different options available when deploying software, Windows Installer, Group Policy, and ZAP files is required. Test yourself with the review questions and the sample exam questions in this chapter.

▶ Be familiar with the features and rules surrounding Group Policy, specifically inheritance, filtering, and precedence.

▶ "Practice makes perfect." As the old saying goes, practicing using Group Policy, creating software packages, deploying them, upgrading them, and removing them will hold you in good stead to deal with the issues presented on the exam.

Introduction

In the preceding chapter, you were introduced to Windows 2000 Group Policy and how it can be used to configure computer and user environments. Group Policy also has a number of additional capabilities, making it an indispensable tool for the Windows 2000 network administrator. One of these is the capability to distribute software applications to the users requiring them or for the purpose of enforcing a corporate standard. This feature also enables you to upgrade software after a new release comes out or forcibly remove software from the user's computer should the organization no longer desire to use the software.

This chapter first defines the software distribution life cycle, including the four phases of any manual or automated software deployment. Next you will look at each of the four phases and discuss how Group Policy can help you deploy software more accurately, in a more timely fashion, and with greater ease. The chapter concludes with a case study and a section with exercises and review and sample exam questions. Using the exercises and exams, you are able to apply the skills presented in this chapter. This should help you better grasp how Group Policy can be used to manage software deployment.

The Software Distribution Life Cycle

When deploying software in an enterprise or in a central location as can be done with Group Policy, you typically go through four stages: preparation, deployment, maintenance, and removal. Each of these stages is characterized by a distinct series of steps that need to take place before the next deployment phase commences. As you already have seen in the preceding chapter, Group Policy is a powerful tool for the administrator; the fact that it also assists in the deployment of software just makes it that much better.

The stages of the software distribution life cycle are as follows:

◆ **Preparation.** The preparation stage deals with all the elements that need to be put in place prior to the software deployment ever taking place. These elements include the creation of a

Windows Installer Package for deployment, the creation of a network share folder to hold the software to be installed, and copying the files for the software application to be deployed to the network shared folder. In some cases, software might not come in a format that can be used by the Windows Installer component of Windows 2000. You might need to use a third-party tool to create the package or, as an alternative, to create a ZAP file to install the software application. All these elements will be dealt with in the "Preparing Software for Deployment Using Group Policy" section of this chapter.

◆ **Deployment.** The deployment stage is when you actually get the software out to the user and/or computer. At this stage, you create a *Group Policy object* (GPO) automating the installation of the software and linking it to the appropriate Active Directory container (site, domain, or OU). You also decide whether the software is to be published or assigned. A decision needs to made concerning whether software should be deployed for the computer or the user. You also have to determine how much interaction the user will have during the installation process. This, in many ways, is the easiest part of software deployment. The hard work was done in the preparation stage. If software has been properly configured, this process will run well. The different ways to deploy software and the creation of a GPO are covered in the "Software Deployment Using Group Policy" section of this chapter.

◆ **Maintenance.** As you are probably already well aware, nothing stays static in this industry. Software is no exception. Would you be reading this book if Microsoft didn't upgrade NT 4 to Windows 2000? Over time, you might need to configure and deploy an upgrade to some of the software on users' machines. Other times, software that has been deployed might need to be redeployed; patches or a service pack might need to be applied to bring software up to the most current incarnation and/or to repair any deficiencies (bugs or anomalies—undocumented features) that might exist. The "Maintaining Software Packages Using Group Policy" section discusses how to upgrade software in the field and the upgrade options available.

◆ **Removal.** Sometimes, software loses its usefulness and might need to be removed. How many of your users still need Microsoft Word 2.0 on their machines? The "Removing a Package" section deals with the issues surrounding the removal of software, forced or not, from users' desktops.

Microsoft Windows 2000 Group Policy enables an administrator to automate the deployment, removal, and maintenance of software packages on users' desktops. Let's start by looking at preparing software for deployment.

PREPARING SOFTWARE FOR DEPLOYMENT USING GROUP POLICY

Before you can make use of the features of Group Policy that make deploying software such an easy task, preparation must take place to ensure that the software to be deployed is in a format that can be used by Windows 2000 Group Policy. Next, a software distribution share must be created on a server from which the software will be installed, and the necessary files must be copied to that location. You are then ready to create the GPO to deploy the software. This section looks at the technologies involved in deploying software using Windows 2000 Group Policy: Windows Installer Packages (MSI) files and ZAP files. It then briefly discusses the process of creating a Windows Installer Package for legacy applications or those software packages that do not come in a format that can be used by Windows Installer.

Packaging Software for Deployment

As previously mentioned, the first step in deploying software using Group Policy is to package the software in a format that Windows Installer can use to automate the distribution process. If the software you are deploying is a newer application that has been certified to work with Windows 2000 (for example, Microsoft Office 2000), you might not have all that much work to do. Newer applications most likely come in a format that can be used by Windows Installer. However, if your application is older (such as Microsoft Office 97), you might need to perform some additional tasks to make sure the automated installation proceeds as it should. You might need to repackage the application in a format compatible with Windows Installer or create a text file (that is, a ZAP file) to tell Windows Installer how to install the application.

Windows Installer Technology

First introduced on a large scale with Microsoft Office 2000, Windows Installer is the technology that enables Group Policy to deploy and manage software. It consists of two main components:

◆ Windows Installer Service

◆ Windows Installer Package

The Windows Installer Service is a service that is installed and runs on all Windows 2000 machines. This service facilitates the automated installation and deployment of software. It also provides the capability to automatically repair or modify existing applications when files are overwritten or removed. In this way, it ensures that the software both is properly installed and stays in working order. You can use the Windows Installer Service to install an application directly from a CD-ROM or other distribution media or through Group Policy.

The Windows Installer Package contains all the necessary information that the Windows Installer Service needs to install or remove an application. This includes the files required by the software as well as registry and INI file changes that need to be made. It also includes any additional support files that are required, summary information on the package and the application that can be shown to the user, and a reference to the location of the product files (that is, where to install the software from). The majority of this information is contained in a single file with an .MSI extension, which is the package file itself. As previously mentioned, the full package to be installed may also include other supplementary files. (For example, MS Office 2000 includes an MSI but also has many files in folders that the Windows Installer will copy to the hard drive.)

NOTE

Windows Installer on NT 4.0
Windows Installer is also installed on Windows NT 4.0 when you install Microsoft Office 2000 or any application that makes use of it. It can be incorporated into the Setup program of an application by the developer. It is installed on the target machine when the Setup program is launched, if it is not found. Just because the Windows Installer Service is installed on Windows NT 4.0, it does not mean you can deploy software onto Windows NT 4.0 desktops. You cannot.

Windows NT 4.0 does not support Windows 2000 Group Policy and, as such, cannot make use of the software deployment features of Group Policy. Both support of Group Policy and support of the Windows Installer Service are required on the target desktop to make use of Group Policy to automate software deployment.

Windows Installer provides the administrator, as well as the end user, with the following three major benefits over what has existed previously:

◆ **Resilient software.** With the Windows Installer Service, should a critical file for an application be accidentally deleted or modified in any way (for example, virus on the system), the Windows Installer Service connects to the software distribution share and replaces the file with a known good copy. This ensures that software applications are always available to the user and are in fact self-repairing.

◆ **Clean removal.** One of the many problems that exist with past Windows software is that removing one piece of software may actually remove a file needed by another piece. You probably have seen a prompt from a package uninstall asking if you would like to remove some shared files. You have no way of knowing whether you should say yes or no. Will saying yes cause another program to fail? Will saying no leave a bunch of orphaned files on your hard drive? Windows Installer runs as a service on each Windows 2000 computer and keeps track of which files are needed by which applications. This ensures that any shared critical files are not removed and that files no longer needed are removed. It does this for all applications in which it was used to perform the installation.

◆ **Elevated security.** In many situations, software applications require that the user performing the installation have administrative rights and permissions on the machine where the application is being installed. As an administrator, you do not want your users to have administrative permissions on their machines, enabling them to perform tasks that might make the computer inoperable. Automating the installation of these packages presented a challenge prior to Windows Installer. Because Windows Installer runs as a service under the LocalSystem account by default, it already has elevated privileges on the system. Applications that require the capability to make changes to the machine component of Windows 2000 can do so during the installation process while still not allowing the user to have administrative privileges. In this way, applications can be deployed that make changes to critical operating system settings (for example, registering

DLLs and COM objects or changing the HKEY_LOCAL
_MACHINE registry hive) without giving the end user the
same capability.

Windows Installer is a component that can provide many benefits
to the administrator in automating software deployment. The
Windows Installer Service is required to perform automated
installation, upgrades, and removal of software using Group Policy.
Windows Installer Package files are the preferred method of having
software prepared for automated deployment.

What if you do not have a package for the software to be deployed?
In Windows 2000, you can still configure software to be deployed
even if you do not have a ready-made Windows Installer Package
file. There are two ways to do this: You can create a ZAP file to tell
Windows Installer how to install the application, or you can create a
Windows Installer Package using a third-party tool. Let's look at
both of these methods, starting with the ZAP file.

Creating a ZAP File to Deploy Software with Group Policy

In some cases, it might be necessary to deploy software on Windows
2000 computers that have been around for a while. The computers
might have been developed in-house or simply do not follow the
Windows Installer conventions Microsoft has outlined. As the
number of the applications far outstrips the number that actually
use the Windows Installer Package format, Microsoft has provided a
way to deploy these software packages as well: the ZAP file format.

The ZAP file is a plain-text file created with any text editor
(Notepad will work) that specifies a number of things about the
software to be installed. The ZAP file might contain the application
name, the name of the setup program, any parameters to be used
for setup, as well as any file extensions to be associated with the
application, and tech support Web site. Not all of this information
needs to be included in the ZAP file, only the application
name (FriendlyName) and the setup executable filename
(SetupCommand). The sample ZAP file in the following
code block shows a simple set of tags that can be used.

```
[Application]
FriendlyName = Microsoft Office 97
SetupCommand = setup.exe /unattend
```

```
DisplayVersion = 8.0
Publisher = Microsoft Corporation
URL = http://www.microsoft.com/office

[Ext]
DOC=
DOT=
XLS=
PPT=
RTF=
```

ZAP File Sections

The ZAP file is made up of two sections, as shown in the preceding code block: the Application section and the Ext (or extensions) section. The Application section outlines information about the software package and how to install it. The Ext section specifies which file extensions should be associated with the application in Active Directory.

The Application section has a number of tags that can be applied. They are described in Table 7.1.

TABLE 7.1

APPLICATION TAGS

Tag	Description	Required or Optional
FriendlyName	This is the name visible to the user and administrator when the application is installed. It also appears in Add/Remove Programs in Control Panel if the application is published or the user wants to remove the application. This is a name describing the application and should not be the name of an executable file. In other words, use something like Microsoft Word97 as a FriendlyName instead of WINWORD.EXE. The name should be friendly to the user.	Required

Tag	*Description*	*Required or Optional*
SetupCommand	This is the name of the executable program used to install the application. This could be an EXE file or a BAT or CMD file, as long as it performs the necessary steps to install the application. The filename specified should be relative to the physical location of the ZAP file containing it. In other words, if both the ZAP file and the setup program are in the same folder, do not precede the filename with the name of the folder. If the program is in a different folder than the ZAP file, you can use a relative path name from the location of the ZAP file as the SetupCommand. For example, the ZAP file and the SETUP.EXE are both in a folder called Office97 on the network distribution share. You only need to configure the tag to read SetupCommand=setup.exe /unattend with no path name preceding the filename. If, on the other hand, the ZAP file is in the software distribution shared folder and the setup program is in a subfolder called Office97, then the tag should include the path name, as in SetupCommand=Office97\ setup.exe /unattend.	Required
DisplayVersion	This is the version number of the application. This number appears in Add/Remove Programs and in the Software Installation portion of Group Policy. This is used to identify the different versions of an application that might have similar names. For example, Office97 is version 8.0; Office2000 is version 9.0.	Optional

continues

TABLE 7.1	*continued*

APPLICATION TAGS

Tag	Description	Required or Optional
Publisher	This is the name of the company or individual that publishes the software application. The publisher of the application also appears in Add/Remove Programs and in the Software Installation portion of Group Policy.	Optional
URL	This is the URL containing additional information about the application and/or technical support details. The URL also appears in Add/Remove Programs and the Software Installation portion of Group Policy.	Optional

A ZAP file needs to contain only the Application section and the FriendlyName and SetupCommand tags. All other portions, including the Ext section, are optional. Specifying the Ext section might be a good idea, however.

The Ext, or extensions, section of the ZAP file is used to associate the application with a file extension in Windows 2000 Active Directory. Windows 2000 uses the Ext section to determine which application should be installed when a user decides to open, or double-click, an operating system file. If the extension of the file does not match a list of applications on the computer that can be used to open the file, the setup program for the application that defined a particular extension as belonging to or supported by itself is called and the application is installed, allowing the user to view the file.

For example, you use Windows Explorer to browse files on a CD-ROM sent to you by Microsoft. Browsing through the files in a folder on the CD-ROM, you locate ZAP file Explained.RTF and decide you want to view its contents. You double-click the file, and the setup program from Word 97 starts up. After you complete the installation of Word 97, the RTF document is displayed on the screen for you. The fact that the .RTF extension was included in the Ext section of the ZAP file allowed it to be published in Active

Directory and to automatically invoke the Word 97 Setup program, which allowed you to see the contents of the file.

To add the Ext section to the ZAP file, simply type the Ext heading on a line by itself. On lines below it, specify the extensions to be associated with the application without the leading period. See the following code block for an example.

```
[Application]
FriendlyName = Microsoft Office 97
SetupCommand = setup.exe /unattend
DisplayVersion = 8.0
Publisher = Microsoft Corporation
URL = http://www.microsoft.com/office

[Ext]
DOC=
DOT=
XLS=
PPT=
RTF=
```

ZAP File Limitations

ZAP files do have some limitations and are not as good as Windows Installer Packages. It should be noted that the preferred method of installing any piece of software is to create a Windows Installer Package using a third-party tool. With packages, all options are available. Applications deployed using ZAP files have the following limitations:

◆ **ZAP files cannot be assigned to users, only published.** As you will see later in this chapter, there are two ways to deploy applications using Group Policy: assign them to a user or computer, or publish them. Assignment is a mandatory installation of a software package, whereas publishing is voluntary (that is, the user might decide not to install the application after all). The fact that you can only publish applications with a ZAP file limits the flexibility of the administrator in ensuring that all users have the required software on their machines.

◆ **ZAP files are not self-repairing.** With applications installed using a Windows Installer Package, a critical application file that is deleted or becomes corrupt automatically is replaced with a known good copy. This behavior is not available to applications deployed using a ZAP file; Windows Installer recognizes one file for the application: the setup program. Windows Installer does not track what was installed by the application's setup program and, hence, cannot tell whether the application is damaged.

◆ **ZAP files usually require user intervention to be installed.**
The ZAP file simply invokes the install program for the application. Unless the software package has a fully unattended mode and this mode has been properly configured, the user has to provide some information for the install to complete. This might be all right in environments in which users are somewhat technically savvy, but it might prove difficult and create additional support headaches in environments in which users do not have a lot of computer experience.

◆ **ZAP files cannot be installed using elevated privileges.**
As previously mentioned, Windows Installer enables you to deploy applications to users even if the user does not necessarily have full privileges to install software on his or her computer. This can be done because, during the installation of Windows Installer Packages, the process runs within the context of Windows Installer. Windows Installer is the one doing the install, not the user. Because Windows Installer is a service that typically has administrative privileges on the computer, any piece of software can be installed, including those requiring administrative rights during installation.

With ZAP files, the program used to install a particular piece of software is invoked by the user and runs within the security context of the user. If the user does not have sufficient permissions to install the program, the installation fails and the application is not installed. This might also cause more support calls and not be the desired result.

So, after all of this, you're probably asking yourself, "Self, when would I decide to use a ZAP file?" The answer you're most likely to receive is, "Hardly ever." ZAP files are a perfectly acceptable way to publish software that is not required to be installed on a machine. It is a method that can be used to deploy optional software, such as utilities, within an enterprise. Examples of applications that can be safely deployed using ZAP files include WinZip32 or file decompressors, Adobe Acrobat Reader, and others. These applications are useful, though not required, on a user's machine; the user has the choice of whether to install the product.

ZAP files should not be used to deploy a critical line of business applications or any pieces of software that all users require and that need to be maintained at a consistent level for all users at all times. If an application you need to deploy fits into one of these categories but does not have a Windows Installer Package available, you can create a Windows Installer Package for the application using a third-party tool.

Creating a Windows Installer Package Using Third-Party Tools

In some cases, you might need to repackage an application so it can be deployed using Windows Installer. As previously shown, it is often preferable to create a Windows Installer Package to deploy an application than to use a ZAP file to perform the same task. Packages offer a fair bit more flexibility for deployment and are also self-repairing, a feature you will find to be almost the best thing since sliced bread.

The process of repacking an application and creating a Windows Installer Package to be used to deploy a piece of software involves several steps and, preferably, two computers. It is performed using WinINSTALL LE, which is shipped with Windows 2000, or any other third-party program that supports the creation of packages such as InstallShield and others. Using WinINSTALL LE shall be assumed for the rest of this section.

The steps involved in repackaging an application include preparing a reference computer, preparing a network installation shared folder, installing Veritas WinINSTALL LE, and taking a "before" image of the system configuration. Several Step by Step tutorials walk you through the process of repackaging an application.

Prepare a Windows 2000 computer to be a reference computer. To repackage an application to be used to deploy software using Group Policy, you need to install the application on a computer as part of the repacking process. You typically use a Windows 2000 Professional computer, although Windows 2000 Server, or any variant, should also work. Use the version of the operating system that will be used by clients receiving the deployed package.

> **NOTE**
>
> **Location of WinINSTALL LE**
> Microsoft, on the Windows 2000 installation CD-ROM, provides a third-party application called WinINSTALL LE by Veritas Software to repackage an application. The program can be found in the VALUEADD\3RDPARTY\MGMT\WINSTLE folder on any of the Windows 2000 versions (Professional, Server, and Advanced Server) and is, itself, a Microsoft Windows Installer Package file.

The first step required to be able to install the application to be repackaged is the preparation of a machine to be the computer on which to install the application. The reference computer should only have Windows 2000 on it and no other software. Other software installed on the machine might cause parts of the application to be repackaged to not install (for example, if the files already exist on the hard drive), which might provide incorrect information to WinINSTALL LE during the repackaging process.

Prepare a network installation shared folder to store the Windows Installer Packages and their supporting files. Users will connect to this shared folder to install the application. The shared folder name also is specified in the Group Policy Software Installation section so that Windows Installer knows where to find it when Group Policy assigns or publishes the application to the user or computer.

The next step is to install Veritas WinINSTALL LE on a second Windows 2000 machine. You should not install WinINSTALL LE on the same machine you are using as a reference computer because this might contaminate the clean environment you have configured. Always install WinINSTALL LE on a second Windows 2000 machine.

To install WinINSTALL LE on the second computer, follow Step by Step 7.1.

STEP BY STEP

7.1 Installing and Configuring WinINSTALL LE

1. Insert the Windows 2000 CD-ROM in the machine's CD-ROM drive and select Browse This CD when the Windows 2000 splash screen appears.

2. Double-click the folders presented in sequence starting with VALUEADD, then 3RDPARTY, then MGMT, and finally, WINSTLE.

3. In the WINSTLE folder, right-click SWIADMLE and select Install or double-click the file. This starts the installation of WinINSTALL LE and a screen similar to Figure 7.1 is presented.

4. WinINSTALL LE installs itself into two folders on the volume where you installed Windows 2000. These folders are located from the root under Program Files\VERITAS Software and include the WINSTALL folder and the WINCONSOLE folder. You need to share the WINSTALL folder by right-clicking it in Windows Explorer and selecting Sharing. Click Share This Folder and leave the configured permissions and the share name as required for your enterprise. In the example, the share is called WINSTALL.

5. You have successfully installed WinINSTALL LE and have prepared it to be used to repackage an application.

FIGURE 7.1
The WinINSTALL LE initial screen.

After installing WinINSTALL LE and sharing the WINSTALL folder, you are ready for the first major step in repackaging an application. You are ready to take the before image of the reference computer.

Taking the before image involves using the WinINSTALL Discover program to take a snapshot of the system configuration of your reference computer before the software is installed. To take the before snapshot, perform the steps shown in Step by Step 7.2.

STEP BY STEP

7.2 Taking a Before Image of the Reference Computer

1. From the reference computer, connect to the WINSTALL share of the machine where you installed WinINSTALL LE. Execute DISCOZ.EXE to start WinINSTALL Discover. A dialog box similar to Figure 7.2 is presented.

FIGURE 7.2
The WinINSTALL Discover startup dialog box.

2. Click Next to continue creating the snapshot. You will be presented with a dialog box asking you to specify the name of the package you are creating, the location and name of the file to be created, and the language in which messages will be presented to the user, as shown in Figure 7.3.

continues

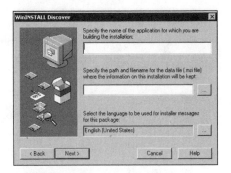

FIGURE 7.3
The WinINSTALL Discover package specification screen.

FIGURE 7.4
The WinINSTALL temporary drive selection screen.

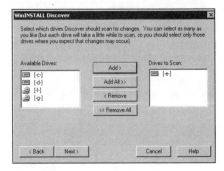

FIGURE 7.5
The WinINSTALL Discover drive scan selection screen

continued

In the name box, type the name of the application you are repackaging. In the path and filename box, type the name of the file to create. The Windows Installer (that is, MSI) file to be created should reside on a network drive in the shared installation folder you created earlier. At this point, you might want to specify a different folder in which to store the file and move the MSI file to the final destination folder later. This is so you can test to make sure the resulting MSI file works correctly before it is placed in a location that might be accessible to users. Click Next to continue.

3. On the following screen, shown in Figure 7.4, select the drive where the Discover Wizard can store its temporary files. This should not be the same drive where you are installing the software. Click Next to continue.

4. Figure 7.5 shows the next screen. Select the drives to be included in the before image. The list of drives you select should include the drive where Windows 2000 is installed as well as the drive where you intend to install the software. Both need to be tracked because many software applications also install files on the Windows 2000 system drive (in addition to the drive where you decide to install them). After making your selection, click Next.

5. On the screen that follows (see Figure 7.6), you are presented with a choice of specifying which files to exclude from the before image scan. The preselected list includes the Windows 2000 page file, Index Server catalog files, and most temporary files. If you know of other files to be added to the list, specify them here and click Next when done; if you are not sure, do not add any additional files.

6. The WinINSTALL LE Discover Wizard starts to scan the hard drives you specified and creates the before image. Figure 7.7 shows the dialog box shown as the scan proceeds.

7. After the before snapshot is created, as shown in Figure 7.8, the Discover Wizard prompts you for the name and location of the setup program of the application you want to install and then launches it.

Now that you have taken the before image of the reference computer and the setup program has been launched for the application you want to repackage, you simply go through the normal application configuration as if you were installing it on any machine. You should choose the settings that make sense for all users who should have this package installed. If this requires you to create additional desktop icons as shortcuts, do this as well. If the install program calls for reboots, perform them. In other words, go through the same process you would use to set up the application.

After the application has been configured, you need to take an after image of the reference computer. This will be scanned for differences, and the Discover Wizard will determine the necessary contents of the package. Connect the reference computer to the WINSTALL share and launch the Discover Wizard again to start the process of creating an after image. Step by Step 7.3 guides you through the process.

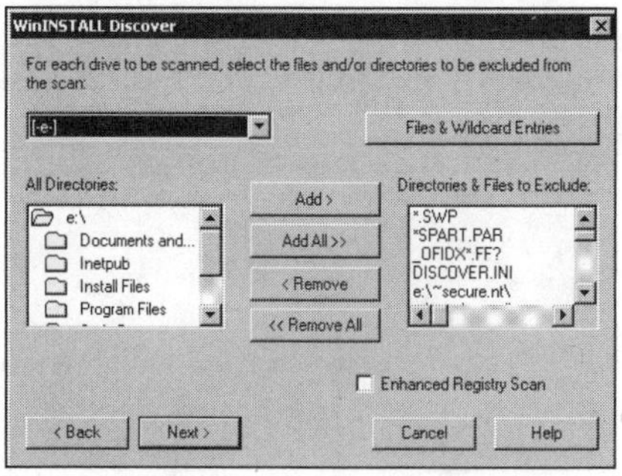

STEP BY STEP

7.3 Taking an After Image of the Reference Computer

1. Connect the reference computer to the WINSTALL share of the machine where you installed WinINSTALL LE. Execute DISCOZ.EXE to start WinINSTALL Discover. A dialog box similar to Figure 7.9 is presented.

continues

FIGURE 7.6
WinINSTALL Discover Wizard file exclusion screen.

FIGURE 7.7
The WinINSTALL Discover Wizard scanning progress dialog box.

FIGURE 7.8
The WinINSTALL Discover before snapshot completion dialog box.

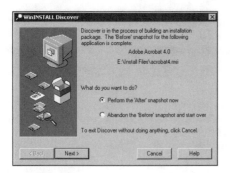

FIGURE 7.9
The WinINSTALL Discover Wizard after image selection dialog box.

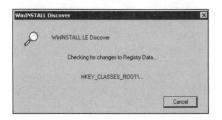

FIGURE 7.10
The WinINSTALL Discover Wizard after image progress dialog box.

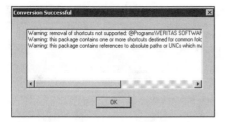

FIGURE 7.11
The WinINSTALL Discover Wizard after image warning and errors dialog box.

FIGURE 7.12
The WinINSTALL Discover Wizard after image completion dialog box.

continued

2. At this point, you need to determine whether you would like to create the after image or abandon the old before image for the application you are repackaging. The name of the application you specified earlier is also shown as a guide (for example, Adobe Acrobat 4.0 for the Adobe Acrobat 4.0 Reader being repackaged in the figure). Select Perform the 'After' snapshot now and click Next to continue.

3. The WinINSTALL LE Discover Wizard starts scanning the hard drive and registry to determine what changes took place during the application installation. During this scanning process, you are presented with a status screen, as shown in Figure 7.10. When complete, you are presented with any errors or warnings encountered, as shown in Figure 7.11. Make a note of the warnings or errors and click OK to continue.

4. The after snapshot is now complete, as the next dialog box shows (see Figure 7.12). You also are told where the package file was created. Click OK to complete the creation of the after image and exit the Discover Wizard.

You have now successfully repackaged an application. You should, at this point, copy the package file to the software distribution share you created earlier so it can be made available for installation.

When copying packages to the software distribution point, keep the following in mind:

◆ Create individual folders for each package on the software distribution share. In other words, put each package and all its associated files in a separate folder on the software distribution share. This makes it easy to maintain the packages and reduces any potential problems associated with figuring out which files belong with which package.

◆ Make the software distribution share a hidden share so users won't be able to see it when browsing the network or searching Active Directory. This ensures that software can still be deployed and that users won't be installing the package just because they found it on the network. Any file with an .MSI extension can be installed using Windows Installer, so hiding the share from users enables you to control through Group Policy which packages are installed by which users.

◆ Use *Distributed File System* (DFS) to provide a single logical share point for all applications, even if the files are physically located on a different machine. Using DFS also enables you to configure replicas of shared folders on multiple machines, thereby ensuring that software can be installed even if a single machine is down.

If you want to make further modifications to the package, you might want to do so prior to copying it to the software distribution share. This ensures that no users install the application before it is ready. You can make these modifications later if the application will only be installed using Group Policy.

Modifying a Windows Installer Package File Using Third-Party Tools

After you have created a package for the software you will be deploying to users and computers using Group Policy, you might want to modify the contents of the package. This can be done using a third-party tool such as Veritas WinINSTALL LE, found on the Windows 2000 CD-ROM. Modifying a package can include adding desktop shortcuts to start the application, providing technical support Web site addresses and names, adding more files to the package, or removing some that might not be required. A great many options are available.

To modify a package, start the Veritas Software Console for WinINSTALL LE and open the package to make the necessary changes as outlined in Step by Step 7.4.

STEP BY STEP

7.4 Modifying an Application Package Using WinINSTALL LE Software Console

1. On the machine where you installed WinINSTALL LE, click Start, Programs, Veritas Software, Veritas Software Console. This launches the Software Console, as shown in Figure 7.13. Note that the Software Console is also subtitled the Windows Installer Package Editor.

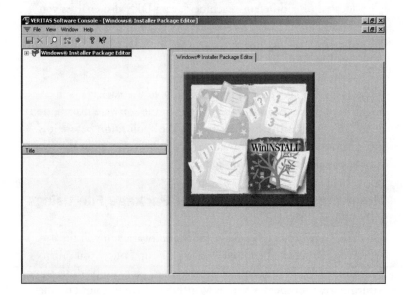

FIGURE 7.13
The Veritas Software Console main screen.

2. To open the package file you created, select Open on the File menu and, in the Browse dialog box, locate the MSI file created by the Discover Wizard. After you have done this, click Open to load the MSI file into the editor.

3. Figure 7.14 shows the Summary tab in the details pane after you have opened your package. As is evident, opening a package populates three panes on the Software Console:

- The details pane on the right side of the screen shows detailed information based on the selections made in the two panes on the left side of the screen.

- The package components listing pane in the top left corner shows the package. As you expand the package itself, each of the components that make up the package, such as the files installed and their GUIDs, are also shown.

- The component properties pane is in the bottom left of the screen. This pane is used to determine the focus of the details pane. For example, if you click on the GUID of a component of the package in the top left pane and then select Registry in the bottom left, the details pane shows registry changes made for that component.

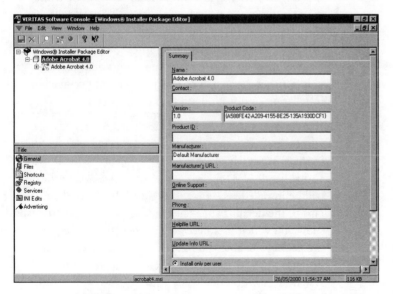

FIGURE 7.14
The Veritas Software Console summary properties screen for the package.

continues

continued

4. To provide additional information about the software
included in the package, click the package name in the
top left pane. Select General in the bottom left pane. A
screen similar to Figure 7.15 displays. If you want to
specify a contact for the package, the URL of the vendor,
version information, the online support site URL, and
other factors, you can do so here. Make changes on the
screen that will assist users if they have problems with
the software package.

Certain options available on this screen have special signif-
icance. The Version field can be used by Group Policy to
help determine whether a software application should be
updated. You can also use this option to tell Group Policy
which application should be replaced by a newer version.

The three radio buttons, close to the bottom of the details
pane, determine how the package can be installed using
Group Policy. Selecting Install only per user does not
allow a package to be assigned to a machine but requires
the user to install it. Selecting Install only per machine has
the opposite meaning. Attempt per machine, if fails, per
user tries to assign an application to a machine first. If this
fails, because the application requires some user settings to
be configured in install, it has the application installed per
user. Further discussion of the per-user and per-machine
installation options follows in the next section.

5. If you want to see a list of files included in the package,
select the package name in the top left pane and the files
in the bottom left. At this point, the details pane provides
a total list of files for the package as well as where they
will be installed, as shown in Figure 7.16. Note the three
tabs in the details pane. The Add, Remove, and Fonts tabs
show you which files need to be added and are required by
the package, enable you to specify which files to remove
during the installation, and specify fonts to add to the
system if they do not already exist.

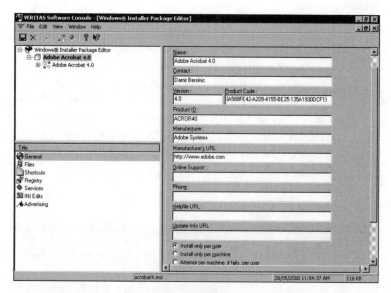

FIGURE 7.15
The Veritas Software Console package general summary information.

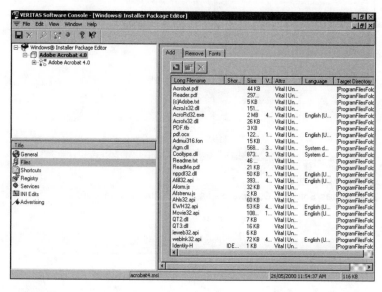

FIGURE 7.16
The Veritas Software Console package files listing.

continues

continued

6. To review which shortcuts will be added or to add a shortcut for the application, click on Shortcuts in the bottom left pane. The details pane will resemble Figure 7.17. For detailed information about a shortcut, double-click the shortcut about which you want to have more information. At this point, a dialog box similar to the one shown in Figure 7.18 displays. To add a shortcut, click the icon in the top left corner of the list of shortcuts in the details pane.

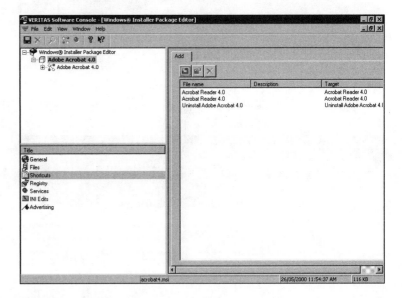

FIGURE 7.17
The Veritas Software Console package shortcuts information.

7. If you want to make other changes, explore the Veritas Software Console for WinINSTALL LE to see what choices are available. Help is available from the Help menu, explaining the different choices available.

8. When you have completed your changes, save them by clicking on the disk icon below the File menu. You can also save your changes by exiting Veritas Software Console and responding in the affirmative when asked if you want to save your changes.

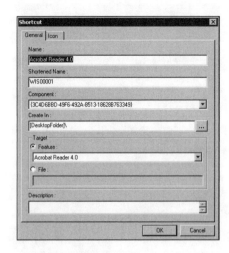

Preparing software to be deployed is an important task that should be performed to make sure what gets installed on a user's computer looks and behaves the way you want it to. Repackaging applications into an MSI file and the associated files to be installed using Windows Installer is the best way to ensure that software works as needed. Placing the completed packages on a Windows 2000 computer, sharing the folder, and applying the required permissions to the folder ensures that software can be deployed using Group Policy and be accessible to users and computers.

FIGURE 7.18
The Veritas Software Console application shortcut details dialog box.

SOFTWARE DEPLOYMENT USING GROUP POLICY

Manage and troubleshoot software by using Group Policy.

• **Deploy software by using Group Policy.**

Now that you've repackaged the software to be deployed, created software distribution share points, and applied permissions to the shares, you are ready to configure Group Policy to deploy the software. In doing so, you have the option to assign a package to a user or computer or to publish a package to a user.

Publishing Software

Publishing software makes the software available for installation for users. Users are able to initiate the installation of the software package in one of two ways:

◆ **Using Add/Remove Programs from within Control Panel.** When you select Add/Remove Programs in Control Panel, you are presented with a list of software available to you based on your group membership and the Group Policy created by the administrator and in effect for you. You then can select the software you want to install, and Windows Installer will install the application for you.

◆ **Using file or document activation.** File or document activation is the automatic invocation of the installation of a software package when a user double-clicks a document whose file extension matches the file extensions configured for the application. By double-clicking the file and not having the software application already installed on the hard disk, you have signaled to Windows Installer that you want to install the program configured to read and interpret a file whose extension matches the one on which you have double-clicked. For example, you double-click a file called GroupPolicy.PDF on a CD-ROM in your CD-ROM drive. If you did not have Adobe Acrobat Reader installed on your computer, Windows 2000 would check to see if a published application is configured to read PDF files. It would find that Adobe Acrobat Reader is configured to read PDF files. Windows 2000 would then invoke the Windows Installer to install Adobe Acrobat Reader so you can read the file. Automatically, the installation of the program (Adobe Acrobat Reader) was invoked by the document you double-clicked (GroupPolicy.PDF). This happened because the extension (.PDF) of the file did not have a reader installed. The extension was published in Active Directory and was mapped to the software package.

Publishing of software is useful when you want to give the user a choice of which software products to install. Publishing is also useful when you want to ensure that users can view documents, but not all users need to have support to view all document types. Publishing software enables you to give the user more choice and is, therefore, only really useful for noncritical applications. Software that all users should have installed on their machines or that is critical to certain users performing their designated tasks within the enterprise should not be published but should be assigned.

Assigning Software to Users and Computers

Software can be assigned to either users or computers. Assigning software to either users or computers ensures that the software is always available.

Assigning software to users enables the software to be advertised on the user's desktop. This means icons for the application will be available even though the application is not currently installed. Double-clicking the software icon, or a file extension associated with the software applications, causes the installation to take place automatically. If the user never double-clicks the software icon or a file with the software extension associated with the package, the software is not installed, thus saving disk space, network bandwidth, and administrative load.

Assigning software to computers ensures that the software is installed when the computer is turned on and connects to the network. The next time the computer processes its Group Policy settings, it finds that software has been assigned to it, and the software is automatically installed. Any software assigned to a computer is available to all users on the computer.

Any software that must be installed in all cases should be assigned to a computer. Software needed by all users that is not required to be on the machine initially can be assigned to the user or group and be installed when required. Either method ensures that the software is available when required.

Deploying Software Using Group Policy

To publish or assign software, you make use of Group Policy. Determining which method shall be used to deploy the software occurs when the software application is associated with the GPO.

To deploy software using Group Policy, follow Step by Step 7.5.

STEP BY STEP

7.5 Deploying Software Using Group Policy

1. Start Active Directory Users and Computer or Active Directory Sites and Services (depending on which container you want to configure the GPO for software deployment) and expand the folder list until you reach the container for which you want to configure software deployment. (The figures in this section show Active Directory Users and Computers.)

2. Right-click the container (domain, OU, or site) for which you want to configure the GPO and select Properties.

3. Click the Group Policy tab and select an existing GPO to be used for software deployment, or click New to create a new GPO, or click Add to link an existing GPO to this container.

4. Click the GPO you will use to deploy software and then click Edit to open the Group Policy Editor MMC, as shown in Figure 7.19.

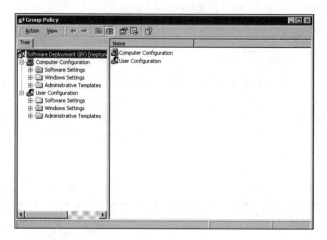

FIGURE 7.19
The GPO Editor MMC main console screen.

5. To configure software deployment for the computer, expand the Software Settings folder under the Computer Configuration folder in Group Policy. To configure software deployment for the user or group, expand the Software Settings folder under User Configuration, as shown in Figure 7.20.

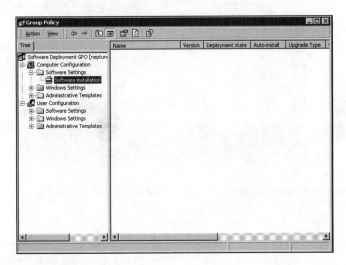

FIGURE 7.20
Software deployment can be configured for the computer or the user portion of Group Policy.

6. To configure a package for deployment, right-click the Software Installation icon and select New, Package. You are presented with a browse box. Browse the network to locate the software distribution shared folder you created earlier. The path to the package is stored in the Group Policy as the point from which to install the software package and should be a network share point.

Do not choose a local drive because users cannot connect to a local path on your machine. You will be presented with a dialog box, similar to Figure 7.21, stating that you are choosing a local path.

continues

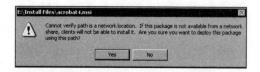

FIGURE 7.21
You receive a warning if the path to the package you have chosen is not a shared folder.

continued

Figure 7.22 shows a network share location used to locate the package file. After you have located the package you want to install, click it.

FIGURE 7.22
Selecting a package using a network share path.

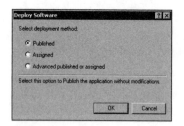

FIGURE 7.23
Package options when attaching to the user configuration in Group Policy.

7. If you have decided to attach the software package to the user portion of Group Policy, you will see a dialog box similar to Figure 7.23. If you are attaching the package to the computer configuration portion of the GPO object, you will see a dialog box similar to the one in Figure 7.24. As previously mentioned, packages cannot be published to computers; hence, the Publish option is grayed-out on the Computer Configuration. The third option presented simply enables you to configure further options (that is, modify the package) when you decide to assign or publish it. This option is discussed in more detail in the next section.

Make your selection to publish or assign and click OK.

8. You have now published or assigned your software package to users or computers. The Group Policy Editor is similar to Figure 7.25 and shows you some information about the package you have deployed. Information presented for each package includes the name of the package and its version number, as specified in the package file. The deployment state (published or assigned) and whether the package should be automatically installed using file extension (that is, document) activation is summarized here. You also can determine the upgrade or installation type (optional or required) and whether the package is an upgrade for an existing other package. You can configure these yourself and modify the package information.

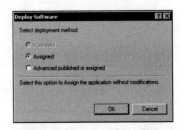

FIGURE 7.24
Package options when attaching to the computer configuration in Group Policy.

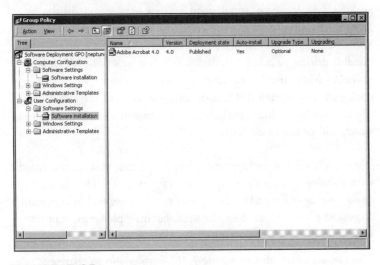

FIGURE 7.25
Clicking on Software installation presents general information for packages currently configured to be deployed using Group Policy.

9. Close the Group Policy Editor and click OK to close the Group Policy Container Properties dialog box. Exit the MMC console you were using to complete the configuration.

Package Deployment Options

Manage and troubleshoot software by using Group Policy.

- **Configure deployment options.**

After you have deployed a package, you can configure some options for the package that change its behavior and enable you to set additional options. You do this by right-clicking the Software Installation object in the Software Settings folder of the Group Policy where you configured the package.

The Software Installation Properties dialog box, as shown in Figure 7.26, enables you to configure general settings for all packages within the scope of that container. These settings include the default installation location for packages, (that is, the network share where packages can be found in case the package location is not available) and the default type of installation for new packages (Publish, Assign, Advanced Published or Assigned, or Present the Dialog Box Shown Earlier). You can determine the amount of user interaction possible during package installation (Basic interaction, which is not much, or Maximum). You have the option to specify whether a package is uninstalled if it falls outside the scope of the GPO. You can also configure file extension preferences and software categories, which will be discussed later.

If you right-click a package and select Properties, you are presented with a dialog box similar to the one in Figure 7.27. The General tab of the package's Properties dialog box provides general information about the package including the manufacturer, platform, support URL, and contact information.

The Deployment tab (see Figure 7.28) enables you to change the deployment information for this package. You can change the Deployment type from Published to Assigned and vice versa. This changes how the package is deployed to users or computers (for example, assigned to users or computers or published to users).

FIGURE 7.26
The Software Installation Properties dialog box in Group Policy Editor.

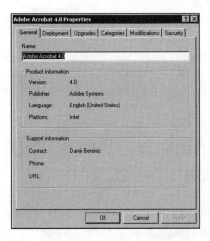

FIGURE 7.27
The package's general Properties dialog box in Group Policy.

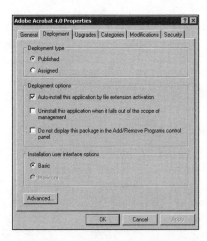

FIGURE 7.28
The package's Deployment tab in the Properties dialog box in Group Policy.

The Deployment options portion of this tab determines what happens when deployment takes place, including auto-installing the application when activated through file extension (that is, document invocation). If you uncheck this box, the file extensions associated with this package are not published, and document invocation will not take place. You can also uninstall the application if the GPO no longer applies to the user (that is, he or she moved to another OU within the Active Directory hierarchy). You also have the option to not advertise the package in Add/Remove Programs so that a user will not know if the package exists to install it.

The Installation user interface options enable you to specify how much user interaction is available to the user during installation. The default setting of Basic simply lets the user watch as the application is installed with default configuration settings. The Maximum setting prompts the user to enter values during installation.

The Upgrades, Categories, Modifications, and Security tabs are discussed later in this chapter.

You have now added the package to a Group Policy, so it can be deployed to users or computers. You have configured the package's deployment options and have outlined how it will be presented to the user. You have also determined whether the package needs to be

NOTE

Conflicting Options It is not a good idea to uncheck both the Auto-Install This Application by File Extension and the Do Not Display This Package in the Add/Remove Programs Control Panel boxes at the same time. Doing so prevents installation of the software when a matching document is invoked; it does not allow the package to be advertised in Add/Remove Programs. The package is configured to be available to the user, but the user never knows to install it or invoke the installation program. The package takes up disk space and causes additional processing for the GPO, but it never is installed. The only time this is useful is prior to a software release. You might want to keep the package unavailable until you are ready to flip the switch.

installed on all computers, in which case you configured the package in the Computer Configuration portion of Group Policy, or whether it will be assigned or published to users. Over time, however, you might need to modify these options or even upgrade packages. The issue of maintaining software packages is presented next.

MAINTAINING SOFTWARE PACKAGES USING GROUP POLICY

Manage and troubleshoot software by using Group Policy.

- **Maintain software by using Group Policy.**

As you know by now, the only constant in this industry is change. Invariably, at some point after deploying your package using Group Policy, you most likely will have to provide an update to keep the software applications on user machines current. This section shows you how to configure an upgrade for a package using Group Policy and how to provide both mandatory and optional upgrades. Finally, you will learn how to remove software that is no longer needed by the organization or whose licenses have expired.

Upgrading a Package

In Microsoft Windows 2000 Group Policy, upgrades to existing packages can be one of two types: mandatory or optional.

Mandatory upgrades are those that must be installed where the previous version of the software exists. For example, you repackaged Microsoft Office 97 and then received notification that the version on users' desktops is not the most recent one. You decide to upgrade all users to the most recent version of Office 97 to correct any deficiencies in the software. To do so, you configure the upgrade to be mandatory. The upgrade package is automatically installed on users' machines the next time the user logs on (if the package was assigned to the user or was published) or the machine is restarted (if the software was assigned to the computer). Mandatory upgrades are an ideal way to make sure all users have the most recent version of critical business applications installed.

Optional upgrades enable the user to continue to use the older version of the software or, optionally, to upgrade to the most recent version. Optional upgrades provide users with a message indicating that a newer version is available and asking if they would like to upgrade now. If the user agrees to the upgrade, the new version of the software is installed, and the old version is replaced. If the user does not agree to the upgrade, he or she will continue to work with the older version of the software. The user will continue to be prompted to install the new version. You can also configure a "drop-dead date" by which users must install the upgrade, or it will be installed on their machine whether they like it or not (a kind of optional upgrade with a mandatory ending).

To perform either type of upgrade, follow Step by Step 7.6.

STEP BY STEP

7.6 Upgrading Software Using Group Policy

1. Repackage the upgraded version of the software or acquire a Windows Installer Package with the upgraded software. To upgrade an existing package to a newer version, the newer version must also be in the form of a Windows Installer Package (or ZAP file). The first step in upgrading software is to either repackage the upgraded version, as previously shown, or to acquire a Windows Installer Package.

2. Place the upgrade package in the shared folder to which users will connect and install the upgraded application.

3. Edit or create a GPO that will hold the new package. You can add the package to the same container in the GPO in which the earlier version was created. This is shown in Figure 7.29 for the sample Adobe Acrobat software package.

continues

continued

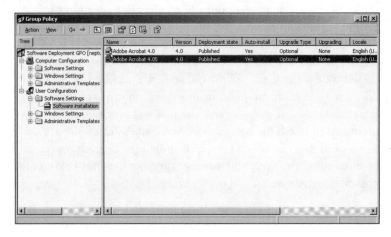

FIGURE 7.29
Adding a package to the GPO is required for the package to upgrade
another package.

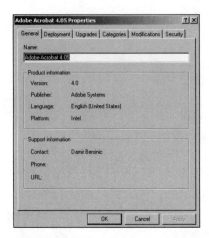

FIGURE 7.30
The package's Properties dialog box.

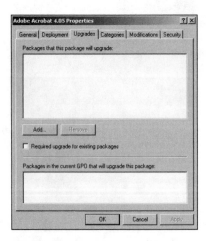

FIGURE 7.31
The Upgrades tab of the package's
Properties dialog box in Group Policy.

4. Modify the package to indicate that it will be used to
upgrade an existing one. To do this, right-click the new
package and select Properties. You are presented with
the Properties dialog box for the package, as shown in
Figure 7.30.

5. Click the Upgrades tab to show a list of other packages
that this package will update, as shown in Figure 7.31.

6. Click Add to add a package to the list of what can be used
to upgrade the initial package. You are presented with a
screen similar to Figure 7.32. This provides you with
several choices, including where to look for the upgrade
package: in the current GPO or another GPO. You can
then browse for a package to be used for the upgrade
among the other GPOs available in the company. You also
have the capability to specify how the upgrade will take
place: by uninstalling the existing package and then
installing the upgrade or by leaving the old software
package intact and simply installing the upgrade over it.

Care should be taken in setting the appropriate options to make sure the software works correctly after the upgrade. When deciding whether to uninstall the previous version, you should test the overwrite if that is the direction you want to go. It is generally a better idea to uninstall the previous version.

Click OK when done to return to the package's Properties dialog box.

7. You now have the option to make the upgrade a required or optional upgrade for an existing package. To make the upgrade package required, click the Required upgrade for existing packages check box, as shown in Figure 7.33. This causes the package to be installed automatically when a user logs on or a computer starts, based on how the initial package was deployed. When you have made your decision, click OK to close the Properties dialog box and save your changes.

8. As shown in Figure 7.34, you now have two packages in the Group Policy software packages details pane. The most recent package installed is designated as a required upgrade for the previous one in our example. Any new user installing the software gets the most recent package; existing users have their software upgraded automatically because the upgrade is marked as required. Close the Group Policy Editor MMC to have the GPO settings take effect.

FIGURE 7.32
Specifying a package to be used to upgrade an existing package.

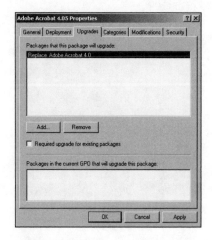

FIGURE 7.33
Package replacement information in the Upgrades tab of the package's Properties dialog box in Group Policy.

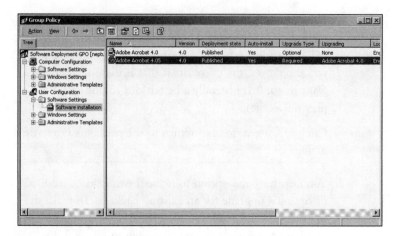

FIGURE 7.34
The Software package screen in Group Policy.

Configuring upgrades to packages is quite simple except for making sure the upgrade is in the proper format (that is, an MSI file). You can configure the upgrade to be mandatory or optional. Mandatory upgrades force the user to replace the previous package with the new one. New users always receive the most recent version. However, what if you only need to replace certain files in a package, not upgrade it?

Redeploying Software

In some situations, instead of upgrading a package, you might simply want to reinstall it on all users' machines. This method is known as redeploying, the reinstallation of an existing package. This method is preferable if you modified a package without changing its name (for example, you added or removed files from the package, which would include a patch to the software), added shortcuts, changed registry settings, or in any other way changed an existing package. To ensure that all users have the updated software, you might want to redeploy the package.

You might also create a new package (MSI) file with the exact same name as the existing package and put it in the same location as the original package. Using this method, you can incorporate more widespread changes to the software than simply by modifying an existing package. As long as the version and package name are identical, it is considered to be the same software. You then can redeploy the package as needed.

To redeploy a package, after making your modification, perform the steps shown in Step by Step 7.7.

STEP BY STEP

7.7 Redeploying a Package Using Group Policy

1. Open Active Directory Users and Computers (or Active Directory Sites and Services), right-click the container where the GPO is located, and select Properties.

2. Go to the Group Policy tab, select the GPO containing information on deploying the package, and click Edit. This opens the Group Policy Editor.

3. Expand the container withing the Software Installation folder where the original package was specified and locate the package you want to redeploy, as shown in Figure 7.35.

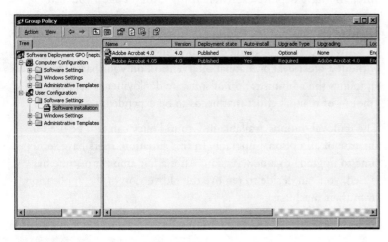

FIGURE 7.35
The package list in the Software installation folder of the Group Policy Editor.

continues

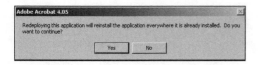

FIGURE 7.36
The redeployment confirmation Dialog box in
Group Policy.

continued

4. To redeploy a package, right-click the package, choose All
Tasks, and then click Redeploy Application. Figure 7.36
shows the dialog box that asks you to confirm that you
want to redeploy the application. Click Yes to do so.

5. Close the Group Policy Editor to commit to your
changes.

6. Click OK to close the container Properties dialog box and
then exit Active Directory Users and Computers.

As you have seen, redeployment is quite simple in cases in which
certain files for an application have been updated but the rest of
the package stays largely intact. You should remember, however,
that redeploying a package causes it to be reinstalled on all client
machines, which can use up large amounts of network bandwidth.

Removing a Package

After you have deployed software using Group Policy, you also
have the option to have Group Policy automate the removal of the
software for you. In this way, applications that are no longer needed
or software that is out-of-date can be removed from users' computers
without a great deal of manual intervention on your part. This
simplifies the administration of software deployment and the
amount of manual effort that needs to be expended.

The removal options available in Group Policy can also be used in
the case of an optional upgrade. In this situation, users have some
time to upgrade to a new version. After a fair amount of time has
lapsed, you can decide to remove the old version of the application
from their machines.

Removal of software has two options:

◆ Mandatory or forced removal, in which the software is
removed from the user's computer whether or not he or she
still requires it. This is selected by specifying the Immediately
uninstall software from users and computers option when
configuring removal of a package for the GPO. The software

is removed prior to the user's desktop being presented and is transparent to the user, if it was assigned to the user. If the package was assigned to the computer, it is removed the next time the computer restarts. If an upgrade of the software exists, the user can install the upgraded version to continue to have the functionality of the software; if not, the software becomes unavailable.

◆ Optional removal enables the user to continue to use the software. This option is selected when you specify the Allow users to continue to use the software but prevent new installations option when configuring removal. The software does not appear in the list of applications under Add/Remove Programs in Control Panel but does remain installed. After the user manually removes the software through Add/Remove Programs on his or her computer, he or she no longer can install it. This is considered the nice method of removing software, but it can be problematic if you want to maintain standard corporate software applications.

To configure removal of a package, perform the steps shown in Step by Step 7.8.

STEP BY STEP

7.8 Removing a Package Using Group Policy

1. Open Active Directory Users and Computers (or Active Directory Sites and Services), right-click the container where the GPO is locate, and select Properties.

2. Go to the Group Policy tab, select the GPO containing information on the package you want to configure the removal of, and click Edit. This opens the Group Policy Editor.

3. Expand the container withing the Software Installation folder where the original package was specified and locate the package you want to remove.

continues

continued

FIGURE 7.37
The package removal options selection dialog box in Group Policy.

4. To remove a package, right-click the package, choose All Tasks, and then click Remove. Figure 7.37 shows the dialog box that will ask you choose the type of removal (forced or optional). Choose the method of removal and click OK to save your choice. You are then returned to the Group Policy Editor. Note that the package no longer appears on the list.

5. Close the Group Policy Editor to commit to your changes.

6. Click OK to close the container Properties dialog box and then exit Active Directory Users and Computers.

Removing software using Group Policy is relatively simple. Keep in mind that, after you choose whether you want to use an optional removal or a forced removal, you cannot change your mind. The package is removed from the GPO and is also removed from the user's machine, either forcibly or by the user agreeing to have it removed. If the user chooses to leave the package on the machine, you cannot force its removal later; the package is no longer in the GPO.

Managing Software Deployment

The process of deploying software in large organizations might require that additional tasks be performed to make the deployment process more friendly by recognizing geographic and language differences. Deployment can be designed to help users select which software to install by creating software categories for similar packages. It also can be designed to automatically initiate the installation of software when a particular file is invoked by the user. The deployment process itself can encounter problems, and the administrator needs to be aware of how to correct some of the common problems encountered in software deployment. Repackaging applications can also present problems during deployment, and an administrator should be familiar these issues as well.

Configuring Package Modifications

Windows 2000 Group Policy allows the use of software modification, or transform files, to deploy several configurations of the same application. Transform files have an .MST extension and are associated with an existing package. In combination with several GPOs, transform files are used to change the behavior of a package when it is deployed in different regions.

For example, your organization, with offices in the United States, Canada, England, and France, wants to deploy Microsoft Office 2000 worldwide. However, you want to make sure users in Paris and Quebec receive French dictionaries, as well as English, when Office 2000 is installed. To solve this problem, you create one package file for Office 2000. To deal with the different dictionaries that need to be supported, you create transform (MST) files for each dictionary. You then create a separate GPO for the Parisian site to include the Office 2000 package as well as the French dictionary MST file. For Quebec, you could use the same or another GPO to also roll out the French dictionary. For Canada, the United States, and England, you might create one or more GPOs that would include the English dictionary transform file.

To add modifications to a software package, perform the steps in Step by Step 7.9.

NOTE

Transform (MST) Files A transform file modifies what is installed on a user's computer based on the GPO used to deploy the software. After the software has been installed on a user's machine, it cannot be modified using an MST file. Only prior to the installation taking place on a computer will the transform file have any effect. For example, 20 users have already installed application X, and you decide to specify a modification using a transform file of application X. Any users who already have application X installed cannot have the modification deployed to them. Only users who do not have application X installed get the software modification specified in the MST file. To apply an MST file to all users (old and new), you also need to redeploy the package.

STEP BY STEP

7.9 Modifying a Package with an MST file

1. Open Active Directory Users and Computers (or Active Directory Sites and Services), right-click the container where the GPO is located, and select Properties.

2. Go to the Group Policy tab, select the GPO containing information on the package you want to modify, and click Edit. This opens the Group Policy Editor.

3. Expand the container within the Software Installation folder where the original package was specified and locate the package to which you want to add a transform file.

continues

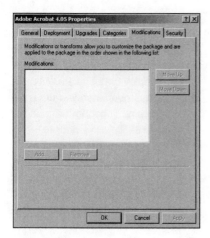

FIGURE 7.38
Modifications to a package can be added from this dialog box.

continued

4. To add modifications, right-click the package, select Properties, and then click the Modifications tab. A screen similar to Figure 7.38 displays.

5. Click Add to add an MST file and then, in the Open dialog box, select the path and filename of the MST file to be used to modify this package and click OK.

6. It is possible to specify more than one MST file for the same package by repeating the preceding step. If specifying more than one MST file for the same package, they will be processed according the order presented on the Modifications tab for the package. You can use the Move Up and Move Down buttons to specify the order of processing.

7. Click OK to close the package Properties dialog box.

8. Close the Group Policy Editor to commit to your changes.

9. Click OK to close the container Properties dialog box and then exit Active Directory Users and Computers.

Using software modifications within the scope of software deployment in a GPO enables you to modify the settings for an application package being deployed. This is a good way to have the same package deployed to different users or computers without having to repackage the software for each specific configuration. Transform files enable you to store only the specific changes to be applied against a package and to have those deployed with a specific GPO.

Creating Software Categories

In large organizations, or even in smaller ones in which many different software applications are in use, it might be beneficial to create software categories to make it easier for users to install the package they want. Creating software categories changes the display in Add/Remove Programs in Control Panel (see Figure 7.39) and enables the user to locate software of the type he or she needs.

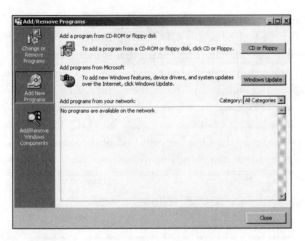

FIGURE 7.39
Add/Remove Programs in Control Panel lists packages Available on the
network in categories.

For example, using Group Policy, you decide to deploy many
different packages including accounting applications, word processors, utilities, spreadsheets, and Internet browsers. By default, all the
software available on the network is listed under a single category.
If many applications are available, this requires the user to scroll
down until he or she finds the needed package, and it could make
the process more difficult. By creating software categories, the user is
able to select the category of software he or she wants to install from
the Category drop-down list box. This display can be limited to only
the software placed in the category.

A single application can appear in more than one category. For
example, Microsoft Office 2000 can be placed in the Office
Packages category as well as in Word Processors, Spreadsheets, and
Presentation Software because it includes all of these. Specifying a
category for a particular package only makes it easier for the user
to find the application. It does not, in any way, change the behavior
of the Group Policy in which the package is configured for deployment. Furthermore, if you add new categories or if you decide to
start using categories, you can modify the software category under
which a package should be listed at any time. This makes it easy to
redefine and streamline categories should this be required.

One very important point that needs to be conveyed is that categories configured in any GPO on the domain are available throughout the domain. This means that software categories function on a domain-wide basis. You can access the Categories tab from any GPO within any OU in the domain. Any changes made to the categories listed are reflected throughout the domain. You cannot have one set of categories in the Sales OU, for example, and another set in the Development OU of the same domain. All categories in all OUs are available throughout the domain. However, you can have a different set of categories in different domains.

To create software categories, follow the steps in Step by Step 7.10.

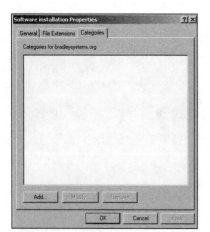

FIGURE 7.40
The Categories tab of the Software Installation Properties dialog box in Group Policy.

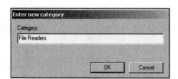

FIGURE 7.41
Clicking Add opens the Enter new category dialog box.

STEP BY STEP

7.10 Creating Software Categories for the Domain

1. Open Active Directory Users and Computers (or Active Directory Sites and Services), right-click the container where the GPO is located, and select Properties.

2. Go to the Group Policy tab, select the GPO containing information on the package you want to modify, and click Edit. This opens the Group Policy Editor.

3. Expand either Computer Configuration or User Configuration and then the Software Settings folder.

4. Right-click Software Installation and select Properties.

5. Click the Categories tab to see the list of categories currently configured, if any, as shown in Figure 7.40.

6. To add a category, click the Add button. A dialog box similar to Figure 7.41 is presented. Type in the name of the category you want to add and click OK to save the category.

7. You are now returned to the Software Installation Properties dialog box where the new category will be listed (see Figure 7.42). Click Add to add more categories, Modify to change the name of an existing category, or Remove to remove a category. When you are done, click Apply and then OK to save you changes.

8. Close the Group Policy Editor to commit to your changes.

9. Click OK to close the container Properties dialog box and then exit Active Directory Users and Computers.

After you have created the categories, they can be used to categorize existing or new packages you have configured for deployment. To assign a software category to a package, follow the steps in Step by Step 7.11.

STEP BY STEP

7.11 Assigning a Software Package to a Category

1. Open Active Directory Users and Computers (or Active Directory Sites and Services), right-click the container where the GPO is located, and select Properties.

2. Go to the Group Policy tab, select the GPO containing information on the package you want to modify, and click Edit. This opens the Group Policy Editor.

3. Expand either Computer Configuration or User Configuration and then the Software Settings folder.

4. Select the package to which you want to assign a category from the list presented when you click Software Installation. Right-click the package and select Properties.

5. Click the Categories tab to see the list of categories available and assigned to this package, as shown in Figure 7.43.

6. Click the category to which you want to assign this package under Available categories and then click Select to assign this package to the category. To remove this package from a category, select the category to remove under Selected categories and click Remove. When you are done, click OK to save your changes.

continues

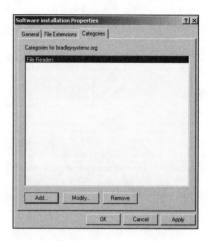

FIGURE 7.42
The Categories tab of the Software Installation Properties dialog box in Group Policy after adding a software category.

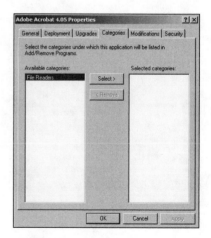

FIGURE 7.43
The Categories tab of the package shows the list of available categories and the ones selected for this package.

continued

> **7.** Close the Group Policy Editor to commit to your changes.
>
> **8.** Click OK to close the container Properties dialog box and then exit Active Directory Users and Computers.

You have now created categories and have assigned a package to one or more categories. When you go to Control Panel and select Add/Remove Programs, the list of available software that can be installed is revealed. This enables you to select the category of software you want to install and shows only the packages configured within that category.

As you have seen, creating categories for software is quite easy. It is of great benefit to organizations that want to publish many applications using Group Policy. It makes it easier for users to find the applications they want to install. Administrators categorize the packages available, and then users can use these categories to browse what is available. As noted, the same package can exist in multiple categories.

But what if users did not have access to Add/Remove Programs in Control Panel?

Associating File Extensions with Applications

Windows 2000 Active Directory provides great new functionality when deploying software applications using Group Policy. When you obtain a package (MSI) file or after you repackage an application using third-party products such as Veritas WinINSTALL LE, you might find that the package will publish file extensions supported by the software.

For example, Adobe Acrobat 4.05 was published in the previous example, it told Windows 2000 Active Directory that it could be used to open files with a .PDF extension. This is very handy. It can provide for automatic installation of the software application on a user's machine whenever he or she double-clicks a PDF file to open it and the software is not yet installed on the machine. In this way, users can invoke the installation of a particular software application when they attempt to open an associated file and the software is not yet installed.

The list of file extensions and applications (packages) that support these extensions is published and tracked by Windows 2000 Active Directory. The mapping of file extension to software package is kept domain-wide, but the determination of which software package is installed when a user attempts to open a file of a particular extension can be configured at an OU or other level. This means users in one particular branch of Active Directory (the Sales OU, for example) can install one application when they activate a document by double-clicking it, while users in another OU (the Development OU) can have a different application installed.

It might be necessary, for example, to support both Microsoft Word 2000 and WordPerfect 2000 in your organization for files with a .DOC extension. Users in your legal department, for historical reasons, prefer to use WordPerfect 2000 to edit their documents. The WordPerfect application has templates and other useful tools to be used by the lawyers and clerks in that part of the organization. Users in other departments within the company, however, prefer to use Word 2000 because this is the corporate standard for word processing. You can configure the priority of the application to be used in the legal department when a file with the .DOC extension is activated by adjusting the GPO used to deploy software in the Legal OU. All other parts of the company have Microsoft Word 2000 associated with the .DOC extension at a higher priority than WordPerfect 2000 and, therefore, have that application installed when they open a DOC file.

Filename extension priorities are configured on a per-GPO basis. You configure the priority of a particular application to be installed through document activation within the GPO, and it only affects users that have the GPO applied to them. Other users are not affected by the priority established in a GPO and might, in fact, install different applications for the same file extension. For example, if you set WordPerfect 2000 as the default application for the DOC extension in the Legal GPO, only users in the Legal OU will have WordPerfect 2000 installed when they activate a DOC file.

NOTE **Windows 2000 Only** File extension priority can only be configured for applications being deployed using Windows 2000 Group Policy (that is, that are configured as a Windows Installer Package). Even though another application that might be a standard component of Windows 2000 might support opening a file with a particular extension, the application cannot be associated with the extension within the GPO. For example, WordPad in Windows 2000 can be used to open a file with a .DOC extension, but WordPad cannot be associated with the .DOC extension within the GPO. This is because there is no package used to deploy WordPad through a GPO. If you want to associate WordPad with the DOC extension, you need to create a package to deploy WordPad.

The main point here is that file extension priority only applies to packages deployed using Windows 2000 Group Policy. It does not apply to software deployed using any other method.

To modify and configure filename extension priorities, perform the steps in Step by Step 7.12.

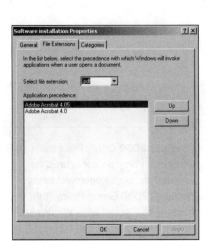

FIGURE 7.44
The File Extensions tab of the Software Installation Properties dialog box.

STEP BY STEP

7.12 Configuring File Extension Priority for a GPO

1. Open Active Directory Users and Computers (or Active Directory Sites and Services), right-click the container where the GPO is located, and select Properties.

2. Go to the Group Policy tab, select the GPO containing information on the package you want to modify, and click Edit. This opens the Group Policy Editor.

3. Expand either Computer Configuration or User Configuration and then the Software Settings folder.

4. Right-click the Software Installation container and select Properties.

5. Click the File Extensions tab to see a list of packages and file extensions currently configured, as shown in Figure 7.44.

6. Select the extension whose application priority you want to modify by using the drop-down list box to see a list of software applications associated with that extension.

7. Use the Move Up and Move Down buttons to bring the application that should be installed by default to the top of the list. Click OK when done to save your changes.

8. Close the Group Policy Editor to commit to your changes.

9. Click OK to close the container Properties dialog box and then exit Active Directory Users and Computers.

If you're wondering how the file extension got associated with a particular package, think back to the "Packaging Software for Deployment" section of this chapter. If you recall, when repackaging an application, you were able to specify with which file extensions that application would be associated. In the same vein, when a software developer creates a package to be used to install his software, he also associates certain file extensions with his application. In this way, users are able to make use of the application as intended.

Whichever way is used to associate an extension with an application, this association is published within Active Directory and is maintained on each client machine. This is so the files can be opened, and the users are not left in the situation in which they have files that cannot be used.

Troubleshooting Software Deployment

Maintain and troubleshoot software by using Group Policy.

- **Troubleshoot common problems that occur during software deployment.**

After you have configured software deployment, especially if you have a large organization with many GPOs used to deploy software, there might be occasions when the deployment is not working exactly as you would expect. Some of the more common problems and their causes are listed in the following table.

TABLE 7.2

COMMON DEPLOYMENT PROBLEMS

Problem	*Cause and Resolution*
Application cannot be installed.	The most likely cause of this problem is that the user cannot reach the network share where the application package is located. Verify that the share is, in fact, available and that the user has permissions to access the package files. The permissions required are Read on the share and Read & Execute at the NTFS level on the volume where the package files are located. The NTFS permissions are required for all files and folders that make up the package.

continues

TABLE 7.2	*continued*

COMMON DEPLOYMENT PROBLEMS

Problem	*Cause and Resolution*
Applications do not appear as expected on the user's desktop.	The most likely cause of this problem is in the way the application was deployed. If the application was assigned to the user, the shortcuts for the application should appear on the user's desktop. If they do not, log on as the user and check to see if the application is listed under Add/Remove Programs in Control Panel. If it is, then the application was published, not assigned. In this case, the user must install the application manually or have the installation begin through document activation.

If the application is not listed in Add/Remove Programs and no shortcuts appear on the desktop, it might be that the application was never deployed or was deployed in another OU. It is also possible that the application was deployed in the correct OU, but the user has been filtered out of the scope of the GPO where the application deployment is defined. Check the security settings for the GPO to make sure the user is not filtered from the GPO settings. |
| Deployed applications do not work properly after installation. | In some cases in which applications are repackaged using a third-party packaging program such as Veritas WinINSTALL LE, the process might not have taken place properly. If during repackaging the setup program of the application did not install certain files on the hard drive of the reference computer, for example, these files will not be in the package file created and will need to exist on the user's hard drive. If they are not found, the application might not work properly after it is deployed. To correct the problem, repackage the application or add the necessary files to the package. |

Problem	*Cause and Resolution*
Package installation removes other files.	This is also a repackaging problem. When an application is repackaged, the period between the before and after snapshot can cause other changes to be made on the system if other programs are launched. This can cause the final package, after the after snapshot is created, to include instructions to remove files from the hard drive. If this is the case, when the package is deployed, it will cause those same files to be removed from the user's computer and might cause other software to stop functioning. To solve this problem, modify the package to remove any reference to file deletion or repackage the software to make sure it is correctly configured.
Applications are not deployed as expected or are not deployed at all.	The most likely cause of this is Group Policy conflicts. GPOs can be created at different levels of Active Directory, and these same GPOs can have application deployment configured within them. It is possible that a setting in one GPO associated with an Active Directory container might conflict with a setting in another GPO in a lower-level Active Directory container. Furthermore, because software can be assigned to both computers and users, computer settings can override user settings depending on the AD level at which they are applied.
	For example, if a user has been assigned Microsoft Word 2000 at the domain GPO level, but this same application has been denied to him at the OU level, the application will not be installed. Furthermore, if a user has been assigned an application like Microsoft Excel 2000 at the domain level, but Microsoft Excel 2000 has been marked for mandatory removal from his computer, then Microsoft Excel 2000 will not be available to the user.
	It is always a good idea to check the inheritance of GPOs within the Active Directory structure.

As you have read in the preceding table, many of the common problems associated with software deployment deal with either improper repackaging or Group Policy issues. Understanding how GPOs work in general (whether or not you are using GPOs for software deployment) is critical. Testing software deployment on a few machines before rolling it out on a large scale reduces the chances of experiencing a large-scale problem.

CASE STUDY: USING GROUP POLICY TO DEPLOY SOFTWARE APPLICATIONS AT SUNSHINE BREWING

ESSENCE OF THE CASE

Sunshine Brewing has purchased a new *enterprise resource planning* (ERP) application that needs to be deployed to all executives and administrative users. Sales people need to have the *Customer Relationship Management* (CRM) component of the application installed on their computers as well because they will use the intelligence of the system to process orders, profile customers, and check on the status of client orders and other elements. Furthermore, Microsoft Office 2000 has been purchased as the corporate office suite standard, and it needs to be installed on all users desktops. Because the company operates in a multi-national environment, specific settings for Office 2000, such as dictionary components used for spell checking, need to conform to local requirements.

It has also been decided that Windows Installer Package files for utility software, including WinZIP, Adobe Acrobat Reader, and RealAudio Player, that have been acquired from your software supplier will be available for users as an optional installation. If the users attempt to open a file of a type supported by the utility, they should be asked whether they want to install the package.

Historically, large-scale deployments of software of this nature have been handled by the IT staff with the help of co-op or summer students to perform the bulk of the grunt work. When calculating the budget for using this approach, the figure presented to the CEO was rejected, and the IT department has been told to perform the deployment using existing resources within a three-month period. As the champion of Windows 2000 in the organization, you have been told to make sure this can be done or face the consequences.

After looking at the requirements, you decide to contact the ERP vendor to see whether the software has any specific installation capabilities that could assist in a deployment of this scale. The third-party vendor of the ERP application has stated that an installation program must be run on each client computer even though the end result is always the same, assuming the same components are installed. A Windows Installer Package does not exist for the ERP system nor does the vendor plan to offer one without Sunshine Brewing paying a hefty price. (They admit they have not tried it and would be starting from scratch.)

CASE STUDY: USING GROUP POLICY TO DEPLOY SOFTWARE APPLICATIONS AT SUNSHINE BREWING

SCENARIO

In this chapter, you were shown how Group Policy can be used to deploy software packages across the enterprise or to a specific set of users. You were also introduced to methods that can be used to upgrade packages that have been deployed, and you learned how to repackage software that does not come in a format compatible with Windows Installer. Here you will determine how this can be used to solve a specific problem at Sunshine Brewing.

ANALYSIS

Although the initial challenge presented by the scope of this software deployment might seem somewhat daunting, using Group Policy to perform the deployment easily solves this problem.

On the ERP side, you would require at least two different software configurations: one for the sales personnel who will have a subset of the ERP package (the CRM component only) and the other for all admin users who will have the entire ERP client software installed on their desktops. Because the ERP vendor does not have the application in a Windows Installer Package format and because this would not help you with the sales requirement, you first need to create two Windows Installer Packages with the correct configuration.

To create the Windows Installer Package for the admin users, you would start with a clean Windows 2000 Professional computer and use Veritas WinINSTALL LE (or another third-party product) to create a before snapshot of the computer. You would then install and configure the ERP application as it should exist on all admin users' machines. During this period, you would create any shortcuts and configure any software settings as they will be required. After configuring the ERP software as needed, you would use the Discover Wizard of Veritas WinINSTALL LE (or the third-party tool) to create the package file with the correct configuration.

To create a Windows Installer Package file for the sales users, you would perform similar steps as for the admin package creation but only include those components of the application required by sales (CRM). At this point, you would have two Windows Installer Packages that you would place on a network share in their own separate folders. You would also place Microsoft Office 2000 on the same share point in its own folder.

To deploy the software, you would need to create three GPOs: one for the Admin OU for the ERP package, a second for the Sales OU for the CRM component of the ERP package, and a third for Microsoft Office 2000. The Microsoft Office 2000 GPO would be created at each site and would include transform (MST) files that would modify the package to include local settings.

You would have the ERP package GPO applied to Authenticated Users in the Admin OU, the CRM package applied to Authenticated Users in the Sales OU, and Microsoft Office 2000 applied to Authenticated Users at the site level with No Override to make sure all users get Microsoft Office 2000.

For the utility software, you would publish all the packages to Authenticated Users using a GPO at the domain level and would enable document activation on each package.

CHAPTER SUMMARY

KEY TERMS

- Assigning software
- Forced (mandatory) package removal
- GPO scope
- Group Policy filtering
- Group Policy inheritance
- Group Policy object (GPO)
- Group Policy precedence
- Mandatory upgrade
- Optional removal
- Optional upgrade
- Package modifications
- Publishing software
- Redeployment
- Repackaging an application
- Repackaging software
- Software categories
- Transform files
- Windows Installer
- Windows Installer Service
- ZAP file

In this chapter, you learned how to use Group Policy to deploy software applications within your enterprise. Software to be deployed using Group Policy must be in a format compatible with Windows Installer. These formats include Windows Installer Package (MSI) files and ZAP files, which the Windows Installer service can parse to start the software installation process.

Software can be delivered to users through Group Policy either by assigning or by publishing. Assigning a software package to a computer automatically installs that package. Assigning a software package to a user automatically places icons on the desktop. When a package is assigned to a user, the software installation process is triggered when the user clicks on an icon or a document whose file extension matches one associated with the package.

Publishing software makes the application available to the user but does not immediately install the software. The software is installed either through Control Panel Add/Remove Programs or by document activation. Document activation involves an attempt by the user to open a file with an extension associated with a particular package. Windows 2000 checks to see if an application is available to open the file on the user's machine. If not, Active Directory is checked for a list of applications and their priority. After the list is reviewed, Group Policy is used to trigger Windows Installer to install the application.

Only Windows Installer Package files can be either assigned or published to users. These files contain the information necessary to install the application without user intervention. ZAP files can only be published. ZAP files require the user to perform the normal install process for the software application. For this reason, third-party tools are available to repackage an application that is not provided in a Windows Installer Package file format. One such tool included on the Windows 2000 CD-ROM is Veritas WinINSTALL LE.

CHAPTER SUMMARY

Administrators can use transform files to deploy the same software package with different options to different OUs within the enterprise. Transform files modify an existing package to meet specific requirements such as language or geographic location. Administrators can also categorize software applications to make it easier for users to select which software to install through Add/Remove Programs in Control Panel.

After some time, it might be necessary for users to receive a newer version of an application or to remove other applications that are no longer required. The administrator can designate a software package as either a required or an optional upgrade for an existing application. Required upgrades are installed without the user having a choice in this decision; optional upgrades enable the user to decide whether he or she wants to upgrade to the most recent version. Software removal can also be forced or optional. Forced removal requires that the software package be removed from the user's machine. An optional removal enables the user to continue to use the application after it has been designated to be removed. Even though the user might decide to leave the package on the system, after he or she removes the application, it no longer is available for installation because it no longer is being published in Active Directory.

Most problems with deploying software using Group Policy result from network errors such as not being able to reach the software distribution point. Some problems are due to the application of Group Policy. When deciding the nature of a problem, you must adhere to all the rules governing policy inheritance, filtering, and other elements outlined in Chapter 6, "Using Group Policy to Manage Users." Deployment is an extremely useful aspect of Group Policy, and it does not change the way Group Policy works in general.

APPLY YOUR KNOWLEDGE

Exercises

All the exercises for this chapter assume you have installed Windows 2000 Server (or Advanced Server) on a computer. Your Windows 2000 Server must be configured as a domain controller of a domain for the exercises to work properly. You need to be able to log on to the domain as an administrator (that is, your user account must be either a member of the Enterprise Admins group or the Domain Admins group). If you know the password for the user Administrator, this will be sufficient.

For these exercises, you need at least two Windows Installer Package files. If you do not have enough, you can use Veritas WinINSTALL LE to repackage an application of your choice and then use that application, or you can use one of the applications on the Windows 2000 CD-ROM that already come packaged in the proper format. A ready-made MSI file that can be used is the Windows 2000 Resource Kit found in the SUPPORT\TOOLS folder on the Windows 2000 CD-ROM.

Exercises in this chapter build on those in Chapter 6, "Using Group Policy to Manage Users." You should have completed the exercises in Chapter 6 prior to starting the following exercises.

7.1 Using Group Policy to Deploy Software

In this exercise, you will first configure software deployment for the Research OU. Then you will test to make sure the published application is available in Add/Remove Programs in Control Panel. If the published application is available in Add/Remove Programs, you will install the package.

Estimated time: 20 minutes.

To add software installation components to the Research Script Policy Research OU, follow these steps:

1. While logged on as a Domain Administrator, start Active Directory Users and Computers.

2. Expand your domain, right-click the Sales OU, and select Properties.

3. Select the Research Script Policy you created in Exercise 6.1 and click Edit. This starts the Group Policy Editor MMC.

4. In the Group Policy console tree, expand User Configuration and then expand Software Settings.

5. Right-click Software Installation and select New and then Package. In the Open dialog box that appears, locate the package file for the software application you want to deploy and select Open. Make sure the package is located on a network share so that all users that need it can access it.

6. In the Deploy Software dialog box that appears, select Published as the deployment method and click OK.

7. Close the Group Policy Editor to save your changes.

8. Click OK on the Research Properties dialog box to close it.

9. Log off your computer after closing the Active Directory Users and Computers MMC.

To test software deployment using Group Policy, follow these steps:

1. Log on to the computer as a user in the Developers Group to whom the Group Policy applies (TimC).

APPLY YOUR KNOWLEDGE

2. From the Start menu, select Settings and then Control Panel.

3. Double-click Add/Remove Programs to start the application.

4. Click Add New Programs to see a list of available applications on the network. Does the package you configured earlier appear on the list?

_____

_____

_____

5. Click the Add button to install the package on the machine. How much user interaction takes place during the installation?

_____

_____

_____

6. Try to start the application and test to make sure it is working properly. Does it appear to function correctly?

_____

_____

_____

7. Log off the computer when you have finished testing the application's functionality.

7.2 Configuring Software Deployment Options

In this exercise, you configure a default software installation shared folder for all applications configured for the Research OU Group Policy. You then create software categories that are available throughout the domain and will assign your package to two categories.

Estimated time: 20 minutes.

To create software categories, assign software to categories, and describe a default installation share for packages, follow these steps:

1. While logged on as a Domain Administrator, start Active Directory Users and Computers.

2. Expand your domain, right-click the Sales OU, and select Properties.

3. Select the Research Script Policy you created earlier and click Edit. This starts the Group Policy Editor MMC.

4. In the Group Policy console tree, expand User Configuration and then expand Software Settings.

5. Right-click Software Installation and select Properties.

6. On the General tab in the General package location field, enter your share name in the format \\SHARE\FOLDER (for example, \\TORONTO\PACKAGES). This configures the default location for all packages in this GPO. The actual full path to the package is retained in the package setting. Placing packages that have been moved in this folder enables them to be located during deployment.

7. Click the Categories tab to add software categories to this GPO and the domain.

8. Click the Add button to add a new category called Utilities and click OK when done. Repeat this step to create two more categories called File Readers and Office Suites. If the software package you are using does not fall under these category headings, add additional categories that can be used to describe your software.

APPLY YOUR KNOWLEDGE

9. When done adding categories, click Apply and then OK to close the Software Installation Properties dialog box.

10. To assign your package to software categories, select the package, right-click it, and then select Properties.

11. Click the Categories tab to see into which categories the software has been placed. From the list of available categories, select File Readers and Utilities and click on Select. Click OK when you have completed your category selection.

12. Close the Group Policy Editor to save your changes.

13. Click OK on the Research Properties dialog box to close it.

14. Close the Active Directory Users and Computers MMC.

To verify placement of software in categories, follow these steps:

1. Log on to the computer as a user in the Developers Group to whom the Group Policy applies (TimC).

2. From the Start menu, select Settings and then Control Panel.

3. Double-click Add/Remove Programs to start the application.

4. Click Add New Programs to see a list of available applications on the network. Which categories are available in the Categories drop-down list box?

_____

_____

_____

5. Select one of the categories in which you placed your package (Utilities or File Readers). Does your package appear in the list when the Utilities category is selected? Is it also listed in the File Readers category? (Substitute your own categories here if appropriate.)

_____

_____

_____

6. Close Add/Remove Programs and then close Control Panel.

7. Log off the computer when done.

7.3 Configuring Software Upgrades

In this exercise, you will configure an upgrade to your package. You will first add another package to your GPO and then will configure it as an upgrade to your existing package. You will make the upgrade required. Finally, you will test the upgrade to make sure it succeeds.

Estimated time: 20 minutes.

To add a package as an upgrade for your existing package, follow these steps:

1. While logged on as a Domain Administrator, start Active Directory Users and Computers.

2. Expand your domain, right-click the Sales OU, and select Properties.

3. Select the Research Script Policy you created earlier and click Edit. This starts the Group Policy Editor MMC.

4. In the Group Policy console tree, expand User Configuration and then expand Software Settings.

APPLY YOUR KNOWLEDGE

5. Right-click Software Installation and select New and then Package. In the Open dialog box that appears, locate the package (MSI) file for the software application that will be used to upgrade your existing package and select Open. This must be a different file than your original application.

6. In the Deploy Software dialog box that appears, select Published as the deployment method and click OK.

7. Right-click the package you just added and select Properties.

8. Click the Categories tab and select the categories that apply to this package. These should be similar (if not identical) to the categories you selected for your original package.

9. Click the Upgrades tab and then click the Add button to add a package of which the new package will be an upgrade.

10. From the list presented, select the first application package and select either Uninstall the existing package, then install the upgrade package or Package can upgrade over the existing package, as it applies to your software application. Click OK.

11. On the Upgrades tab, make sure Required upgrade for existing packages is selected and click Apply and then OK to exit the package Properties dialog box.

12. Close the Group Policy Editor to save your changes.

13. Click OK on the Research Properties dialog box to close it.

14. Log off your computer after closing the Active Directory Users and Computers MMC.

To verify the package upgrade, follow these steps:

1. Log on to the computer as a user in the Developers Group to whom the Group Policy applies (TimC).

2. From the Start menu, select Settings and then Control Panel.

3. Invoke your first application package by double-clicking it or by opening a file extension mapped to it. What happens?

_____

_____

_____

4. Is the older version of your application still installed? Why or why not?

_____

_____

_____

5. Close all programs and log off the computer when done.

7.4   Removing Deployed Packages Using Group Policy

In this exercise, you will configure the mandatory removal of the last package installed (that is, the previous upgrade). You will then test the upgrade to make sure it succeeds.

Estimated time: 20 minutes.

APPLY YOUR KNOWLEDGE

To configure the removal of a package using Group Policy, follow these steps:

1. While logged on as a Domain Administrator, start Active Directory Users and Computers.

2. Expand your domain, right-click the Sales OU, and select Properties.

3. Select the Research Script Policy you created earlier and click Edit. This starts the Group Policy Editor MMC.

4. In the Group Policy console tree, expand User Configuration and then expand Software Settings. Click Software Installation to display a list of packages for this GPO.

5. Right-click the older package and select All Tasks and then Remove.

6. On the Remove Software dialog box, select Immediately uninstall the software from users and computers and click OK. Repeat this step for the upgrade as well. Notice that both packages are removed from the Software Installation list.

7. Close the Group Policy Editor to save your changes.

8. Click OK on the Research Properties dialog box to close it.

9. Log off your computer after closing the Active Directory Users and Computers MMC.

To verify forced package removal using Group Policy, follow these steps:

1. Log on to the computer as a user in the Developers Group to whom the Group Policy applies (TimC).

2. What new messages are presented to you during the logon process?

_____

_____

_____

3. Do the icons or shortcuts for any of your packages appear or are they still available? Why or why not?

_____

_____

_____

4. Close all programs and log off the computer when done.

Review Questions

1. How must software be configured for it to be deployed using Group Policy?

2. You need to make sure that all users in your organization have Microsoft Outlook 2000 installed as their email client. How would you accomplish this?

3. Users in your office in Germany are complaining that they do not have Microsoft Outlook 2000 prompts and other information in German. How would you correct this problem?

4. If a software application is not shipped as a Windows Installer Package file, what alternatives are available for deploying it using Group Policy?

5. If your organization has many software packages deployed, how can you make it easier for users to find the application they want?

6. When would you assign an application to a computer rather than a user?

APPLY YOUR KNOWLEDGE

7. What software deployment options are not available when using ZAP files?

8. How would you add a support telephone number and Web site location to an existing MSI file?

9. Why would a software package remove files from the user's machine when it is deployed?

10. How could you be sure that users would still be able to use an application after it has been removed from the GPO?

Exam Questions

1. You are the administrator of a large multinational organization with offices in Paris, London, Berlin, Moscow, Tokyo, and Sydney, as well as the corporate head office in New York. Your CIO has concluded negotiations with Microsoft, making Microsoft Office 2000 the corporate standard for office suites. He needs you to make sure the software gets deployed.

The requirements for the deployment are as follows:

- Microsoft Office 2000 must be installed on all desktops throughout the enterprise.

- Users in each office must be able to use Microsoft Office 2000 with localized dictionaries and interfaces.

- The corporate legal department in New York, which has its own OU in the Active Directory structure, will not have Microsoft Office 2000 installed on its desktops because all of its documents rely on a third-party add-on to another office suite.

- Travel and other costs for the deployment must be kept as low as possible.

You conclude that the best way to satisfy the requirements is the following:

- Use Microsoft Windows 2000 Group Policy to deploy the software.

- Create a GPO object at the domain level (your organization consists of only one domain) that would assign the software to computers.

- Create transform files for each localized version needed and add them to the package configured in the GPO.

- Block policy inheritance for the legal department OU.

Which of these requirements will be met by your solution? (Choose all that apply.)

A. Microsoft Office 2000 will be installed on all desktops throughout the enterprise.

B. Users in each office will be able to use Microsoft Office 2000 with localized dictionaries and interfaces.

C. The corporate legal department in New York will not have Microsoft Office 2000 installed on its desktops.

D. Travel and other costs for the deployment will be kept as low as possible.

E. The solution will not satisfy any of the outlined objectives.

APPLY YOUR KNOWLEDGE

2. You are the administrator of a large multinational organization with offices in Paris, London, Berlin, Moscow, Tokyo, and Sydney, as well as the corporate head office in New York. Your CIO has concluded negotiations with Microsoft, making Microsoft Office 2000 the corporate standard for office suites. He needs you to make sure the software gets deployed.

   The requirements for the deployment are as follows:

   - Microsoft Office 2000 must be installed on all desktops throughout the enterprise.

   - Users in each office must be able to use Microsoft Office 2000 with localized dictionaries and interfaces.

   - The corporate legal department in New York, which has its own OU in the Active Directory structure, will not have Microsoft Office 2000 installed on its desktops because all of its documents rely on a third-party add-on to another office suite.

   - Travel and other costs for the deployment must be kept as low as possible.

   You conclude that the best way to satisfy the requirements is the following:

   - Use Microsoft Windows 2000 Group Policy to deploy the software.

   - Create GPO objects at the site level (each office is its own site) that would assign the software to computers.

   - Create transform files in each site GPO for the localized version needed at that site and add them to the package configured in the GPO.

   - At the New York site, filter the GPO to not include any computers in the legal department OU.

   Which of these requirements will be met by your solution? (Choose all that apply.)

   A. Microsoft Office 2000 will be installed on all desktops throughout the enterprise.

   B. Users in each office will be able to use Microsoft Office 2000 with localized dictionaries and interfaces.

   C. The corporate legal department in New York will not have Microsoft Office 2000 installed on its desktops.

   D. Travel and other costs for the deployment will be kept as low as possible.

   E. The solution will not satisfy any of the outlined objectives.

3. When comparing Windows Installer Package files and ZAP files, which of the following is true? (Choose the best answer.)

   A. ZAP files cannot be used to deploy software, but package files can.

   B. Package files can publish extensions associated with the application, but ZAP files cannot.

   C. ZAP files can be installed with elevated privileges just like package files.

   D. Package files include shortcuts, registry settings, and the files required to be installed; ZAP files do not.

E. There is no difference in the functionality available in ZAP and package files.

4. You need to make a software application available to users in your sales department. The application is not provided in a Windows Installer Package file format. Users can choose to have the software installed on their computers. What is the best way to deploy this application using Group Policy? (Choose the best answer.)

A. Repackage the application using WinINSTALL LE and assign it to the user.

B. Repackage the application using WinINSTALL LE and publish it to the user.

C. Create a ZAP file for the application and assign it to the user.

D. Create a ZAP file for the application and publish it to the user.

E. It is not possible to deploy software using Group Policy unless it is provided as a Windows Installer Package file.

5. When publishing a package to a user using Group Policy, how can the user initiate the installation of the software application in the package? (Choose two correct answers.)

A. By opening a file whose extension is associated with the package (document activation).

B. By starting the setup program for the package (install activation).

C. By logging on, which starts the setup program for the application (logon activation).

D. By using Add/Remove Programs in Control Panel (user activation).

E. By starting his or her computer, which installs the application (computer activation).

6. In the GPO for the sales department OU, you have configured a package for forced removal for all users. When visiting users in the sales department, you determine that the application was removed from some users' computers but not all. What would be the reason some users in sales still have the package on their machines? (Choose the best answer.)

A. When asked whether they wanted to remove the application, they said no.

B. Their computers were filtered out of the GPO scope.

C. They marked the package as critical on their computers, which overrode the forced removal.

D. They are sales managers and therefore are not subject to the regular sales GPO.

E. They reinstalled the application using Add/Remove Programs in Control after it was removed.

7. You want to deploy an upgrade to an existing application. You want to make sure that all users receive the upgrade and that the old version of the software no longer is available. How should you configure the upgrade? (Choose two correct answers.)

A. Make the upgrade required.

B. Make the upgrade optional.

C. Allow users to keep the existing version.

D. Uninstall the previous version when installing the upgrade.

E. Have the upgrade overwrite the existing version.

8. What are the benefits of using Windows Installer Package files to deploy software? (Choose all correct answers.)

A. You can install software on a user's computer only when the user has permission to do so.

B. Critical files can be automatically replaced if they become corrupt or deleted.

C. Shared files in use by other applications are not removed when the package is removed.

D. You can assign software to users and computers.

E. You can publish software to users and computers.

Answers to Exercises

7.1   Using Group Policy to Deploy Software

Test Software Deployment Using Group Policy

4. Yes, the package is displayed on the list of available programs on the network.

5. For a package file, the amount of interaction is minimal. You are shown status information as the installation proceeds but are not asked to enter any application configuration options. The installation succeeds and uses the parameters indicated in the package file.

If you use a ZAP file instead of a package file, the amount of interaction will be as much as is needed by the setup program for the application being installed.

6. The application should function normally. In other words, it should function the same way it did prior being repackaged, if you repackaged an application using Veritas WinINSTALL LE, or as required by the vendor for all other applications. Windows Installer simply performs the tasks indicated by the software developer to install and make the application workable. If there is a fault in this configuration, check with your software vendor or the person who repackaged the software.

7.2   Configuring Software Deployment Options

Verifying Placement of Software in Categories

4. Utilities, File Readers, and Office Suites. Other categories might also appear if you created them.

5. Your package should be listed in all categories you selected for it including the ones indicated in the exercise, Utilities and File Readers.

7.3   Configuring Software Upgrades

Verifying the Package Upgrade

3. Windows Installer installs the upgrade.

4. The older version of the application is no longer installed because the upgrade either removed it or overwrote it.

APPLY YOUR KNOWLEDGE

7.4   Removing Deployed Packages Using Group Policy

Verifying Forced Package Removal Using Group Policy

2. You will receive messages stating that the deployed software is being removed during the logon process.

3. Icons and shortcuts for the software deployed using Group Policy are no longer available. The packages have been completely removed from your computer.

Answers to Review Questions

1. Software must be in the form of a Windows Installer Package file or you must create a ZAP file if you want to deploy the software using Group Policy.

   The MSI file is in native Windows Installer format and contains the files, registry settings, and shortcuts that make up an application as well as information on where these elements should be installed.

   A ZAP file is a text file that specifies information on the program to be invoked to install the application including any parameters, as well as file extensions, that should be associated with the application. See the section "Preparing Software for Deployment Using Group Policy."

2. Configure a GPO at the domain level and create the Microsoft Outlook 2000 package in the Users Configuration container of the GPO. Assign, rather than publish, the application to make sure it is installed on all users' desktops. See the section "Software Deployment Using Group Policy."

3. Create a GPO at the German users OU in Active Directory and assign the package to it. Configure a transform (MST) file with the German language characteristics required and associate it with the package. This ensures that Microsoft Outlook 2000 is still installed (it is assigned), but the language requirements of the German users are also taken into consideration through the transform (MST) file. See the section "Managing Software Deployment."

4. You can create a ZAP file to install the application and then publish the software product in Group Policy. You can also repackage the application using a third-party repackaging tool such as Veritas WinINSTALL LE, which creates a Windows Installer Package file, providing you with greater flexibility in deployment. See the section "Preparing Software for Deployment Using Group Policy."

5. Create software categories that will be available domain-wide. Then modify your packages in the various GPOs and assign them to one or more categories. In this way, when a user wants to install an application that has been published, he or she can view the list of all software or only the categories in which he or she is interested when going to Add/Remove Programs in Control Panel. See the section "Managing Software Deployment."

APPLY YOUR KNOWLEDGE

6. You would assign an application to a computer rather than a user when the application is required to be available to all users on one or more machines. In this way, users will always have critical software available. See the section "Software Deployment Using Group Policy."

7. When using ZAP files, you cannot assign the package to computers or users; you can only publish them. This is because a ZAP file simply tells Windows Installer what program to invoke to start the installation process. Windows Installer has no control over what actually occurs during the application installation and, therefore, cannot control it. Because of this, packages cannot be assigned because this would require Windows Installer to automate the installation of a software application. See the section "Preparing Software for Deployment Using Group Policy."

8. To add a support telephone number and Web site location to an existing MSI file, you would modify the package (MSI) file using a third-party repackaging product such as Veritas WinINSTALL LE. See the section "Windows Installer Technology."

9. A software package can remove files from a user's machine when it is deployed if it was repackaged and, during the repackaging, files were removed. Because repackaging takes a before and after snapshot of the user's computer to determine what has changed during the software installation process, any files that were removed or modified by either the product's setup program or the user will be incorporated in the package. If the administrator did not carefully examine the resulting package file created and correct any items that should not be passed on to users' machines, it is possible for a repackaged application to make

unwanted changes to a user's system. To correct this problem, either modify the package or repackage the application. See the section "Troubleshooting Software Deployment."

10. To ensure that users will still be able to use an application after it has been removed from a GPO, make the package removal optional. If the removal is optional, users can still make use of the application until they themselves decide to remove it, after which time the application is no longer available. See the section "Maintaining Software Packages Using Group Policy."

Answers to Exam Questions

1. **A, C, D.** Your solution would ensure that all computers in the domain were assigned Microsoft Office 2000 and had it installed. Any GPO defined at the domain level will apply to all containers and OUs within the domain unless blocked. Because you blocked policy inheritance at the legal department OU, the legal department will not have the software installed. The transform files you created will have no effect because they were all added in the one GPO (they will actually cause all the different language versions to be installed) and will not localize the software for each office. Costs were kept down because the deployment was handled through Group Policy and did not require anyone to really travel. See the sections "Software Deployment Using Group Policy" and "Maintaining Software Packages Using Group Policy." Also see the section "Group Policy Inheritance" in Chapter 6, "Using Group Policy to Manage Users."

APPLY YOUR KNOWLEDGE

2. **A, B, C, D.** By defining the GPO at the site level and creating different transform files for each site, you were able to localize the package for each location. Furthermore, by blocking policy inheritance at the legal department OU, you made sure the legal department was exempt from this corporate policy. Finally, by doing all the work using Windows 2000 Group Policy, you kept costs down. See the sections "Software Deployment Using Group Policy" and "Maintaining Software Packages Using Group Policy." Also see the section "Group Policy Inheritance" in Chapter 6, "Using Group Policy to Manage Users."

3. **D.** Package files include shortcuts, registry settings, and the files required to be installed; ZAP files do not. ZAP files are text files that describe the extensions associated with an application and the program to be run when installing the software application. Windows Installer cannot execute ZAP files with elevated privileges because you actually need to run the setup program for the application, and this program runs in the security context of the user initiating the installation. Both ZAP and package (MSI) files can be used in software deployment with a few restrictions. See the section "Preparing Software for Deployment Using Group Policy."

4. **B.** Although both B and D would work, it is better to repackage the application and publish it to the user rather than use a ZAP file. If the user does not have permission to modify the registry or place files in system folders, the ZAP file method may fail because the application cannot be installed using elevated privileges. Windows Installer Package files, even the ones repackaged using WinINSTALL LE, can be installed using elevated privileges.

Assigning the repackaged application to all users would install it on their computers whether or not they wanted the application, and you said you wanted to give them a choice. It is not possible to assign ZAP files; you can only publish them. See the sections "Preparing Software for Deployment Using Group Policy" and "Software Deployment Using Group Policy."

5. **A, D.** When a package is published to a user, it can be installed either through document activation (the user opens a file whose extension is associated with the application) or through user activation in which the user goes to Control Panel and selects Add/Remove Programs to install the software application. The package will not be installed when the user logs on or the computer starts up because it was published and not assigned. For an automatic install to take place, you would need to assign the package to the user or computer. See the section "Software Deployment Using Group Policy."

6. **B.** The most likely reason the application is still installed on their machines is that they were filtered out of the GPO scope where the forced removal was configured. Because the removal of the application was forced, they could not say no because they were never prompted. Whether or not they are sales managers, the Group Policy still applies to them. (Position has no priority in Group Policy.) They could not have reinstalled the package using Add/Remove Programs because it was not available any longer. It was removed. There is no way to make an application "critical" on a machine and therefore have it override GPO settings; this functionality does not exist. See the section "Software Deployment Using Group Policy." Also see the section "Group Policy Security" in Chapter 6, "Using Group Policy to Manage Users."

APPLY YOUR KNOWLEDGE

7. **A, D.** To make sure all users only have the new version, you need to make the upgrade required and uninstall the previous version when performing the upgrade. Making the upgrade optional and allowing users to keep the old version is the same thing. Overwriting the old version might leave portions of that application still around, which is not what you said you wanted. See the section "Maintaining Software Packages Using Group Policy."

8. **B, C, D.** Windows Installer Package files enable you to assign software to users and computers. Furthermore, when removing software, the uninstall process will be smart enough to know which shared files are still in use by other application because the Windows Installer Service keeps track of this information. Finally, Windows Installer Packages provide for resilient software in which Windows Installer automatically replaces critical files that become damaged or corrupted. Publishing of software can be done using either ZAP files or Windows Installer Package files, so this answer is not 100% accurate when it comes to packages. Windows Installer Package files enable you to install software on users' machines even though they might not have the necessary privileges to do so because Windows Installer can perform an installation using its privileges (that is, an elevated privileges install). See the section "Preparing Software for Deployment Using Group Policy."

Suggested Readings and Resources

1. *Microsoft Windows 2000 Resource Kit. Deployment Planning Guide.* Microsoft Press, 2000.

2. *Automated Deployment Options: An Overview White Paper* on Microsoft's Web site at `http://www.microsoft.com/windows2000/library/planning/client/deployops.asp`.

3. *Software Installation and Maintenance* on Microsoft's Web site at `http://www.microsoft.com/windows2000/library/operations/management/siamwp.asp`.

4. *Automating the Deployment of Windows 2000 Professional and Office 2000* on Microsoft's Web site at `http://www.microsoft.com/windows2000/library/planning/incremental/sysprep.asp`.

5. *Desktop Deployment Solutions from Third-Party Companies* on Microsoft's Web site at `http://www.microsoft.com/windows2000/guide/server/partners/DesktopSolutions.asp`.

6. *Software Deployment Using Windows 2000 and Systems Management Server 2.0* on Microsoft's Web site at `http://www.microsoft.com/windows2000/library/planning/management/smsintell.asp`.

7. *Windows Installer* on Microsoft's Web site at `http://www.microsoft.com/windows2000/library/howitworks/management/installer.asp`.

The following objectives from the "Configuring, Managing, Monitoring, and Troubleshooting Active Directory Security Solutions" section of the exam are addressed by this chapter.

Configure and troubleshoot security in a directory services infrastructure.

- **Apply security policies by using Group Policy.**

- **Create, analyze, and modify security configurations by using Security Configuration and Analysis and Security Templates.**

- **Implement an audit policy.**

▶ Your ability to configure and troubleshoot security within an Active Directory structure is addressed on the exam. Microsoft wants to make sure you are familiar with the process of modifying security settings using Group Policy security templates. Knowing what security elements can be configured and applied, where they apply (user or computer), and the end result of a security policy are also tested. You need to know the capabilities and features of the Security Configuration and Analysis MMC snap-in and how it can be used to apply and verify your security policies.

Monitor and analyze security events.

▶ Microsoft also tests your ability to track security policy settings through auditing and your ability to set an audit policy to determine the actual outcome of that security policy. You need to know where to locate security event information and how to analyze the details to determine the cause of a security breach.

CHAPTER 8

Managing Security Using Group Policy

▶ The best way to prepare for this portion of the exam is to use the appropriate tools mentioned in this chapter. Using Security Configuration and Analysis to analyze security on a computer interactively and to create a template provides you with critical hands-on experience that will aide you in answering questions dealing with these tools. Also, exporting security settings through Security Configuration and Analysis should be attempted.

▶ You should configure SECEDIT.EXE through Task Scheduler to analyze security settings on one or more computers and then review the database information that was created.

▶ You should be familiar with the options available in Security Templates and configure one or more Group Policy objects to test these settings. Microsoft requires you to know what kind of security settings can be configured using Group Policy for both the computer and the user.

▶ Testing what happened and knowing the options available in configuring an audit policy also are tested, so you should configure one or more audit settings as well as use Windows Explorer to enable file and object access.

▶ Finally, being able to answer the review and exam questions in this chapter and working through the exercises and Step by Steps will also assist you in preparing for the exam. As always, working through the practice exam in the book and on the CD will also help.

INTRODUCTION

You have seen how Group Policy can be used to configure user and computer settings using administrative templates and scripts. You've also seen how Group Policy can be used to deploy software applications and to minimize the amount of time spent installing software on computers within the enterprise. Group Policy enables the administrator to configure elements of security for different parts of the organization to make sure key resources are used by authorized individuals only.

In this chapter, you find out what security settings are configurable through Windows 2000. Information on security settings that can be configured for the computer, as well as for the user, is presented. The functionality and usefulness of security settings are examined. A discussion on the use and types of security templates available, as well as how security templates can be created, is presented. You also are introduced to the Security Templates snap-in for *Microsoft Management Console* (MMC) and how to make use of it to create and modify security settings in templates.

Next you will be shown how to analyze and configure security settings for a computer using Security Configuration and Analysis, another MMC snap-in. The creation of security templates using Security Configuration and Analysis is also shown. A discussion of the benefits and limitations of using this MMC snap-in is included. Using Group Policy to apply security settings to a number of computers is outlined.

After configuring these security settings using Group Policy, it would be helpful if there were some way to make sure they were in fact being applied as necessary. To find out how this can be accomplished, you will be presented with information on auditing and shown how to configure and audit policy and the options available therein.

SECURITY SETTINGS AVAILABLE IN WINDOWS 2000 GROUP POLICY

Configure and troubleshoot security in a directory services infrastructure.

- **Apply security policies by using Group Policy.**

As you have seen in the two preceding chapters, Group Policy can be used to apply both computer and group settings. This remains true for applying security policy. However, because the more important element in security is to make sure access to resources is restricted to only those individuals who should have it, Group Policy in the security context is overwhelmingly slanted toward the computer side of Group Policy.

As is evident in Figure 8.1, the number of items that can be specified in the Computer Configuration of Group Policy is quite extensive as compared to the User Configuration portion. The User Configuration portion lists only one entry: Public Key Policies. The settings that can be configured in Group Policy for the computer are outlined in the following table.

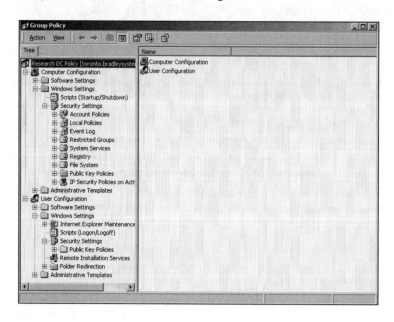

FIGURE 8.1
Group Policy security configuration options.

Setting	*Description*
Account Policies	Enables you to specify password and account lockout policy settings.
	Password policy settings include the password age (minimum and maximum), the number of passwords that will be remembered to prevent reuse of a favorite password by users for a time (that is, until the number of remembered passwords has been reached), the minimum password length, and password complexity. You also have the option to configure storing the password using reversible encryption.
	Account lockout policy settings include the duration of account lockout, the number of incorrect login attempts before invoking lockout, and the account lockout interval—the time between failed login attempts before the counter is reset.
Local Policies	Enables you to configure local computer settings for auditing, user rights assignment (for example, Logon Locally or Logon as a Service), and specific computer security options (such as message text to present to the user prior to logon, whether the last user logon name should display when logging on, and others).
Event Log	Enables the configuration of log file sizes for the three main event logs (system, security, and application), whether logs should be overwritten after their maximum size is reached, and any restrictions on who is allowed to read the log files.
Restricted Groups	Enables you to manage which users can be members of certain security groups and to configure in which other groups these groups can also be members. In other words, this setting enables you to configure group membership using the security policy to ensure that users are always members of certain groups and that certain groups are members of other groups when the policy is applied.
System Services	Enables the administrator to specify how services and devices will be started on the computer. In this way, you can ensure that required services are started on the target computers, while services that may cause problems are prevented from starting.
Registry	Enables you to configure security on registry keys. Through the security policy, you can set who is able to modify keys, read keys, and add new keys to the registry.
File System	Through this security setting, you are able to specify file system security settings for folders and files on NTFS partitions and be sure they will apply when the policy is in effect.

continues

continued

Setting	Description
Public Key Policies	Enables you to set which users will be data recovery agents for the *Encrypting File System* (EFS). Recovery agents are able to decrypt files when the user who created them is not available or has been deleted. Here you can also import certificate files from root certification authorities that will be trusted by Windows 2000, configure trust settings for authorities and certificates they have issued, and specify automatic certificate request settings. Windows 2000 has come a long way to ensure that secure communication takes place and that only those computers and users that have valid proof of authentication, such as certificates, are allowed access. These key security functions are implemented through Group Policy.
IP Security Polices on Active Directory	Enables you to configure how clients, servers, and domain controllers communicate and what level of security is requested, required, or declined. These settings apply to TCP/IP traffic between the various types of Windows 2000 computers.

On the User Configuration side, only one area of configuration exists within Group Policy: public key policies.

Public key policies that can be configured have only a single area: enterprise trusts. This enables the administrator to specify for the user which root certification authorities will be trusted and ensures that no other authorities are allowed by the user.

As is evident, Windows 2000 enables you to configure security in many areas including password management and account policies, local computer policies, restricted group memberships, registry settings, and file system settings. You can also configure public key policies for the Encrypting File System, for example, and network communication through IPSec policies. These can be configured for the computer primarily, with a subset available for the user.

IMPLEMENTING SECURITY POLICIES

Configure and troubleshoot security in a directory services infrastructure.

- **Create, analyze, and modify security configurations by using Security Configuration and Analysis and Security Templates.**

In Windows 2000, there are two main ways to implement security policies: using Security Templates or using Group Policy. The difference is not that great. Templates make it easier to reapply similar settings to many systems. A selection of settings also can be saved using a text file and then be reapplied in different areas if needed.

Security Templates in Windows 2000

A security template is a text file with an .INF extension (for example, SECSERVR.INF). This file includes security settings that can be applied to a single computer using the Security Configuration and Analysis MMC snap-in. These settings can be imported into Group Policy and be applied at the site, domain, or OU level. Security templates are a preconfigured list of settings and might include one or more of the sections previously described.

Microsoft Windows 2000 ships with a number of preconfigured security templates designed to be used in domain controllers, servers, and workstations. These templates include four levels of security that can impact the level of application functionality available. For example, if you decide to use a high level of security, some applications that make use of other portions of the operating system might not function correctly because the user might not have access to these secured areas of the operating system. Security templates are stored in the WINNT\Security\Templates folder on Windows 2000 computers. The four levels of security templates are as follows:

- ◆ **Basic.** Basic templates are the default security level of Windows 2000. They provide a high degree of application functionality but prevent basic security problems such as users configuring blank passwords or reusing the same passwords over and over again.

As shown in Figure 8.2, Microsoft ships default basic templates for domain controllers (basicdc), servers (basicsv), and workstations (basicwk).

◆ **Compatible.** Compatible templates provide more security, such as restricted access to certain parts of the registry, but still ensure that business applications run as required. Windows 2000 includes only one compatible template for workstations by default (compatws).

◆ **Secure.** Secure templates begin to make security more important than business application functionality. This means that business applications are not guaranteed to function in a secure environment because they might attempt to make use of portions of the operating system that have been secured. For example, business applications might put messages in the application log of Event Viewer without proper permissions. Secure templates are included for domain controllers (securedc) and workstations (securews).

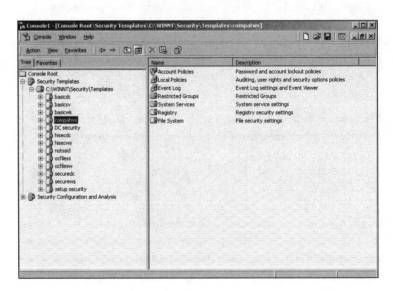

FIGURE 8.2

Preconfigured default security templates shipped with Windows 2000.

◆ **High.** High templates enforce the maximum-security settings in Windows 2000 and do not guarantee that line-of-business applications (such as Microsoft Word 2000, accounting systems, and so on) will work. They are not normally used in a Windows 2000 environment because they might break too many applications, but they are useful in the development of high-security Windows 2000 applications. High-security templates include the signing of IP packets between server and workstation, lockout and disconnection of users, protection of registry and file system components, and many other settings. Windows 2000 ships with high-security templates for domain controller (hisecdc) and workstations (hisecws).

In addition to the four basic template settings, Microsoft Windows 2000 also ships with other templates for specific tasks. These are all variations of the four basic levels but are not named as such in the Security Templates MMC snap-in. You will find out how to open and use the Security Templates snap-in in the next section. These additional templates are as follows:

◆ **DC Security.** This template includes the default security settings applied on all domain controllers. It includes file system and registry protection to ensure that domain controllers function properly. DC Security template is automatically configured and installed on all domain controllers in the domain and is part of the default domain controller policy in the Domain Controller container in Active Directory.

◆ **notssid.** The notssid template removes the Terminal Server SID from the Windows 2000 Server computer. Users will have their access to the Terminal Server defined by their SID and group memberships, not the Terminal Server account SID.

◆ **ocfiless.** The ocfiless template is used to provide additional file security on Windows 2000 Server machines. The files included on the policy may not be installed, which can be problematic because the policy removes permissions to install the files for most users, including Administrator and System.

This template should not be applied prior to installing the files protected by it. (That is, install all the software first and then apply the policy.) To modify the installed files, you need to remove the policy or filter it out.

◆ **ocfilesw.** This policy template is similar to ocfiless except it applies to Windows 2000 Professional computers. The main difference between these two templates is the files included; a number of files on Windows 2000 Server machines do not exist on Windows 2000 Professional.

◆ **Setup Security.** This template is the default, out-of-the-box settings applied to Windows 2000 Professional and Server computers.

Creating and Modifying Security Templates

The creation and modification of security templates in Windows 2000 is performed using the Security Templates MMC snap-in. This snap-in is not preconfigured in any MMC console available in either Administrative Tools or Control Panel. To open MMC and add the Security Templates snap-in to the console, follow Step by Step 8.1.

STEP BY STEP

8.1 Configuring MMC with the Security Templates Snap-In

1. Log on to your Windows 2000 computer as Administrator.

2. From the Start menu, select Run. In the Run dialog box, enter **mmc** as shown in Figure 8.3.

3. From the Console menu of the MMC Console window presented, select Add/Remove Snap-in, as shown in Figure 8.4.

4. In the Add/Remove Snap-in dialog box that is opened, click the Add button to open the Add Standalone Snap-in dialog box (see Figure 8.5), which enables you to choose the snap-in to add.

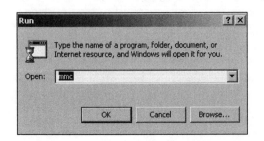

FIGURE 8.3
Invoking Microsoft Management Console from the Run option of the Start menu.

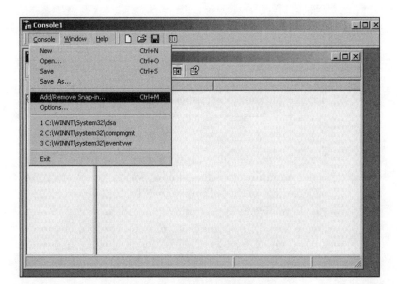

FIGURE 8.4
To add a snap-in, select Add/Remove Snap-in from the Console menu of the MMC Console window.

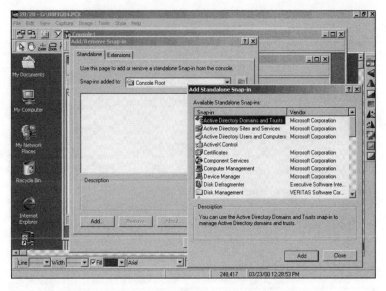

FIGURE 8.5
Clicking Add presents you with a list of snap-ins that are available.

5. Scroll down until you find Security Templates and then double-click Security Templates or click the Add button to add the Security Templates snap-in to the MMC console, as shown in Figure 8.6.

continues

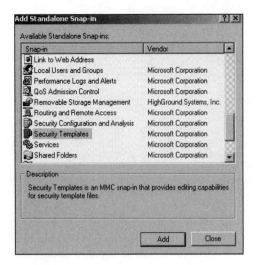

FIGURE 8.6
Click Add to add the Security Templates snap-in to the MMC console.

continued

6. Click Close to close the Add Standalone Snap-in dialog box.

7. Click OK to close the Add/Remove Snap-in dialog box.

8. To save your console settings, from the Console menu, select Save As (see Figure 8.7). Then type the filename in the Save As dialog box.

   Note that the default location to save your console settings is the Administrative Tools folder, which would put your new console in the Administrative Tools program group. An alternative location can be specified, as shown in Figure 8.8, by using the Save in drop-down list box to select it. Your desktop might be a good choice, as shown in Figure 8.9.

9. If you are finished, close the MMC console.

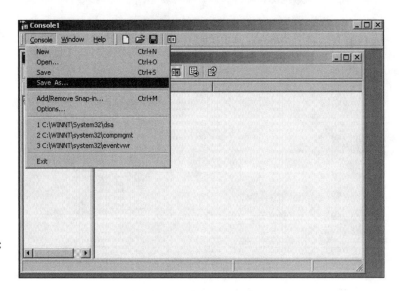

FIGURE 8.7
Select Save As from the Console menu in MMC to save your console with the Security Templates snap-in for use later.

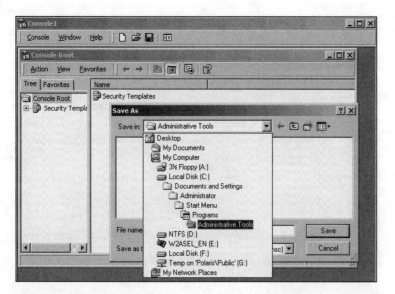

FIGURE 8.8
The default location to save MMC console settings is the Administrative Tools folder. You can select another location from this drop-down list box.

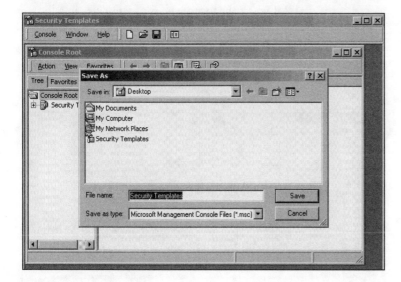

FIGURE 8.9
Saving the Security Templates MMC on your desktop.

After you have configured an MMC console you can use and reuse to create and modify security templates, you are ready to create a template. To create a security template, perform the steps in Step by Step 8.2.

STEP BY STEP

8.2 Creating a Security Template Using the Security Templates MMC Snap-In

1. After logging on to a Windows 2000 computer as Administrator, double-click the Security Templates MMC shortcut you created on your desktop to open Microsoft Management Console.

2. Expand Security Templates in the MMC console to be shown a location. After expanding the default location of C:\WINNT\Security\Templates, you will see a list of the currently available templates, as displayed in Figure 8.10.

3. If you would like to add a new location to store security templates, as shown in Figure 8.11, right-click Security Templates and select New Template Search Path. This can be useful if you want to store a set of templates in a location while developing them and not have them available on this machine right away. It is also useful in cases in which a set of security templates used in an enterprise can be stored on a network share.

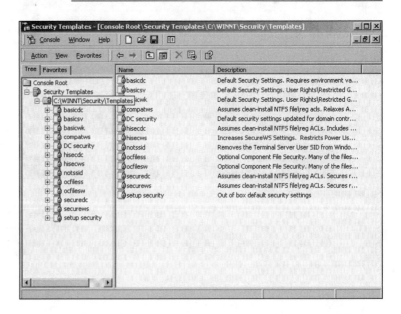

FIGURE 8.10

Displaying available security templates in the default location.

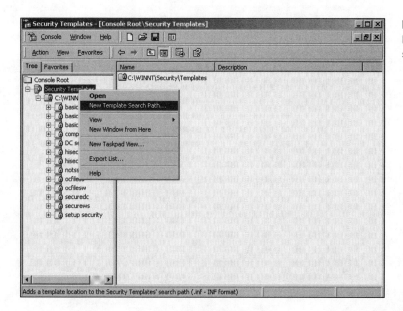

FIGURE 8.11
Right-click Security Templates to add a new security template search path.

4. To add a new security template, right-click the default location listed (because this is where you will be creating the template) and, as shown in Figure 8.12, select New Template.

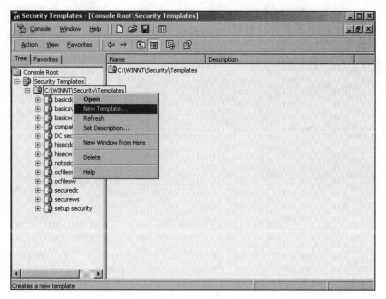

FIGURE 8.12
Right-click the template location path to create a new security template.

continues

continued

NOTE

Using an Existing Security Template Instead of creating a security template from scratch, as shown in Step By Step 8.2, you can take an existing security template and use it as a basis for creating a new template. To do this, right-click the template you want to copy and select Save As. In the Save As dialog box, enter a filename for the copy of the template you want to create. The security templates location will now be updated to include the copy of the template you made.

Copying rather than creating security templates from scratch does have some advantages as well as disadvantages. A main advantage of copying a security template is that, if most of the settings you want to enforce already exist in the template you are copying, making modifications to include a few more will not take as long as adding all changes from scratch. Copying an existing template without being fully aware of its contents, however, can also lead to settings being applied that you did not anticipate.

No matter which method you choose, creating a template from scratch or copying an existing template, always be sure you are aware of the contents of the template in question and thoroughly verify that the changes being made will result in the behavior you expect and desire. As with all things, testing is a key requirement.

5. In the dialog box shown in Figure 8.13, specify a name for the security template and, optionally, a brief description that will appear in the MMC snap-in. Click OK when finished.

6. You have now created a security template that can be used on this machine or, as you will see later, imported into a Group Policy object. The security template you created will have all the options available but nothing set. The default configuration for each item in the template will be Not defined, thereby enabling you to configure and put in effect only those elements of the template that you would like enforced.

7. Close the Security Templates MMC when finished.

After you have created the security template, you need to modify its settings to make sure the security policy reflects the behavior you want. To modify a security template, follow the steps presented in Step by Step 8.3.

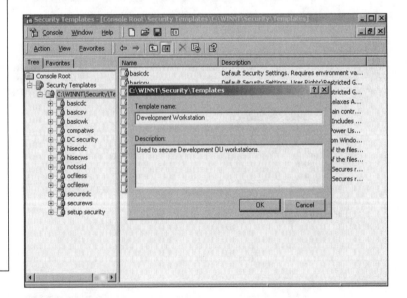

FIGURE 8.13
Enter a name and description for the template you are creating.

STEP BY STEP

8.3 Modifying Security Template Settings Using the Security Templates MMC Snap-In

1. After logging on to a Windows 2000 computer as Administrator, double-click the Security Templates MMC shortcut you created on your desktop to open Microsoft Management Console.

2. Expand Security Templates in the MMC console until you are shown a list of templates and can locate the one you want to modify.

3. Expand the template to be shown a list of settings you can change, as shown in Figure 8.14. This list corresponds to the areas identified in the table previously presented in this chapter.

4. Choose the area where you want to change a setting such as Account Policies. You will encounter a further set of categories for settings. Continue to expand the settings until you locate the one you want to change such as Minimum Password Length in the Password Policy, as shown in Figure 8.15.

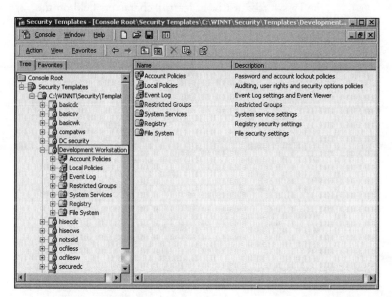

FIGURE 8.14
Expanding a security template presents a list of settings that can be modified.

continues

continued

FIGURE 8.15
To change the minimum length of a password,
expand Account Policies and then Password
Policy in the security template you are modifying.

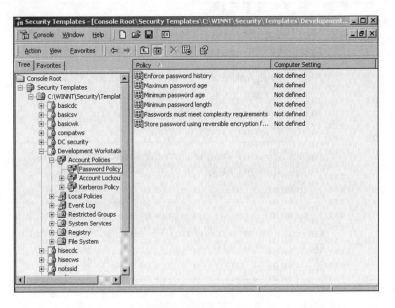

NOTE

**Template Security Policy Setting
Dialog Box**   The information presented in the Template Security Policy
Setting dialog box varies depending
on the available options for the setting and how it was defined in the
template. Although the dialog box
might have the same name, the information to be modified might differ.

5. Double-click Minimum password length in the details
   pane to be presented with a dialog box, as shown in
   Figure 8.16. To set the policy, click Define this policy setting in the template and then set the minimum password
   length to the desired number of characters by changing
   the Password must be at least: n characters field on the
   screen. When finished, click OK.

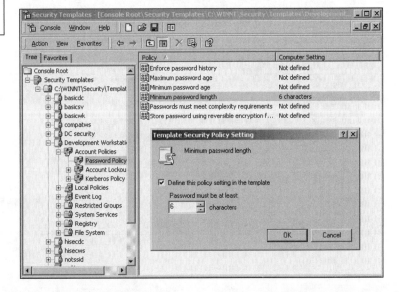

FIGURE 8.16
The Template Security Policy Setting dialog box
enables you to modify security policy settings
such as minimum password length.

6. To save your changes, select Save from the Console menu in MMC or, as shown in Figure 8.17, right-click the template and select Save.

7. Close the MMC console when finished.

Although not yet stated, you can also delete security templates that no longer are of use. This can be done by deleting the file directly from the folder in which it resides (C:\WINNT\Security\Templates, for example) or by using the Security Templates MMC snap-in.

To delete the unwanted security template from the Security Template MMC snap-in, as shown in Figure 8.18, right-click the template to delete and select Delete. When asked if you are sure you want to delete the template, click Yes and it will be gone.

As you have seen, creating, modifying, and deleting security templates is a relatively simple process. The most difficult part is determining exactly which setting should be applied. However, this is something most often based on business requirements rather than technical capabilities and might require discussion with other parts of the enterprise.

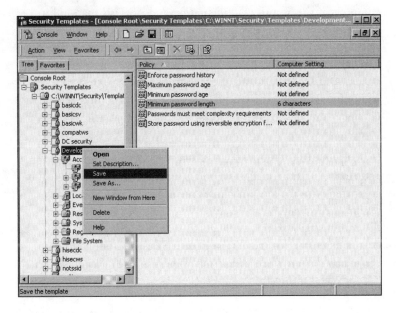

FIGURE 8.17
Save your changes to the security template to make sure they will take effect.

FIGURE 8.18
To delete a security template in MMC, right-click the template to delete and select Delete.

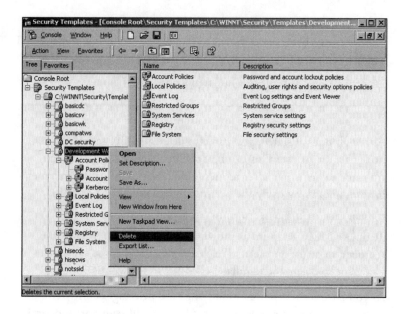

Using Security Configuration and Analysis

Another tool that can be used to configure security settings on a computer is the Security Configuration and Analysis snap-in for MMC. The Security Templates snap-in was used to configure settings, which will later be imported into Group Policy. Security Configuration and Analysis is primarily designed to analyze local system security settings and apply security templates to the local computer. It can also be used to retrieve the local computer security configuration and to create a security template that will reflect the computer's settings.

In analyzing your system's security settings, Security Configuration and Analysis can be used to import a security template. This will be compared with the local machine's security configuration. The results of the analysis can be stored in a database, which enables the administrator to track changes in security settings over time. The default extension for the database file is SDB, and one SDB file is created by default when you install Windows 2000, although you cannot access it directly.

In configuring system security, Security Configuration and Analysis can be used to import security template settings and then apply them directly on the local computer. Unlike Group Policy, Security Configuration and Analysis cannot be used to apply the template settings to more than one computer at a time. If you need to do this, you should import a security template into Group Policy in the Active Directory container where the machines are located.

To open Microsoft Management Console (MMC) and add the Security Configuration and Analysis snap-in to the console, follow the steps presented in Step by Step 8.4.

STEP BY STEP

8.4 Configuring MMC with the Security Configuration and Analysis Snap-In

1. Log on to your Windows 2000 computer as Administrator.

2. From the Start menu, select Run. In the Run dialog box, enter **mmc**.

3. From the Console menu of the MMC console window presented, select Add/Remove Snap-in.

4. In the Add/Remove Snap-in dialog box opened, click the Add button to be shown the Add Standalone Snap-in dialog box, which enables you to choose the snap-in to add.

5. Scroll down until you find Security Configuration and Analysis and then double-click Security Templates or click the Add button to add the Security Configuration and Analysis snap-in to the MMC console, as shown in Figure 8.19.

6. Click Close to close the Add Standalone Snap-in dialog box.

7. Click OK to close the Add/Remove Snap-in dialog box.

8. To save your console settings, from the Console menu, select Save As and then type the filename in the Save As dialog box.

9. If you are finished, close the MMC console.

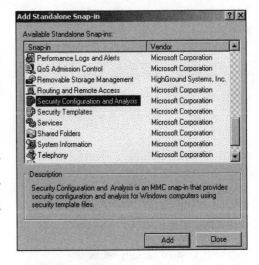

FIGURE 8.19

Click Add to add the Security Configuration and Analysis snap-in to the MMC console.

A database to hold security settings must be created when using the Security Configuration and Analysis snap-in. You can then use this database to perform analysis of your settings against a security template as well as to store your current configuration.

To create a database to be used to analyze your computer against a template, follow the steps shown in Step by Step 8.5.

STEP BY STEP

8.5 Configuring a Database for Analyzing Your Computer in Security Configuration and Analysis

1. Log on to your Windows 2000 computer as Administrator and open the Security Configuration and Analysis MMC console you created in Step by Step 8.4.

2. Click Security Configuration and Analysis to display database requirements, as shown in Figure 8.20.

3. To create a database, follow the instructions displayed. Right-click Security Configuration and Analysis and select Open database, as shown in Figure 8.21.

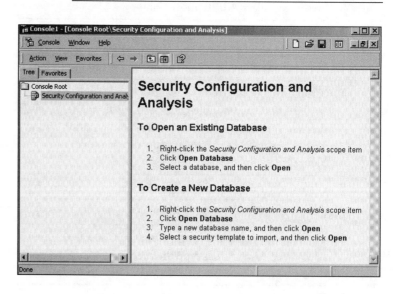

FIGURE 8.20
Security Configuration and Analysis requires a database to store security settings.

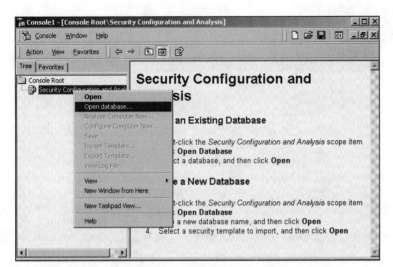

FIGURE 8.21
To create a database, select Open database after right-clicking Security Configuration and Analysis.

4. In the File name field of the Open database dialog box (see Figure 8.22), type the name of the database file you want to create and click Open.

   Note that the default location of the database file being created is in your user profile in a folder called Security. If you would like to change the location of the database file, change the target folder by using the Look in drop-down list box.

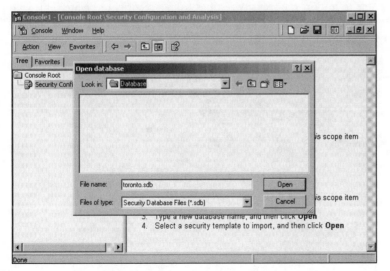

FIGURE 8.22
Select the filename and location of the Security Analysis and Configuration database.

continues

continued

5. You are next presented with a dialog box similar to Figure 8.23, in which you are asked to import a security template to be used to compare the computer's security settings against those in the template. You should select the template whose security settings are desired for the computer on which you are running Security Configuration and Analysis. For example, if you wanted to configure a domain controller with basic security settings, you would select basicdc as the security template file to import. Choose a template and click Open to load its settings.

6. After selecting a template, Security Configuration and Analysis imports its settings and then changes the details pane of MMC to display information on how to configure your computer to use those settings or how to analyze your computer settings, as shown in Figure 8.24.

7. At this point, you have created a database that you can later use to analyze your computer against template settings. Close the MMC console when finished.

At this point, you have configured an MMC console with the Security Configuration and Analysis snap-in and have used that console to import the security settings from a security template. This will enable you to determine how close your computer's current settings are to those in the template, as you will learn in the next section.

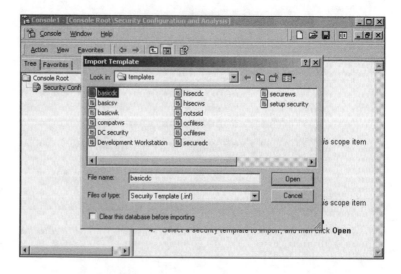

FIGURE 8.23
Click on the security template whose settings should be used as the basis for analyzing the local computer and click Open.

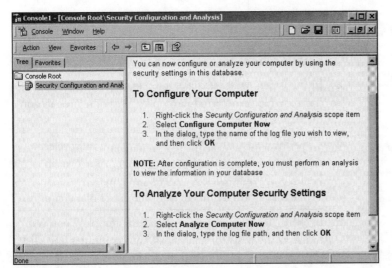

FIGURE 8.24
After importing a template, you can use it to configure your computer's security settings or to analyze your settings using the template as a point of comparison.

Analyzing Your Computer Using Security Configuration and Analysis

Analyzing a computer's security settings means comparing the current configuration of the computer to the desired configuration as stored in a security template. The tool used is the Security Configuration and Analysis MMC snap-in. You can compare security settings against a template to make sure the computer's settings are in compliance with a corporate security policy or to determine whether the settings have changed since the last time you performed the analysis.

To analyze a computer's security, perform the steps included in Step by Step 8.6.

STEP BY STEP

8.6 Analyzing a Computer's Security Configuration Using Security Configuration and Analysis

1. Log on to your Windows 2000 computer as Administrator and open the Security Configuration and Analysis MMC console you created in Step by Step 8.5.

continues

continued

2. Right-click Security Configuration and Analysis and select Open database.

3. In the Open database dialog box, locate the name of the database file you created in Step by Step 8.5, click it, and then click Open.

4. To perform an analysis of your system, you must select a security template to use as a comparison. As shown in Figure 8.25, right-click Security Configuration and Analysis and select Import Template from the list of menu choices.

5. In the dialog box presented, select the template you want to use as the basis for analysis of your computer and click Open. As previously mentioned, choose a template that closely matches the desired settings.

6. To perform the analysis, right-click Security Configuration and Analysis and select Analyze Computer Now, as shown in Figure 8.26.

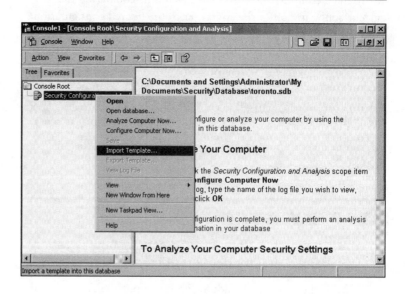

FIGURE 8.25
Right-click Security Configuration and Analysis and choose Import Template to import a template to be used as the basis for analysis.

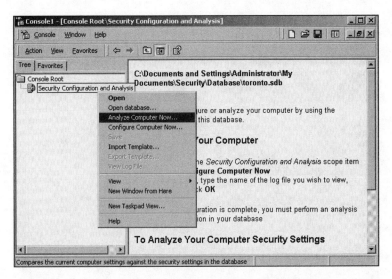

7. You are prompted to select the location of an error log file that might be generated during the analysis process (see Figure 8.27). Keep the default path or choose another one you desire and then click OK.

8. The analysis of the computer's security settings begins and you are presented with the Analyzing System Security progress dialog box, as shown in Figure 8.28.

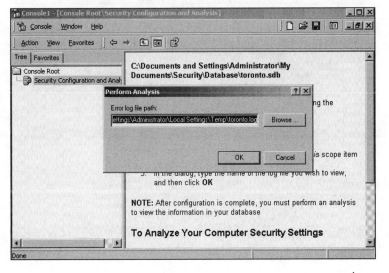

FIGURE 8.27
Choose a path and filename for the analysis error log file.

continues

continued

FIGURE 8.28
As analysis proceeds, the Analyzing System
Security dialog box shows status information.

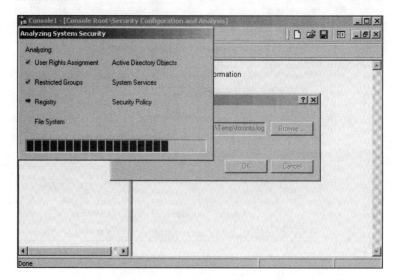

9. After the analysis has been completed, the console appearance changes to show all the areas that were included in
the template and compared against current computer settings, as shown in Figure 8.29. You have a number of
choices available at this point.

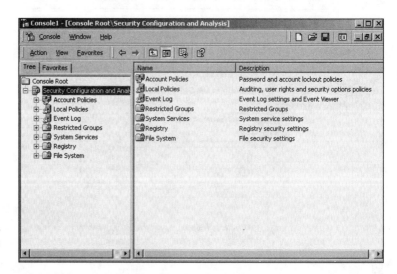

FIGURE 8.29
After the analysis is completed, all security settings in the template will be visible in the MMC
console.

10. To view the analysis log file, right-click Security Configuration and Analysis and make sure the View Log File menu option is checked. As shown in Figure 8.30, the display in the details pane now changes to show the log file. You can review the log file to determine whether any serious errors occurred during the analysis.

11. To review the results of the analysis and to see how the computer settings compare to the database settings, expand the area you want to compare and click it, as shown in Figure 8.31.

For example, to determine the differences between the computer's settings and those in the database (that is, the settings in the template used for comparison) for the Password Policy, you would expand Account Policies and then click Password Policy. The details pane would have three columns: Policy, for the name of the setting; Database Setting, the template setting in the database based on the template you imported; and Computer Setting, the current running configuration of the system.

12. Review the analysis to get a full picture of how closely your system resembles the template and where changes need to be made. Close the MMC console when finished.

NOTE

Analyzing Many Computers In situations in which frequent analysis of a large number of computers is required, Windows 2000 provides a command-line utility called SECEDIT. This utility can be passed the database filename, log location, and other parameters specified within Security Configuration and Analysis. The utility performs the security analysis as you did in the MMC, but you still need to use the Security Configuration and Analysis snap-in to view the results of the analysis.

The command-line SECEDIT.EXE utility can be of value in environments in which scheduling the analysis to occur at off-peak hours is useful. In fact, it is primarily intended to be used through the Task Scheduler and not from the command prompt per se. Administrators can configure a central location for database files for many computers and then also have the results placed there. Following the overnight analysis, the administrator can review each of the database's contents using the Security Configuration and Analysis snap-in to determine whether problems exist.

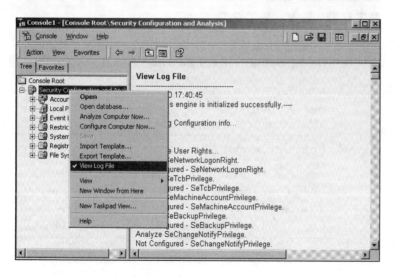

FIGURE 8.30
To view the analysis log file, right-click Security Configuration and Analysis and select View Log File.

FIGURE 8.31
After analysis is complete, you can compare template settings to the actual running settings of the computer.

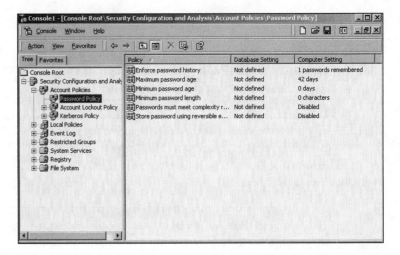

Configuring a Computer with Security Settings

Using Security Configuration and Analysis, you can take the results of analysis and then determine whether template settings are properly configured. Through Security Configuration and Analysis, you can also apply security templates settings to the local computer. To do this, perform the following steps in Step by Step 8.7.

STEP BY STEP

8.7 Configuring a Computer with Security Settings Using Security Configuration and Analysis

1. Log on to your Windows 2000 computer as Administrator and open the Security Configuration and Analysis MMC console you created in Step by Step 8.5.

2. Right-click Security Configuration and Analysis and select Open database.

3. In the Open database dialog box, locate the name of the database file you previously created or create a new database to hold the template settings and then click Open.

4. To configure your computer with the template settings you have just loaded or those stored in the database, right-click Security Configuration and Analysis and select Configure Computer Now from the list of menu choices (see Figure 8.32).

5. In the dialog box presented, select the location of the error log file for the configuration and click OK, as shown in Figure 8.33.

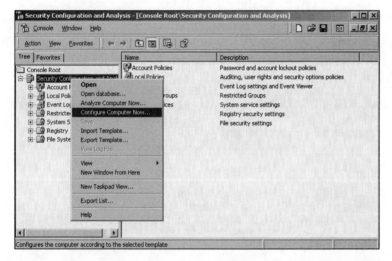

FIGURE 8.32
Right-click Security Configuration and Analysis and select Configure Computer Now to apply template settings to the computer.

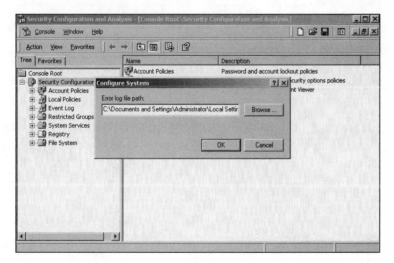

FIGURE 8.33
An error log path and filename must be specified prior to configuration of the computer commencing.

continues

continued

6. Just as you saw with the analysis process, configuration of the computer presents a status screen, as shown in Figure 8.34, to provide you with progress information on the application of security settings on the local computer. When finished, the Security Configuration and Analysis MMC console screen no longer has the different settings displayed.

7. After configuration is complete, you can review the results by looking at the log file as you did for analysis (see Figure 8.35).

8. Close the MMC console when finished.

FIGURE 8.34
As configuration proceeds, a status screen shows you progress.

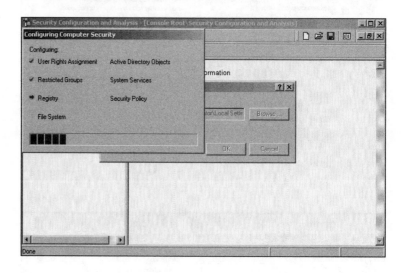

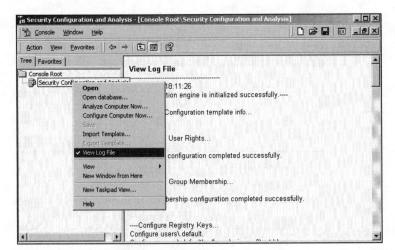

Exporting Security Settings into a Template File

One of the other features of Security Configuration and Analysis is the capability to export current settings presented within the console into a security template file. In this way, you can take the configuration of an existing system and export it to a template that can be imported into other systems or applied using Group Policy.

To export a security configuration into a security template using Security Configuration and Analysis, follow Step by Step 8.8.

STEP BY STEP

8.8 Exporting Security Settings and Creating a Security Template Using Security Configuration and Analysis

1. Log on to your Windows 2000 computer as Administrator and open the Security Configuration and Analysis MMC console you created in Step by Step 8.5.

2. Right-click Security Configuration and Analysis and select Open database.

continues

continued

3. In the Open database dialog box, locate the name of the database file holding the computer settings you want to export and then click Open.

4. To export the computer configuration into a security template file, right-click Security Configuration and Analysis and then select Export Template, as shown in Figure 8.36.

5. In the Export Template To dialog box shown in Figure 8.37, type the name of the template file you want to create and then click OK. If you need to change the folder location of the file, modify this using the Save in drop-down list box.

6. Close the MMC console when finished.

Although Security Configuration and Analysis is a useful tool to analyze, apply, and export a single computer's security settings, the simple fact that it only works on one computer at a time can be problematic for administrators of large Windows 2000 networks. Another method that can be used to apply security settings to a number of computers is Group Policy.

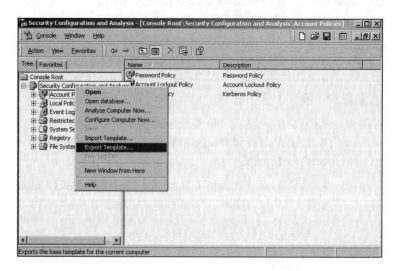

FIGURE 8.36
Right-click Security Configuration and Analysis and select Export Template to export the current computer settings into a security template file.

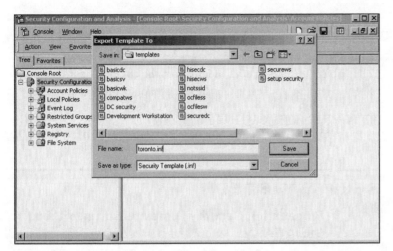

FIGURE 8.37
Specify the location and filename of the security template you are creating in the Export Template To dialog box.

Using Group Policy to Apply Security Settings

As you have seen in previous chapters, Group Policy is an Active Directory object that can be used to apply a large number of configuration settings to a collection of objects located within an Active Directory container such as an OU, domain, or site. Just as you can use Group Policy to apply Administrative Template settings or software deployment to a number of computers within an Active Directory container at one time, the same holds true for security settings.

When applying security settings to computers using Group Policy, you still make use of templates. Group Policy has default templates that have no preconfigured settings and can be modified manually. It is a better approach to create a template file and then import it into Group Policy to make sure all settings that are required to conform to a corporate security policy are properly defined. This also enables the administrator to create and test security settings outside of Group Policy (for example, using Security Configuration and Analysis) before rolling them out to a large number of computers on the domain, OU, or site level.

To apply security policies for an Active Directory container using Group Policy, you import one or more security templates into security settings in Group Policy. Importing a security template into a Group Policy object ensures that all members of the container automatically have the settings applied when the Group Policy propagates.

To apply security settings using Group Policy and to import a security template into a GPO, follow the steps presented in Step by Step 8.9.

STEP BY STEP

8.9 Propagating Security Template Settings Using Group Policy

1. Log on to your Windows 2000 computer as Administrator and start the MMC console where the Group Policy object whose security settings you want to modify is located (either Active Directory Users and Computer or Active Directory Sites and Services).

2. Right-click the container whose GPO will be modified to apply security settings and click Properties.

3. Click the Group Policy tab and select the GPO that will have security settings propagated to objects within its scope. Click Edit to open the Group Policy Editor.

4. Expand Computer Configuration (or User Configuration if changing user security elements), Windows Settings, and then Security Settings to show the areas that can be modified (see Figure 8.38). You can modify the settings manually here, although they will not be saved as a security template. You can import an existing template and have its settings applied within the GPO.

5. To import a security template's settings, right-click Security Settings and choose Import Policy, as shown in Figure 8.39.

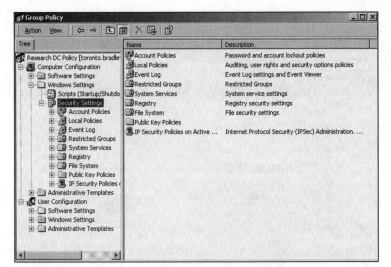

FIGURE 8.38
Expand Windows Settings and then Security Settings in the Computer Configuration container of the Group Policy Editor to see which security settings can be applied.

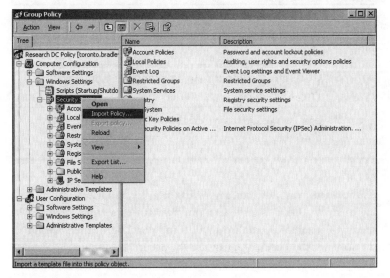

FIGURE 8.39
Right-click Security Settings and choose Import Policy to import a security template into the GPO.

6. In the Import Policy From dialog box presented (see Figure 8.40), locate the path and filename of the security template you want to apply and then click Open. The security template settings will be imported, and you will be returned to the Group Policy Editor. At this point, you might want to review the settings to make sure they are as you expect and as specified in the template.

continues

continued

FIGURE 8.40
Locate the security template you want to import and Click Open.

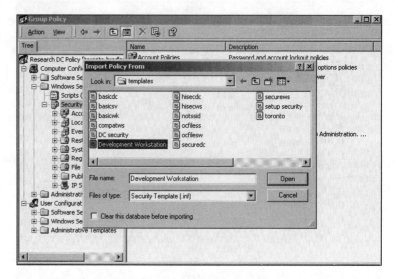

7. When finished, close the Group Policy Editor to save your changes.

8. Click OK to close the Active Directory Container Properties dialog box.

9. Exit Active Directory Users and Computers (or Active Directory Sites and Services) when finished.

As the discussion indicates, importing security templates and applying them in a GPO is quite straightforward. The settings included in the template are now applied to all computers and/or users within the scope of the GPO. You can use the Security Configuration and Analysis MMC snap-in to verify settings on individual computers.

Windows 2000 provides the administrator with a great deal of flexibility in implementing a security policy for both users and computers. As you have seen, Security Templates enable you to configure the settings that should be in place for a computer or user. Security Configuration and Analysis enables you to compare the currently running settings to those in a template, enabling you to compare the current security settings against those that should be in place (that is, those in the security template). To implement the same security settings on a number of different computers or for a number of users, you can make use of Group Policy to assign those settings at the site, domain, or OU level.

CONFIGURING AND IMPLEMENTING AN AUDIT POLICY

Configure and troubleshoot security in a directory services infrastructure.

- **Implement an audit policy.**

As you have seen, you can configure a security policy either in Security Configuration and Analysis or by using Group Policy. One very important element that must be considered is tracking security-related events to determine whether your settings are effective and to thus prevent unauthorized access to resources.

Security auditing policy is a portion of security policy that enables you to configure which security-related events to monitor or have the potential to monitor. By monitoring these security-related system events, you are able to detect attempts by intruders to compromise data on the system or to gain access to resources they should not be able to reach.

When you perform auditing, you are tracking user and operating system activities, or events, on a computer. This information is stored in the security log of Event Viewer. Each entry, or record, in the security log consists of the action performed, the user who performed the action, and whether the action was successful.

The events to be audited are configured in an audit policy, which is a component of security policy. As mentioned, an audit policy can be configured within the Security Settings of Group Policy or by using Security Configuration and Analysis to configure which events to monitor on a single computer. The events that can be monitored and may be part of the audit policy are quite diverse. The following table lists the types of events. For each event, you can track the success or failure.

Event	*Description*
Account logon	Account logon events take place on a domain controller and deal with the domain controller receiving a request to validate a user account. This is different from the logon event, which is discussed later in this table. This type of event takes place when a user attempts to log on to a computer and specifies a domain-level logon account. When the domain controller receives a request from the client machine to log on to the network, an account logon event is said to have occurred. It should be noted that computers as well as users can request account logon.
Account management	An account management event occurs when an administrator creates, changes, or deletes a user account or group. It is also used to track an administrator renaming, disabling, enabling, or modifying the password of a user account.
	Using this event, you can track changes to users and groups within the site, domain, or OU. This event can also be used to track changes in local users and groups on Windows 2000 Server and Windows 2000 Professional computers.
Directory services access	This event tracks user access to a specific Active Directory object. Enabling this audit event in Windows 2000 does not automatically turn on tracking of access to all Active Directory objects. You must specify which users and groups should have access to a specific Active Directory container tracked by modifying entries in the Auditing tab of the Advanced Security settings for an Active Directory object.
Logon	The logon event is triggered when a user logs on to or logs off of a local computer. It can also be used to track network access to a computer because connecting through the network to a machine requires the user to log on to establish the connection. Logon events take place on the computer where access is required, in contrast to Account Logon events, which always occur on domain controllers.
Object access	Object access events include a user attempting to gain access to a file or folder on an NTFS partition or to a printer. Enabling the object access event, such as directory service access, does not turn it on automatically for the computer; rather, it turns on the possibility of auditing for files and printers on the machine. To specify which files, folders, and printers will be audited, you would modify the security settings of the object for which you want to track access.
Policy change	The policy change event tracks success or failure on attempts to change user security options such as password policy, user rights assignment, account lockout settings, or audit policies. In other words, this series of events tracks changes to security settings on the computer or GPO including which events to audit.

Event	*Description*
Privilege use	Privilege use events track the use of certain privileges and user rights by an individual. These include taking ownership of a file or folder, changing the system time, loading and unloading device drivers, and modifying quotas. With the exception of logon and logoff rights and events that affect the Windows 2000 security log, such as shutting down or restarting the computer, this event can be used to track almost all the user rights that can be assigned.
Process tracking	This event is used to track the execution of processes on the system. This includes invoking and stopping an application as well as which other programs an application itself opened. Generally, you would not turn on process tracking unless you were a programmer and wanted to see the flow of execution of your programs and process identification information tracked by Windows 2000.
System	This event deals with the user shutting down or restarting the computer. Other events include anything that would affect the security elements of Windows 2000, such as clearing out the security log in Event Viewer, or other security-related settings on the computer.

Looking at the preceding table, you should now understand that it is possible to track almost any action taken on a system, should one desire to do so. Generally, however, too much auditing is not recommended. Auditing can severely impact the performance of the target system. On the other hand, although no auditing is great for performance, it provides no information on any attempts to gain access to resources by intruders. The ideal amount of auditing is the fine line between performance and security and is different for each organization. Planning is the key.

Planning an Audit Policy

When deciding whether to implement an audit policy and to what extent, planning is the most important aspect of the decision. As previously stated, too much auditing can bring systems to a crawl and can cause users to perceive the network and their machines as being too slow to perform their jobs. On the other hand, too little or no auditing can leave systems vulnerable to threats and can help rather than hinder an intruder. The general rule of thumb is to audit only those events that make sense in your environment.

When planning an audit policy, consider the following guidelines:

◆ **Determine which computers should have auditing configured.** Auditing can be turned on or off for individual computers; therefore, you should determine which ones should have the success or failure of user actions tracked. For example, file servers and domain controllers, which contain sensitive or critical data, are good candidates for auditing. However, users' desktop computers, except in very high-security environments such as national security agencies, the military, or certain parts of financial institutions, should probably not be audited. These computers normally do not contain sensitive or critical data. As always, exceptions can be found and should be treated as such.

◆ **Determine the types of events to audit for each computer.** Some computers should have certain types of events audited that might not apply to other computers. For example, domain controllers are great candidates for the auditing of account logon, account management, and directory service access events. Windows 2000 servers are more likely to have file and folder access, as well as Privilege use events, tracked. All computers may be good candidates for System (startup and shutdown) and Logon events tracking. For each computer, evaluate which events make sense to be tracked on the target computer.

◆ **Do you need to track successful access to or use of a resource, failure to do so, or both?** Obviously, tracking both provides more data, but will this data be useful information or just make it more difficult to locate attempts to bypass security settings on the computer? Success and failure together can be used for resource planning, while failure alone can alert you to possible breaches of security.

◆ **Determine for which objects and users you want to track events.** As previously outlined, some events, such as object (file, folder, and printer) access and directory service access, need to be configured for the object in question as well as the users whose access you want to monitor. Tracking success and failure by the Everyone system group includes all users but might, once again, provide too much data and not much useful information. You need to decide which users and for which objects you want to monitor access.

◆ **Determine whether you need to track usage trends over time.** If so, this requires that you archive security logs on a regular basis and maintain them for longer periods. This won't necessarily have an impact on what you decide to monitor; rather, it will introduce another administrative element into the equation. Factors involved include how long to keep the logs, where to keep them, whether they should be rolled up periodically to track trends, and how this should be done.

◆ **Review the logs frequently and regularly.** Configuring an audit policy and never looking at the security logs is about as useful as winning the lottery but failing to cash in the winning ticket. It might make you feel good to know you have the winning ticket, but it won't let you have the $10 million. In making sure everything is running as it should be, administrators need to check the logs on a regular basis (daily is good) and be on the lookout for any events that should not be there.

A lengthy planning process focusing on auditing has resulted in the agreement of management and everyone else involved. Now that you have determined what auditing needs to occur, you need to implement the policy.

Setting Up an Audit Policy

In setting up an audit policy, you can use one of two tools, depending on the scope of the policy. To configure an audit policy for a single computer, you can make use of the Security Configuration and Analysis snap-in on the local machine where the policy is to be implemented. However, doing so only ensures that the audit policy affects that one machine and might not provide as much value as having similar settings applied to a whole range of machines.

To configure an audit policy for several machines at once, you can make use of Group Policy. To set an audit policy using Group Policy, follow the steps outlined in Step by Step 8.10.

STEP BY STEP

8.10 Configuring an Audit Policy Using Group Policy

1. Log on to your Windows 2000 computer as Administrator and start the MMC console on which the Group Policy object for which you want to configure an audit policy is located (either Active Directory Users and Computer or Active Directory Sites and Services).

2. Right-click the container whose GPO will be modified to install an audit policy and click Properties.

3. Click the Group Policy tab and select the GPO that will have security settings propagated to objects within its scope. Click Edit to open the Group Policy Editor.

4. Expand Computer Configuration, Windows Settings, Security Settings, and then Local Policies to show the areas of the system to which the audit policy can be applied (see Figure 8.41).

5. Select the type of event to audit and double-click to open the setting definition dialog box, as shown in Figure 8.42.

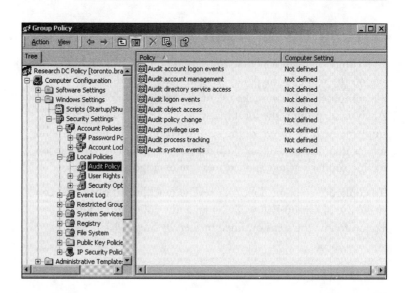

FIGURE 8.41

Expand Windows Settings, Security Settings, and then Local Policies in the Computer Configuration container of the Group Policy Editor to configure an audit policy.

6. Click the Define these policy settings check box and select whether to audit Success, Failure, or both for the event by checking the appropriate check box(es). Click OK to save your changes. The Group Policy Editor will reflect your changes, as shown in Figure 8.43.

7. Repeat steps 5 and 6 for any additional events you want to audit. When finished, close the Group Policy Editor.

8. Click OK to close the Active Directory Container Properties dialog box.

9. Exit Active Directory Users and Computers.

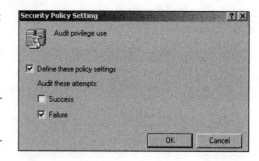

FIGURE 8.42
Double-click the event where you want to configure auditing to open the Security Policy Setting dialog box.

As you can see, setting up auditing is quite simple. Remember, however, that for object access and directory service access, you still need to configure which objects (files, folders, or printers) or Active Directory containers you want to monitor access to and by whom.

Auditing Access to Resources

After you have configured the audit policy to audit object access or Directory Service access, you need to perform additional steps and perform more planning to ensure that events on key resources are monitored. These resources include file system objects, printer objects, and Active Directory objects.

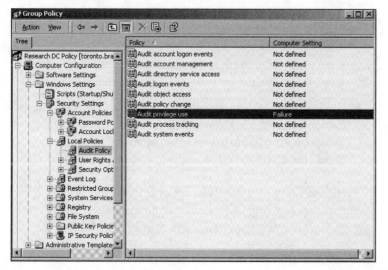

FIGURE 8.43
Changing event configuration for auditing is immediately reflected in the Group Policy Editor.

Auditing Access to File System Objects

When you configure auditing on file system files and folders, you are doing so for files and folders on NTFS file systems only. Auditing of files on FAT or FAT32 file systems is not available; these file systems do not provide any type of security, which is required for auditing.

When you specify auditing on file system objects, keep the following in mind:

◆ Audit failure events for Read operations on critical or sensitive files to determine which users are attempting to gain access to files for which they have no permissions.

◆ Audit success and failure for Delete operations on confidential or archival files to monitor which users might be attempting malicious activities and to track which files were deleted by which users.

◆ Audit success and failure operations for Change Permissions and Take Ownership permission usage for confidential and personal files of users. These events might indicate that someone is trying to change security settings on files to which he does not have access to gain access to data to which he does not currently have the rights. This also records an Administrator taking ownership of a user's file or modifying permissions on a file so he or she can gain access. Even though Administrators might be able to cover their tracks a little better than most, the event is still recorded in the log.

◆ Audit success and failure of all events performed by members of the Guests group. This should be done on the folders to which Guests should not have access. You can verify that no attempts by unauthorized users took place and, if they did, when they occurred (so you can locate a pattern).

◆ Audit file and folder access (both success and failure) on all computers containing shared data that should normally be secured. This way, shared folder activities can be tracked to make sure no unwanted attempts to breach security were made.

To specify auditing on a particular file or folder on an NTFS partition, after enabling Object access auditing (success and failure), perform the following steps detailed in Step by Step 8.11.

STEP BY STEP

8.11 Configuring Auditing on Files and Folders

1. Log on to your Windows 2000 computer as an Administrator and start Windows Explorer from the Accessories program group.

2. Locate the folder or file on an NTFS partition that you want to audit access for and right-click and select Properties. You are presented with a dialog box similar to Figure 8.44.

3. Click the Security tab to show current permissions, as shown in Figure 8.45.

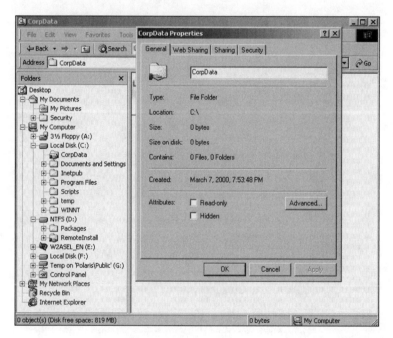

FIGURE 8.44
Selecting Properties for the NTFS folder whose access you want to audit presents this dialog box.

continues

continued

FIGURE 8.45
The Security tab of the NTFS folder shows
currently assigned permissions.

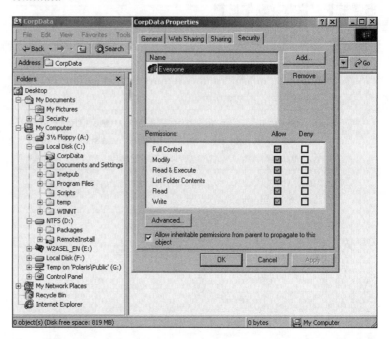

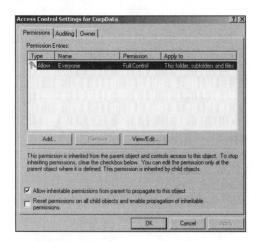

FIGURE 8.46
Clicking on the Advanced button opens the
Access Control Settings dialog box.

4. Click the Advanced button to go to advanced security configuration, as shown in Figure 8.46.

5. Click the Auditing tab to display the currently configured auditing settings for the folder, as shown in Figure 8.47.

6. Click the Add button and select a group or user for whom you want to monitor activity to this folder. After making a selection, you are presented with a dialog box, similar to Figure 8.48, that enables you to specify for which events you want to audit successful or failed access.

Note that you can use the Apply onto drop-down list box to determine whether these auditing settings should be applied to this folder only, this folder and its children, or other combinations.

7. Make your selection by checking the appropriate boxes under Success or Failure and click OK when finished.

8. Repeat steps 6 and 7 to add more groups and users and configure their auditing settings.

9. After you have made your choices, you are returned to the Access Control Settings dialog box. Click Apply and then OK to save your changes.

10. Exit Windows Explorer if you are finished. Otherwise, repeat the preceding steps for any other folders and files for which you need to configure auditing.

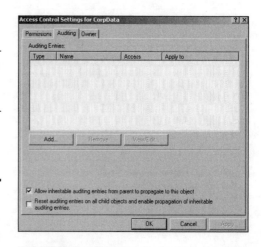

FIGURE 8.47
The Auditing tab lists the currently configured auditing options for the folder.

As the preceding Step by Step shows, it is necessary to use Windows Explorer to enable auditing on the particular files and folders you want to track. This process might take some time to configure all audit settings for all files and folders of a sensitive nature, but it can be critical to ensuring proper secure operation of your network.

Auditing Access to Printer Objects

You can configure auditing on printer objects to track usage as well as to determine whether attempts to make use of sensitive printers (for example, MICR printers that can be used to create checks) are taking place. Although most printers do not require auditing, those that are specialized or expensive to run, such as high-end color laser printers, might require some auditing.

When auditing printers, use these guidelines:

◆ Audit failure events for Print operations on sensitive printers such as those used to print or encode sensitive company documents or preprinted forms. For example, a record store using printers to create gift certificates might want to limit access to the printer that has the gift certificate stock in it.

◆ Audit failure and success for Print operations on expensive printers so you can track usage and possibly use this information to charge back costs to a department or user.

◆ Audit success and failure events for use of Full Control permissions on all printers to track administrative changes to the printer. This includes updating the printer driver as well as creating and removing shares.

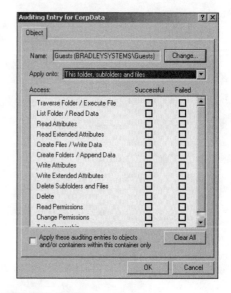

FIGURE 8.48
Selecting a group or user opens the Auditing Entry selection dialog box, enabling you to select which events for this NTFS folder to audit the success or failure of.

◆ Audit success events on Delete permissions on commonly used printers so that purging of documents can be seen as an administrative correction rather than printer failure.

◆ Audit success and failure events on Change Permissions and Take Ownership permissions on sensitive printers to have a record of who was assigned or removed from the access control list for the printer. In this way, you can determine whether an administrator might have inadvertently given permissions to a user who should not have them and can track security breaches.

To specify auditing on a printer, after enabling Object access auditing (success and failure), perform the following steps shown in Step by Step 8.12.

STEP BY STEP

8.12 Configuring Auditing on Printers

1. Log on to your Windows 2000 computer as an Administrator and click Start, Settings, and then Printers. You will be shown a list of printers on the machine similar to those in Figure 8.49.

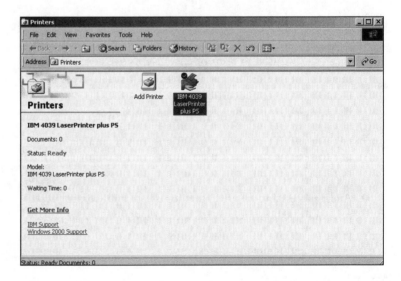

FIGURE 8.49
Selecting Printers from the Settings menu displays printers installed on the computer.

2. Right-click the printer for which you want to enable auditing and select Properties. As shown in Figure 8.50, the printer Properties dialog box displays.

3. Click the Security tab and then the Advanced button to bring up the Access Control Settings dialog box, as shown in Figure 8.51.

4. Click the Auditing tab of the Access Control Settings dialog box to see a list of auditing entries for the printer.

5. To add an entry, click the Add button. You will be prompted to select the user or group whose printer actions you want to audit, as shown in Figure 8.52.

6. After selecting the user or group whose actions you want to audit, the Auditing Entry dialog box is presented (see Figure 8.53). Select the actions you want to audit and click OK when finished.

Note that you can apply your auditing actions to the printer and documents, the printer only, or documents only.

It is also important to note that auditing the Print permission also requires auditing the Read permissions because users need to be able to locate the printer to print to it.

7. Repeat steps 5 and 6 to add more groups and users and configure their auditing settings.

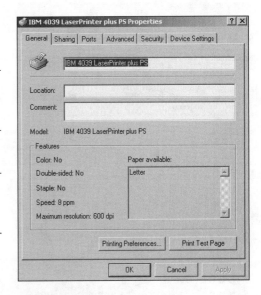

FIGURE 8.50
The printer Properties dialog box opened by right-clicking the printer and selecting Properties.

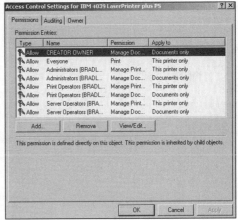

FIGURE 8.51
The Access Control Settings dialog box is opened by clicking Advanced from the Security tab in the printer Properties dialog box.

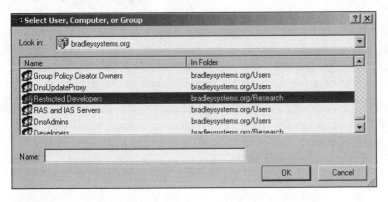

FIGURE 8.52
Clicking the Auditing tab and then Add enables you to insert additional auditing entries for the printer.

continues

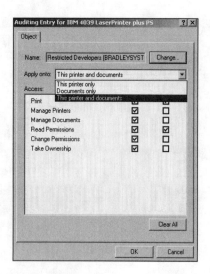

FIGURE 8.53
Selecting Printers from the Settings menu displays printers installed on the computer.

continued

8. After you have made your choices, you are returned to the Access Control Settings dialog box. Click Apply and then OK to save your changes.

9. Click OK to exit the printer Properties dialog box.

10. Close the Printers folder if you are finished. Otherwise, repeat the preceding steps for any other printers for which you need to configure auditing.

Similar to files and folders, auditing access to printers requires that you specify which actions should be audited for which users and on which printers. It is a good idea to audit access to very specific or critical printers (such as check-printing printers or expensive color printers) but not to basic printers used by everyone or those on a user's desk.

Auditing Access to Active Directory Objects

When you configure auditing on Active Directory objects, you are able to track changes, or even simply read access, to a component of Active Directory. The objects that can be tracked are virtually everything in Active Directory.

When auditing Active Directory object access, be sure to audit both the success and failure for critical objects such as user accounts and any groups whose membership is sensitive. You should do this for all administrative users and especially for those to whom you might have delegated control of an Active Directory object. This enables you to determine whether any of the individuals entrusted with maintaining parts of your network infrastructure are attempting to gain more access than they have been assigned.

To audit Active Directory object access, set the audit policy to track directory service access and use. Enable auditing of the object by using the appropriate MMC console such as Active Directory Users and Computers, Active Directory Sites and Services, or Active Directory Domains and Trusts. For example, to enable auditing for the Users container in Active Directory, perform the steps described in Step by Step 8.13.

STEP BY STEP

8.13 Configuring Auditing on Active Directory Objects

1. Log on to your Windows 2000 computer as an Administrator and open Active Directory Users and Computers from the Administrative Tools program group.

2. Expand your domain, right-click the container for which you want to configure auditing (such as the Users container), and select Properties.

3. From the Properties screen, click the Security tab and select Advanced. A screen similar to Figure 8.54 is displayed.

   If the Advanced option is not available, click the View menu in the MMC console and choose Advanced to enable the viewing of advanced options within the console.

4. Click the Auditing tab to see a list of current auditing entries. To add a new entry, click the Add button and select a user or group to audit, as shown in Figure 8.55.

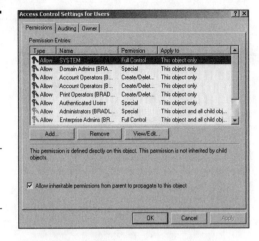

FIGURE 8.54
The Access Control Settings dialog box for the Active Directory Users container enables you to access the audit settings for the Active Directory object.

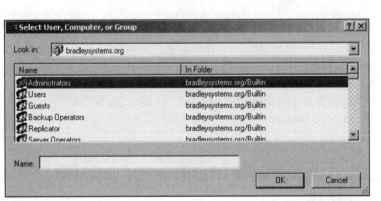

FIGURE 8.55
Clicking the Auditing tab displays a list of current auditing entries.

continues

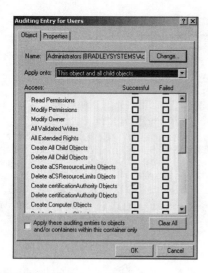

FIGURE 8.56
Adding an audit entry to an Active Directory object presents a long list of possible actions that can be tracked.

NOTE

Focus Auditing at Precise Levels Be careful when applying auditing to all objects and children. This might create auditing entries for a great many objects if set at a very high container in Active Directory. It is usually a good idea to focus auditing of Active Directory objects only at the precise levels required and not allow it to propagate throughout the whole structure.

---

continued

5. From the dialog box presented, select the action you want to audit, success or failure, and the scope to apply the auditing to, as shown in Figure 8.56. Click OK when finished to save your changes.

Note that Active Directory objects have many different permissions that can be audited such as Create Computer Objects or Delete Contact Objects. Active Directory objects can have more permissions than you have seen in either files and folders or printers.

6. If you have completed configuring audit settings for the object, click Apply and then OK to close the Access Control Settings dialog box. If not, add the necessary entries and then exit the dialog box.

7. Click OK to close the Properties dialog box.

8. If you want to audit additional objects, repeat steps 2 through 7 for those containers or objects. When finished, exit Active Directory Users and Computers.

One of the wonderful features of Windows 2000 for administrators is the flexibility and control provided by Active Directory. However, ensuring that only those individuals that need it have access to a particular part of Active Directory is critical to ensuring that it operates properly. Configuring of auditing for access to Active Directory objects, as shown in the Step by Step, enables you to track improper attempts at access.

Reviewing and Monitoring Security Events

Monitor and analyze security events.

After configuring an audit policy, it is of no use to simply let it run without checking to see if there are any events of concern. The whole point of auditing actions is to be able to review and analyze them later; not doing so makes auditing pointless and a waste of resources.

The tool you use to view security records is Event Viewer. You already were introduced to this tool in Chapter 5, "Managing Servers," and should be familiar with how it works. Audit entries are stored in the security log in Event Viewer in chronological order. Events are always stored in the machine local to where the event occurred, except for account logon events, which are stored in the security event log of the domain controller that processed the request. In other words, to see what activities have taken place, you need to review the log of the machine in which you are interested.

To view the security event log of a computer, you can use the Computer Management MMC console from Administrative Tools, or you can use the Event Viewer MMC console directly. For example, to view the security event log on your domain controller, follow the steps described in Step by Step 8.14.

STEP BY STEP

8.14 Reviewing Auditing Events Using Event Viewer

1. Log on to your Windows 2000 computer as an Administrator and open the Event Viewer MMC from the Administrative Tools program group.

2. On the screen displayed (see Figure 8.57), click the Security Log item in the left pane to see a list of audit entries.

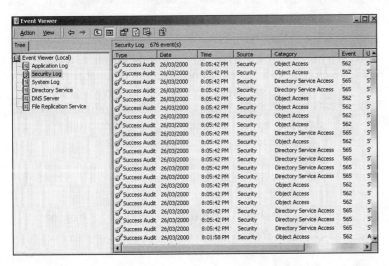

FIGURE 8.57
The Event Viewer security log contains a list of events audited on the local computer.

continues

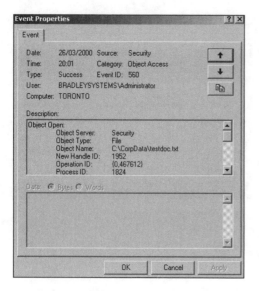

FIGURE 8.58
More detail about the action is visible by double-clicking the event and displaying the Event Properties dialog box.

continued

3. To get more details about the action that took place, double-click the individual entry in the details pane. You will be presented with an Event Properties dialog box, similar to the one in Figure 8.58.

4. Continue to review log entries as desired. When finished, exit Event Viewer.

Using Event Viewer to review any audit events that have occurred on a computer is the only way an administrator can tell whether the security settings implemented through Group Policy or Security Configuration and Analysis are working. By enabling auditing on those parts of Windows 2000 that have been configured through security templates, you are able to track any unauthorized attempts and determine who is trying to gain access to your network or computer. Furthermore, enabling auditing to track the success of an action also enables you to have a log of activity on parts of the system such as files or printers as well as Windows 2000 components such as Active Directory.

CASE STUDY: USING GROUP POLICY TO ENFORCE SECURITY REQUIREMENTS AT SUNSHINE BREWING

ESSENCE OF THE CASE

The CEO of Sunshine Brewing has just returned from a conference on business in the twenty-first century. While being wowed by the possibilities of e-commerce and its offerings, he was also introduced to the problem of ensuring safe transmission of data and protecting internal corporate assets from internal tampering. He has called you into his office to outline his concerns and to ask for your input on how to protect the network from external and internal tampering as well as how to track what is taking place.

Specifically, he is concerned about the following:

▶ He wants to track any authorized attempts to access servers on the intranet and extranet. He would like to know where these attempts are coming from and when as well as which user accounts are being used to attempt to gain access.

▶ He wants to have a historical record of all security-related events on all key servers in the organization, whether used for internal use only or for external access as well.

CASE STUDY: USING GROUP POLICY TO ENFORCE SECURITY REQUIREMENTS AT SUNSHINE BREWINGCASE

▶ He wants to make sure users have to log on to their workstations with a password, and he wants to make sure passwords are not reused over and over again. Users should have to change their password periodically (such as every month) and should not be able to reuse them for a year.

▶ For critical corporate servers, such as the main R&D server, accounting, customer service, and any machines where sensitive data is stored, the list of users who can administer these machines should be centrally controlled. The list of these servers will change from time to time, so it should be easy to modify the list of users.

▶ Any attempt to log on to the domain with a user account that fails three times within 30 minutes should lock the user out. Only administrators should be allowed to unlock the user account.

▶ Users in the R&D department will require smart cards to access their computers, and any removal of a smart card from the machine should log the user off immediately.

▶ The Telnet service on all critical servers should always be disabled, and the list of users who can log on locally to these servers needs to be centrally controlled.

He outlines the preceding and asks whether this can be accomplished with minimal overhead. You reply, "Absolutely." He gives you a week to come up with a plan and submit it to him.

SCENARIO

Ensuring that proper security policies are applied uniformly across an enterprise, or a portion thereof, is critical to the safe transmission and access of data. Being able to track who is attempting to use a resource without authorization, as well as having a method of verifying that the guardians of these policies are not abusing their position, is something that can be enforced using security templates in Group Policy. In this case study, you will see how Group Policy can be used to solve a specific problem at Sunshine Brewing.

ANALYSIS

The security requirements outlined by the CEO of Sunshine can all be accomplished through the use of Group Policy security settings. Because these can be applied at different levels of Active Directory and, through Group Policy filtering, to specific machines on the enterprise network, you feel confident.

Your first recommendation should be to create a domain audit policy that enables auditing of failure of account logon and logon events to track which user accounts are being used to attempt unauthorized access to key servers. This policy would be applied to a specific list of computers. This list could be kept in a global security group maintained by an administrator and with the GPO filtered to be applied to that security group only. In this way, other noncritical servers would not have their logon events audited. The Group Policy should have the No Override option enabled.

continues

CASE STUDY: USING GROUP POLICY TO ENFORCE SECURITY REQUIREMENTS AT SUNSHINE BREWING

continued

To maintain a historical record of security events, you can configure the event log settings, using the security policy for those key servers, to never overwrite the security log. You would naturally increase the log size using the GPO to a size (100MB or so) that would enable you to capture many events for those intervals between the clearing of the log file. You would also restrict guest access to the security log using the same policy and, for maximum security, configure the settings so the computer shuts down if the security log fills up. The GPO should be configured with No Override at the domain level.

Because the list of administrators for key corporate servers needs to be centrally controlled, you could create another GPO that would use the Restricted Groups portion of the security settings to add users to the SecureServerAdmins security group you create through the GPO. This GPO would also be applied to a list of specific servers and would be filtered so it does not restrict administration of other servers in the organization. The GPO should be created at the domain level and be configured with No Override.

For password enforcement, create another domain-level policy with the appropriate settings (maximum password age of 30 days and remember 12 passwords, for example). The policy should also have a minimum password age of at least 1 day to prevent users from changing their passwords in less than 12 days back to the original. Password length, although not specified, should be set to at least one character (although five or six might be a better length), so that users are required to have a password. This policy could also hold the account lockout settings of no more than three attempts within 30 minutes. The GPOs should also be configured with No Override so they are uniformly enforced throughout the company. They should be filtered to include all users.

It is possible to disable the Telnet service through the System Services portion of security settings. The policy should also be created at the domain level and be filtered to those servers considered critical.

Finally, to ensure that when an R&D user removes his or her smart card from the computer he or she is immediately logged off, configure the smart card removal behavior in the security options of local policies in a GPO at the R&D OU level. This automatically logs off the user when the card is removed.

Because you have implemented all these security requirements through GPOs, they can easily be centrally administered and will be applied throughout the domain, or at the OU level, as needed.

CHAPTER SUMMARY

In this chapter, you learned how to create a security policy and how to monitor the effectiveness of that security policy using auditing. It should be noted that auditing itself is a component of security policy and should be considered and planned while you are planning your security policy as a whole. (How would you know if your security policy works otherwise?)

In setting up a security policy, you can use one of two tools: the Security Configuration and Analysis MMC snap-in or Group Policy within Active Directory. Security Configuration and Analysis enables you to configure the security policy for the local computer. It also enables you to retrieve current security settings for the computer and compare them against a security template containing a preconfigured collection of security settings. In this way, you are able to compare your computer's current security configuration settings with the list of desired ones contained in the template. You can also export your current security settings on the computer to a template using Security Configuration and Analysis. Finally, you can import a security template into Security Configuration and Analysis and then apply its settings against your computer to enable a local policy.

To apply a security policy against several computers at the same time, you can make use of Group Policy. It should be noted once again that computers can be members of security groups in Windows 2000, and the easiest way to apply the same settings to a number of computers is to add them to a security group. Like other Group Policy settings, once configured, a security policy applies to all machines within the scope of the Group Policy. In this way, you can apply the same security configuration at the same time to computers with sensitive information and be sure that the security configuration will take effect. When using Group Policy to apply and configure a security policy, you also import security templates and modify them as required. The template settings are applied to all machines within the scope of the policy. When using Group Policy to enforce a security policy, the same rules regarding Group Policy inheritance and filtering still apply.

KEY TERMS

- Active Directory
- Audit policy
- Auditing
- Blocking policy inheritance
- Disk quotas
- GPO inheritance
- GPO scope
- Group Policy filtering
- Registry
- Security Configuration and Analysis
- Security template

CHAPTER SUMMARY

NOTE **Security and Usability** When deciding on the application of security settings to users and computers in Windows 2000, you should always create a balance between security and usability. What this means is that too high a level of security can make the system difficult for individuals to use; too little security can make it vulnerable to attack.

An example of too much security at the expense of usability is requiring the user to change his or her password each day. Users will get tired of changing their passwords and will often forget the newest password. This will make the system secure (nobody can get on) but will not provide good usability.

An example of insufficient security with great usability is not requiring passwords for users. This makes it easy for the individual to use the system but also leaves it completely vulnerable to attack by those who should not have access. Clearly, this is not a good solution.

The best configuration is one that provides good security with appropriate usability. What this exactly means depends on each situation and each company. Security should satisfy corporate requirements to minimize risk but should be aware of the user's legitimate need to have a workable system.

Security templates are text files with preset security configuration information that can imported into Security Configuration and Analysis and/or Group Policy. Windows 2000 ships with a number of default security templates providing preconfigured settings at various security levels from none to highly secure. When choosing a template, consider whether you need the level of protection provided and why you are making use of the protection. Security should only be as tight as required—no more, no less.

To determine whether your security configuration is working or if unauthorized access is being attempted on key resources, you can configure an audit policy. An audit policy is a subset of security policy and is configured using the same tools. The types of events that can be audited include file and folder access, logon and logoff activity, and use of privileges. When configuring auditing, it might be necessary to be more precise than simply configuring the audit policy using Group Policy or Security Configuration and Analysis. You might actually have to modify object permissions to further refine your audit policy. This is required for files and folders, printers, and Active Directory objects because turning auditing on for everything would present too high a level of overhead. When configuring auditing for these objects or in general, audit only as much as is required so as not to introduce too high an overhead on the system.

APPLY YOUR KNOWLEDGE

Exercises

The following exercises have you configure a security policy using Group Policy. A component of the security policy will be an audit policy. You will then verify whether your security and audit policy had the desired effect.

You will need a second computer that is a member of your domain on which to test the policy. This computer needs to belong to the Research OU you created in Chapter 6, "Using Group Policy to Manage Users."

8.1 Implementing a Security Policy for the Research OU

This exercise makes use of the groups and policies you have implemented in the exercises in Chapters 6 and 7. You will need a Research OU and a Restricted Developers security group.

Estimated time: 20 minutes.

To create a GPO for the security policy and set permissions for the policy, follow these steps:

1. If you have not already done so, log on to your computer as the Administrator for your domain.

2. Start Active Directory Users and Computers and expand your domain to reveal the Research OU.

3. Right-click the Research OU and select Properties.

4. In the Properties dialog box, select the Group Policy tab and click on New to add a new policy called Research Security Policy.

5. Click the Research Security Policy and then click Properties.

6. Click the Security tab and then click the Add button to add a new security entry. Add the Developers group and assign it Read and Apply Group Policy permission to the Research Security Policy. Also, make sure your computer to be used for logon testing (the computer name TORONTO, for example) is also assigned the Read and Apply Group Policy permission.

   If the Security tab is not available, click the View menu in the MMC console and choose Advanced to enable the viewing of advanced options within the console.

7. Click OK to save your changes.

8. Click Close to close the Research OU Properties dialog box.

To configure settings for the Research Security Policy, follow these steps:

1. Open Active Directory Users and Computers and locate the Research OU. Right-click the Research OU and select Properties.

2. Click the Group Policy tab and select the Research Security Policy. Click Edit to open the Group Policy Editor MMC console.

3. Expand Computer Configuration, Windows Settings, and then Security Settings.

4. Right-click Security Settings, select Import Policy, select BASICDC.INF as the Security Template to load, and then click Open.

5. Expand Account Policies and then click Account Lockout. In the details pane, double-click Account Lockout Duration.

APPLY YOUR KNOWLEDGE

6. In the Security Policy Setting dialog box, click Define this policy setting, set the duration to 5 minutes, and click OK. Notice that this also changes the values for the two other settings in Account Lockout.

7. Double-click Account lockout threshold, change the setting to 3 invalid logon attempts, and click OK.

8. Expand Local Policies and click Account Policy.

9. Double-click Audit account logon events and enable both success and failure tracking. Do the same for Audit logon events.

10. Close the Group Policy Editor MMC window. Notice that you will be prompted to save the template settings. Choose the default path indicated and click OK.

11. Click Close to exit the Research Properties dialog box and then exit Active Directory Users and Computers.

12. Restart Windows 2000.

8.2   Testing Security Policy

In this exercise, you will attempt to log on as TimC with an incorrect password to trigger the account lockout setting in the security policy. You will then log on as Administrator and review the Event Viewer security log to test the audit policy settings.

Estimated time: 20 minutes.

To trigger the account lockout in the security policy, follow these steps:

1. Attempt to log on to the domain from the second computer as user TimC with a password of Microsoft. The attempt should fail. If it does not, pick a different password and make sure it fails.

2. Continue to have invalid logons until the Group Policy kicks in and you are told your account is locked out.

3. On your domain controller, log on as a domain administrator.

4. Open Event Viewer from the Administrative Tools program group and select Security Log.

5. Review the entries in the log, starting at the top showing the administrator logging on and then further down indicating the lockout of the user.

6. Close Event Viewer and log off.

Review Questions

1. You want to ensure that only users of the MANAGERS security group are able to access files and folders on a server called CORPSECURE. You have not yet created the MANAGERS security group. The list of users who will be members of the managers group needs to be protected at all times, and the assignment of users to this group cannot be delegated to others. How can you accomplish this?

2. You suspect that co-op students hired by the software development department have been trying to gain access to the CORPSECURE server from the network. How can you determine whether this is the case?

3. Your company has just installed a new $35,000 color printer whose use should be limited to only the graphic arts department. You want to track any attempts to use this printer by others as well as which users in the graphic arts department make the greatest use of the printer. How would you accomplish this?

APPLY YOUR KNOWLEDGE

4. For what can you use Security Configuration and Analysis?

5. You want to ensure that all communication between Windows 2000 member servers in your finance department is encrypted. You also want to ensure that client computers in the finance department communicate with the payroll server in a secure manner. How would you accomplish this?

6. You need to configure the same audit policy for three Windows 2000 Server computers in the development department. You also want to enforce the same audit policy for a Windows 2000 member server in the quality assurance department. How can you accomplish this?

7. What is the default extension of the database files created by Security Configuration and Analysis?

8. You want to ensure that all users in your Windows 2000 domain change their passwords every 30 days. Members of the Sales Clerks OU do not need to change their passwords because they are assigned passwords by the IS department. How would you satisfy these requirements?

Exam Questions

1. You need to configure security settings that will be applied to several domain controllers within the Toronto site of your organization and to an additional three member servers in the New York site. Which Windows 2000 Administrative Tools would you use to accomplish your goals? (Choose all correct answers.)

   A. Security Configuration and Analysis

   B. Security Templates

   C. Active Directory Users and Computer

   D. Active Directory Sites and Services

   E. Active Directory Domains and Trusts

2. You need to track attempts to access files on a network share called SOURCECODE on the ENGINEERING member server in your domain. Which of the following tasks must you perform to accomplish your goals? (Choose all correct answers.)

   A. Audit logon activity on ENGINEERING.

   B. Audit file and folder access on SOURCE-CODE.

   C. Audit object access on the ENGINEERING.

   D. Audit directory access on ENGINEERING

   E. Audit file and folder access on ENGINEERING.

   F. Audit object access on SOURCECODE.

3. You have been asked to create a new security template that will be used to implement security settings on a number of machines in your organization. Most of the required settings exist in two other security templates called PasswordTemplate and AuditTemplate that were created by your predecessor. Several other settings do not exist in any templates and need to be specified.

   What steps must you perform to create the security template? (Choose four correct answers.)

   A. Open the Group Policy Editor and import the PasswordTemplate and AuditTemplate templates.

APPLY YOUR KNOWLEDGE

B. Open Security Configuration and Analysis and import the PasswordTemplate and AuditTemplate templates after creating a new database.

C. Use Security Configuration and Analysis to export the security database settings to a new security template.

D. Use Security Configuration and Analysis to analyze the computer against the security database.

E. Use the Group Policy Editor to modify the security settings to match those required.

F. Use Security Configuration and Analysis to modify the security settings to match those required.

G. Use Security Configuration and Analysis to manually create the template.

H. Use Security Configuration and Analysis to review the security settings for the PasswordTemplate and AuditTemplate templates after creating a new database.

I. Copy the PasswordTemplate and Audit-Template files to the NewTemplate file.

J. Use Security Configuration and Analysis to import the NewTemplate file after creating a new database.

4. Which of the following audit policy settings, when enabled, will by default not result in any audit entries in the security event log. (Choose two correct answers.)

A. Audit Object Access

B. Audit Logon Events

C. Audit System Events

D. Audit Directory Service Access

E. Audit Account Logon Events

F. Audit File and Print Access

5. You need to analyze the security configuration of all computers in the development and finance departments on a regular basis. What two tools would enable you to accomplish this in the most efficient manner? (Choose two correct answers.)

A. Active Directory Users and Computers

B. Task Scheduler

C. Windows Explorer

D. Security Configuration and Analysis

E. SECEDIT

F. NTDSUTIL

6. You want to keep track of the amount of time users spend logged on to the network. Which of the following audit events should you enable? (Choose the best answer.)

A. Audit account logon events - Success

B. Audit account management - Success

C. Audit account logon events - Failure

D. Audit logon events - Success

E. Audit logon events - Failure

F. Audit account management - Failure

APPLY YOUR KNOWLEDGE

7. The management of conciliar.com has decided that password policy maintenance should be determined by each area of the company. The only corporate requirement is that all users must have a password of at least five characters.

   The Active Directory structure of conciliar.com includes a top-level domain called conciliar.com and four additional subdomains called namerica.conciliar.com, europe.conciliar.com, samerica.conciliar.com, and specific.conciliar.com that have been created for administrative purposes. Because the migration to Windows 2000 has just recently been completed, no new Group Policy objects have been created yet.

   How would you configure Group Policy to enforce the corporate password policy setting while allowing all other elements of password management to be controlled locally? (Choose all correct answers.)

   A. Modify the default domain policy at the conciliar.com domain with the password settings.

   B. Create a GPO called Password Policy Settings in each domain with the password policy settings.

   C. Create a GPO at the conciliar.com domain called Password Policy Settings with the password policy settings.

   D. Link the Password Policy Settings GPO from the conciliar.com domain to each subdomain.

   E. Configure Block Policy Inheritance for the Password Policy Settings GPO.

   F. Move all users in the subdomains to the Users container of the conciliar.com domain.

   G. Configure No Override for the Password Policy Settings GPO.

   H. Configure No Override for the Default Domain Policy GPO at the conciliar.com domain.

8. You decide to implement an audit policy to satisfy the following requirements:

   - All user attempts to log on to the network must be audited.

   - Users failing to log on locally to the FINDATA file server should be tracked.

   - Actions by administrators to add, delete, and modify users in the default Users container should be tracked.

   - Any access to the Information Services OU in Active Directory should be tracked.

   - Any attempts by any member of the SalesPersons security group to access the Commissions folder on the SALESDATA file server should be tracked.

   To satisfy these requirements, you decide to perform the following tasks:

   - Create a GPO default domain audit policy at the domain level.

   - Assign the Apply Group Policy permission to Authenticated Users and leave all other permissions at their default settings for the default domain audit policy.

   - Configure the default domain audit policy to audit the success and failure of account logon events.

APPLY YOUR KNOWLEDGE

- Configure the default domain audit policy to audit the success and failure of account management events.

- Configure the default domain audit policy to audit the success of object access.

- Configure the default domain audit policy to audit the success and failure of directory service access.

Which of the outlined requirements were satisfied by your solution? (Choose all correct answers.)

A. All user attempts to log on to the network must be audited.

B. Users failing to log on locally to the FIND-ATA file server should be tracked.

C. Actions by administrators to add, delete, and modify users in the default Users container should be tracked.

D. Any access to the Information Services OU in Active Directory should be tracked.

E. Any attempts by any member of the SalesPersons security group to access the Commissions folder on the SALESDATA file server should be tracked.

9. You have configured auditing to satisfy the following requirements:

   - All user attempts to log on to the network must be audited.

   - Actions by administrators to add, delete, and modify users in the default Users container should be tracked.

   - Unsuccessful attempts to change Group Policy on the domain must be tracked.

- Users receiving an error when attempting to shut down a computer should be tracked.

- Failure of users to connect to the CONFIDENTIAL share on the EXECUTIVE member server should be tracked.

You configure an audit policy with the following settings:

Audit account logon events – Failure

Audit account management – Success, Failure

Audit directory services access – Not configured

Audit logon events – Success and Failure

Audit object access – Not configured

Audit policy change – Success and Failure

Audit privilege use – Not configured

Audit process tracking – Failure

Audit system events – Success and Failure

After putting these settings into effect by using Group Policy at the domain level, you notice that some aspects of what you want to track are not appearing in the security event log, and others you did not want to track are.

Which of the audit policy settings do you need to change to correct the problem? (Choose all that apply.)

A. Audit account logon events – Failure

B. Audit account management – Success, Failure

C. Audit directory services access – Not configured

D. Audit logon events – Success and Failure

E. Audit object access – Not configured

APPLY YOUR KNOWLEDGE

F. Audit policy change – Success and Failure

G. Audit privilege use – Not configured

H. Audit process tracking – Failure

I. Audit system events – Success and Failure

10. You decide to implement an audit policy to satisfy the following requirements:

    - All user attempts to log on to the network must be audited.

    - Users failing to log on locally to the FINDATA file server should be tracked.

    - Actions by administrators to add, delete, and modify users in the default Users container should be tracked.

    - Any access to the Information Services OU in Active Directory should be tracked.

    - Any attempts by any member of the SalesPersons security group to access the Commissions folder on the SALESDATA file server should be tracked.

    To satisfy these requirements, you decide to perform the following tasks:

    - Create a GPO called Default Domain Audit Policy at the domain level.

    - Assign the Apply Group Policy permission to Authenticated Users, FINDATA, and SALESDATA and deny the Apply Group Policy permission for the Domain Admins security group for the default domain audit policy.

    - Configure the default domain audit policy to audit the failure of logon events.

    - Configure the default domain audit policy to audit the success and failure of account management events.

    - Configure the default domain audit policy to audit the success and failure of object access.

    - Use Windows Explorer on the SALESDATA server to track the success and failure of the List Folder/Read Data access on the Commissions folder for the SalesPersons security group.

    Which of the outlined requirements were satisfied by your solution? (Choose all correct answers.)

    A. All user attempts to log on to the network must be audited.

    B. Users failing to log on locally to the FINDATA file server should be tracked.

    C. Actions by administrators to add, delete, and modify users in the default Users container should be tracked.

    D. Any access to the Information Services OU in Active Directory should be tracked.

    E. Any attempts by any member of the SalesPersons security group to access the Commissions folder on the SALESDATA file server should be tracked.

Answers to Review Questions

1. The best way to accomplish your desired goals is to create a security policy on CORPSECURE with Restricted Groups settings to include the MANAGERS group. Assign users to the MANAGERS group through the security policy only, thereby not allowing other users to be added except through the policy. Assign the MANAGERS group the

APPLY YOUR KNOWLEDGE

Access this computer from the network user right and remove it from the group Everyone and the group Authorized Users. See "Implementing Security Policies."

2. To determine whether co-op students are attempting to gain access to the CORPSECURE server, create an audit policy configured to audit privilege use for the Everyone group (because it could be some other users) and failure to use the privilege in question (Access This Computer from the Network). See "Configuring and Implementing an Audit Policy."

3. Enable object access auditing on the Windows 2000 computer where the printer is defined. Assign appropriate permissions to the shared printer to ensure that only members of the graphic arts department have access. Configure auditing on the printer for Failure to Print and Read the Printer for the Everyone group and Success and Failure for members of the graphic arts department. The former enables you to track unauthorized attempts to access the printer. The latter tracks printer usage within the graphic arts department. See "Configuring and Implementing an Audit Policy."

4. Security Configuration and Analysis can be used to analyze system security by creating a security database and comparing the settings to a security template. It can also be used to configure system security by applying template settings to the computer. Finally, it can be used to create new templates for the current computer configuration or to merge existing settings with a template to create a new security template. See "Implementing Security Policies."

5. You would first create two security groups: one for all the member servers in the finance department and another for the client computers in the finance department. Next you would create an OU for the finance department, if an OU for the finance department did not already exist, and place the computers in the OU as well as the security groups. You would then create a GPO at the Finance OU level with the required settings and assign the GPO to the two security groups. See "Implementing Security Policies." See also "Group Policy Scope" in Chapter 6, "Using Group Policy to Manage Users."

6. The best way to accomplish your goals is to create a GPO at the Development OU level. Configure a security template with the appropriate settings and import the template into the GPO. Then assign the GPO to the computers in the Development OU. This assigns the template settings to the development department computers. To have the same settings on the computer in quality assurance, you would use Security Configuration and Analysis on the quality assurance computer to import the template and configure the settings on the quality assurance computer. See "Implementing Security Policies." See also "Group Policy Scope" in Chapter 6, "Using Group Policy to Manage Users."

7. The default extension for the security database files created by Security Configuration and Analysis is .SDB. See "Implementing Security Policies."

8. To force all users in the domain to change their passwords every 30 days, you would create a GPO at the domain level with the appropriate password policy settings. You would assign this GPO to the Authenticated Users group. To not

have the policy apply to the sales clerks, you would create a security group and place all users who are sales clerks in the security group. You would then Deny the Apply Group Policy permission to the sales clerks security group. See "Implementing Security Policies." See also "Group Policy Scope" in Chapter 6, "Using Group Policy to Manage Users."

Answers to Exam Questions

1. **A, B, D.** You would need to use Security Templates to create the template that will be applied to domain controllers in the Toronto site and the other servers. You would then use Active Directory Sites and Services to create a GPO for the site and import the security template. Finally, you would use Security Configuration and Analysis to import the template into the other servers and apply its settings. See "Implementing Security Policies."

2. **B, C.** To determine who is trying to gain unauthorized access to the SOURCECODE share on the server called ENGINEERING, you need to enable auditing of object access on the computer (ENGINEERING) and then enable auditing of files and folders on the SOURCECODE share. Logon activity auditing will tell you who is trying to log on to the computer but not for what purpose. It might help but is not the ideal solution. You cannot audit file and folder access on the machine or object access on the share. Auditing directory access will have no effect here. See "Configuring and Implementing an Audit Policy."

3. **B, C, D, F.** To satisfy the requirements of creating a new template from two existing ones with additional settings, you would make use of Security Configuration and Analysis to create the new template. This makes any answer using the Group Policy Editor incorrect. In using Security Configuration and Analysis, you would first import both templates after having created a new security database. You would then analyze your computer against the database settings. This step is required so you can export the database settings as a template. You would next configure any settings that were not in the PasswordTemplate and AuditTemplate templates as required. Finally, you would export the database settings to a security template using the Export Template menu option in Security Configuration and Analysis. See "Implementing Security Policies."

4. **A, D.** When enabling auditing of object access and directory services access, no events appear in the Windows 2000 security event log. This is because you need to further specify which objects (such as files, folders, and printers) or Active Directory elements (OUs, users, groups, and so on) you want audited and by whom. This is accomplished using Windows Explorer in the case of files, folders and printers; Control Panel in the case of printers; or Active Directory Users and Computer or Active Directory Sites and Services in the case of Active Directory. See "Configuring and Implementing an Audit Policy."

5. **B, E.** The two tools that would enable you to analyze the security configuration on the required computers on a regular basis are SECEDIT.EXE and the Task Scheduler. SECEDIT.EXE can be used to perform the analysis of a computer's

APPLY YOUR KNOWLEDGE

security configuration; Task Scheduler can be used to schedule when secedit should be run. See "Implementing Security Policies."

6. **A.** To track the amount of time users spend logged on to the network, you would enable audit the success of account logon events. Account logon events deal with a user logging on to a workstation and requesting a logon to the domain. This is different than a logon event in which the user is requesting access to a resource on a member server or is logging on locally to a computer. The requirement was to track users' time on the network, which requires a domain-level logon. Auditing success of account logon events would place an entry in the security event log on a domain controller when a user logs on to the network and another when he or she logs off. This would enable you to track the time spent online. See "Configuring and Implementing an Audit Policy."

7. **C, D, G.** This question is a bit tricky because it tests your knowledge of Group Policy more than anything else. The issue here is how to you enforce a corporate policy in a structure in which subdomains exist. As you learned in Chapter 6, domains are an administrative barrier, and GPOs do not cross domain boundaries unless configured at a site. Sites are not mentioned here, so it won't help much. Then the best way to satisfy the requirements is to create the "Password Policy Settings" GPO at the concilar.com domain level with the appropriate settings. You would then link it to each subdomain so it is available there. Finally, you would configure No Override to ensure that these minimum settings are applied throughout the company. See "Implementing

Security Policies." See also "Group Policy Scope" in Chapter 6, "Using Group Policy to Manage Users."

8. **A, C.** The only requirements satisfied by your solution would be the tracking of all logon attempts on the network and administrator modification of user accounts in the default Users container. In fact, the policy you implemented would track any account management activity by any user because the GPO was applied to the Authenticated Users group, which includes all users. Even though the configuration you decided on will have other things occur, the two requirements that will definitely be satisfied are A and C. Note that Microsoft might also provide you with answers on an exam that do more than is required, but as long as they accomplish the stated goal, they might be the correct answer. See "Configuring and Implementing an Audit Policy." Also see "Group Policy Security" in Chapter 6, "Using Group Policy to Manage Users."

9. **A, D, F, I.** To satisfy the requirements and not have extra information in the security log, you would need to change the auditing of account logon events to audit both success and failure to track all logons to the network. You would also need to change logon event auditing to only failure in order to track unsuccessful attempts to connect to the EXECUTIVE file server. To track unsuccessful attempts to change policy settings, you only need failure set on audit policy changes. Finally, you can also reduce system event auditing to only failure if all you want to track is which users received an error when attempting to shut down their computer. See "Configuring and Implementing an Audit Policy."

APPLY YOUR KNOWLEDGE

10. **B, E.** Your solution will track any unsuccessful attempts by users to log on to the FINDATA server because you have configured auditing of the logon event. Because the GPO is created at the domain level and you have granted the Apply Group Policy permission to the FINDATA server, the policy will apply at that server and will track failure to log on to the machine. You have also properly configured auditing of the Commissions folder of the SALES-DATA server using Windows Explorer and have enabled auditing the success and failure of object access at the domain GPO. This will track attempts by members of the SalesPersons security group to access this folder. See "Configuring and Implementing an Audit Policy."

Suggested Readings and Resources

1. Windows 2000 Resource Kit. *Deployment Planning Guide.* Microsoft Press, 2000.

2. *Security Configuration Toolset* on Microsoft's Web site at `http://www.microsoft.com/windows2000/library/howitworks/security/sctoolset.asp`.

3. *Securing Windows 2000 Network Resources* on Microsoft's Web site at `http://www.microsoft.com/windows2000/library/planning/incremental/securenetworkresources.asp`.

4. *Step-by-Step Guide to Using the Security Configuration Toolset* on Microsoft's Web site at `http://www.microsoft.com/windows2000/library/planning/incremental/securenetworkresources.asp`.

5. *Step-by-Step Guide to Configuring Enterprise Security Policies* on Microsoft's Web site at `http://www.microsoft.com/windows2000/library/planning/security/entsecsteps.asp`.

6. *Default Access Control Settings* on Microsoft's Web site at `http://www.microsoft.com/windows2000/library/planning/security/secdefs.asp`.

7. *Secure Networking Using Windows 2000 Distributed Security Services* on Microsoft's Web site at `http://www.microsoft.com/windows2000/library/howitworks/security/distsecservices.asp`.

8. *IP Security for Windows 2000 Server* on Microsoft's Web site at `http://www.microsoft.com/windows2000/library/howitworks/security/ip_security.asp`.

This chapter covers the two objectives from the unit "Installing, Configuring, Managing, Monitoring, Optimizing, and Troubleshooting Change and Configuration Management" that are concerned with Remote Installation Services.

Deploy Windows 2000 by using Remote Installation Services (RIS).

- **Install an image on a RIS client computer.**

- **Create a RIS boot disk.**

- **Configure remote installation options.**

- **Troubleshoot RIS problems.**

- **Manage images for performing remote installations.**

▶ The purpose of this objective is to make sure you know how to install and configure Remote Installation Services on a Windows 2000 member server computer. This includes making sure you have the prerequisites for both the RIS server and the client, being able to create CD-based and RIPrep images, knowing how to create a RIS boot disk and when to use one, and using RIS to deploy Windows 2000. You also need to know what common problems might be encountered with RIS and how to solve them.

Configure RIS security.

- **Authorize a RIS server.**

- **Grant computer account creation rights.**

- **Prestage RIS client computers for added security and load balancing.**

CHAPTER 9

Deploying Windows 2000 Using Remote Installation Services

▶ In testing you on deploying Windows 2000 using RIS, Microsoft wants to make sure you are completely familiar with the security aspects of RIS including how to authorize a RIS server to respond to client requests, how and when to delegate the creation of computer accounts to other users in the organization, and finally, how to ensure that only those computers whose identification is known are allowed to deploy Windows 2000 using RIS (that is, prestaging a client computer).

The specific subobjectives appear in two sections of the chapter with authorizing and granting computer creation rights in the "Setting Up a RIS Server" section and prestaging client computers in its own section of the chapter. This should not be a concern because Microsoft will probably test you on these, and other topics, in the same question. Just be aware of the issues involved with security and RIS.

OUTLINE

STUDY STRATEGIES

▶ The best way to prepare for the Remote Installation Services portion of the exam is to fully understand the requirements for both the RIS server and clients. Working through the exercises in this chapter and having two computers available will help you prepare for the exam because you will be able to configure a RIS server and use RIS to deploy Windows 2000 Professional on the second computer. If you do not have a computer with a PXE-enabled network card, you should create a RIS boot disk for your network card.

▶ You should also practice prestaging a client as well as authorizing a RIS server in Active Directory. Knowing how to configure client-machine naming and how to authorize users to create computer accounts in the domain is also required. Generally, this can be accomplished by working through the Step by Steps in this chapter as well as the exercises.

▶ Being able to answer the review questions and the exam questions will help in your preparation for the exam. What can go wrong with a RIS deployment should be understood as well because Microsoft tends to ask you questions on this topic.

▶ Once again, the best way to prepare for this portion of the exam is to work with the product and perform a rollout of at least one machine using RIS.

INTRODUCTION

As you have seen, after you have configured Active Directory using Group Policy, you have a lot of features you can make use of, including Group Policy to control the user environment, deploy software and updates to users and computers, and configure and monitor security settings. However, you still need to install Windows 2000 Professional, or other Windows 2000 variants, on computers to be able to use these wonderful features.

When installing Windows 2000 on client computers, you have several methods available to you. First, you can install Windows 2000 by using the CD-ROM and configuring all settings manually for each machine. The problem here is that this process can become quite time consuming and requires a lot of user interaction to be performed properly.

Another method that can be used is to create an unattended installation file and then automate the installation, either from a network share or using the CD-ROM, so that less user interaction is required. This process makes it easier to install multiple machines simultaneously and may be a viable root.

A third method is to create an image of a Windows 2000 reference computer using a third-party imaging product such as Symantec Ghost or PowerQuest Disk Image Pro and then copy the image to other machines with the exact same *hardware abstraction layer* (HAL) characteristics. This process is quite quick and can also be a viable solution.

A fourth method is to make use of the new Windows 2000 feature called *Remote Installation Service* (RIS), which enables the automated installation of Windows 2000 Professional on client machines from a network share. It also provides additional security and other features, which might make it the right choice for a deployment in many organizations.

OVERVIEW OF REMOTE INSTALLATION SERVICES

Deploy Windows 2000 by using Remote Installation Services (RIS).

Remote Installation Services is a Windows 2000 component that enables automatic installation of Windows 2000 Professional on client computers. Computers connect to the RIS server during the initial boot phase and start the installation of Windows 2000 Professional remotely. The installation of Windows 2000 Professional can make use of either the Windows 2000 Professional installation files found on the CD-ROM or a RIPrep image containing the operating system as well as the configuration of other applications. The image files are stored on the RIS server and are downloaded at boot time to the client machine to start the installation.

The remote installation process relies upon a number of key technologies in both the server and client machines. On the server side, RIS requires the following:

◆ An NTFS partition containing the images of Windows 2000 Professional that will be installed on client computers. More than one image can exist on the same partition.

◆ Images to be used to perform the installation of Windows 2000 Professional on client computers. Images can be the Windows 2000 Professional installation files found on the CD-ROM or *Remote Installation Preparation* (RIPrep) images. RIPrep images represent a fully configured computer, including additional application software, desktop settings, and network connections, and represent an easy way to install the same configuration on several computers quickly.

◆ The Remote Installation Service, which listens for and responds to client requests to install Windows 2000 Professional on a client computer. Remote Installation Services makes use of three other Windows 2000 networking components, which must be installed and running on the RIS server.

NOTE

Windows 2000 Professional Only Remote Installation Services in Windows 2000 only supports the installation of Windows 2000 Professional client software through RIS. It is not currently possible to use RIS to install Windows 2000 Server or Advanced Server on a target machine through RIS. To install the Server variants of Windows 2000 on a computer, you need to perform either a CD-based installation or an unattended installation from a network share.

- *Boot Information Negotiation Layer* (BINL), which responds to client requests and helps service client computers.

- *Single Instance Store* (SIS), which helps minimize disk space used by RIS images by replacing duplicate copies of files on the disk with a link to the common store location for those files shared by multiple images.

- *Trivial File Transfer Protocol* (TFTP), which is used to download the images to the client computers and start the installation of Windows 2000 Professional.

◆ The Dynamic Host Configuration Protocol (DHCP) service installed and activated on a Windows 2000 Server, Advanced Server, or Data Center Server computer to respond to client requests for an IP address. Clients are assigned a DHCP address to use when connecting to the RIS server to start the install. The DHCP server must be authorized within Active Directory for it to be allowed to lease IP addresses to client machines on which a RIS install will be performed.

◆ Windows 2000 Active Directory to be installed and configured with at least one Windows 2000 domain. RIS requires Active Directory to install and manage its configuration and locate computer accounts allowed to use RIS to install Windows 2000 Professional.

◆ Domain Name Service (DNS) to locate Active Directory services within the domain.

On the client side, to perform an installation of Windows 2000 Professional using RIS, the client must have a network card or computer conforming to a particular set of specifications. The client-side requirements include the following:

◆ A Pentium 166 or higher CPU-based computer. Pentium 233 or better, including Celeron, Pentium II, or Pentium III is recommended. The client computer that will use RIS to install Windows 2000 Professional must meet at least the minimum specifications required for the Windows 2000 Professional operating system.

◆ A hard disk with at least 1GB of free space configured as a primary partition. It is recommended that you have a larger hard disk on the client computer if you want to install other applications. A 2GB hard disk is preferred.

◆ 64MB of RAM required, 128MB recommended. The more memory on the computer, the better the performance of Windows 2000 Professional.

◆ A 10Mbps network adapter, 100Mbps recommended. The network adapter must conform to the *Pre-Boot Execution Environment* (PXE) specification version 0.99c or later or be a PCI-based network adapter supported by a RIS boot disk. Computers conforming to the NetPC specification or computers that have been tested and verified to comply with the PC98 and later specifications should be compliant.

◆ The *Basic Input/Output System* (BIOS) of the client computer must be configured to boot from the network card if using a PXE-compliant card. If you are using a RIPrep image, the client computer must be configured to boot from the floppy.

If your client machine meets the preceding outlined requirements and you have properly configured and installed a RIS server after meeting all the server-based requirements, you will be able to use RIS to deploy Windows 2000 Professional images on client computers.

NOTE	**PCMCIA/PC Card Not Supported** PC Card or PCMCIA network cards found in notebook computers are not supported by RIS. This means it is not possible to use RIS to roll out a large-scale notebook deployment except by using a docking station with a compliant network card installed. When the notebook computer is docked, it uses the docking station network card to access the LAN; if this card is PXE-compliant or supported by the RIS boot disk, you can then use RIS to deploy Windows 2000 Professional to the notebook.

The Process of Installing Windows 2000 Professional Using RIS

Deploy Windows 2000 by using Remote Installation Services (RIS).

• **Install an image on a RIS client computer.**

The actual process of performing an installation of Windows 2000 Professional after configuring a RIS server and creating an image is quite elegant. During the boot process, using either a PXE-compliant network card or the RIS boot disk, the user presses F12. This initiates the process of configuring the computer using RIS. A number of steps then take place to perform the install.

1. The client computer sends out a DHCP Discover packet to locate a DHCP server and request an IP address. The packet also includes the *globally unique identifier* (GUID) for the computer as well as a request to be serviced by a RIS server. The GUID is an important element, as you will soon see.

2. The DHCP server assigns the client an IP address so it can communicate on the network.

3. The client computer is directed to and connects to a RIS server.

4. After the client connects to the RIS server, the RIS server checks Active Directory to see whether the client computer has been prestaged (that is, preconfigured to receive a specific list of images for a particular RIS server in the enterprise). To determine whether the client computer is prestaged, the RIS server contacts Active Directory to locate the computer's GUID. If it is found, the computer is considered to be prestaged.

5. If the client computer is found to be prestaged, the RIS server directs the client to contact its designated RIS server as specified in Active Directory and then provides a username and password to log on.

   If the computer is not prestaged, the RIS server that the user contacted prompts him to provide his username and password to log on.

6. After the user logs on to the RIS server, the user is presented with a list of available images to choose to install and is required to select one.

7. After selecting an image, the installation process begins to configure the computer with Windows 2000 Professional.

The configuration and use of Remote Installation Services is a four-step process:

1. The installation of Remote Installation Services

2. The configuration of the RIS server and the starting of the RIS, including creating the necessary images to be used to install Windows 2000 Professional

3. The authorization of the RIS server in DHCP Manager so that clients getting a DHCP address can also make a request to use a RIS server during the initial boot-up process

4. The granting of the right to create computer accounts in the domain to users who will be using RIS to install Windows 2000 on their computer and adding the computers to the domain

The first step in this chain is to install the RIS server.

INSTALLING AND CONFIGURING A RIS SERVER

The process of installing Remote Installation Services is actually quite straightforward. First you need to make sure the requisite hardware and software requirements are taken care of, and then you can add Remote Installation Services to one of your Windows 2000 Server, Advanced Server, or Data Center Server computers that is a member of your domain. It is possible to have more than one RIS server that can be used to deploy Windows 2000 Professional, although only one will ever be used to install the operating system to a machine at one time.

Remote Installation Services Prerequisites

Prior to installing Windows 2000 Remote Installation Services, you need to ensure that your server meets the requirements for RIS. These include the hardware requirements for the server computer itself as well as other Windows 2000 components needed by Remote Installation Services.

Server Hardware Requirements

The hardware requirements for your RIS server are almost identical to those for Windows 2000 Server itself with one minor difference. The hardware needed to run Remote Installation Services includes the following:

◆ A Pentium 166 or higher CPU. A Pentium II 300 or better is recommended.

◆ A 10Mbps network adapter (for example, 10BASE-T). A 100Mbps network adapter (for example, 100BASE-TX) is recommended.

◆ 256MB of RAM minimum, although a 128MB RAM configuration is supported. Additional memory is required if you plan to run DHCP, DNS, or other services on the same server as RIS.

◆ 2GB of hard disk space minimum (4GB recommended) split into two partitions on the hard disk. One partition is used to store the RIS images and must use NTFS; the other is used for the Windows 2000 Server operating system. It is recommended that all partitions be NTFS. The RIS image partition must have sufficient space to hold all images that will be available on the server.

◆ A VGA video card with 800×600 resolution.

◆ A mouse and keyboard.

◆ A CD-ROM drive is recommended so you can copy the Windows 2000 Professional CD contents to the image location if using CD-based images.

The only major difference in requirements when installing a RIS server on Windows 2000 Server or Advanced Server computers is the need for a minimum of two volumes on the hard disk: one to hold the RIS images, which must be formatted for the NTFS file system; and the other for the server operating system.

RIS Software Requirements

Before you can install and make use of Remote Installation Services on your LAN, a number of other pieces of software must be installed. You can install these components on the same server as

Remote Installation Services or, for better performance, on another Windows 2000 Server or Advanced Server computer.

The software components that need to be installed and configured prior to installing Remote Installation Services are as follows:

◆ **Domain Name System (DNS).** DNS is required to locate objects in Active Directory. Any DNS server that can be used with Active Directory will work. The RIS computer needs to be configured with the IP address of the DNS server.

◆ **Active Directory.** RIS requires Active Directory to locate computer accounts and to manage the RIS configuration. It is not possible to install Remote Installation Services in an environment in which Active Directory is not installed and configured—Active Directory is a required component.

◆ **DHCP service.** RIS uses DHCP to assign IP addresses to client machines. As previously mentioned, clients issue a DHCP Discover packet to be assigned an IP address, which also contains the request to be connected to a RIS server. DHCP servers authorize RIS server machines and forward the client's request to connect to a RIS server to the one it knows about or the one to which the client has been prestaged.

After these software components have been installed and configured, it is possible to start the installation of Remote Installation Services on a Windows 2000 Server, Advanced Server, or Data Center Server computer.

Setting Up a RIS Server

To set up a RIS server, after meeting the preceding hardware and software requirements, you perform four tasks:

1. Install Remote Installation Services on the Windows 2000 Server computer. You can install RIS during the installation of Windows 2000 Server or afterwards. Installation of RIS does not configure it; it only installs the files required to make RIS workable.

2. Configure the RIS server and start it by using the Remote Installation Services Setup Wizard. This step also requires you to create an initial CD-based image and requires that you have the Windows 2000 Professional CD-ROM available.

3. Authorize the RIS server in Active Directory by using DHCP Manager. Upon doing so, the RIS server is able to respond to client requests to start a remote install.

4. Grant the rights to create computer accounts on the domain to users who will be performing remote installations using RIS.

Installing RIS on a Windows 2000 Server Computer

If you did not select RIS to be installed during your Windows 2000 Server installation, you can always install it after the fact by using Add/Remove Programs from Control Panel or the Configure Your Server Wizard. You need to have the Windows 2000 Server or Advanced Server CD-ROM available or a path to the source files on your network.

To install Remote Installation Services using the Configure Your Server Wizard, follows the steps in Step by Step 9.1.

STEP BY STEP

9.1 Installing RIS Using the Configure Your Server Wizard

1. Log on to your Windows 2000 computer as a Domain Administrator.

2. From the Start menu, select Programs, Administrative Tools and then Configure Your Server. A screen similar to Figure 9.1 displays.

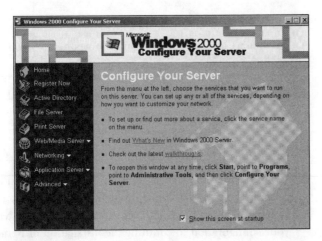

FIGURE 9.1
Using the Configure Your Server Wizard is one way to install Remote
Installation Services.

3. From the Configure Your Server Wizard, select Advanced
and then click Optional Components, from which you
can start the Windows Components Wizard, as shown in
Figure 9.2.

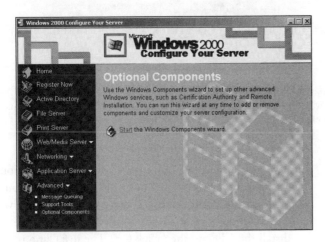

FIGURE 9.2
The Windows Components Wizard can be opened by selecting Advanced,
Optional Components in the Configure Your Server Wizard.

continues

N O T E

More Than One Way to Install RIS
Another way to install Remote
Installation Services is to use
Add/Remove Programs from Control
Panel. If you want to use this method,
substitute the following steps in
place of steps 1 through 4 in Step
by Step 9.1.

1. Log on to your Windows 2000
   computer as a Domain
   Administrator.

2. From the Start menu, select
   Settings and then Control Panel.

3. From Control Panel, double-click
   Add/Remove Programs.

4. From Add/Remove Programs,
   select Add/Remove Windows
   Components to open the
   Windows Component Wizard.

Follow the rest of the steps (5 and
on) to complete the installation of
Remote Installation Services. The
rest of the screens are identical using
either method.

continued

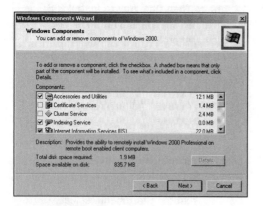

FIGURE 9.3
The Windows Components Wizard enables you
to install additional Windows 2000 components
on the computer.

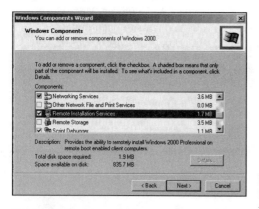

FIGURE 9.4
Select Remote Installation Services from the
list and click Next to start the install.

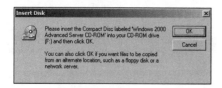

FIGURE 9.6
If the Windows 2000 CD-ROM is not in
the CD-ROM drive, you will be prompted to
insert it.

4. Click Start to open the Optional Components Wizard, resulting in a display similar to Figure 9.3.

5. As shown in Figure 9.4, scroll down the list of available components and select Remote Installation Services by checking the box next to it. Then click Next to start the installation.

6. If you previously installed Terminal Services, you will be prompted to confirm the setup of Terminal Services, as shown in Figure 9.5. Click Next after you have selected your configuration to continue the installation of Remote Installation Services.

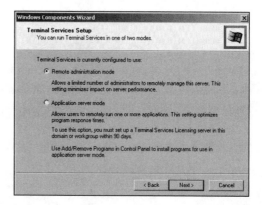

FIGURE 9.5
If previously installed, confirm your Terminal Services configuration and then click Next.

7. If you did not install Terminal Services, the installation commences and, as shown in Figure 9.6, prompts you to install the Windows 2000 Server or Advanced Server CD-ROM if it is not already in the CD-ROM drive. Install the CD and then click OK. The installation continues as shown in Figure 9.7.

8. When the installation is done, a screen similar to Figure 9.8 displays. Click Finish to complete the installation.

9. You will be promoted to restart your computer, as shown in Figure 9.9. Click Yes to restart the Windows 2000 Server and finalize the Remote Installation Services installation.

You have now installed Remote Installation Services. You cannot make use of RIS at this point, however; you need to configure it first.

Configuring Remote Installation Services

After installing Remote Installation Services on a Windows 2000 Server, Advanced Server, or Data Center Server computer, you need to configure it to make it usable. Configuration consists of specifying the folder on an NTFS partition that will be used to store RIS images as well as configuring initial settings for how the RIS server will respond to client requests. You also need to provide the location of the Windows 2000 Professional source files that will be copied to the RIS folder and will be used to create the initial CD-based image. You can configure Remote Installation Services using one of three methods.

First, after rebooting your Windows 2000 Server computer and logging on as an Administrator, the Configure Your Server Wizard will start automatically (unless you turned this feature off). Then, as shown in Figure 9.10, it prompts you to Finish Setup, which starts the Remote Installation Services Setup Wizard and enables you to complete RIS configuration.

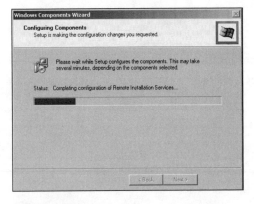

FIGURE 9.7
The Windows Components Wizard will install Remote Installation Services on your computer.

FIGURE 9.8
After the Windows Components Wizard has installed Remote Installation Services, click Finish to complete the installation.

FIGURE 9.9
Restart your computer when prompted to finalize the installation of Remote Installation Services.

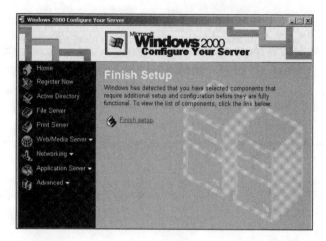

FIGURE 9.10
The Configure Your Server Wizard prompts you to Finish Setup, which can be used to configure Remote Installation Services on your computer.

Second, you can open the Remote Installation Services Setup Wizard and configure RIS by going to Control Panel, Add/Remove Programs and selecting Add/Remove Windows Components. You will be prompted to configure RIS, as shown in Figure 9.11. Click the Configure button to start the configuration of Remote Installation Services.

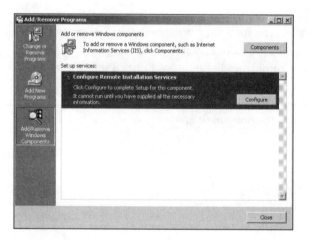

FIGURE 9.11
Going to Control Panel, Add/Remove Programs and selecting Add/Remove Windows Components also prompts you to configure Remote Installation Services on your computer.

The third method that can be used to configure RIS is to open the Remote Installation Services Setup Wizard by using the risetup.exe utility, as shown in the following Step by Step.

STEP BY STEP

9.2 Configuring RIS Using the Remote Installation Services Setup Wizard

1. Log on to your Windows 2000 computer as a Domain Administrator.

2. From the Start menu, select Run and then type **risetup.exe** in the Run box, as shown in Figure 9.12, to open the Remote Installation Services Setup Wizard. The Remote Installation Services Setup Wizard can also be opened from a command prompt instead of Start, Run.

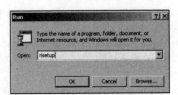

FIGURE 9.12
You can configure Remote Installation Services by running risetup.exe from the Run command of the Start menu.

3. When started, the Remote Installation Services Setup Wizard presents a screen similar to Figure 9.13, indicating that DNS, DHCP, and the Windows 2000 Professional CD-ROM are required during the configuration process. Note that client computer requirements are indicated as well. Click Next to continue.

FIGURE 9.13
When started, the Remote Installation Services Setup Wizard reminds you of the requirements for RIS.

continues

continued

NOTE

Dedicated Disk Recommended It is recommended that the disk containing the initial image, as well as all other images, be dedicated to RIS. In this way, you will have the best performance and not impact other OS activity by clients reading files from the RIS disk.

The disk used to store images must also be a basic disk. The *Single Instance Store* (SIS) Service does not support dynamic disks, so only basic disks can be used to store RIS images. To provide fault tolerance in case of disk loss, it is recommended that you have more than one RIS server in a location; this also enables you to distribute the workload between the RIS servers during deployment.

4. The next screen prompts you for the location of a folder to store the RIS images, as shown in Figure 9.14. Type the name of a folder located on an NTFS partition that is not the system drive and click Next to continue the configuration.

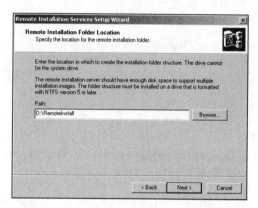

FIGURE 9.14
Specify the location of the Remote Installation Services folder to be located on an NTFS partition (not your system drive) on your computer.

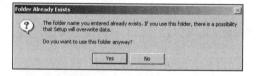

FIGURE 9.15
If the folder already exists on your computer, you will be prompted to overwrite it.

If the folder you specify already exists on the volume, you will be prompted as to whether you would like to overwrite it, as shown in Figure 9.15. Click Yes to overwrite the contents of the folder or No to select a different folder.

5. By default, RIS servers do not respond to client requests right after they are initially set up. If you would like to start using the RIS server right away to perform remote installations of Windows 2000 Professional using default settings, select the Respond to client computers requesting service check box, as shown in Figure 9.16.

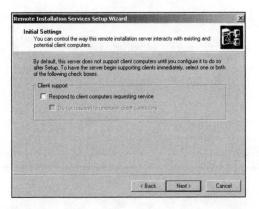

FIGURE 9.16
Decide whether the RIS server should become active immediately by
checking the Respond to client computers requesting service check box.

> If you decide to make the RIS server active immediately,
> you also have the option to respond to only known
> computers requesting RIS (by checking the Do not
> respond to unknown client computers option) or any
> computer (the default and unchecked option). If you
> make the RIS server immediately active, you should let
> any client make use of it. Not allowing this will have the
> same effect as configuring it later. Click Next.

6. You are next prompted to specify the location of the
   Windows 2000 Professional installation files, as shown in
   Figure 9.17. This defaults to your CD-ROM drive, but
   you can specify a different path by using the Browse
   button and locating the files or by typing in the path
   yourself. When you have selected the proper path,
   click Next.

continues

continued

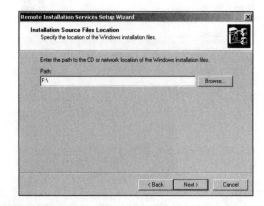

FIGURE 9.17
Specify the location of the Windows 2000 Professional files to create the initial CD image for Remote Installation Services.

FIGURE 9.18
If you insert a CD-ROM other than Windows 2000 Professional, an error message will remind you that RIS only supports Windows 2000 Professional.

If you install the Windows 2000 Server CD or any other CD besides the Windows 2000 Professional CD, you will be reminded, as shown in Figure 9.18, that RIS only supports the installation of Windows 2000 Professional.

7. After providing a path to the correct product, you are asked to indicate the name of the folder where the CD-based image files will be copied, as shown in Figure 9.19. Usually it is best to use the default of win2000.pro for the initial image and name other images differently later.

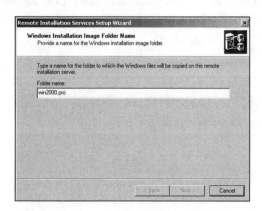

FIGURE 9.19
Provide the name of the Windows 2000 Professional image folder on the RIS partition.

If the folder already exists, an error occurs and a dialog box similar to Figure 9.20 asks whether you would like to overwrite the contents of the folder. Click Yes to overwrite the folder. Click No to return to the Select a Folder dialog box to type in a new name.

Click Next to continue.

8. You are now prompted to provide a friendly name and description for the image created by the Remote Installation Services Setup Wizard, as shown in Figure 9.21. This is the name users will see when they boot computers and are prompted to select the image they want to install. Leave the default name intact or overwrite the information with your own choices. Click Next to continue.

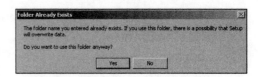

FIGURE 9.20
An error appears if the folder already exists. Click Yes to overwrite the folder or No to specify another folder name.

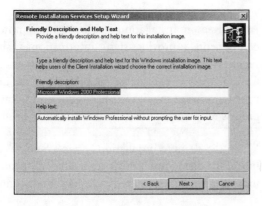

FIGURE 9.21
Provide a friendly name to the Windows 2000 Professional image being created. It will be shown to users initiating a remote install.

9. You will now see a summary screen showing the actions to be performed, as shown in Figure 9.22. Click Finish to complete the configuration of Remote Installation Services.

continues

continued

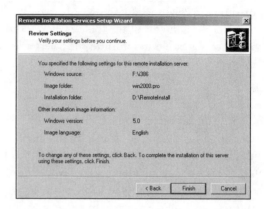

FIGURE 9.22
The Remote Installation Services summary screen shows the actions to be performed.

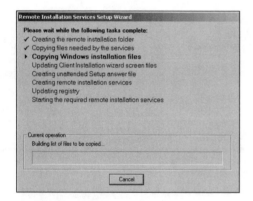

FIGURE 9.23
The Remote Installation Services Setup Wizard provides progress information during the configuration process.

10. As the Remote Installation Services Setup Wizard installs components, it provides status information, as shown on Figure 9.23. If you want to cancel the setup of RIS, click Cancel; otherwise, monitor the progress of the install. You might also want to take a coffee break now because the process takes some time (about 15 minutes or so).

11. When the Remote Installation Services Setup Wizard finishes, a dialog box similar to Figure 9.24 is presented, indicating that the required tasks have been completed.

FIGURE 9.24
The Remote Installation Services Setup Wizard provides information on tasks performed at completion.

The Remote Installation Services Setup Wizard has
created the RIS folder, copied the files needed for RIS,
copied the Windows 2000 Professional installation files
from the CD-ROM or the location you indicated,
updated the Client Installation Wizard files, created an
unattended Setup answer file, updated the registry, started
the required services such as TFTP, and created a Single
Instance Storage volume.

Click Done to complete the configuration and exit
the wizard.

By running the Remote Installation Services Setup Wizard, you have
created the initial configuration of RIS. You now need to authorize
the RIS server and can add additional images and further refine the
installation.

Authorizing the RIS Server

Configure RIS security.

- **Authorize a RIS server.**

After you have configured RIS on a computer, you must authorize
the RIS server in Active Directory. If your RIS is also the DHCP
server and the DHCP server has been authorized in Active
Directory, this step has already been completed; if not, you need
to authorize the server.

To authorize your RIS server, you use the DHCP console, which is
part of Administrative Tools. If you do not have Administrative
Tools installed on the RIS server, you need to do so to be able to
authorize the server. To install the Administrative Tools, double-click
Adminpak.msi in the WINNT\SYSTEM32 folder on your machine.
The Adminpak.msi package contains all the Administrative Tools,
including the DHCP console.

After installing Administrative Tools, to authorize your server,
perform the following steps.

STEP BY STEP

9.3 Authorizing the RIS Server in Active Directory

1. Log on to your Windows 2000 computer as a Domain Administrator.

2. From the Start menu, select Programs, Administrative Tools and then DHCP to open the DHCP console, as shown in Figure 9.25.

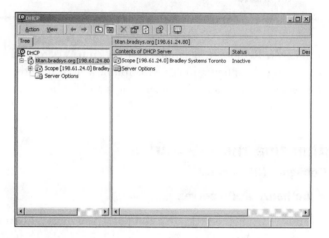

FIGURE 9.25
Open the DHCP console from Administrative Tools to authorize your RIS server.

3. In the DHCP console, right-click DHCP and then select Manage authorized servers, as shown in Figure 9.26.

4. If your server does not appear in the list of authorized servers, click Authorize to add it to the list.

5. In the Authorize DHCP Server dialog box (see Figure 9.27), type your RIS server name or IP address in the Name or IP address box and then click OK. When asked to confirm your selection, click Yes.

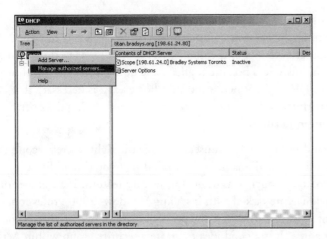

FIGURE 9.27
Enter the name or IP address of your RIS server in the Authorize DHCP Server dialog box to add your RIS server to the list of authorized servers.

FIGURE 9.26
Select Manage authorized servers by right-clicking DHCP in the DHCP console to add your RIS server to the list of authorized servers.

6. Click Close to exit the Authorize DHCP Server dialog box after confirming that your RIS server has been added to the list of authorized servers.

7. Exit the DHCP console to complete your task.

You have now successfully authorized your RIS server in Active Directory and have enabled it to respond to client requests. At this point, clients are able to contact the RIS server to start the remote installation of Windows 2000 Professional using the default image created when you configured your RIS server. However, they are not able to create computer accounts in the domain or have their workstations join the domain, which effectively means they cannot install Windows 2000 Professional using Remote Installation Services.

Granting the Right to Create a Computer Account in the Domain

Configure RIS security.

• **Grant computer account creation rights.**

For users to be able to make use of RIS and install an operating system image on their computer, they need to be able to create computer accounts in the domain. This privilege is normally limited to Administrators because it affects the domain structure within Active Directory. When using RIS, however, it is necessary that this permission be granted to those users performing the operating system installation.

When deciding to which users to grant the right to create computer accounts in the domain, keep in mind that you should limit this capability as much as possible for security reasons. If a number of individuals are tasked with installing Windows 2000 Professional on client machines, these are the people to whom this privilege should be granted. It is a good idea to create a security group within Active Directory, add the users who will be using RIS to install Windows 2000 Professional to the group, and then grant the right to the group.

To grant the right to create computer accounts in the domain to a security group, follow these steps.

FIGURE 9.28
Open the Delegation of Control Wizard from Active Directory Users and Computers to start the process of granting users the Create a Computer Account in the Domain right.

FIGURE 9.29
The Delegation of Control Wizard displays an information dialog box. Click Next to continue.

STEP BY STEP

9.4 Granting the Create Computer Account in the Domain Right to Users

1. Log on to your Windows 2000 computer as a Domain Administrator.

2. From the Administrative Tools program group, open Active Directory Users and Computers.

3. Right-click the OU or domain where you want to enable users to create computer accounts and select Delegate Control to open the Delegation of Control Wizard, as shown in Figure 9.28.

4. When the Delegation of Control Wizard starts, it displays an information dialog box, as shown in Figure 9.29. Click Next to continue.

5. You are now prompted to add users or groups to which you want to delegate control, as shown in Figure 9.30. Click Add to bring up the list of users, select the users or groups for which you want to be able to create computer accounts in the domain, and then click Add. When you have finished adding the users and/or groups to whom you want to delegate control, click Next.

6. In the next dialog box, you have the choice to delegate common tasks or to specify a custom set of privileges you want to delegate, as shown in Figure 9.31. In the list of common tasks displayed, check the Join a computer to the domain task and click Next. This is the only permission required to enable users to create computer accounts in the domain using RIS.

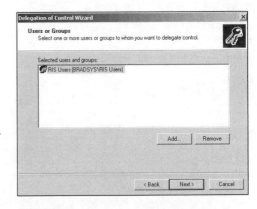

FIGURE 9.30
Click Add to add users and/or groups to whom you want to delegate control for adding computer accounts to the domain. After you have completed your selections, click Next to continue.

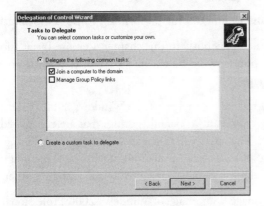

FIGURE 9.31
Select the Join a computer to the domain common task to grant the right to create computer accounts in the domain using the Delegation of Control Wizard.

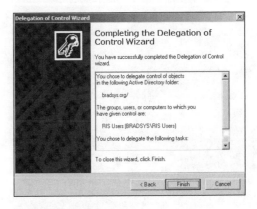

FIGURE 9.32
The Delegation of Control Wizard summary screen displays a list of tasks to be performed. Click Finish to give the Create Computer Account in the Domain right to the delegated users and/or groups.

7. The Delegation of Control Wizard presents a summary screen, as shown in Figure 9.32. If all tasks are correct, click Finish to perform the actions and exit the Delegation of Control Wizard.

8. Exit Active Directory Users and Computers.

At this point, you have performed all the necessary tasks for other users to use Remote Installation Services to install a default configuration of Windows 2000 Professional on client computers and to have those computers join the domain. However, you might want to enable users to select from a list of Windows 2000 Professional images so that different users can install different configurations of Windows 2000 Professional. To do this, you need to create the appropriate images.

CREATING REMOTE INSTALLATION SERVICES IMAGES

Deploy Windows 2000 by using Remote Installation Services (RIS).

- **Manage images for performing remote installations.**

As mentioned previously in this chapter, Remote Installation Services supports two different image types: CD-based images and RIPrep images.

CD-based images are images of the Windows 2000 Professional operating system and its default settings that are configured using an answer file. The answer file is created manually or by using Windows Setup Manager. Remote Installation Services, when configured, installs a default CD-based image. You can configure others as well.

A RIPrep image is an image of Windows 2000 Professional preconfigured on a reference or source computer; it can include the operating system as well as additional applications. When a RIPrep image is deployed, a copy of the reference computer is made on a target machine by using Remote Installation Services. You create a RIPrep image by using the Remote Installation Preparation Wizard, which is included with Windows 2000 Server, Advanced Server, or Data Center Server.

Creating a CD-Based Image for Remote Installation Services

As you already have seen, Remote Installation Services installs a default CD-based image when you configure RIS. This image is a copy of the Windows 2000 Professional installation files from the CD-ROM and a standard answer file called Ristandard.sif. You can modify the default answer file (also known as a setup information file, or SIF) using Windows Setup Manager, or you can create additional answer files using the same tool.

Installing Windows Setup Manager

Windows Setup Manager is part of the Windows 2000 Resource Kit and can be found in the SUPPORT\TOOLS folder of the Windows 2000 Server, Advanced Server, or Professional CD-ROM. To install Windows Setup Manager on your computer if it is not already installed, follow these steps.

STEP BY STEP

9.5 Installing Windows Setup Manager

1. Log on to your Windows 2000 computer as a Domain Administrator.

2. Insert the Windows 2000 Server (or Professional or Advanced Server) CD-ROM into your CD-ROM drive.

3. From the Start menu, select Programs, Accessories, and then Windows Explorer.

4. Using Windows Explorer, click your CD-ROM drive letter and then expand the SUPPORT and TOOLS folders on the CD-ROM. You can also double-click the My Computer icon on your desktop, then your CD-ROM drive, then SUPPORT, and finally TOOLS. This accomplishes the same task.

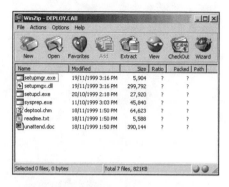

FIGURE 9.33
DEPLOY.CAB in the SUPPORT\TOOLS folder of
the Windows 2000 CD-ROM contains the
files for the Setup Manager Wizard.

5. Double-click DEPLOY.CAB in the TOOLS folder to look
at the contents of the CAB file, as shown in Figure 9.33.
(Note: The figure shows WinZIP being used to open the
CAB file. This was used for this example only. WinZIP is
not required to display the contents of DEPLOY.CAB.)

6. Select both setupmgr.exe and setupmgx.dll and then right-
click them and select Extract.

7. Determine the location to which you want to extract
the files on your hard disk (WINNT\SYSTEM32, for
example). Browse the location and then click Extract to
extract the files

8. Close Windows Explorer when done.

Using Windows Setup Manager to Create an Unattended Installation File

After you have installed Windows Setup Manager, you can use it to
configure an unattended installation file for a CD-based image that
you will use to install Windows 2000 Professional using Remote
Installation Services. In creating an unattended installation or SIF
file with Windows Setup Manager, you are preconfiguring the
settings that will be used on the target computer when Windows
2000 Professional is deployed using RIS.

To create and configure an unattended installation file using
Windows Setup Manager, follow these steps.

STEP BY STEP

9.6 Configuring an Unattended Installation File for RIS Using Windows Setup Manager

1. Log on to your Windows 2000 computer as a Domain
Administrator.

2. Click Start and then Run. In the Run dialog box, type **setupmgr** to start the Windows Setup Manager, as shown in Figure 9.34. If you did not place the Windows Setup Manager files in a folder in your path, select the Browse button and browse to the location of the file to open it.

3. The Setup Manager Wizard starts and displays the information dialog box as shown in Figure 9.35. Click Next to continue.

4. The next screen gives you the choice of creating a new answer file, modifying an existing one, or creating one that duplicates the current computer's configuration (see Figure 9.36). If you want to modify the default Ristandard.sif answer file created when you configured RIS, use the Browse button to locate the file. Because you are creating a new answer file for a different image, select Create a new answer file and click Next.

5. The Product to Install screen in Figure 9.37 gives you the choice of what type of answer file to create. The choices are a Windows 2000 Unattended Installation, Sysprep Install, or Remote Installation Services. Select Remote Installation Services and click Next to continue.

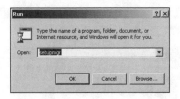

FIGURE 9.34
Open Windows Setup Manager from the Start, Run menu option.

FIGURE 9.35
Windows Setup Manager starts and displays the information dialog box.

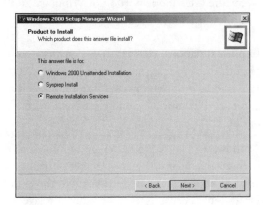

FIGURE 9.37
Select Remote Installation Services from the Windows Setup Manager Wizard to create an answer file to be used with RIS.

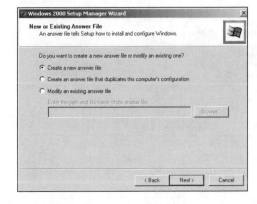

FIGURE 9.36
Windows Setup Manager enables you to create a new answer file, create an answer file to duplicate the current computer's configuration, or modify an existing answer file.

continues

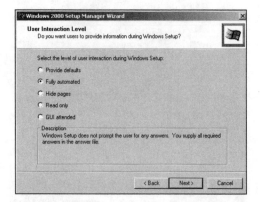

FIGURE 9.38
To fully automate the installation of Windows 2000 Professional using RIS, select Fully Automated from the User Interaction Level screen.

continued

6. The next screen, shown in Figure 9.38, prompts you to specify the level of user interaction to take place during the installation. The choices are as follows:

- **Provide defaults.** The SIF file includes default choices, which the user can override during the installation process.

- **Fully automated.** The installation process installs Windows 2000 Professional without any user interaction.

- **Hide pages.** The installation process does not display pages that have all options configured via the answer file to the user. Any pages requiring user interaction are displayed.

- **Read only.** The pages displayed during setup are not hidden from the user, but the user also cannot make changes to the selections contained in the answer file. This tells the user what is going on but does not let his or her change the options.

- **GUI-attended.** The Text-mode portion of setup is fully automated, but the user is able to make all the choices for the GUI-mode portion of Windows 2000 Professional installation.

In most situations, you will create an answer file that will perform the entire installation of Windows 2000 Professional without any user interaction. Select Fully automated from the list and click Next to configure this option.

7. As shown in Figure 9.39, you are prompted to accept the license agreement on the next screen. Because you have selected a fully automated installation, the Windows 2000 Professional license agreement is not displayed to the user. However, someone with the authority to agree to the license agreement must do so to make the installation of Windows 2000 Professional legal. Review the license

agreement and check the I accept the terms of the License Agreement check box to agree to it. Click Next to continue.

8. You next are prompted for the password to use for the Administrator account on the target computer, as shown in Figure 9.40. If you selected a fully automated installation, this is the only option available; if user interaction is possible during the setup process, you also have the option of enabling the user to select the Administrator password him- or herself. Specifying a password makes the password used for all computers using this answer file the same (that is, the same administrator password will exist on all machines using this answer file); enabling the user to select one gives the user administrative control of his or her desktop. Choose the option that follows your company's policies and is available for the installation type you have selected. For this example, type a password of your choosing in the Password and Confirm Password fields.

   If you leave the Administrator password blank, you also have the option to automatically log on to the machine as Administrator during the first boot. This is the least secure option and is not recommended.

9. As shown in Figure 9.41, you are now prompted to select display settings for the target machine. If you leave all choices as the Windows default, your target machine will be set up to use 16 colors at 640×480 resolution at the default refresh frequency for the card and monitor. If you want to change this to a new default to be used on the target computer, make the changes here. You also have the option to select custom settings from here. Change the defaults to the settings shown in Figure 9.41 and click Next to continue.

continues

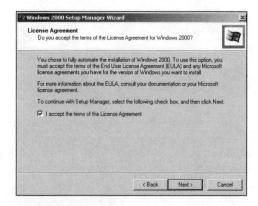

FIGURE 9.39
You must agree to the Windows 2000 Professional license agreement to perform a fully automated installation and to create the SIF file.

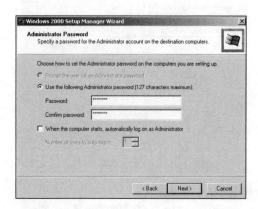

FIGURE 9.40
Specify a password to be used for the Administrator account on the target computer.

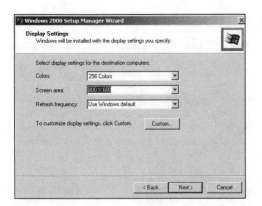

FIGURE 9.41
Modify the display settings to those you want
the target computer to have on this screen.

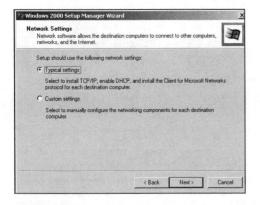

FIGURE 9.42
Choose the network configuration of the target
computer by selecting Typical or Custom
Settings on this screen.

continued

10. The Network Settings dialog box (see Figure 9.42) appears next, asking you whether you want the target computer to have Typical Settings or Custom Settings, which you configure. Typical settings include a DHCP-enabled machine with TCP/IP only and Client for Microsoft Networks. If you want to specify more than one network adapter or additional network protocols (such as IPX/SPX or NetBEUI) or services, you must choose Custom Settings. To choose Typical Settings, select the radio button and click Next.

11. Windows 2000 requires proper time zone settings on all computers. From the dialog box displayed in Figure 9.43, select whether the client computers should have the same time zone configuration as the RIS server or, using the drop-down list box, different time zone settings. Click Next after making your choice.

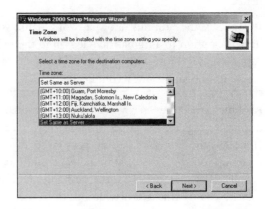

FIGURE 9.43
Determine whether the time zone settings for the target computer should
be the same as the RIS server from this screen.

12. The next screen, as shown in Figure 9.44, enables you to specify whether to configure additional settings or leave them at the default values. Additional settings that can be configured include the following:

- **Telephony.** This option configures the area code, country, and telephone properties for the target machine. These would be used when dialing out with a modem (see Figure 9.45).

- **Regional Settings.** These settings include date format, currency, numbers, and keyboard layout (see Figure 9.46).

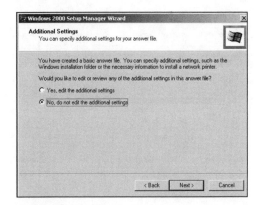

FIGURE 9.44
Choose whether to install Windows 2000 Professional using the default settings or customize the computer environment from this screen.

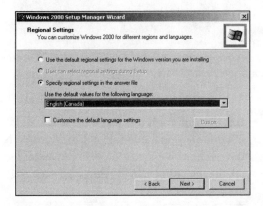

FIGURE 9.46
Regional Settings for the computer can be configured using custom settings.

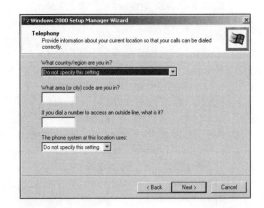

FIGURE 9.45
Telephony properties can be configured using custom settings.

- **Languages.** This option enables you to install support for additional languages on the client computer (see Figure 9.47).

continues

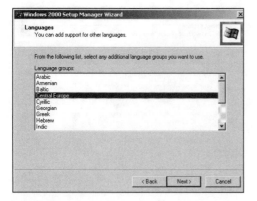

FIGURE 9.47
The computer's Language settings can be configured using custom settings.

- **Browse and Shell Settings.** Here you can configure proxy settings for Internet Explorer (see Figure 9.48).

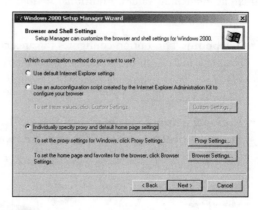

FIGURE 9.48
Internet Explorer proxy settings and the contents of the Favorites folder in IE can be configured using custom settings.

- **Installation Folder.** If you want to install Windows 2000 Professional in a folder other than WINNT on the system drive, you can select the folder location for the operating system here (see Figure 9.49).

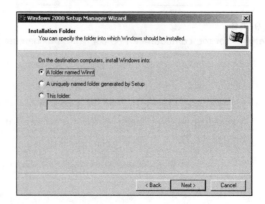

FIGURE 9.49
To install Windows 2000 Professional in a different folder when using RIS, configure the location using custom settings.

- **Network Printers.** If you want the target computer to be automatically configured to connect to one or more network printers after installation, specify the name and location of the printers using this dialog box (see Figure 9.50).

- **Run Once.** The Run Once dialog box enables you to input the names of programs to be run after the installation completes. This enables you to start the installation of additional programs for the user after Windows 2000 Professional is installed. This can be used to install applications that are not part of Windows 2000 but are required by the user (see Figure 9.51).

If you do not want to specify any additional custom settings, click Next to accept the Windows 2000 Professional defaults.

13. As shown in Figure 9.52, you now need to provide a name and description for the answer file you are creating. The name is displayed to users when they initiate Windows 2000 setup through RIS. It should be descriptive enough and distinctive enough to let users know what they are installing. Type the name and description on this screen and then click Next to continue.

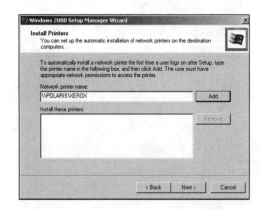

FIGURE 9.50
To automatically install network printers on the target computer, use custom settings to configure which printers to install.

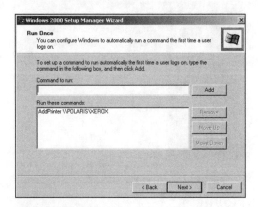

FIGURE 9.51
Additional programs can be run after installation completes by specifying the path and executable filename custom settings.

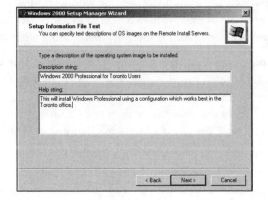

FIGURE 9.52
Enter a descriptive name and additional information about the SIF file being created to advise the user of the contents of this Windows 2000 Professional configuration.

continues

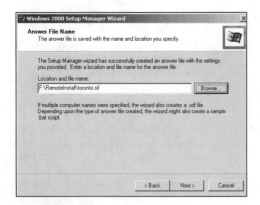

FIGURE 9.53
Specify the name and location of the answer file.

FIGURE 9.54
After you have completed your answer file configuration, click Finish to exit Windows Setup Manager.

continued

14. The next screen, shown in Figure 9.53, prompts you to specify the name and location of the answer file. You can name the file anything you like, but you should place it in the RIS server image folder created during the configuration of Remote Installation Services. Multiple files can exist in the same folder. Type the name and location of the SIF file and then click Next to save it.

15. The final screen for Setup Manager, shown in Figure 9.54, indicates which files were created and tasks performed. Click Finish to exit Windows Setup Manager and complete the creation of your answer file.

After creating the answer file, you might want to modify the file to include additional changes. For example, you might not want to install games on the client computers in a business environment. To modify the answer file, use Notepad and make the necessary changes.

Associating an Answer File with a CD-Based Image

After creating an answer file configured to use Remote Installation Services to perform the installation of Windows 2000 Professional, it is necessary to associate this answer file with a CD-based image. Associating an answer file with a CD-based image makes the settings in the answer file available for use when performing a remote install.

It is possible to associate several answer files with the same CD-based image because the files used to install Windows 2000 Professional on a computer are the same for a given CPU family (for example, Intel processors). You would have more than one CD-based image if other CPU families were used or if a locale-specific version of Windows 2000 Professional needed to be used (for example, Canadian French).

To associate an answer file with a CD-based image, perform the steps in Step by Step 9.7.

STEP BY STEP

9.7 Associating an Answer File with a CD-Based Image

1. Log on to your Windows 2000 computer as a Domain Administrator.

2. From the Start menu, select Programs, Administrative Tools, and then Active Directory Users and Computers.

3. In Active Directory User and Computers, expand the appropriate folder containing your RIS server.

4. Right-click your RIS server computer and select Properties.

5. In the Properties dialog box, click the Remote Install tab to display the Remote Installation Services options for the computer, as shown in Figure 9.55.

6. Click Advanced Settings from the Remote Install tab to view the advanced configuration information for RIS, as shown in Figure 9.56.

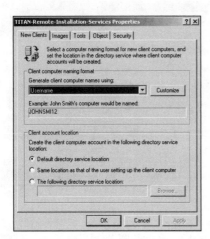

FIGURE 9.56
Clicking Advanced on the Remote Install tab of the computer Properties dialog box in Active Directory Users and Computers displays the advanced properties for the RIS server.

N O T E **Understand Changes** The answer file created by Windows Setup Manager has all the default sections and tags required to perform an unattended installation using Remote Installation Services. A thorough understanding of the section tags and options available should exist prior to making changes to the file because errors in your changes could make the answer file unusable. The document unattend.doc, located in DEPLOY.CAB on the Windows 2000 CD-ROM in the SUPPORT\TOOLS folder, provides information on answer file sections and tags. This file should be reviewed prior to making any manual changes to answer files.

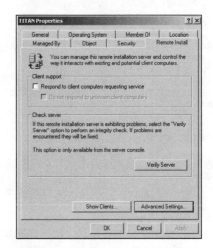

FIGURE 9.55
The Remote Install tab of the computer Properties dialog box in Active Directory Users and Computers displays the RIS settings for the server.

continues

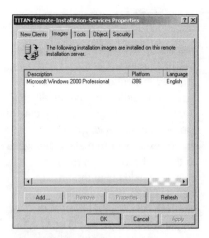

FIGURE 9.57
To display a list of images and to add or remove images to be used by RIS, select the Images tab in the advanced Properties dialog box.

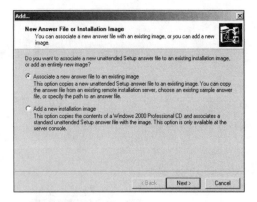

FIGURE 9.58
To add a new image or to associate an answer file with an existing image, click Add on the Images tab.

continued

7. In the Remote Installation Services advanced Properties dialog box, click the Images tab, as shown in Figure 9.57.

8. In the Images tab, click Add to add another image to the list of available images. This displays the screen shown in Figure 9.58.

9. In the New Answer File or Installation Image dialog box, you have the option to add a new CD-based image or to associate a new answer file with an existing image. Select Associate a new answer file to an existing image and click Next.

10. In the dialog box that follows (see Figure 9.59), you need to specify the location from which the answer file will be copied. Choices are Windows image sample files provided with Windows 2000 and created during the initial RIS setup, another RIS server, or an alternate path, which includes any location. Select An alternate location and click Next.

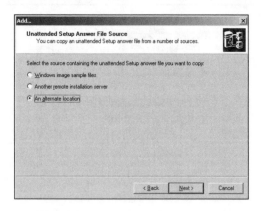

FIGURE 9.59
Specify the general location of the answer file to be used, either a sample answer file, one located on another RIS server, or an answer file on disk (alternate location).

11. In the dialog box presented in Figure 9.60, browse to the location of the answer file you created and select the file. When done, click Next to continue.

12. As shown in Figure 9.61, you are then prompted for the Windows 2000 image on the RIS server with which you want to associate this answer file. Select the image by clicking it and then click Next to continue.

13. You next are prompted to confirm the name and description of the image to be installed using this answer file (see Figure 9.62). This is the same name and description you provided when you created the answer file using Windows Setup Manager. If you want to make changes, do so and then click Next.

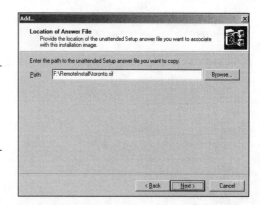

FIGURE 9.60
Browse your disk to locate the answer file and click Next to continue.

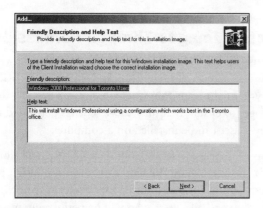

FIGURE 9.62
Specify the name and description of the image to be installed and click Next.

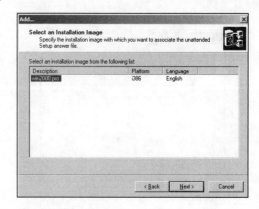

FIGURE 9.61
Select the image with which to associate the answer file and click Next.

14. Review the settings for the answer file you will be installing to use the image and click Finish to copy the file to the template location, as shown in Figure 9.63.

continues

FIGURE 9.63
Confirm your settings in the review screen and click Finish to copy the answer file to the Templates folder.

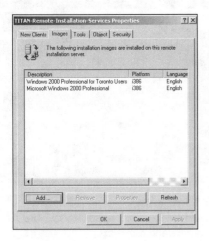

FIGURE 9.64
The Images tab is updated with the new answer file image information after you click Finish.

continued

15. As shown in Figure 9.64, the new answer file is added to the list of images that can be installed from this server using RIS. Click OK to close the advanced Properties dialog box and again to close the RIS server Properties dialog box.

16. Exit Active Directory Users and Computers.

You have now installed a new answer file that can be used to perform a remote install of Windows 2000 Professional with the settings of the answer file. However, you might want to restrict which users can use this image to ensure that only authorized users have privileges to install the image.

Restricting Images Through Permissions

After an image is created and an answer file is associated with the image, it is available to all users who can connect to the RIS server. However, you might want to restrict which users are able to use certain images to ensure that only those settings permitted to be installed by a user can be installed on a computer.

Permissions to images are set by assigning NTFS permissions to the SIF (that is, answer) file on the hard drive. You can assign permissions directly to a SIF file to limit its use. Typically, you would create a security group and add users who will be performing installs of a particular image to the group. You would then assign permissions to the group so its members have access to the image, while other users and groups do not.

To assign permissions to the SIF file you just associated with an image, follow this Step by Step.

STEP BY STEP

9.8 Assigning Permissions to Images

1. Log on to your Windows 2000 computer as a Domain Administrator.

2. From the Start menu, select Programs, Accessories, and then Windows Explorer.

3. Using Windows Explorer, navigate to the drive and folder where you installed your images when you configured Remote Installation Services. The answer file is located in a folder called Templates under the folder containing the image you installed on the RIS server, as shown in Figure 9.65.

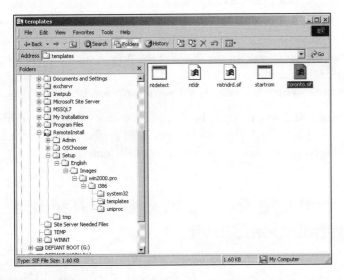

FIGURE 9.65
Navigate to the Templates folder in the path where you installed the image to locate the answer file to which you want to assign permissions.

4. Right-click the SIF file whose permissions you want to modify and then select the Security tab to show the current permissions on the file, as shown in Figure 9.66.

5. As you will note, permissions currently assigned to the file are grayed in the security box. This means they have been inherited from the parent folder. To assign specific permissions to a group, you need to remove the inherited permissions. To do so, uncheck Allow inheritable permissions from parent to propagate to this object. This presents the dialog box shown in Figure 9.67. Select Copy to copy the existing permissions to the file.

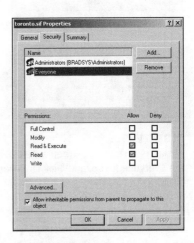

FIGURE 9.66
Right-click the SIF file whose permissions you want to change and select Security to display the Security tab and existing permissions.

continues

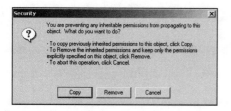

FIGURE 9.67
To remove inherited permissions, uncheck Allow inherited permissions from parent to propagate to this object and click Copy to copy the inherited permissions to the file.

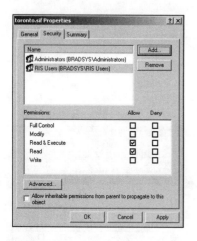

FIGURE 9.68
Assign permissions as required, remove the Everyone group, and click OK when done.

continued

6. Click Add to add the security group or users to whom you want to assign permissions for the image and make sure they are assigned Read and Read & Execute permissions on the file. Remove permissions for the Everyone group, as shown in Figure 9.68.

7. Click OK to confirm permission assignment on the file.

8. Exit Windows Explorer.

You have now restricted the image to the Administrators group plus any additional users who should make use of this image. To assign permissions on other images, follow the same procedure.

At this point, you are ready to allow users with appropriate permissions to install the image of Windows 2000 Professional with the settings specified in your answer file on their computers.

Creating a RIPrep Image for Remote Installation Services

An alternative to CD-based images with Remote Installation Services is to use a *Remote Installation Preparation* (RIPrep) image. RIPrep images enable you to deploy not only Windows 2000 Professional but a preconfigured computer installation including other applications and other PC settings. Furthermore, RIPrep images are a compressed form of the operating system and applications copied onto computers by RIS; therefore, they allow a quick installation of all required components for a user's desktop.

For example, if your company has a standard set of applications that all users need to have available when a new machine is installed, you have two ways to ensure that the computer is configured properly. First, you can use a CD-based image to install Windows 2000 Professional using Remote Installation Services and then manually install the applications or deploy them using Group Policy if possible. The second method is to install Windows 2000 Professional on a computer, install all the applications, make any changes to the environment as necessary, and then image the entire thing to create a RIPrep image. The RIPrep image can then be deployed using Remote Installation Services and, in this way, install the operating system, applications, and all required settings on the machine at the same time.

Determining whether to use a CD-based image or a RIPrep image depends on a number of factors including frequency of changes. If the standard user desktop configuration changes frequently, a RIPrep image would have to be updated and installed on a RIS server whenever a change took place. This would require the preparation of a source computer with the new settings quite frequently (that is, whenever the configuration changed). Doing this might require more work than using a CD-based image and installing the software manually or through Group Policy. However, if the standard applications used in the organization are not updated too frequently (such as every three months or even less frequently), RIPrep could provide an easy way to deploy fully configured desktops. Any minor changes to the computer configuration and application settings can be deployed using Group Policy or through SMS or some other method.

When creating a RIPrep image to be used to install Windows 2000 Professional and applications, you need two computers:

◆ The source computer onto which you will install Windows 2000 Professional and all applications. The source computer is the basis for the creation of the RIPrep image using a tool provided with Remote Installation Services.

◆ A RIS server onto which the RIPrep image will be copied and from which it will be available to be installed onto other machines to clone the source computer applications and settings.

> **NOTE**
>
> **CD-Based Image Needed** To install a RIPrep image on a RIS server and have that image available for installation on other machines, the RIS server must already contain a CD-based image. This should not normally be a problem because the configuration of RIS creates a default CD-based image. If the CD-based image is for a different CPU family than the RIPrep image, however, you need to install a CD-based image from the same CPU family as the RIPrep image prior to installing the RIPrep image on the RIS server for the deployment to work.

Configuring the Source Computer

The first thing you need to do to create a RIPrep image is to configure the source computer with the same configuration and applications that will be deployed on the additional workstations. This involves five tasks:

1. Install Windows 2000 Professional on the source machine. Because you are only able to deploy Windows 2000 Professional using RIS, the operating system installed on the source machine must be Windows 2000 Professional.

2. Configure Windows 2000 components and settings as required for the source and all target machines. This means that, if you want to have a specific desktop look and feel, it should be configured the way you want all users to have their desktops looking when they install the image. Also, if you want users to have a DHCP-assigned TCP/IP address or additional protocols or network services installed, this should be performed on the source computer. You are mirroring the configuration of the source computer on the target machines, so make sure all settings on the source are as you want them to be on the targets.

3. Install and configure the applications required for this desktop configuration. When installing the applications, use the normal setup programs or Windows Installer packages to copy the necessary files and then add any additional items, such as desktop shortcuts, menu items, or company templates, onto the hard drive of the source computer. You can have Windows 2000 Group Policy also automatically install assigned applications. Alternatively, at this time, you can install published applications on the source computer that might later be deployed using Group Policy. This minimizes the amount of network traffic—that is, if Group Policy later checks to make sure the target computer has an application installed; installing it on the source and deploying it using RIS when the computer is configured saves time later when the machine is restarted and the user logs on.

4. Test the operating system and applications to make sure everything works as expected. This is a very important step. It is not very useful to create a RIPrep image of a source computer and applications, have it be deployed, and then realize things are

not working as they should. Test, test, and test again to be sure all the applications and the operating system work as required on the target computers after being deployed using RIS.

5. Copy the Administrator profile of the source computer to the default User profile. This is required because all the configuration and installation of applications on the source machine are typically performed while logged on as Administrator. For these same settings to be available to the user of the target computer after the image is deployed, you need to have it configured as the default User profile because this profile is copied when a user logs on to the machine.

To copy the Administrator profile to the default User profile, perform these steps.

STEP BY STEP

9.9 Copying the Administrator Profile to the Default User Profile on the Source Machine

1. Log on to your source Windows 2000 Professional computer as an Administrator.

2. Create a new user on the computer by copying the Administrator user. If you copy the Administrator user when creating another user, this also copies group membership for the user. You need to be a member of the Administrators group on the source machine to copy the profile.

3. Log off the machine and log on again as the new administrative user you created in step 2.

4. Right-click My Computer and then click Properties.

5. In the System Properties dialog box, click the User Profiles tab.

6. Select the profile for Administrator and then click Copy To.

continues

continued

7. In the Copy To dialog box, copy the profile to the C:\Document and Settings\Default User path where the default User profile is stored.

8. In the Permitted to Use This Profile section of the Copy To dialog box, click the Change button to change who is allowed to use this profile.

9. In the List Names From box, click the local computer.

10. In the Names box, click Everyone and then click Add to give the Everyone group (that is, all users) permission to use this profile.

11. Click OK to close this dialog box and then click OK again to close the Copy To dialog box.

12. Close the System Properties dialog box.

13. Log off as the new administrative user and log on again as Administrator.

14. Delete the new administrative user you created to make a copy of the Administrator profile.

After you have configured the source computer with Windows 2000 Professional, configured the applications to be used on the machine, and copied the Administrator user profile to the default User profile, the hard work is mostly over. At this point, you need to create an image of the source computer configuration so that it can be deployed on other machines.

Creating the RIPrep Image and Copying It to a RIS Server

The final step in making the RIPrep image available to users is to use a tool to image the source computer and copy the image to the RIS server. To do this, you run the Remote Installation Preparation Wizard across the network on the source computer itself. A RIS server must be available and be configured with a CD-based image of the same CPU family as the source computer for this step to work.

The Remote Installation Preparation Wizard does the following:

◆ It configures the source computer to a generic state by removing all unique settings such as a *security identifier* (SID) for the machine, the name of the computer, and any registry settings that need to be unique on each target computer.

◆ It creates a RIPrep image with the computer settings and copies the image to the RIS server you specify.

◆ It creates an answer (SIF) file and associates the answer file with the RIPrep image.

To create a RIPrep image and install it on a RIS server by running the Remote Installation Preparation Wizard, perform the following steps.

STEP BY STEP

9.10 Using the Remote Installation Preparation Wizard to Create a RIPrep Image on a RIS Server

1. Log on to your source Windows 2000 Professional computer as an Administrator.

2. From the Start menu, select Run.

3. In the Run dialog box, start the Remote Installation Wizard from the RIS server by running the riprep.exe file, for example:

```
\\<RIS_SERVER>\reminst\admin\i386\riprep.exe
```

where <RIS_SERVER> is the name of your RIS server. Click OK.

4. In the dialog box that appears, specify the required options as follows:

Option	Description
Server name	Enter the name of the RIS server on which you want to store this RIPrep image; that will be used to deploy the image to target machines.

continues

continued

Option	Description
Folder name	Enter the name of the folder on the RIS server that will be used to store this image.
Friendly description	Enter the name you want users to see when they start a remote installation to install an image. The name should provide information about what is contained on the image (such as "Standard Sales Desktop").
Help text	Enter descriptive information on what the image contains and its intended purpose or audience.

5. To start imaging, click Finish. The Remote Installation Preparation Wizard performs its tasks and notifies you when done.

NOTE

Manual Load Balancing of RIPrep Images The Remote Installation Preparation Wizard creates and installs the RIPrep image of the source computer on only one RIS server. In many organizations, you might find that you require multiple RIS servers to balance the load in deploying Windows 2000 Professional or to have the same set of images available in many geographic locations. To make the RIPrep image you created available on other RIS servers, copy the image to other RIS servers and users can deploy it.

You are now ready to deploy this image on target computers with all applications and desktop settings mirroring the source computer. If you want to limit the RIPrep image to a select group of users, as with the CD-based image, modify the NTFS permissions on the SIF file associated with the image to restrict access to the image.

Creating the RIPrep image and installing it on a RIS server is the final step in the process of imaging a source computer. As you have seen, steps involved include installing Windows 2000 Professional and all applications on the source computers, copying the Administrator profile to the default user profile, and finally, using the Remote Installation Preparation Wizard to create the image and install it on a RIS server. You are now ready to perform a remote installation of the image as well as any image on the RIS server.

PERFORMING A REMOTE INSTALLATION

After installing Remote Installation Services on a target server, authorizing the RIS server in Active Directory, configuring the server and installing the initial CD-based image, creating additional images, granting permissions for users to create computer accounts in the domain, and setting the required permissions on the image files, you are ready to enable users to install a Windows 2000 Professional image on a target computer. As always, when deploying a new technology, it is a good idea to test the RIS installation of each image on a test computer before making it available to all users. If you have multiple configurations of computers to which you will deploy Windows 2000 Professional using either a CD-based or RIPrep image, each configuration should be thoroughly tested before a large-scale deployment.

Configuring Server Installation Options

Deploy Windows 2000 by using Remote Installation Services (RIS).

- **Configure remote installation options.**

Before enabling clients to make use of RIS, you might want to configure options on the RIS server to set how computer account names are generated. You can also specify the directory service context in Active Directory where the computer account will be created. This is done by invoking the Properties dialog box for the RIS Server in Active Directory Users and Computers.

To configure client computer-naming options and Active Directory computer context for clients using the RIS server, follow these steps.

STEP BY STEP

9.11 Configuring Client Computer-Naming Options and Directory Context

1. Log on to your Windows 2000 computer as a domain Administrator.

2. From the Start menu, select Programs, Administrative Tools, and then Active Directory Users and Computers.

3. Locate your RIS server within the Active Directory tree, right-click it, and select Properties.

continues

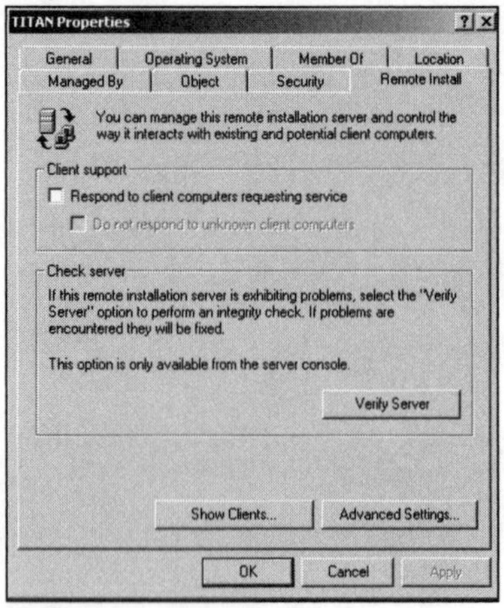

FIGURE 9.69
Configure RIS server settings on the Remote Install tab of your RIS server's Properties dialog box.

continued

4. From the Properties dialog box, click the Remote Install tab to display the RIS server settings, as shown in Figure 9.69.

5. Click the Advanced Settings button to open the advanced properties for the RIS server. The Remote-Installation-Services Properties dialog box, similar to Figure 9.70, displays.

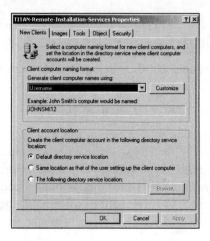

FIGURE 9.70
The Remote-Installation-Services Properties dialog box enables you to specify computer naming options, among other things.

> **NOTE**
>
> **Disabling All Images on a RIS Server**
> Note that you can globally enable whether your server responds to client requests by checking the Respond to client computers requesting service check box on the Remote Install tab of the server's Properties dialog box. Unchecking it makes the images on the server unavailable, and clients will not be able to use this RIS server.

6. The New Clients tab of the Remote-Installation-Services Properties dialog box enables you to change the way computer names are generated when clients install Windows 2000 Professional on their machines using RIS. The default naming format is UserName. (The user's first and last name is used to create the computer name.)

7. To select a computer-naming format, select one of the preconfigured naming formats in the drop-down list box or, if you want to have full control over the way names are created, click the Customize button, which displays a dialog box similar to Figure 9.71.

8. To specify in which Active Directory context to create the computer account when installing Windows 2000 Professional using RIS, select one of the options in Client account location. The available options are as follows:

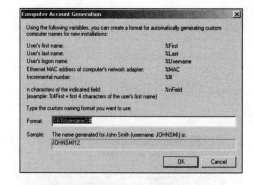

Option	*Active Directory Location*
Default directory location	Create the new computer account in the Computers container for the domain in Active Directory. Use this option, the default, when the person installing RIS is different from the user who will eventually make use of the machine. In this way, all computers are placed in the Computers container and can be moved to another OU by the administrator for Group Policy application.
Same location as the user setting up the client computer	Create the new computer account in the same OU as the domain user account for the user installing Windows 2000 Professional using RIS. This enables all users and computers to be created in the same OU and enables you to configure uniform Group Policy settings for both. If the user installing Windows 2000 Professional using RIS will be the one using the machine, this is a good choice.
A specific directory service location	Create the computer account in an OU specified in the Browse box. If you want all RIS-deployed computers to be placed in a specific OU to indicate that they were installed using RIS, this might be a good choice. In this way, you can determine which machines have been deployed using RIS and then move them to the appropriate container later for Group Policy and/or organization reasons.

9. After you have configured the naming conventions to be used for computers and the Active Directory context into which to place the RIS-deployed machines, click OK to close the Remote-Installation-Services Properties dialog box.

continues

continued

10. Click OK to close the RIS server properties dialog box and save your changes.

11. Exit Active Directory Users and Computers.

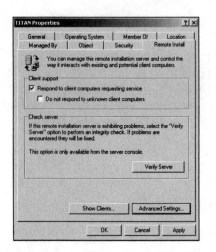

FIGURE 9.72
Make sure to check the Respond to client computers requesting service check box on the Remote Install tab of the RIS server.

Now you can truly say you are ready to deploy your Windows 2000 Professional images. Do not forget to check the Respond to client computers requesting service check box on the RIS server computer Remote Install tab of the Properties dialog box (see Figure 9.72); otherwise, clients are not able to connect to the RIS server and be given a list of images to install. If you have done this, make sure you have clients meeting the system requirements and start to deploy.

Configuring Client Installation Options

Deploy Windows 2000 by using Remote Installation Services (RIS).

- **Install an image on a RIS client computer.**

During the installation of Windows 2000 Professional from a RIS server, you might want to give certain users performing the installation the capability to specify settings or to force the installation to operate completely without user interaction. The characteristics of the installation are specified in a *Group Policy object* (GPO) assigned to the user performing the installation. If more than one GPO applies to the user, the settings at the OU or lowest level take effect unless No Override has been configured at a higher level.

To configure client installation options in Group Policy for users performing the install, follows these steps.

STEP BY STEP

9.12 Configuring Client Installation Options Using Group Policy

1. Log on to your Windows 2000 computer as a Domain Administrator.

2. From the Start menu, select Programs, Administrative Tools, and then Active Directory Users and Computers.

3. Locate the OU (that is, the container) for the users that will be performing the installation (or select the domain to apply these settings to all users), right-click the container, and select Properties.

4. In the Properties dialog box for the container, select Group Policy.

5. In the Group Policy screen, select an existing Group Policy whose settings you want to modify or create a new Group Policy for RIS client settings. Click Edit to open the Group Policy Editor.

6. In the Group Policy Editor, expand User Configuration, Windows Settings, and then Remote Installation Services, as shown in Figure 9.73.

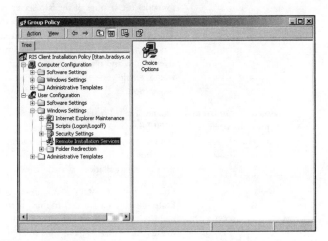

FIGURE 9.73
To change client installation options for RIS, configure the Remote Installation Services settings in Group Policy for the users who will perform the installations.

7. In the details pane, double-click Choice Options to display the RIS client installation options, as shown in Figure 9.74.

continues

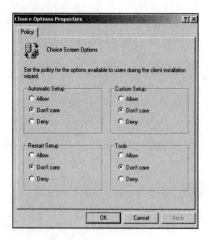

FIGURE 9.74
Double-clicking Choice Options enables you
to set the RIS client options.

continued

8. Modify the settings in the Choice Options dialog box as
   required for your organization. You have three choices for
   each setting: Allow, Don't care, and Deny. Allow turns the
   setting on; Don't care leaves it as set by a previous policy
   or at the default specified in the RIS server
   configuration; Deny explicitly disallows the setting.

   The settings available to be changed include:

Setting	*Description*
Automatic Setup	Install Windows 2000 Professional using the computer-naming rules and computer account location indicated in the RIS server configuration (which you performed in the preceding Step by Step).
Custom Setup	Enables the user to specify the computer name and Active Directory container where the computer account will be created. This overrides the settings of the RIS server and enables clients to name their machines using another naming convention. For example, if client machines in an office were named after moons and planets, setting this option would enable you to support that convention.
Restart Setup (from a previous attempt)	Enables a failed installation of Windows 2000 Professional using RIS to restart on the computer without the user being prompted to reenter information previously specified in the Client Installation Wizard.
Tools	Enables the user installing Windows 2000 Professional to have access to third-party maintenance and troubleshooting tools on the machine, such as being able to upgrade the BIOS. This is intended to be used by technical support personnel and should be allowed in GPOs applied to tech support users; it should not, however, normally be assigned to users.
	The tools that can be used for maintenance and troubleshooting through RIS are specified on the Tools tab of the Remote-Installation-Services Properties dialog box invoked by the Advanced Settings button on the Remote Install tab of the RIS server's Properties dialog box (see Figure 9.75).

The default settings for RIS only allow Automatic Setup. If you desire any other configuration, you need to specify it in the GPO. Do so.

9. Click OK to save your option settings and close the Choice Options dialog box.

10. Close the Group Policy Editor to save the GPO settings.

11. Click OK to close the container Properties dialog box.

12. Exit Active Directory Users and Computers.

Group Policy, once again, is a powerful tool in specifying the behavior of Windows 2000 services, RIS in this case. Group Policy can be used to make sure corporate policies on the deployment of Windows 2000 using RIS are adhered to.

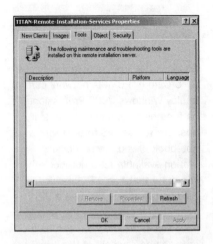

FIGURE 9.75
The Tools tab of the Remote-Installation-Services Properties dialog box is where you specify third-party troubleshooting and maintenance tools.

Client Computer Requirements

The first step in deploying Windows 2000 Professional on a computer using Remote Installation Services is to make sure the computer meets the hardware requirements for Windows 2000 Professional as well as RIS. Installing Windows 2000 using RIS does not change the requirements for the operating system, only the method used to install the operating system on a machine.

The hardware requirements for a client computer using Windows 2000 Professional are as follows:

Hardware Component	*Requirement*
CPU	Pentium 166 or greater. Pentium II 300 or better recommended.
Memory	64MB of RAM minimum; 128MB of RAM recommended.
Hard disk space	1GB of hard disk space minimum; 2GB of hard disk space recommended. SCSI and IDE hard disks are supported.

continues

continued

Hardware Component	Requirement
Network adapter	A PCI network adapter operating at 10MBps minimum (such as 10BASE-T); 100MBps recommended (100BASE-TX). The adapter should either have a PXE-based boot ROM (version .99c or greater) or be supported by a RIS boot disk. PC Card/PCMCIA network adapters are not supported.
Boot device	The computer should be configured to boot from the PXE-enabled network card.

If your target computer meets the hardware requirements, you are now ready to deploy Windows 2000 Professional to the machine using RIS.

Using RIS to Install an Image on a Computer With a PXE-Compliant Network Card

To install Windows 2000 Professional on a computer with a PXE-enabled network card, make sure the computer is configured to boot from the network card. To verify this, during the computer's *Power-On Self Test* (POST), press the key combination that enables you to enter BIOS setup and verify that the first boot device is the network card.

After making sure the network card is the first boot device, restart the computer. When the network card indicates that it is trying to boot from the network, press F12. After the client computer establishes a connection with a RIS server (and after it has been assigned an IP address by a DHCP server and referred to a RIS server), the user is prompted to press F12 again to download the Client Installation Wizard.

After the Client Installation Wizard has been downloaded, the user is prompted to log on to the domain. If the logon is successful, the user is provided with a list of options.

NOTE

Notebooks Can Be Deployed Using RIS Although Remote Installation Services does not enable you to use a PC Card or PCMCIA network card to deploy Windows 2000 Professional on a notebook computer, it is still possible to use RIS to deploy to a notebook. If you have a docking station available for a notebook computer that has a PCI network card installed, you can use a RIS boot disk. If the card is PXE-enabled, boot across the network and then start the deployment of Windows 2000 Professional. This is the only way to deploy Windows 2000 using RIS to a notebook computer.

As an aside, some newer notebook computers available on the market today have integrated PCI-based network cards. If these cards are supported by a RIS boot disk or are PXE-enabled, it might be possible to deploy Windows 2000 Professional to these notebook computers using RIS without the requirement for a docking station.

Option	*Description*
Automatic Setup	Users are allowed to choose which image to install, and if the user has permission to access the image, the one chosen is installed on the client computer without user intervention. If just a single image is available on the RIS server, the user is not prompted and the installation starts automatically.
Custom Setup	Users might be able to override the computer name and Active Directory container in which the computer will be stored. This option works only if the user has not been denied Custom Setup permissions in a Group Policy that applies to him.
Restart Setup (from a previous attempt)	The user can restart a failed attempt to install the image on the computer. This option restarts the entire installation process from the beginning but does not prompt the user to provide options that were already registered during the initial installation attempt.
Maintenance and Troubleshooting	The user can use third-party maintenance tools to perform troubleshooting on the target computer.

> **NOTE**
>
> **Multilingual Deployment**
> The menu presented to the user when he presses F12 is based on the contents of a file called WELCOME.OSC located in the OSChooser folder in the RIS shared folder on the RIS server. By default, this file is in English and assumes that all user prompts should be in English. Microsoft provides a sample file called MULTILNG.OSC in the same location that shows you how to make your prompts and user interaction with RIS multilingual. This file should be used as a template to create your own multilingual menu of deployment options should your requirements dictate it.

After you have made your selection, the installation process commences. If you selected a custom setup, you are prompted for the name to be used for the computer and the location of the Active Directory container in which to create the computer account.

Using RIS to Install an Image on a Computer Using a RIS Boot Disk

Deploy Windows 2000 by using Remote Installation Services (RIS).

- **Create a RIS boot disk.**

In situations in which the network card on a machine is not PXE compliant, you are still able to use RIS to deploy a Windows 2000 Professional image on a target machine. If the target machine has a PCI network card supported by the RIS boot disk, you can create the disk and have it emulate the PXE environment.

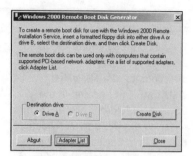

FIGURE 9.76
The Windows 2000 Remote Boot Disk
Generator can be used to create a
Remote Installation Services boot disk.

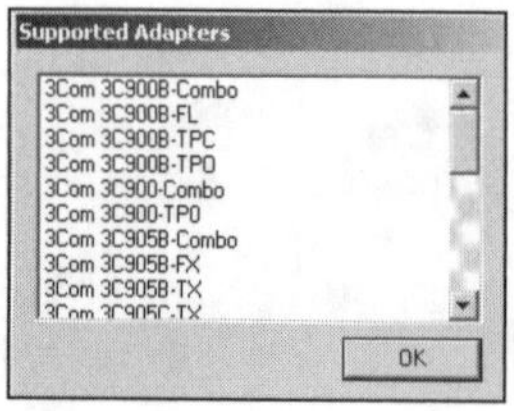

FIGURE 9.77
Clicking on Adapter List shows the
list of network cards supported by
the RIS boot disk. Verify that your
network card is on the list.

To create a RIS boot disk, follow these steps.

STEP BY STEP

9.13 Creating a RIS Boot Disk

1. Log on to any Windows 2000 computer as an Administrator.

2. From the Start menu, select Run.

3. In the Run dialog box, type

   \\<RIS_SERVER>\reminst\admin\i386\rbfg.exe

   where <RIS_SERVER> is the name of your RIS server. Click OK. This starts the Windows 2000 Remote Boot Disk Generator, as shown in Figure 9.76.

4. If you want to verify that the network adapter in your machine is supported by the RIS boot disk process, click Adapter List to display a dialog box similar to Figure 9.77.

   If you find that the network card on the target computer is not on the list of supported cards and is not PXE compliant, you cannot use RIS to deploy Windows 2000 Professional. You need to acquire a network card compatible with RIS or one that is PXE compliant. There are no other alternatives if you want to use RIS.

5. Insert a blank, formatted floppy disk in your floppy drive and click Create Disk to create the RIS boot disk.

After you have created the RIS boot disk, make sure the floppy drive is the default boot device on the target computer, insert the RIS boot disk in the floppy drive, and power on the machine. Similar to a PXE-compliant network boot, when the boot process starts, press F12 when prompted to do so. The rest of the steps to deploy a Windows 2000 Professional image using RIS are the same as a PXE-compliant network card boot (shown in Step by Step 9.12).

Prestaging Client Computers

Configure RIS security.

- **Prestage RIS client computers for added security and load balancing.**

By default, after a RIS server is installed, unless you specifically indicated that the RIS server should only respond to requests from known computers, the RIS server responds to requests from any client machine given an IP address through DHCP and requests the location of a RIS server in the DHCP Discover packet. Clearly, this presents a potential security hole and might allow the installation of a Windows 2000 Professional image by any user with a valid domain account that has permissions to the answer file.

To restrict the computers to which a RIS server responds, you need to prestage the client computers so that their identity will be known to the RIS server. Prestaging a client computer also designates which RIS server is used by the client to provide a list of images and to act as the source of the deployment image.

To prestage a client computer, you need to know the GUID of the client computer and then create the computer account in the domain before the RIS install takes place. The GUID of a client computer is provided by the manufacturer as part of the P XE specification and is commonly found on a label either inside or outside the computer case or might also commonly be found by looking at the BIOS settings. The GUID is always 32 characters long and has the format

$$\{dddddddd\text{-}dddd\text{-}dddd\text{-}dddd\text{-}dddddddddddd\}$$

where d is a hexadecimal value.

If your client computer does not have a PXE-enabled network card and you are using a RIS boot disk to deploy the Windows 2000 Professional image on the client computer, you can still prestage the computer. The GUID of a computer starting with a RIS boot disk is the MAC address of the network card padded with leading 0s to make sure the entire string is 32 characters long. For example:

$$\{00000000\text{-}0000\text{-}0000\text{-}0000\text{-}00104BF91001\}$$

After you have determined the GUID of the client machine, you can prestage the client computer using Active Directory Users and Computers. To prestage a client computer, follow these steps.

STEP BY STEP

9.14 Prestaging a Client Computer with a Known GUID

1. Log on to your Windows 2000 computer as a Domain Administrator.

2. Open Active Directory Users and Computers.

3. Right-click the OU where you want to create the computer account and point to New and then Computer.

4. In the New Object – Computer dialog box shown in Figure 9.78, enter the name of the computer to prestage and click Next.

5. On the next screen, shown in Figure 9.79, click the This is a managed computer check box and enter the GUID of the computer. If you entered the GUID in the proper format, the Next button should be available. When you have entered the GUID, click Next to continue.

FIGURE 9.78
To prestage a client computer, open the New Object – Computer dialog box to create the computer account.

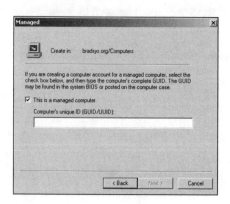

FIGURE 9.79
Enter the GUID of the computer to prestagstage and click Next after checking the This is a managed computer check box.

6. As shown in Figure 9.80, you now have the option of designating to which RIS server the client computer will connect to receive a list of images or whether to allow the client computer to connect to any RIS server to install Windows 2000 Professional. If you want to tie the client computer to a specific RIS server, make that selection and enter the fully qualified DNS name of the RIS server. After you have made your selection, click Next to continue.

7. The next screen, similar to Figure 9.81, displays a summary of settings. If everything is correct, click Finish to complete the prestaging of the client computer.

8. Exit Active Directory Users and Computers.

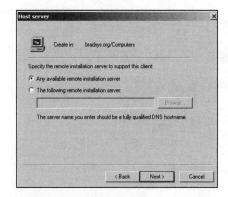

FIGURE 9.80
Determine whether the client computer will contact a specific RIS server for deployment or any available RIS server on this screen.

The preceding Step by Step guided you through the process of prestaging a client computer when the GUID is known. In some situations, especially on older computers, the GUID might not be known, such as when you are using a RIS boot disk and the MAC address of the network card cannot be easily found. However, it is still possible to prestage these computers. To prestage a computer for which the GUID is not known, follow these steps.

FIGURE 9.81
The summary screen shows a list of actions to be performed and the settings you supplied. Click Finish to prestage the computer.

STEP BY STEP

9.15 Prestaging a Client Computer with an Unknown GUID

1. Start the RIS client computer using a RIS client boot disk and log on to the domain as requested.

2. When prompted, select a setup option and press Enter.

3. Select an image when provided with a list and press Enter.

4. When you receive a warning, press Enter. The GUID for the client computer appears on the screen, and the computer is now prestaged.

5. Turn off the computer to prevent the initiation of a RIS image download.

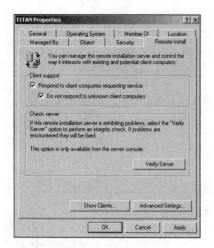

FIGURE 9.82
To make sure the RIS server only responds to requests from prestaged clients, select the Do not respond to unknown client computers check box on the Remote Install tab for the RIS Server.

At this time, the RIS client has been prestaged and can receive an image from any RIS server. If you want to assign the client computer to a specific RIS server, do so in the Properties dialog box of the RIS client computer in Active Directory Users and Computers.

A final task you might want to complete is to configure the RIS server to respond only to requests from clients that have been prestaged. This is accomplished by selecting the Do not respond to unknown client computers check box in the Remote Install tab for the RIS server, as shown in Figure 9.82.

Up to this point, you have gone through the process of installing and configuring, including authorizing, Remote Installation Services on a Windows 2000 Server, Advanced Server, or Data Center Server computers. You also have created a CD-based image and have walked through the process of creating a RIPrep image based on a source computer configuration. You then applied permissions to the images and prestaged computers to make sure only those machines whose GUIDs are known in Active Directory can make use of RIS, and then from a specific server and using a particular image. You also determined the necessary hardware requirements for RIS client computers and walked through the process of creating a RIS boot disk for those computers without a PXE-enabled network card. However, knowing all this and making sure all requirements are met, you might still encounter problems.

TROUBLESHOOTING REMOTE INSTALLATION SERVICES

> **Deploy Windows 2000 by using Remote Installation Services (RIS).**
>
> • **Troubleshoot RIS problems.**

Even though we all try to make sure problems do not occur, sometimes things go wrong despite our best efforts. The following table outlines a number of common problems, as well as the most likely cause and solution, that can be encountered with Remote Installation Services.

TABLE 9.1

PROBLEMS ENCOUNTERED WITH REMOTE INSTALLATION SERVICES

Problem	Cause	Solution
Client computers are not being assigned an IP address. No DHCP message appears during the boot process.	The most likely cause of this problem is that a Windows 2000 DHCP server is not available.	First, check to see if non-RIS clients are being assigned an IP address through DHCP. If not, check to make sure your DHCP server is running. If so, verify that your DHCP server is a Windows 2000 DHCP server, that it has been authorized in Active Directory, and that it is not a Windows NT 4.0 DHCP server. If so, verify that the client and the DHCP server are on different physical subnets and that a DHCP relay agent is available and functioning on the same subnet as the RIS client computer. Finally, ensure that the DHCP server has available addresses to lease and that the DHCP scope has been activated.
Clients are assigned an IP address but do not display the BINL message indicating a connection to the RIS server.	The most likely cause for this problem is that the RIS server is not online. Another possible problem could be that the RIS server is online but has not been authorized in Active Directory.	Bring the RIS server online and authorize it.
Client computers cannot start the download of an image.	This is most likely caused by a hung NetPC Boot Service Manager (BINLSVC) on the RIS server. In this situation, the BINL message is displayed to the client, indicating that a RIS server has been contacted, but nothing else will happen.	To correct the problem, stop and restart the NetPC Boot Service Manager Service.

continues

| TABLE 9.1 | *continued* |

PROBLEMS ENCOUNTERED WITH REMOTE INSTALLATION SERVICES

Problem	*Cause*	*Solution*
Clients using the RIS boot disk cannot connect to the RIS server.	The most likely cause of this problem is that the client computer has a network card that is not supported by the RIS boot disk.	Verify that the network card appears on the adapter list in the Remote Boot Disk Generator utility. If it does not, replace it with a network adapter on the list.
Pressing F12 initiates a remote boot, but the client cannot connect to the RIS server.	The most likely cause of this problem is that the PXE-based network card has a boot ROM earlier than version .99c. The PXE boot ROM must be version .99c or later and, with some network cards, might need to be version .99i to work properly.	Replace the network card or the boot ROM to solve this problem. It is also possible that this problem occurs when a RIS server is down. Verify that the RIS server is operational.
Expected installation options are not available to a user.	The most likely cause of this problem is Group Policy conflicts. If a GPO is defined for the user at the OU level, a higher-level GPO may have had a No Override setting applied, and it also contains configuration settings for RIS.	Verify the GPO precedence for the user.

As you have seen, the majority of problems with RIS deal with necessary supporting servers not being available or client components not working quite right. As always, careful planning of all aspects of RIS, as well as the Group Policy elements that affect it, will ensure a robust and problem-free installation (for the most part).

CASE STUDY: USING REMOTE INSTALLATION SERVICES TO DEPLOY WINDOWS 2000 PROFESSIONAL TO NEW DESKTOP COMPUTERS AT SUNSHINE BREWING

ESSENCE OF THE CASE

A number of the desktops at Sunshine Brewing are starting to become outdated, and it has been decided that a capital acquisition strategy will be implemented to replace these aging machines. The number of new desktops to be purchased is estimated at 2,500 with about 500 of these machines used to replace R&D desktops, 235 for the executives, 500 for IT, and the remainder for admin. Sales recently received a new group of notebooks, so no new machines are needed for them. All machines are Pentium III 650MHz and on the Windows 2000 Hardware Compatibility List. Each of the machines has at least 256MB of memory and a 12GB hard disk. The new computers all have Intel Pro/100+ PCI 100BASE-TX network cards, which have a PXE boot ROM at version .99c or later.

The R&D machines should only include the base Windows 2000 Professional operating system because additional applications to be installed by R&D are specialized. Common corporate applications, such as Office 2000, will be deployed after the machines are configured with Windows 2000 Professional using Group Policy. The names of R&D machines should be prestaged in the R&D OU to make sure only the machines targeted for R&D will be created and assigned the inherited permissions of the OU.

Executives' machines should include Office 2000 Professional and the reporting software for the ERP package. Other applications that need to be installed will be handled manually or via Group Policy. The machines should be prestaged.

The IT machines also should only contain Windows 2000 Professional and the Administrative Tools for Active Directory as well as the Windows 2000 Resource Kit.

Admin machines should mimic their current desktop configuration and do not need to be prestaged.

The deployment of all machines, with the exception of R&D, will be performed by IT staff at the various locations using an over-the-network install. You want to make sure the wide area network is not used to transfer the files needed for the OS installation. (That is, each site should have its own server to act as a source for the operating system deployment.)

continues

CASE STUDY: USING REMOTE INSTALLATION SERVICES TO DEPLOY WINDOWS 2000 PROFESSIONAL TO NEW DESKTOP COMPUTERS AT SUNSHINE BREWING

continued

SCENARIO

Deployment of Windows 2000 Professional on new desktop computers, either by itself or with additional applications, can be a time-consuming process. In this chapter, you were introduced to Remote Installation Services and how it can speed up the process of operating system deployment as well as, through the use of RIPrep images, additional applications. You will see how this can be applied to solve a problem at Sunshine Brewing.

ANALYSIS

The simple solution for this problem is the Remote Installation Services component of Windows 2000. Because all new computers have a PXE-enabled network card of the appropriate version and all components of the machines are on the HCL, you do not need to worry about strange problems during the deployment (unless they're hardware related).

To make sure the deployment succeeds, you would perform the following:

- Install and configure a RIS server at each site.

- Load an initial CD-based image of Windows 2000 Professional on each RIS server during the configuration and call it Standard Windows 2000 Professional Install.

- Authorize each RIS server in Active Directory.

- Make sure a DHCP server exists at each location and is authorized in Active Directory.

- Create a RIPrep image of a typical executive's machine (including the additional applications) and copy it to each RIS servers where executive machines will be located.

- Use Active Directory Users and Computers to prestage the executives' machines with the GUID of the machine.

- Create a RIPrep image for the admin users by creating an image of a typical admin machine as it currently exists. Place the image of all RIS servers in all sites where admin machines will be created.

- Create a RIPrep image with the configuration of the IT users and place the image in all sites where IT staff is located.

- Grant the R&D security group permissions to create computer accounts in the R&D OU and have them prestage the computers.

- Boot each machine from the network card and select the appropriate image to install.

Using the preceding list of steps and configuration settings will enable you to deploy Windows 2000 Professional and all the necessary applications to each class of user computer as necessary.

CHAPTER SUMMARY

Remote Installation Services is a component of the IntelliMirror technology of Windows 2000 that enables you to deploy Windows 2000 Professional images during the boot phase on a client computer.

RIS supports clients meeting the NetPC specification, which requires a PXE-enabled network card with a PXE-enabled boot ROM that is version .99c or later. Client computers that do not have a PXE-enabled network card can still be deployed using RIS by creating a RIS boot disk. These clients must have one of the network cards supported by the RIS boot disk.

On the server side, RIS needs to be installed on a Windows 2000 Server, Advanced Server, or Data Center Server computer. The RIS Server depends on other Windows 2000 technologies, including Active Directory and DHCP. A RIS server must be authorized in Active Directory for it to be able to provide images to clients who want to install Windows 2000 Professional.

Installation of RIS server is performed by using the Add/Remove Windows components of Add/Remove Programs in Control Panel or by using Configure Your Server. When you install RIS, all the necessary files required by RIS are installed; however, you must also configure the RIS server. Configuring the RIS server creates an initial CD-based image on the server and starts all the required services for RIS including Trivial File Transfer Protocol, Single Instance Store, and the Boot Service Manager Service.

Images used to deploy Windows 2000 Professional using RIS can be CD-based images or Remote Installation Preparation images. CD-based images are a copy of the files needed for installation of Windows 2000 Professional, and they provide the same process as an unattended installation using the Windows 2000 Professional CD. RIPrep images enable you to configure Windows 2000 Professional as well as other applications on a source computer, create an image on a RIS shared folder that contains the entire computer configuration, and then deploy it to target machines. RIPrep images provide the fastest deployment of both the operating system and applications.

KEY TERMS
- Active Directory
- Answer file
- Authorizing a RIS server
- CD-based image
- Dynamic Host Configuration Protocol (DHCP)
- Domain Name System (DNS) server
- Globally unique identifier (GUID)
- Media Access Layer (MAC) address
- Prestaging
- Pre-boot execution environment (PXE)
- RBFG.EXE (Remote Boot Disk Generator)
- Restricting images
- Remote Installation Preparation (RIPrep)
- Remote Installation Services (RIS)
- RIS boot disk
- RIS image
- Remote Installation Services Installation and Configuration Wizard (RISETUP)
- Setup Manager

CHAPTER SUMMARY

KEY TERMS

- Single Instance Store (SIS) Service
- Source computer
- SYSPREP utility
- Target computer
- Trivial File Transfer Protocol (TFTP)

A single RIS server is able to hold several images. Images must be stored on a separate partition formatted with NTFS, although storing images on a separate physical disk is recommended for performance reasons. You might also have several RIS servers on the same network. It is a good idea to copy the common images to more than one server for load balancing.

Client computers might be prestaged, which requires that you know the GUID of the client computer. Prestaging involves creating the client computer in the proper Active Directory container in Active Directory Users and Computers. The GUID can be found in the BIOS of the computer or on a label provided by the vendor. Computers for whom a RIS boot disk is needed can also be prestaged by using the MAC address of the network card and padding it leading 0s so that it matches the same format as a GUID.

Assigning permissions to the answer file used by a particular image enables you to restrict who is able to install a particular image. Users installing Windows 2000 Professional on a computer that has not been prestaged must have the Create Computer Object privilege within the container where the computer account will be created. The container where the computer account will be created can be configured on the advanced properties of the RIS server in Active Directory Users and Computers, as can the naming format used to create the computer accounts.

To start the installation of Windows 2000 Professional through RIS, you need to make sure the PXE-enabled network card is the first boot device on the machine or, in the case of a RIS boot disk, that the floppy drive is the boot device. During the boot phase, the user presses F12 to indicate a staged boot, at which point the DHCP server is contacted to assign the computer an IP address and connect it to a RIS server. Prestaged clients can be configured to download their image directly from a specific RIS server to make sure the client receives the image it needs.

APPLY YOUR KNOWLEDGE

Exercises

In the following exercises, you will install Remote Installation Services on your Windows 2000 Server computer, configure RIS and create the initial CD-based image, apply permissions on the image, create a RIS boot disk, and deploy the image on a client computer with a PXE-enabled network card or a network card supported by the RIS boot disk.

Exercises 1 through 4 can be performed on a single Windows 2000 Server, Advanced Server, or Data Center Server computer that is a member server or a domain controller in an Active Directory domain. Exercise 5 requires another computer with a PXE-enabled network card or a network card supported by the RIS boot disk. The hard drive on the client computer in Exercise 5 should not have any partitions created.

For your RIS server computer, make sure the DHCP server service has been installed and authorized in Active Directory (this is required for the RIS server to respond to client requests) and that the DHCP server has been configured with at least one scope with a valid range of IPs for your LAN. You might also configure other settings such as a gateway address, DNS server, and so on. Also, make sure you have at least two partitions on your hard disk and that one is formatted with NTFS and is not the same partition on which Windows 2000 Server is installed.

The exercises assume you have a Research OU and a Restricted Developers security group (which were used in the exercises in Chapters 6 through 8). If not, create the OU and the security group and create a user who will be a member of the Restricted Developers security group.

9.1 Installing Remote Installation Services

In this exercise, you will install RIS on your Windows 2000 Server computer.

Estimated time: 20 to 25 minutes.

1. Log on to your computer as a Domain Administrator.

2. From the Start menu, select Settings and then Control Panel.

3. From Control Panel, double-click Add/Remove Programs.

4. From Add/Remove Programs, click Add Windows Components.

5. In the Windows Components page, under Components, scroll down until you see Remote Installation Services. Select it and click Next.

6. When the Files Needed dialog box opens, insert the Windows 2000 Server CD-ROM into your CD-ROM drive or specify the location of the Windows 2000 Server files and click OK.

7. When the Completing the Windows Components Wizard opens, click Finish.

8. When prompted to restart your computer, click Yes.

9.2 Configuring RIS and Installing the Initial Image

In this exercise, you will configure Remote Installation Services and install the initial Windows 2000 Professional CD-based image.

Estimated time: 20 to 25 minutes.

APPLY YOUR KNOWLEDGE

1. Log on to your RIS server as a Domain Administrator.

2. From the Start menu, select Settings and then Control Panel.

3. From Control Panel, double-click Add/Remove Programs. The Add/Remove Windows Components screen displays.

4. Under Setup services, click Configure next to Configure Remote Installation Services.

5. When the Remote Installation Services Setup Wizard starts, click Next to bypass the introductory screen.

6. When prompted for the location of your installation folder, make sure the default path of d:\remoteinstall (or whatever drive letter is presented) points to an NTFS partition on your computer that is not the system partition. If you want to specify a different location, do so. Click Next to continue.

7. When the Initial Settings dialog box opens, clear the Respond to client computers requesting service check box and click Next.

8. Insert the Windows 2000 Professional CD-ROM in your CD-ROM drive. If the Windows 2000 professional CD window appears, close it.

9. When prompted for the location of the Windows 2000 Professional files, type *drive:*\i386 where drive is the letter for your CD-ROM drive (for example, e:\i386). Click Next to continue.

10. When prompted for the folder in which to store the Windows 2000 Professional initial CD-based image, leave the default of win2000.pro and click Next.

11. When prompted to enter a friendly name and description for the image, enter a name and description that will identify the default image or leave the predefined text and click Next.

12. When the Review Settings dialog box opens, make sure the settings are correct and then click Finish.

13. The Remote Installation Setup Wizard then creates the RIS shared folder, copies files needed by RIS, copies the Windows 2000 Professional files to the image folder, creates an answer file for the image, configures RIS, updates the registry, creates a Single Instance Store volume, and starts the RIS services.

    When all tasks are completed, click Done.

14. Exit Add/Remove Programs.

15. Close Control Panel.

9.3 Securing the Image and Granting the Right to Create a Computer Account in the Research OU

In this exercise, you will configure RIS server options to place the computer account that will be created during the deployment of Windows 2000 Professional in the Research OU (that is, the same OU as the user account). You will then assign permissions to create the computer account to the Restricted Developers security group. Finally, you will assign permissions to the answer file for the image to the Restricted Developers security group and remove it from Everyone so that only members of that security group can install the image.

Estimated time: 20 to 25 minutes.

APPLY YOUR KNOWLEDGE

To configure RIS to create the computer account in the Research OU, follow these steps:

1. Log on to your RIS server as a Domain Administrator.

2. From the Start menu, select Programs, Administrative Tools, and then Active Directory Users and Computers.

3. In the MMC console, locate your RIS server, right-click it, and select Properties.

4. In the computer's Properties dialog box, select the Remote Install tab.

5. In the Remote Install tab, click Advanced Settings.

6. In the Remote-Installation-Services Properties dialog box, in the Create the client computer account in the following directory services location section on the New Clients tab, select Same location as that of the user setting up the client computer and click OK.

7. Click OK to close the RIS server properties dialog box.

8. Close Active Directory Users and Computers.

Grant the Restricted Developers Security Group the Right to Create Computer Accounts in the Research OU

1. Log on to your RIS server as a Domain Administrator.

2. From the Start menu, select Programs, Administrative Tools, and then Active Directory Users and Computers.

3. Locate the Research OU, right-click it, and select Delegate Control.

4. When the Delegation of Control Wizard starts, click Next.

5. On the Users and Groups screen, click Add, select the Restricted Developers security group from the list, click Add, and then click OK. You will be retuned to the Users and Groups screen. Click Next.

6. In the Active Directory Object Type dialog box, select This folder, existing objects in this folder, and creation of new objects in this folder and click Next.

7. On the Permissions screen, make sure General and Creation and deletion of specific child objects are checked. Scroll down the permissions dialog box until you locate Create Computer objects. Select it and then click Next.

8. Review your settings in the Completing the Delegation of Control Wizard screen and select Finish to make the changes.

9. Exit Active Directory Users and Computers.

Securing the Windows 2000 Professional Image

1. Log on to your RIS server as a Domain Administrator.

2. From the Start menu, select Programs, Accessories, and then Windows Explorer.

APPLY YOUR KNOWLEDGE

3. Using Windows Explorer, navigate your RIS folder until you locate a file called ristndrd.sif under the folder holding the default image. A possible location for this could be

   ```
   d:\remoteinstall\setup\English\images\win2000
   pro\i386\templates
   ```

   if you installed the image in a folder called win2000.pro and named the RIS folder RemoteInstall.

4. Right-click ristndrd.sif and select Properties.

5. In the Properties dialog box, select the Security tab.

6. In the Security tab, uncheck Allow inheritable permissions from parent to propagate to this object and then select Copy in the Security dialog box that opens.

7. In the Security tab, remove the Everyone group and add the Restricted Developers security group. Confirm that the Restricted Developers security group has Read and Read & Execute permissions on the file.

8. Click OK to close the Properties dialog box for the file.

9. Exit Windows Explorer.

9.4   Creating a RIS Boot Disk (Optional)

This exercise needs to be performed if your client computer does not have a PXE-enabled boot ROM. If your client computer has this capability, you do not need to create a RIS boot disk.

Estimated time: 20 to 25 minutes.

1. Log on to any Windows 2000 computer as an Administrator.

2. From the Start menu, select Run.

3. In the Run dialog box, type

   \\<RIS_SERVER>\reminst\admin\ i386\rbfg.exe

   where <RIS_SERVER> is the name of your RIS server. Click OK. This starts the Windows 2000 Remote Boot Disk Generator.

4. Click Adapter List to display a list of supported adapters and to verify that your network adapter is supported.

5. Insert a blank formatted floppy disk into your floppy drive and click Create Disk to create the RIS boot disk.

9.5   Deploying Windows 2000 Using Remote Installation Services

In this exercise, you deploy Windows 2000 by using Remote Installation Services.

Estimated time: 20 to 25 minutes.

1. On the client computer, enter **BIOS Setup** and verify that the PXE-enabled network card is the first boot device. If you are using a RIS boot disk, verify that the floppy drive is the first boot device.

2. If using a RIS boot disk, insert the disk into the floppy drive. Start the client computer.

3. During the boot phase on a PXE-enabled computer, press F12. For a RIS boot disk, press F12 when prompted.

APPLY YOUR KNOWLEDGE

4. When prompted, press F12 again to download and start the Client Installation Wizard.

5. When you are asked to log on, log on as user TimC with a password of password. TimC is a user in the Restricted Developers security group. If you have created another user in the security group, log on as that user.

6. In the list of available installation options, select Automatic Setup to install Windows 2000 Professional with the default settings.

7. If prompted for the image to install, select the one on which you have defined permissions. You should not be prompted for an image to install because the previous exercises only installed a single image on your RIS server.

8. Follow the prompts during installation if any.

Review Questions

1. What types of images can be deployed using Remote Installation Services?

2. What permission must a user have before he can use Remote Installation Services to configure a client computer?

3. What advantages does prestaging clients provide the Administrator?

4. By default, which RIS server responds to a client request to install an operating system on the client computer?

5. You need to name client computers based on the MAC address of the network adapter preceded by PC-. How can this be accomplished?

6. You need to make sure network shared printers are also installed on a client computer deployed using RIS. How can you accomplish this?

7. You want to deploy Windows 2000 Professional on new computers that will be used in your accounting department. Management has decided that games should not be installed on any computer in the organization. How can you configure RIS to not install games on these new machines?

8. Your company just purchased 100 new notebook computers for your sales staff. You want to simplify the deployment of Windows 2000 Professional with Microsoft Office 2000 and several proprietary applications developed by your in-house programmers on these notebook computers. How will RIS help you to simplify the deployment?

9. What key needs to be pressed on a client computer to start the deployment of Windows 2000 Professional?

10. When configuring Remote Installation Services, what actions are performed by the Remote Installation Setup Wizard?

Exam Questions

1. You have just been hired by SoftLogic Inc. to help in the configuration and deployment of client computers using RIS. It has been decided that all computers on the network will have their 1GB hard disks replaced by new 10GB hard disks and will have a CD-ROM installed. The existing machines are Pentium 166 computers with 32MB of RAM and 10MB ISA network cards.

APPLY YOUR KNOWLEDGE

These machines were purchased several years ago, but funds have not been allocated for their replacement. However, in addition to the hard drive and CD-ROM drives, additional funds exist to upgrade these systems.

What minimum additional upgrades to the client computers would you recommend to make sure a RIS-based deployment succeeds? (Choose two answers.)

A. Pentium 233 CPU

B. 128MB RAM

C. 100MB ISA network card

D. 10MB PCI network card

E. 64MB RAM

2. What services must be running before RIS can be installed and configured? (Choose three correct answers.)

A. WINS

B. DHCP

C. DNS

D. Trivial File Transfer Protocol

E. Active Directory

F. Single Instance Storage

3. You have decided to use a RIS-based deployment on 50 computers in your marketing department. You verify that all the machines have been recently purchased and have a PXE-enabled boot ROM. You create and configure the image on the RIS server and assign the proper permissions. You boot the client computer and press F12 to initiate a RIS installation; however, you do not seem to be able to connect to the RIS server. You

verify that the DHCP server, RIS server, and DNS server are all running and that a domain controller is available on the network. What is the most likely cause of the problem? (Choose the best answer.)

A. The BINLSVC is not started on the RIS server.

B. The PXE boot ROM is earlier than version .99c.

C. The PXE boot ROM is earlier than version .99i.

D. The network card does not contain a PXE boot ROM.

E. The network cable is unplugged from the client computer.

4. What operating systems can be deployed using RIS? (Choose all correct answers.)

A. Windows 2000 Server

B. Windows NT 4.0 Workstation

C. Windows 98

D. Windows 2000 Professional

E. Windows 2000 Advanced Server

F. Windows Millennium

5. What benefits does prestaging of client computers provide? (Choose all correct answers.)

A. Only IT staff can deploy a computer when it is prestaged.

B. A client computer can be configured to talk to a specific RIS server.

C. If the RIS server goes down, prestaging automatically selects another RIS server to continue the installation.

D. The load can be balanced between RIS servers.

E. Prestaging creates an image specific to the computer.

6. You need to deploy 200 computers using Remote Installation Services. The computers that need to be deployed have the following configurations:

- 50 Pentium II 300MHz notebook computers with PC Card network cards, 10GB hard disks, and 128MB of RAM

- 20 Pentium 233MHz desktop computers with PCI network cards, 4GB hard disks, and 64MB of RAM

- 30 Pentium III 800MHz desktop computers with PXE-enabled network cards, 20GB hard disks, and 32MB of RAM

- 40 Pentium Pro 200MHz dual-processor desktop computers with PCI network cards, 4GB hard disks, and 256MB of RAM

- 60 AMD K6-3 500MHz notebook computers with no network cards, 8GB hard disks, 64MB of RAM, and a docking station with a PCI network card and sound card

Which computers can be deployed using RIS? (Choose all correct answers.)

A. 50 Pentium II 300MHz notebook computers with PC Card network cards, 10GB hard disks, and 128MB of RAM

B. 20 Pentium 233MHz desktop computers with PCI network cards, 4GB hard disks, and 64MB of RAM

C. 30 Pentium III 800MHz desktop computers with PXE-enabled network cards, 20GB hard disks, and 32MB of RAM

D. 40 Pentium Pro 200MHz dual-processor desktop computers with PCI network cards, 4GB hard disks, and 256MB of RAM

E. 60 AMD K6-3 500MHz notebook computers with no network cards, 8GB hard disks, 64MB of RAM, and a docking station with a PCI network card and sound card

7. What Windows 2000 tool or technology would you use to prestage client computers? (Choose the best answer.)

A. Remote Installation Services Setup Wizard

B. Active Directory Users and Computers

C. Group Policy

D. Setup Manager Wizard

E. Remote Installation Preparation Wizard

8. What advantages does using a RIPrep image offer over using a CD-based image? (Choose all correct answers.)

A. RIPrep images can include applications as well as the operating system.

B. RIPrep images can be deployed on machines with a different HAL than the source computer.

C. RIPrep images perform a full install of the operating system, enabling the user to choose all settings.

APPLY YOUR KNOWLEDGE

D. RIPrep images can be easily updated by copying only changes files to the image folder.

E. RIPrep images are faster than CD-based images.

9. What services are installed by RIS and used during software deployment? (Choose three correct answers.)

A. Single Instance Storage Service

B. DHCP

C. DNS

D. Trivial File Transfer Protocol

E. Boot Service Manager Service

10. You are the domain administrator for your organization running a Windows 2000 Active Directory domain. You are about to receive 200 new desktop computers that will be used to replace existing systems. All the computers coming in have a PXE-enabled network card, 10GB hard disk, CD-ROM drive, and 128MB of memory.

The new computers will be used in four departments: finance, sales, IT, and executive. Each of these departments is represented in Active Directory with its own OU. The IT department is short-staffed and is unable to keep up with the workload.

You need to ensure the following:

- That all new computers have Windows 2000 Professional installed

- That users in finance, sales, and IT have the company accounting application installed

- That users in all departments have Microsoft Office 2000 installed on their computers

- That only members of the Domain Admins group are allowed to join computers to the domain

- That the deployment takes as little time as possible

- That the deployment uses minimal IT resources

To satisfy these requirements, you decide to do the following:

- Install Remote Installation Services on a Windows 2000 member server and authorize the server in Active Directory.

- Create a CD-based image on the RIS server for Windows 2000 Professional.

- Repackage the corporate accounting application using a third-party repackaging tool.

- Create a Group Policy object at the domain level filtered to assign the corporate accounting package to members of the executive, sales, and finance global security groups.

- Have IT users who are members of the Domain Admins group use RIS to install Windows 2000 Professional on the new machine by booting off the network card.

- Instruct IT software deployment staff to manually install Microsoft Office 2000 on all client computers.

Which of the following requirements were satisfied by your solution? (Choose all correct answers.)

A. All new computers have Windows 2000 Professional installed.

B. Users in finance, sales, and IT have the company accounting application installed.

C. Users in all departments have Microsoft Office 2000 installed on their computers.

D. Only members of the Domain Admins group are allowed to join computers to the domain.

E. The deployment takes as little time as possible.

F. The deployment uses minimal IT resources.

11. You are the domain administrator of a secretive branch of the Canadian federal government. Your department has just received a shipment of 500 new computers that need to have Windows 2000 Professional installed on them. Each of the new machines comes with 64MB of memory, 13GB hard disk, CD-ROM drive, and a PXE-enabled network card.

   To minimize the effort required to deploy Windows 2000 Professional on the new computers, you decide to use RIS. You properly configure the RIS server and authorize it in Active Directory. Users begin the installation properly, and everything seems fine until a user telephones you stating that he does not understand the prompts on the screen. Digging deeper, you realize that this user is more comfortable with French prompts rather than the default English ones presented by RIS. Your manager also reminds you that all user interfaces in the Canadian government must be bilingual.

What is the easiest way to accomplish this requirement? (Choose the best answer.)

A. Install RIS on a second server configured with the French Canadian version of Microsoft Windows 2000 Server; prestage all the French client machines in Active Directory, making sure they only connect to the new server; and then have the user start the deployment.

B. Copy Multilng.osc to welcome.osc in the OSChooser folder of your existing RIS server.

C. Copy welcome.osc to multilng.osc in the OSChooser folder of your existing RIS server.

D. Provide each of your francophone users with a RIS boot disk containing French menus.

E. Create a new CD-based image on the RIS server using the French Canadian version of Windows 2000 Professional.

12. You are the domain administrator for your organization running a Windows 2000 Active Directory domain. You are about to receive 200 new desktop computers that will be used to replace existing systems. All the computers coming in have a PXE-enabled network card, 10GB hard disk, CD-ROM drive, and 128MB of memory.

   The new computers will be used in four departments: finance, sales, IT, and executive. Each of these departments is represented in Active Directory with its own OU. The IT department is short-staffed and is unable to keep up with the workload.

APPLY YOUR KNOWLEDGE

You need to ensure the following:

- That all new computers have Windows 2000 Professional installed

- That users in finance, sales, and IT have the company accounting application installed

- That users in all departments have Microsoft Office 2000 installed on their computers

- That only members of the Domain Admins group are allowed to join computers to the domain

- That the deployment takes as little time as possible

- That the deployment uses minimal IT resources

To satisfy these requirements, you decide to do the following:

- Create a WINNT.SIF file using Setup Manager and copy the file to a floppy disk. Make sufficient copies of the floppy for each IT user who is also a domain administrator.

- Copy the Microsoft Office 2000 distribution files and MSI file to a network share.

- Repackage the corporate accounting application using a third-party repackaging tool.

- Create a Group Policy object at the domain level filtered to assign the corporate accounting package to members of the executive, sales, and finance global security groups.

- Create a GPO at the domain level that assigns Microsoft Office 2000 to Authenticated Users.

- Have IT users who are members of the Domain Admins group use a Windows 2000 Professional CD-ROM and the floppy with the WINNT.SIF file to install Windows 2000 on the client computers.

Which of the following requirements were satisfied by your solution? (Choose all correct answers.)

A. All new computers have Windows 2000 Professional installed.

B. Users in finance, sales, and IT have the company accounting application installed.

C. Users in all departments have Microsoft Office 2000 installed on their computers.

D. Only members of the Domain Admins group are allowed to join computers to the domain.

E. The deployment takes as little time as possible.

F. The deployment uses minimal IT resources.

13. Which utility can be used to create a RIS boot disk? (Choose the best answer.)

A. RISETUP.EXE

B. SYSPREP.EXE

C. RBFG.EXE

D. Active Directory Users and Computers

E. RIPREP.EXE

14. You are the domain administrator for your organization running a Windows 2000 Active Directory domain. You are about to receive 200 new desktop computers that will be used to replace existing systems. All the computers coming in have a PXE-enabled network card, 10GB hard disk, CD-ROM drive, and 128MB of memory.

The new computers will be used in four departments: finance, sales, IT, and executive. Each of these departments is represented in Active Directory with its own OU. The IT department is short-staffed and is unable to keep up with the workload.

You need to ensure the following:

- That all new computers have Windows 2000 Professional installed

- That users in finance, sales, and IT have the company accounting application installed

- That users in all departments have Microsoft Office 2000 installed on their computers

- That only members of the Domain Admins group are allowed to join computers to the domain

- That the deployment takes as little time as possible

- That the deployment uses minimal IT resources

To satisfy these requirements, you decide to do the following:

- Install and configure a RIS server, authorize it in Active Directory, and install the initial CD-based image.

- Install Windows 2000 Professional and the accounting application on one new computer.

- Create a RIPrep image of the new computer and place it on the RIS server in its own folder.

- Copy the Microsoft Office 2000 distribution files and MSI file to a network share.

- Create a GPO at the domain level that assigns Microsoft Office 2000 to Authenticated Users.

- Instruct members of the Domain Admins group to boot from the PXE-enabled network card on the new client computers and deploy the RIPrep image to computers for finance, sales, and executives.

- Instruct members of the Domain Admins group to boot from the PXE-enabled network card on the new client computers and use a CD-based image to deploy Windows 2000 Professional on all other machines.

Which of the following requirements were satisfied by your solution? (Choose all correct answers.)

A. All new computers have Windows 2000 Professional installed.

B. Users in finance, sales, and IT have the company accounting application installed.

C. Users in all departments have Microsoft Office 2000 installed on their computers.

D. Only members of the Domain Admins group are allowed to join computers to the domain.

APPLY YOUR KNOWLEDGE

E. The deployment takes as little time as possible.

F. The deployment uses minimal IT resources.

15. You have decided to use RIS to deploy Windows 2000 to 1,750 new computers in your organization. For the sake of expediency, it has been decided that members of the Domain Users group will be able to create computer accounts in their own OU. You configure RIS to create computer accounts in the same OU as the user installing Windows 2000. You want to make sure corporate naming policies for new computers are not compromised. What is the best way to accomplish this? (Choose the best answer.)

A. Prestage all client computers.

B. Do not allow users to restart an interrupted installation.

C. Remove the Read permission from the answer file for the OU.

D. Do not allow users to create computer accounts.

Answers to Review Questions

1. You can deploy CD-based and RIPrep images using Remote Installation Services. At least one CD-based image needs to be on the RIS server before a RIPrep image can be placed on the server. See "Overview of Remote Installation Services."

2. The user must have the Create Computer Object permission in the Active Directory container where the computer account will be created. If the user performing the installation does not have this permission, the installation fails. See "Performing a Remote Installation" and "Installing and Configuring a RIS Server."

3. Prestaging client computers enables the administrator to create the client computer in Active Directory before the deployment and specify which RIS server will be used as a source for the images presented to the user performing the deployment. Prestaging clients, along with a RIS server configuration that only allows the RIS server to respond to known clients, will ensure that RIS can't be used to deploy Windows 2000 Professional on machines that should not have it installed. See "Performing a Remote Installation."

4. The RIS server that responds to service a client request is the one that has been configured to do so. If the client is prestaged and configured to receive an image from a specific RIS server, that RIS server responds. If the client has not been prestaged, any server that is allowed to respond to unknown client requests will respond and start the installation after a users successfully logs on. In the latter case, it most likely will be the server nearest to the client and least busy; however, this cannot always be predicted, which is why prestaging is recommended. See "Installing and Configuring a RIS Server."

5. To name clients with the MAC address of the network card preceded by "PC-," you would configure custom client naming options in the RIS server's Remote-Installation-Services Properties dialog box in Active Directory Users and Computers. The string you would enter to allow this naming is PC-%MAC%. See "Performing a Remote Installation."

6. To ensure that network printers are also installed when an operating system is deployed using RIS, create a new answer file that includes the network printers in the settings and associate it with an existing CD-based image, or modify the existing answer file to include the printers using the Setup Manager Wizard or Notepad. See "Creating Remote Installation Services Images."

7. To make sure games are not installed on the new machines that will be deployed using RIS, manually modify the answer file for the image to be deployed on the machines and modify the Component section to not include games as follows:

```
[Components]
    freecell=off
    minesweeper=off
    pinball=off
    solitaire=off
```

See "Creating Remote Installation Services Images."

8. This is a tough question to answer. If the notebook computers have a PC Card or PCMCIA network adapter, you cannot use RIS to deploy a RIPrep image including both the operating system and Office 2000. However, if the notebook computers have docking stations with a PCI-based network card with a PXE boot ROM or if the network card is on the supported list for a RIS boot disk, you could use RIS to deploy the RIPrep image. See "Performing a Remote Installation."

9. You need to press F12 when booting a client computer to connect to the RIS server and initiate a RIS deployment of Windows 2000 Professional on the computer. See "Performing a Remote Installation."

10. When configuring RIS, the Remote Installation Setup Wizard creates the RIS shared folder, copies files needed by RIS, copies the Windows 2000 Professional files to the image folder, creates an answer file for the image, configures RIS, updates the registry, creates a Single Instance Store volume, and starts the RIS services. See "Installing and Configuring a RIS Server."

ANSWERS TO EXAM QUESTIONS

1. **D, E.** For a RIS deployment to succeed, the machines need to have at least 64MB of RAM (the minimum requirement for Windows 2000 Professional) and a PCI network card (ideally with a PXE boot ROM). More memory would help, but you were asked to provide the minimum additional requirements, which is also why a faster CPU is not the right answer. See "Performing a Remote Installation."

2. **B, C, E.** A DHCP server, DNS server, and Active Directory domain controller must exist on the network before you can install and configure a RIS server. See "Installing and Configuring a RIS Server."

3. **B.** Although all the requirements on the server side have been met and the card has a PXE boot ROM, it is most likely earlier than version .99c, which is required for RIS to function correctly. You can discern that a PXE boot ROM is indeed on the network card because the question points out that you can start the deployment by pressing F12 during the boot phase on the computer, which is why D is not correct in this case. See "Troubleshooting Remote Installation Services."

APPLY YOUR KNOWLEDGE

4. **D.** RIS can be used to deploy Windows 2000 Professional only. None of the other operating systems can be deployed using RIS. Windows Millennium has not been released as of this writing, so this answer might be correct by the time you read this book (although at press time it was not known if it would be supported by RIS). See "Overview of Remote Installation Services."

5. **B, D.** Prestaging a client computer enables it to be assigned to a specific RIS server. If you prestage all client computers, you are able to balance the load on multiple RIS servers, thereby ensuring that no one server becomes overworked. See "Performing a Remote Installation."

6. **B, C, D, E.** The only computers that cannot be deployed using RIS are the notebook computers with PC Card network cards. Because all other computers either meet the minimum hardware requirements for Windows 2000 Professional or have a PCI card, with a PXE boot ROM or one that can be used with a RIS boot disk, they can all be deployed using RIS. See "Performing a Remote Installation."

7. **B.** To prestage client computers, you would use Active Directory Users and Computers to create the computer account in the appropriate OU by specifying the GUID. See "Performing a Remote Installation."

8. **A, E.** RIPrep images can include applications as well as the operating system because they are a copy of the source computer used to create the RIPrep image. Furthermore, RIPrep images might be smaller in size than a CD-based image and are quicker to deploy because the entire image gets copied on the client computer instead of going through the normal Windows 2000

Professional installation process, which is what happens with a CD-based image. Also, a CD-based image requires you to install the applications using Group Policy or manually, taking even more time. See "Creating Remote Installation Services Images."

9. **A, D, E.** After running the Remote Installation Setup Wizard, the Single Instance Storage, Trivial File Transfer Protocol, and Boot Service Manager Service are installed. DHCP and DNS are required to install RIS on a server in a network. See "Installing and Configuring a RIS Server."

10. **A, B, C, D.** The solution you have chosen ensures that Windows 2000 is installed on all client machines and that only the Domain Admins group creates computer accounts in the domain. This is because you created a CD-based image when you installed the RIS server and properly authorized it. You also directed Domain Admins to perform the task. Creating a GPO with the repackaged accounting application assigned to users in the appropriate groups will have it deployed the next time the user logs on and clicks on an icon for the accounting program. Manually installing Office 2000 also ensures that it is available to all users on the new machines. However, this is not the easiest or quickest way to satisfy these requirements. (Microsoft will ask you this type of question.) See "Creating Remote Installation Services Images" and "Installing and Configuring a RIS Server."

11. **B.** The easiest way to make the menu interface multilingual is to copy the Multilng.osc file over top of the welcome.osc file in the OSChooser folder. The default file that gets displayed to the user is welcome.osc, which by default is English

only. Multilng.osc has options for choosing a language and so on. Note also that you need to create answer files in the appropriate language because images themselves have a language associated with them. See "Installing and Configuring a RIS Server."

12. **A, B, C, D.** The answer to this question is similar to the one for question 10. The method chosen installs Windows 2000 Professional on all client computers but requires Domain Admins to do it manually for all computers. Creating a package for the accounting application and taking the MSI file for Microsoft Office also ensures that, through the GPOs created, these applications will be installed on all machines. However, this is not the easiest or the least resource-intensive way of doing so. See "Creating Remote Installation Services Images" and "Installing and Configuring a RIS Server."

13. **C.** The Remote Boot Floppy Generator is the tool used to create a RIS boot disk. Sometimes questions on Microsoft exams can be this simple, though not very often. See "Performing a Remote Installation."

14. **A, B, C, D, E, F.** By using a RIPrep image created from a source computer with the accounting application and Windows 2000 Professional, you have killed two birds with one stone. Because all users need to have Microsoft Office 2000 installed, creating a GPO to assign the package to Authenticated Users ensures that

this product gets installed the first time a user logs on and makes use of the program. Using RIS also made it easy to perform the deployment, minimizing the IT resources needed perform the task. See "Creating Remote Installation Services Images" and "Performing a Remote Installation." Also see "Group Policy Scope" in Chapter 6, "Using Group Policy to Manage Users."

15. **B.** The best way to make sure users cannot change the computer name during the RIS deployment is to make sure it restarts from scratch every time because an interrupted installation might ask the user for further input. You need to allow users to create computer accounts because there are too many computers to prestage. Removing Read permissions on the answer file would not allow users to use that answer file and allow them to perform the deployment. See "Troubleshooting Remote Installation Services" and "Performing a Remote Installation."

Suggested Readings and Resources

1. Microsoft Windows 2000 Resource Kit. *The Deployment Planning Guide.* Microsoft Press, 2000.

2. *Automated Deployment Options: An Overview White Paper* on Microsoft's Web site at http://www.microsoft.com/windows2000/library/planning/client/deployops.asp.

3. *Windows 2000 Professional Automated Deployment Options: An Introduction* on Microsoft's Web site at http://www.microsoft.com/windows2000/library/planning/client/autodeploy.asp.

4. *Automating the Deployment of Windows 2000 Professional and Office 2000* on Microsoft's Web site at http://www.microsoft.com/windows2000/library/planning/incremental/sysprep.asp.

5. *Desktop Deployment Solutions from Third-Party Companies* on Microsoft's Web site at http://www.microsoft.com/windows2000/guide/server/partners/DesktopSolutions.asp.

FINAL REVIEW

Fast Facts

Study and Exam Preparation Tips

Practice Exam

Now that you have read through this book, worked through the exercises, and gotten as much hands-on experience administering Active Directory as you could, you're ready for the exam. This last section is designed as a "final cram in the parking lot" before you walk into the exam. You can't reread the whole book in an hour, but you will be able to read this section in that time.

This section is organized by objective category, giving you not just a summary but a review of the most important points from each chapter. Remember that this is meant to be a review of concepts and a trigger for you to remember the tidbits of information you'll need when taking the exam. If you know this information and the concepts that stand behind it, chances are the exam will be a snap.

Fast Facts

EXAM 70-217
INSTALLING AND ADMINISTERING
WINDOWS 2000 DIRECTORY
SERVICES INFRASTRUCTURE

INSTALLING, CONFIGURING, AND TROUBLESHOOTING ACTIVE DIRECTORY

As you review this section, it is imperative that you remember the purpose of the different components of Active Directory. You need to know what each component is, where it is defined, and most importantly, why you would use it. The exam is based very much on real-world scenarios, and as such, you have to try to bring to mind where you would use each piece of Active Directory in the real world.

The two main sections of this objective break down into many parts.

Install, Configure, and Troubleshoot the Components of Active Directory

Microsoft will test you on your understanding of the prerequisites, the use, and the installation of the various parts of Active Directory. There are a number of subpoints in this section, but primarily they all key-in on these three points.

Install Active Directory

Things to consider before installing Active Directory include the following:

◆ The system needs to meet the Windows 2000 minimum for installation: 64MB RAM, 1.2GB disk available, and 166MHz processor.

◆ You will need a DNS server that supports SRV records.

◆ If the DNS server does not support dynamic updates, you need to add the entries in the NETLOGON.DNS to make sure the services can be found.

◆ You can start the promotion using the DCPROMO command or from the Configure Your Server wizard.

◆ You should have a domain name and all the other configuration information worked out in advance.

◆ When you create the first domain controller, you are creating a *new* domain controller for a *new* root domain in a *new* forest. At this point, that single domain controller is the forest.

Create Sites

Things to consider when creating sites include the following:

◆ The biggest thing to remember about sites is that they control replication inside a domain.

◆ Sites are part of the physical network, not the logical structure.

◆ Each site should have a domain controller and a global catalog server.

◆ Clients will always look for a server in the site first, and then they will look in the domain and then in the forest. The best response time is achieved by keeping server in the sites with the users.

◆ Sites are connected using a site link to all the other sites.

◆ You create a site in Active Directory Sites and Services. Right-click and choose New Site. You need to give a site name and select the default site link it will use.

◆ A site is defined as a collection of IP subnets connected by a high-speed network.

◆ Sites can have Group Policy objects placed on them. If there is a GPO on a site, then a domain controller for the domain where the GPO was created should be placed in the site.

Create Subnets

When creating subnets, consider the following:

◆ To create a subnet, use Sites and Services. You will need to enter an IP address and subnet mask for a system on the subnet.

◆ A subnet is a physical subnet from a network.

◆ Subnets are added to sites, and you must specify one when you create a subnet.

◆ In the subnet properties, you can provide a location that will be used in Active Directory.

◆ When a subnet is created, the notation you will see is the subnet ID/number of bits to get the ID.

Create Site Links

Consider the following when creating site links:

◆ A site link represents a physical connection between two sites. This connection is a network path that is either permanent or temporary.

◆ Site links are created in Sites and Services.

◆ For most connections, you will use RPC over IP for site links. For a nonpermanent connection, you can use SMTP.

◆ SMTP site links require a certificate from a certificate authority.

◆ There are three variables you can set for a site: schedule (what times the link is available), interval (how often to check for new information), and cost (used to decide which link to use if there is more than one between sites).

◆ You can ignore site link schedules to force replication by setting the Ignore Schedules option under the protocol, IP or SMTP, properties.

◆ You can specify a server as a bridgehead server for a site in the properties for the server.

◆ Two sites can be linked by more than one site link. The lower cost link will be used first. The default cost is 100.

Create Site Link Bridges

When creating site link bridges, consider the following:

◆ Site link bridges are used to connect sites that are not physically connected by creating a path through an intermediary site.

◆ Site link bridges will not have any effect unless Automatic site link bridging is turned off in the properties for the protocol. Automatic site link bridging is referred to as transitive site links on the exam.

◆ Two or more site links can participate in a site link bridge.

◆ Site link bridges are created in Active Directory Sites and Services.

Create Connection Objects

Consider the following when creating connection objects:

◆ The *Knowledge Consistency Checker* (KCC) normally creates connections.

◆ Connection objects represent a connection or association between two servers.

◆ Within a site, the KCC will create a link from each server to at least (if you have more than two) two other servers.

◆ Using the site links and site link bridging if Transitive site links is turned off, the KCC will also create the connections between servers in different sites.

◆ You can manually create connections, but KCC will never remove one you create or update it even if a better path becomes available at some later time.

◆ Connection objects are found in the NTDS Settings container for each server.

Create Global Catalog Servers

Things to consider when creating global catalog servers include the following:

◆ The global catalog is a list of all objects in the enterprise with a subset of objects.

◆ Global catalog servers are really LDAP servers that provide the list of objects to the clients.

◆ The global catalog servers also play a key role in the replication of the schema partition and the configuration partition.

◆ The global catalog houses the universal groups that you define.

◆ There should be at least one global catalog server per domain and one per site.

◆ Global catalog servers are domain controllers. In Sites and Services, there is a check box under the NTDS Settings for each server, controlling whether or not it is a global catalog server.

Move Server Objects Between Sites

When moving server objects between sites, consider the following:

◆ To give the best client response, servers should be in the same site as the client. This is why you want to be able to move servers.

◆ The server you move into a site should be on the physical subnet.

◆ You move a server by right-clicking on the server and choosing move.

Transfer Operations Master Roles

Consider the following points when transferring operations master roles:

◆ Each operations master has a special role.

• **Schema master**. This is the only write-enabled copy of the schema. The capability to write to the schema has to be turned on; this is done in the Operations Master Properties found in the Active Directory Schema snap-in. This snap-in has to be added using ADMINPAK.MSI. There is only one schema master in the forest. If any part of an organization needs a different schema, you will need more than one forest.

• **Domain naming master.** This is the system that ensures that your domain tree or forest structure stays in shape. This server is also responsible for configuring all the transitive trusts in the enterprise. The trusts will be implemented automatically by the PDC emulators. There is only one domain naming master in a forest.

- **PDC emulator.** This is the server that will implement the trust relationships. It is also used to service down-level logon requests and down-level domain controllers requests for directory database replication. There is one in each domain. Remember that "down level" refers to any non-Active Directory system, including Windows NT 4.0.

- **Relative identifier master.** The RID master generates random sequences that are combined with the domain's unique identifier to create the SID for objects created on a domain controller. The RID master sends batches of RID to each domain controller it will use until they're gone. Then it will get the next batch from the RID master. There is a separate RID master for each domain.

- **Infrastructure master.** This system makes sure the user-to-group mappings are correct for users from its domain. There is one per domain.

◆ The schema operations role is controlled in the Active Directory Schema. First connect to the server that will take over the role and then in Operations Master click Change.

◆ The domain naming master role is controlled in Active Directory Domains and Trusts. As with the schema master, connect to the controller that will take the role and then, under Operations Master, change the role.

◆ The domain-level roles are controlled in Active Directory Users and Computers. Connect to the domain controller and then move the role or roles using operations masters.

◆ The NTDSUTIL can be used to transfer the role from the command line. It can also be used to seize a role (take it forcefully). If a schema master, domain naming master, or RID master role has to be seized, the old server can never be brought back online or Active Directory could be corrupted.

Verify Active Directory Installation

When verifying Active Directory installation, consider the following:

◆ Verifying the installation is not a big exam topic.

◆ Check that the database and log files are present.

◆ Check that the SYSVOL share is present.

◆ Check that the tools are in the Program menu.

◆ Check that you see your domain controller in Active Directory Users and Computers.

◆ You should also check that the correct DNS records are registered for the Netlogon service.

Implement an Organizational Unit Structure

Consider the following when implementing an OU structure:

◆ The key here is to remember that OUs are used to delegate authority and to logically group users, computers, groups, and other objects that delegates can manage.

◆ You can create an OU within an OU, but Microsoft recommends that you don't go beyond three levels (that is, an OU in an OU in an OU).

◆ All you need to do to create an OU is right-click on the object you want it under—the domain or other OU—and then use New, Organizational Unit from the context menu.

◆ OUs affect permissions. Sites affect replication. Domains contain both.

Back Up and Restore Active Directory

Being able to back up and restore Active Directory is very important. You will need to know when to do a restore, when to do an authoritative restore, and when to just reinstall the domain controller.

Perform an Authoritative Restore of Active Directory

Consider the following when performing an authoritative restore of Active Directory:

◆ Every change made either through replication or by a user incrementally changes the *Update Sequence Number* (USN) for a domain controller.

◆ Only changes made by a user will incrementally change the USN on an object.

◆ Authoritative restores are required only if you are trying to bring back a deleted object. There is no other reason to perform an authoritative restore. It restores the object and incrementally changes the USN to such a point that it is higher than the update number for the deletion.

◆ An authoritative restore is like a normal restore on a domain controller except that you will use the NTDSUTIL to increment the USN of the object you want to recover after the backup is restored.

◆ The authoritative restore will recover the object and all subobjects it held.

◆ You need to know the distinguished name of the deleted object (for example, cn=Techs,cn=Users, dc=ScrimTech,dc=local).

◆ After an authoritative restore, you will need to wait until replication occurs before the object will be restored to other domain controllers.

Recover from a System Failure

Consider the following when attempting to recover from a system failure:

◆ You can recover a domain controller in one of three ways:

• Reinstall the O/S and promote the system to be a domain controller. Allow replication to bring the Active Directory information back. This is the simplest method, and it is best applied to systems that are only domain controllers, notably if there isn't a recent backup.

• Reinstall the O/S and then restart in Active Directory Restore mode using the F8 key. Restore the information from the system and the system state data. Finally, restart the controller in normal mode and let replication bring the system up-to-date.

• Perform an authoritative restore. This is used only if you are trying to bring a deleted object and its subobjects back. In this case, restore as noted in the previous point, but before you restart to normal mode, use the NTDSUTIL to recover the object.

◆ Unless the backup was recent, you should not restore an operations master because the information could be out-of-date. In this case, it is better to seize the role. Fault tolerance for operations masters should be done by having another domain controller on the same segment to receive replicated changes immediately.

◆ The Knowledge Consistency Checker will automatically rebuild the connections when a domain controller is offline.

INSTALLING, CONFIGURING, MANAGING, MONITORING, AND TROUBLESHOOTING DNS FOR ACTIVE DIRECTORY

As was stated in the introduction to this text, DNS provides the hierarchy for Active Directory. You need to make sure DNS is working. A good portion of the exam is dedicated to this topic.

Install, Configure, and Troubleshoot DNS for Active Directory

Generally, the installation is simple. Remember that you use Add/Remove Programs to get to the Windows components. From there, you use the Network Services item to install DNS.

Integrate Active Directory DNS Zones with Non-Active Directory DNS Zones

When integrating an Active Directory DNS with a non-Active Directory DNS, consider the following:

◆ The Windows 2000 DNS server is a standard DNS server. This means you can have primary and secondary zones. It also means the other servers you use (either the secondary or primary) can be any type of server.

◆ The DNS server provides for incremental transfers (IXFR), which are RFCs and are based on the serial number of the zone file.

◆ The DNS server can be set to send data to any DNS server, to the DNS servers you list as name servers in the domain, or to specific servers that you enter. It can also be set to notify these servers of changes.

◆ The *Start of Authority* (SOA) record for a domain sets the frequency with which secondary servers must refresh. The value is 15 minutes by default but can be changed.

◆ If you create an Active Directory–integrated zone, that zone belongs to one domain. For this reason, it should be created at the root of the tree.

◆ In Active Directory–integrated zones, any domain controller in the zone with which the DNS is integrated can be a "primary" server. That is, you will have the capability to register a computer at any of the domain controllers rather than the one primary server.

◆ In AD-integrated zones, the data for the zone is stored in Active Directory and is therefore an object. This means that the computer account must have permissions to update that object to be able to register when it starts.

◆ To create a subdomain that is not Active Directory, you can delegate a part of the namespace to another server. This creates the required *Name Server* (NS) records.

◆ An AD-integrated zone can have a standard secondary server.

Configure Zones for Dynamic Updates

When configuring zones for dynamic updates, consider the following:

◆ You can configure both standard and Active Directory-integrated zones to allow updates.

◆ If the zone is AD integrated, you can specify that the updates be secure. (Check the permissions on the object.)

◆ Scavenging is the process of taking records that have not been refreshed out of the DNS server's zone. This can be done on both types of zones. The times can be set on the server object and the zone object.

◆ The client, the DHCP server, or both can do dynamic updates. Normally, the client registers the forward zone name, and the DHCP server registers the reverse lookup name.

◆ Remember that if the domain controller or any other server does not have the DNS server configured in its TCP/IP settings, it will not register with DNS.

◆ You can still use a referral to WINS to create a dynamic DNS environment for down-level clients and servers.

Manage, Monitor, and Troubleshoot DNS

In general, you should know the options available on the DNS server and how to create zones. This particular objective is design to ensure that you understand the replication process, but there could be questions that are just related to managing the server.

Manage Replication of DNS Data

Consider the following when managing the replication of DNS data:

◆ If you are using an Active Directory-integrated zone, the replication is handled by Active Directory. This means you can control replication using the site links and site link bridges you create.

◆ If there is a secondary server to a standard zone, an Active Directory-integrated zone, or a zone on another server, the refresh for that transfer is set in the SOA record.

◆ Zone transfers can be done from a primary, secondary, or Active Directory–integrated server. The server that provides the records is the master server.

◆ Any DNS server that supports SRV records can act as a secondary for an Active Directory-integrated zone.

◆ You can restrict zone transfers to servers in the Name Server page or to specific servers, or you can leave the zone so that any server can transfer the zone.

◆ You can configure the primary server or any master server to notify the secondary servers of changes.

◆ Windows 2000 DNS servers can use IXFR, or incremental zone transfers. This will send all the changes since the last version the secondary had based on serial number. This means the master server must track the changes made between zone file updates.

INSTALLING, CONFIGURING, MANAGING, MONITORING, OPTIMIZING, AND TROUBLESHOOTING CHANGE AND CONFIGURATION MANAGEMENT

You should be familiar with what Group Policy is and how it can help you implement uniform standards across the enterprise.

Group Policy enables you to specify how a computer will be configured, whether or not users are able to make changes to certain computer configurations, which software will be automatically or optionally installed on users' computers, and how security settings will be applied.

Group Policy applied to a user will lock down the desktop and other characteristics of a user's environment no matter from where he logs on to the domain: his usual workstation, a remote machine through dial-up, another node in the same location, or a computer halfway around the world.

Implement and Troubleshoot Group Policy

In general, you should know what Group Policy is composed of, how to create a new Group Policy, how to link an existing GPO to an Active Directory container, how to modify a GPO, how to block GPO inheritance, how to filter the application of Group Policy using permissions, and how to delegate the administration of Group Policy to lower-level administrators.

Create a Group Policy Object

Group Policy objects are composed of two parts:

◆ **Group Policy containers (GPCs).** GPCs are Active Directory containers where the GPO version information and *globally unique identifier* (GUID) are stored such as a site, domain, or OU.

◆ **Group Policy templates (GPTs).** GPTs are physical files, including Administrative Templates and Scripts, that are stored within the Policies container for the SYSVOL share on domain controllers. Each GPT is stored in a folder with the same name as the GUID of the GPO for which it is a template.

When creating a GPO, consider the following:

◆ Group Policy can be created at a site, domain, or OU level.

◆ Once created, the GPO settings are modified using the Group Policy Editor MMC snap-in.

◆ Only Domain Admins or those users who have been granted the Create Group Policy Object permissions can create a GPO at any level.

◆ Windows NT 4.0 System Policies do not migrate to Group Policy when upgrading a domain controller to Windows 2000.

◆ Group Policy application can be audited and the results viewed in the Event Viewer. This is a good troubleshooting tool when needed.

Link an Existing GPO

Consider the following when linking an existing GPO:

◆ Linking an existing GPO to an Active Directory container enables its settings to be applied to computers and users within the OU.

◆ The same GPO can be linked to any number of Active Directory containers.

◆ The GPT contains a common collection of settings that will be applied to all Active Directory containers to which the GPO has been linked.

Delegate Administrative Control of Group Policy

When delegating administrative control of Group Policy, consider the following:

◆ Delegating administrative control of a GPO enables other users to modify the GPO settings.

◆ For a user to be delegated administrative control of a GPO, he or she needs to have Read and Write permissions on the GPO to modify it.

◆ Delegation of administrative control is done by setting appropriate permissions through the Security tab for the GPO properties.

Modify Group Policy Inheritance

When modifying Group Policy inheritance, consider the following:

◆ Group Policy settings specified at a higher level, such as a domain or a site, are automatically inherited by all lower-level Active Directory objects such as subdomains and OUs.

◆ Group Policy is processed in the following order:

• Site

• Domain

• Organizational unit

◆ A local administrator responsible for a subdomain or OU can block policy inheritance from higher levels, thereby ensuring that only his or her GPOs will be processed.

◆ Higher-level administrators have the option to override the blocking of GPO application at lower levels, thereby forcing GPO settings even if they are blocked at a lower level.

◆ Group Policy conflict refers to the same setting being applied at different levels of Active Directory. The last GPO process will be the one whose setting will apply unless No Override has been specified at a higher-level GPO.

◆ Group Policy precedence in the same container will determine which conflicting settings will be applied based on the order in the Group Policy tab for the Active Directory Container. The GPO at the top of the list wins.

Filter Group Policy Settings by Associating Security Groups to GPOs

To filter Group Policy settings by associating security groups to GPOs, consider the following:

◆ Group Policy filtering is the assignment of permissions to a GPO to ensure that it is only processed by those users for whom it was intended. In this way, it is possible to selectively implement Group Policy for a security group, computer, or user.

◆ It is possible to disable processing of the user or computer component of a GPO by selecting Properties in the Group Policy tab.

◆ For the GPO to be applied, the user must have the Read and Apply Group Policy permission on the GPO.

◆ To deny Group Policy processing and filter it so that it is not applied to the user, group, or computer, select the Deny option for the Apply Group Policy privilege for the user, group, or computer.

Modify Group Policy

To modify Group Policy, consider the following:

◆ Modifying Group Policy involves changing its settings using the Group Policy Editor MMC snap-in.

◆ Only users with both Read and Write permissions on the GPO can modify it.

◆ After modifying a GPO, the new settings will be replicated to domain controllers within 5 minutes and applied to users and computers within 90 minutes, although this setting can be changed using Group Policy.

◆ The administrator can disable processing of the unused portion of a GPO (either the user or computer portion) to speed up downloads of the GPO template to computers. Disabling both user and computer configuration will disable the GPO.

Manage and Troubleshoot User Environments by Using Group Policy

In general, you should be familiar with the difference between scripts and administrative templates.

GPO settings can be applied through administrative templates or scripts.

Administrative templates and scripts can be configured for both the computer and the user.

Control User Environments by Using Administrative Templates

To use administrative templates for controlling user environments, consider the following:

◆ Administrative templates modify the registry for the user or computer to apply policy settings.

◆ Administrative template settings are applied according to Group Policy inheritance unless inheritance has been blocked or No Override has been specified.

◆ If a conflict exists in the application of an administrative template setting between a user and a computer, computer settings always override user settings.

Assign Script Policies to Users and Computers

When assigning script policies to users and computers, consider the following:

◆ Scripts can be BAT, CMD, or any file supported by Windows Script Host.

◆ Scripts are used to configure users and/or settings that cannot be configured using other elements of Group Policy.

◆ If a conflict exists in the application of scripts, the last script to execute will be the one whose settings are applied, regardless of whether the script is a user logon script or a system startup script.

Manage and Troubleshoot Software by Using Group Policy

For this objective, you need to be familiar with the methods that can be used to deploy software to users and computers (publishing and assigning), how to upgrade software packages using Group Policy, how to redeploy packages to include patched files, and how to remove software using Group Policy.

Deploy Software by Using Group Policy

When deploying software by using group policy, consider the following:

◆ Software to be deployed using Group Policy must be in a format compatible with Windows Installer—that is, either a Windows Installer Package (MSI) file or a ZAP file.

◆ Software can be delivered to users through Group Policy either by publishing it or by assigning it.

◆ Assigning a software package to either a computer or a user will automatically install that package (in the case of a computer) or will place icons on the desktop if the package was installed (in the case of a user).

◆ Publishing software makes the application available to the user but does not immediately install the software. The software will be installed either through Control Panel Add/Remove Programs or by document activation.

◆ Document activation involves an attempt by the user to open a file with an extension associated with a particular package and then installing the software.

◆ Only Windows Installer Package (MSI) files can be either assigned or published to users because they contain the information necessary to install the application without user intervention.

◆ ZAP files can only be published, and they require the user to perform the normal install process for the software application.

◆ Third-party tools are available to repackage an application that is not provided in a Windows Installer Package (MSI) file format. Veritas WinINSTALL LE is included on the Windows 2000 CD-ROM.

◆ Administrators can use transform (MST) files to deploy the same software package with different options to different OUs within the enterprise.

◆ Transform files (MST) modify an existing package to meet specific requirements such as language or geographic location.

◆ Software categories enable administrators to categorize software applications to make it easier for users to select which software to install through Add/Remove Programs in Control Panel.

Maintain Software by Using Group Policy

Consider the following when maintaining software by using Group Policy:

◆ Software upgrades can be deployed using Group Policy. Upgrades may be either required or optional for an existing application.

◆ Required upgrades are installed without the user having a choice in this decision.

◆ Optional upgrades enable the user to decide whether he or she wants to upgrade to the most recent version.

◆ Software removal can also be configured through Group Policy and can be forced or optional.

◆ Forced removal requires that the software package be removed from the user's machine, whereas an optional removal enables the user to continue to use the application after it has been designated to be removed.

Configure Deployment Options

When configuring deployment options, consider the following:

◆ Software can be delivered to users through Group Policy either by publishing it or by assigning it.

◆ Assigning a software package to either a computer or a user will automatically install that package (in the case of a computer) or will place icons on the desktop if the package was installed (in the case of a user).

◆ Publishing software makes the application available to the user but does not immediately install the software. The software will be installed either through Control Panel Add/Remove Programs or by document activation.

◆ Document activation involves an attempt by the user to open a file with an extension associated with a particular package and then installing the software.

◆ Only Windows Installer Package (MSI) files can be either assigned or published to users because they contain the information necessary to install the application without user intervention.

◆ ZAP files can only be published, and they require the user to perform the normal install process for the software application.

Troubleshoot Common Problems That Occur During Software Deployment

When troubleshooting common problems that occur during software deployment, consider the following:

◆ Most problems with deploying software using Group Policy are the result of network errors, such as not being able to reach the software distribution point, or have to do with the application of Group Policy.

◆ When determining the nature of a problem, you must still adhere to all the rules governing policy inheritance, filtering, and other elements.

Manage Network Configuration by Using Group Policy

In testing your knowledge of managing network configuration using Group Policy, Microsoft will deal with the computer portion of Group Policy templates. You should be familiar with what types of settings can be applied and what happens when user and computer settings conflict. You will also be tested on other elements of Group Policy in general (inheritance, filtering, and so on) when applied to computers.

◆ Settings that can be configured for the computer are outlined in the following table.

Setting Type	Used to Control
Windows components	Parts of Windows 2000 and its tools. Here you are able to configure the behavior of parts of Windows 2000, including Internet Explorer, Microsoft NetMeeting, Windows Installer, Task Scheduler. The types of things that can be configured include whether the program can be installed, configuration of the program on the computer, which portions of the program can be used, and how the program will behave once launched.
System	How parts of Windows 2000 will operate including what happens at logon or logoff, DNS client suffix configuration, whether disk quotas will be enforced, and Group Policy characteristics such as refresh internal. It also controls Windows File Protection, the capability of Windows 2000 to automatically replace critical system files that may have been overwritten by other programs.
Network	Attributes of network connections such as whether connection sharing will be enabled on the computer and the behavior of offline files, including how and when synchronization takes place.
Printer	Configuration of printers such as whether they can be published in Active Directory, whether to publish printers automatically, whether published or not-Web-based printing is permitted, and as other settings such as computer location, the polling frequency for printers, and others.

◆ Any Administrative Template setting that exists in both the computer portion as well as the user portion of Group Policy will always have the computer setting apply.

Deploy Windows 2000 by Using Remote Installation Services

Remote Installation Services (RIS) is a component of the IntelliMirror technology of Windows 2000 that enables you to deploy Windows 2000 Professional images during the boot phase on a client computer.

Microsoft will test your knowledge of Remote Installation Services on the exam in several areas. You will need to know the requirements for configuring a RIS server, the client requirements, how to create a CD-based image as well as a RIPrep image, and how to troubleshoot common problems with Remote Installation Services.

Install an Image on a RIS Client Computer

Consider the following when installing an image on a RIS client computer:

◆ RIS supports client computers meeting the NetPC specification or computers with a *Pre-Boot Execution Environment* (PXE) network card with a PXE-enabled boot ROM that is version .99c or later.

◆ Client computers that do not have a PXE-enabled network card can still be deployed using RIS by creating a RIS boot disk. These clients must have one of the network cards supported by the RIS boot disk.

◆ To start the installation of Windows 2000 Professional through RIS, you need to make sure that the PXE-enabled network card is the first boot device on the machine or, in the case of a

RIS boot disk, that the floppy drive is the boot device. During the boot phase, the user presses F12 to indicate a staged boot at which point the DHCP server is contacted to assign the computer an IP address and connect it to a RIS server.

Create a RIS Boot Disk

When creating a RIS boot disk, consider the following:

◆ Client computers that do not have a PXE-enabled network card can still be deployed using RIS by creating a RIS boot disk. These clients must have one of the network cards supported by the RIS boot disk.

◆ The RIS boot disk is created by running RBFG.EXE from the REMINST\ADMIN\ i386 folder of the RIS server.

◆ A RIS boot disk can be configured for supported PCI adapters, a list of which is available when the RBFG.EXE utility is run.

Configure Remote Installation Options

When configuring remote installation options, consider the following:

◆ The RIS server depends on other Windows 2000 technologies, including Active Directory, DNS, and DHCP.

◆ RIS needs to be installed on a Windows 2000 Server, Advanced Server, or Data Center Server computer. Two hard disk partitions are required. The partition used to store disk images must be formatted with NTFS and cannot be the same as the system partition.

◆ Installation of a RIS server is performed by using Add/Remove Windows Components of Add/Remove Programs in Control Panel, or Configure Your Server. When you install RIS, all the necessary files required by RIS are installed; however, you must also configure the RIS server.

◆ Configuring a RIS server is performed by using the Remote Installation Setup Wizard after you install RIS. It can be invoked from the command line by typing **risetup** at the command prompt or from Start/Run, or through Add/Remove Programs.

◆ Configuring the RIS server creates an initial CD-based image on the server and starts all the required services for RIS including *Trivial File Transfer Protocol* (TFTP), *Single Instance Store* (SIS), and the *Boot Service Manager Service* (BINLSVC) .

Troubleshoot RIS Problems

Common RIS problems are shown in the following table.

Problem	Cause and Solution
Client computers are not being assigned an IP No DHCP message appears during the boot process.	The most likely cause of this problem is that a Windows 2000 DHCP server is not available.
	To solve the problem, begin by checking to see if non-RIS clients are being assigned an IP address through DHCP. If not, check to make sure your DHCP server is running; if so, verify that your DHCP server is a Windows 2000 DHCP server, that it has been authorized in Active Directory, and that it is not a Windows NT 4.0 DHCP server. If so, verify whether the client and the DHCP server are on different

continues

Problem	Cause and Solution
	physical subnets and that a DHCP relay agent is available and functioning on the same subnet as the RIS client computer. Finally, check that the DHCP server has available addresses to lease and that the DHCP scope has been activated.
Clients are assigned an IP address but do not display the BINL message indicating a connection to the RIS server	The most likely cause for this problem is that the RIS server is not online. Another possible problem could be that the RIS server is online but has not been authorized in Active Directory. Bring the RIS server online and authorize it to solve this problem.
Client computers cannot start the download of an RIS server.	This is most likely caused by hung NetPC Boot Service Manager on the image. In this situation, the BINL message will be displayed to the client, indicating that a RIS server has been contacte but nothing else will happen.
	To correct the problem, stop and restart the NetPC Boot Service Manager Service.
Clients using the RIS boot disk cannot connect to the RIS server.	The most likely cause of this problem is that the client computer has a network card that is not supported by the RIS boot disk.
	Verify that the network card appears on the adapter list in the Remote Boot Disk Generator utility. If it does not, replace it with a network adapter on the list.

Problem	Cause and Solution
Pressing F12 initiates a remote boot, but the client cannot connect to that RIS server.	The most likely cause of this problem is that the PXE-based network card has a boot ROM earlier than version .99c. The PXE boot ROM must be version .99c or later and, with some network cards, may need to be version .99i to work properly.
	Replace the network card or the boot ROM to solve this problem.
	It is also possible that this problem occurs when a RIS server is down. Verify that the RIS server is operational.
Expected installation options are not available to a user.	The most likely cause of this problem is Group Policy conflicts. If a GPO is defined for the user at the OU level, a higher-level GPO may have had a No Override setting applied, and it also contains configuration settings for RIS.
	Verify the GPO precedence for the user.

Manage Images for Performing Remote Installations

When managing images for performing remote installations, consider the following:

❖ Configuring the RIS server creates an initial CD-based image on the server and starts all the required services for RIS including Trivial File Transfer Protocol, Single Instance Store, and the Boot Service Manager Service.

◆ Images used to deploy Windows 2000 Professional using RIS can be CD-based images or *Remote Installation Preparation* (RIPrep) images.

◆ CD-based images are a copy of the files needed for installation of Windows 2000 Professional and provide the same process as an unattended installation using the Windows 2000 Professional CD.

◆ RIPrep images enable you to configure Windows 2000 Professional as well as other applications on a source computer, create an image on a RIS shared folder that contains the entire computer configuration, and then deploy it to target machines. RIPrep images provide the fastest deployment of both the operating system and applications.

◆ RIPrep images require a reference Windows 2000 Professional computer with all the applications installed and the Sysprep utility to prepare the image.

◆ All images are associated with an answer (SIF) file, which is created using the Setup Manager utility available with the Windows 2000 Resource Kit located in the TOOLS folder of the Windows 2000 CD-ROM.

◆ Assigning permissions to the answer (SIF) file used by a particular image enables you to restrict who is able to install a particular image.

◆ A single RIS server is able to hold several images. Images must be stored on a separate partition formatted with NTFS. You can also have several RIS servers on the same network, each of which may contain the same or different images. Common images should be copied to more than one server for load balancing.

Configure RIS Security

For RIS to work, you need to authorize the RIS server and apply proper permissions on the images so they are filtered to the users that need to make use of them. Microsoft will test your knowledge of how to authorize a RIS server, set permissions on images, and define which users can create computer accounts on the domain.

Authorize a RIS Server

Consider the following when authorizing a RIS server:

◆ A RIS server must be authorized in Active Directory for it to be able to provide images to clients who want to install Windows 2000 Professional.

◆ Authorizing a RIS server is performed from the DHCP MMC snap-in.

◆ If the RIS server is also a DHCP server, it is automatically authorized because the same process is used for DHCP servers to be allowed to hand out IP addresses.

Grant Computer Account Creation Rights

Consider the following when granting computer account creation rights:

◆ For a user who is deploying an image to a computer using RIS to create a computer account in the domain, he or she must have the Create Computer Objects permission in the Active Directory container where he or she wants to create the computer account.

◆ Users can be granted the required privileges through the Security tab of the Properties screen for the Active Directory container or by using the Delegation of Control Wizard.

◆ Domain Admins and Enterprise Admins have the Create Computer Object on all Active Directory containers within the domain by default.

◆ Users installing Windows 2000 Professional on a computer that has not been prestaged must have the Create Computer Object privilege within the container where the computer account will be created.

◆ The container where the computer account will be created can be configured on the advanced properties of the RIS server in Active Directory Users and Computers, as can the naming format to be used to create the computer accounts.

Prestage RIS Client Computers for Added Security and Load Balancing

When prestaging RIS client computers for added security and load balancing, consider the following:

◆ Client computers may be prestaged. Prestaging involves creating the client computer in the proper Active Directory container in Active Directory Users and Computers.

◆ The globally unique identifier of the computer is needed to pre-stage a client and can be found in the BIOS of the computer or on a label provided by the vendor.

◆ Prestaged clients can be configured to download their image directly from a specific RIS server to ensure that the client receives the image it needs.

◆ Computers for whom a RIS boot disk is needed can also be prestaged by using the MAC address of the network card and padding it with leading 0s so that it matches the same format as a GUID.

MANAGING, MONITORING, AND OPTIMIZING THE COMPONENTS OF ACTIVE DIRECTORY

In this section, we get to the nitty-gritty of management. This is where you need to know how to add objects to Active Directory. You will also need to know how to work objects in Active Directory. Although the actions are simple, Microsoft will present some unique situations on the exam, and you should be prepared to use elimination to help narrow the choices.

Manage Active Directory Objects

This is a broad topic because there are many types of objects and a number of things you can do with them. Remember, though, that the reason everything is an object is so you can treat them all the same. Therefore, if the exam asks about moving a user, remember that it is the same as moving a computer or any other object.

Move Active Directory Objects

To move Active Directory objects, consider the following:

◆ Moving includes moving not only within Active Directory but also between Active Directory and other directory services. This includes using the LDIFDE and CSVDE utilities. This can be used to move data between different types of systems.

◆ Moving an object is limited to the domain within Active Directory Users and Computers because the domain's unique ID makes up the first part of object's SID. To be able to move an object to a different domain, you need to use MOVETREE, which is included for that purpose.

◆ Within a domain, you can use the **Move** command on the context menu.

◆ Remember that if you move (or delete) a container such as an OU on one controller while another user creates new objects in that container, the new objects will end up in Lost and Found. Check this container occasionally.

Publish Resources in Active Directory

When publishing resources in Active Directory, consider the following:

◆ Remember that a *distributed file system* (DFS) can be a standalone system or a fault-tolerant system. This is not published in Active Directory. Publishing takes an existing share and makes it available in Active Directory.

◆ Printers are published by default for Windows 2000. Whether it is published or not depends on the List in Directory check box.

◆ Non-Windows 2000 printers can be published by using Active Directory Users and Computers to create the printer object.

◆ A non-Windows 2000 printer can also be published if you add the printer as a local printer to a Windows 2000 server and configure the port as the network address of the current share. Sharing the Windows 2000 printer now lists the printer in Active Directory by default.

◆ Shares are added to Active Directory using the Active Directory Users and Computers tool.

Locate Objects in Active Directory

Consider the following when locating objects in Active Directory:

◆ You should know where both the administrator and users can search. Administrators can search in the Active Directory Users and Computers console. Users can search for objects in Start Search and in My Network Places.

◆ You should know what the tabs do for the main objects: users, computers, printers, and groups. Although you aren't really expected to memorize every option, you should know where to go to find an option.

◆ After you have found an object or a group of objects, you should then be able to manipulate those objects as a group by selecting them from the list and then choosing an option from the context menu.

Create and Manage Accounts Manually or by Scripting

When creating and managing accounts manually or by scripting, consider the following:

◆ Know how to create an object using Active Directory Users and Computers and the other AD tools.

◆ You should know that the programming interface is called ADSI and that it works with a COM object called LDAP://. This object will enable you to connect to the directory tree in different-based locations and perform operations.

◆ Remember that LDIFDE and CSVDE can be used to copy objects in and out. The file can be edited outside Active Directory and then imported back in.

◆ You can use a Microsoft Exchange connector to connect to Exchange Server 5.5 Service Pack 3 and exchange users, groups, and contacts.

◆ You can still use the **NET USER** and **NET GROUP** commands to manage users.

Control Access to Active Directory Objects

Consider the following when controlling access to Active Directory objects:

◆ Remember that one of the key properties stored for every object is the *access control list* (ACL). The ACL will determine what users can do to the object. The access control list is made up of access control entries.

◆ The objects created within container objects inherit the permissions of those container objects. This inheritance can be turned off. If you turn off inheritance, you will be asked what you want to do with the existing permissions: keep or remove.

◆ The user's credentials are attached to the user process. When the process attempts an access the SID from the credentials (access token) is compared to the entries in the access control list.

◆ When you set permissions, you will normally have the option of applying them to the object, the object and subobjects, or just subobjects.

Delegate Administrative Control of Objects in Active Directory

When delegating administrative control of objects in Active Directory, consider the following:

◆ When you delegate control, you are setting permissions on the object and subobjects.

◆ The Delegation of Control Wizard should be used to make the delegation simple. It will set the permissions for you including advanced permissions.

◆ Delegation is normally done on organizational units. This is their main purpose.

◆ You should know the main permissions and on what they can be set. Remember, there are both object permissions and properties permissions that can be set.

Manage Active Directory Performance

For this objective, you need to primarily remember which tools you should use to manage servers and to look at Active Directory overall.

Monitor, Maintain, and Troubleshoot Domain Controller Performance

When monitoring, maintaining, and troubleshooting domain controller performance, consider the following:

◆ The key tools here are Performance, which is called the System Monitor snap-in; Network Monitor; and Task Manager.

◆ Performance can measure any detail about the computer and can be used to log the current performance so you can compare it to later performance. It is used to create a baseline of performance as well.

◆ In Performance, objects are the parts of the system you can monitor. The object will have several counters that represent the aspects of the object you can measure, and instances represent each occurrence of an object.

◆ Network Monitor lets you trap and view network traffic and will help you by breaking down the traffic into usable information. This can be used with communications problems to see the information on the wire.

◆ Task Manager is a way to get a quick peek at the current system performance, but it does not track performance over a period of time. It can also be used to change the priority and processor affinity of an executing program.

◆ Remember that you should occasionally compact the database. This is done using the NTDSUTIL.

Monitor, Maintain, and Troubleshoot Active Directory Components

Consider the following when monitoring, maintaining, and troubleshooting Active Directory components:

◆ Remember the preceding information about the operations masters.

◆ Remember that everything requires that DNS be operational.

◆ Remember these utilities:

• **ACLDiag**. This utility will let you determine whether a user has been given access to a directory object. It can also reset access control lists to their default state.

• **ADSIEdit.** This is an MMC snap-in that lets you view all objects in the directory and modify the objects or set access control lists on them.

• **DNSCMD.** This utility checks the dynamic registration of DNS resource records.

• **DOMMAP**. This utility checks the replication topology and domain relationships.

• **DSACLS.** This enables you to check and edit the access control list on directory objects.

• **DSAStat.** This will compare the information on domain controllers looking for differences.

• **ESEUtil.** This utility works on the extensible storage engine and can repair, check, compact, move, and dump database files. The NTDSUTIL calls these functions to perform various tasks.

• **NETDOM5.** This utility handles the batch management of trusts, joining computers to domains, and verifying trusts and secure channels.

• **NETTest.** This utility can check end-to-end network connectivity as well as distributed services functions.

• **NLTest.** This program checks to see if the locator service and secure channel are functioning.

• **NTDSUtil.** In addition to managing operations masters and allowing authoritative restores, this utility manages the database files (using ESEUtil) and lists site, domain, and server information.

• **REPAdmin.** This checks replication consistency between replication partners, monitors replication status, displays replication metadata, and forces replication events and Knowledge Consistency Checker recalculation.

- **REPLMon.** This program displays replication topology, monitors replication status, and can force replication events and Knowledge Consistency Checker recalculation.

- **SDCheck.** This tool enables an administrator to determine whether access control lists are being inherited correctly and whether access control list changes are being replicated from one domain controller to another.

- **SIDWalker.** This utility lets you set the ACL on objects that were owned by accounts that have been moved, deleted, or orphaned.

Manage and Troubleshoot Active Directory Replication

This topic is basically a matter of knowing how the connections, site link, and site link bridges work, and the tools that can be used to monitor replication. Most of this has already been reviewed.

Manage Intersite Replication

When managing intersite replication, consider the following:

◆ Intersite replication is managed by the KCC. You should not create manual connections.

◆ KCC configures servers with two partners in site and possibly a partner in another site.

Manage Intrasite Replication

When managing intrasite replication, consider the following:

◆ The key utilities are REPAdmin and REPLMon. The Admin program lets you administer the replication from the command line, and the REPLMon snap-in lets you monitor replication.

CONFIGURING, MANAGING, MONITORING, AND TROUBLESHOOTING ACTIVE DIRECTORY SECURITY SOLUTIONS

After configuring Group Policy and setting up your Active Directory structure, you need to ensure that proper precautions are taken so that unauthorized access to computers is prevented. In doing so, you need to be familiar with how Group Policy can be used to configure security settings for both users and computers as well as how to create an audit policy that enables you to detect and track unauthorized access.

Configure and Troubleshoot Security in a Directory Services Infrastructure

For this objective, Microsoft will test your knowledge of the process of setting up and analyzing security settings for components of Active Directory. Knowing how to analyze security on Windows 2000 computers using Security Configuration and Analysis and how to load and create templates using the same tool will be tested. Also, your knowledge of how to configure a security policy using templates will also be judged. Finally, Microsoft will test you on how to implement and configure auditing to provide information of any attempts at unauthorized access to computers, files, printers, and other resources. Thoroughly understanding Group Policy inheritance, filtering, and blocking, which was explained in Chapter 6, "Using Group Policy to Manage Users," is assumed here.

Apply Security Policies by Using Group Policy

When applying security policies by using Group Policy, consider the following:

◆ Security settings that can be managed through group policy include the following:

Setting	Description
Account Policies	Enables you to specify password and account lockout policy settings. Password policy settings include the password age (minimum and maximum), the number of passwords that will be remembered to prevent reuse of a favorite password by users, minimum password length, and password complexity. You also have the option to configure storing the password using reversible encryption. Account lockout policy settings include the duration of account lockout, the number of incorrect logon attempts before invoking lock out, and the account lockout interval, which is the time between failed logon attempts before the counter is reset.
Local Policies	Enables you to configure local computer settings for auditing, user rights assignment (such as Logon Locally, Logon as a Service, and so on), and specific computer security options such as message text to present to the user prior to logon, whether the last user logon name should be displayed when logging on, and others.
Event Log	Enables the configuration of log file sizes for the three main event logs (system, security, and application), whether logs should be overwritten, and any restrictions on who is allowed to read the log files.
Restricted Groups	Enables you to manage which users can be members of certain security groups. It also enables you to configure of which other groups these groups can be members. In other words, this setting enables you to configure group membership using the security policy to ensure that users are always members of certain groups and also that certain groups are members of other groups when the policy is applied.

Setting	Description
Registry	Enables you to configure security on registry keys. Through the security policy, you can set who is able to modify keys, read keys, and add new keys to the registry.
File System	Through this security setting, you are able to specify file-system security settings for folders and files on NTFS partitions and be sure that they will apply when the policy is in effect.
Public Key Policies	Enables you to set which users will be data recovery agents for the *Encrypting File System* (EFS). Recovery agents are able to decrypt files when the user who created them is not available or has been deleted. Here you can also import certificate files from root certification authorities that will be trusted by Windows 2000, will configure trust settings for authorities and certificates they have issued, and will specify automatic certificate request settings. Windows 2000 has come a long way to ensure that secure communication takes place and also that only those computers and users that have valid proof of authentication, such as certificates, are allowed access. These key security functions are implemented through Group Policy.
IP Security Directory Policies on Active Directory	Enables you to configure how clients, servers, and domain controllers will communicate and what level of security will be requested, required, or declined. These settings apply to TCP/IP traffic between the various types of Windows 2000 computers.

◆ Two tools can be used in managing security policy: Security Configuration and Analysis MMC snap-in or Group Policy within Active Directory.

◆ To apply a security policy against several computers at the same time, you can make use of Group Policy. Like other Group Policy settings, once configured, a security policy will apply against all machines within the scope of the Group Policy. When using Group Policy to enforce a security policy, the same rules regarding Group Policy inheritance and filtering still apply.

Create, Analyze, and Modify Security Configurations by Using Security Configuration and Analysis and Security Templates

Consider the following when creating, analyzing, and modifying security configurations by using Security Configuration and Analysis and Security Templates:

◆ Security Configuration and Analysis enables you to configure the security policy for the local computer. It also enables you to retrieve current security settings for the computer and compare them against a security template containing a preconfigured collection of security settings.

◆ Security Templates are text files with preset security configuration information that can be imported into Security Configuration and Analysis and/or Group Policy. Windows 2000 ships with a number of default Security Templates providing preconfigured settings at various security levels from none to highly secure. When choosing a template, consider whether you need the level of protection provided and why you are making use of it. Security should only be as tight as required. No more, no less.

Implement an Audit Policy

When implementing an audit policy, consider the following:

◆ Audit policy is a subset of security policy, is configured using the same tools, and enables you to track the usage of privileges on different parts of the system. The types of events that can be audited include file and folder access, logon and logoff activity, and use of privileges.

◆ For certain types of auditing (such as file and folder access, printer access, and Active Directory object access), you will have to modify object permissions to further refine your audit policy. When configuring auditing for these objects, or in general, audit only as much as is required so as not to introduce too high an overhead on the system.

Monitor and Analyze Security Events

When monitoring and analyzing security events, consider the following:

◆ Event Viewer is the tool to be used to monitor security-related events such as those configured through auditing.

◆ The security log of Event Viewer contains all security-related events.

◆ Filtering the log enables you to find events of interest more easily.

◆ If the security log fills up, the administrator can configure the computer to shut down. This ensures that no security-related information is lost.

This element of the book provides you with some general guidelines for preparing for a certification exam. It is organized into four sections. The first section addresses your learning style and how it affects your preparation for the exam. The second section covers your exam preparation activities and general study tips. This is followed by an extended look at the Microsoft Certification exams, including a number of specific tips that apply to the various Microsoft exam formats and question types. Finally, changes in Microsoft's testing policies, and how these might affect you, are discussed.

LEARNING STYLES

To better understand the nature of preparation for the test, it is important to understand learning as a process. You probably are aware of how you best learn new material. You may find that outlining works best for you, or, as a visual learner, you may need to "see" things. Whatever your learning style, test preparation takes place over time. Obviously, you shouldn't start studying for these exams the night before you take them; it is very important to understand that learning is a developmental process. Understanding it as a process helps you focus on what you know and what you have yet to learn.

Thinking about how you learn should help you recognize that learning takes place when you are able to match new information to old. You have some previous experience with computers and networking. Now you are preparing for this certification exam. Using this book, software, and supplementary materials will not just add incrementally to what you know; as you study, the organization of your knowledge actually restructures as you integrate new information into your existing knowledge base. This will lead you to a more comprehensive understanding of the tasks and concepts

Study and Exam Prep Tips

outlined in the objectives and of computing in general. Again, this happens as a result of a repetitive process rather than a singular event. Keep this model of learning in mind as you prepare for the exam, and you will make better decisions concerning what to study and how much more studying you need to do.

STUDY TIPS

There are many ways to approach studying, just as there are many different types of material to study. However, the tips that follow should work well for the type of material covered on the certification exams.

Study Strategies

Although individuals vary in the ways they learn information, some basic principles of learning apply to everyone. You should adopt some study strategies that take advantage of these principles. One of these principles is that learning can be broken into various depths. Recognition (of terms, for example) exemplifies a more surface level of learning in which you rely on a prompt of some sort to elicit recall. Comprehension or understanding (of the concepts behind the terms, for example) represents a deeper level of learning. The ability to analyze a concept and apply your understanding of it in a new way represents a further depth of learning.

Your learning strategy should enable you to know the material at a level or two deeper than mere recognition. This will help you perform well on the exams. You will know the material so thoroughly that you can easily handle the recognition-level types of questions used in multiple-choice testing. You will also be able to apply your knowledge to solve new problems.

Macro and Micro Study Strategies

One strategy that can lead to this deeper learning includes preparing an outline that covers all the objectives and subobjectives for the particular exam you are working on. You should delve a bit further into the material and include a level or two of detail beyond the stated objectives and subobjectives for the exam. Then expand the outline by coming up with a statement of definition or a summary for each point in the outline.

An outline provides two approaches to studying. First, you can study the outline by focusing on the organization of the material. Work your way through the points and sub-points of your outline with the goal of learning how they relate to one another. For example, be sure you understand how each of the main objective areas is similar to and different from another. Then, do the same thing with the subobjectives; be sure you know which subobjectives pertain to each objective area and how they relate to one another.

Next, you can work through the outline, focusing on learning the details. Memorize and understand terms and their definitions, facts, rules and strategies, advantages and disadvantages, and so on. In this pass through the outline, attempt to learn detail rather than the big picture (the organizational information that you worked on in the first pass through the outline).

Research has shown that attempting to assimilate both types of information at the same time seems to interfere with the overall learning process. Separate your studying into these two approaches, and you will perform better on the exam.

Active Study Strategies

The process of writing down and defining objectives, subobjectives, terms, facts, and definitions promotes a more active learning strategy than merely reading the material. In human information-processing terms, writing forces you to engage in more active encoding of the information. Simply reading over it exemplifies more passive processing.

Next, determine whether you can apply the information you have learned by attempting to create examples and scenarios on your own. Think about how or where you could apply the concepts you are learning. Again, write down this information to process the facts and concepts in a more active fashion.

The hands-on nature of the step-by-step tutorials and exercises at the ends of the chapters provide further active learning opportunities that will reinforce concepts as well.

Common-Sense Strategies

Finally, you should also follow common-sense practices when studying. Study when you are alert, reduce or eliminate distractions, and take breaks when you become fatigued.

Pre-Testing Yourself

Pre-testing allows you to assess how well you are learning. One of the most important aspects of learning is what has been called "meta-learning." Meta-learning has to do with realizing when you know something well or when you need to study some more. In other words, you recognize how well or how poorly you have learned the material you are studying.

For most people, this can be difficult to assess objectively on their own. Practice tests are useful in that they reveal more objectively what you have learned and what you have not learned. You should use this information to guide review and further studying. Developmental learning takes place as you cycle through studying, assessing how well you have learned, then reviewing, and then assessing again until you feel you are ready to take the exam.

You may have noticed the practice exam included in this book. Use it as part of the learning process. The *ExamGear, Training Guide Edition* test simulation software included on the CD also provides you with an excellent opportunity to assess your knowledge.

You should set a goal for your pre-testing. A reasonable goal would be to score consistently in the 90-percent range.

See Appendix C, "Using the ExamGear, Training Guide Edition Software," for more explanation of the test simulation software.

Exam Prep Tips

Having mastered the subject matter, the final preparatory step is to understand how the exam will be presented. Make no mistake: A Microsoft Certified Professional (MCP) exam will challenge both your knowledge and your test-taking skills. This section starts with the basics of exam design, reviews a new type of exam format, and concludes with hints targeted to each of the exam formats.

The MCP Exam

Every MCP exam is released in one of three basic formats. What's being called exam format here is really little more than a combination of the overall exam structure and the presentation method for exam questions.

Understanding the exam formats is key to good preparation because the format determines the number of questions presented, the difficulty of those questions, and the amount of time allowed to complete the exam.

Each exam format uses many of the same types of questions. These types or styles of questions include several types of traditional multiple-choice questions, multiple-rating (or scenario-based) questions, and simulation-based questions. Some exams include other types of questions that ask you to drag and drop on the screen, reorder a list, or categorize things. Still other exams ask you to answer these types of questions in response to a case study you have read. It's important that you understand the types of questions you will be asked and the actions required to properly answer them.

The rest of this section addresses the exam formats and then tackles the question types. Understanding the formats and question types will help you feel much more comfortable when you take the exam.

Exam Format

As mentioned above, there are three basic formats for the MCP exams: the traditional fixed-form exam, the adaptive form, and the case study form. As its name implies, the fixed-form exam presents a fixed set of questions during the exam session. The adaptive form, however, uses only a subset of questions drawn from a larger pool during any given exam session. The case study form includes case studies that serve as the basis for answering the various types of questions.

Fixed-Form

A fixed-form computerized exam is based on a fixed set of exam questions. The individual questions are presented in random order during a test session. If you take the same exam more than once, you won't necessarily see the exact same questions. This is because two or three final forms are typically assembled for every fixed-form exam Microsoft releases. These are usually labeled Forms A, B, and C.

The final forms of a fixed-form exam are identical in terms of content coverage, number of questions, and allotted time, but the questions are different. You may notice, however, that some of the same questions appear on, or rather are shared among, different final forms. When questions are shared among multiple final forms, the percentage of sharing is generally small. Some forms share no questions, but some forms have a 10–15 percent duplication of questions on the final exam forms.

Some forms also have a fixed time limit in which you must complete the exam. The *ExamGear, Training Guide Edition* software on the CD-ROM that accompanies this book provides fixed-form exams.

Finally, the score you achieve on a fixed-form exam, which is always reported for MCP exams on a scale of 0 to 1,000, is based on the number of questions you answer correctly. The passing score is the same for all final forms of a given fixed-form exam.

The typical format for the fixed-form exam is as follows:

- ◆ 50–60 questions.

- ◆ 75–90 minute testing time.

- ◆ Question review is allowed, including the opportunity to change your answers.

Adaptive Form

An adaptive-form exam has the same appearance as a fixed-form exam, but its questions differ in quantity and process of selection. Although the statistics of adaptive testing are fairly complex, the process is concerned with determining your level of skill or ability with the exam subject matter. This ability assessment begins with the presentation of questions of varying levels of difficulty and ascertaining at what difficulty level you can reliably answer them. Finally, the ability assessment determines whether that ability level is above or below the level required to pass that exam.

Examinees at different levels of ability will see quite different sets of questions. Examinees who demonstrate little expertise with the subject matter will continue to be presented with relatively easy questions. Examinees who demonstrate a high level of expertise will be presented progressively more difficult questions. Individuals of both levels of expertise may answer the same number of questions correctly, but because the higher-expertise examinee can correctly answer more difficult questions, he or she will receive a higher score and is more likely to pass the exam.

The typical design for the adaptive form exam is as follows:

◆ 20–25 questions.

◆ 90–minute testing time (although this is likely to be reduced to 45–60 minutes in the near future).

◆ Question review is not allowed, providing no opportunity for you to change your answers.

The Adaptive-Exam Process

Your first adaptive exam will be unlike any other testing experience you have had. In fact, many examinees have difficulty accepting the adaptive testing process because they feel that they were not provided the opportunity to adequately demonstrate their full expertise.

You can take consolation in the fact that adaptive exams are painstakingly put together after months of data gathering and analysis and that adaptive exams are just as valid as fixed-form exams. The rigor introduced through the adaptive testing methodology means that there is nothing arbitrary about the exam items you'll see. It is also a more efficient means of testing, requiring less time to conduct and complete than traditional fixed-form exams.

As you can see in Figure 1, a number of statistical measures drive the adaptive examination process. The measure most immediately relevant to you is the ability estimate. Accompanying this test statistic are the standard error of measurement, the item characteristic curve, and the test information curve.

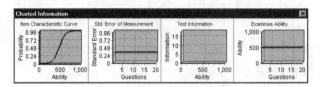

FIGURE 1
Microsoft's adaptive testing demonstration program.

The standard error, which is the key factor in determining when an adaptive exam will terminate, reflects the degree of error in the exam ability estimate. The item characteristic curve reflects the probability of a correct response relative to examinee ability. Finally, the test information statistic provides a measure of the information contained in the set of questions the examinee has answered, again relative to the ability level of the individual examinee.

When you begin an adaptive exam, the standard error has already been assigned a target value below which it must drop for the exam to conclude. This target value reflects a particular level of statistical confidence in the process. The examinee ability is initially set to the mean possible exam score (500 for MCP exams).

As the adaptive exam progresses, questions of varying difficulty are presented. Based on your pattern of responses to these questions, the ability estimate is recalculated. At the same time, the standard error estimate is refined from its first estimated value of one toward the target value. When the standard error reaches its target value, the exam is terminated. Thus, the more consistently you answer questions of the same degree of difficulty, the more quickly the standard error estimate drops, and the fewer questions you will end up seeing during the exam session. This situation is depicted in Figure 2.

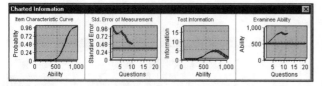

FIGURE 2
The changing statistics in an adaptive exam.

As you might suspect, one good piece of advice for taking an adaptive exam is to treat every exam question as if it were the most important. The adaptive scoring algorithm attempts to discover a pattern of responses that reflects some level of proficiency with the subject matter. Incorrect responses almost guarantee that additional questions must be answered (unless, of course, you get every question wrong). This is because the scoring algorithm must adjust to information that is not consistent with the emerging pattern.

Case Study Form

The case study format first appeared with the advent of the 70-100 exam (Solution Architectures). The questions in the case study format are not the independent entities that they are in the fixed and adaptive formats. Instead, questions are tied to a case study, a long scenario-like description of an information technology situation. As the test taker, your job is to extract from the case study the information that needs to be integrated with your understanding of Microsoft technology. The idea is that a case study will provide you with a situation that is more like a "real-life" problem situation than the other formats provide.

The case studies are presented as "testlets." These are sections within the exam in which you read the case study, then answer 10 to 15 questions that apply to the case study. When you finish that section, you move on to another testlet with another case study and its associated questions. There may be as many as five of these testlets that compose the overall exam. You will be given more time to complete such an exam because it takes time to read through the cases and analyze them. You may have as much as three hours to complete the exam—and you may need all of it. The case studies are always available through a linking button while you are in a testlet. However, once you leave a testlet, you cannot come back to it.

Figure 3 provides an illustration of part of a case study.

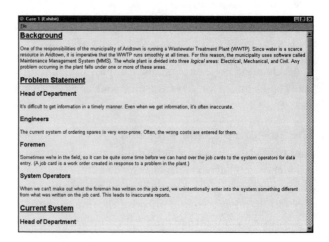

FIGURE 3
An example of a case study

Question Types

A variety of question types can appear on MCP exams. Examples of many of the various types appear in this book and the *ExamGear, Training Guide Edition* software. We have attempted to cover all the types that were available at the time of this writing. Most of the question types discussed in the following sections can appear in each of the three exam formats.

The typical MCP exam question is based on the idea of measuring skills or the ability to complete tasks. Therefore, most of the questions are written so as to present you with a situation that includes a role (such as a system administrator or technician), a technology environment (100 computers running Windows 98 on a Windows 2000 Server network), and a problem to be solved (the user can connect to services on the LAN, but not the intranet). The answers indicate actions that you might take to solve the problem or create setups or environments that would function correctly from the start. Keep this in mind as you read the questions on the exam. You may encounter some questions that just call for you to regurgitate facts, but these will be relatively few and far between.

In the following sections we will look at the different question types.

Multiple-Choice Questions

Despite the variety of question types that now appear in various MCP exams, the multiple-choice question is still the basic building block of the exams. The multiple-choice question comes in three varieties:

◆ **Regular multiple-choice.** Also referred to as an alphabetic question, it asks you to choose one answer as correct.

◆ **Multiple-answer multiple-choice.** Also referred to as a multi-alphabetic question, this version of a multiple-choice question requires you to choose two or more answers as correct. Typically, you are told precisely the number of correct answers to choose.

◆ **Enhanced multiple-choice.** This is simply a regular or multiple-answer question that includes a graphic or table to which you must refer to answer the question correctly.

Examples of such questions appear at the end of each chapter.

Multiple-Rating Questions

These questions are often referred to as scenario questions. Similar to multiple-choice questions, they offer more extended descriptions of the computing environment and a problem that needs to be solved. Required and desired optional results of the problem-solving are specified, as well as a solution. You are then asked to judge whether the actions taken in the solution are likely to bring about all or part of the required and desired optional results. There is, typically, only one correct answer.

You may be asking yourself, "What is multiple about multiple-rating questions?" The answer is that rather than having multiple answers, the question itself may be repeated in the exam with only minor variations in the required results, optional results, or solution introduced to create "new" questions. Read these different versions very carefully; the differences can be subtle.

Examples of these types of questions appear at the end of the chapters.

Simulation Questions

Simulation-based questions reproduce the look and feel of key Microsoft product features for the purpose of testing. The simulation software used in MCP exams has been designed to look and act, as much as possible, just like the actual product. Consequently, answering simulation questions in an MCP exam entails completing one or more tasks just as if you were using the product itself.

The format of a typical Microsoft simulation question consists of a brief scenario or problem statement, along with one or more tasks that you must complete to solve the problem. An example of a simulation question for MCP exams is shown in the following section.

A Typical Simulation Question

It sounds obvious, but your first step when you encounter a simulation question is to carefully read the question (see Figure 4). Do not go straight to the simulation application! You must assess the problem that's presented and identify the conditions that make up the problem scenario. Note the tasks that must be performed or outcomes that must be achieved to answer the question, and then review any instructions you're given on how to proceed.

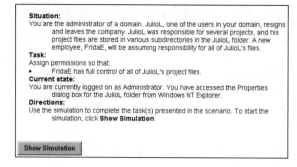

Situation:
You are the administrator of a domain. JulioL, one of the users in your domain, resigns and leaves the company. JulioL was responsible for several projects, and his project files are stored in various subdirectories in the JulioL folder. A new employee, FridaE, will be assuming responsibility for all of JulioL's files.
Task:
Assign permissions so that:
- FridaE has full control of all of JulioL's project files.
Current state:
You are currently logged on as Administrator. You have accessed the Properties dialog box for the JulioL folder from Windows NT Explorer.
Directions:
Use the simulation to complete the task(s) presented in the scenario. To start the simulation, click **Show Simulation**.

Show Simulation

FIGURE 4
A typical MCP exam simulation question with directions.

The next step is to launch the simulator by using the button provided. After clicking the Show Simulation button, you will see a feature of the product, as shown in the dialog box in Figure 5. The simulation application will partially obscure the question text on many test center machines. Feel free to reposition the simulator and to move between the question text screen and

the simulator by using hotkeys or point-and-click navigation, or even by clicking the simulator's launch button again.

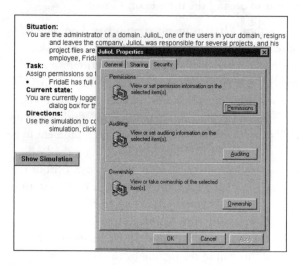

FIGURE 5
Launching the simulation application.

It is important for you to understand that your answer to the simulation question will not be recorded until you move on to the next exam question. This gives you the added capability of closing and reopening the simulation application (using the launch button) on the same question without losing any partial answer you may have made.

The third step is to use the simulator as you would the actual product to solve the problem or perform the defined tasks. Again, the simulation software is designed to function—within reason—just as the product does. But don't expect the simulator to reproduce product behavior perfectly. Most importantly, do not allow yourself to become flustered if the simulator does not look or act exactly like the product.

Figure 6 shows the solution to the example simulation problem.

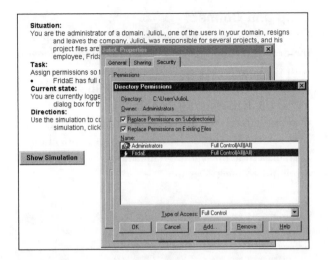

FIGURE 6
The solution to the simulation example.

Two final points will help you tackle simulation questions. First, respond only to what is being asked in the question; do not solve problems that you are not asked to solve. Second, accept what is being asked of you. You may not entirely agree with conditions in the problem statement, the quality of the desired solution, or the sufficiency of defined tasks to adequately solve the problem. Always remember that you are being tested on your ability to solve the problem as it is presented.

The solution to the simulation problem shown in Figure 6 perfectly illustrates both of those points. As you'll recall from the question scenario (refer to Figure 4), you were asked to assign appropriate permissions to a new user, FridaE. You were not instructed to make any other changes in permissions. Thus, if you were to modify or remove the administrator's permissions, this item would be scored wrong on an MCP exam.

Hot Area Question

Hot area questions call for you to click on a graphic or diagram in order to complete some task. You are asked a question that is similar to any other, but rather than clicking an option button or check box next to an answer, you click the relevant item in a screen shot or on a part of a diagram. An example of such an item is shown in Figure 7.

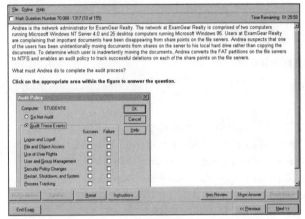

FIGURE 7
A typical hot area question.

Drag-and-Drop Questions

Microsoft has utilized two different types of drag-and-drop questions in exams. The first is a select-and-place question. The other is a drop-and-connect question. Both are covered in the following sections.

Select and Place

Select-and-place questions typically require you to drag and drop labels on images in a diagram so as to correctly label or identify some portion of a network. Figure 8 shows you the actual question portion of a select-and-place item.

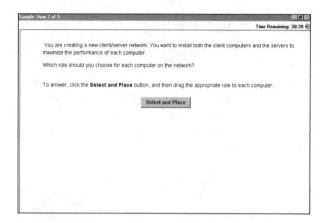

FIGURE 8
A select-and-place question.

Figure 9 shows the window you would see after you chose Select and Place. It contains the actual diagram in which you would select and drag the various server roles and match them with the appropriate computers.

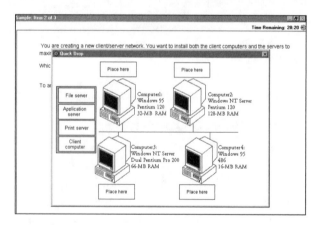

FIGURE 9
The window containing the diagram.

Drop and Connect

Drop-and-connect questions provide a different spin on the drag-and-drop question. The question provides you with the opportunity to create boxes that you can label, as well as connectors of various types with which to link them. In essence, you are creating a model or diagram in order to answer the question. You might have to create a network diagram or a data model for a database system. Figure 10 illustrates the idea of a drop-and-connect question.

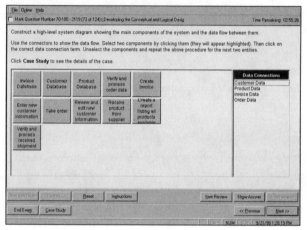

FIGURE 10
A drop-and-connect question.

Ordered-List Questions

Ordered-list questions simply require you to consider a list of items and place them in the proper order. You select items and then use a button to add them to a new list in the correct order. You have another button that you can use to remove the items in the new list in case you change your mind and want to reorder things. Figure 11 shows an ordered-list item.

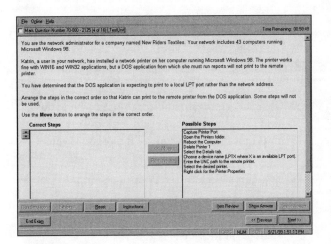

FIGURE 11
An ordered list question.

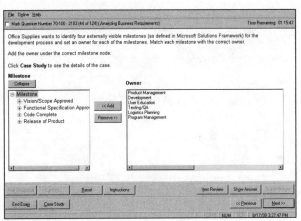

FIGURE 12
A tree question.

Tree Questions

Tree questions require you to think hierarchically and categorically. You are asked to place items from a list into categories that are displayed as nodes in a tree structure. Such questions might ask you to identify parent-child relationships in processes or the structure of keys in a database. You might also be required to show order within the categories, much as you would in an ordered list question. Figure 12 shows a typical tree question.

As you can see, Microsoft is making an effort to utilize question types that go beyond asking you to simply memorize facts. These question types force you to know how to accomplish tasks and understand concepts and relationships. Study so that you can answer these types of questions rather than those that simply ask you to recall facts.

Putting It All Together

Given all these different pieces of information, the task now is to assemble a set of tips that will help you successfully tackle the different types of MCP exams.

More Exam Preparation Tips

Generic exam-preparation advice is always useful. Tips include the following:

◆ Become familiar with the product. Hands-on experience is one of the keys to success on any MCP exam. Review the exercises and the Step by Steps in the book.

◆ Review the current exam-preparation guide on the Microsoft MCP Web site (www.microsoft.com/mcp/examinfo/exams.htm). The documentation Microsoft makes available over the Web identifies the skills every exam is intended to test.

◆ Memorize foundational technical detail, but remember that MCP exams are generally heavier on problem solving and application of knowledge than on questions that require only rote memorization.

◆ Take any of the available practice tests. We recommend the one included in this book and the ones you can create using the *ExamGear* software on the CD-ROM. As a supplement to the material bound with this book, try the free practice tests available on the Microsoft MCP Web site.

◆ Look on the Microsoft MCP Web site for samples and demonstration items. These tend to be particularly valuable for one significant reason: They help you become familiar with new testing technologies before you encounter them on MCP exams.

During the Exam Session

The following generic exam-taking advice that you've heard for years also applies when you're taking an MCP exam:

◆ Take a deep breath and try to relax when you first sit down for your exam session. It is very important that you control the pressure you may (naturally) feel when taking exams.

◆ You will be provided scratch paper. Take a moment to write down any factual information and technical detail that you committed to short-term memory.

◆ Carefully read all information and instruction screens. These displays have been put together to give you information relevant to the exam you are taking.

◆ Accept the non-disclosure agreement and preliminary survey as part of the examination process. Complete them accurately and quickly move on.

◆ Read the exam questions carefully. Reread each question to identify all relevant detail.

◆ Tackle the questions in the order in which they are presented. Skipping around won't build your confidence; the clock is always counting down (at least in the fixed-form exams).

◆ Don't rush, but also don't linger on difficult questions. The questions vary in degree of difficulty. Don't let yourself be flustered by a particularly difficult or wordy question.

Fixed-Form Exams

Building from this basic preparation and test-taking advice, you also need to consider the challenges presented by the different exam designs. Because a fixed-form exam is composed of a fixed, finite set of questions, add these tips to your strategy for taking a fixed-form exam:

◆ Note the time allotted and the number of questions on the exam you are taking. Make a rough calculation of how many minutes you can spend on each question, and use this figure to pace yourself through the exam.

◆ Take advantage of the fact that you can return to and review skipped or previously answered questions. Record the questions you can't answer confidently on the scratch paper provided, noting the relative difficulty of each question. When you reach the end of the exam, return to the more difficult questions.

◆ If you have session time remaining after you complete all the questions (and if you aren't too fatigued!), review your answers. Pay particular attention to questions that seem to have a lot of detail or that require graphics.

◆ As for changing your answers, the general rule of thumb here is *don't*! If you read the question carefully and completely and you felt like you knew the right answer, you probably did. Don't second-guess yourself. If, as you check your answers, one clearly stands out as incorrect, however, of course you should change it. But if you are at all unsure, go with your first impression.

Adaptive Exams

If you are planning to take an adaptive exam, keep these additional tips in mind:

◆ Read and answer every question with great care. When you're reading a question, identify every relevant detail, requirement, or task you must perform and double-check your answer to be sure you have addressed every one of them.

◆ If you cannot answer a question, use the process of elimination to reduce the set of potential answers, and then take your best guess. Stupid mistakes invariably mean that additional questions will be presented.

◆ You cannot review questions and change answers. When you leave a question, whether you've answered it or not, you cannot return to it. Do not skip any question, either; if you do, it's counted as incorrect.

Case Study Exams

This new exam format calls for unique study and exam-taking strategies. When you take this type of exam, remember that you have more time than in a typical exam. Take your time and read the case study thoroughly. Use the scrap paper or whatever medium is provided to you to take notes, diagram processes, and actively seek out the important information. Work through each testlet as if each were an independent exam. Remember, you cannot go back after you have left a testlet. Refer to the case study as often as you need to, but do not use that as a substitute for reading it carefully initially and for taking notes.

FINAL CONSIDERATIONS

Finally, a number of changes in the MCP program will impact how frequently you can repeat an exam and what you will see when you do.

◆ Microsoft has instituted a new exam retake policy. The new rule is "two and two, then one and two." That is, you can attempt any exam twice with no restrictions on the time between attempts. But after the second attempt, you must wait two weeks before you can attempt that exam again. After that, you will be required to wait two weeks between subsequent attempts. Plan to pass the exam in two attempts or plan to increase your time horizon for receiving the MCP credential.

◆ New questions are being seeded into the MCP exams. After performance data is gathered on new questions, the examiners will replace older questions on all exam forms. This means that the questions appearing on exams will regularly change.

◆ Many of the current MCP exams will be republished in adaptive form. Prepare yourself for this significant change in testing; it is entirely likely that this will become the preferred MCP exam format for most exams. The exception to this may be the case study exams because the adaptive approach may not work with that format.

These changes mean that the brute-force strategies for passing MCP exams may soon completely lose their viability. So if you don't pass an exam on the first or second attempt, it is likely that the exam's form will change significantly by the next time you take it. It could be updated from fixed-form to adaptive, or it could have a different set of questions or question types.

Microsoft's intention is not to make the exams more difficult by introducing unwanted change, but to create and maintain valid measures of the technical skills and knowledge associated with the different MCP credentials. Preparing for an MCP exam has always involved not only studying the subject matter, but also planning for the testing experience itself. With the recent changes, this is now more true than ever.

This exam consists of 65 questions reflecting the material you have covered in the chapters. These questions are representative of the types you should expect to see on the actual exam.

The answers to all questions appear in a section following the exam. It is strongly suggested that, when you take this exam, you treat it just as you would the actual exam at the test center. Time yourself, read carefully, and answer all the questions to the best of your ability.

Most of the questions do not simply require you to recall facts; they require deduction on your part to come up with the best answer. Most questions require you to identify the best course of action to take in a given situation. Many of the questions are verbose, requiring you to read them carefully and thoroughly before you attempt to answer them. Run through the exam. When you miss questions, review any material associated with them.

Practice Exam

Exam Questions

1. Sally is currently working on configuring the DNS at Scriberco Ltd. so that it will be able to handle Windows 2000. The server is running on a Windows 2000 Advanced Server, and Sally will be using this server for the initial setup of the Active Directory infrastructure. After she configures the server, she attempts to install the first domain controller. The installation asks if she would like to install a DNS server; she chooses not to install the DNS server. After the system restarts, she receives errors about the Netlogon service not being able to start. What should she do to correct this problem?

   A. Install a DNS server on the domain controller.

   B. Configure the TCP/IP properties.

   C. Use DCPROMO to demote the server and then use DCPROMO to bring the server back up as a domain controller accepting the DNS server this time.

   D. She needs to manually start the DNS service on the new domain controller because it is marked for manual startup by default.

2. Joan is a consultant helping New Riders Vineyards upgrade their network from Windows NT 4.0 to Windows 2000. The network consists of 70 domain controllers and 3,400 clients. The clients have been upgraded to Windows 2000 Professional, and the member servers, including the DNS and WINS servers, have been upgraded to Windows 2000 Server or Windows 2000 Advanced Server. The process to date has been going well, and the final step in the process will be to upgrade the domain controllers, which is expected to take about 10 days. Joan starts the process on a Saturday morning by upgrading the PDC; after the system restarts, the system cannot start the Netlogon service. Joan checks all the settings on the system, and they are fine. What should she check next?

   A. She needs to verify that the DNS server allows updates.

   B. She needs to install the DNS service on the domain controller.

   C. She should have started the upgrade with a BDC.

   D. She needs to run the Sysprep utility before she performs the upgrade.

3. Factron Inc. is in the process of upgrading their network to Windows 2000. They started by upgrading their DNS servers from a combination of BIND- and Windows NT–based DNS servers to Windows 2000–based DNS servers. The company has seven locations across North America, and the main DNS server is in their Vancouver office. The other locations are in Calgary and Toronto. There are three DNS servers in the Vancouver office, two in Calgary, and four in Toronto. Currently, all the secondary servers are retrieving the zone file from the primary. The DNS servers will be changed to Active Directory integrated once there are domain controllers in all three offices; until then, though, the standard primary zone will be used. The administrator of the Factron Inc. network asks you what they can do to reduce the number of updates taking place across the WAN links while they are upgrading to Windows 2000?

   A. Configure a secondary in each site as a master.

   B. Change the time to live on the entries.

   C. Configure all the systems in the network to use a central server.

D. There is nothing that can be done until the zone is configured to be Active Directory integrated.

4. Beth is designing the DNS structure that will support the move from Windows NT 4.0 and Solaris 2.7 to a pure Windows 2000 environment. Currently, the DNS servers are on a Solaris 2.7 system running a version of BIND that supports SRV records and dynamic updates. She plans to use the existing DNS servers during the upgrade and then switch to Windows 2000 servers version of DNS. She wants to use an Active Directory-integrated zone on the DNS servers when Windows 2000 domain controllers are completely deployed. She configures the DNS servers to transfer the zone files every two hours rather than the default 15 minutes. Later, after the domain controllers are upgraded and she has switched the zone to Active Directory integrated, she notices that updates in the zone files are be transferred in less than two hours; in some cases, the changes seem to be appearing in less than 5 minutes. What should she do?

A. When the zone was reconfigured as Active Directory integrated, the default transfer schedule was put back; all she needs to do is change the information again.

B. Because the zone is Active Directory integrated, the replication is now being handled by Active Directory; therefore, there is nothing she needs to do.

C. Because the zone is now Active Directory integrated, she will need to set the replication time for the DNS records using the NTDS settings in the Active Directory Sites and Services snap-in.

D. Because the zone is now Active Directory integrated, she will need to set the replication time for the DNS records using the NTDS settings in the Active Directory Users and Computers snap-in.

5. You are a consultant working with Scriberco Importers. You have been working with the administration during the transition to Windows 2000. The network is broken down into geographical areas, and users will occasionally transfer from one office to another. In the previous network, the user would be deleted from one domain and added to another using a piece of third-party software. Heidi, one of the network administrators, has just received a request to move a user from the Seattle office to the New York office. This involves moving the user from the NAWest domain to the NAEast domain. Heidi has asked you for help because she does not seem to be able to do this in Active Directory Users and Computers. What should you tell her to do?

A. She will need to get the upgrade to the third-party utility they were using.

B. She will need to type the fully distinguished name for the new location in the Move dialog box.

C. She will need to use the MOVETREE utility to move the user.

D. She will need to delete the user and then re-create the user in the other domain.

6. Jenna has just created a new site and added the subnets to the site in the Wingtip Toys network. The users are complaining that the logon process is now taking longer than it should. What should Jenna do to correct this problem?

A. She needs to add a DNS server to the new site.

B. She needs to add a DC to the new site.

C. She needs to add a logon proxy to the site.

D. She doesn't need to do anything; this is a consequence of using sites.

7. You are having a problem with a computer on the network that will not register with the DNS server. The system is part of an organizational unit, and you are working with a user that has been given administrative rights to the OU to solve the problem. If the computer starts and tries to register its name on the DNS server, you get a permissions error in the event log on the DNS server and a failure listed in the Event Viewer for the system. If, however, you log on and use the IPCONFIG utility to register the name, it works fine. What should you check next?

A. You should check whether the system is a DHCP client.

B. You should check the permissions on the Active Directory object.

C. You should check that the DNS server is configured to accept updates.

D. You should check that the computer account exists in Active Directory.

8. You are the administrator of the Scriberco Ltd. network. You have just finished replacing a system that crashed due to a hard-disk failure. You replaced the system and used DCPROMO to make it a domain controller again. Later in the day, you are attempting to install a new personnel management system, and the installation fails. The failure reports that it cannot create a class that is required to run the software on the network. What should you do to enable you to install the software? (Choose two.)

A. You should log on as the local system account on the computer on which you are attempting to install the software.

B. You should log on using an Enterprise admin account to install the software.

C. You should make sure the schema master is available and allows modifications.

D. You should seize the schema master role because the system that died must have been the schema master.

E. You should logon as an Enterprise admin and check the permissions.

9. You are the administrator of a Windows 2000 network. The network is a small network with five domain controllers and a dozen Windows 2000–based servers. There are 400 clients in the network, all of which are running Windows 2000 Professional. The users are complaining that logons are taking longer than they used to and that accessing network servers is slow at times as well. You need to correct these problems, and you suspect the replication is the problem. What should you do to correct the problem?

A. Divide the network into two or more sites.

B. Divide the network into two or more domains.

C. Divide the network into two or more organizational units.

D. Reduce the number of servers by two.

10. You are going to take the server that is currently the schema and domain naming operations masters offline. The system will be offline for a significant period of time, and you want to transfer the operations master roles to another computer. Which of the following tools will you need to use to accomplish this? (Choose all that apply.)

A. Active Directory Users and Computers

B. Active Directory Sites and Services

C. Active Directory Domains and Trusts

D. Active Directory schema

E. The NTDSUTIL command-line utility

F. The Computer Management snap-in

G. The DNS snap-in

11. After several meetings with the engineering department at New Riders Research, the executive staff has decided to allow the engineering department to have control of the computers and users in that department. There are 280 computers and users all located in the engineering facility that you must now move to a newly created organizational unit. You will have the entire weekend to perform the move. How should you do it?

A. Use Drag and Drop to drag the users to the new OU.

B. Use the **Move** command in the context menu.

C. Create a group that contains all the engineers and then move the group to the new OU.

D. Use the **Find** command to find the users in the engineering facility, verify the names, and then use **Move** from the context menu to move them.

12. You are running your Windows 2000 domain in mixed mode because you still have several domain controllers running Windows NT 4.0. There are currently eight Windows 2000 domain controllers in the domain and four Windows NT 4.0 backup domain controllers. Many systems have been upgraded over the last couple days to Windows 2000, including both member servers and client workstations.

A user calls and complains that he is not able to log on to the domain. He changed his password 10 minutes ago and then the power in their office failed. The user needs to be able to get on the network because he is expecting an important message from the Athens office. The user is on a segment that has not been upgraded, meaning the nearest domain controller is a Windows NT 4.0 domain controller and the client is running Windows 98. What should you do next to get the user logged on to the network?

A. Force replication within the entire domain using Active Directory Sites and Services.

B. Force the Windows NT 4.0 domain controllers to replicate with the global catalog.

C. Force replication between the domain controllers and the PDC emulator.

D. Force the replication across site links using Active Directory Sites and Services.

13. You are an administrator on a network, and your supervisor has asked you to upgrade a computer from the Engineering domain in the West7 site to a global catalog server. What must you do?

A. Edit the NTDS Settings for a suitable controller.

B. Edit the Group Policy for the Engineering organizational unit and only give Apply permissions to that one computer.

C. This has to be done in the registry.

D. You must reinstall the system.

14. The network has been slow for the last three days. At first you thought this was due to the amount of traffic generated during the upgrades. However, you haven't done any upgrades today, and the network is still slow. What tool should you use to determine what is causing the problem?

A. Use Performance on the global catalog servers.

B. Use Performance on the domain controllers.

C. Use Network Monitor on any computer.

D. Use Network Monitor on a domain controller.

15. Your company is located in five cities across the state of New Jersey. There is the head office where the IT department is located, and there are four branch offices that deal with sales and delivery. The company wants to keep central control of resources and users in the head office but wants each office to have users who will have control over changing passwords and who will be able to deal with printer and share problems. What is the best way to implement this?

A. Create a root domain in the head office and then create a child domain for each of the branch offices.

B. Create a root domain in the head office and then another root domain in a separate forest in each of the branches.

C. Create a root domain in the head office and one for the branches. Then create an organizational unit for each branch in the branches domain. Delegate some control of the OU to a member in the local offices.

D. Create a root domain in the head office and then create a site for each local office. Delegate control of each site as required.

16. During a recent cleanup of old accounts, one of the junior administrators accidentally deleted an entire OU that contained the accounts for users that are currently on extended leave but will be returning. You know that some of the users used EFS and others had very specialized permissions, so trying to re-create the accounts will take a long time and might not be feasible. You want to recover the accounts. What should you do? (Choose two.)

A. Perform a restore from a system backup.

B. Perform a restore from a system state backup.

C. Use the directory services utility to increment the USN on the object.

D. Use Activity Directory Users and Computers to re-create the OU before you restore.

E. Use the directory services utility to store the re-created OU.

17. Your network is broken down into 12 different sites. Of the 12 sites, 11 are on the same network at one location, and one is at a remote location that uses RRAS and demand-dial routing to access the main office through a VPN on the Internet. You want to make sure the replication will work between all sites. What should you do?

A. Create connection objects between controllers in each site.

B. Create the site links and assign the correct cost and availability.

C. Create the required site links and site link bridge.

D. Create the required site links and site link bridges and then create connections between servers at different locations.

18. You have a remote office on your network that will be connected to the main office using a 256Kbps frame relay link before you roll out Windows 2000. You are planning the connections to the office for Active Directory. Looking at the current traffic between the offices, you anticipate the traffic in the day will consume 90% of the bandwidth, and the overnight traffic (between 6 p.m. and 6 a.m.) will use 20%. You want to make sure your users get all the bandwidth they require. What should you configure?

A. Create a script that adds the connection object at night and then removes it in the morning. Use the Task Scheduler to run the script.

B. Create a site link and configure the site link with two schedules.

C. Create a site link bridge and change the site involved every morning and every evening.

D. Create two site links with different schedules.

19. One of the domain controllers on your network has just crashed. The domain controller was part of the Production site in the Toronto domain; thankfully, it was not an operations master. You have another server with the same configuration, and you need to restore the domain controller quickly because it was one of only two at that site. You take the server to the site and install Windows 2000 Server. What must you do to restore the server?

A. Use DCPROMO to promote the server to a domain controller.

B. Use DCPROMO to promote the server to a domain controller and then perform a restore from backup.

C. Use directory services Restore mode from the F8 menu and then restore the domain controller from tape backup.

D. Use directory services Restore mode and then perform an authoritative restore.

20. You are an administrator on the Scriberco Ltd. network. You have been assigned an area of the physical network that you are responsible for; it includes 10 sites. The users in one of the sites are complaining that the logon process is taking much longer than it should. There are two

domain controllers in that particular site: one from the root domain, which is primarily for DNS and the global catalog, and one for the Human Resources domain. What should you do next to troubleshoot the problem?

A. Use Performance to check the domain controllers.

B. Use the Network Monitor to see what traffic in on the network.

C. Use the NBTSTAT command-line utility to check the server status.

D. Rebuild the two servers.

21. You are attempting to install the first domain controller in the first domain for your Windows 2000 rollout. There is currently a Windows NT 4.0 domain named ScribercoNT. However, over the years, that domain has had many different administrators, and at this point, you decide to start clean with your organization of 100 people.

You start the DCPROMO utility and begin to install the domain after entering the domain name as **SCRIBERCO.LOCAL**. The system pauses for a long while and then comes back with a warning that the down-level domain name will be Scriberco0 because there is already a Scriberco domain on the network. What should you do to correct this?

A. Change the name of the new domain.

B. Change the protocols you have installed in the NT 4.0 domain so that it doesn't use TCP/IP.

C. Locate the domain controller(s) for the Scriberco domain and take it (them) offline.

D. Accept the suggested name.

22. You want to upgrade the hardware on a domain controller that is in use in a domain you manage. You obtain the parts, and on the weekend, you perform the upgrade. After the upgrade, your boss asks you to quantify the value of the upgrade. What tool should you use?

    A. You should use the Performance tool.

    B. You should use the Network Monitor.

    C. You should use the Monitoring tab on the servers Properties dialog box.

    D. You should use the Task Manager.

23. You are about to monitor the performance of a domain controller. The controller has been slow lately, and the disk light is on most of the time. What counters should you include in Performance? (Choose two.)

    A. Memory

    B. CPU

    C. Physical Disk

    D. Network Segment

    E. Task Manager

24. You are trying to create a site in the Active Directory Sites and Services snap-in. The site you are trying to create is called Minn. What piece of information other than the name will you need?

    A. You will need the site link to which it will belong.

    B. You will need the information on the first subnet that will be in this site.

    C. You will need the name of a domain controller that will be in the site.

    D. You don't need to know anything but the name.

25. You will be upgrading your network to Windows 2000 in the next few months. You are reading up on the requirements for the DNS server that will be used for the Windows 2000 domain because you will still have several servers running UNIX. You want to know whether you need to move the DNS servers to the Windows 2000 system or whether you can continue to run them on UNIX. What are the requirements for DNS to work with Active Directory?

    A. The DNS server must support SRV records.

    B. The DNS server must support incremental transfers.

    C. The DNS server must support updates.

    D. The DNS server must support secure updates.

26. You have been adding printers to a print server you recently upgraded from Windows NT 4.0 Server to Windows 2000 Server. The five new printers you just added are all working, and when you check Active Directory, you find they are all listed. You notice that the other two printers on the system are not listed. What should you do to include these printers in Active Directory?

    A. In the Properties dialog box for the printers on the Active Directory tab, make sure that List in the Directory is checked.

    B. In the Properties dialog box for the printers on the Sharing tab, make sure that List in the Directory is selected.

    C. You will need to install the printer in Active Directory User and Computers.

    D. You will need to remove and then add back the printers.

27. An older Windows 98 system is running on a Pentium 133, meaning you cannot upgrade the system to Windows 2000. During the upgrade process that will take several months, you want to make sure the existing users will be able to use this printer; however, you also want Windows 2000 users to be able to work with it. What action should you take?

   A. Create the printer as a local printer on a Windows 2000 server and set the port to the network name of the existing printer.

   B. Create the printer as a network printer on a Windows 2000 server and set the network address to the network name of the existing printer.

   C. Create the printer object in the Windows 2000 Active Directory.

   D. You cannot share the printer from a Windows 98 system and will need to move it at least to a Windows NT Server.

28. You are configuring the backup schedule for a Windows 2000 server. You will be backing up all the data, including system state data, to a remote server with sufficient room. The policy states that you must have a full backup once a week and differential backups Monday, Tuesday, Wednesday, Thursday, and Friday. You configure the full backup to run once a week and to overwrite the previous week's backup. You then test it and everything is fine. You now are configuring the differential backups. How many tasks should you configure?

   A. 1

   B. 2

   C. 5

   D. 260

29. It's Thursday, and one of the member servers on your network has crashed. You need to restore the server from backup. You have replaced the drives and have reloaded Windows 2000 Advanced Server. You join the server to the domain and are ready now to restore from tape. There is a normal backup from Sunday morning and differential backups from Monday, Tuesday, and Wednesday nights. What should you reload? (Choose two.)

   A. You should reload the normal backup.

   B. You should reload the Monday backup.

   C. You should reload the Tuesday backup.

   D. You should reload the Wednesday backup.

30. Your company currently has DNS servers that are used with the UNIX servers and workstations used across the organization. You will be adding Windows 2000 with Active Directory to the network shortly, and you need to provide resolution for the current UNIX servers and workstations in addition to being able to work with Windows 2000. You already know that the BIND version you are using does not support SRV records and will not work with Active Directory. What is the easiest way to resolve this problem?

   A. Use Windows 2000 servers as the DNS servers for your company.

   B. Upgrade the BIND version so you will be able to use it Active Directory.

   C. Create a secondary zone file for the existing zone on the Windows 2000 servers. Have the other Windows 2000 DNS servers use that one as the master server.

   D. Configure the Windows 2000 DNS server to use the UNIX server as a forwarder.

31. You are finding that you frequently need to create new users for the sales department, about one or two per week. You want to make the creation of the accounts as simple as possible. What should you do?

    A. Create a text file with all the sales settings and import this to Active Directory Users and Computers for each new account after you edit the text file.

    B. Create a fake sales account that is disabled; copy the account when you need to create a new sales user.

    C. Use the group policies to set the account information for the entire organizational unit and then just create basic users.

    D. Write a batch file using the **NET USER** command.

32. You want to look at the CPU time that a process is using. What is the quickest way to determine this value?

    A. Use the Performance tool.

    B. Use the **NET STATISTICS** command.

    C. Use the Task Manager.

    D. Use the System Information tool.

33. One of the junior operators was attempting to make a schema modification but could not do so. He assumed the schema master was down and figured he had better seize the schema master role. You find out about this, and after giving the junior operator 80,000 disks to format, you go off to fix the problem. What do you need to do?

    A. You need to take the previous schema master offline and reformat the drive; then you need to verify the schema.

    B. You need to undo the change the junior operator made and then seize the role back on the schema master. After that, you need to make the modification that needed to be made initially.

    C. You need to seize the role on the previous schema master and then format the drive on the system that had seized the role.

    D. You need to reinstall the entire Active Directory.

34. You have just installed the first domain controller in your Active Directory forest. After you restart the system, you verify that the Active Directory tools are on the Administrative Tools menu and that you can find you computer in the Domain Controllers container in Active Directory.

    You open the DNS console and expand your server, which is in the list. You see the name of your forward lookup zone, and you expand this. There are a couple entries, but the Active Directory entries are not listed. What should you do? (Choose all that apply.)

    A. Use **IPConfig /registerdns** command to register your computer.

    B. Stop and start the DNS server service.

    C. Stop and start the server service.

    D. Stop and start the Netlogon service.

    E. Verify your Network Identification.

    F. Verify your TCP/IP settings and point to yourself as a DNS server.

    G. Use the **NSLookUp /registerdns** command to register your domain.

35. You are in the process of delegating administrative control of an OU to a user named Sandra who will be helping manage user accounts in the domain. Using the Delegation of Control Wizard, you allow the user to reset passwords and to change the attributes of users. Later, when the user is trying to reset a password, she is not able to although she could for other users. She calls to tell you this and to have you reset the password. You are able to reset the password, and you tell her you'll look into it. What should you check?

   A. You should check the permissions on the OU that you delegated.

   B. You should check the permissions on Sandra's account.

   C. You should check the permissions on the Users account.

   D. You should rerun the Delegation of Control Wizard.

36. You are in the process of creating computer objects in the domain so the junior technicians will be able to install the systems. As you are adding the computer accounts, you get to a point at which the system will not let you add any more computers. What could the problem be?

   A. You have reached the limit to the number of objects Active Directory can contain.

   B. You have reached the limit to the number of objects an organizational unit can hold.

   C. You have run out of relative identifiers and should check the operations master.

   D. Your session on the domain controller has been dropped.

37. You attempt to install Remote Installation Services on your Windows 2000 Server computer, and you receive an error stating that RIS cannot be installed on the machine. What is the most likely cause of the problem?

   A. DHCP is not installed on the server.

   B. The computer is not a member of an Active Directory domain.

   C. DNS is not installed on the computer.

   D. The computer is not a member of a workgroup.

   E. The computer does not have a PXE-enabled network card.

38. You design a Group Policy structure with two GPOs, one at the domain level and the other at the Sales OU level.

   • At the domain level, you specify a background wallpaper and assign the policy to Authenticated Users.

   • At the Sales OU level, you disable Control Panel and assign the policy to the SalesPeople security group.

   • At the Sales OU level, you specify a background wallpaper and assign it to the Salespeople security group.

   • At the domain level, you specify that users can only make use of the Add/Remove Programs and Display portions of Control Panel.

   • You configure the Sales OU GPO to block policy inheritance.

   • You configure the domain-level GPO with No Override.

A user in the Sales OU logs on to the network after you have saved your changes and a refresh of the GPO has taken place on all domain controllers affected. What will be the result of your GPO settings on the user desktop? (Choose all correct answers.)

A. Control Panel will be disabled for the user.

B. Only Add/Remove Programs and Display properties will be available in Control Panel.

C. The user will have the domain-level background wallpaper.

D. The user will have the background wallpaper specified in the Sales OU GPO.

39. You have installed Remote Installation Services on a Windows 2000 member server in your domain that is also a DHCP server. The DHCP server has been authorized in Active Directory.

   What minimum set of additional tasks must you perform to enable the server to respond to RIS requests from clients? (Choose two).

   A. Authorize the RIS server in Active Directory.

   B. Make sure the network card in the RIS server is PXE enabled.

   C. Install an initial CD-based image on the RIS server.

   D. Run the RISETUP utility.

   E. Install an initial RIPrep image on the RIS server.

   F. Prestage the RIS server.

40. You have configured software deployment using Group Policy at the domain level on a domain controller in the scriberco.com domain as follows:

   • You assign Adobe Acrobat to computers in the domain.

   • You publish Microsoft Office 2000 to users in the domain.

   • You assign Microsoft Word 2000 to computers in the domain.

   • Permissions on the GPO are left at default.

   RobS, a member of the Domain Admins group, logs on to the domain after installing Windows 2000 Professional on a brand new computer. What software configuration will take place as a result of the GPO settings? (Choose all correct answers.)

   A. Adobe Acrobat will be installed on the computer.

   B. Microsoft Office 2000 will be installed on the computer.

   C. Microsoft Word 2000 will be installed on the computers.

   D. Adobe Acrobat will be listed in Add/Remove Programs.

   E. Microsoft Office 2000 will be listed in Add/Remove Programs.

   F. Microsoft Word 2000 will be listed in Add/Remove Programs.

   G. No software will be installed on the computer.

41. What are the default Group Policy refresh intervals for computers in the domain? (Choose two correct answers.)

   A. Group Policy is refreshed on domain controllers every 15 minutes.

   B. Group Policy is refreshed on member servers and workstations every 15 minutes.

   C. Group Policy is refreshed on member servers and workstations every 90 minutes.

D. Group Policy is refreshed on domain controllers every 90 minutes.

E. Group Policy is refreshed on member servers and workstations every 5 minutes.

F. Group Policy is refreshed on domain controllers every 5 minutes.

42. You have configured software deployment using Group Policy at the domain level on a domain controller in the scriberco.com domain as follows:

- You assign Adobe Acrobat to computers in the domain.

- You publish Microsoft Office 2000 to users in the domain.

- You assign Microsoft Word 2000 to computers in the domain.

- Permissions on the GPO are left at default. RoryM, a member of the Developers group, logs on to the domain after installing Windows 2000 Professional on a brand new computer. What software configuration will take place as a result of the GPO settings? (Choose all correct answers.)

A. Adobe Acrobat will be installed on the computer.

B. Microsoft Office 2000 will be installed on the computer.

C. Microsoft Word 2000 will be installed on the computer.

D. Adobe Acrobat will be listed in Add/Remove Programs.

E. Microsoft Office 2000 will be listed in Add/Remove Programs.

F. Microsoft Word 2000 will be listed in Add/Remove Programs.

G. No software will be installed on the computer.

43. You modify the Offline folder settings for users on an existing GPO that has been assigned to the SalesPeople security group. NatashaR, a member of the SalesPeople security group, is already logged on to the domain on a Windows 2000 Professional computer. When will the updated settings for Offline folders take effect on her computer?

A. The next time she logs on to the domain.

B. Within 5 minutes.

C. Within 90 minutes.

D. Within 15 minutes.

E. The next time the computer restarts.

F. The new settings will not take effect.

44. You have an existing Group Policy called Sales Desktop Policy that has been created in the Sales OU of the factron.com domain. You want to apply the same settings to the Sales OU of the scriberco.com domain, which is in the same forest as the factron.com domain. What would be the easiest way to accomplish this?

A. Copy the Sales Desktop Policy to the Sales OU of the scriberco.com domain.

B. Create a new policy called Scriberco Sales Desktop Policy on the Sales OU of the scriberco.com domain and manually copy the settings from the Sales Desktop Policy on the factron.com domain.

C. Create a new policy called Scriberco Sales Desktop Policy on the Sales OU of the scriberco.com domain and link it to the Group Policy template of the Sales Desktop Policy on the factron.com domain.

D. Link the Sales Desktop Policy to the Sales OU of the scriberco.com domain.

45. You are the administrator of the factron.com domain. You have created the following Active Directory containers:

    - A Sales Organizational Unit

    - A Development Organizational Unit

    - A Finance Organizational Unit

    In which Active Directory containers are you unable to create a Group Policy? (Choose all that apply.)

    A. Users

    B. Sales OU

    C. Finance OU

    D. Computers

    E. Development OU

    F. factron.com domain

    G. Domain Controllers

46. You have configured a domain-level Group Policy on the scriberco.com domain with the following settings:

    - You have enabled the Windows Installer setting Always install with elevated privileges for computers in the domain.

    - You have disabled registry editing tools for users in the domain.

    - You have disabled new task creation in the Task Scheduler for users in the domain.

    - You have disabled the Windows Installer setting Always install with elevated privileges for users in the domain.

    - You have enabled Drag and Drop for the Task Scheduler for computers in the domain.

NatashaR logs on to a Windows 2000 Professional computer in the domain. What will be her effective settings based on your Group Policy configuration? (Choose all that apply.)

A. Windows Installer will install applications with elevated privileges.

B. Windows Installer will install applications using the same privileges as the logged-on user.

C. Registry editing tools will be enabled.

D. Registry editing tools will be disabled.

E. She will be able to create a task in the Task Scheduler using drag and drop.

F. She will not be able to create a task in the Task using Drag and Drop.

47. You modify the Offline folder settings for users on an existing GPO that has been assigned to the SalesPeople security group. NatashaR, a member of the SalesPeople security group, is already logged on to the domain on a Windows NT Workstation 4.0 computer. When will the updated settings for Offline folders take effect on her computer? (Choose the best answer.)

    A. The next time she logs on to the domain.

    B. Within 5 minutes.

    C. Within 90 minutes.

    D. Within 15 minutes.

    E. The next time the computer restarts.

    F. The new settings will not take effect.

48. Which of the following audit policy settings, when enabled, require no further action on your part for auditing to commence? (Choose all correct answers.)

    A. Audit Object Access

    B. Audit Logon Events

C. Audit System Events

D. Audit Directory Service Access

E. Audit Account Logon Events

F. Audit File and Print Access

G. Audit User Names

49. Which of the following are required tags within the Application section in a ZAP file? (Choose two correct answers.)

A. DisplayVersion

B. ApplicationName

C. FriendlyName

D. Publisher

E. URL

F. SetupCommand

50. Scriberco.com has made extensive use of Group Policy to publish and assign software to users and computers throughout the enterprise. Recently, users have been complaining that, when they use Add/Remove Programs in Control Panel to install an application, the list of applications is so long that they cannot find the software package they want to install very easily. How can you make it easier for users to find software packages they want to install?

A. Assign applications to specific users.

B. Publish applications to specific users.

C. Associate applications with specific file extensions and have users search for applications by file extension.

D. Create software categories for the published applications.

E. Reduce the number of applications available.

F. Do nothing. This is just the way it works.

51. You need to make a software application available to users in your sales department. The application is not provided in a Windows Installer Package file format. Users may choose to have the software installed on their computers. What is the best way to deploy this application using Group Policy?

A. Repackage the application using WinINSTALL LE and assign it to the user.

B. Repackage the application using WinINSTALL LE and publish it to the user.

C. Create a ZAP file for the application and assign it to the user.

D. Create a ZAP file for the application and publish it to the user.

E. It is not possible to deploy software using Group Policy unless it is provided as a Windows Installer Package file.

52. The management of scriberco.com has decided that a uniform password policy needs to exist for all users in the enterprise. The policy should enforce a minimum password length of 6 characters, a maximum password age of 30 days, a minimum password age of 1 day, and a password history of 12 passwords.

The Active Directory structure of scriberco.com includes four additional subdomains. These subdomains are called namerica.scriberco.com, europe.scriberco.com, samerica.scriberco.com, and specific.scriberco.com and have been created for administrative purposes. Because the migration to Windows 2000 has just recently been completed, no new Group Policy objects have yet been created.

What would be the easiest way to enforce the password policy settings throughout the enterprise?

A. Modify the default domain policy with the password settings.

B. Create a GPO in each domain with the password policy settings.

C. Create a GPO at the scriberco.com domain called Password Policy Settings with the password policy settings.

D. Link the Password Policy Settings GPO from the scriberco.com domain to each subdomain.

E. Move all users in the subdomains to the Users container of the scriberco.com domain.

53. Through an acquisition, scriberco.com has merged with factron.com to create a new company called FactroScriberco International Limited. Both scriberco.com and factron.com have a Windows 2000 Active Directory structure in place in their own forest.

The Active Directory structure of scriberco.com includes four additional subdomains These subdomains are called namerica.scriberco.com, europe.scriberco.com, samerica.scriberco.com, and specific.scriberco.com and have been created for administrative purposes.

The Active Directory structure of factron.com includes no additional subdomains.

The new management of FactroScriberco International Limited has decided that a uniform password policy needs to exist for all users in the enterprise. The policy should enforce a minimum password length of 6 characters, a maximum password age of 30 days, a minimum password age of 1 day, and a password history of 12 passwords.

What tasks need to be performed to enforce a uniform password policy across all Active Directory domains that are part of FactroScriberco International Limited? (Choose two correct answers.)

A. Modify the default domain policy for scriberco.com with the password settings.

B. Create a GPO in each domain with the password policy settings.

C. Create a GPO at the scriberco.com domain called Password Policy Settings with the password policy settings.

D. Link the Password Policy Settings GPO from the scriberco.com domain to each subdomain and the factron.com domain.

E. Create an explicit two-way trust relationship between scriberco.com and factron.com.

F. Modify the default domain policy for factron.com with the password settings.

54. In what order are Group Policy settings applied through the structure of Active Directory?

A. OU, site, domain

B. Site, domain, OU

C. Computers, users

D. OU, domain, site

E. Domain, site, OU

F. Asynchronously

55. Where are Group Policy template settings stored?

A. On each Windows 2000 computer's %SystemRoot%\GPO folder

B. On each domain controller's %SystemRoot%\GPO folder

C. On each domain controller's SYSVOL share in a folder with the same name as the GPO

D. On each domain controller's SYSVOL share in a folder with the same name as the GUID of the GPO

E. On each Windows 2000 computer's SYSVOL share in a folder with the same name as the GPO

F. On each Windows 2000 computer's SYSVOL share in a folder with the same name as the GUID of the GPO

56. You suspect that users at the Operations OU level that have been delegated administrative permissions to the OU are allowing users to become administrators of their own computers. Corporate security policy states that only Domain Admins and members of the ComputerAdmins security group should be granted administrative rights on all users computers. What steps would you need to take to enforce the corporate security policy? (Choose all that apply.)

A. Create a GPO at the domain level.

B. Create a GPO at the Operations OU level.

C. Set No Override for the GPO.

D. Set Block Policy Inheritance for the GPO.

E. Configure Administrators as a restricted group in the GPO.

F. Add Domain Admins and ComputerAdmins to the Administrators restricted group.

G. Add Group Admins and ComputerAdmins to the Administrators restricted group.

H. Create a new group for security purposes.

57. As the domain administrator of factron.com, you have been asked to configure user desktop settings for the domain. The domain consists of the following organizational units:

- Information Services, which also includes three other OUs: Help Desk, Development, and Network Admin

- Corporate Logistics, which also includes two other OUs: Finance and Operations

- Sales, which includes two other OUs: Inside Sales and Outside Sales

- Executives

A GPO exists at the domain level that requires all users to change their passwords every 30 days.

A GPO exists at the Sales OU level that removes the **Run** command from the desktop and installs a desktop wallpaper with the current month's promotions on the computers.

A GPO exists at the Executive OU that assigns Microsoft Office 2000 to all users within the scope of the GPO.

A GPO exists at the Finance OU that assigns Microsoft Excel 2000 and the company accounting application to computers within the scope of the GPO.

What would user BradT, whose user account is created in the Executive OU, need to do to start Microsoft Word 2000 for the first time? (Choose two correct answers.)

A. When prompted, install Microsoft Office 2000.

B. Double-click on a file with an .XLS extension.

C. Connect to the network share on which Microsoft Word 2000 is installed and start the Setup program.

D. Click on the Microsoft Word icon from the Start menu, Programs.

E. Double-click on a file with a .DOC extension.

58. As the Domain Administrator of factron.com, you have been asked to configure user desktop settings for the domain. The domain consists of the following organizational units:

   - Information Services, which also includes three other OUs: Help Desk, Development and Network Admin

   - Corporate Logistics, which also includes two other OUs: Finance and Operations

   - Sales, which includes two other OUs: Inside Sales and Outside Sales

   - Executives

A GPO exists at the domain level that requires all users to change their passwords every 30 days.

A GPO exists at the Sales OU level that removes the **Run** command from the desktop and installs a desktop wallpaper with the current month's promotions on the computers.

A GPO exists at the Executive OU that assigns Microsoft Office 2000 to all users within the scope of the GPO.

A GPO exists at the Finance OU that assigns Microsoft Excel 2000 and the company accounting application to computers within the scope of the GPO.

Recently, you have been asked to satisfy the following requirements:

   - The CEO has decided that all users should have the same desktop wallpaper installed on their machines.

   - The CIO wants to track Domain Administrators using their inherited permissions to delete security logs on computers belonging to Executives.

   - The VP of Sales wants to make sure that salespeople's documents stored in the MyDocuments folder of users in the OU are backed up during the normal backup cycle.

   - The VP of Sales wants to make sure that any changes made to documents by salespeople when using their notebook computers show up on the network version of the file.

   - No user in the Operations department should have access to Control Panel.

To satisfy these requirements, you perform the following tasks:

   - Create a GPO at the domain level that configures the corporate logo as the default desktop wallpaper for all users. Assign the Authenticated Users group Read and Apply Group Policy permission to the GPO. Configure No Override for the GPO.

   - Create a security group called SalesComputers in the SalesOU and add each computer in the SalesOU to the security group.

   - Create a GPO at the domain level that copies the contents of the MyDocuments folder from each computer to which the policy has been applied to a network share with a script executed at user logon and user logoff.

- Create a GPO at the Information Services OU level that enables Audit Privilege Use and Audit System Events. Grant the Authenticated Users Read and Apply Group Policy permissions.

- Create a GPO at the Operations OU that disables Control Panel for all Authenticated Users.

Which of the outlined requirements have been satisfied by your solution? (Choose all that apply.)

A. All users have the same desktop wallpaper installed on their machines.

B. The CIO is able to track Domain Administrators using their inherited permissions to delete Security logs on computers belonging to Executives.

C. Salespeople's documents stored in the MyDocuments folder of users in the OU are backed up during the normal backup cycle.

D. Changes made to documents by salespeople when using their notebook computers show up on the network version of the file.

E. No user in the Operations department has access to Control Panel.

59. As the Domain Administrator of factron.com, you have been asked to configure user desktop settings for the domain. The domain consists of the following organizational units:

- Information Services, which also includes three other OUs: Help Desk, Development and Network Admin

- Corporate Logistics, which also includes two other OUs: Finance and Operations

- Sales, which includes two other OUs: Inside Sales and Outside Sales

- Executives

A GPO exists at the domain level that requires all users to change their passwords every 30 days.

A GPO exists at the Sales OU level that removes the **Run** command from the desktop and installs a desktop wallpaper with the current month's promotions on the computers.

A GPO exists at the Executive OU that assigns Microsoft Office 2000 to all users within the scope of the GPO.

A GPO exists at the Finance OU that assigns Microsoft Excel 2000 and the company accounting application to computers within the scope of the GPO.

Recently, you have been asked to satisfy the following requirements:

- The CEO has decided that all users should have the same desktop wallpaper installed on their machines.

- The CIO wants to track Domain Administrators using their inherited permissions to delete Security logs on computers belonging to Executives.

- The VP of Sales wants to make sure that salespeople's documents stored in the MyDocuments folder of users in the OU are backed up during the normal backup cycle.

- The VP of Sales wants to make sure that any changes made to documents by salespeople when using their notebook computers show up on the network version of the file.

- No user in the Operations department should have access to Control Panel.

To satisfy these requirements, you perform the following tasks:

- Create a GPO at the domain level that configures the corporate logo as the default desktop wallpaper for all users. Assign the Authenticated Users group Read and Apply Group Policy permission to the GPO. Configure No Override for the GPO.

- Create a GPO at the Sales OU level that copies the contents of the MyDocuments folder from each computer to which the policy has been applied to a network share with a script executed at user logon and user logoff.

- In the same GPO where you created in the Sales OU, enable Offline files to automatically enable offline files on key folders on the sales server.

- Create a GPO at the Executive OU level that enables Audit Privilege Use and Audit System Events. Grant the Executives security group Read and Apply Group Policy permissions. Remove the Authenticated Users group from the list of groups to which the GPO settings apply.

- Create a GPO at the Operations OU that disables Control Panel for all Authenticated Users.

Which of the outlined requirements have been satisfied by your solution? (Choose all that apply.)

A. All users have the same desktop wallpaper installed on their machines.

B. The CIO is able to track Domain Administrators using their inherited permissions to delete security logs on computers belonging to Executives.

C. Salespeople's documents stored in the MyDocuments folder of users in the OU are backed up during the normal backup cycle.

D. Changes made to documents by salespeople when using their notebook computers show up on the network version of the file.

E. No user in the Operations department has access to Control Panel.

60. As the Domain Administrator of factron.com, you have been asked to configure user desktop settings for the domain. The domain consists of the following organizational units:

- Information Services, which also includes three other OUs: Help Desk, Development, and Network Admin

- Corporate Logistics, which also includes two other OUs: Finance and Operations

- Sales, which includes two other OUs: Inside Sales and Outside Sales

- Executives

After configuring Group Policy to satisfy various requirements identified by management, you find that users in the Finance OU are complaining that the time it takes to log on to the domain has increased considerably. What is the most likely cause of the problem?

A. Finance computers are too slow to process Group Policy.

B. Finance computers are running Windows NT 4.0, which requires time to convert Group Policy to System Policy.

C. You are using logon scripts, which are processed after all other policy is applied.

D. Finance computers have a large number of GPOs to process because they are the lowest-level OU.

E. Finance computers have to process Group Policy and System Policy because the domain is in mixed mode.

61. If you wanted to ensure that an application was always available to all users in the enterprise, how would you configure the application in Group Policy?

A. Publish the application to computers.

B. Assign the application to computers.

C. Publish the application to users.

D. Assign the application to users.

E. It is not possible to ensure an application is available to all users with Group Policy.

62. You configure a startup script in a GPO for the Sales OU that maps LPT1 to the \\SALESSERVER\HPLaser printer. You configure a logon script that maps LPT1 to the \\SALESSERVER\Lexmark printer for user HeesH, whose user account is in the Sales OU. You disable access to Control Panel in the same GPO for Authenticated Users. What printers will be available to HeesH and to which printer port will they be mapped?

A. The \\SALESSERVER\HPLaser printer will be mapped to LPT1 and available to HeesH.

B. The \\SALESSERVER\Lexmark printer will be mapped to LPT1 and available to HeesH.

C. The \\SALESSERVER\HPLaser printer will be mapped to LPT2 and available to HeesH.

D. The \\SALESSERVER\LexMark printer will be mapped to LPT2 and available to HeesH.

E. HeesH will not have access to any printers.

63. Users have had Microsoft Office 97 deployed to their computers using Group Policy. You now need to upgrade Microsoft Office 97 to Microsoft Office 2000 for all users in the enterprise; however, users should still be able to use Microsoft Office 97 for 30 days. After the 30-day period, users will be required to upgrade to Microsoft Office 2000. How can you accomplish this using Group Policy? (Choose two correct answers.)

A. Make Microsoft Office 2000 a required upgrade.

B. Make Microsoft Office 2000 a required upgrade with a 30-day delay period.

C. Make Microsoft Office 2000 an optional upgrade.

D. Make Microsoft Office 2000 an optional upgrade configured with a 30-day conversion required.

E. After 30 days, change the upgrade type for Microsoft Office 2000 to required from optional.

F. After 30 days, change the upgrade type for Microsoft Office 2000 to optional from required.

64. What advantages does using a RIPrep image offer over using a CD-based image? (Choose two correct answers.)

A. RIPrep images can include applications as well as the operating system.

B. RIPrep images can be deployed on machines with a different HAL than the source computer.

C. RIPrep images perform a full install of the operating system, allowing the user to choose all settings.

D. RIPrep images can be easily updated by copying only changes files to the image folder.

E. RIPrep images are faster than CD-based images.

65. You need to deploy 150 computers using Remote Installation Services. The computers that need to be deployed have the following configurations:

- 10 Pentium II 600MHz notebook computers with integrated PCI network cards with PXE boot ROMs, a 10GB hard disk, and 128MB of RAM

- 20 Pentium 233MHz desktop computers with PCI network cards, a 4GB hard disk, and 32MB of RAM

- 50 Pentium III 800MHz desktop computers with PCI network cards, a 20GB hard disk, and 32MB of RAM

- 5 Pentium Pro 200MHz dual-processor desktop computers with PCI network cards, a 4GB hard disk, and 256MB of RAM

- 65 AMD Athlon 800MHz desktop computers with a PXE-enabled network card, an 8GB hard disk, and 64MB of RAM

Which computers can be deployed using RIS without a boot disk? (Choose two correct answers.)

A. 10 Pentium II 600MHz notebook computers with integrated PCI network cards with PXE boot ROMs, a 10GB hard disk, and 128MB of RAM

B. 20 Pentium 233MHz desktop computers with PCI network cards, a 4GB hard disk, and 32MB of RAM

C. 50 Pentium III 800MHz desktop computers with PCI network cards, a 20GB hard disk, and 32MB of RAM

D. 5 Pentium Pro 200MHz dual-processor desktop computers with PCI network cards, a 4GB hard disk, and 256MB of RAM

E. 65 AMD Athlon 800MHz desktop computers with a PXE-enabled network card, an 8GB hard disk, and 64MB of RAM

ANSWERS TO EXAM QUESTIONS

1. **B.** The DNS service is by default set to start automatically on a Windows 2000 server, so answer D is wrong. The DNS service can be on a Windows 2000 server in any configuration, or even on a BIND server, as long as it supports SRV records, so answer A is wrong. Answer C just doesn't make sense. This would be very bad if you had to constantly DCPROMO down and then up again to register the services, meaning answer C is out of the running. This leaves answer B, which could be the problem if the DNS entry does not point at the server Sally created. Additionally, she would check the DNS server to make sure it allows updates. See the "Cannot Create Dynamic Entries" section in Chapter 2, "Configuring DNS for Active Directory."

2. **A.** In this question, like the last, the DNS server can be any DNS server that supports SRV records. The only time that DNS must be on a domain controller is if the zone is Active Directory integrated, meaning answer B is wrong. Answer C is definitely wrong because the only write-enabled copy of the domain database in Windows NT is on the PDC. Answer D has

nothing to do with the DCPROMO process. It is used to enable you to work with disk-imaging utilities with Windows 2000 Professional. Answer A is the correct answer because the Netlogon service must be able to register its records to start properly. If the DNS server didn't support dynamic updates, the SRV records would need to be added manually from the NETLOGON.DNS file. See the "Integrating DNS and Active Directory" section in Chapter 2, "Configuring DNS for Active Directory."

3. **A.**   By choosing a local master server in Calgary and Toronto and then having the other local secondary servers get the zone file from it, you will reduce the WAN traffic. The secondary you choose as the master in each location will get the file from the Vancouver primary server, and then the other local secondary servers can get the zone file from the local master. Answer B would help if the concern were with other companies' records because this affects the minimum time you will cache an entry. Answer C will reduce the zone file traffic over the WAN links but will in all likelihood increase dramatically the resolution traffic over the link, in effect trading one type of traffic for another. Answer D is negated because answer A is correct. For more information, see the "Transferring Zone Information" section in Chapter 2, "Configuring DNS for Active Directory."

4. **B.**   In this case, it is not a problem because the Active Directory zone will use Active Directory replication. This will actually give Beth tools like site links to control the replication. When a zone is converted to Active Directory integrated, the zone no longer has a zone transfer schedule, and it therefore could not have been reset. This means answer A is wrong. Although it is true that Active Directory replication will now be used, you cannot set the values in the NTDS settings. The only

settings you can change are in the site links, so answers C and D are also wrong. For more information, see the "Integrating DNS and Active Directory" section in Chapter 2, "Configuring DNS for Active Directory."

5. **C.**   In this case, Heidi will not be able to move the user in Active Directory Users and Computers, meaning answer B is wrong. The object in this case is moving between domains, so she will need the MOVETREE utility. She could use a third-party utility if she wanted to, but there is no need, and she certainly doesn't need to wait for one. This means answer A is wrong. There would be a need for the third-party utility if you had to delete the user and then re-create them; because this isn't the case, though, answer D is also wrong. See the "Moving Objects Within the Directory" section in Chapter 4, "Administering Active Directory Services."

6. **B.**   The clients will first query the DNS server for a logon server in the local site, waiting for this to fail until it looks for a logon server in the domain. Because the domain controller could now be nearly anywhere on the network, the logon request could now have to jump across several routers. In this case, the best solution is to add a local domain controller, which will address both of these issues. Adding a DNS server might speed up the resolution, but it will not address the other issues. There is a DCHP relay agent and a WINS proxy, but there is no logon proxy; therefore, answer C is wrong. Sites should have a domain controller and a global catalog server to facilitate all forms of logon and to ensure that there are no effects from using sites, so answer D is wrong. Remember that sites are used to control replication, not to slow logons or other network traffic. For more information, see the "Working in the Physical Network" section in Chapter 3, "Building Your Active Directory Structure."

7. **B.** In this case, the clue lies in the fact the user can register the entry but the computer (or rather, its account) cannot. The fact that you can register the account yourself means answer C is wrong. If it were a DHCP problem, this would be a lot larger of a problem and not tied to this one computer. The computer account must exist because you were able to update the record, so answer D is wrong. See the "Integrating DNS and Active Directory" section in Chapter 2, "Configuring DNS for Active Directory."

8. **B, C.** The local system account would not have the right to modify the schema on the schema master and would probably not have any rights outside the local computer. This means answer A is wrong. Answer D might be necessary as the very last resort; however, there are many other possibilities that you need to be aware of that should be checked first. Answer E makes no sense. Answer B could be the problem because you need to be Enterprise Admin or Schema Admin to change the schema, and answer C is possible because schema modifications should normally not be enabled. For more information, see the "Server Roles" section in Chapter 5, "Managing Servers."

9. **A.** Sites are used to control replication traffic in Active Directory. In this case, there is no justification to go to a domain model because there are not enough systems to justify it; therefore, answer B is wrong. Dividing the network into different organizational units will increase the capability to manage the network; however, this is a logical construct and will do nothing in the physical world. Reducing the number of servers might help, but obviously, if the servers are there, they are serving some purpose. Removing them just to reduce bandwidth would probably cause other problems. For more information, see the "Working in the Physical Network" section in Chapter 3, "Building Your Active Directory Structure."

10. **C, D, E.** You can transfer the roles through the graphical interface using the Active Directory schema to transfer the schema master role and using Active Directory Domains and Trusts to transfer the domain naming master role. You could also use the NTDSUTIL to transfer the roles. Active Directory Users and Computers can be used to transfer the other three roles through the graphical interface but not those specified in the question; this means that answer A is wrong. Active Directory Sites and Services does manage Active Directory, but it cannot transfer any roles; therefore, answer B is also incorrect. The Computer Management and DNS snap-ins do not manage Active Directory, making answers F and G incorrect. For more information, see the "Server Roles" section in Chapter 5, "Managing Servers."

11. **D.** Unfortunately, there is no drag-and-drop capability in the MMC for move computers, so answer A is wrong. The **Move** command on the context menu will move the users; however, you will need to move each individually. Therefore, B is not the best answer. Putting the users in a group is probably a good idea overall; however, it does not accomplish the goal of moving the user accounts. The best choice is to use the **Find** command to then verify the system and users that are found. Once you have verified the users and computers, you can move the users and computers en masse. For more information, see the "Moving Objects Within the Directory" section in Chapter 4, "Administering Active Directory Services."

12. **C.** In this case, just like Windows NT 4.0, the password change that needed to take place on the PDC emulator has not had a chance to replicate to the BDC that is near the client. In this case, you would want to force the BDC near the user to replicate with the PDC emulator. You can force computers to replicate in Windows 2000,

but you force a computer to replicate with another computer. To force widespread replication as suggested in answer A, you would need to spend a great deal of time forcing replication over every connection for every server. The global catalog server does contain some extra information and by default is also be the PDC emulator; however, because there is an option that listed the PDC emulator, this is not the best answer. The PDC emulator is the system that will bring the NT domain controllers up to speed. Although D would help if the server the user was attempting to use was a Windows 2000 domain controller, because it is not, this answer is wrong. See the "Server Roles" section in Chapter 5, "Managing Servers."

13. **A.**   This is not a hard task, but you should remember that it's done by editing the NTDS Settings properties and enabling the global catalog on the server. The Group Policy might be able to perform this task because it has the capability to modify the domain controller's registry. However, Group Policy is not intended to be used for a single user or computer. This means answer B is wrong. This does not have to be done in the registry, and therefore answer C is wrong. Answer D is obviously overkill. See the "Global Catalog Servers" section in Chapter 3, "Building Your Active Directory Structure."

14. **C.**   In this case, you want to look at the traffic on the network. The System Monitor (Performance) will let you see how busy the network is, but it can't really tell you what protocols are on the network; therefore, answers A and B are wrong. Answer D means you need to run Network Monitor, this can be done on any Windows 2000 computer, not just domain controllers. This means answer D is wrong. See the section "Monitoring a Domain Controller" section in Chapter 5, "Managing Servers."

15. **D.**   In this case, there is no known reason to go to multiple domains, so the best way to keep control at the head office level while still allowing some control at the branch level is to have a single domain with three organizational units. All the other answers involve breaking the network up with domains. You would have done this in NT 4.0; however, Microsoft is pressing the fact that this is no longer a requirement. See the "Creating an Organizational Unit" section in Chapter 4, "Administering Active Directory Services."

16. **B, C.**   In this case, you are being asked how to perform an authoritative restore. This, of course, involves starting the system in directory services Restore mode, restoring the system state data, using NTDSUTIL (the directory services utility) to perform the authoritative restore, and then restarting the server in normal mode. The trick to this question is that, rather than asking you to perform an authoritative restore, the result of an authoritative restore is given: Increment the USN. Obviously, Answer A is wrong because a system backup does not necessarily contain the Active Directory, and answer D does not make sense as you will overwrite the OU in the restore. For more information, see the "Backing Up and Restoring Servers" section in Chapter 5, "Managing Servers."

17. **B.**   All you need to do is create the site links and the KCC will create the connections. The KCC will use transitive bridging (automatic bridging) to connect all the sites. You could create a site link bridge and turn off transitive bridging, but there is no stated reason to do either in the question. This means answers C and D are incorrect. Answer A is also incorrect because you want the KCC to deal with this so it can adapt the connections to network conditions. See the "Replicating Active Directory Information" section in Chapter 3, "Building Your Active Directory Structure."

18. **D.** The best way to deal with this is to create a site link that is active during the day with a long interval between replications. Then create a second site link that is active at night with a short interval. Answer A could perhaps work in theory, but it is certainly not the best way to deal with this. Answer B would be okay if you could create two schedules on the same site link, but you cannot. Answer C just wouldn't work because there are only two sites and the two links between the same two sites would be automatically bridged. For more information, see the "Replicating Active Directory Information" section in Chapter 3, "Building Your Active Directory Structure."

19. **A.** Because the server was not an operations master and there is no mention of any other special services as the quickest way to bring the other server up, this will force it to replicate all the information from the remaining server. If the server that crashed was an operations master, you could have seized the role, assuming it hadn't crashed immediately after a backup. The other options are all more involved and therefore are not the best answer. For more information, see the "Backing Up and Restoring Servers" section in Chapter 5, "Managing Servers."

20. **A.** The next check would be the event logs on the two systems. Then you will check whether the domain controllers are accepting logon requests and how the four main resources are. The main resources are memory, disk, CPU, and network, for which you should use System Monitor (Performance). If these were all okay, you would then move on to the network to see what requests were being sent on the local network. This could be something as silly as the domain controller for the local domain is not configured with the right IP address for a DNS server and, as such, is not registered. Answer B is probably something you will have to get to in

some cases but not the first item from this list. Answer C could be useful if this was a TCP/IP problem, but it's not. Answer D is overkill, is very time consuming, and does not help you the next time the same problem occurs. For more information, see the "Monitoring a Domain Controller" section in Chapter 5, "Managing Servers."

21. **C.** What is happening is that the installation is checking for a down-level domain name, which in this case would be Scriberco. Because it is finding that name on the network, it will give you the option of Scriberco1, which you could accept; however, it would be better to locate the rogue domain controller and remove it from the network. Answer A is not an option because you want to use the domain name. Answer B would work, but changing the protocols on all the computers in the domain just to manage the down-level name wouldn't be worth the aggravation of the old and new domains not being able to communicate. Answer D will also work; however, the best answer is to find the rogue domain controller and the users that installed it. See the "Installing the First Domain" section in Chapter 3, "Building Your Active Directory Structure."

22. **A.** The best tool to measure the performance of a system is the Performance tool (System Monitor). This will let you monitor the four key system resources: disk, CPU, memory, and network subsystem. The Network Monitor only deals with network traffic and would not be overly useful in this case; therefore, answer A is wrong. There is no Monitoring tab in the server's Properties dialog box (there is for the DNS service, though), so answer C is wrong. Task Manager could be used, but it does not provide the same level of information as a log of system

counters, so answer D is wrong. For more information, see the "Monitoring a Domain Controller" section in Chapter 5, "Managing Servers."

23. **A, C.**   In this case, you will want to see what types of read and writes the system is doing, and you will also want to see the memory usage. The most common cause of the disk light flashing is a memory problem that causes excessive paging. This will cause a dramatic slowdown in the system response because it needs to swap both data and instructions between RAM and disk. The CPU is certainly worth monitoring, but the disk light hint in the question leads to memory and disk; the same is true of the network segment making answers B and D incorrect. Answer E makes no sense. For more information, see the "Monitoring a Domain Controller" section in Chapter 5, "Managing Servers."

24. **A.**   When you create a site, the two pieces of information you need are the name of the site and the site link that will service the site. After you create the site, you can then move or create subnets in the site. This means answer B is wrong. After the subnets, you can then move a domain controller into the site. This means answer C is wrong. Because answer A is correct, answer D is incorrect. See the "Replicating Active Directory Information" section in Chapter 3, "Building Your Active Directory Structure."

25. **A.**   The only actual requirement is that the DNS server must support SRV records. The ability to support incremental transfers (answer B) and the ability to support updates of any kind (answers C and D) are not required. You should consider, however, the ability to perform dynamic updates to be required in the real world. See the "Integrating DNS and Active Directory" section in Chapter 2, "Configuring DNS for Active Directory."

26. **B.**   All you need to do to list a printer from a Windows 2000 computer is select the List in the Directory option from the Sharing tab. There is no Active Directory tab in the Printers dialog box, so answer A is incorrect. The only time you will need to add the printer in Active Directory User and Computers is if the printer is shared from a non-Windows 2000 computer. Because answer B is correct, you will not need to remove and re-add the printer as answer D suggests. For more information, see the "Publishing Printers" section in Chapter 4, "Administering Active Directory Services."

27. **C.**   Although answer A is close, it does not share the printer after it is created. In the real world, you would do this and then share the printer so that the printer driver would be available to the users that want to use the printer. Answer B is wrong because it is only connecting to a network printer, and you would not be able to share the printer after connecting to it. Answer D is not correct because you can add the printer to the Active Directory. For more information, see the "Publishing Printers" section in Chapter 4, "Administering Active Directory Services."

28. **A.**   With the new scheduling capabilities in Windows 2000, you can create a single task that will run on the required days rather than creating a separate task for each backup. For more information, see the "Backing Up and Restoring Servers" section in Chapter 5, "Managing Servers."

29. **A, D.**   Because a differential backup copies all information since the last normal (full) backup, all you need to do is restore the full backup and the last differential. For more information, see the "Backing Up and Restoring Servers" section in Chapter 5, "Managing Servers."

30. **A.** When you are writing the exam, remember the more Microsoft the better. Therefore, if there is no requirement to use a BIND DNS server, you should consider that the answer is to use a Microsoft DNS server. Upgrading a BIND server so that it will be compliant would work, but it is not a Microsoft solution, so answer A is a better answer. Although answer C would work, you would not be able to use dynamic updates; therefore, answer A is better. Again, answer D would work because you could create an Active Directory-integrated zone and then just forward queries for UNIX server. See the "Integrating DNS and Active Directory" section in Chapter 2, "Configuring DNS for Active Directory."

31. **B.** Although it is possible to import a text file, this is not the best answer because you would need to use a test editor to edit the file and then use a utility to import the account; therefore, answer A is not correct. Answer C would allow you to control some aspect of the user information but not all of it. Answer D will also work, but again, this is a clumsy way to create users. Answer B is the best answer because using templates is an easy way to create users. See the "Performing Basic Administration" section in Chapter 4, "Administering Active Directory Services."

32. **C.** When you need to measure the internal workings of Windows 2000, you should use the Performance tool (System Monitor). However, you can use the Task Manager in this case, and it's faster and easier, so answer A is not the best answer. While the **NET** command will let you get some statistics on the server and workstation services, it cannot profile a process so answer B is wrong. The System Information tool doesn't exit, so answer D is wrong. For more information, see the "Monitoring a Domain Controller" section in Chapter 5, "Managing Servers."

33. **A.** In this case, the damage is done, and the best you can do is getting the network back to being stable. Because the junior operator was able to grab the role, you can assume that the schema master was offline, so you should remove the old server so it doesn't come back online. Formatting the drive will ensure that it doesn't come back online in the future. Answers B and C are likely to cause more damage, and you could not do either unless the new schema master is offline. Answer D is just overkill, but if the schema is corrupted, you may just have to do it. For more information, see the "Server Roles" section in Chapter 5, "Managing Servers."

34. **A, D, F.** In this case, you need to verify that you are pointing at the correct DNS server, and then you should try to register the computer name and the services. Stopping and starting the DNS or the server services serves no point in this case, so answers B and C are not correct. The network identification will be set by DCPROMO during the promotion, so answer E is correct. There is no **registerdns** command in the **nslookup** command, so answer G is wrong. See the "Troubleshooting DNS" section in Chapter 2, "Configuring DNS for Active Directory."

35. **C.** It is possible that the specific object has different permissions that are blocking the permissions set using the Delegation of Control Wizard. You will probably check the permissions on the OU that you delegated, but because she could reset password for other users, this wouldn't be the first choice. This means answer A isn't the best answer. Answer B isn't likely because her account is working. Rerunning the wizard might fix the problem, but its not likely because it didn't work the first time. This means answer D is wrong. See the "Permissions in Active Directory" section in Chapter 4, "Administering Active Directory Services."

36. **C.**   Unless you are adding billions and billions (apologies to Carl Sagan) of computers, you're not going to fill up the Active Directory. There isn't a limit on sessions, so that is not likely, and it leaves us with answer C. If the RID master is offline for a long period of time, the domain control could run out of RIDs and will not be able to create new objects. For more information, see the "Server Roles" section in Chapter 5, "Managing Servers."

37. **B.**   The most likely reason is that the computer is not a member of an Active Directory domain. Active Directory is required to be installed and a domain created before you can install a RIS server. For more information, see the sections "Installing and Configuring a RIS Server," "Remote Installation Services Prerequisites," and "RIS Software Requirements," in Chapter 9, "Deploying Windows 2000 Using Remote Installation Services."

38. **A, C.**   Because you configured the domain-level GPO with No Override, the settings that were specified at the Sales OU GPO will be ignored if they conflict with the domain-level OU settings. This means that the user will have the domain-level wallpaper because these settings directly conflict. However, disable Control Panel set at the Sales OU will also be the effective GPO setting because this is specified at the OU level, which is closest to the user logging on. However, in actuality, if the user were able to start Control Panel, his or her only choice would be Add/Remove Programs and Display, as configured in the domain-level GPO. Because the user is not able to start Control Panel, this is the effective setting. For more information, see the "Group Policy Security" and "Group Policy Inheritance" sections in Chapter 6, "Using Group Policy to Manage Users."

39. **C, D.**   The additional steps that must be performed are to run RISETUP.EXE, which starts the Remote Installation Services Setup Wizard and installs an initial CD-based image. The Remote Installation Service Setup Wizard will prompt you to install an initial CD-based image, although you can decide not to perform this task, which is why both C and D are the correct answers. It is not required to authorize the RIS server in Active Directory because it is running on the same machine that is a DHCP server, in which case it is already authorized. See the "Setting Up a RIS Server" and "Configuring Remote Installation Services" sections in Chapter 9, "Deploying Windows 2000 Using Remote Installation Services."

40. **A, C, E.**   Because Adobe Acrobat and Microsoft Word 2000 were assigned to computers, these applications will be automatically installed on the computers when they are started. Microsoft Office 2000 has been published to users, which means it will be listed in Add/Remove Programs, allowing RobS to install it when he needs it or by document invocation. Even though he is a member of the Domain Admins group, the default policy permissions are Read and Apply Group Policy to Authenticated Users, of which all logged-on users are members including Domain Admins. For more information, see Chapter 7, "Software Distribution Using Group Policy" and Chapter 6, "Using Group Policy to Manage Users."

41. **C, F.**   The default Group Policy refresh internal is 5 minutes on domain controllers and 90 minutes, plus or minus a 30-minute stagger interval, on member servers and workstations. For more information, see the "Group Policy Scope" and "Group Policy Processing" sections in Chapter 6, "Using Group Policy to Manage Users."

42. **A, C, E.** Because Adobe Acrobat and Microsoft Word 2000 were assigned to computers, these applications will be automatically installed on the computers when they are started. Microsoft Office 2000 has been published to users, which means it will be listed in Add/Remove Programs, allowing RobS to install it when he needs it or by document invocation. Even though he is a member of the Domain Admins group, the default policy permissions are Read and Apply Group Policy to Authenticated Users, of which all logged-on users are members including Domain Admins. For more information, see Chapter 7, "Software Distribution Using Group Policy," and Chapter 6, "Using Group Policy to Manage Users." The answer to this question is the same as for number 40. The question was asked twice to test your knowledge of permission settings and how they apply to GPO processing.

43. **A.** Offline files settings do not follow the normal refresh internal for Group Policy. For these GPO settings to be applied, the user will need to log off and log back on to the domain. For more information, see the "Group Policy Scope" and "Group Policy Processing" sections in Chapter 6, "Using Group Policy to Manage Users."

44. **D.** The easiest way to have the settings of one Group Policy apply to another OU outside the original scope of the GPO is to link it to the new OU. This way, whatever changes get made to the original GPO will be applied to in all OUs to which the GPO has been linked. If you want to maintain different settings in each OU, you can create a separate GPO at each OU level and configure the settings manually, although this would not be the easiest way to have the same settings as the original GPO. See the "Creating and Managing Group Policy" section in Chapter 6, "Using Group Policy to Manager Users."

45. **A, D, G.** You cannot create a GPO in the Users, Computers, or Domain Controllers containers in Active Directory. These containers are not organizational units and therefore cannot have a GPO attached to them. See the "Creating and Managing Group Policy" section in Chapter 6, "Using Group Policy to Manager Users."

46. **A, D, F.** In Group Policy processing, when the same setting is specified for the computer and the user, the computer setting will always win. In this situation, this means that Windows Installer will always use elevated privileges. Other settings specified will not conflict. Even though for Task Scheduler you enabled Drag and Drop for the computer, because you disabled new task creation for the user, she will not be able to create a task. Registry editing tools will be disabled, as configured for the user. See the "Group Policy Scope," "Combining Group Policies," and "Group Policy Processing Rules" sections in Chapter 6, "Using Group Policy to Manager Users."

47. **F.** Because NatashaR is using a computer running Windows NT Workstation 4.0, Group Policy settings will not take affect. This is because Group Policy settings only take affect on Windows 2000 computers. See the note in the "Introduction to Group Policy" section in Chapter 6, "Using Group Policy to Manager Users."

48. **B, C, E.** Audit Logon Events, Audit Account Logon Events, and Audit System Events require no further action and will be reflected in the security log automatically. Audit Object Access and Audit Directory Service Access require that the administrator assign which users will have their actions audited on which objects, and must be configured on the required objects. See the "Setting Up and Audit Policy" in Chapter 8, "Managing Security Using Group Policy."

49. **C, F.** The FriendlyName and SetupCommand tags are required in a ZAP file. They specify the name of the application and the program to run to start the installation of an application. Publisher, URL, and DisplayVersion are valid tags but are not required for the ZAP file to be used. ApplicationName is not a valid tag in a ZAP file. For more information, see the sections "Preparing Software for Deployment Using Group Policy," "Packaging Software for Deployment," "Creating a ZAP File to Deploy Software with Group Policy," and "ZAP File Sections" in Chapter 7, "Software Distribution Using Group Policy."

50. **D.** The best way to make it easier for users to find the applications they want to install is to create software categories and put applications into categories. This will enable a user to change a category of application he wants to install and see only the applications in the specified category instead of the entire list of all applications. See the "Managing Software Deployment" and "Creating Software Categories" sections in Chapter 7, "Software Distribution Using Group Policy."

51. **B.** The best way to make the application to users in the sales department is to repackage it using a third-party repackaging tool, such as WinINSTALL LE, and then publish it to users. Because you want users to be able to choose to install the application, you should not assign it to the user or computer. For more information, see the "Preparing Software for Deployment Using Group Policy," "Packaging Software for Deployment," "Windows Installer Technology," and "Modifying a Windows Installer Package File Using Third-Party Tools" sections in Chapter 7, "Software Distribution Using Group Policy."

52. **A.** To have the same password policy on all domains in scriberco.com, modify the default domain policy at the top-level domain. Because you did not create any additional GPOs at the subdomain and because the default behavior for the default domain policy is to have it copied to all subdomains in an Active Directory structure, modifying the default domain policy on scriberco.com will accomplish all the required goals. See Chapter 6, "Using Group Policy to Manager Users," and especially note the "Introduction to Group Policy" and "Group Policy Components" sections.

53. **A, F.** The answer to this question is similar to the preceding one, except for the new wrinkle of having another Active Directory forest. Because there are two forests involved in this scenario, you would need to modify the default domain policy for each forest involved: scriberco.com and fac-tron.com. Creating an explicit trust between the two forests is not required for the enforcement of Group Policy, nor would it necessarily help. See Chapter 6, "Using Group Policy to Manager Users," and especially note the "Introduction to Group Policy" and "Group Policy Components" sections.

54. **B.** The order of Group Policy application is always site, domain, and then OU. In this way, the policies closest to the user or computer will be applied last because they are assumed to be the most applicable. See the sections "Group Policy Scope," "Combining Group Policies," and "Group Policy Processing Rules" in Chapter 6, "Using Group Policy to Manager Users."

55. **D.** Group Policy templates are stored on each domain controller in the SYSVOL share in a folder with the same name as the globally unique identifier of the Group Policy object. See the "Introduction to Group Policy" and "Group Policy Components" sections in Chapter 6, "Using Group Policy to Manager Users."

56. **B, C, E, F.**   To ensure that only members of the Domain Admins and ComputerAdmins security groups have administrative control of computers in the Operations OU, you should first create a GPO at the Operations OU level. You would then configure the Administrators group as a restricted group in the GPO and add Domain Admins and ComputerAdmins as members of the Administrators group in the GPO. This would override the default membership of the Administrators group on each computer in the Operations OU. You should set No Override for the GPO to ensure that lower-level administrators cannot override the setting by blocking policy inheritance. For more information, see the section "Security Settings Available in Windows 2000 Group Policy" in Chapter 8, "Managing Security Using Group Policy," and the sections "Group Policy Security" and "Group Policy Inheritance" in Chapter 6, "Using Group Policy to Manager Users."

57. **D, E.**   Because Microsoft Office 2000 has been assigned to users in the Executives OU, it will automatically be installed on all computers within the scope of the policy including BradT's computer. To start Microsoft Word 2000, all he has to do is start the program from the Programs menu or double-click on a file with the .DOC extension. See the "Software Deployment Using Group Policy" section in Chapter 7, "Software Distribution Using Group Policy."

58. **A, C, E.**   The GPOs you created will ensure that all users in the domain have the same desktop wallpaper because this policy was created at the domain level and was configured with No Override. Through the logoff script, the contents of MyDocuments for users in the Sales OU will be copied to a network share and be backed up using the normal backup cycle. Finally, by creating a GPO at the Operations OU, you have disabled Control Panel for all users in Operations. You will not be able to track who is accessing Executives machines because you created the GPO with the correct settings in the Information Services OU instead of the Executives OU. See the sections "Creating and Managing Group Policy" and "Group Policy Security" in Chapter 6, "Using Group Policy to Manager Users." Also see the section "Configuring and Implementing and Audit Policy" in Chapter 8, "Managing Security Using Group Policy."

59. **A, C, D, E.**   The GPOs and settings you have configured will satisfy all the requirements outlined by management except for being able to track which administrators are deleting the security logs on Executives computers. The domain-level GPO configured with No Override will ensure that all users have the same desktop wallpaper. The GPO with a script at the Sales OU will ensure that MyDocuments is backed up during normal backup cycles. Enabling Offline files at the Sales OU GPO for the folders used by salespeople will ensure that they always have required documents on their machines and that they become synchronized when users log off. Creating a GPO at the Executives OU level with the appropriate auditing settings would have tracked attempts by Admins to access Executives PCs without permission if you had assigned the GPO to the Domain Admins group instead of Executives. Finally, in creating a GPO at the Operations OU, you have disabled Control Panel for all users in Operations. For more information, see the "Creating and Managing Group Policy" and "Group Policy Security" sections in Chapter 6, "Using Group Policy to Manager Users." Also see the "Configuring and Implementing and Audit Policy" section in Chapter 8, "Managing Security Using Group Policy."

60. **D.**   The most likely cause of the problem is that the Finance OU is at the lowest level of the policy processing chain. This means that users in Finance may have to process site, domain, and other OU policies during the logon process, which could make logging on a lengthy process. The best way to solve this problem is to minimize the number of GPOs that need to be processed. See the "Group Policy Scope" and "Group Policy Processing" sections in Chapter 6, "Using Group Policy to Manager Users."

61. **B.**   The best way to ensure that an application is available to everyone in a domain is to assign the application to computers. In this way, it will be installed on all computers within the scope of the GPO and will be installed during computer start-up. See the sections, "Software Deployment Using Group Policy" and "Assigning Software to Users and Computers" in Chapter 7, "Software Distribution Using Group Policy."

62. **B.**   Logon scripts are processed after startup scripts for computers. Because of this, LPT1 will be mapped to the \\SALESSERVER\Lexmark printer, which is the one specified for the user. See the "Configuring and Using Scripts in Group Policy" and "Group Policy Script Processing Order" sections in Chapter 6, "Using Group Policy to Manager Users."

63. **C, E.**   Because there is no way to configure an upgrade as optional with a 30-day conversion to required, this process will need to be two steps. You would first configure the upgrade to be optional and then manually change it to required after 30 days. This will enable users to keep Office 97 on their desktops for the 30-day

interval, but then all users will be required to install Office 2000 if they have not yet done so. See the "Maintaining Software Packages Using Group Policy" section in Chapter 7, "Software Distribution Using Group Policy."

64. **A, E.**   RIPrep images can include applications as well as the operating system because they are a copy of the source computer used to create the RIPrep image. Furthermore, RIPrep images may be smaller in size than a CD-based image and are quicker to deploy because the entire image gets copied on the client computer instead of going through the normal Windows 2000 Professional installation process, which is what happens with a CD-based image. Also, a CD-based image would require you to install the applications using Group Policy or manually, taking even more time. See the sections "Creating Remote Installation Services Images" and "Creating a RIPrep Image for Remote Installation Services" in Chapter 9, "Deploying Windows 2000 Using Remote Installation Services."

65. **A, E.**   Because only the 10 600MHz notebook computers with a PCI network card and the 800MHz AMD Athlon computers have a PXE-enabled network card, they are the only ones that can be installed using Remote Installation Services without requiring a boot disk. The other computers can most likely be deployed using RIS, but will require a RIS boot disk See the sections "Performing a Remote Installation" and "Client Computer Requirements" in Chapter 9, "Deploying Windows 2000 Using Remote Installation Services."

APPENDIXES

Glossary

A

access control list (ACL) An access control list is used to verify the permissions of a process to access an object. The credentials of the process are compared to the entries in the access control list to determine whether access is granted and what permissions are available if access is granted.

Active Directory (AD) Active Directory is a hierarchical directory service used in Windows 2000. It organizes users into organizational units and domains that are all part of a common namespace.

Active Directory–integrated zone An Active Directory–integrated zone is a type of DNS zone that uses Active Directory to store the records. The records will then be replicated using Active Directory replication and will have an ACL. This will also enable a computer to register with any integrated domain controller.

Administrative Templates Administrative Templates are a portion of Group Policy that applies registry settings to users and/or computers to enforce corporate rules. Settings include which programs can be run, how offline folders are treated, desktop settings, and others.

Administrator This is the principal account in a Windows 2000 domain or on a Windows 2000 standalone computer. This account has the capability to perform any action within its scope (domain or computer by virtue of being a member of the appropriate administrators group).

Answer file An ASCII text file created by Windows Setup Manager, the SYSPREP utility, or manually using any text editor, specifying the installation configuration of Windows 2000 on a target computer. In RIS, Answer files are used to specify how the deployment of Windows 2000 Professional will take place.

assigning software packages Assigning software packages is the forced deployment of a software package to a user or computer as configured in Group Policy. Users or computers that have a package assigned to them will have it installed and cannot decide not to have it installed.

attributes Attributes describe an object in the same way an adjective describes a noun (for example, the green door). In the case of an object such as a file, the file type would be an attribute.

audit policy Security auditing policy is a portion of security policy that enables you to configure which security-related events to monitor or which to potentially monitor. By monitoring these security-related system events, you are able to detect attempts by intruders to compromise data on the system or to gain access to resources they should not be able to reach.

auditing Auditing is the process of tracking execution of user rights, file access, or other security elements on a computer. Group Policy can be used to configure auditing settings for a computer.

authentication   This is the process of verification that takes place when a user logs on to a computer or when a computer logs on to the domain. The authentication proves that the user or computer is the correct user or computer. This does not provide any encryption.

authoritative restore   When an object is deleted, the deletion is replicated to other domain controllers with an updated USN on the object. If the object is restored from backup, the normal replication process will cause it to be removed because the delete has a higher USN. To force the object back into Active Directory, you perform an authoritative restore. This will increase the object USN by 10,000, which will make the update higher than the delete USN.

authorizing a RIS server   This refers to registering a RIS server within Active Directory and thereby permitting it to service client requests for a RIS image. This is performed through the DHCP MMC snap-in.

B–D

background process   A background process is any process, either a service or user initiated, that is not currently interacting with the user. In simple terms, if the process is not able to receive input from the keyboard or mouse, it is a background process.

backup domain controller (BDC)   This is a type of computer found in Windows NT 4.0 domains. This computer kept a copy of the domain accounts database and was able to authenticate user logons. No changes could be made at a BDC, however, because the copy of the database that was kept was read only.

backup   The process of backing up system and user files to tape or disk or any other media supported by the backup program in use.

Banyan   Banyan VINES was one of the first PC network operating systems to provide enterprise-wide directory services. In Banyan, these services were based on the Network Information System that was originally developed in the UNIX world, upon which all of Banyan was based.

blocking policy inheritance   Blocking GPO inheritance means configuring a GPO at a lower-level Active Directory container so that any policies set at a higher level of Active Directory are not applied. You would typically block policy inheritance at an OU to ensure that only OU GPO settings are applied to users and computers.

caching server   A caching server is a type of DNS server that caches name resolutions that it retrieves. All Windows 2000 DNS servers are caching servers. If a server does not contain any zone files, however, it will be considered a caching-only server.

CD-based image   An image of Windows 2000 Professional that is a copy of the installation files found on the Windows 2000 Professional CD-ROM. CD-based images are deployed using RIS.

child domain   A child domain is a domain that exists as subdomain of another domain. For example RD.ScrimTech.local would be a child of ScrimTech.local.

class   A class of objects is one type of object. For example, a file is a class of object. Different classes of objects will have different extended attributes and will normally have different methods that can be applied. All classes of objects have some common attributes and methods such as name and type for attributes and create and delete for methods.

collection   A collection is a special type of object attribute in which there could be one or more entries for the same attribute. An example of a collection is the access control list, which is a made up of one or more access control entries.

computers   Within the Windows 2000 domain structure, computers are one of the object classes defined in Active Directory. This facilitates the management and location of computer objects on the network.

configuration partition   This is the Active Directory partition that contains information about the domains and trusts between them. The information is replicated from the domain naming master to all domain controllers in the enterprise.

connection objects   A connection object represents network path through which Active Directory replication will flow. These are normally created by the Knowledge Consistency Checker.

container object   This is an object in directory services, such as a group, that exists primarily to contain other Active Directory objects.

credentials   In simple terms, credentials are the information you use to connect to the remote computer. Within the Windows 2000 domain, credentials are stored in an access token and include the user information along with a list of groups to which the user belongs. The access token can then be attached to each process the user starts, and when a process attempts to access an object, these credentials can be compared to the ACL on the object to determine if access is allowed.

database   A database is a structure that stores data in a series of tables (lists) that have a given set of columns. Each table defines a single entity, a class in Windows 2000, with each row holding the information about one of those entities. For example, there is a user class in Windows 2000 that is a table in the Active Directory database. For each user, a row is added to the table. There is a single column that contains a unique identifier, and all the other columns contain attributes or collections about the entity.

DCPROMO   This utility is used to promote and demote computers. Promotion will make the system a domain controller, and demotion will reset it to a member server or standalone server.

directory   In simple terms, this is a list, a simple database that contains a list of items that a person might search. In Windows 2000, the directory is the collection of information about the object that can be found on the network.

Disk Quotas   Disk Quotas are settings on an NTFS volume used to enforce the amount of disk space that can be used by each user for files they create and/or own. Disk Quotas help ensure that users do not hog a disk and that enough space is available for all users.

distinguished name   A distinguished name is the full name of an object within Active Directory. This will include the domain name and the names of the organizational units to which a user belongs. For example, if there is a user named BehelerS in the users container of a domain called technical.newriders.local, the distinguished name for the user would be cn=BehelerS, cn=users, dc=technical, dc=newriders, dc=local. For another user in the same container, the relatively distinguished name of cn=BehelerS could be used because all other parts of the name are the same.

distribution group   A distribution group is a group you create so you will be able to send it email. Distribution groups cannot be assigned permissions or rights and can only contain users.

domain   In terms of DNS, this is a name given to an organization on the Internet. In truth, it is only part of the namespace for the Internet. In Windows 2000, a domain is a part of the namespace, but it is also a logical division that can be used to separate a large group of users from the rest of the network, providing a security and replication boundary.

domain controller   A domain controller is a computer that has a copy of the domain database. Domain controllers are able to authenticate user logon requests. Domain controllers in Windows 2000 are also able to modify the domain account database.

domain local group   A domain local group is normally used to assign rights or permissions to resources. Domain local groups are local to all domain controllers and member servers in native mode.

domain name system (DNS)   The domain name system is the system used on the Internet and on many private networks to resolve the names of computers. DNS is made up of namespace, name servers, and resolvers.

domain naming master   The domain naming master is one of the operation master roles. This computer is responsible for ensuring that the name-space of the domain is correct, and it is also responsible for the configuration of trust relationships that will be configured on the PDC emulators within the domains of the Active Directory forest. There is only one domain naming master per forest.

domain partition   The domain partition represents all the information about all the objects in a domain. The domain partition is replicated only within a domain and not between domains.

dynamic domain name system (DDNS)   This is an extension of the DNS standard that enables hosts to register names with the DNS server dynamically.

Dynamic Host Configuration Protocol (DHCP)
DHCP enables computers on the network to receive an automatic TCP/IP configuration including options. DHCP servers in Windows 2000 need to be authorized in Active Directory, which is intended to stop other users from installing DHCP. The Windows 2000 DHCP server is able to update the DNS server as the addresses are assigned; however, in normal behavior, it will only update the reverse lookup information and enable the client to register its forward lookup information.

dynamic updates   Dynamic updates are fairly new to DNS. They enable a client computer or the DHCP server to register records in the DNS. This enables a network to use DHCP, which reduces management of the network, and still be able to update the DNS server as the client address changes.

E–H

enterprise   A general term that describes a scope including the entire organization.

entity   An entity is the subject of a table within a database. In Windows 2000, an entity is any of the types or classes of objects stored in Active Directory.

Event Viewer   The Event Viewer is used to look at the system log files for various parts of the system including system, security, application, and DNS. This is the first place you should look when troubleshooting a problem.

extensible architecture   This is a type of architecture that can be added to or extended. The Windows 2000 Active Directory is said to be extensible because the tables that make up the directory database can have columns (attributes) added to them.

folder redirection   Folder redirection is the selective placement of folders of which all users will make use on different volumes of local computers or on shared network volumes where they may be backed up. Folder Redirection is enforced through Group Policy.

forced package removal   Mandatory or forced removal is the removal (uninstallation) of a software package from the user's computer. Forced package removal cannot be cancelled by the user. In a forced removal, the software package is always removed from the computer.

forcing Group Policy Forcing Group Policy is the opposite of blocking—not allowing a lower-level Active Directory container's GPO settings to overwrite a GPO setting at a higher level. You would normally force Group Policy at the domain level to ensure that company rules are uniformly applied to all users, regardless of their OU settings.

foreground process The active process on a computer. The process the user is interacting with is said to be the foreground process.

forest A forest is logically any single Active Directory domain or any grouping of domains. Notably, a structure is said to be a forest if it contains two or more trees—that is, two or more discontinuous namespaces.

forward lookup Forward lookups are the simplest type of resolution that will be performed. In a forward lookup, the system is trying to find the IP address for a computer name.

fully qualified domain name (FQDN) An FQDN is the full name of the computer and is a combination of the host name and the domain to which it belongs.

global catalog The global catalog in Active Directory is made up of a list of all objects within all domains along with a subset of common attributes for each of the objects. The global catalog is used to locate objects in Active Directory and is accessed using the Active Directory services interface or LDAP.

global catalog server This is the system that will contain the global catalog and will replicate with the other global catalog servers to build the full global catalog. This server should be designed with this extra workload in mind.

global group A global group is used to gather users from a domain so they can be added en mass to local groups in the domain or in other domains.

GPO inheritance Group Policy object inheritance is the set of rules by which higher-level GPO settings are applied or overwritten by lower-level GPOs in Active Directory. The default GPO inheritance hierarchy is site-domain-OU, which means that settings at a site level may be overwritten at a domain level, which may then be overwritten at the OU level. In this way, settings applied closest to the user or computer will have precedence by default.

GPO scope GPO scope deals with which Active Directory containers a GPO is associated. Group Policy objects may be associated with a single Active Directory container (for example, an OU) or may also be added to other containers at the same or a different level. The same settings will be applied at all containers to which the GPO is linked.

Group Policy container A Group Policy container is an Active Directory container that includes GPO attributes (such as the GUID) and version information.

Group Policy filtering Filtering a GPO is the assignment of permissions to a Group Policy, thereby determining to which users and/or computers the policy will be applied.

Group Policy object (GPO) A Group Policy object is an object within Active Directory that enables an administrator to configure software deployment settings, security settings, and administrative templates, thereby enforcing corporate rules for users and computers. Group Policy is composed of Group Policy containers and Group Policy templates.

Group Policy precedence Precedence is the order in which GPOs within the same container are processed. Because it is possible to link more than one GPO to the same Active Directory container, precedence determines which GPO will have the final say.

Group Policy template A Group Policy template is a set of folders and subfolders in the SYSVOL share on Windows 2000 domain controllers containing the scripts, security templates, and administrative settings for Group Policy to be downloaded on client computers.

groups A group is a container-type object found in Active Directory. Groups are used primarily for collect rights and permissions or for collecting users for the purposes of management.

globally unique identifier (GUID) A GUID is a 32-character string used to uniquely identify a computer for pre-staging. In RIS, it is usually the identity of the PXE-enabled network card, but it can also be the MAC address of a non-PXE-compliant network card padded to 32 characters and using the proper format.

hierarchy A hierarchy is any structure that has a single starting point from which the structure expands. This includes organizational charts within a company and the domain namespace. The hierarchy in Windows 2000 describes the namespace that starts with a root domain that then flows down through children domains and the grandchildren.

I–L

infrastructure master The infrastructure master is a domain-level operations master. It is responsible for updating the group membership of the domain users across the entire enterprise.

inheritance In Active Directory, permissions are inherited from parent objects. This process is called inheritance and can be blocked if desired.

Internet A worldwide network used to join various corporate and public networks into a single network.

iterative query DNS server performs iterative queries as it performs a name resolution. This type of query will look for the best answer possible, including a redirection to another name server.

Knowledge Consistency Checker (KCC) The KCC is responsible for creating the intrasite connections to ensure that each computer will have at least two replication partners. It will also use the site links you create to make connections between servers at different sites so that replication can take place between the sites.

LAN Manager A network operating system developed by IBM and Microsoft. This network was one of the first to use domain controllers to centralize the authentication of users on a network.

leaf-level objects This is an object in directory services such as a user object that holds a place but does not contain other objects.

Lightweight Directory Access Protocol (LDAP) LDAP is a protocol that was originally defined for accessing an X.500 directory structure. It has been expanded to access many of the directories using a defined set of object attribute identifiers that are controlled by the International Standards Organization.

local group A local group is the same as a domain local group. It is used for rights and permissions, but it exists on standalone servers and Windows 2000 Professional computers. These are also used on member servers in mixed mode.

logon/logoff scripts Logon/logoff scripts are BAT, CMD, or Windows Script Host files (VBScript or JScript) that are run at logon or logoff time by each user that has the GPO applied. Logon/logoff scripts enable the administrator to configure other settings for the user that cannot be set through Group Policy.

M–P

Media Access Layer (MAC)   The MAC address is the physical address assigned to a network card and is used to identify it on the network.

mandatory upgrade   A mandatory upgrade is an upgrade to an existing software package deployed through Group Policy that must be installed. Mandatory upgrades can be set for the user or the computer and will remove the previous version of the package.

master server   A master server is the server from which a secondary DNS will retrieve a copy of a zone file. The master can be a primary or secondary server.

method   A method is an action that can be performed on an object. Common methods include create and delete. Methods are important because they are used when you are programmatically accessing objects such as Active Directory.

mixed mode   In this mode, Active Directory will still allow the use of Windows NT 3.51 and 4.0 BDC computers. If you are running in this mode, you will not be able to nest groups nor will you be able to work with universal security groups.

MOVETREE   This utility can be used to move objects between domains. Within a domain, an object can be moved in Users and Computers using the context menu command Move.

name server   This is a component of DNS name servers that is responsible for receiving resolution requests from other servers or from clients and processing the requests.

namespace   This is an entire tree of names that starts with a root and branches from there. The namespace is like a directory structure on a drive. The entire Internet is controlled using a single namespace, whereas each Active Directory tree will be a single namespace.

native mode   Native mode allows for nesting of security groups and the use of universal security groups. No Windows NT BDC can be on the network if you are in native mode.

Netlogon   The Netlogon or Network Logon service is the service that will handle the request for network authentication from users.

NetWare   NetWare is a popular network operating system that was originally designed to use a separate user database on each server. Later, NetWare was improved with Novell Directory Services, which enabled it to compete more easily in the enterprise-networking arena.

Network Monitor   The Network Monitor is a utility that will enable you to capture and view network traffic. This will enable you troubleshoot network problems.

network operating system (NOS)   An operating system or extension to an operating system will enable clients to use a redirector to determine if a request is for the local machine or a remote system. The NOS can then expose the required network interface or can access it on behalf of the user application to pass the request to another service running, normally, on another computer connect to the network.

No Override   Same as forcing Group Policy.

notification   Master DNS servers can notify secondary servers when there is a change in the zone file. This is done using a notification.

NSLOOKUP   The NSLOOKUP utility can be used to query a DNS server either from the command line or by creating a session with the DNS server.

NTDSUTIL   This utility is used for several different functions. Notably, it is used to seize a single-operations master role and to perform authoritative restores.

NTFS NTFS is the file system in Windows 2000. It provides many benefits, including the capability to set file and folder permissions, making it a requirement for the SYSVOL share.

object An object is a general term used for any resource or other entity that exists. By using the object model, programming is simplified through the ability to use and reuse code.

object-level permissions Permission can be set on objects to control who can manage the object. This is the basis of delegating control of an OU because the permissions are inherited by child objects.

operating system An operating system is a program or set of programs that provides basic services to the user of a computer. The operating system should at least be able to start the computer, manage memory on the computer, interact with the basic input/output system of the computer, and schedule the execution of programs on the system.

optional package removal Optional removal enables the user to decide whether to remove an application from his or her computer or leave it installed.

optional upgrade An optional upgrade is an upgrade to a Group Policy–deployed software package that a user may decide to install on his or her computer but is not obliged to do so.

organization An organization is a term that refers to the company or enterprise that is implementing Active Directory. In X.400 and X.500 terms, the organization (O) is the name of the company.

organizational unit (OU) An organizational unit is a subgrouping within a domain that can be used to delegate administrative control of the objects it contains. In X.400 and X.500, an organizational unit is a subdivision of the organization.

originating write An originating write is a change to an object in Active Directory caused by a process other than replication. For example, a user changing his or her password is an originating write. The originating write will update the update sequence number of the object.

package modifications Package modifications are changes applied to a software package, and they are contained in transform (MST) files. Transform files are associated with an existing package. They, in combination with several GPOs, are used to change the behavior of a package when it is deployed in different regions.

PDC emulator This is a operations master role on the domain level. The PDC emulator will handle replication with down-level domain controllers and authentication of down-level clients. It also creates the trust relationships between domains.

Performance This utility enables you to monitor and view the performance of all the parts of the system at a very low level. It can be used to troubleshoot general system problems and to troubleshoot performance problems.

permissions Permissions provide a user with the capability to work with an object. The permissions that a user or other security principal has for an object are contained in the discretionary access control list (DACL). This is set by the owner or a user with the Permissions permission on the object.

prestaging The process of creating computer accounts in Active Directory by using the GUID of the computer. Prestaging enables the administrator to configure a client computer to receive its image list from a specified RIS server, and it also can be used to ensure that only those computers that have been prestaged can use RIS.

primary domain controller (PDC)   In a Windows NT 4.0 network, the PDC is the main domain controller. It contains the only write-enabled version of the domain database. This system then needs to replicate that database to the backup domain controllers so that they are also able to authenticate user logon requests.

primary server   The primary name server is the server where the zone file is created. Changes to the zone file will be made on this server only and then will be sent to the secondary servers. If the zone is Active Directory integrated, there will no longer be a primary server because all domain controllers with DNS installed will be able to make modifications.

Printers   This is a class of objects in Active Directory that is used to publish or list printers in the Active Directory so that users will be able to search for and use a printer anywhere in the enterprise if they have permissions.

process   A process is a combination of assigned virtual memory and at least one execution thread that is used to run an application. Services each run in a process as do all programs that users run, including the initial user process (Explorer.exe). Every process will have a set of credentials attached in the form of an access token, which will determine the rights and permissions of the process.

properties   Properties describe an object in the same way an adjective describes a noun (for example, the green door). In the case of an object such as a file, the file type would be a property.

publishing software packages   Publishing software packages is the capability to enable a user to optionally install a Group Policy–deployed software package by document activation through Add/Remove Programs in Control Panel.

PXE   Pre-Boot Execution Environment (PXE) is a standard by which a network card with a boot ROM complying with the standard can request a TCP/IP address from a DHCP server and the IP address of a RIS server to start the installation of a Windows 2000 Professional image.

R–S

Remote Access Service (RAS)   RAS enables users to dial in to a Windows 2000 network. The old version in Windows NT 4.0 had to allow users fully into the network and then authenticate them. In Windows 2000, this is avoided.

recursive query   A recursive query is a query between a client and the DNS server that requests the name resolution or a failure notification.

redeployment   Redeployment is the reinstallation of an existing software package through Group Policy, usually to distribute a patch for an existing application.

redirector   A redirector is part of the network operating system that is responsible for formulating requests that will be passed to a server service. The redirector in Windows 2000 is called the Workstation service.

registry   The registry is a collection of settings that exists on each computer for both the computer and the users who log on to that computer. The registry is broken down into a series of subtrees of which KEY_LOCAL_MACHINE and HKEY_USERS are the most important because they deal with computer, COM+, and user settings. Group Policy Administrative Templates modify the registry to enforce GPO settings at the user and computer level.

relative identifier (RID) master   This is a operations master on the domain level. The RID master creates and distributes RIDs that are used in conjunction with domain SIDs to create the SIDs for new objects in the domains.

Remote Installation Services (RIS) This is a Windows 2000 service that facilitates the deployment of Windows 2000 Professional to computers by means of a RIS boot disk or a PXE-compliant network adapter.

Remote Procedure Call (RPC) RPCs are one of the methods that can be used for interprocess communications. This method uses an external redirector andserver that many services and clients can use at the same time. Server-to-server RPC communications should have at least 64KB of network bandwidth.

repackaging an application Repackaging an application is the creation of a Windows installer package for an application by use of a third-party repackaging tool such as Veritas WinInstall LE.

replication This is the process of copying data from one location to another. Replication is important in Active Directory. Active Directory replicates schema information, configuration information, domain information, and the global catalog.

resolver This is a small piece of code that is built in to an application or the operating system that performs the recursive query to the DNS server.

resources Any file, folder, printer, service, or other portion of a computer that is available for use. Network resources are those that are shared to the network so that they are available to the users on the network.

restore The process of restoring files from a backup.

restricting images Restricting images is the act of assigning NTFS permissions on answer files for RIS images. Restricting images enables the administrator to specify which user or group accounts will be allowed to make use of a specific image through RIS.

reverse lookup A reverse lookup is the process of asking for the name of a server based on an IP address.

rights In the same way that permissions control what a user can do to a file, rights control what system actions a user can perform, for example changing the system time.

Remote Installation Preparation (RIPrep) image RIPrep images contain the entire configuration of a source computer including the operating system and all installed applications and shortcuts. They are deployed to target computers with the same HAL as the source using Remote Installation Services.

RIS boot disk A disk created by the Remote Boot Disk Generator program (Rbfg.exe) that emulates a PXE-based environment on a computer without a PXE-compliant network card. The RIS boot disk can be used to start the installation of a RIS image on a target computer.

RIS image An operating system image that can be deployed to computers from a RIS server. RIS images can be CD based or RIPrep images and are stored on a RIS server.

RIS server A Windows 2000 server that is part of an Active Directory domain and has Remote Installation Services installed.

root domain The starting point for a hierarchy. There is a root domain on the Internet that is the starting point of the namespace for the entire Internet. In the Windows 2000 world, the root domain is the first domain that is installed to which all other domains will be joined as other branches of the namespace.

scavenging This is a process that is required on a server that performs dynamic registration. The process will look for outdated records and remove them.

schema This is the term used to describe the rows and columns that make up the tables in a database. The schema in Windows 2000 refers to the definition of classes (tables) and attributes (columns) within the directory database.

schema master   This is one of the operation master roles, and it contains the only write-enabled copy of the schema of the directory database. When changes are made, this system will ensure that all the other domain controllers in the enterprise are updated. There is only one schema master in an Active Directory forest, and all changes to the schema are made across the entire forest.

schema partition   This is the where the schema information is contained. The schema partition is replicated from the schema master to all domain controllers in the network.

second-level domains   In the DNS namespace, a second-level domain is a domain that an organization will use. For example, the second-level domain in www.newriders.com would be newriders.

secondary server   This is a DNS server that can provide an authoritative answer to a client because it has a copy of the zone file. In standard mode, it cannot make a change to the zone file that is copied from a master server.

Security Configuration and Analysis   Security Configuration and Analysis is an MMC snap-in primarily designed to analyze local system security settings and apply security templates to the local computer. It can also be used to retrieve the local computer security configuration and to create a security template that will reflect the computer's settings.

security context   This is the user credentials under which a process is running.

security group   A security group is used to set permissions. You can also use a security group for email; however, security groups are approximately 2,600 bytes larger.

security principal   Security principal is a term applied to any object that you can give permissions or rights to, such as users, computers, and groups.

Security Templates   Security Templates are text files containing the rules used to enforce security settings for users and computers. They form the basis for a security policy for users and computers.

service   This is background application that is started automatically when the computer starts or is started manually by an operator. Services typically do not interact with the desktop but run as a background process providing services to other processes.

service (SRV) records   The SRV record is a new type of record in DNS that enables a service to register a DNS name so that users can search for a service rather than a particular computer.

shares   A share is a class of objects that is available in Active Directory. Share objects enable share folder resources to be published to Active Directory so that users can search for them more easily.

security identifier (SID)   This is the unique number that will identify every object in the Active Directory. The SID for objects in Windows 2000 is made up of a combination of the domain SID from the domain where they were created and a unique relative identifier.

Simple Mail Transfer Protocol (SMTP)   SMTP is a simple protocol normally used to move information from one computer to another. In Windows 2000, this protocol can be used for replication between sites.

Single Instance Store (SIS) Service   The Single Instance Store Service runs on a RIS server and is responsible for ensuring that the files required for a CD-based RIS image can be found. It also helps minimize disk space used by ensuring that multiple copies of the same file required by multiple RIS images do not exist and that a single copy of the file is instead shared.

site   A site is a group of IP subnets connected using high-speed networking. Sites can be used to control replication.

site link bridges   This is a connection between two or more site links acting as a path for Active Directory replication between sites not directly linked. Bridges are ignored unless you turn off automatic site link bridging.

site links   A site link is a logical connection between two or more sites. A site link lets the KCC know about other sites in your network so that it can create the required links.

software categories   Software categories are logical groupings of published software packages that enable a user to more easily browse the available software to determine which package to install. The same software package may appear in more than one category.

source computer   The computer onto which Windows 2000 Professional, applications, and other settings are applied that will be used as the source for a RIPrep image.

Start of Authority (SOA)   The SOA record sets the refresh interval and the name of the primary server for a standard zone.

startup/shutdown scripts   Startup/shutdown scripts are BAT, CMD, or Windows Script Host files (VBScript or JScript) that run at startup and shutdown time for the computers that have the GPO applied. Startup/shutdown scripts enable the administrator to configure other settings for the computer that cannot be set through Group Policy.

subnet   A subnet is a single segment of a routed network. It is normally identified using the subnet ID followed by a slash and the number of bits in the netmask. For example, 148.53.64.0/18 would be a subnet for hosts 148.53.64.1 through 14.53.127.254.

SYSTEM account   The SYSTEM account is a special account that can be used to start services that will be available on a computer. The SYSTEM account is really the computer account that has complete control of the local system.

system state data   The system state data is the core of the operating system and represents Active Directory, the registry, the certificate database, and other key files. The system state data should be backed up on a schedule.

SYSVOL   This is the system volume share. It is the connection point that will be used to authenticate user logons and store logon scripts, group policies, and similar files.

T–Z

table   A table is a structure in a database that contains data. A table is made of columns, which represent attributes or properties, and rows, which represent entities.

target computer   The computer onto which RIPrep or CD-based images will be installed using Remote Installation Services. The target computer must meet Windows 2000 Professional hardware requirements and must have a PXE-enabled network card or be supported by the RIS boot disk.

Task Manager   This is a basic utility that can give a quick look at the current performance of the system, including which processes are running and the overall statistics for CPU and memory. You can use this application to end a task that is not responding or to change the priority of a running task.

Trivial File Transfer Protocol (TFTP)   TFTP is a protocol that runs on a RIS server and is used to transfer files to the target computer during deployment. This is not the same as the FTP protocol you might use to connect to an FTP site on the Internet. TFTP differs from FTP in that it does not require any user interaction, which is why it is used for Remote Installation Services.

time to live (TTL) When a DNS server resolves an address, it will cache this address for the time given in the returned information. This time is the TTL for the DNS cache entry.

top-level domains On the Internet, top-level domains are used as the first division of the name space. The best known is probably the com top-level domain.

traffic Traffic is a general term in computing that refers to data that is traveling or must travel across the network. A great concern is that a network will have more traffic than it can handle.

transform files Same as package modifications.

tree A root domain and all its children of a single contiguous namespace is considered a tree in Active Directory.

trust relationships A trust relationship is a relationship between two Microsoft domains in which one of the domains will trust the other to perform authentication. The domain that trusts the other will accept logon requests for the users who exist in the other domain. The local domain controller will forward the logon request to the trusted domain controller, which will perform the authentication and return the information to the trusting domain controller.

universal group A universal group is a special type of group that exists in the global catalog and can span domains easily. Security groups should be used sparingly because they increase the interdomain replication.

Update Sequence Number (USN) A number used on the domain controller to keep track of the number of updates the controller has made and on the object to keep track of the number of updates made to it. These numbers make multimaster replication possible.

user (username) A user is a class of objects in the Active Directory database that is used to represent the people who will be able to log on and use resources from the network.

user process A user process is a process started by a user. The user's credentials will be attached to the process to ensure that the process does not access information it should not access.

Windows 2000 The current network operating system from Microsoft. Windows 2000 will eventually ship in four versions: Professional, Server, Advanced Server, and Data Center.

Windows Installer Package The Windows Installer Package contains all the necessary information that the Windows Installer Service needs to install or remove an application. This includes the files required by the software, registry and INI file changes that need to be made, any additional support files that are required, summary information on the package and the application that can be shown to the user, and a reference to the location of the product files—that is, where to install the software from. The majority of this information is contained in a single file with an .MSI extension, which is the package file itself.

Windows Installer Service The Windows Installer Service is a service that is installed and runs on all Windows 2000 machines. This service facilitates the automated installation and deployment of software. It also provides the capability to automatically repair or modify existing applications in cases in which files are overwritten or removed.

Windows Internet Naming System (WINS) A WINS server is similar to a DNS server but is especially designed for NetBIOS names, which are hierarchical. These servers are required for Windows NT 4.0 and other down-level clients.

Windows NT This is the previous version of Microsoft's network operating system. Windows NT Terminal Server edition served as the foundation for the current Windows 2000.

workstation Workstation is the general term for a computer on a network. It is also the Windows 2000 service that will be responsible for connecting to remote resources across the network.

X.500   The X.500 standard is a theoretical standard that describes how to create and manage a hierarchical directory structure. Microsoft's Active Directory is loosely based on X.500.

ZAP file   A ZAP file is an ASCII text file created with any text editor (Notepad will work) and that specifies a number of things about the software to be installed including the application name, the name of the setup, program, any parameters to be used for setup as well as any file extensions to be associated with the application, the tech support Web site address, and so on. ZAP files are used to deploy software using Group Policy for which no Windows Installer Package exists.

zone   The zone, or zone file, is the group of resource records for a domain. Servers that have a copy of the zone file can service requests for authoritative answers about the system in the domain.

zone transfer   This is the process of copying a zone file from a master server to a secondary server. This process is not used in Active Directory–integrated zones.

Overview of the Certification Process

You must pass rigorous certification exams to become a Microsoft Certified Professional. These closed-book exams provide a valid and reliable measure of your technical proficiency and expertise. Developed in consultation with computer industry professionals who have experience with Microsoft products in the workplace, the exams are conducted by two independent organizations. *Virtual University Enterprises* (VUE) testing centers offer exams at more than 2,700 locations in 128 countries. Sylvan Prometric offers the exams at more than 2,000 authorized Prometric Testing Centers around the world as well.

To schedule an exam, call Sylvan Prometric Testing Centers at 800-755-EXAM (3926) (or register online at http://www.2test.com/register) or VUE at 888-837-8734 (or register online at http://www.vue.com/ms/msexam.html). At the time of this writing, Microsoft offered eight types of certification, each based on a specific area of expertise. Please check the Microsoft Certified Professional Web site for the most up-to-date information (www.microsoft.com/mcp/).

TYPES OF CERTIFICATION

❖ **Microsoft Certified Professional (MCP).** Persons with this credential are qualified to support at least one Microsoft product. Candidates can take elective exams to develop areas of specialization. MCP is the base level of expertise.

❖ **Microsoft Certified Professional+Internet (MCP+Internet).** Persons with this credential are qualified to plan security, install and configure server products, manage server resources, extend service to run CGI scripts or ISAPI scripts, monitor and analyze performance, and troubleshoot problems. Expertise is similar to that of an MCP but with a focus on the Internet.

❖ **Microsoft Certified Professional+Site Building (MCP+Site Building).** Persons with this credential are qualified to plan, build, maintain, and manage Web sites using Microsoft technologies and products. The credential is appropriate for people who manage sophisticated, interactive Web sites that include database connectivity, multimedia, and searchable content.

◆ **Microsoft Certified Database Administrator (MCDBA).** Qualified individuals can derive physical database designs, develop logical data models, create physical databases, create data services by using Transact-SQL, manage and maintain databases, configure and manage security, monitor and optimize databases, and install and configure Microsoft SQL Server.

◆ **Microsoft Certified Systems Engineer (MCSE).** These individuals are qualified to analyze the business requirements for a system architecture; design solutions; deploy, install, and configure architecture components; and troubleshoot system problems.

◆ **Microsoft Certified Systems Engineer+Internet (MCSE+Internet).** Persons with this credential are qualified in the core MCSE areas and also are qualified to enhance, deploy, and manage sophisticated intranet and Internet solutions that include a browser, proxy server, host servers, database, and messaging and commerce components. An MCSE+Internet–certified professional is able to manage and analyze Web sites.

◆ **Microsoft Certified Solution Developer (MCSD).** These individuals are qualified to design and develop custom business solutions by using Microsoft development tools, technologies, and platforms. The new track includes certification exams that test the user's ability to build Web-based, distributed, and commerce applications by using Microsoft products such as Microsoft SQL Server, Microsoft Visual Studio, and Microsoft Component Services.

◆ **Microsoft Certified Trainer (MCT).** Persons with this credential are instructionally and technically qualified by Microsoft to deliver Microsoft Education Courses at Microsoft-authorized sites. An MCT must be employed by a Microsoft Solution Provider Authorized Technical Education Center or a Microsoft Authorized Academic Training site.

NOTE For up-to-date information about each type of certification, visit the Microsoft Training and Certification Web site at http://www.microsoft.com/mcp. You can also contact Microsoft through the following sources:

- Microsoft Certified Professional Program: 800-636-7544

- mcp@msource.com

- Microsoft Online Institute (MOLI): 800-449-9333

CERTIFICATION REQUIREMENTS

The following sections describe the requirements for the various types of Microsoft certifications.

NOTE An asterisk following an exam in any of the following lists means that it is slated for retirement.

How to Become a Microsoft Certified Professional

To become certified as an MCP, you need only pass any Microsoft exam (with the exceptions of Networking Essentials, #70-058* and Microsoft Windows 2000 Accelerated Exam for MCPs Certified on Microsoft Windows NT 4.0, #70-240).

How to Become a Microsoft Certified Professional+Internet

To become an MCP specializing in Internet technology, you must pass the following exams:

◆ Internetworking with Microsoft TCP/IP on Microsoft Windows NT 4.0, #70-059*

◆ Implementing and Supporting Microsoft Windows NT Server 4.0, #70-067*

◆ Implementing and Supporting Microsoft Internet Information Server 3.0 and Microsoft Index Server 1.1, #70-077*

   OR Implementing and Supporting Microsoft Internet Information Server 4.0, #70-087*

How to Become a Microsoft Certified Professional+Site Building

To be certified as an MCP+Site Building, you need to pass two of the following exams:

◆ Designing and Implementing Web Sites with Microsoft FrontPage 98, #70-055

◆ Designing and Implementing Commerce Solutions with Microsoft Site Server 3.0, Commerce Edition, #70-057

◆ Designing and Implementing Web Solutions with Microsoft Visual InterDev 6.0, #70-152

How to Become a Microsoft Certified Database Administrator

There are two MCDBA tracks: one tied to Windows 2000, the other based on Windows NT 4.0.

Windows 2000 Track

To become an MCDBA in the Windows 2000 track, you must pass three core exams and one elective exam.

Core Exams

The core exams required to become an MCDBA in the Windows 2000 track are as follows:

◆ Installing, Configuring, and Administering Microsoft Windows 2000 Server, #70-215

   OR Microsoft Windows 2000 Accelerated Exam for MCPs Certified on Microsoft Windows NT 4.0, #70-240 (only for those who have passed exams #70-067*, #70-068*, and #70-073*)

◆ Administering Microsoft SQL Server 7.0, #70-028

◆ Designing and Implementing Databases with Microsoft SQL Server 7.0, #70-029

Elective Exams

You must also pass one elective exam from the following list:

◆ Implementing and Administering a Microsoft Windows 2000 Network Infrastructure, #70-216 (only for those who have *not* already passed #70-067*, #70-068*, and #70-073*)

OR Microsoft Windows 2000 Accelerated Exam for MCPs Certified on Microsoft Windows NT 4.0, #70-240 (only for those who have passed exams #70-067*, #70-068*, and #70-073*)

◆ Designing and Implementing Distributed Applications with Microsoft Visual C++ 6.0, #70-015

◆ Designing and Implementing Data Warehouses with Microsoft SQL Server 7.0 and Microsoft Decision Support Services 1.0, #70-019

◆ Implementing and Supporting Microsoft Internet Information Server 4.0, #70-087*

◆ Designing and Implementing Distributed Applications with Microsoft Visual FoxPro 6.0, #70-155

◆ Designing and Implementing Distributed Applications with Microsoft Visual Basic 6.0, #70-175

Windows NT 4.0 Track

To become an MCDBA in the Windows NT 4.0 track, you must pass four core exams and one elective exam.

Core Exams

The core exams required to become an MCDBA in the Windows NT 4.0 track are as follows:

◆ Administering Microsoft SQL Server 7.0, #70-028

◆ Designing and Implementing Databases with Microsoft SQL Server 7.0, #70-029

◆ Implementing and Supporting Microsoft Windows NT Server 4.0, #70-067*

◆ Implementing and Supporting Microsoft Windows NT Server 4.0 in the Enterprise, #70-068*

Elective Exams

You must also pass one elective exam from the following list:

◆ Designing and Implementing Distributed Applications with Microsoft Visual C++ 6.0, #70-015

◆ Designing and Implementing Data Warehouses with Microsoft SQL Server 7.0 and Microsoft Decision Support Services 1.0, #70-019

◆ Internetworking with Microsoft TCP/IP on Microsoft Windows NT 4.0, #70-059*

◆ Implementing and Supporting Microsoft Internet Information Server 4.0, #70-087*

◆ Designing and Implementing Distributed Applications with Microsoft Visual FoxPro 6.0, #70-155

◆ Designing and Implementing Distributed Applications with Microsoft Visual Basic 6.0, #70-175

How to Become a Microsoft Certified Systems Engineer

You must pass operating system exams and two elective exams to become an MCSE. The MCSE certification path is divided into two tracks: Windows 2000 and Windows NT 4.0.

The following lists show the core requirements for the Windows 2000 and Windows NT 4.0 tracks and the electives.

Windows 2000 Track

The Windows 2000 track requires you to pass five core exams (or an accelerated exam and another core exam). You must also pass two elective exams.

Core Exams

The Windows 2000 track core requirements for MCSE certification include the following for those who have *not* passed #70-067, #70-068, and #70-073:

◆ Installing, Configuring, and Administering Microsoft Windows 2000 Professional, #70-210

◆ Installing, Configuring, and Administering Microsoft Windows 2000 Server, #70-215

◆ Implementing and Administering a Microsoft Windows 2000 Network Infrastructure, #70-216

◆ Implementing and Administering a Microsoft Windows 2000 Directory Services Infrastructure, #70-217

The Windows 2000 track core requirements for MCSE certification include the following for those who have passed #70-067*, #70-068*, and #70-073*:

◆ Microsoft Windows 2000 Accelerated Exam for MCPs Certified on Microsoft Windows NT 4.0, #70-240

All candidates must pass one of these three additional core exams:

◆ Designing a Microsoft Windows 2000 Directory Services Infrastructure, #70-219

OR Designing Security for a Microsoft Windows 2000 Network, #70-220

OR Designing a Microsoft Windows 2000 Infrastructure, #70-221

Elective Exams

Any MCSE elective exams that are current (not slated for retirement) when the Windows 2000 core exams are released can be used to fulfill the requirement of two elective exams. In addition, core exams #70-219,

#70-220, and #70-221 can be used as elective exams, as long as they are not already being used to fulfill the "additional core exams" requirement outlined previously. Exam #70-222 (Upgrading from Microsoft Windows NT 4.0 to Microsoft Windows 2000) can also be used to fulfill this requirement. Finally, selected third-party certifications that focus on interoperability may count for this requirement. Watch the Microsoft MCP Web site (www.microsoft.com/mcp) for more information on these third-party certifications.

Windows NT 4.0 Track

The Windows NT 4.0 track is also organized around core and elective exams.

Core Exams

The four Windows NT 4.0 track core requirements for MCSE certification are as follows:

◆ Implementing and Supporting Microsoft Windows NT Server 4.0, #70-067*

◆ Implementing and Supporting Microsoft Windows NT Server 4.0 in the Enterprise, #70-068*

◆ Microsoft Windows 3.1, #70-030*

OR Microsoft Windows for Workgroups 3.11, #70-048*

OR Implementing and Supporting Microsoft Windows 95, #70-064*

OR Implementing and Supporting Microsoft Windows NT Workstation 4.0, #70-073*

OR Implementing and Supporting Microsoft Windows 98, #70-098

◆ Networking Essentials, #70-058*

Elective Exams

For the Windows NT 4.0 track, you must pass two of the following elective exams for MCSE certification:

◆ Implementing and Supporting Microsoft SNA Server 3.0, #70-013

   OR Implementing and Supporting Microsoft SNA Server 4.0, #70-085

◆ Implementing and Supporting Microsoft Systems Management Server 1.2, #70-018

   OR Implementing and Supporting Microsoft Systems Management Server 2.0, #70-086

◆ Designing and Implementing Data Warehouse with Microsoft SQL Server 7.0, #70-019

◆ Microsoft SQL Server 4.2 Database Implementation, #70-021*

   OR Implementing a Database Design on Microsoft SQL Server 6.5, #70-027

   OR Implementing a Database Design on Microsoft SQL Server 7.0, #70-029

◆ Microsoft SQL Server 4.2 Database Administration for Microsoft Windows NT, #70-022*

   OR System Administration for Microsoft SQL Server 6.5 (or 6.0), #70-026

   OR System Administration for Microsoft SQL Server 7.0, #70-028

◆ Microsoft Mail for PC Networks 3.2-Enterprise, #70-037*

◆ Internetworking with Microsoft TCP/IP on Microsoft Windows NT (3.5–3.51), #70-053*

   OR Internetworking with Microsoft TCP/IP on Microsoft Windows NT 4.0, #70-059*

◆ Implementing and Supporting Web Sites Using Microsoft Site Server 3.0, #70-056

◆ Implementing and Supporting Microsoft Exchange Server 4.0, #70-075*

   OR Implementing and Supporting Microsoft Exchange Server 5.0, #70-076

   OR Implementing and Supporting Microsoft Exchange Server 5.5, #70-081

◆ Implementing and Supporting Microsoft Internet Information Server 3.0 and Microsoft Index Server 1.1, #70-077*

   OR Implementing and Supporting Microsoft Internet Information Server 4.0, #70-087*

◆ Implementing and Supporting Microsoft Proxy Server 1.0, #70-078

   OR Implementing and Supporting Microsoft Proxy Server 2.0, #70-088

◆ Implementing and Supporting Microsoft Internet Explorer 4.0 by Using the Internet Explorer Resource Kit, #70-079

   OR Implementing and Supporting Microsoft Internet Explorer 5.0 by Using the Internet Explorer Resource Kit, #70-080

◆ Designing a Microsoft Windows 2000 Directory Services Infrastructure, #70-219

◆ Designing Security for a Microsoft Windows 2000 Network, #70-220

◆ Designing a Microsoft Windows 2000 Infrastructure, #70-221

◆ Upgrading from Microsoft Windows NT 4.0 to Microsoft Windows 2000, #70-222

How to Become a Microsoft Certified Systems Engineer+Internet

You must pass seven operating system exams and two elective exams to become an MCSE specializing in Internet technology.

Core Exams

The following seven core exams are required for MCSE+Internet certification:

◆ Networking Essentials, #70-058*

◆ Internetworking with Microsoft TCP/IP on Microsoft Windows NT 4.0, #70-059*

◆ Implementing and Supporting Microsoft Windows 95, #70-064*

   OR Implementing and Supporting Microsoft Windows NT Workstation 4.0, #70-073*

   OR Implementing and Supporting Microsoft Windows 98, #70-098

◆ Implementing and Supporting Microsoft Windows NT Server 4.0, #70-067*

◆ Implementing and Supporting Microsoft Windows NT Server 4.0 in the Enterprise, #70-068*

◆ Implementing and Supporting Microsoft Internet Information Server 3.0 and Microsoft Index Server 1.1, #70-077*

   OR Implementing and Supporting Microsoft Internet Information Server 4.0, #70-087*

◆ Implementing and Supporting Microsoft Internet Explorer 4.0 by Using the Internet Explorer Resource Kit, #70-079

   OR Implementing and Supporting Microsoft Internet Explorer 5.0 by Using the Internet Explorer Resource Kit, #70-080

Elective Exams

You must also pass two of the following elective exams for MCSE+Internet certification:

◆ System Administration for Microsoft SQL Server 6.5, #70-026

   OR Administering Microsoft SQL Server 7.0, #70-028

◆ Implementing a Database Design on Microsoft SQL Server 6.5, #70-027

   OR Designing and Implementing Databases with Microsoft SQL Server 7.0, #70-029

◆ Implementing and Supporting Web Sites Using Microsoft Site Server 3.0, # 70-056

◆ Implementing and Supporting Microsoft Exchange Server 5.0, #70-076

   OR Implementing and Supporting Microsoft Exchange Server 5.5, #70-081

◆ Implementing and Supporting Microsoft Proxy Server 1.0, #70-078

   OR Implementing and Supporting Microsoft Proxy Server 2.0, #70-088

◆ Implementing and Supporting Microsoft SNA Server 4.0, #70-085

How to Become a Microsoft Certified Solution Developer

The MCSD certification has undergone substantial revision. Listed below are the requirements for the new track (available fourth quarter 1998) as well as the old.

New Track

For the new track, you must pass three core exams and one elective exam.

Core Exams

The core exams are as follows. You must pass one exam in each of the following groups:

Desktop Applications Development (one required)

◆ Designing and Implementing Desktop Applications with Microsoft Visual C++ 6.0, #70-016

 OR Designing and Implementing Desktop Applications with Microsoft Visual FoxPro 6.0, #70-156

 OR Designing and Implementing Desktop Applications with Microsoft Visual Basic 6.0, #70-176

Distributed Applications Development (one required)

◆ Designing and Implementing Distributed Applications with Microsoft Visual C++ 6.0, #70-015

 OR Designing and Implementing Distributed Applications with Microsoft Visual FoxPro 6.0, #70-155

 OR Designing and Implementing Distributed Applications with Microsoft Visual Basic 6.0, #70-175

Solution Architecture (required)

◆ Analyzing Requirements and Defining Solution Architectures, #70-100

Elective Exam

You must pass one of the following elective exams:

◆ Designing and Implementing Distributed Applications with Microsoft Visual C++ 6.0, #70-015

◆ Designing and Implementing Desktop Applications with Microsoft Visual C++ 6.0, #70-016

◆ Designing and Implementing Data Warehouses with Microsoft SQL Server 7.0, #70-019

◆ Developing Applications with C++ Using the Microsoft Foundation Class Library, #70-024

◆ Implementing OLE in Microsoft Foundation Class Applications, #70-025

◆ Implementing a Database Design on Microsoft SQL Server 6.5, #70-027

◆ Implementing a Database Design on Microsoft SQL Server 7.0, #70-029

◆ Designing and Implementing Web Sites with Microsoft FrontPage 98, #70-055

◆ Designing and Implementing Commerce Solutions with Microsoft Site Server 3.0, Commerce Edition, #70-057

◆ Programming with Microsoft Visual Basic 4.0, #70-065*

◆ Application Development with Microsoft Access for Windows 95 and the Microsoft Access Developer's Toolkit, #70-069

◆ Designing and Implementing Solutions with Microsoft Office 2000 and Microsoft Visual Basic for Applications, #70-091

◆ Designing and Implementing Database Applications with Microsoft Access 2000, #70-097

◆ Designing and Implementing Collaborative Solutions with Microsoft Outlook 2000 and Microsoft Exchange Server 5.5, #70-105

◆ Designing and Implementing Web Solutions with Microsoft Visual InterDev 6.0, #70-152

◆ Designing and Implementing Distributed Applications with Microsoft Visual FoxPro 6.0, #70-155

◆ Designing and Implementing Desktop Applications with Microsoft Visual FoxPro 6.0, #70-156

◆ Developing Applications with Microsoft Visual Basic 5.0, #70-165

◆ Designing and Implementing Distributed Applications with Microsoft Visual Basic 6.0, #70-175

◆ Designing and Implementing Desktop Applications with Microsoft Visual Basic 6.0, #70-176

Old Track

For the old track, you must pass two core technology exams and two elective exams for MCSD certification. The following lists show the required technology exams and elective exams needed for MCSD certification.

Core Exams

You must pass the following two core technology exams to qualify for MCSD certification:

◆ Microsoft Windows Architecture I, #70-160*

◆ Microsoft Windows Architecture II, #70-161*

Elective Exams

You must also pass two of the following elective exams to become an MSCD:

◆ Designing and Implementing Distributed Applications with Microsoft Visual C++ 6.0, #70-015

◆ Designing and Implementing Desktop Applications with Microsoft Visual C++ 6.0, #70-016

◆ Designing and Implementing Data Warehouses with Microsoft SQL Server 7.0, #70-019

◆ Microsoft SQL Server 4.2 Database Implementation, #70-021*

  OR Implementing a Database Design on Microsoft SQL Server 6.5, #70-027

  OR Implementing a Database Design on Microsoft SQL Server 7.0, #70-029

◆ Developing Applications with C++ Using the Microsoft Foundation Class Library, #70-024

◆ Implementing OLE in Microsoft Foundation Class Applications, #70-025

◆ Programming with Microsoft Visual Basic 4.0, #70-065

  OR Developing Applications with Microsoft Visual Basic 5.0, #70-165

  OR Designing and Implementing Distributed Applications with Microsoft Visual Basic 6.0, #70-175

◆ Designing and Implementing Desktop Applications with Microsoft Visual Basic 6.0, #70-176

◆ Microsoft Access 2.0 for Windows-Application Development, #70-051*

OR Microsoft Access for Windows 95 and the Microsoft Access Development Toolkit, #70-069

OR Designing and Implementing Database Applications with Microsoft Access 2000, #70-097

◆ Developing Applications with Microsoft Excel 5.0 Using Visual Basic for Applications, #70-052*

◆ Programming in Microsoft Visual FoxPro 3.0 for Windows, #70-054*

OR Designing and Implementing Distributed Applications with Microsoft Visual FoxPro 6.0, #70-155

OR Designing and Implementing Desktop Applications with Microsoft Visual FoxPro 6.0, #70-156

◆ Designing and Implementing Web Sites with Microsoft FrontPage 98, #70-055

◆ Designing and Implementing Commerce Solutions with Microsoft Site Server 3.0, Commerce Edition, #70-057

◆ Designing and Implementing Solutions with Microsoft Office (code-named Office 9) and Microsoft Visual Basic for Applications, #70-091

◆ Designing and Implementing Collaborative Solutions with Microsoft Outlook 2000 and Microsoft Exchange Server 5.5, #70-105

◆ Designing and Implementing Web Solutions with Microsoft Visual InterDev 6.0, #70-152

Becoming a Microsoft Certified Trainer

To fully understand the requirements and process for becoming an MCT, you need to obtain the Microsoft Certified Trainer Guide document from the following WWW site:

```
http://www.microsoft.com/mcp/certstep/mct.htm
```

At this site, you can read the document as a Web page or display and download it as a Word file. The MCT Guide explains the process for becoming an MCT. The general steps for the MCT certification are as follows:

1. Complete and mail a Microsoft Certified Trainer application to Microsoft. You must include proof of your skills for presenting instructional material. The options for doing so are described in the MCT Guide.

2. Obtain and study the Microsoft Trainer Kit for the *Microsoft Official Curricula* (MOC) courses for which you want to be certified. Microsoft Trainer Kits can be ordered by calling 800-688-0496 in North America. Those of you in other regions should review the MCT Guide for information on how to order a Trainer Kit.

3. Take and pass any required prerequisite MCP exam(s) to measure your current technical knowledge.

4. Prepare to teach a MOC course. Begin by attending the MOC course for which you want to be certified. This is required so that you understand how the course is structured, how labs are completed, and how the course flows.

5. Pass any additional exam requirement(s) to measure any additional product knowledge that pertains to the course.

6. Submit your course preparation checklist to Microsoft so that your additional accreditation may be processed and reflect on your transcript.

If you are interested in becoming an MCT, you can obtain more information by visiting the Microsoft Certified Training WWW site at http://www.microsoft.com/train_cert/mct/ or by calling 800-688-0496.

> **WARNING**
>
> You should consider the preceding steps a general overview of the MCT certification process. The precise steps that you need to take are described in detail on the Web site mentioned earlier. Do not misinterpret the preceding steps as the exact process you must undergo.

What's on the CD-ROM

This appendix is a brief rundown of what you'll find on the CD-ROM that comes with this book. For a more detailed description of the newly developed *ExamGear, Training Guide Edition* exam simulation software, see Appendix D, "Using the ExamGear, Training Guide Edition Software." All items on the CD-ROM are easily accessible from the simple interface. In addition to *ExamGear, Training Guide Edition*, the CD-ROM includes the electronic version of the book in *Portable Document Format* (PDF), several utility and application programs, and a complete listing of the test objectives and where they are covered in the book.

EXAMGEAR, TRAINING GUIDE EDITION

ExamGear is an exam environment developed exclusively for New Riders Publishing. It is, we believe, the best exam software available. In addition to providing a means of evaluating your knowledge of the Training Guide material, *ExamGear, Training Guide Edition* features several innovations that help you to improve your mastery of the subject matter.

For example, the practice tests allow you to check your score by exam area or category to determine which topics you need to study more. In another mode, *ExamGear, Training Guide Edition* allows you to obtain immediate feedback on your responses in the form of explanations for the correct and incorrect answers.

Although *ExamGear, Training Guide Edition* exhibits most of the full functionality of the retail version of *ExamGear,* including the exam format and question types, this special version is written to the Training Guide content. It is designed to aid you in assessing how well you understand the Training Guide material and enable you to experience most of the question formats you will see on the actual exam. It is not as complete a simulation of the exam as the full *ExamGear* retail product. It also does not include some of the features of the full retail product, such as access to the mentored discussion groups. However, it serves as an excellent method for assessing your knowledge of the Training Guide content and gives you the experience of taking an electronic exam.

Again, for a more complete description of *ExamGear, Training Guide Edition* features, see Appendix D, "Using the ExamGear, Training Guide Edition Software."

EXCLUSIVE ELECTRONIC VERSION OF TEXT

The CD-ROM also contains the electronic version of this book in PDF. The electronic version comes complete with all figures as they appear in the book. You will find that the search capabilities of the reader come in handy for study and review purposes.

COPYRIGHT INFORMATION AND DISCLAIMER

New Riders Publishing's *ExamGear* **test simulator**: Copyright ©2000 by New Riders Publishing. All rights reserved. Made in U.S.A.

Using the ExamGear, Training Guide Edition Software

This training guide includes a special version of *ExamGear*—a revolutionary new test engine that is designed to give you the best in certification exam preparation. *ExamGear* offers sample and practice exams for many of today's most in-demand technical certifications. This special Training Guide edition is included with this book as a tool to utilize in assessing your knowledge of the Training Guide material while also providing you with the experience of taking an electronic exam.

In the rest of this appendix, we describe in detail what *ExamGear, Training Guide Edition* is, how it works, and what it can do to help you prepare for the exam. Note that although the Training Guide edition includes nearly all the test simulation functions of the complete, retail version, the questions focus on the Training Guide content rather than on simulating the actual Microsoft exam. Also, this version does not offer the same degree of online support that the full product does.

EXAM SIMULATION

One of the main functions of *ExamGear, Training Guide Edition* is exam simulation. To prepare you to take the actual vendor certification exam, the Training Guide edition of this test engine is designed to offer the most effective exam simulation available.

Question Quality

The questions provided in the *ExamGear, Training Guide Edition* simulations are written to high standards of technical accuracy. The questions tap the content of the Training Guide chapters and help you review and assess your knowledge before you take the actual exam.

Interface Design

The *ExamGear, Training Guide Edition* exam simulation interface provides you with the experience of taking an electronic exam. This enables you to effectively prepare for taking the actual exam by making the test experience a familiar one. Using this test simulation can help eliminate the sense of surprise or anxiety that you might experience in the testing center, because you will already be acquainted with computerized testing.

STUDY TOOLS

ExamGear provides you with several learning tools to help prepare you for the actual certification exam.

Effective Learning Environment

The *ExamGear, Training Guide Edition* interface provides a learning environment that not only tests you through the computer, but also teaches the material you need to know to pass the certification exam. Each question comes with a detailed explanation of the correct answer and provides reasons why the other options were incorrect. This information helps to reinforce the knowledge you have already and also provides practical information you can use on the job.

Automatic Progress Tracking

ExamGear, Training Guide Edition automatically tracks your progress as you work through the test questions. From the Item Review tab (discussed in detail later in this appendix), you can see at a glance how well you are scoring by objective, by unit, or on a question-by-question basis (see Figure D.1). You can also configure *ExamGear* to drill you on the skills you need to work on most.

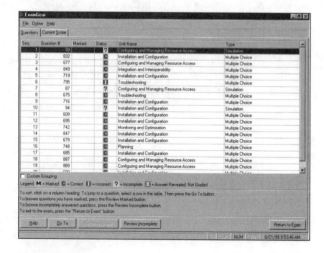

FIGURE D.1
Item review.

HOW EXAMGEAR, TRAINING GUIDE EDITION WORKS

ExamGear comprises two main elements: the interface and the database. The *interface* is the part of the program that you use to study and to run practice tests. The *database* stores all the question-and-answer data.

Interface

The *ExamGear, Training Guide Edition* interface is designed to be easy to use and provides the most effective study method available. The interface enables you to select from the following modes:

◆ **Study Mode.** In this mode, you can select the number of questions you want to see and the time you want to allow for the test. You can select questions from all the chapters or from specific chapters. This enables you to reinforce your knowledge in a specific area or strengthen your knowledge in areas pertaining to a specific objective. During the exam, you can display the correct answer to each question along with an explanation of why it is correct.

◆ **Practice Exam.** In this mode, you take an exam that is designed to simulate the actual certification exam. Questions are selected from all test-objective groups. The number of questions selected and the time allowed are set to match those parameters of the actual certification exam.

◆ **Adaptive Exam.** In this mode, you take an exam simulation using the adaptive testing technique. Questions are taken from all test-objective groups. The questions are presented in a way that ensures your mastery of all the test objectives. After you have a passing score or if you reach a point where it is statistically impossible for you to pass, the exam is ended. This method provides a rapid assessment of your readiness for the actual exam.

Database

The *ExamGear, Training Guide Edition* database stores a group of test questions along with answers and explanations. At least three databases are included for each Training Guide edition product. One includes the questions from the ends of the chapters. Another includes the questions from the Practice Exam. The third is a database of new questions that have not appeared in the book. Additional exam databases may also be available for purchase online and are simple to download. Look ahead to the section "Obtaining Updates" in this appendix to find out how to download and activate additional databases.

INSTALLING AND REGISTERING EXAMGEAR, TRAINING GUIDE EDITION

This section provides instructions for *ExamGear, Training Guide Edition* installation and describes the process and benefits of registering your Training Guide edition product.

Requirements

ExamGear requires a computer with the following:

◆ Microsoft Windows 95, Windows 98, Windows NT 4.0, or Windows 2000.

 A Pentium or later processor is recommended.

◆ Microsoft's Internet Explorer 4.01 or later version.

 Internet Explorer 4.01 (or a later version) must be installed. (Even if you use a different browser, you still need to have Internet Explorer 4.01 or later installed.)

◆ A minimum of 16MB of RAM.

 As with any Windows application, the more memory, the better your performance.

◆ A connection to the Internet.

 An Internet connection is not required for the software to work, but it is required for online registration, product updates, downloading bonus question sets, and for unlocking other exams. These processes are described in more detail later.

Installing ExamGear, Training Guide Edition

Install *ExamGear, Training Guide Edition* by running the Setup program that you found on the *ExamGear, Training Guide Edition* CD. Follow these instructions to install the Training Guide edition on your computer:

1. Insert the CD in your CD-ROM drive. The Autorun feature of Windows should launch the software. If you have Autorun disabled, click Start, and choose Run. Go to the root directory of the CD and choose START.EXE. Click Open and OK.

2. Click the button in the circle, and you see the welcome screen. From here you can install ExamGear. Click the ExamGear button to begin installation.

3. The Installation Wizard appears onscreen and prompts you with instructions to complete the installation. Select a directory on which to install ExamGear, Training Guide Edition (the Installation Wizard defaults to C:\Program Files\ExamGear).

4. The Installation Wizard copies the ExamGear, Training Guide Edition files to your hard drive, adds ExamGear, Training Guide Edition to your Program menu, adds values to your Registry, and installs test engine's DLLs to the appropriate system folders. To ensure that the process was successful, the Setup program finishes by running ExamGear, Training Guide Edition.

5. The Installation Wizard logs the installation process and stores this information in a file named INSTALL.LOG. This log file is used by the uninstall process in the event that you choose to remove ExamGear, Training Guide Edition from your computer. Because the ExamGear installation adds Registry keys and DLL files to your computer, it is important to uninstall the program appropriately (see the section "Removing ExamGear, Training Guide Edition from Your Computer").

Registering ExamGear, Training Guide Edition

The Product Registration Wizard appears when *ExamGear, Training Guide Edition* is started for the first time, and *ExamGear* checks at startup to see whether you are registered. If you are not registered, the main menu is hidden, and a Product Registration Wizard appears. Remember that your computer must have an Internet connection to complete the Product Registration Wizard.

The first page of the Product Registration Wizard details the benefits of registration; however, you can always elect not to register. The Show This Message at Startup Until I Register option enables you to decide whether the registration screen should appear every time *ExamGear, Training Guide Edition* is started. If you click the Cancel button, you return to the main menu. You can register at any time by selecting Online, Registration from the main menu.

The registration process is composed of a simple form for entering your personal information, including your name and address. You are asked for your level of experience with the product you are testing on and whether you purchased *ExamGear, Training Guide Edition* from a retail store or over the Internet. The information will be used by our software designers and marketing department to provide us with feedback about the usability and usefulness of this product. It takes only a few seconds to fill out and transmit the registration data. A confirmation dialog box appears when registration is complete.

After you have registered and transmitted this information to New Riders, the registration option is removed from the pull-down menus.

Registration Benefits

Remember that registration allows you access to download updates from our FTP site using *ExamGear, Training Guide Edition* (see the later section "Obtaining Updates").

Removing ExamGear, Training Guide Edition from Your Computer

In the event that you elect to remove the *ExamGear, Training Guide Edition* product from your computer, an uninstall process has been included to ensure that it is removed from your system safely and completely. Follow these instructions to remove *ExamGear* from your computer:

1. Click Start, Settings, Control Panel.

2. Double-click the Add/Remove Programs icon.

3. You are presented with a list of software that is installed on your computer. Select ExamGear, Training Guide Edition from the list and click the Add/Remove button. The ExamGear, Training Guide Edition software is then removed from your computer.

It is important that the INSTALL.LOG file be present in the directory where you have installed *ExamGear, Training Guide Edition* should you ever choose to uninstall the product. Do not delete this file. The INSTALL.LOG file is used by the uninstall process to safely remove the files and Registry settings that were added to your computer by the installation process.

USING EXAMGEAR, TRAINING GUIDE EDITION

ExamGear is designed to be user friendly and very intuitive, eliminating the need for you to learn some confusing piece of software just to practice answering questions. Because the software has a smooth learning curve, your time is maximized because you start practicing almost immediately.

General Description of How the Software Works

ExamGear has three modes of operation: Study Mode, Practice Exam, and Adaptive Exam (see Figure D.2).

All three sections have the same easy-to-use interface. Using Study Mode, you can hone your knowledge as well as your test-taking abilities through the use of the Show Answers option. While you are taking the test, you can expose the answers along with a brief description of why the given answers are right or wrong. This gives you the ability to better understand the material presented.

The Practice Exam section has many of the same options as Study Mode, but you cannot reveal the answers. This way, you have a more traditional testing environment with which to practice.

The Adaptive Exam questions continuously monitor your expertise in each tested topic area. If you reach a point at which you either pass or fail, the software ends the examination. As in the Practice Exam, you cannot reveal the answers.

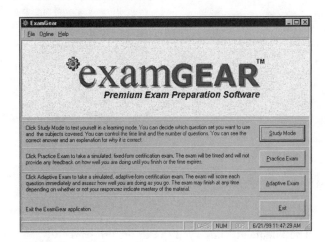

FIGURE D.2
The opening screen offers three testing modes.

Menu Options

The *ExamGear, Training Guide Edition* interface has an easy-to-use menu that provides the following options:

Menu	Command	Description
File	Print	Prints the current screen.
	Print Setup	Allows you to select the printer.
	Exit ExamGear	Exits the program.
Online	Registration	Starts the Registration Wizard and allows you to register online. This menu option is removed after you have successfully registered the product.
	Check for Product Updates	Downloads product catalog for Web-based updates.
	Web Browser	Opens the Web browser. It appears like this on the main menu, but more options appear after the browser is opened.
Help	Contents	Opens *ExamGear, Training Guide Edition's* help file.
	About	Displays information about *ExamGear, Training Guide Edition*, including serial number, registered owner, and so on.

File

The File menu allows you to exit the program and configure print options.

Online

In the Online menu, you can register *ExamGear, Training Guide Edition*, check for product updates (update the *ExamGear* executable as well as check for free, updated question sets), and surf Web pages. The Online menu is always available, except when you are taking a test.

Registration

Registration is free and allows you access updates. Registration is the first task that *ExamGear, Training Guide Edition* asks you to perform. You will not have access to the free product updates if you do not register.

Check for Product Updates

This option takes you to *ExamGear, Training Guide Edition's* Web site, where you can update the software. Registration is required for this option to be available. You must also be connected to the Internet to use this option. The *ExamGear* Web site lists the options that have been made available since your version of *ExamGear* was installed on your computer.

Web Browser

This option provides a convenient way to start your Web browser and connect to the New Riders Web site while you are working in *ExamGear, Training Guide Edition*. Click the Exit button to leave the Web browser and return to the *ExamGear* interface.

Help

As it suggests, this menu option gives you access to *ExamGear's* help system. It also provides important information like your serial number, software version, and so on.

Starting a Study Mode Session

Study Mode enables you to control the test in ways that actual certification exams do not allow:

◆ You can set your own time limits.

◆ You can concentrate on selected skill areas (units).

◆ You can reveal answers or have each response graded immediately with feedback.

◆ You can restrict the questions you see again to those missed or those answered correctly a given number of times.

◆ You can control the order in which questions are presented—random order or in order by skill area (unit).

To begin testing in Study Mode, click the Study Mode button from the main Interface screen. You are presented with the Study Mode configuration page (see Figure D.3).

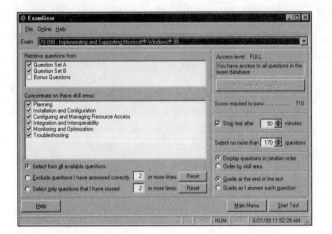

FIGURE D.3
The Study Mode configuration page.

At the top of the Study Mode configuration screen, you see the Exam drop-down list. This list shows the activated exam that you have purchased with your *ExamGear, Training Guide Edition* product, as well as any other exams you may have downloaded or any Preview exams that were shipped with your version of *ExamGear*. Select the exam with which you want to practice from the drop-down list.

Below the Exam drop-down list, you see the questions that are available for the selected exam. Each exam has at least one question set. You can select the individual

question set or any combination of the question sets if there is more than one available for the selected exam.

Below the Question Set list is a list of skill areas or chapters on which you can concentrate. These skill areas or chapters reflect the units of exam objectives defined by Microsoft for the exam. Within each skill area you will find several exam objectives. You can select a single skill area or chapter to focus on, or you can select any combination of the available skill areas/chapters to customize the exam to your individual needs.

In addition to specifying which question sets and skill areas you want to test yourself on, you can also define which questions are included in the test based on your previous progress working with the test. *ExamGear, Training Guide Edition* automatically tracks your progress with the available questions. When configuring the Study Mode options, you can opt to view all the questions available within the question sets and skill areas you have selected, or you can limit the questions presented. Choose from the following options:

◆ **Select from All Available Questions.** This option causes *ExamGear, Training Guide Edition* to present all available questions from the selected question sets and skill areas.

◆ **Exclude Questions I Have Answered Correctly *X* or More Times.** *ExamGear* offers you the option to exclude questions that you have previously answered correctly. You can specify how many times you want to answer a question correctly before *ExamGear* considers you to have mastered it (the default is two times).

◆ **Select Only Questions That I Have Missed *X* or More Times.** This option configures *ExamGear, Training Guide Edition* to drill you only on questions that you have missed repeatedly. You may specify how many times you must miss a question before *ExamGear* determines that you have not mastered it (the default is two times).

At any time, you can reset *ExamGear, Training Guide Edition*'s tracking information by clicking the Reset button for the feature you want to clear.

At the top-right side of the Study Mode configuration sheet, you can see your access level to the question sets for the selected exam. Access levels are either Full or Preview. For a detailed explanation of each of these access levels, see the section "Obtaining Updates" in this appendix.

Under your access level, you see the score required to pass the selected exam. Below the required score, you can select whether the test will be timed and how much time will be allowed to complete the exam. Select the Stop Test After 90 Minutes check box to set a time limit for the exam. Enter the number of minutes you want to allow for the test. (The default is 90 minutes.) Deselecting this check box allows you to take an exam with no time limit.

You can also configure the number of questions included in the exam. The default number of questions changes with the specific exam you have selected. Enter the number of questions you want to include in the exam in the Select No More than *X* Questions option.

You can configure the order in which *ExamGear, Training Guide Edition* presents the exam questions. Select from the following options:

◆ **Display Questions in Random Order.**
This option is the default option. When selected, it causes *ExamGear, Training Guide Edition* to present the questions in random order throughout the exam.

◆ **Order by Skill Area.** This option causes *ExamGear* to group the questions presented in the exam by skill area. All questions for each selected skill area are presented in succession. The test progresses from one selected skill area to the next, until all the questions from each selected skill area have been presented.

ExamGear offers two options for scoring your exams. Select one of the following options:

◆ **Grade at the End of the Test.** This option configures *ExamGear, Training Guide Edition* to score your test after you have been presented with all the selected exam questions. You can reveal correct answers to a question; but if you do, that question is not scored.

◆ **Grade as I Answer Each Question.** This option configures *ExamGear* to grade each question as you answer it, providing you with instant feedback as you take the test. All questions are scored unless you click the Show Answer button before completing the question.

You can return to the *ExamGear, Training Guide Edition* main startup screen from the Study Mode configuration screen by clicking the Main Menu button. If you need assistance configuring the Study Mode exam options, click the Help button for configuration instructions.

When you have finished configuring all the exam options, click the Start Test button to begin the exam.

Starting Practice Exams and Adaptive Exams

This section describes practice exams and adaptive exams, defines the differences between these exam options and the Study Mode option, and provides instructions for starting them.

Differences Between the Practice and Adaptive Exams and Study Mode

Question screens in the practice and adaptive exams are identical to those found in Study Mode, except that the

Show Answer, Grade Answer, and Item Review buttons are not available while you are in the process of taking a practice or adaptive exam. The practice exam provides you with a report screen at the end of the exam. The adaptive exam gives you a brief message indicating whether you've passed or failed the exam.

When taking a practice exam, the Item Review screen is not available until you have answered all the questions. This is consistent with the behavior of most vendors' current certification exams. In Study Mode, Item Review is available at any time.

When the exam timer expires, or if you click the End Exam button, the Examination Score Report screen comes up.

Starting an Exam

From the *ExamGear, Training Guide Edition* main menu screen, select the type of exam you want to run. Click the Practice Exam or Adaptive Exam button to begin the corresponding exam type.

What Is an Adaptive Exam?

To make the certification testing process more efficient and valid and therefore make the certification itself more valuable, some vendors in the industry are using a testing technique called *adaptive testing*. In an adaptive exam, the exam "adapts" to your abilities by varying the difficulty level of the questions presented to you.

The first question in an adaptive exam is typically an easy one. If you answer it correctly, you are presented with a slightly more difficult question. If you answer that question correctly, the next question you see is even more difficult. If you answer the question incorrectly, however, the exam "adapts" to your skill level by presenting you with another question of equal or lesser difficulty on the same subject. If you answer that question correctly, the test begins to increase the difficulty level again. You must correctly answer several questions at a predetermined difficulty level to pass the exam. After you have done this successfully, the exam is ended and scored. If you do not reach the required level of difficulty within a predetermined time (typically 30 minutes) the exam is ended and scored.

Why Do Vendors Use Adaptive Exams?

Many vendors who offer technical certifications have adopted the adaptive testing technique. They have found that it is an effective way to measure a candidate's mastery of the test material in as little time as necessary. This reduces the scheduling demands on the test taker and allows the testing center to offer more tests per test station than they could with longer, more traditional exams. In addition, test security is greater, and this increases the validity of the exam process.

Studying for Adaptive Exams

Studying for adaptive exams is no different from studying for traditional exams. You should make sure that you have thoroughly covered all the material for each of the test objectives specified by the certification exam vendor. As with any other exam, when you take an adaptive exam, either you know the material or you don't. If you are well prepared, you will be able to pass the exam. *ExamGear, Training Guide Edition* allows you to familiarize yourself with the adaptive exam testing technique. This will help eliminate any anxiety you might experience from this testing technique and allow you to focus on learning the actual exam material.

ExamGear's Adaptive Exam

The method used to score the adaptive exam requires a large pool of questions. For this reason, you cannot use this exam in Preview mode. The adaptive exam is presented in much the same way as the practice exam. When you click the Start Test button, you begin answering questions. The adaptive exam does not allow item review, and it does not allow you to mark questions to skip and answer later. You must answer each question when it is presented.

Assumptions

This section describes the assumptions made when designing the behavior of the *ExamGear, Training Guide Edition* adaptive exam.

◆ You fail the test if you fail any chapter or unit, earn a failing overall score, or reach a threshold at which it is statistically impossible for you to pass the exam.

◆ You can fail or pass a test without cycling through all the questions.

◆ The overall score for the adaptive exam is Pass or Fail. However, to evaluate user responses dynamically, percentage scores are recorded for units and the overall score.

Algorithm Assumptions

This section describes the assumptions used in designing the *ExamGear, Training Guide Edition* adaptive exam scoring algorithm.

Unit Scores

You fail a unit (and the exam) if any unit score falls below 66%.

Overall Scores

To pass the exam, you must pass all units and achieve an overall score of 86% or higher.

You fail if the overall score percentage is less than or equal to 85% or if any unit score is less than 66%.

Inconclusive Scores

If your overall score is between 67 and 85%, it is considered to be *inconclusive*. Additional questions will be asked until you pass or fail or until it becomes statistically impossible to pass without asking more than the maximum number of questions allowed.

Question Types and How to Answer Them

Because certification exams from different vendors vary, you will face many types of questions on any given exam. *ExamGear, Training Guide Edition* presents you with different question types to allow you to become familiar with the various ways an actual exam may test your knowledge. The Solution Architectures exam, in particular, offers a unique exam format and utilizes question types other than multiple choice. This version of *ExamGear* includes cases—extensive problem descriptions running several pages in length, followed by a number of questions specific to that case. Microsoft refers to these case/question collections as *testlets*. This version of *ExamGear, Training Guide Edition* also includes regular questions that are not attached to a case study. We include these question types to make taking the actual exam easier because you will already be familiar with the steps required to answer each question type. This section describes each of the question types presented by *ExamGear* and provides instructions for answering each type.

Multiple Choice

Most of the questions you see on a certification exam are multiple choice (see Figure D.4). This question type asks you to select an answer from the list provided. Sometimes you must select only one answer, often indicated by answers preceded by option buttons (round selection buttons). At other times, multiple correct answers are possible, indicated by check boxes preceding the possible answer combinations.

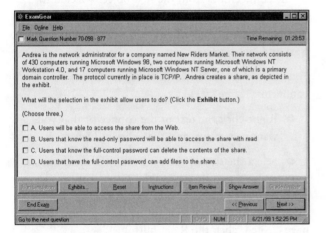

FIGURE D.4
A typical multiple-choice question.

You can use three methods to select an answer:

◆ Click the option button or check box next to the answer. If more than one correct answer to a question is possible, the answers will have check boxes next to them. If only one correct answer to a question is possible, each answer will have an option button next to it. *ExamGear, Training Guide Edition* prompts you with the number of answers you must select.

◆ Click the text of the answer.

◆ Press the alphabetic key that corresponds to the answer.

You can use any one of three methods to clear an option button:

◆ Click another option button.

◆ Click the text of another answer.

◆ Press the alphabetic key that corresponds to another answer.

You can use any one of three methods to clear a check box:

◆ Click the check box next to the selected answer.

◆ Click the text of the selected answer.

◆ Press the alphabetic key that corresponds to the selected answer.

To clear all answers, click the Reset button.

Remember that some of the questions have multiple answers that are correct. Do not let this throw you off. The *multiple-correct* questions do not have one answer that is more correct than another. In the *single-correct* format, only one answer is correct. *ExamGear, Training Guide Edition* prompts you with the number of answers you must select.

Drag and Drop

One form of drag-and-drop question is called a *drop-and-connect* question. These questions present you with a number of objects and connectors. The question prompts you to create relationships between the objects by using the connectors. The gray squares on the left side of the question window are the objects you can select. The connectors are listed on the right side of the question window in the Connectors box. An example is shown in Figure D.5.

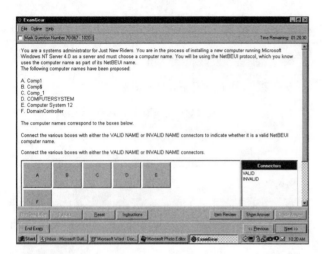

FIGURE D.5
A typical drop-and-connect question.

FIGURE D.6
The error message.

To select an object, click it with the mouse. When an object is selected, it changes color from a gray box to a white box. To drag an object, select it by clicking it with the left mouse button and holding the left mouse button down. You can move (or drag) the object to another area on the screen by moving the mouse while holding the left mouse button down.

To create a relationship between two objects, take the following actions:

1. Select an object and drag it to an available area on the screen.

2. Select another object and drag it to a location near where you dragged the first object.

3. Select the connector that you want to place between the two objects. The relationship should now appear complete. Note that to create a relationship, you must have two objects selected. If you try to select a connector without first selecting two objects, you are presented with an error message like that illustrated in Figure D.6.

Initially, the direction of the relationship established by the connector is from the first object selected to the second object selected. To change the direction of the connector, right-click the connector and choose Reverse Connection.

You can use either of two methods to remove the connector:

◆ Right-click the text of the connector that you want to remove, and then choose Delete.

◆ Select the text of the connector that you want to remove, and then press the Delete key.

To remove from the screen all the relationships you have created, click the Reset button.

Keep in mind that connectors can be used multiple times. If you move connected objects, it will not change the relationship between the objects; to remove the relationship between objects, you must remove the connector that joins them. When *ExamGear, Training Guide Edition* scores a drag-and-drop question, only objects with connectors to other objects are scored.

Another form of drag-and-drop question is called the *select-and-place* question. Instead of creating a diagram as you do with the drop-and-connect question, you are asked a question about a diagram. You then drag and drop labels onto the diagram in order to correctly answer the question.

Ordered-List Questions

In the *ordered-list* question type (see Figure D.7), you are presented with a number of items and are asked to perform two tasks:

1. Build an answer list from items on the list of choices.

2. Put the items in a particular order.

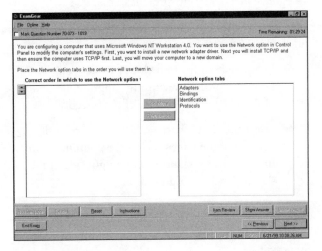

FIGURE D.7
A typical ordered-list question.

You can use any one of the following three methods to add an item to the answer list:

◆ Drag the item from the list of choices on the right side of the screen to the answer list on the left side of the screen.

◆ From the available items on the right side of the screen, double-click the item you want to add.

◆ From the available items on the right side of the screen, select the item you want to add; then click the Move button.

To remove an item from the answer list, you can use any one of the following four methods:

◆ Drag the item you want to remove from the answer list on the left side of the screen back to the list of choices on the right side of the screen.

◆ On the left side of the screen, double-click the item you want to remove from the answer list.

◆ On the left side of the screen, select the item you want to remove from the answer list, and then click the Remove button.

◆ On the left side of the screen, select the item you want to remove from the answer list, and then press the Delete key.

To remove all items from the answer list, click the Reset button.

If you need to change the order of the items in the answer list, you can do so using either of the following two methods:

◆ Drag each item to the appropriate location in the answer list.

◆ In the answer list, select the item that you want to move, and then click the up or down arrow button to move the item.

Keep in mind that items in the list can be selected twice. You may find that an ordered-list question will ask you to list in the correct order the steps required to perform a certain task. Certain steps may need to be performed more than once during the process. Don't think that after you have selected a list item, it is no longer available. If you need to select a list item more than once, you can simply select that item at each appropriate place as you construct your list.

Ordered-Tree Questions

The *ordered-tree* question type (see Figure D.8) presents you with a number of items and prompts you to create a tree structure from those items. The tree structure includes two or three levels of nodes.

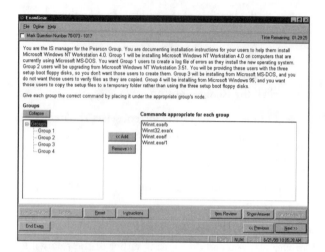

FIGURE D.8
A typical ordered-tree question.

An item in the list of choices can be added only to the appropriate node level. If you attempt to add one of the list choices to an inappropriate node level, you are presented with the error message shown in Figure D.9

FIGURE D.9
The Invalid Destination Node error message.

Like the ordered-list question, realize that any item in the list can be selected twice. If you need to select a list item more than once, you can simply select that item for the appropriate node as you construct your tree.

Also realize that not every tree question actually requires order to the lists under each node. Think of them as simply tree questions rather than ordered-tree questions. Such questions are just asking you to categorize hierarchically. Order is not an issue.

You can use either of the following two methods to add an item to the tree:

◆ Drag the item from the list of choices on the right side of the screen to the appropriate node of the tree on the left side of the screen.

◆ Select the appropriate node of the tree on the left side of the screen. Select the appropriate item from the list of choices on the right side of the screen. Click the Add button.

You can use either of the following two methods to remove an item from the tree:

◆ Drag an item from the tree to the list of choices.

◆ Select the item and click the Remove button.

To remove from the tree structure all the items you have added, click the Reset button.

Simulations

Simulation questions (see Figure D.10) require you to actually perform a task.

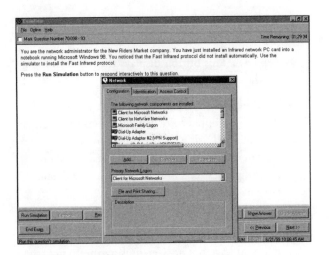

FIGURE D.10
A typical simulation question.

The main screen describes a situation and prompts you to provide a solution. When you are ready to proceed, you click the Run Simulation button in the lower-left corner. A screen or window appears on which you perform the solution. This window simulates the actual software that you would use to perform the required task in the real world. When a task requires several steps to complete, the simulator displays all the necessary screens to allow you to complete the task. When you have provided your answer by completing all the steps necessary to perform the required task, you can click the OK button to proceed to the next question.

You can return to any simulation to modify your answer. Your actions in the simulation are recorded, and the simulation appears exactly as you left it.

Simulation questions can be reset to their original state by clicking the Reset button.

Hot Spot Questions

Hot spot questions (see Figure D.11) ask you to correctly identify an item by clicking an area of the graphic or diagram displayed. To respond to the question, position the mouse cursor over a graphic. Then press the right mouse button to indicate your selection. To select another area on the graphic, you do not need to deselect the first one. Just click another region in the image.

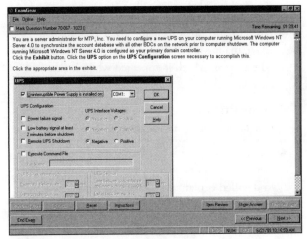

FIGURE D.11
A typical hot spot question.

Standard ExamGear, Training Guide Edition Options

Regardless of question type, a consistent set of clickable buttons enables you to navigate and interact with questions. The following list describes the function of each of the buttons you may see. Depending on the question type, some of the buttons will be grayed out and will be inaccessible. Buttons that are appropriate to the question type are active.

◆ **Run Simulation.** This button is enabled if the question supports a simulation. Clicking this button begins the simulation process.

◆ **Exhibits.** This button is enabled if exhibits are provided to support the question. An *exhibit* is an image, video, sound, or text file that provides supplemental information needed to answer the question. If a question has more than one exhibit, a dialog box appears, listing exhibits by name. If only one exhibit exists, the file is opened immediately when you click the Exhibits button.

◆ **Reset.** This button clears any selections you have made and returns the question window to the state in which it appeared when it was first displayed.

◆ **Instructions.** This button displays instructions for interacting with the current question type.

◆ **Item Review.** This button leaves the question window and opens the Item Review screen. For a detailed explanation of the Item Review screen, see the "Item Review" section later in this appendix.

◆ **Show Answer.** This option displays the correct answer with an explanation of why it is correct. If you choose this option, the current question will not be scored.

◆ **Grade Answer.** If Grade at the End of the Test is selected as a configuration option, this button is disabled. It is enabled when Grade as I Answer Each Question is selected as a configuration option. Clicking this button grades the current question immediately. An explanation of the correct answer is provided, just as if the Show Answer button were pressed. The question is graded, however.

◆ **End Exam.** This button ends the exam and displays the Examination Score Report screen.

◆ **<< Previous.** This button displays the previous question on the exam.

◆ **Next >>.** This button displays the next question on the exam.

◆ **<< Previous Marked.** This button is displayed if you have opted to review questions that you have marked using the Item Review screen. This button displays the previous marked question. Marking questions is discussed in more detail later in this appendix.

◆ **<< Previous Incomplete.** This button is displayed if you have opted to review questions that you have not answered using the Item Review screen. This button displays the previous unanswered question.

◆ **Next Marked >>.** This button is displayed if you have opted to review questions that you have marked using the Item Review screen. This button displays the next marked question. Marking questions is discussed in more detail later in this appendix.

◆ **Next Incomplete>>.** This button is displayed if you have opted to review questions, using the Item Review screen, that you have not answered. This button displays the next unanswered question.

Mark Question and Time Remaining

ExamGear provides you with two methods to aid in dealing with the time limit of the testing process. If you find that you need to skip a question or if you want to check the time remaining to complete the test, use one of the options discussed in the following sections.

Mark Question

Check this box to mark a question so that you can return to it later using the Item Review feature. The adaptive exam does not allow questions to be marked because it does not support item review.

Time Remaining

If the test is timed, the Time Remaining indicator is enabled. It counts down minutes remaining to complete the test. The adaptive exam does not offer this feature because it is not timed.

Item Review

The Item Review screen allows you to jump to any question. *ExamGear, Training Guide Edition* considers an *incomplete* question to be any unanswered question or any multiple-choice question for which the total number of required responses has not been selected. For example, if the question prompts for three answers and you selected only A and C, *ExamGear* considers the question to be incomplete.

The Item Review screen enables you to review the exam questions in different ways. You can enter one of two *browse sequences* (series of similar records): Browse Marked Questions or Browse Incomplete Questions. You can also create a custom grouping of the exam questions for review based on a number of criteria.

When using Item Review, if Show Answer was selected for a question while you were taking the exam, the question is grayed out in item review. The question can be answered again if you use the Reset button to reset the question status.

The Item Review screen contains two tabs. The Questions tab lists questions and question information in columns. The Current Score tab provides your exam score information, presented as a percentage for each unit and as a bar graph for your overall score.

The Item Review Questions Tab

The Questions tab on the Item Review screen (see Figure D.12) presents the exam questions and question information in a table. You can select any row you want by clicking in the grid. The Go To button is enabled whenever a row is selected. Clicking the Go To button displays the question on the selected row. You can also display a question by double-clicking that row.

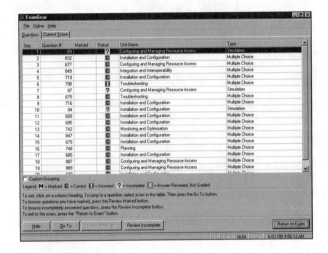

FIGURE D.12
The Questions tab on the Item Review screen.

Columns

The Questions tab contains the following six columns of information:

- ◆ **Seq.** Indicates the sequence number of the question as it was displayed in the exam.

- ◆ **Question Number.** Displays the question's identification number for easy reference.

- ◆ **Marked.** Indicates a question that you have marked using the Mark Question check box.

- ◆ **Status.** The status can be M for Marked, ? for Incomplete, C for Correct, I for Incorrect, or X for Answer Shown.

◆ **Unit Name.** The unit associated with each question.

◆ **Type.** The question type, which can be multiple choice, drag and drop, simulation, hot spot, ordered list, or ordered tree.

To resize a column, place the mouse pointer over the vertical line between column headings. When the mouse pointer changes to a set of right and left arrows, you can drag the column border to the left or right to make the column more or less wide. Simply click with the left mouse button and hold that button down while you move the column border in the desired direction.

The Item Review screen enables you to sort the questions on any of the column headings. Initially, the list of questions is sorted in descending order on the sequence number column. To sort on a different column heading, click that heading. You will see an arrow appear on the column heading indicating the direction of the sort (ascending or descending). To change the direction of the sort, click the column heading again.

The Item Review screen also allows you to create a *custom grouping*. This feature enables you to sort the questions based on any combination of criteria you prefer. For instance, you might want to review the question items sorted first by whether they were marked, then by the unit name, then by sequence number. The Custom Grouping feature allows you to do this. Start by checking the Custom Grouping check box (see Figure D.13). When you do so, the entire questions table shifts down a bit onscreen, and a message appear at the top of the table that reads `Drag a column header here to group by that column`.

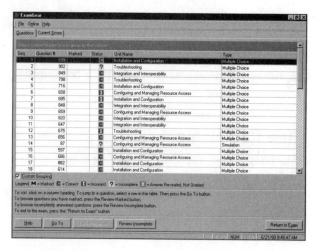

FIGURE D.13
The Custom Grouping check box allows you to create your own question sort order.

Simply click the column heading you want with the left mouse button, hold that button down, and move the mouse into the area directly above the questions table (the custom grouping area). Release the left mouse button to drop the column heading into the custom grouping area. To accomplish the custom grouping previously described, first check the Custom Grouping check box. Then drag the Marked column heading into the custom grouping area above the question table. Next, drag the Unit Name column heading into the custom grouping area. You will see the two column headings joined together by a line that indicates the order of the custom grouping. Finally, drag the Seq column heading into the custom grouping area. This heading will be joined to the Unit Name heading by another line indicating the direction of the custom grouping.

Notice that each column heading in the custom grouping area has an arrow indicating the direction in which items are sorted under that column heading. You can reverse the direction of the sort on an individual column-heading basis using these arrows. Click the column heading in the custom grouping area to change the direction of the sort for that column heading only. For example, using the custom grouping created previously, you can display the question list sorted first in descending order by whether the question was marked, in descending order by unit name, and then in ascending order by sequence number.

The Custom Grouping feature of the Item Review screen gives you enormous flexibility in how you choose to review the exam questions. To remove a custom grouping and return the Item Review display to its default setting (sorted in descending order by sequence number), simply uncheck the Custom Grouping check box.

The Current Score Tab

The Current Score tab of the Item Review screen (see Figure D.14) provides a real-time snapshot of your score. The top half of the screen is an expandable grid. When the grid is collapsed, scores are displayed for each unit. Units can be expanded to show percentage scores for objectives and subobjectives. Information about your exam progress is presented in the following columns:

◆ **Unit Name.** This column shows the unit name for each objective group.

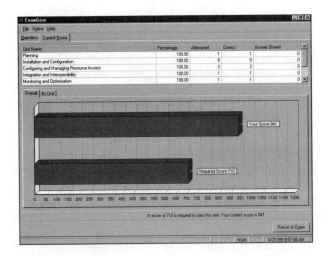

FIGURE D.14
The Current Score tab on the Item Review screen.

◆ **Percentage.** This column shows the percentage of questions for each objective group that you answered correctly.

◆ **Attempted.** This column lists the number of questions you answered either completely or partially for each objective group.

◆ **Correct.** This column lists the actual number of questions you answered correctly for each objective group.

◆ **Answer Shown.** This column lists the number of questions for each objective group that you chose to display the answer to using the Show Answer button.

The columns in the scoring table are resized and sorted in the same way as those in the questions table on the Item Review Questions tab. Refer to the earlier section "The Item Review Questions Tab" for more details.

A graphical overview of the score is presented below the grid. The graph depicts two red bars: The top bar represents your current exam score, and the bottom bar represents the required passing score. To the right of the bars in the graph is a legend that lists the required score and your score. Below the bar graph is a statement that describes the required passing score and your current score.

In addition, the information can be presented on an overall basis or by exam unit. The Overall tab shows the overall score. The By Unit tab shows the score by unit.

Clicking the End Exam button terminates the exam and passes control to the Examination Score Report screen.

The Return to Exam button returns to the exam at the question from which the Item Review button was clicked.

Review Marked Items

The Item Review screen allows you to enter a browse sequence for marked questions. When you click the Review Marked button, questions that you have previously marked using the Mark Question check box are presented for your review. While browsing the marked questions, you will see the following changes to the buttons available:

◆ The caption of the Next button becomes Next Marked.

◆ The caption of the Previous button becomes Previous Marked.

Review Incomplete

The Item Review screen allows you to enter a browse sequence for incomplete questions. When you click the Review Incomplete button, the questions you did not answer or did not completely answer are displayed for your review. While browsing the incomplete questions, you will see the following changes to the buttons:

◆ The caption of the Next button becomes Next Incomplete.

◆ The caption of the Previous button becomes Previous Incomplete.

Examination Score Report Screen

The Examination Score Report screen (see Figure D.15) appears when the Study Mode, practice exam, or adaptive exam ends—as the result of timer expiration, completion of all questions, or your decision to terminate early.

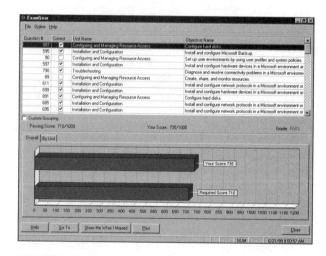

FIGURE D.15
The Examination Score Report screen.

This screen provides you with a graphical display of your test score, along with a tabular breakdown of scores by unit. The graphical display at the top of the screen compares your overall score with the score required to pass the exam. Buttons below the graphical display allow you to open the Show Me What I Missed browse sequence, print the screen, or return to the main menu.

Show Me What I Missed Browse Sequence

The Show Me What I Missed browse sequence is invoked by clicking the Show Me What I Missed button from the Examination Score Report or from the configuration screen of an adaptive exam.

Note that the window caption is modified to indicate that you are in the Show Me What I Missed browse sequence mode. Question IDs and position within the browse sequence appear at the top of the screen, in place of the Mark Question and Time Remaining indicators. Main window contents vary, depending on the question type. The following list describes the buttons available within the Show Me What I Missed browse sequence and the functions they perform:

◆ **Return to Score Report.** Returns control to the Examination Score Report screen. In the case of an adaptive exam, this button's caption is Exit, and control returns to the adaptive exam configuration screen.

◆ **Run Simulation.** Opens a simulation in Grade mode, causing the simulation to open displaying your response and the correct answer. If the current question does not offer a simulation, this button is disabled.

◆ **Exhibits.** Opens the Exhibits window. This button is enabled if one or more exhibits are available for the question.

◆ **Instructions.** Shows how to answer the current question type.

◆ **Print.** Prints the current screen.

◆ **Previous or Next.** Displays missed questions.

Checking the Web Site

To check the New Riders home page or the *ExamGear, Training Guide Edition* home page for updates or other product information, choose the desired Web site from the Web Sites option of the Online menu. You must be connected to the Internet to reach these Web sites. When you select a Web site, the Internet Explorer browser opens inside the *ExamGear, Training Guide Edition* window and displays the Web site.

OBTAINING UPDATES

The procedures for obtaining updates are outlined in this section.

The Catalog Web Site for Updates

Selecting the Check for Product Updates option from the Online menu shows you the full range of products you can either download for free or purchase. You can download additional items only if you have registered the software.

Product Updates Dialog Box

This dialog box appears when you select Check for Product Updates from the Online menu. *ExamGear, Training Guide Edition* checks for product updates from the New Riders Internet site and displays a list of products available for download. Some items, such as *ExamGear* program updates or bonus question sets for exam databases you have activated, are available for download free of charge.

Types of Updates

Several types of updates may be available for download, including various free updates and additional items available for purchase.

Free Program Updates

Free program updates include changes to the *ExamGear, Training Guide Edition* executables and runtime libraries (DLLs). When any of these items are downloaded, *ExamGear* automatically installs the upgrades. *ExamGear, Training Guide Edition* will be reopened after the installation is complete.

Free Database Updates

Free database updates include updates to the exam or exams that you have registered. Exam updates are contained in compressed, encrypted files and include exam databases, simulations, and exhibits. *ExamGear, Training Guide Edition* automatically decompresses these files to their proper location and updates the *ExamGear* software to record version changes and import new question sets.

CONTACTING NEW RIDERS PUBLISHING

At New Riders, we strive to meet and exceed the needs of our customers. We have developed *ExamGear, Training Guide Edition* to surpass the demands and expectations of network professionals seeking technical certifications, and we think it shows. What do you think?

If you need to contact New Riders regarding any aspect of the *ExamGear, Training Guide Edition* product line, feel free to do so. We look forward to hearing from you. Contact us at the following address or phone number:

New Riders Publishing
201 West 103 Street
Indianapolis, IN 46290
800-545-5914

You can also reach us on the World Wide Web:

    http://www.newriders.com

Technical Support

Technical support is available at the following phone number during the hours specified:

317-581-3833

Monday through Friday, 10:00 a.m.–3:00 p.m. Central Standard Time.

Customer Service

If you have a damaged product and need a replacement or refund, please call the following phone number:

800-858-7674

Product Updates

Product updates can be obtained by choosing *ExamGear, Training Guide Edition*'s Online pull-down menu and selecting Products Updates. You'll be taken to a private Web site with full details.

Product Suggestions and Comments

We value your input! Please email your suggestions and comments to the following address:

certification@mcp.com

LICENSE AGREEMENT

YOU SHOULD CAREFULLY READ THE FOLLOWING TERMS AND CONDITIONS BEFORE BREAKING THE SEAL ON THE PACKAGE. AMONG OTHER THINGS, THIS AGREEMENT LICENSES THE ENCLOSED SOFTWARE TO YOU AND CONTAINS WARRANTY AND LIABILITY DISCLAIMERS. BY BREAKING THE SEAL ON THE PACKAGE, YOU ARE ACCEPTING AND AGREEING TO THE TERMS AND CONDITIONS OF THIS AGREEMENT. IF YOU DO NOT AGREE TO THE TERMS OF THIS AGREEMENT, DO NOT BREAK THE SEAL. YOU SHOULD PROMPTLY RETURN THE PACKAGE UNOPENED.

LICENSE

Subject to the provisions contained herein, *New Riders Publishing* (NRP) hereby grants to you a nonexclusive, nontransferable license to use the object-code version of the computer software product (Software) contained in the package on a single computer of the type identified on the package.

SOFTWARE AND DOCUMENTATION

NRP shall furnish the Software to you on media in machine-readable object-code form and may also provide the standard documentation (Documentation) containing instructions for operation and use of the Software.

LICENSE TERM AND CHARGES

The term of this license commences upon delivery of the Software to you and is perpetual unless earlier terminated upon default or as otherwise set forth herein.

TITLE

Title, ownership right, and intellectual property rights in and to the Software and Documentation shall remain in NRP and/or in suppliers to NRP of programs contained in the Software. The Software is provided for your own internal use under this license. This license does not include the right to sublicense and is personal to you and therefore may not be assigned (by operation of law or otherwise) or transferred without the prior written consent of NRP. You acknowledge that the Software in source code form remains a confidential trade secret of NRP and/or its suppliers and therefore you agree not to attempt to decipher or decompile, modify, disassemble, reverse engineer, or prepare derivative works of the Software or develop source code for the Software or knowingly allow others to do so. Further, you may not copy the Documentation or other written materials accompanying the Software.

UPDATES

This license does not grant you any right, license, or interest in and to any improvements, modifications, enhancements, or updates to the Software and Documentation. Updates, if available, may be obtained by you at NRP's then-current standard pricing, terms, and conditions.

LIMITED WARRANTY AND DISCLAIMER

NRP warrants that the media containing the Software, if provided by NRP, is free from defects in material and workmanship under normal use for a period of sixty (60) days from the date you purchased a license to it.

THIS IS A LIMITED WARRANTY AND IT IS THE ONLY WARRANTY MADE BY NRP. THE SOFTWARE IS PROVIDED "AS IS" AND NRP SPECIFICALLY DISCLAIMS ALL WARRANTIES OF ANY KIND, EITHER EXPRESS OR IMPLIED, INCLUDING, BUT NOT LIMITED TO, THE IMPLIED WARRANTY OF MERCHANTABILITY AND FITNESS FOR A PARTICULAR PURPOSE. FURTHER, COMPANY DOES NOT WARRANT, GUARANTEE, OR MAKE ANY REPRESENTA-TIONS REGARDING THE USE, OR THE RESULTS OF THE USE, OF THE SOFTWARE IN TERMS OR CORRECTNESS, ACCURACY, RELIABILITY, CURRENTNESS, OR OTHERWISE AND DOES NOT WARRANT THAT THE OPERATION OF ANY SOFTWARE WILL BE UNINTERRUPTED OR ERROR FREE. NRP EXPRESSLY DISCLAIMS ANY WARRANTIES NOT STATED HEREIN. NO ORAL OR WRITTEN INFORMATION OR ADVICE GIVEN BY NRP, OR ANY NRP DEALER, AGENT, EMPLOYEE, OR OTHERS SHALL CREATE,

MODIFY, OR EXTEND A WARRANTY OR IN ANY WAY INCREASE THE SCOPE OF THE FOREGOING WARRANTY, AND NEITHER SUBLICENSEE OR PURCHASER MAY RELY ON ANY SUCH INFORMATION OR ADVICE. If the media is subjected to accident, abuse, or improper use, or if you violate the terms of this Agreement, then this warranty shall immediately be terminated. This warranty shall not apply if the Software is used on or in conjunction with hardware or programs other than the unmodified version of hardware and programs with which the Software was designed to be used as described in the Documentation.

LIMITATION OF LIABILITY

Your sole and exclusive remedies for any damage or loss in any way connected with the Software are set forth below.

UNDER NO CIRCUMSTANCES AND UNDER NO LEGAL THEORY, TORT, CONTRACT, OR OTHERWISE, SHALL NRP BE LIABLE TO YOU OR ANY OTHER PERSON FOR ANY INDIRECT, SPECIAL, INCIDENTAL, OR CONSEQUENTIAL DAMAGES OF ANY CHARACTER INCLUDING, WITHOUT LIMITATION, DAMAGES FOR LOSS OF GOODWILL, LOSS OF PROFIT, WORK STOPPAGE, COMPUTER FAILURE OR MALFUNCTION, OR ANY AND ALL OTHER COMMERCIAL DAMAGES OR LOSSES, OR FOR ANY OTHER DAMAGES EVEN IF NRP SHALL HAVE BEEN INFORMED OF THE POSSIBILITY OF SUCH DAMAGES, OR FOR ANY CLAIM BY ANOTHER PARTY. NRP'S THIRD-PARTY PROGRAM SUPPLIERS MAKE NO WARRANTY, AND HAVE NO LIABILITY WHATSOEVER, TO YOU. NRP's sole and exclusive obligation and liability and your exclusive remedy shall be: upon NRP's election, (i) the replacement of our defective media; or (ii) the repair or correction of your defective media if NRP is able, so that it will conform to the above warranty; or (iii) if NRP is unable to replace or repair, you may terminate this license by returning the Software. Only if you inform NRP of your problem during the applicable warranty period will NRP be obligated to honor this warranty. SOME STATES OR JURISDICTIONS DO NOT ALLOW THE EXCLUSION OF IMPLIED WARRANTIES OR LIMITATION OR EXCLUSION OF CONSE-QUENTIAL DAMAGES, SO THE ABOVE LIMITATIONS OR EXCLUSIONS MAY NOT APPLY TO YOU. THIS WARRANTY GIVES YOU SPECIFIC LEGAL RIGHTS AND YOU MAY ALSO HAVE OTHER RIGHTS WHICH VARY BY STATE OR JURISDICTION.

MISCELLANEOUS

If any provision of the Agreement is held to be ineffective, unenforceable, or illegal under certain circumstances for any reason, such decision shall not affect the validity or enforceability (i) of such provision under other circumstances or (ii) of the remaining provisions hereof under all circumstances, and such provision shall be reformed to and only to the extent necessary to make it effective, enforceable, and legal under such circumstances. All headings are solely for convenience and shall not be considered in interpreting this Agreement. This Agreement shall be governed by

and construed under New York law as such law applies to agreements between New York residents entered into and to be performed entirely within New York, except as required by U.S. Government rules and regulations to be governed by Federal law.

YOU ACKNOWLEDGE THAT YOU HAVE READ THIS AGREEMENT, UNDERSTAND IT, AND AGREE TO BE BOUND BY ITS TERMS AND CONDITIONS. YOU FURTHER AGREE THAT IT IS THE COMPLETE AND EXCLUSIVE STATE-MENT OF THE AGREEMENT BETWEEN US THAT SUPERSEDES ANY PROPOSAL OR PRIOR AGREEMENT, ORAL OR WRITTEN, AND ANY OTHER COMMUNICATIONS BETWEEN US RELATING TO THE SUBJECT MATTER OF THIS AGREEMENT.

U.S. GOVERNMENT RESTRICTED RIGHTS

Use, duplication, or disclosure by the Government is subject to restrictions set forth in subparagraphs (a) through (d) of the Commercial Computer-Restricted Rights clause at FAR 52.227-19 when applicable, or in subparagraph (c) (1) (ii) of the Rights in Technical Data and Computer Software clause at DFARS 252.227-7013, and in similar clauses in the NASA FAR Supplement.

Index

A

C

F

H

Q–R

X–Z

Additional Tools for Certification Preparation

Taking the author-driven, no-nonsense approach that we pioneered with our *Landmark* books, New Riders proudly offers something unique for Windows 2000 administrators—an interesting and discriminating book on Windows 2000 Server, written by someone in the trenches who can anticipate your situation and provide answers you can trust.

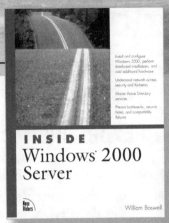

INSIDE
Windows 2000 Server

William Boswell

ISBN: 1-56205-929-7

Windows 2000
ESSENTIAL REFERENCE

Includes coverage of Server, Workstation, and Professional

Steven Tate, et al.

ISBN: 0-7357-0869-X

Architected to be the most navigable, useful, and value-packed reference for Windows 2000, this book uses a creative "telescoping" design that you can adapt to your style of learning. It's a concise, focused, and quick reference for Windows 2000, providing the kind of practical advice, tips, procedures, and additional resources that every administrator will need.

Understanding the Network is just one of several new titles from New Riders' acclaimed *Landmark* series. This book addresses the audience in practical terminology, and describes the most essential information and tools required to build high-availability networks in a step-by-step implementation format. Each chapter could be read as a standalone, but the book builds progressively toward a summary of the essential concepts needed to put together a wide area network.

Understanding the Network
A Practical Guide to Internetworking

Michael J. Martin

ISBN: 0-7357-0977-7

New Riders
Windows 2000 Resources

Advice and Experience for the Windows 2000 Networker

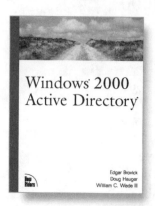

LANDMARK SERIES

We know how important it is to have access to detailed, solution-oriented information on core technologies. *Landmark* books contain the essential information you need to solve technical problems. Written by experts and subjected to rigorous peer and technical reviews, our *Landmark* books are hard-core resources for practitioners like you.

ESSENTIAL REFERENCE SERIES

The *Essential Reference* series from New Riders provides answers when you know what you want to do but need to know how to do it. Each title skips extraneous material and assumes a strong base of knowledge. These are indispensable books for the practitioner who wants to find specific features of a technology quickly and efficiently. Avoiding fluff and basic material, these books present solutions in an innovative, clean format—and at a great value.

CIRCLE SERIES

The *Circle Series* is a set of reference guides that meet the needs of the growing community of advanced, technical–level networkers who must architect, develop, and administer Windows NT/2000 systems. These books provide network designers and programmers with detailed, proven solutions to their problems.

The Road to MCSE Windows 2000

The new Microsoft Windows 2000 track is designed for information technology professionals working in a typically complex computing environment of medium to large organizations. A Windows 2000 MCSE candidate should have at least one year of experience implementing and administering a network operating system.

MCSEs in the Windows 2000 track are required to pass **five core exams and two elective exams** that provide a valid and reliable measure of technical proficiency and expertise.

See below for the exam information and the relevant New Riders title that covers that exam.

Core Exams

w MCSE Candidates (Who Have Not Already Passed Windows NT 4.0 Exams) st Take All 4 of the Following Core Exams:

am 70-210: Installing, Configuring d Administering Microsoft ndows 2000 Professional

am 70-215: Installing, Configuring d Administering Microsoft ndows 2000 Server

am 70-216: Implementing d Administering a Microsoft ndows 2000 Network rastructure

am 70-217: Implementing d Administering a Microsoft ndows 2000 Directory rvices Infrastructure

ISBN 0-7357-0965-3   ISBN 0-7357-0968-8

ISBN 0-7357-0966-1   ISBN 0-7357-0976-9

or

MCPs Who Have Passed 3 Windows NT 4.0 Exams (Exams 70-067, 70-068, and 70-073) Instead of the 4 Core Exams at Left, May Take:

Exam 70-240: Microsoft Windows 2000 Accelerated Exam for MCPs Certified on Microsoft Windows NT 4.0.

(This accelerated, intensive exam, which will be available until September, 2001, covers the core competencies of exams 70-210, 70-215, 70-216, and 70-217.)

ISBN 0-7357-0979-3

MCSE Training Guide: Core Exams (Bundle)

ISBN 0-7357-0988-2

PLUS - All Candidates - 1 of the Following Core Elective Exams Required:

xam 70-219: Designing a Microsoft Windows 2000 Directory rvices Infrastructure

xam 70-220: Designing Security for a Microsoft Windows 2000 Network

xam 70-221: Designing a Microsoft Windows 2000 etwork Infrastructure

ISBN 0-7357-0983-1   ISBN 0-7357-0984-X   ISBN 0-7357-0982-3

LUS - All Candidates - 2 of the Following Elective Exams Required:

ny current MCSE electives (visit www.microsoft.com for a list of current electives)

elected third-party certifications that focus on interoperability will be accepted as an alternative to one ective exam. Please watch for more information on the third-party certifications that will be acceptable.)

Exam 70-219: Designing a Microsoft Windows 2000 Directory Services Infrastructure

Exam 70-220: Designing Security for a Microsoft Windows 2000 Network

Exam 70-221: Designing a Microsoft Windows 2000 Network Infrastructure

xam 70-222: Upgrading from Microsoft Windows NT 4.0 to Microsoft Windows 2000

ISBN 0-7357-0983-1   ISBN 0-7357-0984-X   ISBN 0-7357-0982-3

ore exams that can also be used as elective exams may only be counted once toward a certification; that is, if a candidate receives edit for an exam as a core in one track, that candidate will not receive credit for that same exam as an elective in that same track.

New Riders

WWW.NEWRIDERS.COM

New Riders | # Books for Networking Professionals

Windows NT/2000 Titles

Windows 2000 TCP/IP
By Karanjit Siyan, Ph.D.
2nd Edition
900 pages, $39.99
ISBN: 0-7357-0992-0

Windows 2000 TCP/IP cuts through the complexities and provides the most informative and complex reference book on Windows 2000-based TCP/IP topics. The book is a tutorial-reference hybrid, focusing on how Microsoft TCP/IP works, using hands-on tutorials and practical examples. Concepts essential to TCP/IP administration are explained thoroughly, and are then related to the practical use of Microsoft TCP/IP in a serious networking environment.

Windows 2000 DNS
By Roger Abell, Herman Knief, Andrew Daniels, and Jeffrey Graham
2nd Edition
450 pages, $39.99
ISBN: 0-7357-0973-4

The Domain Name System is a directory of registered computer names and IP addresses that can be instantly located. Without proper design and administration of DNS, computers wouldn't be able to locate each other on the network, and applications like email and Web browsing wouldn't be feasible. Administrators need this information to make their networks work. *Windows 2000 DNS* provides a technical overview of DNS and WINS, and how to design and administer them for optimal performance in a Windows 2000 environment.

Windows 2000 Server Professional Reference
By Karanjit Siyan, Ph.D.
3rd Edition
1800 pages, $75.00
ISBN: 0-7357-0952-1

Windows 2000 Server Professional Reference is the benchmark of references available for Windows 2000. Although other titles take you through the setup and implementation phase of the product, no other book provides the user with detailed answers to day-to-day administration problems and tasks. Real-world implementations are key to help administrators discover the most viable solutions for their particular environments. Solid content shows administrators how to manage, troubleshoot, and fix problems that are specific to heterogeneous Windows networks, as well as Internet features and functionality.

Windows 2000 Professional

By Jerry Honeycutt
350 pages, $34.99 US
ISBN: 0-7357-0950-5

Windows 2000 Professional explores the power available to the Windows workstation user on the corporate network and Internet. The book is aimed directly at the power user who values the security, stability, and networking capabilities of NT alongside the ease and familiarity of the Windows 95/98 user interface. This book covers both user and administration topics, with a dose of networking content added for connectivity.

Windows NT Power Toolkit

By Stu Sjouwerman and Ed Tittel
1st Edition
800 pages, $49.99
ISBN: 0-7357-0922-X

This book covers the analysis, tuning, optimization, automation, enhancement, maintenance, and troubleshooting of Windows NT Server 4.0 and Windows NT Workstation 4.0. In most cases, the two operating systems overlap completely. Where the two systems diverge, each platform is covered separately. This advanced title comprises a task-oriented treatment of the Windows NT 4.0 environment. By concentrating on the use of operating system tools and utilities, resource kit elements, and selected third-party tuning, analysis, optimization, and productivity tools, this book will show you how to carry out everyday and advanced tasks.

Windows 2000 User Management

By Lori Sanders
300 pages, $34.99
ISBN: 1-56205-886-X

With the dawn of Windows 2000, it has become even more difficult to draw a clear line between managing the user and managing the user's environment and desktop. This book, written by a noted trainer and consultant, provides comprehensive, practical advice to managing users and their desktop environments with Windows 2000.

Windows 2000 Deployment & Desktop Management

By Jeffrey A. Ferris, MCSE
1st Edition
400 pages, $34.99
ISBN: 0-7357-0975-0

More than a simple overview of new features and tools, *Windows 2000 Deployment & Desktop Management* is a thorough reference to deploying Windows 2000 Professional to corporate workstations. Incorporating real-world advice and detailed excercises, this book is a one-stop resource for any system administrator, integrator, engineer, or other IT professional.

Planning for Windows 2000

By Eric K. Cone, Jon Boggs, and Sergio Perez
1st Edition
400 pages, $29.99
ISBN: 0-7357-0048-6

Windows 2000 is poised to be one of the largest and most important software releases of the next decade, and you are charged with planning, testing, and deploying it in your enterprise. Are you ready? With this book, you will be. *Planning for Windows 2000* lets you know what the upgrade hurdles will be, informs you of how to clear them, guides you through effective Active Directory design, and presents you with detailed rollout procedures. Eric K. Cone, Jon Boggs, and Sergio Perez give you the benefit of their extensive experiences as Windows 2000 Rapid Deployment Program members by sharing problems and solutions they've encountered on the job.

SQL Server System Administration

By Sean Baird, Chris Miller, et al.
1st Edition
352 pages, $29.99
ISBN: 1-56205-955-6

How often does your SQL Server go down during the day when everyone wants to access the data? Do you spend most of your time being a "report monkey" for your coworkers and bosses? *SQL Server System Administration* helps you keep data consistently available to your users. This book omits introductory information. The authors don't spend time explaining queries and how they work. Instead, they focus on the information you can't get anywhere else, like how to choose the correct replication topology and achieve high availability of information.

Inside Windows 2000 Server

By William Boswell
2nd Edition
1533 pages, $49.99
ISBN: 1-56205-929-7

Finally, a totally new edition of New Riders' best-selling *Inside Windows NT Server 4*. Taking the author-driven, no-nonsense approach pioneered with the *Landmark* books, New Riders proudly offers something unique for Windows 2000 administrators—an interesting, discriminating book on Windows 2000 Server written by someone who can anticipate your situation and give you workarounds that won't leave a system unstable or sluggish.

Internet Information Services Administration
By Kelli Adam
1st Edition,
200 pages, $29.99
ISBN: 0-7357-0022-2

Are the new Internet technologies in Internet Information Services giving you headaches? Does protecting security on the Web take up all of your time? Then this is the book for you. With hands-on configuration training, advanced study of the new protocols, the most recent version of IIS, and detailed instructions on authenticating users with the new Certificate Server and implementing and managing the new e-commerce features, *Internet Information Services Administration* gives you the real-life solutions you need. This definitive resource prepares you for upgrading to Windows 2000 by giving you detailed advice on working with Microsoft Management Console, which was first used by IIS.

SMS 2 Administration
By Michael Lubanski and Darshan Doshi
1st Edition
350 pages, $39.99
ISBN: 0-7357-0082-6

Microsoft's new version of its Systems Management Server (SMS) is starting to turn heads. Although complex, it allows administrators to lower their total cost of ownership and more efficiently manage clients, applications, and support operations. If your organization is using or implementing SMS, you'll need some expert advice. Michael Lubanski and Darshan Doshi can help you get the most bang for your buck with insight, expert tips, and real-world examples. Michael and Darshan are consultants specializing in SMS and have worked with Microsoft on one of the most complex SMS rollouts in the world, involving 32 countries, 15 languages, and thousands of clients.

SQL Server 7 Essential Reference
By Sharon Dooley
1st Edition
500 pages, $35.00 US
ISBN: 0-7357-0864-9

SQL Server 7 Essential Reference is a comprehensive reference of advanced how-tos and techniques for SQL Server 7 administrators. This book provides solid grounding in fundamental SQL Server 7 administrative tasks to help you tame your SQL Server environment. With coverage ranging from installation, monitoring, troubleshooting security, and backup and recovery plans, this book breaks down SQL Server into its key conceptual areas and functions. This easy-to-use reference is a must-have for any SQL Server administrator.

Networking Titles

Network Intrusion Detection: An Analyst's Handbook
By Stephen Northcutt
1st Edition
267 pages, $39.99
ISBN: 0-7357-0868-1

Get answers and solutions from someone who has been in the trenches. The author, Stephen Northcutt, original developer of the Shadow intrusion detection system and former director of the United States Navy's Information System Security Office at the Naval Security Warfare Center, gives his expertise to intrusion detection specialists, security analysts, and consultants responsible for setting up and maintaining an effective defense against network security attacks.

Understanding Data Communications, Sixth Edition
By Gilbert Held
Sixth Edition
600 pages, $39.99
ISBN: 0-7357-0036-2

Updated from the highly successful fifth edition, this book explains how data communications systems and their various hardware and software components work. More than an entry-level book, it approaches the material in textbook format, addressing the complex issues involved in internetworking today. A great reference book for the experienced networking professional that is written by the noted networking authority, Gilbert Held.

Lotus Notes and Domino Titles

Domino System Administration
By Rob Kirkland, CLP, CLI
1st Edition
850 pages, $49.99
ISBN: 1-56205-948-3

Your boss has just announced that you will be upgrading to the newest version of Notes and Domino when it ships. How are you supposed to get this new system installed, configured, and rolled out to all of your end users? You understand how Lotus Notes works—you've been administering it for years. What you need is a concise, practical explanation of the new features and how to make some of the advanced stuff work smoothly by someone like you, who has worked with the product for years and understands what you need to know. *Domino System Administration* is the answer—the first book on Domino that attacks the technology at the professional level with practical, hands-on assistance to get Domino running in your organization.

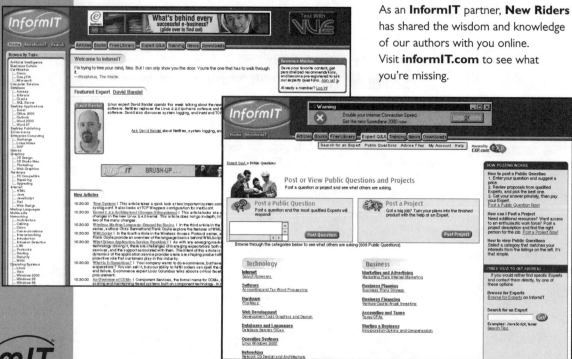
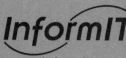

Other Books By New Riders

MICROSOFT TECHNOLOGIES

ADMINISTRATION

Inside Windows 2000 Server
1-56205-929-7 • $49.99 US / $74.95 CAN

Windows Windows 2000 Essential Reference
0-7357-0869-X • $35.00 US / $52.95 CAN

Windows 2000 Active Directory
0-7357-0870-3 • $29.99 US / $44.95 CAN

Windows 2000 Routing and Remote Access Service
0-7357-0951-3 • $34.99 US / $52.95 CAN

Windows 2000 Deployment & Desktop Management
0-7357-0975-0 • $34.99 US / $52.95 CAN

Windows 2000 DNS
0-7357-0973-4 • $39.99 US / $59.95 CAN

Windows 2000 User Management
1-56205-886-X • $34.99 US / $52.95 CAN

Windows 2000 Professional
0-7357-0950-5 • $34.99 US / $52.95 CAN

Planning for Windows 2000
0-7357-0048-6 • $29.99 US / $44.95 CAN

Windows 2000 Server Professional Reference
0-7357-0952-1 • $75.00 US / $111.95 CAN

Windows 2000 Security
0-7357-0991-2 • $39.99 US / $59.95 CAN

Windows 2000 TCP/IP
0-7357-0992-0 • $39.99 US / $59.95 CAN

Windows NT/2000 Network Security
1-57870-253-4 • $45.00 US / $67.95 CAN

Windows NT/2000 Thin Client Solutions
1-57870-239-9 • $45.00 US / $67.95 CAN

Windows 2000 Virtual Private Networking
1-57870-246-1 • $45.00 US / $67.95 CAN
• Available January 2001

Windows 2000 Active Directory Design & Deployment
1-57870-242-9 • $45.00 US / $67.95 CAN

Windows 2000 and Mainframe Integration
1-57870-200-3 • $40.00 US / $59.95 CAN

Windows 2000 Server: Planning and Migration
1-57870-023-X • $40.00 US / $59.95 CAN

Windows 2000 Quality of Service
1-57870-115-5 • $45.00 US / $67.95 CAN

Windows NT Power Toolkit
0-7357-0922-X • $49.99 US / $74.95 CAN

Windows NT Terminal Server and Citrix MetaFrame
1-56205-944-0 • $29.99 US / $44.95 CAN

Windows NT Performance: Monitoring, Benchmarking, and Tuning
1-56205-942-4 • $29.99 US / $44.95 CAN

Windows NT Registry: A Settings Reference
1-56205-941-6 • $29.99 US / $44.95 CAN

Windows NT Domain Architecture
1-57870-112-0 • $38.00 US / $56.95 CAN

SYSTEMS PROGRAMMING

Windows NDIS Miniport Development
1-57870-248-8 • $50.00 US / $74.95 CAN
• Available March 2001

Windows NT/2000 Native API Reference
1-57870-199-6 • $50.00 US / $74.95 CAN

Windows NT Device Driver Development
1-57870-058-2 • $50.00 US / $74.95 CAN

DCE/RPC over SMB: Samba and Windows NT Domain Internals
1-57870-150-3 • $45.00 US / $67.95 CAN

WEB PROGRAMMING

Real World Web Code: Techniques for Structured ASP Programming
0-7357-1033-3 • $39.99 US / $59.95 CAN • Available March 2001

Exchange & Outlook: Constructing Collaborative Solutions
1-57870-252-6 • $40.00 US / $59.95 CAN

APPLICATION PROGRAMMING

Delphi COM Programming
1-57870-221-6 • $45.00 US / $67.95 CAN

Windows NT Applications: Measuring and Optimizing Performance
1-57870-176-7 • $40.00 US / $59.95 CAN

Applying COM+
0-7357-0978-5 • $49.99 US / $74.95 CAN

SCRIPTING

Windows Script Host
1-57870-139-2 • $35.00 US / $52.95 CAN

Windows NT Shell Scripting
1-57870-047-7 • $32.00 US / $45.95 CAN

Windows NT Win32 Perl Programming: The Standard Extensions
1-57870-067-1 • $40.00 US / $59.95 CAN

Windows NT/2000 ADSI Scripting for System Administration
1-57870-219-4 • $45.00 US / $67.95 CAN

Windows NT Automated Deployment and Customization
1-57870-045-0 • $32.00 US / $45.95 CAN

Win32 Perl Scripting: The Administrator's Handbook
1-57870-215-1 • $35.00 US / $52.95 CAN

BACK OFFICE

SMS 2 Administration
0-7357-0082-6 • $39.99 US / $59.95 CAN

Internet Information Services Administration
0-7357-0022-2 • $29.99 US / $44.95 CAN

SQL Server System Administration
1-56205-955-6 • $29.99 US / $44.95 CAN

SQL Server 7 Essential Reference
0-7357-0864-9 • $35.00 US / $52.95 CAN

Inside Exchange 2000 Server
0-7357-1027-9 • $49.99 US / $74.95 CAN
• Available February 2001

WEB DESIGN & DEVELOPMENT

OPEN SOURCE

MySQL
0-7357-0921-1 • $49.99 US / $74.95 CAN

Web Application Development with PHP 4.0
0-7357-0997-1 • $39.99 US / $59.95 CAN

PHP Functions Essential Reference
0-7357-0970-X • $35.00 US / $52.95 CAN
• Available February 2001

Python Essential Reference
0-7357-0901-7 • $34.95 US / $52.95 CAN

Qt: The Official Documentation
1-57870-209-7 • $50.00 US / $74.95 CAN

Berkeley DB
0-7357-1064-3 • $39.99 US / $59.95 CAN
• Available February 2001

GNU Autoconf, Automake, and Libtool
1-57870-190-2 • $40.00 US / $59.95 CAN

CREATIVE MEDIA

Designing Web Usability
1-56205-810-X • $45.00 US / $67.95 CAN

Designing Web Graphics.3
1-56205-949-1 • $55.00 US / $81.95 CAN

Flash 4 Magic
0-7357-0896-7 • $45.00 US / $67.95 CAN

<creative.html design>
1-56205-704-9 • $39.99 US / $59.95 CAN

Creating Killer Web Sites, Second Edition
1-56830-433-1 • $49.99 US / $74.95 CAN

Secrets of Successful Web Sites
1-56830-382-3 • $49.99 US / $74.95 CAN

XML

Inside XML
0-7357-1020-1 • $49.99 US / $74.95 CAN

XHTML
0-7357-1034-1 • $39.99 US / $59.95 CAN
• Available January 2001

LINUX/UNIX

ADMINISTRATION

Networking Linux: A Practical Guide to TCP/IP
0-7357-1031-7 • $39.99 US / $59.95 CAN
• Available February 2001

Inside Linux
0-7357-0940-8 • $39.99 US / $59.95 CAN

Vi iMproved (VIM)
0-7357-1001-5 • $49.99 US / $74.95 CAN
• Available January 2001

Linux System Administration
1-56205-934-3 • $29.99 US / $44.95 CAN

Linux Firewalls
0-7357-0900-9 • $39.99 US / $59.95 CAN

Linux Essential Reference
0-7357-0852-5 • $24.95 US / $37.95 CAN

UnixWare 7 System Administration
1-57870-080-9 • $40.00 US / $59.99 CAN

DEVELOPMENT

Developing Linux Applications with GTK+ and GDK
0-7357-0021-4 • $34.99 US / $52.95 CAN

GTK+/Gnome Application Development
0-7357-0078-8 • $39.99 US / $59.95 CAN

KDE Application Development
1-57870-201-1 • $39.99 US / $59.95 CAN

GIMP

Grokking the GIMP
0-7357-0924-6 • $39.99 US / $59.95 CAN

GIMP Essential Reference
0-7357-0911-4 • $24.95 US / $37.95 CAN

SOLARIS

Solaris Advanced System Administrator's Guide, Second Edition
1-57870-039-6 • $39.99 US / $59.95 CAN

Solaris System Administrator's Guide, Second Edition
1-57870-040-X • $34.99 US / $52.95 CAN

Solaris Essential Reference
0-7357-0023-0 • $24.95 US / $37.95 CAN

Solaris System Management
0-7357-1018-X • $39.99 US / $59.95 CAN
• Available March 2001

Solaris 8 Essential Reference
0-7357-1007-4 • $34.99 US / $52.95 CAN
• Available January 2001

NETWORKING

STANDARDS & PROTOCOLS

Differentiated Services for the Internet
1-57870-132-5 • $50.00 US / $74.95 CAN

Cisco Router Configuration & Troubleshooting, Second Edition
0-7357-0999-8 • $34.99 US / $52.95 CAN

Understanding Directory Services
0-7357-0910-6 • $39.99 US / $59.95 CAN

Understanding the Network: A Practical Guide to Internetworking
0-7357-0977-7 • $39.99 US / $59.95 CAN

Understanding Data Communications, Sixth Edition
0-7357-0036-2 • $39.99 US / $59.95 CAN

LDAP: Programming Directory Enabled Applications
1-57870-000-0 • $44.99 US / $67.95 CAN

Gigabit Ethernet Networking
1-57870-062-0 • $50.00 US / $74.95 CAN

Supporting Service Level Agreements on IP Networks
1-57870-146-5 • $50.00 US / $74.95 CAN

Directory Enabled Networks
1-57870-140-6 • $50.00 US / $74.95 CAN

Policy-Based Networking: Architecture and Algorithms
1-57870-226-7 • $50.00 US / $74.95 CAN

Networking Quality of Service and Windows Operating Systems
1-57870-206-2 • $50.00 US / $74.95 CAN

Policy-Based Management
1-57870-225-9 • $55.00 US / $81.95 CAN
• Available March 2001

Quality of Service on IP Networks
1-57870-189-9 • $50.00 US / $74.95 CAN

Designing Addressing Architectures for Routing and Switching
1-57870-059-0 • $45.00 US / $69.95 CAN

Understanding & Deploying LDAP Directory Services
1-57870-070-1 • $50.00 US / $74.95 CAN
Switched, Fast and Gigabit Ethernet, Third Edition
1-57870-073-6 • $50.00 US / $74.95 CAN
Wireless LANs: Implementing Interoperable Networks
1-57870-081-7 • $40.00 US / $59.95 CAN
Local Area High Speed Networks
1-57870-113-9 • $50.00 US / $74.95 CAN
Wide Area High Speed Networks
1-57870-114-7 • $50.00 US / $74.95 CAN
The DHCP Handbook
1-57870-137-6 • $55.00 US / $81.95 CAN
Designing Routing and Switching Architectures for Enterprise Networks
1-57870-060-4 • $55.00 US / $81.95 CAN
Network Performance Baselining
1-57870-240-2 • $50.00 US / $74.95 CAN
Economics of Electronic Commerce
1-57870-014-0 • $49.99 US / $74.95 CAN

SECURITY

Intrusion Detection
1-57870-185-6 • $50.00 US / $74.95 CAN
Understanding Public-Key Infrastructure
1-57870-166-X • $50.00 US / $74.95 CAN
Network Intrusion Detection: An Analyst's Handbook, 2E
0-7357-1008-2 • $45.00 US / $67.95 CAN
Linux Firewalls
0-7357-0900-9 • $39.99 US / $59.95 CAN
Intrusion Signatures and Analysis
0-7357-1063-5 • $39.99 US / $59.95 CAN
• Available February 2001
Hackers Beware
0-7357-1009-0 • $45.00 US / $67.95 CAN
• Available March 2001

LOTUS NOTES/DOMINO

Domino System Administration
1-56205-948-3 • $49.99 US / $74.95 CAN
Lotus Notes & Domino Essential Reference
0-7357-0007-9 • $45.00 US / $67.95 CAN

PROFESSIONAL CERTIFICATION

TRAINING GUIDES

MCSE Training Guide: Networking Essentials, 2nd Ed.
1-56205-919-X • $49.99 US / $74.95 CAN
MCSE Training Guide: Windows NT Server 4, 2nd Ed.
1-56205-916-5 • $49.99 US / $74.95 CAN
MCSE Training Guide: Windows NT Workstation 4, 2nd Ed.
1-56205-918-1 • $49.99 US / $74.95 CAN
MCSE Training Guide: Windows NT Server 4 Enterprise, 2nd Ed.
1-56205-917-3 • $49.99 US / $74.95 CAN
MCSE Training Guide: Core Exams Bundle, 2nd Ed.
1-56205-926-2 • $149.99 US / $223.95 CAN
MCSE Training Guide: TCP/IP, 2nd Ed.
1-56205-920-3 • $49.99 US / $74.95 CAN
MCSE Training Guide: IIS 4, 2nd Ed.
0-7357-0865-7 • $49.99 US / $74.95 CAN
MCSE Training Guide: SQL Server 7 Administration
0-7357-0003-6 • $49.99 US / $74.95 CAN
MCSE Training Guide: SQL Server 7 Database Design
0-7357-0004-4 • $49.99 US / $74.95 CAN
MCSD Training Guide: Visual Basic 6 Exams
0-7357-0002-8 • $69.99 US / $104.95 CAN
MCSD Training Guide: Solution Architectures
0-7357-0026-5 • $49.99 US / $74.95 CAN
MCSD Training Guide: 4-in-1 Bundle
0-7357-0912-2 • $149.99 US / $223.95 CAN
A+ Certification Training Guide, Second Edition
0-7357-0907-6 • $49.99 US / $74.95 CAN
Network+ Certification Guide
0-7357-0077-X • $49.99 US / $74.95 CAN

Solaris 2.6 Administrator Certification Training Guide, Part I
1-57870-085-X • $40.00 US / $59.95 CAN
Solaris 2.6 Administrator Certification Training Guide, Part II
1-57870-086-8 • $40.00 US / $59.95 CAN
Solaris 7 Administrator Certification Training Guide, Part I and II
1-57870-249-6 • $49.99 US / $74.95 CAN
MCSE Training Guide: Windows 2000 Professional
0-7357-0965-3 • $49.99 US / $74.95 CAN
MCSE Training Guide: Windows 2000 Server
0-7357-0968-8 • $49.99 US / $74.95 CAN
MCSE Training Guide: Windows 2000 Network Infrastructure
0-7357-0966-1 • $49.99 US / $74.95 CAN
MCSE Training Guide: Windows 2000 Network Security Design
0-73570-984X • $49.99 US / $74.95 CAN
MCSE Training Guide: Windows 2000 Network Infrastructure Design
0-73570-982-3 • $49.99 US / $74.95 CAN
MCSE Training Guide: Windows 2000 Directory Svcs. Infrastructure
0-7357-0976-9 • $49.99 US / $74.95 CAN
MCSE Training Guide: Windows 2000 Directory Services Design
0-7357-0983-1 • $49.99 US / $74.95 CAN
MCSE Training Guide: Windows 2000 Accelerated Exam
0-7357-0979-3 • $69.99 US / $104.95 CAN
MCSE Training Guide: Windows 2000 Core Exams Bundle
0-7357-0988-2 • $149.99 US / $223.95 CAN

FAST TRACKS

CLP Fast Track: Lotus Notes/Domino 5 Application Development
0-73570-877-0 • $39.99 US / $59.95 CAN
CLP Fast Track: Lotus Notes/Domino 5 System Administration
0-7357-0878-9 • $39.99 US / $59.95 CAN
Network+ Fast Track
0-7357-0904-1 • $29.99 US / $44.95 CAN
A+ Fast Track
0-7357-0028-1 • $34.99 US / $52.95 CAN
MCSD Fast Track: Visual Basic 6, Exam #70-175
0-7357-0019-2 • $19.99 US / $29.95 CAN
MCSD FastTrack: Visual Basic 6, Exam #70-175
0-7357-0018-4 • $19.99 US / $29.95 CAN

SOFTWARE ARCHITECTURE & ENGINEERING

Designing for the User with OVID
1-57870-101-5 • $40.00 US / $59.95 CAN
Designing Flexible Object-Oriented Systems with UML
1-57870-098-1 • $40.00 US / $59.95 CAN
Constructing Superior Software
1-57870-147-3 • $40.00 US / $59.95 CAN
A UML Pattern Language
1-57870-118-X • $45.00 US / $67.95 CAN

How to Contact Us

IF YOU NEED THE LATEST UPDATES ON A TITLE THAT YOU'VE PURCHASED:

1) Visit our Web site at www.newriders.com.

2) Enter the book ISBN number, which is located on the back cover in the bottom right-hand corner, in the site search box on the left navigation bar.

3) Select your book title from the list of search results. On the book page, you'll find available updates and downloads for your title.

IF YOU ARE HAVING TECHNICAL PROBLEMS WITH THE BOOK OR THE CD THAT IS INCLUDED:

1) Check the book's information page on our Web site according to the instructions listed above, or

2) Email us at userservices@macmillanusa.com, or

3) Fax us at 317-581-4663 ATTN: Tech Support.

IF YOU HAVE COMMENTS ABOUT ANY OF OUR CERTIFICATION PRODUCTS THAT ARE NON-SUPPORT RELATED:

1) Email us at nrfeedback@newriders.com, or

2) Write to us at New Riders, 201 W. 103rd St., Indianapolis, IN 46290-1097, or

3) Fax us at 317-581-4663.

IF YOU ARE OUTSIDE THE UNITED STATES AND NEED TO FIND A DISTRIBUTOR IN YOUR AREA:

Please contact our international department at international@mcp.com.

IF YOU ARE INTERESTED IN BEING AN AUTHOR OR TECHNICAL REVIEWER:

Email us at opportunities@newriders.com. Include your name, email address, phone number, and area of technical expertise.

IF YOU WANT TO PREVIEW ANY OF OUR CERTIFICATION BOOKS FOR CLASSROOM USE:

Email us at nrmedia@newriders.com. Your message should include your name, title, training company or school, department, address, phone number, office days/hours, text in use, and enrollment. Send these details along with your request for desk/examination copies and/or additional information.

IF YOU ARE A MEMBER OF THE PRESS AND WOULD LIKE TO REVIEW ONE OF OUR BOOKS:

Email us at nrmedia@newriders.com. Your message should include your name, title, publication or Web site you work for, mailing address, and email address.

To better serve you, we would like your opinion on the content and quality of this book. Please complete this card and mail it to us or fax it to 317-581-4663.

Name _____

Address _____

City _____ State _____ Zip _____

Phone_____ Email Address _____

Occupation _____

Which certification exams have you already passed? _____

_____

_____

_____

Which certification exams do you plan to take? _____

_____

_____

_____

What influenced your purchase of this book?
- ❑ Recommendation ❑ Cover Design
- ❑ Table of Contents ❑ Index
- ❑ Magazine Review ❑ Advertisement
- ❑ Reputation of New Riders ❑ Author Name

How would you rate the contents of this book?
- ❑ Excellent ❑ Very Good
- ❑ Good ❑ Fair
- ❑ Below Average ❑ Poor

What other types of certification products will you buy/have you bought to help you prepare for the exam?
- ❑ Quick reference books ❑ Testing software
- ❑ Study guides ❑ Other

What do you like most about this book? Check all that apply.
- ❑ Content ❑ Writing Style
- ❑ Accuracy ❑ Examples
- ❑ Listings ❑ Design
- ❑ Index ❑ Page Count
- ❑ Price ❑ Illustrations

What do you like least about this book? Check all that apply.
- ❑ Content ❑ Writing Style
- ❑ Accuracy ❑ Examples
- ❑ Listings ❑ Design
- ❑ Index ❑ Page Count
- ❑ Price ❑ Illustrations

What would be a useful follow-up book to this one for you?_____

Where did you purchase this book? _____

Can you name a similar book that you like better than this one, or one that is as good? Why?_____

_____

_____

How many New Riders books do you own? _____

What are your favorite certification or general computer book titles? _____

_____

What other titles would you like to see us develop?_____

_____

Any comments for us? _____

_____

_____

Fold here and tape to mail

- -

New Riders Publishing
201 W. 103rd St.
Indianapolis, IN 46290